THE REORDERING OF CULTURE

THE REORDERING OF CULTURE:

LATIN AMERICA, THE CARIBBEAN AND CANADA

IN THE HOOD

Alvina Ruprecht, Editor
Cecilia Taiana, Associate Editor

Carleton University Press

Printed and bound in Canada

Canadian Cataloguing in Publication Data

Main entry under title:
Latin America, the Caribbean and Canada in the hood : the reordering of culture

Text in English and French. Includes bibliographical references.
ISBN 0-88629-269-7

1. Latin America—Civilization. 2. Caribbean Area—Civilization. 3. Canada—Civilization—Foreign influences. I. Ruprecht, Alvina Roberta II. Taiana, Cecilia

E40.L38 1995 970 C95-900803-9E

Données de catalogage avant publication (Canada)

Vedette principale au titre:
Latin America, the Caribbean and Canada in the hood : the reordering of culture

Textes en anglais et en français. Comprend des références bibliographiques.
ISBN 0-88629-269-7

1. Amérique latine—Civilisation. 2. Antilles, Région de la mer des—Civilization. 3. Canada—Civilisation—Influence étrangère. I. Ruprecht, Alvina Roberta II. Taiana, Cecilia

E40.L38 1995 970 C95-900803-9F

Cover illustration: *Once upon a time* (Revue Noire, 1993) by M. Victor Ulloa
Typeset: Mayhew & Associates Graphic Communications, Richmond, Ontario

Carleton University Press gratefully acknowledges the support extended to its publishing programme by the Canada Council and the financial assistance of the Ontario Arts Council. The Press would also like to thank the Department of Canadian Heritage, Government of Canada, and the Government of Ontario through the Ministry of Culture, Tourism and Recreation, for their assistance.

CONTENTS

VII HISTORICAL PERSPECTIVES

VIII TOWARD AN ELECTRONIC HOOD

ACKNOWLEDGEMENTS

The idea for this book was inspired by conversations with my colleagues, and particularly with Cecilia Taiana, as we prepared the annual meeting of the Canadian Association for Latin American and Caribbean Studies (CALACS) which took place at Carleton University (Ottawa, Canada) in October 1993. The general theme of that conference was *Culture and Development: Rethinking Modernity.* As the focus of the book moved away from the developmental component of the conference title, many of the articles in this book were rewritten from papers given at that conference. However, since the CALACS conference was the departure point for this book, none of this would have been possible without the generous funding from Carleton University which made the conference possible. I owe much to John ApSimon, Dean of Graduate Studies, Stuart Adam, Dean of Arts, Robin Farqhuar, President of Carleton University, Marilyn Marshall, former Dean of Social Sciences, and Fraser Taylor, Director of Carleton International, as well as the Canadian Association for Latin American and Caribbean Studies. Also, with regard to this early stage of the book, we are indebted to Judy Young and the Department of Canadian Heritage, Multiculturalism, as well as the Canada Council, for their support.

Special thanks must go to Juanita Montalvo, Director of programmes at the Canadian Foundation for the Americas (FOCAL), for her encouragement, sound advice and never failing enthusiasm. We would also like to thank Wendy Drukier (FOCAL) for her research, John Harewood and Jorge Etcheverry for their constant and faithful collaboration; Leonardo Humerez, Hugh Hazelton, Adrian Harewood and Sharen Khan for their translations, and the Centre d'analyse des littératures francophones/créolophones des Amériques (CALIFA) for their interest in our work. John

Flood, director of Carleton University Press was especially helpful with his suggestions, insights.

We are grateful to all the contributors for their patience and good will which carried right through to the end. We would like to thank Hans George Ruprecht who corrected some of the French texts and a very special thanks to the fine judgement and professionalism of Claudia Buckley, who contributed to the editorial process, and to Mary Jean McAleer for her assistance with data entry revisions.

Needless to say, this project would never have come into being without the very generous contributions from Emile Martel, formerly of the Department of External Affairs, from the Canadian Association for Latin American and Caribbean Studies (CALACS), and especially from the International Development Research Centre (IDRC). The increasing importance of Canada's role in the process of the reconfiguration of the Americas makes it essential that support for research in the many areas involving all forms of human activity be continued. We thank these funding bodies for their confidence and we most gratefully acknowledge their contributions.

INTRODUCTION

LATIN AMERICA, THE CARIBBEAN AND CANADA: THE NEW CULTURAL NEIGHBOURHOOD

Alvina Ruprecht

THE RECENT SIGNING of the North American Free Trade Agreement (NAFTA) between Mexico, the United States and Canada, the creation of the *MERCOSUR* with Argentina, Brazil, Paraguay and Uruguay as well as the regrouping of the greater Caribbean in the loosely formed Association of Caribbean States,[1] in preparation for eventual trade relations with the other countries of the Americas, are evidence that geographical, political and economic barriers are crumbling on this side of the Atlantic. The global "tectonic shift" currently transforming the world is leaving its mark on relations between Latin America, the Caribbean and Canada. However, analyses of these forces of globalization that are overwhelming the "territorially based forces of local survival" (Barnet & Cavanagh, 1995, p.22) and even challenging the concept of "nation," have tended to emphasize economic and political questions, disregarding the fact that cultural forces form the very basis on which American identities and consequently inter-American relations are defined.[2]

The most obvious mediators of the cultural dynamics are the technological developments that have given great impetus to the worldwide diffusion of North American culture, to the transfer of knowledge through the so-called electronic highway, as well as to new syncretic forms of mass culture as they appear in television programming and the popular culture industries. But aside from the impact of technology, specialists in the human and social sciences are well aware that the activity of human beings cannot be explained by the hermetically sealed categories of 19th-century Positivist thinking, but rather by the rules of power operating in networks of interrelations subjected to the tensions of domination, exchange and transformation, whether these networks function in local, national, multinational or intra-national spaces.

Long before any cross-continental trade agreements were ever negociated by politicians, the phenomena related to culture acquired special meaning in this geographical context where the globalizing dynamic was acknowledged by anthropologists, art historians, linguists, theologians and specialists in all facets of socio-cultural exchange. The Americas, through the brutal clash of European, African and American indigenous cultures, and more recently of Asian and Middle Eastern peoples, have been defined, ever since the 15th century, by the dynamics of the meeting of differences, the results of which have always depended on the relations of power existing among the groups in question. In this context, military, political and economic forces have always left their marks on and thus become part of the cultural transformations that took place during the whole history of colonial, slave-trading and immigrant activity. To ignore questions of culture would be to show a lack of understanding of the peoples whose histories laid the groundwork for the present day social tensions, visions of the world, and human inter-relations that constitute the Americas.

The present volume, which does not pretend to be an exhaustive study of any one problem or any particular aspect of these cultural dynamics, proposes an interdisciplinary sampling of various forms of inter-American/inter-Caribbean cultural connectedness in an attempt to understand some of the facets and idiosyncracies of the present-day processes of cultural globalization which are playing an important role in defining the new American neighbourhood. We have brought together scholars and artists in a dialogue that crosses the American continents, writing about ourselves and about each other, examining our cultural relations from a variety of disciplinary, theoretical and ideological perspectives.

The majority of the texts were selected from papers presented at the 1993 annual meeting of the Canadian Association for Latin American and Caribbean Studies (CALACS), held at Carleton University, Ottawa, October 21-24, 1993. Other articles are reworked versions of papers given at the annual meeting of the Caribbean Studies Association (CSA) at the Univeristy of Yucatan, Merida, Mexico, May 23-28, 1994.

Several of the authors propose definitions of that slippery notion of culture but a brief overview of the question would be useful here.[3] Much of the misunderstanding and the neglect of the dynamics of culture is no doubt due to the fact that the concept itself has been locked into a "humanities definition" inherited from hierarchical Western and Eurocentric traditions where it had come to mean, as Stuart Hall points out, "a set of texts and artefacts representing an ideal order" (Hall 1980, p.27), dehistoricized and decontextualized objects detached from the human condition and more commonly linked to artistic products of so-called high culture.

However, the emergence of the "cultural studies enterprise"[4] and its reliance on interdisciplinary perspectives involving anthropology, history, sociology and theories of ideology—as well as recent theorization of the relationships between the Americas and the former colonial powers in post-colonial and after colonial theories,[5] have lead to an interdisciplinary and transnational mode of thought where culture is concerned, and have profoundly transformed our understanding of that concept.

If we start with the anthropological definition reformulated by Stuart Hall around the writings of Levi-Strauss, our present understanding of culture, which must go beyond the notion of artistic production, is more appropriately associated with the result of the dialectical interaction between the raw material of life experience at one pole and the complex human disciplines and formalized institutions, which transmit or distort this raw material at the other (Hall, 1986, p.28). In her article, on culture and education in post-colonial development in the southern Andes of Chile, Maria-Inés Arratia, refers to the anthropological definitions of Keesing, "a bounded universe of shared ideas and customs"; of Tylor, "that complex whole which includes knowledge, belief, art, morals, law, custom and any other capabilities and habilities acquired by man"; and of Hatch, "the way of life of a people." Culture is conceived of as the sum of human practices and experiences that not only reflect reality in some way but that also construct reality and give it meaning.

In the context of post-colonial studies, we find that the notion of culture reflects tendencies related to the postmodern breakdown of the dominant cultural models and canons as they are redefined by the multidisciplinary categories of ethnicity, race, class and gender. The result has been the legitimation of varieties of practices hitherto considered marginal, or peripheral, related to popular culture, belief systems, indigenous practices and questions of identity.[6]

This reconfiguration of the Americas as a result of the cultural globalizing phenomena does not necesarily mean a homogenization of differences to produce a super culture of the Americas which will absorb all others, but rather the realignment of these phenomena, a questioning of former practices, and the production of new cultural categories. Given the postmodern epistemological upheaval which has destablized the disciplines of the humanities in the same way that geopolitical boundaries have been displaced, we are seeing the emergence of ambivalent cultural categories, confirmed by the way cultural discourses borrow from many disciplines including biology, geography, geology, history, linguistics, mass communications, physics and psychoanalysis. A new metaphorical vocabulary has emerged in theoretical texts related to Latin America and the Caribbean where critics talk of hybridity, creolization, metissage and migrancy, cannibalism and syncretism, homogeneity, disorder and disjunction, realignement and renegociation. Images of the *repeating island,* the *border,* the *root* and the *rhizome, chaos, mimicry* and *oraliture* characterize the theoretical writings of Homi Bhabha, Benitez-Rojo, Edouard Glissant, Raphaël Confiant, Patrick Chamoiseau, Maximilien Laroche, Elizabeth Hicks, Hortense Spillers and many others.

Related to the multi-disciplinary and cross-border perspective is the fact that simple binary oppositional categories—black/white, rich/poor, dominant/dominated high culture/low culture, traditional/modern, science/humanities—are no longer sufficient to grasp the movement of this evolving new neighbourhood. For this reason, the texts we have chosen reflect various understandings of the notion of culture and a multiplicity of theoretical perspectives.

The eight chapters of this book, consisting of 38 texts, focus on cultural areas rather than on specific geographical locations. The first chapter entitled *Renegotiating Belief Systems,* presents four articles dealing with deeply rooted changes in our inter-American vision of the world. It includes a discussion of the paradigm shift brought about by an American-centered understanding of "humanity," a rethinking of Liberation theology, and descriptions of Rastafari culture in a global perspective. Chapter II, *Writers Between Worlds,* includes testimonies by Canadian writers of Caribbean and Latin American origins who describe their coming to terms with Canadian society. This is followed by a chapter, *Critical Perspectives on Contemporary Writers,* composed of eight essays which analyze literary works from Canada, Cuba, Martinique, Haiti, Chili, Jamaica Mexico and Dominica. Four texts on the emergence of contemporary discourses which attempt to reclaim and regenerate indigenous cultures make up chapter IV, *Indigenous Cultures: Creative Encounters.* This is followed by *Popular Culture in the Hood,* a collection of eight texts analyzing various dynamics related to popular musics, tourism, film, and cartooning. Chapter VI, *Rethinking Identities,* proposes three studies of the representation of identities in America from a contemporary sociological and literary perspective. Chapter VII, *Historical Perspectives,* shows how historical categories are used to shed new light on phenomena of the present as well as the past. The final chapter, *Toward an Electronic Hood,* investigates the possibility of creating a methodology for comparative cross cultural epistemology using as its departure point analysis based on two course outlines from universities in Canada and Argentina.

However, the organization of these essays could very well seem arbitrary because many of these studies are linked in ways that go beyond the specific cultural fields they examine. It is this other linkage which brings to the foreground the interdisciplinary criss-crossing characteristic of cultural enquiry. On the one hand, certain texts are grounded in concepts based on cultural anthropology or cultural studies and post-colonial theory, thus blurring the boundaries of specific disciplines. In the area of popular culture, for example, popular music is seen not only in the context of the multinational music industry (Averill), but also as an instrument of resistance against an educational system that has tended to serve as a vehicle for cultural colonization in the Caribbean (Noguera), while the survival of Calypso music is integrated into a Marxist critique as Embert Charles shows its relevance to the growth of civil society in the Caribbean. As well, theatre peformance and research become a means of psychological healing by exorcising the tensions of exile (Kurapel). G. Yearwood shows how the new Caribbean cinema structures social consciousness and thus calls for a rethinking of mimetic representational models, while H. Ford-Smith demonstrates the way that Caribbean culture experienced as tourism by North Americans, becomes a model for a perverse North/South dialogue that prolongs colonial discourses and perceptions. Certain forms of literature become a means of deconstructing racial fears and stereotyping in North America (Ruprecht) and of renegociationg the place of immigrant populations within Canadian society (Algoo-Baksh, Clarke, Dabydeen). L. Rojas-Trempe, analyzing the works of Mexican women writers, reveals a a demystifying feminine discourse which serves as a counterpoint to the patriarchal ideology found in the poems of the major literary authority figures of the moment. The author traces the evolution of female literary discourse to show the various phases of resistance to the dominant culture as the literature has moved beyond criticism of Manichean and sexist stereotypes to become an independant and defiant semiotic, proclaiming its own system of images through which the feminine subject attempts to overcome every kind of oppression and repression. In other contexts, painting, drawing (Craven) and the act of story-telling (Esteva) offer clues to the reclaiming of an indigenous past and alternative ways of knowing, erased by the official histories of Mexico and Nicaragua While both art and cinema are analyzed as forces of social change (Craven, Yearwood).

Apart from the cultural studies and post-colonial approaches, other articles reclassify information or subject texts to socio-critical, historical, discursive and stylistic analysis to shed new light on cultural and artistic phenomena.

In the context of cultural history, Alain Yacou investigates the role played by the island of Guadeloupe in Columbus'geostrategy of discovery, while syncretic practices of Afro-Caribbean origin such as Rastafari and Vodou are linked to the evolution of political and socio-cultural organization in the Americas, Europe and even Japan (Yawney, Curtius). Liberation theology which originated in Latin America and which is perceived to be based on a critique of the European schools of theology and the central role played by Rome in the church administration, is seen by J. de Lannoy rather as having deep roots in Latin America; according to him it prolongs, up to a certain point, the theological tradition of Spanish baroque scholasticism which is embedded in the major institutions of Latin American society.

Alberto Ciria presents a detailed repertoire of the Argentinian film industry during the Alfonsín years to show the strong influence of the American film industry in Argentina. John Lent has done pioneer work on political cartooning in the Caribbean, creating the possibility of further research on the relationship between this art form and news kinds of political consciousness.

As well, literary texts are given close thematic, historical or structuralist readings by academics from Cuba (Araujo), Jamaica (Allen), Haiti (N'Zengou-Tayo), Chile (Del Pozo) and Canada (Case, Hazelton, Perron) to show how individual writers mediate their relations with their present social context. F.I. Case uses elements of stylistic analysis to show how the poetry of Dionne Brand signifies her revolt against the alienating "Babylon" of Canadian society. C. Allen shows how the female protagonists in works by two writers of English Caribbean origin who lived most of their creative lives in England and United States, produce a "cross-cultural sensitivity" equivalent to a process of "patchworking," an image related to mending and sewing which suggests a dynamic quite different from the geographical and linguistic based notion of *"creolité"* preferred by the French/Creole writers. N. Araújo shows how shifts in thinking with regard to European canonic literature has allowed the emergence of writers such as Dulce Maria Loynaz in Cuba, while J. Del Pozo sheds light on ideological tensions in Chile by analyzing the representation of the relationship between Spanish and Chilean political movements in 1938 as presented by two Chilean novelists. M-J. N'Zengou-Tayo establishes a troubled continuity within the movement of creative writing in the French Caribbean by examining the relationship between Patrick Chamoiseau *(Texaco)* and Eouard Glissant *(Le Discours antillais)*. H. Hazelton justifies the creation of a new category of Latino-québécois literature while S. Perron examines one aspect of the problem of exile and the representation of the critical revision of the past in two recent novels by Canadian/Chilean writers: José Leandro Urbina and Hernán Barrios. From another perspective, Latin American and Caribbean writers residing in Canada give personal testimonies about their lives in exile and their sometimes difficult adaptation to the Canadian cultural milieu.

One of the central essays in this book is the text by Sylvia Wynter. She pinpoints, in a Foucauldian re-reading of modernity inspired by the Haitian crisis, the changing episteme which characterizes a more radical postmodern thinking within Western society. Basing her work on historical research, she shows how the Cenù Indians in 15th-century Spanish America already recognized new conditions for the possibility of acquiring knowledge when they expressed the idea that the Pope and the Spanish King were "mad" and "drunken" because these two lords of the universe thought they had the right to take and give away lands that couldn't possibly belong to them. The Cenù Indians could only interpret the conquest through their own concept of "man," framed by categories of thinking outside those that prompted the political choices of the Spanish King and the Pope and which, according to Wynter, are still in place in a secularized form, in Euro-centred North American thinking, illustrated by the contradictions inherent in the simultaneous American invasion of Haiti and American rejection of the boat people. This thinking, derived from Western religion and philosophy, where one local—i.e., European—interpretation of "man," seen as isomorphic with Europe and her own interests as a continent—became naturalized as the true and authentic understanding of "man" and so synonymous with being "human." It is this biologized, naturalized and unquestioned understanding of Christian European "man," thought of as universally applicable that must be deconstructed by rejecting its supra-cultural premises and accepting the notion of a culture-systemic mode of causality and thus a transculturally constructed actuality; the Americas are the space where "maps of spring have to be redrawn again ... in undared forms." Needless to say, her discussion helps us to understand why many authors in this volume have felt compelled to wrestle, in various ways, with the cultural construction of the multiple facets of identity.

G. Esteva's article takes us beyond the paradigm of progress and the Western project of international development, into the realm of universally applicable laws of culture where he helps us "rediscover" the legitimacy of the vernacular culture in indigenous Mexico.

Pierre Beaucage begins his investigation of American Indian identity by examining the meaning of modernity. He suggests several anthropological approaches: the *"universaliste,"* the *"ethniste"* and the *"re-tribalisant."* He then settles on an approach based on a dialectical relationship between demographic, economic and ecological factors, on the one hand, and the hegemonic and organizational capacities of the groups in question, on the other. Finally, he shows how the actualization of modernity in practical socio-economic terms, corresponds to a specific conception of identity as interpreted by the Nahua Indians in the region of Puebla, Mexico, and not on any notion inherited from the "developed" world.

Daniel Yon delves into opposing notions of "strategic essentialism" and cultural construction of identity to show that blackness is a product of contradiction, ambivalence, desire, denial and constant remapping, forged in reaction to exclusion and racism. He presents interviews with young Canadians of Caribbean origin living in Toronto, to show that many of them do not know what being black means, but that once they are placed in a "tradition of pigmentocracy" by Toronto society, they act according to certain expectations. Yon shows that blackness could be one of those notions that Prakash calls, a category that fails (1995, p.12). In a similar way, *Nègre* is not presented as a socio-biological reality in the novels of Dany Laferrière, in the way that Austin Clarke draws his Caribbean immigrants. Laferrière's black man is a literary construction, a "pernicious act of language"(Gates, 1986, p.5), performing as a stereotype in an ironic mode, in order to expose the discursive dynamics of racism (Ruprecht).

Catharina Vallejo explains how race was related to a series of ideological categories that were classified and manipulated in literary texts of the 19th-century Dominican Republic. In the wake of the Haitian independence struggle, the Spanish-speaking neighbour had to evacuate all Euro-Spanish connections and so it became a political necessity to legitimize a national Indian identity. Milagros Ortiz uncovers a similar process in present day Nicaragua. Analyzing the poetry and songs of the Ladina population of the Pacific coast, she uncovers the complex construction of an ambiguous Indian identity. She shows that what she calls the *indien en moi* identity, corresponds to a collective and official "indianity," while the *indien des autres* a much more problematic concept, is offically denied but legitimized by popular discourses where it is used to identify members of a same ethnic group. This gives rise to a confused and ambiguous notion of identity within that population and within the country as a whole.

The final text in this book represents a category of its own. Cecilia Taiana takes us into the future by defining the notion of the text and the intertext and then going beyond these literary categories to reflect on the cultural consequences of the electronic based hypertext and possible hypertext linkages. Her study of these electronic links, which forsees new forms of cross-cultural analysis based on a diversity of texts, gives us a glimpse into the future of our American neighbourhood. There is no doubt that the new technologies, by the rapidity of exchange, the volume of information exchanged, and the new possibilities for "advances in conceptual navigation"(Taiana) are currently causing a radical transformation of what we currently call culture.

ENDNOTES

1. According to this association, formed in 1994, members of the Caribbean community are: Anguilla, Antigua and Barbuda, Barabados, Belize, Colombia, Costa Rica, Cuba, Dominica, Dominican Republic, El Salvador, Grenada, Guatemala, Guyana, Haiti, Honduras, Jamaica, Mexico, Nicaragua, Panama, St. Vincent, St. Kitts & Nevis, Saint Lucia, Suriname, Trinidad and Tobago and Venezuela. Conspicuously absent are the Dutch possessions, Curaçao and Aruba and the French Departments of Martinique, Guadeloupe and French Guyana.
2. See the special issue of *Theory, Culture & Society* (1990), on the Globalization of Culture.
3. See especially *Relocating Cultural Studies. Developments in Theory and Research*, V. Blundell, J. Shepherd, I. Taylor (Eds.).

4. See works by Stuart Hall, especially *Culture, Media, Language,* Working Papers in Cultural Studies, 1972-79, (Ed.). S.Hall, D. Hobson, Andrew Lowe, P.Willis, 1986, London: Hutchinson; see Tony Bennett (1993). "Useful culture", *Relocating cultural studies,* V. Blundell, J. Shepherd & I.Taylor (Eds.), New York: Routledge, 1993, p.68; see the March 1995 issue of the *Canadian Review of Comparative Literature/Revue canadienne de littérature comparée* which deals with the "disciplinary repositioning associated with the cultural studies movement." (Morrow, 1995, p.1)
5. Within the mass of literature produced in this context, one might mention *The Location of Culture* (Homi Bhabha), *Colonialisms Culture* (Nicholas Thomas), *After colonialism* (Gyan Prakash, Ed.); *The Repeating Island* (Benitez-Rojo); the special issue of *Boundary 2,* New Americanists 2: National Identities and Postnational Narratives, D.E. Pease (Ed.). 19 (1), Spring 1992, Duke University Press; *Hispanic Issues,* Latin American Identity and Constructions of Difference, A. Chanady (Ed.). 10, 1994.
6. In her introduction to volume 10 of *Hispanic Issues* dealing with "Latin American identity and the constructions of difference," Amaryll Chanady refers to the ongoing debate about "the extension of the term Latin American" to include the Spanish, French, Dutch, English, French and English based Creole-speaking peoples of the Caribbean and even French-speaking Canadians, (Chanady, 1994,p. XV). This is an indication of the geo-political boundary shifting currently taking place, resulting from displacement of cultural canons and the legitimization of hitherto marginalized peoples. See also *Forging Identities and Patterns of Development,* H. Diaz, J. Rummens, P.Taylor (Eds.), Toronto: Canadian Scholars Press, 1991.

REFERENCES

Austin-Broos, D.J.(1994). Race/Class: Jamaica's discourse of heritable identity. *New West Indian Guide,* 65 (3-4), pp.213-233.

Barnet, R.J., Cavanagh, J. (1994). *Global dreams. Imperial corporations and the new world order,* New York: Simon & Schuster.

Benitez-Rojo, A. (1992). *The Repeating island. The Caribbean and the postmodern perspective,* Durham: Duke University Press.

Bernabé, J., Chamoiseau, P., Confiant, R., (1989). *Eloge de la créolité,* Paris: Gallimard.

Bhaba, H. (1994). *The Location of culture,* London: Routledge.

Blundell,V., Shepherd, J., Taylor, I., (Eds.), (1993). *Relocating cultural studies,* London and New York: Routledge.

Chambers, I. (1990). *Border dialogues,* London: Routledge.

Chanady, A. (1994). Latin American imagined communities and the postmodern challenge. *Latin American Identity and Constructions of Difference. Hispanic Issues, 10,* A. Chanady (Ed.), pp.IX-XLVI.

Cooper, C. (1993). *Noises in the blood. Orality, gender and the 'vulgar' body of Jamaican popular culture,* London: Macmillan Press.

Diaz, H.P., Rummens, J., Taylor P.(Eds.), (1991). *Forging identities and patterns of development,* Toronto: Canadian Scholars Press.

Featherstone, M. (1990). Global culture: An introduction. *Theory, Culture & Society,* 7, pp.1-14.

Ferguson, M. (1992). The mythology about globalization. *European Journal of Communication,* 7, pp.69-93.

Gates, H.L. (Ed.), (1986). *Race. Writing and difference,* Chicago: The University of Chicago Press.

Glissant, E. (1981). *Le discours antillais,* Paris: Le Seuil.

———. (1992). *Identité comme racine, identité comme relation. Identité, culture, développement. Actes du colloque international organisé par le Comité de la Culture, de l'Education et de l'Environnement de la Guadeloupe, Pointe-à-Pitre 11-13 décembre 1989,* Paris: Editions Caribbéennes, pp.199-204.

Hall, S., Hobson, D., Lowe, A., Willis, P. (Eds.), (1986). *Culture, media, language,* London: Hutchinson.

Hicks, D.E. (1991). *Border writing. The multidimensional text,* Minneapolis: University of Minnesota Press.

Hutcheon, L. (1995). Colonialism and the postcolonial condition. Introduction: Complexities abounding. *Publications of the Modern Language Association of America,* 110 (1), pp.7-16.

Laroche, M. (1991). *La Double Scène de la représentation. Oraliture et littérature dans la Caraïbe.* Québec: Université Laval, Grelca.

Lent, J. (1990). Popular Culture in the Caribbean: A literature review. *Caribbean Popular Culture,* Lent J.(Ed.), Bowling Green: Bowling Green State University Popular Press.

Morrow, R.A. (1995). The challenge of cultural studies. *Canadian Review of Comparative Literature/Revue canadienne de littérature comparée,* 23 (1), pp.1-20.

Prakash, G. (1995). *After Colonialism: Imperial histories and postcolonial displacements,* Princeton: Princeton University Press.

Savishinsky, N. (1994). Transnational popular culture and the global spread of the Jamaican Rastafarian movement. *New West Indian Guide/Nieuwe West-Indische Gids,* 68 (3-4), pp. 259-281

Spillers, H. (1991). Introduction: Who cuts the border? Some readings. *Comparative American Identities,* H.Spillers (Ed.), New York: Routledge.

Wallerstein, I. (1990). Culture as the ideological battleground of the modern world system. *Theory, Culture & Society,* 7, pp. 31-55.

CHAPTER I

RENEGOTIATING BELIEF SYSTEMS

THE POPE MUST HAVE BEEN DRUNK THE KING OF CASTILE A MADMAN: CULTURE AS ACTUALITY, AND THE CARIBBEAN RETHINKING MODERNITY[1]

Sylvia Wynter

On the basis of the Cenù Indians' perception of the Requisition, by means of which the Spaniards legitimated their claim to the indigenous lands, what seemed to the Spaniards to be a universally applicable order of truth, was "mad and drunken speech." The crisis of today's Haiti and the paradox of the United State's response to this crisis are to be understood in the terms of a parallel contradiction.

The crisis of the Caribbean as exemplified in the Haitian situation, is the crisis, too, of our present order of knowledge where the contemporary Western industrialized order, which represents its own local culture and its conception of the human, as natural, supracultural and isomorphic with the human species, is constrasted with the culturality of all other human orders. If this crisis is to be resolved, we must deconstruct this way of thinking and recognize that our contemporary culture, together with the actuality of our Western modernity, to which it gives rise, functions according to the same laws by which all other cultures and their belief systems function. The article concludes by suggesting that the major thinkers of today's Caribbean have challenged these "truths" and opened the way to a new hypothesis—that of the functioning of universally applicable *laws of culture* as the veridical etiology of all the "ills" endemic to Haiti as well as the other ex-slave islands.

Selon les indiens Cenú, le document intitulé la *Réquisition,* qui a permis aux Espagnols d'établir un ordre de vérité universelle et donc de légitimer l'appropriation des terres indigènes, serait un texte conçu par des «fous» et des «ivrognes». La crise actuelle en Haïti et le paradoxe de la réaction américaine devant cette crise, doivent se comprendre dans le contexte d'une contradiction comparable. La crise de la Caraïbe exemplifiée par la situation en Haïti, illustre l'état de notre savoir actuel selon lequel le monde occidental idustrialisé, basé sur une «culture locale,» tient sa propre conception de «l'humain» pour l'état «naturel» des choses. Par conséquent, on a tendance à le considérer isomorphe de l'espèce humain en général et supraculturel, soit au delà de la «spécificité culturelle» par laquelle le savoir occidental caractérise les autres ordres humains.

Pour résoudre cette crise, il faudrait déconstruire ce mode de réflexion et reconnaître que notre culture contemporaine qui englobe l'actualité de notre modernité occidentale, functionne selon les mêmes lois que toutes les autres cultures et leurs systèmes de croyances.

C'est dans ce sens que les penseurs les plus importants de la Caraïbe actuelle ont remis en question ces "vérités" universelles et ouvert la voie vers une nouvelle hypothèse, celle qui propose des *lois de culture* qui fonctionneraient universellement telle une étiologie de tous les «maux» dont souffrent Haïti et les autres îles ex-esclaves de la Caraïbe.

*

About the Pope being the Lord of all the universe in the place of God, and that he had given the lands of the Indies to the King of Castile, the Pope must have been drunk when he did it, for he gave what was not his....The king who asked for and received this gift must have been some madman for he asked to have given to him that which belonged to others.

(The Cenù Indian's reply to the Spaniard "local culture" conception of the legitimacy of the Papal Bull of 1492 as one which "gave" the New World to Spain) (Greenblatt, 1974, p.27).

This objectification of the world continually brings man into conflict with his fellows. This competition, however, is not in Heidegger's view the consequence of political or personal ambition, as Machiavelli or the ancients understood it, nor simply the result of a universal desire for self-preservation, as Hobbes might have characterized it, but the consequence of a new understanding of man's humanity and the subsequent attempt of men to realize it. (Gillespie,1984, p.27)

THE QUOTATION of the first part of the title, i.e., "the Pope must have been drunk, the king of Castile a madman," is taken from a report of the 16th century Cenù Indian's comment on a politico-juridical Spanish document called the Requisition.[2] This document was drawn up about 1512-1513 by a bureaucrat of the Spanish State. It was intended to establish the grounds of legitimacy for that state's expropriation of the lands, and sovereignty of the peoples of the indigenous cultural worlds of the Caribbean and the Americas. More directly, it was intended to legitimate, in dually religio-juridical terms, the then lucrative slave-raiding missions being carried out on the mainland territories by groups of Spanish expeditionaries who had been licensed to "discover and expropriate" *(descubrir y ganar)* lands intended to expand the sovereignty of the state as well as to enrich the expeditionaries and their backers (Wynter, 1991). The direct purpose of the Requisition was to legitimate the process by which the dynamic transfer of wealth and resources from the rest of the world to the Western European enclaves of the world system was set in motion, and be effected within the terms of what made the "real real" and the "normal normal" for the invading European Christians. Consequently, within the logic of the new ethical-political distinctions juridically crafted by the document any group of the indigenous peoples who refused to accept Christian conversion and resisted Spain's sovereignty could be at once classified as *inimicos Christi* (enemies of Christ). On that basis, they could then be captured, enslaved and sold within the prescriptive rules laid down by the Church with respect to what could and could not be accepted as just causes for the enslavement of others.[3]

However, while deploying the classificatory terms of the Church, and its universal narrative, the Requisition now functioned within the particular terms of the new discourse of the incipiently civic humanist reasons of state, and its hegemonically political organization of reality, as effected by the modern European state, in whose primary interest the structure of our present world system was first laid down. The function of the juridical document was therefore to draw the "culturally alien" people of the Caribbean and the Americas within the classificatory logic of the Judaeo-Christian "local culture" theology, and yet to do so in specifically monarchical-juridical terms that could make their subjugation and expropriation by the Spanish state seem "real" and "normal." The central declaration of the document was therefore based on the Church's specific conception of history *(historia rerum gestarum),* in which, because Christ had given the Earth into the Pope's keeping and the Pope had donated the lands to Spain so that the Indians could be evangelized into the only True Faith (and thereby emancipated as "barbarous nations" from their enslavement to "diabolic" religions), any resistance by the indigenous peoples would make their lands justly expropriable and they themselves justly enslavable.

The Cenù Indians, on the other hand, speaking from within the quite different categories of their still polytheistic and divinized nature religious cultures, could only interpret the discourse of the Requisition, as pronounced by the subjects of the Spanish State, as non-sense, as the speech of "drunkards" or "madmen." Their response to the Requisition's reformulation of the Papal Bull of 1493, which had given most of the New World to Spain, (and eventually, Brazil to Portugal), therefore enables us to recognize that, as Richard Rorty was to argue several centuries later, our present "objective" mode of truth is only true within the specific terms of our present culture's self-conception (Rorty, 1985). Equally, the discourse of the Requisition, like the correlated discourses which legitimated the West's global expansion, was only true within the terms of the 16th century variant of the matrix Judaeo-Christian culture of the West, and therefore within the terms of its behavior-motivational belief system and neo-Augustianian principle of explanation.

Keeping this is mind, we now turn our attention to the Caribbean 500 years later, specifially to Haiti which has recently been at the centre of the news. The call for the United States invasion to dislodge the ruling military group was made in the wake of the failure of the policy of sanctions to do the job. History seemed to be repeating itself. The first United States intervention had been effected in 1915, in the context of the First World war. The long term purpose of the American occupation of Haiti (1915-1934) had been to enforce the kind of political stability needed for private foreign investment to continue to function as the integrative mechanism of our present global order of modernity and therefore of our present hegemonic cultural system of whose "form of life" the economic system of capitalism is the central expression.

When the United States intervened in 1915 to protect its investors' "economic interests," it had therefore done so within the prescriptive terms of a specific culturally instituted order of consciousness or belief system, and therefore within the logic of the specific "understanding of man's humanity" with which these terms provided. As indicated in the second phase of my title (i.e., Culture as Actuality), the major thesis of this paper, is that it is the phenomenon of culture, rather than of either "nature" or "history" that provides the ground of all human existential reality or actuality. Hence the inevitability with which the American occupiers of 1915 effected a process of modernization in Haiti in terms that were to benefit largely the Westernized Haitian elite—the mulatto business and political elite, and later, the Duvalieriste Black political elite or Noiriste[4]—thereby strengthening them against the Vodounist peasantry and agro-proletariat. Also acting within the same terms, however, the American occupiers carried out their mandate on the basis of an overt United States Southern anti-black or color line racism, displayed impartially to elite and peasantry, since racism, anti-black and non-white racism is as culturally prescribed by "our present understanding of man's humanity," and its purely biologized "metaphor of the self" (Pandian, 1988) on the model of a natural organism, as is our economically organized order of global reality.[5]

Reactions to the overt brand of United States type "racism" amongst certain sections of the French educated elite in Haiti led to the movement of *Indigénisme* whose thrust was to lay claim to and revalorize the African components of Haitian culture, specifically the popular neo-agrarian religion of Vodoun which, although syncretized with Roman Catholic elements, is essentially African-derived; as a religion that has been made, within the logic of contemporary Western thought, into the byword of an antithetical irrationality to its own ostensibly supra-cultural order of rationality, into the Derridean Fool to its Logos.[6]

TWO UNDERSTANDINGS OF HUMANITY, TWO MODES OF REFLECTIVE THOUGHT: THE NEO-AGRARIAN WORLD OF VODOUN, THE TECHNO-INDUSTRIAL WORLD OF THE WEST

> From the point of view of empirical science, Vodouisants would say that the entire cosmos, including all of the principles inherent in its mechanical, biological, and stellar functions, can be reduced to one higher principle, Bondye, who is the ensurer of universal order and the source of all human actions. The highest wisdom consists not only in recognizing the wholeness of the universal order as contained in Bondye, but also in affirming that same wholeness in the human community. (Desmangles, 1992, p.96)

Before the shock of the United States 1915 occupation, the popular religious culture of Vodoun, even where repressed and stigmatized by the elite as the "price of the ticket" for its assimilation into being "magnificent coloured Frenchmen" (Price-Mars, 1983, p.8), had been nevertheless inscribed in the Haitian collective psyche, because of the unifying role that this counter-belief system had played in making possible Haiti's anti-slavery, independence struggle and victory against the French. The "return" of the elite to a reclaiming of this legacy was therefore part of the intellectual challenge to what most Haitians now saw as their island's neo-imperial occupation by the Americans. There were two variants to this challenge. One thrust, that of Price-Mars, laid the emphasis on the calling into question the distortions of Western ethnographic accounts of Vodoun. The other, that of Francois Duvalier (and his Noiristes), was to manipulate Vodoun, together with its secret society system[7] as a powerful semi-official tool with which to displace the hegemony of the largely mulatto upper-class elite, replacing it with its own socially mobile lower middle black, but no less educationally Westernized, elite.

For the Haitian popular classes, however, the peasantry and agro-proletariats, whose practitioners of Vodoun lived within the terms of its quite different "understanding of man's humanity," the major issue was not the Southern style white racism of the Americans. Rather, it was the issue of the direct impact on their lives of the processes of modernization that the Americans carried out within the terms of a cultural logic and principle of organization directly opposed to their own. This clash would lead to their armed revolt under the leadership of the peasant leader Charlemagne Peralte (Wilentz, 1989). Although Peralte was eventually defeated and executed, semi-lynching style, by the Americans, he became both a national hero for the new Duvalieriste Haitian elite, as well as a revered popular icon for the Vodouisant masses. This armed revolt had therefore been the expression of a profound clash between the Americans, as the bearers of the West's techno-industrial "understanding of man's humanity" and the still hegemonically neo-Agrarian and symbiotic African-cum-Judaeo-Christian "understanding," of which the Haitian Vodouisant were and are the bearers.[8]

For in spite of the far-reaching impact of the techno-industrial mode of reflective thought[9] which the Americans expressed through their modernizing activities, this thought was and is generated from the now purely secularized variant of the matrix Judaeo-Christian "local culture" of the West, as a variant which although now globalized, is itself "one of the forms life has locally taken" (Geertz, 1983). In consequence, the clash between the American occupiers and the Vodouisant Haitian peasantry was one between two ways of life, two orders of consciousness, or modes of being, two modes of the "real and the normal," both of which had until then, coexisted in the hegemonic cultural terms of the former; and therefore within the structural logic of the world system put in place by the West from the 16th century on (Wallerstein, 1974).

Hence the paradox that it was to be the modernizing and debt-collecting imperative of the first 1915 United States intervention that was to lead directly to today's escaping-only-to-be repatriated-again-by the patrolling American coast guard vessels—boat-people—that is, as refugees that were only secondarily economic refugees (as they are classified as being, in order to be denied asylum status), but rather primarily escapees from the global effects of the implacable logic of our present techno-industrial mode of "reflective thought." It is this mode of thought that motivates and legitimates the economic policies, not only of the Americans but also of Haiti's Westernized elites, while these are the very policies that have set in train the world-systemic uprooting and jobless impoverishment of today's escaping boat peoples of the G.7's satellite worlds.

One needs to point out here that the Haitian boat people are, in their majority, the descendants of African slaves rather than, as in the case of Cuba, primarily of European settlers and their mixed descendants. Therefore, unlike the Cubans, the Haitians are black and not fleeing from a Communist, but only from a neo- or peripheral-capitalist, military dictatorship.

This is not to say that the call by both white and black Americans for the intervention to "restore democracy" by restoring Aristide to power is not sincerely meant. But rather that it is, in the larger context of the now fully effected shift to a consumer-driven, as distinct from the earlier production-driven, phase of the global-systemic accumulation of capital that the goals of blocking the entrance of a large mass of black Haitians refugees into the United States and of "restoring democracy" in its Western bourgeois definition[10] to Haiti coincide. A democratically elected and restored Aristide or his like, together with a new cadre of technocrats, in the place of the military elite and/or dictators such as the Duvaliers, are now needed to enable the re-modernization of Haiti, in the new terms required by the ongoing re-ordering of the Western world system.

New prescriptive rules are now needed by the global economic system as a function of the stable replication of our present "local culture" and its Western bourgeois "understanding of man's humanity." If we see our present "understanding" as a transumed form (i.e., a new form which nevertheless carries over the old meanings) (Bloom, 1983) of the original matrix "understanding" put in place by the rise of the Judaeo-Christianity's then new conception of being human),[11] a culture-historical continuity can here be identified. For while even refugees from Castro's Cuba are also being detained, it is against the would-be migrants of Haiti as the largest nation-state island of the ex-slave, and therefore in its majority, black Caribbean, that the most total exclusion is being carried out. The continuity here is that it had also been on these islands and specifically on the island shared today between Haiti and the Dominican Republic that the initial culturally legitimized division of labour, based on the West's 16th century "invention of man" (Foucault, 1973, p.386), had established the hierarchical structures that were to be founding both to the Caribbean and to what is today's world system. This first hierarchical structural pattern, one that had been based on the dominance/subordinate relationships of settler to natives or of Europeans to *indios,* on the one hand and of masters to slaves, Europeans to "negros"[12] on the other, had been put in place on the basis of two forms of forced labor institutions. These had been that of the neo-serf, the *encomienda* system[13] manned by indios, and that of the slave plantation system manned by "negros," both of which had been put in place by the Europeans, in the terms of their then specific 16th century "local culture" "understanding of man's humanity."

Another culture-historical continuity was to underlie the more total degree of exclusion being inflicted today on the Haitians, as contrasted to the Cubans. This was that, in the wake of the abolition of slavery and in the context of the West's second invention of Man in a now totally secularized form, it was to be, as Jacob Pandian, the anthropologist further points out, the peoples of African hereditary descent, who were to be made into the physical referent of the ostensibly genetically dysselected Human Other (or nigger/nègre) to Man's[14] new self-conception (Pandian, 1988). That is, as the Eugenic (i. e., genetically selected) Self within the now biologized "understanding of man's humanity."

It is, therefore, within the terms of this now globalized "understanding" that the black popular majority of the ex-slave Caribbean and centrally of Haiti now find themselves imprisoned today, driving them to seek escape by migration as boat people to the United States at the same time as they are blocked by United States Coast Guard vessels.

There is another central continuity here. At the time of the initial putting in place of the founding structures of the post-1492 Caribbean by the Spaniards, who had then coercively (with *their ships* hovering offshore), put these structures in place, these Spaniards too would have understood their own actions as *aculturally* as we understand our actions, too, today. That is, as actions/behaviours prescribed and legitimated by a universally applicable "understanding of man's humanity" and its mode of truth.

The proposed parallel here is that the legitimating speech put forward by President Clinton to defend the paradox of both attempting to "restore democracy" to Haiti (with warships and marines) at the same time as his Coast guard vessels enforce the exclusion of Haitian migrants to the United States, makes sense and therefore is not a parallel "mad" discourse, only within the terms of our present "understanding of man" and its "local culture" order of truth. Since if for the Americans, Aristide's return (as a popularly elected leader) will, it is believed, serve two purposes (i.e., be the most effective guard against the threat now posed by the boat people to the racial-national interests of the United States, a country that still conceives of itself as being culturally, a Euroamerican, and, biologically, a white nation,[15] and second, provide a stable atmosphere for United States investments), the Haitians themselves, including the boat people stopped at sea, are being asked to believe that the only goal of the Americans is to "restore democracy" represented as the only cure for the "affliction" that ails Haiti. As if Haiti's past ills, exacerbated by its political leadership, are not themselves fundamentally due to the world systemic role of "underdevelopment" imposed upon it within the terms of our present Western bourgeois "understanding of man's humanity" and the attempt of people to realize it; an understanding of which the United States is now the global enforcer.

Yet the issue here, as Heidegger brilliantly implies (1977), is not the issue of those who seek to realize this understanding or to militarily enforce it. The issue here is that of the "understanding" itself, and of those, we the scholars of contemporary academia, who formulate, elaborate and represent this "local culture" understanding as if it were a universally applicable and acultural one.

HISTORY AS "HUMAN ACTUALITY"? OR THE "LOCAL CULTURE" OF THE WEST AS THE GROUND OF CONTEMPORARY HISTORY, OF MODERNITY

As we have seen, the question, 'What is history?' asks whether history is human actuality or merely the product of human imagination, i.e., whether it is the *res gestae* or only the *historia rerum gestarum.* Modernity has come to the conclusion that it is the human actuality....The philosophical development that occurs ... represents the increasing and ultimately utter historicization of Western life and thought.... It is thus not accidental that in our times we note an even more vehement and partisan attachment to particular conceptions of history. (Gillespie,1984, p.24)

The post-1492 Caribbean, the world system of which its islands were to be founding units, and the era of modernity, were all three brought into existence by the same dynamic process of cultural discontinuity, and therefore of historical rupture. This discontinuity/rupture was effected by the intellectual revolution of lay humanism in the context of the rise of the modern European state, as the first, if still partly religious, form of a secularizing mode of human co-existence. While it was in the context of these dual movements of intellectual and socio-systemic transformation that a new order of transculturally applicable truth, that of the natural sciences, was also to gradually emerge.

This new order of truth, which had emerged in the wake of both the 15th-century voyages of the Portuguese and Columbus, and of Copernicus' challenge to the earlier correlated belief system in the ostensibly divinely-ordered non-homogeneity of a universe divided between the moving celestial realm as the realm of the Redeemed Spirit, and the terrestrial realm of the Earth which, as the abode of "fallen" mankind, had to be fixed and unmoving at the centre of the universe, based itself on a new hypothesis. This hypothesis was that nature functioned in the same way "in Europe" as "in America," "in heaven as on earth," and all according to the same laws, to the "same accustomed course of nature" *(cursus solitus naturae).*[16] While given that these laws could now be recognized as governing all parts of the universe, they could be made the basis for the elaboration of a new order of knowledge in whose terms, the knower could now extrapolate from the qualities of bodies that are "found to be within the reach of our experiments," what the qualities of all bodies whatsoever, however distant, would have to be (Funkenstein, 1986, p.29).

This new image of Nature as an autonomously functioning force or cause in its own right was to accompany the parallel process of the secularizing or degodding of the criterion of being human at the public levels of existence that was to be the defining characteristic, both of the process to which we give the name modernity, and of the world system that was to be its condition of existence. The foundations of both modernity and our present world system were therefore laid down in the context of the rise of the post-feudal European state, whose first project of extra-European colonization was to bring into existence the new sociopolitical structures of today's Caribbean. In turn, these structures were to be themselves founding, both to the world system in which we now find ourselves and to the single history within whose dynamic we all now live. At the same time, as both Foucault and Pandian show, the degodding of being, the institution of the post-1943 Caribbean politics and the initiation of modernity, were themselves to be inseparable from the invention both of Man and of its human Others, first that of the indio/negro complex, later, that of the nigger/native complex.[17]

The major point is that if Latin Christian Europe secularized itself in the 15th and 16th centuries, as the West, eventually secularizing all human models of being and behaving, it was to do so in the transumed specific terms of its own "local culture." This is nowhere more evident than by the term "secular" itself. For as will be noted, I have used the term secular several times here and used it interchangeably, with the term degodding. The term "secular," as given in the Oxford English Dictionary (O.E.D.) is a meaning specific to the religio-cultural field of Judaeo-Christianity, and therefore, to its behavior-motivating Grand Narrative of Emancipation (Lyotard, 1989), based on the explanatory schema of enslavement to Original Sin/Emancipation from Original Sin through the-mediation-of-baptism, and of behaviours oriented toward the goal of Spiritual Redemption. The O.E.D. gives the etymology of the English word "secular" as coming from the Latin term saecularis, that is, from the adjective correlated with the noun saeculum which means "generation, age" and more generally the "World" as opposed to the "Church"(O.E.D. 1971, p.365). By the nature of our shared response to the meaning of the word secular, we are therefore already responding within the terms of a specific cultural field, as enacted by the formal rules of a now global and purely desupernatualized variant of the original feudal Judaeo-Christian culture of Western Europe.

This semantic shift had entailed the increasing hegemony of the secular World at the public levels of existence, together with increasing privatization of religion, and therefore of the Church (in the wake of Luther's "Reformation"). With this shift, the term secular now came to be applied to "literature, history, art" not "concerned with or devoted to the service of religion" (O.E.D., 1971, p.365). In consequence, the new doctrine of secularism which followed from this step, came to function as the new narrative schema on which modernity was to be based. However, although the term secular would now come, within the terms of its new narrative-schematic field, to signify reality as contrasted to the increasingly negatively marked irreality of the Church, it did so in terms that were themselves generated, as variant forms, from the matrix narrative schema that had been founding both to the culture of the Judaeo-Christian West, and that of its precursor, the still polytheistic cultural and philosophical system of the ancient Greek polis.

The new discourse of civic humanism which effected this transfer of hegemony did this by transuming the matrix Judaeo-Christian Grand Narrative of Emancipation and its Augustianian "principle of explanation" of mankind's enslavement to Original Sin and its imperative quest for remission from this sin, and therefore of redemption in the other-worldly City of God. This new schema had been that of mankind's represented enslavement both to the pre-political "state of nature" and the irrational, particularistic and self-interested aspects of its own nature, with remission from this enslavement being only possible by subjecting oneself to the rational order of the political state. Seeing that only the state-as-universal was now empowered to secure the "common good" as against the threatening chaos and disorder of the war of each against all, of the particular and private self interest of the one, against those of the others. It was this behaviour-motivating schema and the correlated "understanding of man's humanity" from which it derived, that had therefore served to revalue the terms of the former Church/World opposition, i.e., to revalue the world as the sphere of a fixed and stable, although temporal, reality—at the same time as it relegated the Church to the private sphere as an increasingly "spiritual" realm of "irreality."

It was to be in the context of this process (one of whose effects was also that of the transformation of the Church into the spiritual arm of the state, as the state had earlier been the temporal and military arm of the Church), that the terms of legitimation on whose basis Spain expropriated the New World, were prescribed and enacted—that is, as terms which although found by the Cenù Indians from their culturally-external observer perspective, to be "mad" and "drunken" and therefore non-sense, were to be indispensable to the specific culture-historical dynamics out of which "Modernity," the contemporary Caribbean, and the Americas were to emerge and on the basis of whose "ground" Europe's conquest of the Americas was both effected and made to seem legitimate and just.

Our shared understanding of the word secular (as academics and scholars all of whom, whatever our cultures of origin, have been *disciplined* in Foucault's sense of the word, in the conceptual models of the epistemological order derived from the original basis of the *studia*), is only made possible by our already enculturation in the specific culture systemic categories in which this word has come to have the same transcultural meaning as other such terms as degodding or de-supernaturalization. However, within the shared field of our mutual understanding, the expression itself, i.e., culture systemic categories, cannot help but strike a jarring note. In that given the acultural premise on which our present shared mode of comprehension is based, i. e., the premise, specific to our present now purely secularized variant of the matrix Judaeo-Christian culture, that we are not in a culture at all, and that our native model of reality (Legesse, 1973, p.274) is reality-in-itself, the term "culture-systemic categories" cannot be "heard" or normally understood to make sense for us within the Focauldian "regime of truth" of our present order of knowledge and its disciplinary paradigms. At the same time, because our present episteme or order of knowledge elaborates itself on the basis of a now purely biological description of the human, in whose terms, man had been invented in its second form, on the model of a "natural organism" (Foucault, 1973, pp.310, 351), and with this model serving as a non-questionable rhetorical a priori (Grassi, 1980), this aprioristic model then enables our present disciplinary paradigms to represent their "local culture" conception of the human as if this conception were isomorphic with the human species itself. This conflation of Man/human then enables the well-being of this specific category of the human, man to be represented as if its well-being, too, were isomorphic with the well-being of the human species as a whole; and by extrapolation, as if the well-being of the West, and of the Westernized "developed" enclaves, were, are, or could ever be, isomorphic with the well-being of their "underdeveloped" satellite areas such as Haiti.

The crisis of the Caribbean as vividly exemplified these past few weeks in the Haitian situation is, therefore, like the overall crisis of modernity, the crisis, too, of our present order of knowledge, as the elaborated expression of our present understanding of man's humanity, and its correlated behavior-motivating schema, in which the culture-systemic conception, Man, is mis-represented as if it were the human itself. If this crisis is to be fundamentally resolved, therefore, this misrepresentation, together with the founding rhetorical strategy which makes it believable, must be deconstructed.

Franz Fanon, Aimé Césaire and other major thinkers of the ex-slave Caribbean have challenged the ostensibly supracultural and therefore value-free nature of the "objective knowledge" of our present episteme. From their liminal perspective of alterity—they have shown that by means of its disciplinary paradigms, one "local culture's" conception of the human Man, is strategically presented as if its referent were the human species itself, as if its culture-systemic "world" were the new "Church," its ground of actuality, supracultural, its speech not as mad and drunken, as inside that ground it is rational, logical, and alone experiencable as true.

In this context and against the central premise of modernity with respect to the *non-homogeneity* of our contemporary Western industrialized order which represents its own actuality as supracultural as contrasted with the *culturality* of all other human orders, we can put forward the following hypothesis: that our contemporary culture, together with the actuality of the Westernized modernity to which it gives rise, functions according to the same laws by which all other cultures, and their behaviour-motivational belief systems, including that of Vodoun, function.

CULTURE AS ACTUALITY: THE EX-SLAVE CARIBBEAN AND THE DISENCHANTING OF CONSCIOUSNESS/BELIEF/IDEOLOGY

> the child does not know
> the map of spring has always to be
> drawn again ...
> the undared form ...
> o fresh source of light
> those who unveiled neither
> gunpowder nor compass
> those who tamed neither a steam nor electricity
> those who explored neither sea nor sky
> but without whom the earth would not be earth. (Césaire, 1938)

Given the role of alterity or of Human Otherness imposed upon the recently freed slaves of the Caribbean and of the Americas (Pandian, 1988) as a function of the West's 19th-century reinvention of Man on the model of a natural organism, it has been precisely this biologized understanding that the major thinkers of the ex-slave Caribbean have been compelled to call into question. This has been so because, as the educated elites of the majority ex-slave but still until the 1960s, colonized population, they also had been socialized by the education system of the European colonial powers, in the terms of the same "understanding of man's humanity" and therefore of the order of consciousness to which it gives rise, that calls for their group negation as both the Native and the Nègre/Negro/Nigger Other to the Western bourgeois criterion of being human, Man. It was this "double consciousness" that led to the Copernican challenge made by the Martinican psychiatrist Franz Fanon in his book *Black Skin, White Masks,* to this "understanding." Faced with the regularity of the autophobic and reflexly aversive responses displayed by his black patients to themselves, their physiognomy, together with their equally reflex preference for "whiteness," Fanon proposed that such an "aberration of affect" could not be an individual problem to be dealt with by psychoanalysis. Fanon set in motion the disenchanting of our present understanding and conception of being human.

Even before Fanon, however, the Negritude poet, Aimé Césaire, had not only confronted the reality of this "aberration of affect" as he himself had experienced it, as the condition of attaining to human status in the terms of our present understanding, but had also called into question the imperative of the techno-industrial world task to which this understanding, and the mode of subjectivity which it embodies prescriptively leads. Césaire did this poetically in his 1938 *Notebook of a Return to My Native Land,* as well as theoretically in his 1955 *Discourse on Colonialism,* so that in the stanza of the poem cited as epigraph to this section, for example, what he reveals in these, normally very much misunderstood lines and the sequence that follows,[18] is that Heidegger's (1977) prescriptive world task, to which all mankind is increasingly subordinated, is a task mandated by a single and relative criterion of what it is to be human, made into an Absolute.

Celebrating and revalorizing non-techno-industrial Agrarian civilizations, including centrally, those of Africa, in his poem "Notebook," as civilizations that the West has been able to see only as the negation and lack of its own techno-industrial imperative, Césaire refers to them, ironically, in the very terms of negation/lack through whose prism, contemporary Western scholarship has consistently seen them "those who unveiled neither gunpowder nor compass/who tamed neither steam nor electricity/who explored neither sea nor sky and yet without whom the earth would not be earth." Here, by his use of this series of inversions, Césaire uncovers the very techno-cultural fallacy that the ethnologist, Asmaron Legesse has also analyzed as the fallacy central to the self-conception of Western modernity. For while, as Legesse argues, it is abundantly clear that technologically inferior societies such as those of the Stone Age Australians had sociologically more stable and viable institutions, contemporary scholars, thinking within the framework of the technocultural fallacy as well as of the evolutionary paradigm which underlies our present order of knowledge, remain unable to confront this fact. Because they use technology as their ultimate criterion of human value, they tend to magnify "tenfold those aspects of society that are ... dependent on the technological order," even going so far as to define culture itself as "an assemblage of tools and human patrimony as a tool-making tradition" (Legesse, 1973).

The duality of the challenge that Césaire makes in *Notebook of a Return to my Native Land* is therefore poetically logical. While the poem revolves about his exorcism of the depths of alienation of his own socialized consciousness—one that induces him to be reflexly aversive to his own physiognomic being, as well as to that of his always already stigmatized nègre population group—and as the prelude to his revalorization of his/their human *isness* or Negritude, this thrust which calls into question our present understanding of man's humanity is linked to its complement. That is, to the thrust which calls into question the effects to which this understanding leads. Following up on the series of ironical inversions cited in the epigraph to this section, Césaire in a great cadenced outburst, revalorizes the very agrarian civilzations and their quite different understandings of man's humanity that Western modernity posits as its Other, as the World to its techno-industrial Church. In doing so, Césaire here effects a radical discontinuity with contemporary Western thought, with therefore, the enabling fiction in the terms of whose behaviour-motivational principle of explanation, the one-sided techno-industrial goal of the mastery of nature/mastering of Natural Scarcity, has been made into the single Absolute criterion of being human:

> Heia for the royal kailcedrate!
> Heia for those who have never invented anything
> those who never explored anything
> those who never tamed anything
> those who give themselves up to the essence of all things
> Ignorant of surfaces but struck by the movement of all things
> free of the desire to tame but familiar with the play of the world. (Césaire, 1938)

Humans, Nietzsche (1971) argued, know their reality only through specific modes of world perception that are the condition of our coming to know the world in a stable and consistent manner. These world perceptions and the consciousness to which they give rise are always, however, relative to specific "local cultures" and therefore to Fanon's always already culturally socialized, individual subject. It is only, therefore, because the individual subject is able to forget the fact of his/her being a represented subject, that he/she can "live with some repose, safety and consequence"; since were this individual subject to get out of the prison walls of his/her faith, even for an instant, his/her "self-consciousness would be destroyed at once." As a result, the human subject is enabled to experience himself/herself as a fixed and stable subject only by repressing the relativity both of his/her mode of being and his/her related mode of cognizing; while because it already "costs him some trouble to admit to himself that the insect and the bird perceive a world different from his own," (that, in effect also the Cenù Indians when culturally autocentric, and today's Haitian Vodouisants "perceive a world" that is also different from our now Westernized own), such a subject must, as the condition of its very being, perceive its world perception as the only possible one. Yet it is clear that the question, "which of the two world perceptions" (that of the Westernized subject, that of the Vodouisant, or that of a bird), is more accurate, is quite a senseless one, since to decide this question it would be necessary to apply a (transculturally and transpecies valid) standard of right perception, i.e., to apply a standard which does and can not exist.

The fact that the 16th-century Cenù Indians had been enabled to "hear" the discourse of the Requisition, within the terms of its own quite different world perception and its standard of right perception and, therefore, outside the terms of the world perception of the hybridly politico-religious 16th century variant of the matrix Judaeo-Christian "local culture" of the West, makes possible a parallel recognition with respect to the paradox of today's Haitian / United States crisis. It is from a parallel reoccupation of the place of both Church and State and their respective ethics, by a new reasons-of-the-economy ethic,[19] and therefore from the "prison-walls" of the latter's world perception, that we must now be liberated. A liberation, however, that cannot be effected, either in the terms of Aristide's politicized and creolized Judaeo-Christian theology, nor, indeed, in that of Marx's revolutionary but still culturally Judaeo-Christian counter-ideology, but rather in the new cognitive terms called for in Césaire's *Notebook of a Return to my Native Land,* as well as in Fanon's *Black Skin, White Masks;* terms, on the one hand, of an exorcism, and, on the other of a sociodiagnostics of our present order of consciousness, its "local culture" understanding of man's humanity, and related behavior-motivational schema, or belief-system. Terms that would therefore call for the disenchanting of all belief—from Vodoun, the "root of all belief" to our contemporary Westernized own.

CONCLUSION

Like the Cenù Indians who most fully paid the price for the "mad and drunken" speech of the then first secularizing variant of the Judaeo-Christian culture of 16th-century Europe, no one more pays the price for the now hegemonic speech and the related behaviour motivational-schema of its second purely secularized variant than the peoples of the ex-slave Caribbean islands. No people more so among these than the peoples of the island of Haiti who, mired in poverty, and in an accelerating environmental degradation (Wilenz, 1989), remain caught in the pincers of three belief systems, one neo-agrarian and religious (that of Vodoun), the other also religious and Judaeo-Christian (the official religion of Roman Catholicism), and the third the now totally hegemonic economic-techno-industrial belief system of our present "understanding of man's humanity," the one that increasingly impels us all to attempt to realize it.

> "Islands," wrote Césaire in his "Notebook,"
> that are scars upon water
> islands that are evidence of wounds
> crumbled islands
> islands that are waste paper torn up and strewn
> upon the water
> islands that are broken blades driven into the
> flaming sword of
> the sun. (Césaire, 1938)

The ex-slave islands, the "waste paper existence" of whose peoples have been nakedly verified by United States coast-guard vessels which move to block all attempts on their parts to flee their "condemned of the earth" status, as those who most bear witness to the "hidden costs" of our present variant of the "mad" and "drunken" speech, will be compelled to move now, not just beyond the local dystopia of the by now anachronistic Haitian military elite, but beyond our now global and hegemonic "understanding of man's humanity." The second "true victory" of a new science of the Word can only be possible when we are able to look at the world from the outsider vantage point of the 16th-century Cenù Indians. When that happens, we will recognize that the history of the last 500 years from the Requisition onwards has been a culturally and not an historically determined one. We will understand that our present behavior motivational constructs and their "programming language"—constructs such as "Natural Scarcity," the "Debt Mechanism," and the "cure" of the "world task" as imperatives of Material Redemption through economic growth—are no more "true" outside our present variant culture's "ground" of actuality than the pronouncements of the Requisition could have counted as true outside the "ground" of actuality of the earlier 16th-century form of the Judaeo-Christian culture of the West. In the same way, the Vodoun's anti-social workers of "witchcraft," irate ancestors and offended loas, and the "ethno-medicine" of houngans and mambos[20] were only able to "cure" the afflictions within its Neo-Agrarian culture's mode of actuality; within the "root" of the Vodouisants' belief.

Human beings are magical. Bios and Logos. Words made flesh, muscle and bone animated by hope and desire,[21] belief materialized in deeds, deeds which crystallize our actualities. "It is man who brings society into being" (Fanon, 1967, p.11). And the maps of spring always have to be redrawn again, in undared forms.

ENDNOTES

1. This article is the condensed version of a longer text that will be published at a later date. (Editor's note)
2. See for this Stephen Greenblatt's *Learning to curse: Essays on early modern culture.* New York: Routledge, 1974, pp.26-31.
3. Liberal historians tend to oversee the implications of the fact that in the variant culture of the 16th century, Europeans still thought in terms of just and unjust titles to sovereignty and slavery. See Sylvia Wynter, "New Seville and the Conversion Experience of Bartolome de las Casas," *Jamaica Journal,* 17: 2 and 3, May and August, 1984.
4. I use the term *Noiristes* to refer to the black Haitian bearers of the cultural nationalist discourse which functioned as the legitimating ideology of Duvalierism. Because "race" and "culture" are collapsed into each other in this discourse, the Noiristes were enabled to invert the racial supremacist theories of Europe and of Euroamerica into a counter-racial supremacy theory used to harness the energies of the popular Black majority of Haitians to the interest of this New class's overriding

aim, as members of the educated lower middle class, of displacing and replacing the hegemony of the traditional mulatto bourgeoisie.

The Noiristes, although no less europhone than the latter, given the French system of education, sought to exploit the popular culture of vodoun, selecting out elements which it manipulated and harnessed to its own socio-political goals.

5. In his *The Order of things: An archeology of the human sciences.* New York: Vintage, 1973, Foucault traces the ways in which our present disciplines which were put in place during the 19th century, were, and still are, articulated on the basis of the new "understanding of man's humanity" on the model of a natural organism, (i.e., "Man" as one who lives (biology), labors (economics), and speaks (linguistics). See "Labour, Life, and Language," pp.250-302.
6. See Jacques Derrida, "Cogito and the History of Madness," *Writing and Difference,* where he argues that every system of thought (or logos) can only articulate itself as true through the mediation of the category of that which functions as its Fool. That is, as the category of the mad functioned for the Logos of the Age of Reason, and as Voodoo economics functions for our present hegemonic logos and its order of objective truth.
7. See Wade Davis (1988). *Passage of darkness: the ethnobiology of the Haitian zombie.* Chapel Hill and London: University of North Carolina Press, pp. 244-262. Duvalier was to harness elements of this system to the keeping in place of his dictatorship.
8. See Harold Morowitz'(1991). "Balancing Species Preservation and Economic Considerations," *Science,* 253, AAAS. 16th August, for a discussion of the different modes of "reflexive thought" of the Agrarian and of the Industrial eras.
9. Ibid., p.753
10. In our present system of thought "democracy" is used as a term of commendation, while the fact that it is both a conception specific to a "local culture," that of the West, as well as to its now middle-class variant (rather than aristocratic and/or popular), is overlooked. See for a critique of this "fallacy" D.B. Redford (1992). *Egypt, Canaan and Israel in ancient times.* Princeton, NJ: Princeton University Press, pp. 372-373.
11. See Peter Brown (1982). *The Cult of saints: Its rise and function in Latin Christianity.* Chicago: University of Chicago Press; Hans Blumenburg (1983). *The legitimacy of the modern age.* (R.M. Wallace Trans.). Cambridge: MIT Press.
12. Both the terms *indios* and *negros* were generated from the semantic field of the Judaeo-christian culture of the West. See Sylvia Wynter (1992). *Do not call us negros: How multicultural textbooks perpetuate racism.* San Francisco: Aspire Publications.
13. The encomienda was a forced labor institution where, Spain in reconquering its territory from Islam, had entrusted large numbers of the Spanish Moors to the overlordship of a Spanish-Christian military commander. In the New World variant of this institution, Indian families were "serfs" rather than slaves, and entrusted as a workforce to Spanish settlers in exchange for their ostensible Christianization.

14. See V. Y. Mudimbe (1988). *The Invention of Africa: Gnosis, philosophy* and the Order of Knowledgy. Bloomington: Indiana Univeristy Press; Anthony Pagden (1982). *The Fall of natural man: The American indian and the origins of comparative ethnology.* Cambridge: Cambridge University Press.
15. While politically the U.S. is defined as North America, inclusive of all its peoples, this is not so at the cultural level where the disciplines, specifically of the Humanities define the U.S.A. in Euroamerican (and thereby racial-national) terms. See "Do Not Call Us Negros", (cited in note 11).
16. See Sylvia Wynter (1995). "1492: A New World View," Vera Hyatt, et. al. (Eds.), *Race, discourse, and the origins of the Americas.* Washington: The Smithsonian Institution Press; see also Sylvia Wynter, "Columbus and the Poetics of the Propter Nos," in (Djelal Kadir, Ed.), *Discovering Columbus in Annals of Scholarship,* 8:2, Spring 1991, pp. 251-286.
17. See Jacob Pandian (1995). *Anthropology and the Western tradition: Towards an authentic Anthropology.* Prospect Heights: Waveland Press. The non-Western and laregly non-white peoples colonized by the West were also defined as natives and placed on a racial-cultural scale defined by the West—Indoeuropeans at the top and Africans at the bottom. The two terms natives/niggers or nègres, are therefore part of the same complex of Otherness that is founding to our present "understanding of man's humanity."
18. Wole Soyinka has been the most strident critic of these lines, which as a Western educated writer and thinker, he interprets in the very terms of the "techno-cultural fallacy" of contemporary Western civilization and its understanding of man's humanity, which Césaire was here calling in question. See Soyinka's extended essay (1980) Myth, literature and the African world. Cambridge: Cambridge University Press.
19. Little has been done on the parallel "reasons-of-the-economy" ethic brought in by the new order of discourse from Adam Smith to Malthus to Ricardo. See in this respect Kenneth Lux (1990). *Adam Smith's mistake: How a moral philosopher invented economics and ended morality.* Boston and London: Shambhala.
20. *Mambo* is the term used for the vodun priestess, the female equivalent of the houngan, the male priest.
21. Dave Wagner uses this phrase in an essay on C.L.R. James whom he quotes: "Hegel," he told the Detroit readers, "is going to make a tremendous organization and analysis of thoughts, categories, etc. But he takes time out to say, and we will forget this at our own peril, that categories, the forms of logic, in Desire, Will, etc., are *human feelings and actions* (James' emphasis). History, in other words, is the animation of muscle and bone by hope and desire." See Dave Wagner (1986). "Philosophy and Culture." P. Buhle (Ed.), C.L.R. *James: His life and work.* London, New York.

REFERENCES

Arnold, A.J. (1981). *Modernism and negritude: The poetry and poetics of Aimé Césaire.* Cambridge/London: Harvard University Press.

Baker, L.R. (1987). *Saving belief?: A critique of physicalism.* Princeton: Princeton University Press.

Bauman, Z. (1989). *Modernity and the holocaust.* Ithaca: Cornell University Press.

Binsbergen, W.J.M. (1981). "Religious change and the problem of evil in western Zambia," *Religious Change in Zambia Explanatory Studies.* London: Kegan Paul International.

Bloom, H. (1982). *The breaking of the vessels.* Chicago: University of Chicago Press.

Blumenberg, H. (1983). *The legitimacy of the modern age.* Cambridge: MIT Press.

Brown, P. (1981). *The cult of the saints: Its rise and function in Latin Christianity.* Chicago: The University of Chicago Press.

Césaire, A. Poetry and Knowledge, Trans. A. J. Arnold in *Lyric and Dramatic Poetry,* 1946-82. Trans. by Clayton Eshleman and Annette Smith. Intro. by A. James Arnold. Charlottesville: Caraf Books, The University Press of Virginia.

———. (1956). *Lettre à Maurice Thorez.* 1926, October 24. Paris: Presence Africaine, 3rd Edition.

———. (1969). *Notebook of a return to my native land.* Trans. Anna Bostock and John Berger. Hamondsworth: Penguin Books.

———. (1972). *Discourse on colonialism.* Trans. *Discours sur le colonialisme.* New York: Monthly Review Press.

Chorover, S. (1979). Genesis: Human nature as a social weapon in *From Genesis to Genocide: The Meaning of Human Nature and the Power of Behavior Control.* Cambridge: MIT Press.

Danielli, J.F. (1980). Altruism: The opium of the people. *The Journal of Social and Biological Structures.* 3:2, pp.87-94.

Davis, W. (1988). *Passage of darkness: The ethnobiology of the Haitian Zombie.* Chapel Hill: The University of North Carolina Press.

Derrida, J. (1992). Cogito and the history of madness in *Writing and Difference.* Chicago & London: The University of North Carolina Press.

Desmangles, L. (1992). *The faces of the gods: Vodou and Roman Catholicism in Haiti.* Chapel Hill & London: The University of North Carolina Press.

Edelman, G. (1987). *Neural Darwinism: The Theory of neuronal group Selection.* New York: Basic Books.

Evans-Pritchard, E.E. (1937). *Witchcraft, Oracles and Magic in among the Azande.* Oxford: The Clarendon Press.

Fanon, F. (1967). *Black skins, white masks.* New York: Grove Press.

Fanon, F. (1963). *The Wretched of the earth,* Preface by Jean-Paul Sartre. Trans. Constance Farrington. New York: Grove Press.

Foucault, M. (1973). *The Order of things: An archeology of the human sciences.* New York: Random House.

Funkenstein, A. (1986). *Theology and the scientific imagination: From the middle ages to the seventeenth century.* Princeton: Princeton University Press.

Geertz, C. (1983). *Local knowledge: Further essays in interpretive anthropology.* New York: Basic Books.

Gillespie, M. (1984). *Hegel, Heidegger, and the ground of history.* Chicago: University of Chicago Press.

Girard, R. (1986). *The scapegoat.* Trans. Yvonne Freccero. Baltimore: The Johns Hopkins University Press.

Goldstein. A. (1994). *Addiction: From biology to drug policy.* New York: W.H. Freeman.

Goveia, E. (1972). The Social Framework, *Savacou.* Mona, Kingston Jamaica, pp.2-15.

Grassi, E. (1980). *Rhetoric and Philosophy: The humanist tradition.* University Park: Pennsylvania University Press.

Greenblatt, S. (1970). *Learning to curse.* New York: Routledge.

Gutting, G. (1989). *Michel Foucault's archeology of scientific reason.* Cambridge: Cambridge University Press.

Habermas, J. (1968). *Knowledge and human interests.* Boston: Beacon Press.

Heidegger, M. (1977). *The Question of technology and other essays.* Trans. William Lovitt. New York: Harper and Row.

Isaacs, G. (1983). Aspects of human evolution, *Evolution from Molecules to Men.* D.S. Bendall (Ed.), Cambridge: Cambridge University Press.

Kelves, D. (1988). *In the name of Eugenics: Genetics and the uses of human heredity.* Berkeley & Los Angeles: University of California Press.

Lamming, G. (1953). *In the castle of my skin.* New York: McMillan Publishing Co.

Landau, M. (1991). *Narratives of human evolution.* New Haven and London: Yale University Press.

Legesse, A. (1973). *Gada: Three approaches to the study of African society.* New York: The Free Press.

Lux, K. (1990). *Adam Smith's mistake: How a moral philosopher Invented economics and ended morality.* Boston and London: Shambhala.

Lyotard, J.F. (1984). *The Postmodern Condition: A report on knowledge.* Trans. by G. Bennington and B. Massumi. Foreword by F. Jameson. Minneapolis: University of Minnesota Press.

Maturana, H., Varela, F. (1987). *The biological roots of human understanding.* Boston: New Science Library.

Maturana, H., Varela, F. (1980). *Autopoeisis and cognition: The realization of living.* Preface by Sir Stafford Beer. Dordrecht/London: D. Reidel Publishing Company.

Morison, E. (1957). *A new and fresh English translation of the letter of Columbus, announcing the discovery of America.* Madrid.

Morowitz, H. (1991). Balancing species preservation and economic consideration, *Science,* 253, AAAS.

Mudimbe, V.Y. (1988). *The invention of Africa: Gnosis philosophy and the order of knowledge.* Bloomington: Indiana University Press.

Nietzsche, F. (1971). On truth and falsity in the ultra-moral sense, Trans. A. Muge, *The Existential Tradition.* N. Languilli (Ed.), New York: Doubleday and Co., Anchor Books.

Oxford English Dictionary. 1971. Glasgow and New York: Oxford University Press.

Pagden, A. (1982). *The Fall of natural man: The American Indian and the origin of comparative ethnology.* Cambridge: Cambridge University Press.

Pagels, H. (1988). *The Dream of reason: The computer and the rise of the sciences of complexity.* New York: Simon and Schuster.

Pandian, J. (1985). *Anthropology and the Western tradition: Towards an authentic anthropology.* Prospect Heights: Waveland Press.

Pocock, J.G.A. (1975). The *Machiavellian moment: Florentine political thought and the Atlantic political tradition.* Princeton: Princeton University Press.

———. (1989). *Politics, language, and time: Essays on political thought and history.* Chicago and London: University of Chicago Press.

Polanyi, K. (1957). *The Great transformation: The political and economic origins of our time.* Boston: Beacon Press.

Price Mars, J. (1983). *So spoke uncle.* Trans. Magdaline W. Shannon. Washington: Three Continents Press.

Redford, D. (1992). *Egypt, Canaan, and Israel in ancient times.* Princeton: Princeton University Press.

Ricoeur, P. (1979). Ideology and utopia as Cultural imagination, *Being Human in a Technological Age.* D.M. Borchert, D. Stewart (Eds.), Athens: Ohio University Press.

Riedl, R., Kasper, J. (1984). *Biology of knowledge: The evolutionary basis of reason.* New York: John & Sons.

Rorty, R. (1985). Solidarity or Objectivity, *Post-Analytic Philosophy,* D.M. Borchert, D. Stewart (Eds.), New York: Columbia University Press.

Soyinka, W. (1980). *Myth, literature, and the African world.* Cambridge: Cambridge University Press.

Taussig, M. (1987). *Shamanism, Colonialism, and the wild man.* Chicago: University of Chicago Press.

Valesio, P. (1980). *Nova Antiqua: Rhetorics as a contemporary theory.* Bloomington: Indiana University Press.

Vattimo, G. (1992). Optimistic nihilism, *Symposium: A Revaluation of the Revaluation of All Values in Common Knowledge.* Winter, 1:3.

Wallerstein, I. (1974). *The modern world system: Capitalist agriculture and that of the world economy in the sixteenth century.* London: Academic Press.

Wheeler, S. (1988). Wittgenstein as deconstructor, *New Literary History,* 19:2.

Wilentz, A. (1989). *The rainy season.* New York: Simon and Schuster.

Wynter, S. (1984). New Seville and the conversion experience of Bartolomé de Las Casas, Parts 1 and 2. *Jamaica Journal* 17:2 and 17:3.

———. (1992). Columbus and the poetics of the propter Nos, *Annals of Scholarship: An International Quarterly in the Humanities and Social Sciences,* 8:2, Discovering Columbus, D.Kadir (Ed.). Detroit: Wayne State University Press.

———. (1995). Is 'development' a purely empirical concept? Or also teleological?: A perspective from 'we-the-underdeveloped', *Prosepects for Recovery and Sustainable Development in Africa.* Yansane (Ed.) Westport: Greenwood Press.

———. (1995). 1492: A new world view, *Race, Discourse, and the Origins of the Americans.* V.L. Hyatt et al.(Eds.). Washington: The Smithsonian Press.

A CONFLICT OF THEOLOGICAL INTERPRETATIONS: BAROQUE SCHOLASTICISM VERSUS LIBERATION THEOLOGY

Jean-Louis de Lannoy

In its concern for achieving a greater adaptation of Christian doctrines to the contemporary social conditions of Latin America, liberation theology offers divergent views on many social conceptions inherited from the Baroque scholastic tradition. It also takes its inspiration from some Marxist theories concerning social structures and institutional violence, in order to respond to the new manifestations of poverty and oppression which are appearing in Latin American societies. Although Baroque scholasticism, Marxism and liberation theology agree on notions such as the "the finality of history," the conflicts of interpretation between Christianism and Marxism have compelled the liberation theologians to reformulate some of their basic conceptions.

En adaptant la doctrine chrétienne aux conditions actuelles de la vie en Amérique latine, la théologie de la libération prend le contrepied de nombreuses conceptions sociales, héritées de la tradition scholastique et/ou baroque. Cette nouvelle théologie s'inspire en partie des théories marxistes concernant les structures sociales et la violence institutionnelle, pour répondre aux nouvelles manifestations de pauvreté et d'oppression qui apparaissent dans les sociétés latino-américaines. Bien qu'une convergence existe entre la tradition scholastique baroque, le marxisme et la théologie de la libération au sujet de la "fin de l'Histoire", les conflits d'interprétation entre christianisme et marxisme ont obligé les théologiens de la libération à reformuler certaines de leurs propositions.

THE EMERGENCE OF LIBERATION THEOLOGY has been perceived as a radically new departure in Roman Catholic thought and as a vigourous effort to adjust the Christian message to the particular problems of Latin American society.

From its very beginnings, liberation theology has been associated with a new current in the social sciences: dependency theory.[1] Both liberation theology and dependency theory originated in Latin America; however both claim universal applicability.

Liberation theology seeks to engage Christians in an active commitment in favour of the poor populations of the world. Dependency theories offer a vision of the world divided between a dominant "centre" of capitalist nations and the subordinate "peripheral" nations. In spite of these world perspectives, the Latin American continent remains the focus of both liberation theology and dependency theory.

Liberation theologians offer an interpretation of the Bible based on a "social scientific" analysis of Latin American history and society. They use dependency theories to analyze the causes of poverty in Latin America and to promote charismatic action among Christian communities.

Most of the leading liberation theologians received part of their formal education in Europe (see Cleary, 1985); in this context, they became more sensitive not only to the centralization in Rome of the Church administration but also to the dominance of the European schools of theology over the doctrinal orientation of the Church.

Their starting point is a critical assessment of the theological tradition which, inspired by Rome, predominates in Latin America. They criticize the prevalent theological orientation of Rome as too abstract and susceptible to function as a screen masking the actual involvement of the Catholic Church with the established structures of power and wealth. Their ambition is to formulate a new theology which would provide a concrete foundation for the Christian doctrines in Latin America and which would consequently address the human problems of an impoverished continent.

My suggestion is that the theological tradition which predominates in Latin America is distinct from the theological currents developed in Europe and that this has been overlooked by the liberation theologians. That theological tradition is Spanish baroque scholasticism: it has an ancient foundation in the religious culture of Latin America and is embedded in the major institutions of Latin American societies.

Richard Morse (1954, 1964) has developed an analysis of the Baroque scholastic doctrines and their relevance to the institutional foundations of Spanish America. The doctrines of Francisco de Vitoria, Molina, Suarez and other 16th-century Spanish theologians were taught in the seminaries and universities of the Spanish colonies from the very beginning and comprised the basic intellectual nourishment of the religious and political elites of the Spanish empire. Morse claims that they provided the foundations for "a deep-lying matrix of thought and attitude" (1964, p.153) which can still be observed today.

Morse pays particular attention to the neo-Thomist doctrines of Francisco Suarez (1548-1617), as they "encapsulated certain assumptions about political man and certain political dilemmas that pervade Hispanic political life to this day" (1964, p.154). Generally speaking, Spanish neo-Thomism presented a theoretical formulation of the ideals of the Spanish state and of its overseas empire.

Thomist socio-political doctrines rested on two central principles which Ernst Troeltsch (1960) identifies as organicism and patriarchalism. The first principle applies to the structuring of society: the social system constitutes an organic unity; its various components participate in the life of the social whole by fulfilling their respective functions. These functions are of unequal importance for the life of the social organism. "Out of the organic idea ... follows only the division of labour and service in general, and something which ... is rational, necessary, and harmonious" (Troeltsch, 1960, p.286). However, in addition to these "functional" inequalities, there are some which, resulting from accidents of nature, of personal destiny and of the arbitrariness of social life, cannot be explained in rational terms but "can only be held to proceed from the inscrutable will of God" (p.286). Accordingly, society is a hierarchical system in which each group or even individual person serves a purpose which derives from the *Corpus mysticum* of the Church and not from changing definitions of purpose according to historical circumstances. Corresponding to that social hierarchy is a scale of social inequalities which has to be accepted as inherent in society. The possible tensions and conflicts resulting from the structure of social inequality are dealt with in light of the second principle of the Thomist socio-political doctrines: what Troeltsch calls "patriarchalism."

The model of all social relationships is the family in which the authority of the *pater familias* must receive the willing subordination of the members of the family. "The sociological ideal of the Family as the original ideal of human relationships is applied to all the conditions of rule and subordination in general" (Troeltsch, 1960, p.287). The harmonious operation of the social organism depends upon the acquiescence of each person in his or her status position with its attendant rights and obligations. Such acquiescence is contingent upon the acceptance by all groups and people of the supreme authority of the sovereign.

In defining the role of the monarch, the Spanish neo-Thomists introduced various elements which inspired and justified the centralization of power in the Spanish crown. Thus in accepting the paternalistic authority in the king, the subjects to do not delegate, but totally renounce their autonomy in favour of their prince. The king's major role is to secure the reign of Christian justice in a hierarchical and compartmentalized society. In the administration of justice, the king's adjudication of particular cases of conflict is more important than the law itself, because the law can deal only with general concerns, but it might not apply or be opportune for specific situations (Morse, 1964).

Those are the doctrines which inspired and informed the legal and political apparatus of the Spanish empire. Their influence was bolstered by the close association of Church and State as well as by the exclusion of any external ideological influence in the Spanish empire.

The regime of *Real Patronato de las Indias* effectively transformed the Church into an agency of the Spanish crown and consolidated the absolute power of the king by providing it with a religious justification. No challenge to the authority of the crown was tolerated. If abuses or injustices occurred, they were supposed to be the effects of the incompetence, or the sinful, criminal actions, of the subordinates.

In return for its collaboration, the Church received from the crown total protection and exclusive control over the religious interests of the "colonies." This regime is at the root of the close identity between the interests of the established church and those of the political and social elites in Latin American societies.

Even after the independence, and in spite of many proclamations by the liberal political leaders, the constitutions of the new Spanish American states retained this non-democratic and moralistic imprint almost intact. Dealy (1968) shows how, for the Spanish American constitutionalists, politics were the achievement of the "common good" in the tradition of Aquinas and not the satisfaction of interests as Locke would have it. Consequently for them "only the morally good man could be a good citizen" and "good government depended upon the recruitment of good men" (Dealy, 1968, p.44). A great number of those constitutions established Catholicism as the state religion, prohibited the free exercise of any other religious cult and seriously abridged, if not altogether abolished, freedom of speech, of the press, and of assembly. Many constitutions provided that children should be taught the fundamentals of the Catholic religion in the schools. The Mexican constitution of 1814 provides that the quality of citizenship is lost "for crimes of heresy, apostasy and *lesa-nacion* (high reason)." A Colombian constitution of 1815 proclaims that there can be no liberty without morality, nor morality without religion (Dealy, 1968, p.48).

The contemporary Latin American constitutions manifest in general an impressive continuity of thought with those of the early 19th century; the same non-democratic, non-liberal vision inspires them. There is no conception of inalienable rights of citizens. "Instead rights in Spanish America are constitutionally qualified and relative.... Necessity of State is a recognized doctrine" (Dealy, 1968, p.52). Individual rights are limited by the requirements of public and social order; Congress is the body which in most cases will define these relative rights in practice. Thus, concludes Dealy, "there is nothing in the way of rights or privileges that may not be constitutionally abridged by passage of a law" (1968, p.53), whereas in the United States, for example, the way the rights of religion, speech and press are safeguarded is by prohibiting Congress from making rules in the area of these rights. Furthermore, many Latin American constitutions grant the President the right to set aside the basic civil rights "for the safeguard of public order" (or for "reason of state"). This is of course the safest way to quash the right of political opposition.

The primacy given in the neo-Thomist doctrines to the body politic over the individual member of society finds its echo in the priority of the "reason of state" embedded in the modern Latin American constitutions, and there is an obvious continuity between the role attributed to the supreme magistrate by these constitutions and the conception of the patriarchal ruler in the baroque scholastic tradition.

Can we observe the same continuity in thought and practice with regard to the Latin American Church?

With the collapse of the Spanish empire, the Church was relieved from the state control imposed by the *Real Patronato.* However, in many cases, it also lost the protection of the State and had to face the anticlerical policies of many "liberal" governments. How did the Church adjust to this new situation?

Although there existed a variety of attitudes toward the new political authorities, ranging from total support to open confrontation, the general orientation of the Catholic authorities toward the governments of the new republics consisted in claiming their total independence from them while at the same time demanding support in the interests of the Church.

The principle of organicism assumes the unity of human society in which the Church is recognized as the soul of the whole organism and its integrity is guaranteed. Whenever that principle was challenged by anticlerical policies, the Church found itself justified in resisting the government. As Troeltsch puts it: "The Church ... is justified in her struggle against godless and insubordinate State authorities, and is therefore justified in revolution" (1960, p.289). In so doing, it is defending the integrity of the Christian social organism.

Thus, during more than a century and a half after independence, the Church in Latin America maintained an attitude of reaction against political and social innovations. Its reactionary attitude was even more total than in the various organizations of the Catholic Church in Europe because the Latin American Church was operating within a context of greater tension between political innovation and a stagnant social and cultural environment. In Europe, impressive efforts of renovation in theological thinking persisted despite the condemnation of the so-called "modernism" by Rome; significant innovation was demonstrated in politics by various forms of liberal Catholicism and later by Catholic action movements. Only feeble echoes of these efforts of Catholic renovation reached Latin America where the clerical structures remained stagnant and the Spanish neo-scholastic doctrines remained dominant.

As the industrial revolution was late in reaching the Latin American continent and remained circumscribed to limited areas, an industrial working class did not appear as a significant component of society for a long time. The Church was thus not prepared to adjust to the sudden growth of an industrial proletariat that came to Latin America in the middle of the 20th century; neither did it understand the new character of poverty brought about by the industrialization process. Until the 1960s, the Church continued to preach acceptance by the poor of their "inferior social status" and to regard their miserable social conditions of life as a sign of God's will. In the line of the patriarchal principle, the Church dealt with poverty by giving alms and providing traditional "charities." However, in this domain, it was losing its traditional monopoly and facing competition on the part of state agencies, first in the field of education, then in the domains of health and welfare services. Furthermore, Protestant and other non-governmental organizations started to penetrate the lower classes of the continent in new fields of social action where the Catholic Church was not prepared to become involved. It is with this more dynamic approach to popular needs and interests that the secular sectors in competition with the Church demonstrated the inadequacy of the traditional Catholic view of the world and mode of operation.

An effort to break down the increasing isolation of the Church from the modern world came in the 1960s with the Second Council of Vatican and the development of liberation theology in Latin America.

Before the Second World War, Pope Pius XI had complained that the loss of the working classes to the Church was the greatest scandal of the 19th century. He was referring to the masses of workers who populated the industrial centres of Europe. Now that the industrialization process was spreading to Latin America, the Church authorities were afraid that a similar loss of the working masses would occur in the Latin American countries. Rural-urban migrations were taking place suddenly and on a large scale; new forms of mass poverty were appearing in the shanty towns around the large cities of the continent. At the same time, new modes of exploitation, of oppression, and of violence were affecting the Latin American populations. Those dramatic changes forced the Latin American Church authorities to recognize the inadequacy of the traditional Catholic doctrines for explaining the new conditions and for coping with them. In this same movement of recognition, they were forced to admit how strongly the material conditions of existence could affect the quality of spiritual life. What sense was there in the neo-scholastic doctrines of poverty when one is confronted with the abject conditions of life in the large shanty towns?

Scholastic organicism represents society as made up of various groups united in the pursuit of the common good under the guidance of the Church. This implies a certain amount of consideration on the part of the groups toward each other. It was somewhat relevant for the traditional forms of social relations in the "estate societies" of pre-modern Latin America.[2] The poor classes were considered as occupying a rightful position at the bottom of the social hierarchy with a dignity of their own. It was the Christian duty of the wealthy to assist the poor because "a position of privilege" became "an opportunity for service" (Troeltsch, 1960, p.288).

The very idea of the dignity of the poor was radically undermined in the context of the shanty towns. For a large population deprived of the most basic necessities of life and living at the margin of public order and morality, the concepts of social order, virtues and sin are hardly significant. The Catholic missionaries who went to live among those poor found the source of "spiritual evil" or sin in the evil conditions of material life and in "sinful social structures." To do otherwise would have amounted to blaming the victims of abject poverty and social chaos for their suffering.[3]

Those perspectives are at the root of "liberation theology." In reaction to the neo-Thomist view of an organic society, this new theological approach calls upon the social sciences for analyzing society. It replaced the concepts of scholastic social philosophy with the sociological concepts and theories elaborated for the analysis of social classes, social conflicts and social dynamism. In the 1960s and 1970s, when liberation theologians started to formulate their first propositions, the Marxist theories and various forms of dependency theories were very much in favour in the departments of social sciences of the Latin American universities. These theories rest on the basic assumption of conflict relationships between social classes and between groups of nations in contrast to the ideal of social unity and harmony postulated by the scholastic organic model. Marx does not envision societies as integrated wholes but as the locus of class conflicts; for him, social life rests not on a unity of purpose but on the opposition of class interests. Marx sees in the ruling classes the agents of oppression who must be destroyed as enemies of mankind's progress. If Marx takes the side of the poor classes, it is not because of their poverty but because, and only if, they represent the future of liberated mankind.

While the liberation theologians want to use the Marxist analysis of class conflict as an explanation for the cause of poverty affecting a large section of the Latin American societies, they find themselves unable to integrate in the Christian message of universal love the views of Marx on the destruction of class enemies. During the second meeting of the Council of Latin American Bishops (CELAM), which took place in Medellin in 1968, liberation theologians were very influential in the passing of the motion of "preferential option for the poor." The "traditionalist" members of the CELAM meeting accepted this motion in the light of the organic doctrine which considers the poor as the bearers of Jesus' love and the agents of God for the exercise of the virtue of charity. The liberation theologians, on their part, wanted to "activate" the poor to become the agents of their own spiritual and material liberation, as they could not conceive one without the other. This was leading many of the liberation theologians toward an interpretation of the "preferential option" in terms of class consciousness and class organization and, in the logic of Marxist analysis, of class conflict: to liberate the poor from their spiritual and material misery, one has to help them towards their organization as a class fighting against the rich.[4]

In view of these developments, the Vatican authorities decided to replace the term "preferential option" with the term "preferential love for the poor" (Marle, 1968, p.533). This marked the insistence of the official Church doctrine on the concept of universal Christian love and the rejection of a conflict conception of society. This left the liberation theologians without the support of the highest Church authorities for whom Christianity does not exclude any particular group or class from the spiritual "liberation." But neither could the liberation theologians count on the support of the Marxists for whom the poor are not *ipso facto* the agents of their liberation.

With regard to the issue of oppression, the liberationists met similar conflicts of theological interpretation. We have seen that the organic idea contains an active, critical element which might justify resistance to oppression, even going up to active rebellion. The scholastic doctrines recognize the right of rebellion as a right of the Christian conscience for the sake of organic harmony: oppressive rulers must amend their ways or else be overthrown; unjust institutions offend the law of God and must be altered or destroyed. The only reserve which scholasticism imposes is that rebellion can be exercised only if it does not cause still greater general disorder. Of course, this restriction is almost impossible to assess in any actual conflict situation.

The centuries of colonial regime in Latin America were relatively free of active violence after the first period of conquest. In such a context, the doctrine of social harmony seemed justified, at least as a model for the New World. It is only during the last decennials of the Bourbon regime that sizeable armies were constituted in the Spanish empire. By contrast, the century and a half after the end of the Spanish rule witnessed long and frequent periods of violence and oppression.

However, since the 1960s, new types of violence and oppression have appeared in Latin America: the systematic practice of terror by governments and by terrorist groups has enhanced the depersonalization of violence. At the same time, the forms of oppression by governments, by economic entrepreneurs or by criminal agents have become more pervasive because of the greater complexity and efficiency of modern organization.

New instruments of analysis are needed for identifying these new forms of oppression. Liberation theologians have borrowed the neo-Marxist concept of "institutional violence." Violence and oppression are no longer strictly political or military issues because they are embedded in the very social fabric of Latin American society. This view leads the liberation theologians toward a generalized revolutionary stance which includes a challenge to the upper hierarchy of the Latin American church. They denounce the active or passive collusion between the upper clergy and the social, the economic and often the political elites of Latin America. Some of these accusations had already been accepted by some members of the church hierarchy. Following the meetings of Medellin (1968) and Puebla (1979), the church authorities embarked on a change of policies in their relations with the wealthy classes and the power elites. Nevertheless, centuries of collusion with those elites have left deep foundations for the exploitation of the poor.

In their sense of urgency for change, several liberationists have advocated the building up of a "church of the poor" for pursuing the combined spiritual and material liberation of the poor and oppressed.[5] Besides the difficulty of defining the practical limits of a class of "poor and oppressed" in a continent where poverty and oppression is pervasive, such a project constitutes a direct challenge to the long established principle of unity of the Catholic Church inspired by the aim of salvation for all the Christians. In the scholastic doctrine, the Church takes its place at the apex of the organic structure of human society and within it all differences of rank (which are, in the secular society, strongly emphasized) vanish in the vision of the ultimate Christian destination.

There is an important point of convergence between scholastic doctrines, liberation theology and Marxism. In all three cases, the ultimate vision is that of reconciliation of conflicting forces and complete harmony.

In the scholastic tradition, the Church is an eternal institution. On this earth, it is called the Church Militant, in which this divine institution has to accept the imperfections of human existence, including social inequality. The sense of injustice felt by the poor should be alleviated by the solidarity of Christian love and the performance of their duty by the privileged groups. At the "end of time," the Church will become the Church Triumphant in which the quality of all human beings as children of God will be achieved. To paraphrase Troeltsch (1960, p.288), the necessity of a patriarchal charity only arises out of the conditions of sinful humanity and it is the task of the Church Militant to secure its accomplishment. In the Church Triumphant, the organic principles of harmony and integration will be supreme.

For Marxism, the socialist society will be reached by the end of the class struggle with the ultimate triumph of the universal proletariat. It will signal the liberation from any alienation and the assumption by the whole mankind of its full humanity.

Liberation theology was taken, during its first period of development (in the 1960s and 1970s), by an infatuation with the hope of a "socialist revolution" for the complete material and spiritual "liberation" of the poor. This utopian vision combined the dream of complete freedom and social equality promised by Marxism with the vision of spiritual salvation pursued by the Christian Church.

In their later writings, the liberation theologians have more moderate expectations.[6] In their desire to use the rational instruments of social science to bring down to earth and up to the modern times the social doctrine of the Catholic Church, they came to recognise the validity of the old scholastic principle of "proportionality," an assessment of the moral and spiritual costs and benefits in their programmes of action. Their doctrinal and missionary programmes are now heavier than ever.

ENDNOTES

1. Cleary (1985, p.75) points out that Gustavo Gutierrez, the man who coined the term "theology of liberation," started its theological system with a critique of (economic) development as an idea which, promoted by non-Latin Americans, was clearly bankrupt in Latin America. What the continent needed was not development but liberation. In his own words, Gutierrez asserts that "dependence and liberation are correlative terms (1973, p.81)." For a systematic analysis of the relations between liberation theology and dependency theory, see Garrett (1988) and McGovern (1989).
2. The term "estate society" refers to a social structure made up of a variety of "privileged" groups; i.e., groups having particular (or private) jurisdictions. Within the corporate State apparatus of the Spanish American empire, broad groups (*Peninsulares, criollos,* ecclesiastics, Indians, etc.) were defined as subjected to particular jurisdictions. More specific privileges were also attached to smaller corporate groups: members of the Inquisition, members of the armed forces, university students, merchants and craftsmen, etc. What inspired this complex legislation and its implementation was the patriarchal spirit which pervaded the Laws of the Indies. (See Morse, 1954; Morse, 1964; and Haring, 1963).

3. The relationship between spiritual life, material well-being, education and political responsibility is discussed in Levi (1989), particularly in chapter 5, *The Liberation Theologians and the Causes of Poverty.*
4. This perspective has been elaborated within what Hewitt (1989) calls the "grass-roots approach" (in opposition to the "institutional approach") to the conception of "preferential option for the poor." Hewitt's study convincingly exposes the deficiencies of the grassroots model.
5. The new emphasis on the poor, initiated by the theology of liberation and assumed by the Church hierarchy reveals one of the most drastic differences between the scholastic tradition (for which poverty has to be accepted both as an expression of God's will and as a source of spiritual elevation) and the theology of liberation which defines poverty as the result of man-made social action. On this point, see Stewart-Gambino (1987).
6. A good summary of the recent evolution of liberation theology can be found in Sigmund 1990, chapter 10, *After Twenty Years: Liberation Theology Today* (pp.176-178).

REFERENCES

Cleary, E.L. (1985). *Crisis and change: The Church in Latin America today.* Maryknoll, NY: Orbis Books.

Dealy, G. (1968). Prolegomena on the Spanish American political tradition. *Hispanic American Historical Review* 48(1), pp.37-58.

Garrett, W.R. (1988). Liberation theology and dependency theory. In R. Rubenstein & J. Roth (Eds.), *The political significance of Latin American liberation theology* (pp.174-198). Washington, DC: Washington Institute Press.

Gutierrez, G. (1973). *A theology of liberation: history, politics, and salvation* (Sister Caridad Inda & J. Eagleson, Trans.). Maryknoll, NY: Orbis Books. (Original work published 1968).

Haring, C.H. (1963). *The Spanish empire in America.* New York: Harcourt, Brace & World.

Hewitt, W.E. (1989). Origins and aspects of the option for the poor in Brazilian Catholicism. *Journal for the Scientific Study of Religion,* 28(2), pp.120-135.

Levi, W. (1989). *From alms to liberation. The Catholic Church, the theologians, poverty and politics.* New York: Praeger.

Marle, R. (1986). La théologie de la libération réhabilitée? *Etudes,* 365(5), pp.521-536.

McGovern, A.F. (1989). Dependency theory, Marxist analysis, and liberation theology. In M.H. Ellis & O. Maduro (Eds.), *The future of liberation theology. Essays in honor of Gustavo Gutierrez* (pp.272-286). Maryknoll, NY: Orbis Books.

Morse, R. (1954). Toward a theory of Spanish American government. *Journal of the History of Ideas,* 15(1), pp.71-93.

———. (1964). The heritage of Latin America. In L. Hartz (Ed.), *The Founding of New Societies* (pp.123-177). New York: Harcourt, Brace & World.

Sigmund, P.E. (1990). *Liberation theology at the cross road. Democracy or revolution?* New York: Oxford University Press.

Steward-Gambino, H. (1987). The evolving role of the Latin American Catholic Church. *Latin American and Caribbean Contemporary Record,* 6, pp.A100-A117.

Troeltsch, E. (1960). *The social teaching of the Christian Churches* (Vol.1) O.Wyon, Trans. New York: Harper Torchbooks. (Original work published 1911).

TELL OUT KING RASTA DOCTRINE AROUND THE WHOLE WORLD: RASTAFARI IN GLOBAL PERSPECTIVE

Carole D. Yawney

This paper discusses the implications for the Rastafari movement, of its spread worldwide in the last two decades. It suggests that further opportunities for Rastafari mobilization, which began in Jamaica in the early 1930s, exist outside the Caribbean, especially in North America and United Kingdom. On the other hand, Rastafari communities abroad have to deal with pressures such as racism, criminalization, and commodification in more intense ways than in the Caribbean. The author argues that all these factors influence the shape that Rastafari takes outside the Caribbean, as well as at its point of origin. It suggests that the impact of this development is most noticeable in the role that orthodox Rastafari culture (Nyahbinghi) plays as well as the position that Rastafari women hold.

Cet article examine la mondialisation récente du mouvement Rastafari, créé en Jamaïque dans les années 1930. Toutefois, les nouvelles communautés Rasta implantées surtout en Amérique du Nord et en Grande Bretagne, doivent affronter le racisme, la criminalité et la commodification d'une manière beaucoup plus intense que les communautés vivant dans la Caraïbe. L'auteur, tout en expliquant que ces sources de conflit ont une influence importante sur l'orientation du mouvement à l'extérieur de la Caraïbe aussi bien qu'en Jamaique, montre que l'impact de cette évolution récente se fait sentir surtout dans les rôles joués par la culture orthodoxe Rastafari (Nyahbinghi) et par les femmes.

THE TITLE OF THIS PAPER is borrowed from a traditional Rastafari chant which exhorts Rastafari to get their Bible, read it with overstanding, and then tell out King Rastafari doctrine around the whole world.[1] Since its genesis in Jamaica in the early 1930s Rastafari has managed to export its culture of resistance around the globe.[2]

This is a rather remarkable achievement for a theocratically oriented religious movement, generally lacking institutional support and centralized forms of organization, which could make proselytization easier.[3] In addition, in most societies where it has manifested, Rastafari has been under siege by the State, by the media, by the dominant culture. Despite all this, and through overcoming its own internal contradictions and sectarian politics, Rastafari continues to be a vibrant and dynamic force for social change, maintaining its potential to confront the dominant society in many ways.

Although caution should be exercised when generalizing about Rastafari, a few observations can be made about it as it has developed in the Jamaican context. Rastafari themselves date their genesis to 1930, the year Ras Tafari was crowned Emperor Haile Selassie I of Ethiopia. While the Bible, in particular the Hebrew Testament and Revelations, is a key text for Rastafari, their orientation is profoundly Afrocentric. The collective repatriation of black people to Africa, to Ethiopia in particular, is a major goal.

This paper addreses some of the implications of the globalization of Rastafari, both for the movement itself, and for the communities in which it has made an impact. I am using the concept of "globalization" here in a counter-hegemonic sense to refer to the world-wide spread of Rastafari.[4] A major issue arises: to what extent has Rastafari the capacity for developing a universal cultural appeal beyond the confines of its local, Caribbean-based, specifically Jamaican, Afrocentric orientation, without fundamentally altering its premises? Moreover, what kinds of contradictions or dynamic tensions (in the sense of creative challenges) does the process of globalization generate within Rastafari?

On the one hand, while many Rastafari claim that theirs is a universal religion for all peoples, some, on the other hand, want to protect it as a predominantly black heritage. The increasing global dissemination of Rastafari, partly through reggae music and active travel, mainly by elders and brethren, has brought this question into sharper focus. In other words, is Rastafari a liberation theology and culture of resistance relevant only to Caribbean people of African descent, or other black folk in the diaspora, or can it be adopted by other people without being appropriated by them?

This dilemma appears to parallel the experience of the First Nations peoples of the Americas. On the one hand, many First Nations elders have taught that their traditional attitudes and practices, particularly regarding "Mother Earth," hold the solution to the current environmental crisis in the West. On the other hand, there is considerable ambivalence about non-Native people taking the Teachings, professing to walk the Way, and in particular, becoming teachers themselves. The globalization of Rastafari raises similar issues—we need to determine precisely what are the specific aspects of Rastafari that form the basis of its resonance where it has gained a footing beyond the black community.

Moreover, now that far more Rastafari are physically present in other states of Africa, in addition to Ethiopia where some have been settled since the 1960s, we need to examine this particular cultural exchange. Although this is not the repatriation on the political scale envisioned by Rastafari, it still constitutes a significant dynamic. While the message of Rastafari was initially spread via the electronic and performance mode of reggae, the implications of more sustained contact between Rastafari and the citizens of various African states such as Ghana, Nigeria, Senegal, Tanzania, Zimbawe, Kenya, and South Africa, needs to be explored. What shape does Rastafari take in new and different contexts? And, what is the feedback effect upon various Rastafari communities in the Caribbean and the North?

In this paper I hope to show that since the early 1980s, with Rastafari communities in the diaspora reaching a kind of critical density, there have been a series of international events which have served to focus and precipitate a self-conscious development within Rastafari, not only to resist ongoing attempts to repress it and other black cultural expressions, but also to actively seek to raise its creative and critical profile. This has both accelerated the pace of international networking and consolidation among Rastafari, and attracted much more positive public attention.

While particular circumstances and an availability of certain kinds of resources have made it possible for the Rastafari communities to take on challenges in the United Kingdom, Canada, and the United States not easily met in the Caribbean context, where Rastafari has been conditioned by a longer history of containment and repression, developments among Rastafari communities in the diaspora of the North have also had a feedback effect on Caribbean-based Rastafari communities.

In this paper I review some of these developments to show how some longheld attitudes and practices have been reinforced at the same time that Rastafari have engaged in new initiatives as part of this globalization process. For example, since the early 1980s several international conferences and cultural events have been held mostly outside the Caribbean, a setting more conducive to examining certain issues within Rastafari than is possible in the more conservative context of the Caribbean, particularly in Jamaica. Here I refer specifically, among other things, to the role of Rastafari women, not only as partners and mothers, but also as artists and organizers, in a movement which traditionally has had male leadership.

John Homiak, a Washington-based anthropologist and long-term researcher of Rastafari, who has also played a role in facilitating some of these international Rastafari cultural exchanges, has argued that this process seems to have highlighted certain contradictory tendencies within Rastafari. such as the tension between egalitarianism and hierarchy (Homiak, forthcoming "b," pp.15-18). Homiak's research in this focusses mainly on the challenges to the concept of leadership or "Eldership" within Rastafari that globalization entails (Homiak, forthcoming "b").

With regard to reinforcing traditional patterns, the process of globalization seems also to have strengthened the foundation of the House of Nyahbinghi, which reprsents the most disciplined and orthodox expression of Rastafari.[5] Homiak has suggested that we are indeed witnessing "something of a revival of Nyahbinghi traditions in Jamaica" (Homiak, forthcoming "b," p.19). There has, in fact, been a conscious effort by Nyahbinghi elders, since the mid-1980s, to travel outside Jamaica to promote this tradition, the result of what many Rastafari regard as the weakening or undermining of Rastafari orthodoxy by the reliance on reggae music as the sole source of Rastafari teachings and "livity," the Rastafari concept for way of life. There has also been a countervaling movement by Rastafari raised in the diaspora who make, in effect, what could be considered pilgrimages to Jamaica to study with seasoned elders and to experience Nyahbinghi livity first hand.[6]

Rastafari communities under siege abroad, where they have to deal with additional forms of oppression, such as institutionalized racism around education issues, immigration practices, the criminal justice system, and so on, may rely increasingly on the more orthodox forms of livity for religious and cultural protection.[7] Rastafari in the diasporas of Birmingham, London, Washington, Philadelphia, New York, and Toronto cannot afford to be casual about their identity when the dominant society seems intent on criminalizing, racializing, commodifying, romanticizing, or trivializing them. These tend to be the primary mechanisms of social control practised upon Rastafari.

The Rastafari response to its globalization is significant then for a number of reasons. It may help to shed further light on the process of how culture changes and adapts to evolving circumstances. As localized as Rastafari was in Jamaica for a number of decades, it was never isolated from the international arena. In fact, if we adopt the perspective that Jamaica itself was never a marginalized hinterland, but rather that it constituted historically an integral part of a much larger picture, then we can partly understand why one of its major exports is its culture. Reggae and Rastafari, for example, resonate globally because they somehow have a universal pulse.

RASTAFARI AS A TRAVELLING CULTURE

My approach in this paper is informed by James Clifford's discussion of the implications for "postmodern" ethnography, in which the cultural informant moves in a far wider field than the anthropologist typically expects (Clifford, 1992). In his article on "Traveling Cultures," Clifford argues that:

> In much traditional ethnography ... the ethnographer has localized what is actually a regional/national/global nexus, relegating to the margins a "culture's" external relations and displacements. This is now increasingly questioned ... Anthropological "culture" is not what it used to be. And once the representational challenge is seen to be the portrayal and understanding of local/global encounters, co-productions, dominations, and resistances, then one needs to focus on hybrid, cosmopolitan experiences as much as on rooted, native ones. (Clifford, 1992, pp.100-101)

Clifford goes to on suggest, after George Marcus and Michael Fisher, that "innovative forms of multi-locale ethnography may be necessary to do justice to transnational political, economic, and cultural forces that traverse and constitute local or regional worlds" (Clifford, 1992, p.102). As ethnographers, this would imply giving up a rigid sense of polarized notions of Rastafari centre and margins—the notion of a baseline orthodoxy in relation to "versions of"—and recognizing the legitimacy of evolving diasporic expressions. However, we also need to pay attention to how Rastafari themselves define the question of cultural authenticity, particularly in light of globalization. Where I prefer to proceed with this discussion with reference to the local and global dialectic, John Homiak has analyzed the same problem in terms of "yard" and "nation"' for the reason that both concepts are themselves used by Rastafari (Homiak, forthcoming "b," p.1).

Marlene Warner-Lewis's approach to African continuities in Rastafari may be helpful in resolving this dilemma of "pure" versus altered cultural forms. She suggests that we think in terms of how:

> At any one period of time, a description of a culture—even a participant understanding of it—will emphasize its major characteristics. But there are always exceptions to rules, deviations, minor tendencies; these are modes which at that point in time are less popular or even suppressed for some social, aesthetic or political reason. But at another point in time, a sub-dominant or residual tendency may assume greater importance and visibility than it previously had. At any period of its evolution, therefore, the cultural history of the group is characterized by variations in the dominance versus marginality of any one of its multiple facets. This variability carries a spacial dimension as well. (Warner-Lewis, 1993, p.109)

From this perspective we could regard Rastafari, both throughout its history and in its contemporary form, as a vast reservoir of interrelated themes and ideas, which vary in the way Warner-Lewis supposes.

The formative history of Rastafari in fact demonstrates that a number of cultural themes were strategically and creatively woven together in response to both local and global events. The influence of Garveyism, Ethiopianism, Hindu culture, Biblical fundamentalism, African beliefs and practices, and Jamaican peasant culture, including Revival, have been discussed elsewhere at some length (Chevannes, 1978; Homiak, 1985; Mansingh and Mansingh, 1985; Post, 1970; Warner-Lewis, 1993). In addition, Rastafari elders and leaders have always been communicators and travellers. In fact, Caribbean peoples have always travelled, mostly as workers rather than as tourists, but this has contributed nevertheless to the possibility of developing enriched syncretic cultural forms. With reference to Rastafari, a variety of orientations which give priority to one or another combination of these themes has always existed within the movement.[8]

We need to address the social as well as the ideological heterogeneity of Rastafari. There have always been various social formations in Rastafari, ranging from loosely knit collectives, to those with official names and a more formal social and ritual calendar, to some that are quite well organized along more hierarchical and bureaucratic lines. Many Rastafari may also be associated with the Ethiopian World Federation or the Ethiopian

Orthodox Church. And individual Rastafari may well involve themselves with more than one group.

While sectarian rivalries may develop between various interests, this diversity could be regarded as a cultural resource. Here I am suggesting that, depending upon the "works" (the Rastafari term for one's cultural/ spiritual mission) which Rastafari might take up, the movement can avail itself of the appropriate format from this "pool." I hope to demonstrate the range of activities into which Rastafari have been thrust since the early 1980s as a result of globalization. It can then be argued that both ideological and social diversity can be used as strengths rather than liabilities.

For academic students of Rastafari several methodological considerations also arise as a result of this heterogeneity. Globalization simply brings them more into focus. Methodologically the prudent course is to locate oneself as a researcher vis-à-vis the movement, and to be specific about one's sources of data. Ethnographers can have widely varying experiences, which affect their perception of Rastafari and the way in which they portray it sociologically. It was contentious enough to try to grasp the range of Rastafari when it was localized in Jamaica, but as it spread into the Caribbean and beyond, it has simply become impossible for any one researcher to keep in touch with all its versions.

Over the years Rastafari has been described in different ways: millenarian movement, culture of resistance, religion, way of life, youth culture, and so on. Following Warner-Lewis's logic, all these perspectives have probably been relevant at one time or another, or indeed, at any one time. However, in terms of contemporary Rastafari there are many local adaptations. For example, we find militant Maori Rastafari in New Zealand and dreadlocks-inspired Rastafari in Japan (McDonald, 1982; Keita, 1991). Horace Campbell reviews manifestations of Rastafari in the Caribbean, the United Kingdom, Canada, and some states of Africa (Campbell, 1987). Terisa Turner has reported on the popularity of Rastafari in East Africa, particularly in Kenya, with an emphasis on the role of Rastafari women there (Turner, 1992). More recently, in an extensive survey of literature on Rastafari, Frank Jan van Dijk has documented reports on the Rastafari influence in Surinam and The Netherlands, as well as the societies noted above (Van Dijk, 1993). Clearly, given the range of Rastafari expression, and the different contextual circumstances to which Rastafari need to adapt, as researchers we cannot presume any one interpretive framework.

Second, globalization increases the difficulty of defining a research community and orienting oneself to the movement. From the beginning Rastafari have been extremely distrustful of outsiders, particularly researchers, whom they consign to the most disparaging category of "pharisees and scribes." Rastafari have both ritual and political strategies for "testing" and "controlling" researchers. This is easily understandable given their history of oppression by the dominant society, which is intensified in racist and reactionary states outside the Caribbean. Rastafari also follow very closely accounts of themselves written by others, and do not hesitate to give critical feedback.[9] Negotiating a long-term research role can be stressful. Most written work on Rastafari is not based on extensive field work at all, a pattern also noted by Van Dijk (1993, p.4). The distancing that results can lead to a very partial take on the Rastafari whole.

Therefore, in addition to critically interrogating the location of the researcher, we also need to use a wide range of materials to develop a more comprehensive perspective on Rastafari. In addition to fieldwork and personally connecting, this would include the abundance of papers, reports, newsletters, pamphlets, and books published from the inside by Rastafari themselves in the Caribbean, the United Kingdom, the United States, and Canada. Many of these sources unfortunately have a limited and local distribution. However, one of the advantages of the globalization of Rastafari is the opportunities that exist outside the Caribbean for access to resources that make it possible for these publishing ventures to take place.

Finally, from a methodological perspective, globalization has also coincided with the coming of age within Rastafari of a generation of scholars, cultural activists, and critical artists who are Rastafari themselves. As Rastafari experts on Rastafari, they have an international presence as much as Elders do, and play key roles in national and international Rastafari assemblies. They too are a part of Rastafari as a "traveling culture." Moreover, their imput also challenges the intellectual hegemony of outsider researchers in a way that raises issues of responsibility and representation. As activist researchers and cultural critics they are in an excellent position to take in the more general sweep of Rastafari.

THE PROCESS OF GLOBALIZATION

While Rastafari have always been international travellers, and can hardly been seen as isolated from international currents in a Jamaican outpost, the 1980s witnessed a new stage in the globalization of Rastafari. In 1980

Rastafari celebrated its "Golden Jubilee," acknowledging the 50 years since its inception. Then, since the early 1980s, Rastafari initiated a series of international missions and assemblies, which heralded another phase in Rastafari history. (The terms "mission" and "assembly" are Rastafari cultural expressions.) With the advent of the 1990s, and the plans to celebrate the centenary of Emperor Haile Selassie's birth in 1992, Rastafari as a "travelling culture" was precipitated from the local into the global field as never before, as the distance between the two collapsed exponentially.

In this section I want to return to my initial question, which is focussed on the issues that globalization raises within the movement. I want to review some of the highlights of this period, which have provided arenas in which to articulate these concerns. However, it should be remembered that while these various missions and conferences both objectively and symbolically represent major events in the life of Rastafari, the international communication and networking that has made them possible are part of a continuous and developing process which cannot be underestimated.

It is also important to have a sense of the local cultural ground which provides the context for these occasions. Since the 1970s Rastafari and reggae musicians have been performing around the world. Substantial Rastafari communities have developed in North America, the United Kingdom, and several African countries. Independently, many Rastafari elders have made tours abroad. For example, Rases Sam Brown, Mortimo Planno, Boanerges, Jah Bones, Doc Bagga, and Ascento Foxe are all well travelled. A subsequent generation of Rastafari cultural activists is equally mobile, especially in various African states. Nor is the communication all one way. For example, in early 1986 two Rastafari brethren from the Universal Rastafari Improvement Association in Tanzania visited Jamaica with the express purpose of building ties that would foster repatriation. In other words, the events described below all occurred in fairly well established and receptive Rastafari communities, which could draw upon a range of resources in order to sponsor them.

In the early 1980s the Rastafari Brethren Organization in Trinidad published an internationally inspired newspaper called *Rastafari Speaks,* against all kinds of odds, which included a persistent pattern of confiscation by the police. It served as both a voice for the Rastafari community and a vechicle for organization. It was especially instrumental in mobilizing Rastafari energies throughout the Eastern Caribbean. And by the account of its editor, Shango Baku, "the international assemblies of

Rastafari in Toronto, Canada (1982), and Kingston, Jamaica (1983), were stimulated and promoted through *Rastafari Speaks,* which by this time had surfaced as the accredited forum for the progress of the movement" (Baku, 1984).

The First International Rastafari Conference, held in Toronto in 1982, issued a report which included several recommendations, among them that a follow-up conference be held in Jamaica the following year (International Rastafarian Conference, no date). A detailed journalistic account of the conference was published in a local cultural magazine, written by Valerie Harris (1982). Harris noted that the role of Rastafari women was the "hot" issue within the Rastafari community, generating much impassioned reasoning, both backstage and frontstage (Harris, p.185). One of the main organizers of the Toronto conference was a Rastafari woman who devoted most of the following year to living in Jamaica and helping to organize the second International Assembly there.

At the Jamaican conference the issue of the role of Rastafari women was raised again, but not in as open and as direct a way as in Toronto. And again, as part of a final report, resolutions were passed which addressed several issues, including the status of women within the movement, repatriation and international Rastafari economic development. Also, suggestions were made that Nyahbinghi elders travel outside the Caribbean on missions to generally educate and inform, since the House of Nyahbinghi was recognized at this conference as the primary spiritual source of Rastafari.[10] In fact, eventually a permanent residential House of Nyahbinghi Centre was established at Scott's Pass near Mandeville, Jamaica.

The following year, therefore, in 1984, the first official elders' mission outside the Caribbean was organized in Toronto. Known as: "Voice of Thunder: Dialogue with Nyahbinghi Elders," it was a 30-day cultural and religious education program, which utilized schools, universities, public libraries, and community centres for its venues, as it was partly sponsored by the Ministry of Citizenship and Culture, as well as educational institutions.[11]

In 1986 a major international Rastafari conference was held as part of Caribbean Focus, a year-long cultural celebration in the United Kingdom. For two weeks at the Commonwealth Institute in London, from July 14 to 27, Rastafari Focus was convened, under the coordinating auspices of the Rastafarian Advisory Service (RAS), just one of many well-organized and active Rastafari organizations in the United Kingdom. The prime movers of this event were two Rastafari women.

In the United Kingdom context, which was much less restrictive than in Jamaica, the role of Rastafari women once more generated controversial reasonings. ("Reasoning" is a Rastafari concept which refers to a form of stylized discourse.) But other themes also provided continuity with the earlier international assemblies: repatriation, Rastafari economic development, and ways of dealing with various forms of repression and attacks on the movement. And once again, Nyahbinghi played the central spiritual role. At the end of the conference, a new initiative called The Nyahbinghi Project generated a series of workshops which were held in several communities in the United Kingdom over the next several months to keep the momentum up and to continue to explore some of the issues raised at Rastafari Focus, including the role of women. By 1988 the Rastafarian Advisory Service had published a detailed report on Rastafari Focus (RAS, 1988).

Then in 1988, 1989, and 1990 official Nyahbinghi elders' missions were made to the eastern United States, again with the partial support of educational institutions. These activities have been discussed at length by John Homiak, who was also involved in organizing these events (Homiak, forthcoming "b"). Not only did such missions consolidate Nyahbinghi as the arbiter of Rastafari spiritual integrity, but they also facilitated the consolidation of Rastafari communities in the areas around Washington, Baltimore, New York, and Philadelphia.

All these events were building momentum toward the celebration of the 1992 centenary of Emperor Haile Selassie's birth. And the central focus of this event was to be in Shashamanee, Ethiopia, where a few dozen Rastafari had settled since the early 1960s into the 1970s, on a land grant given to the "Black Peoples of the West" by Emperor Haile Selassie. During the period of the Dergue, local Ethiopians seized control of much of this land, putting this phase of Shashamanee's development somewhat on hold (Campbell, 1987, p.226).

During the period of my first fieldwork in Jamaica in the early 1970s, I was associated with a group of Rastafari brethren from Local 37 of the Ethiopian World Federation, which was intent on repatriation to Africa and pursued this goal in a very practical way. Some of its members frequently wrote in *African Opinion,* a black nationalist paper published in New York trying to mobilize support for their position. In addition, these same brethren promoted the learning of Amharic and Ethiopian cultural traditions and history, as they were constantly in touch with the developments taking place in Shashamanee. At that same time, in the early 1970s, there were other Houses of Rastafari which actively resisted this initiative, symbolized by their insistence on the use of I-ance or Dread Talk.

However, since the fall of the Dergue and with the impending Centenary of the Emperor's Birth, there was a renewed interest in all aspects of Ethiopian culture. Whereas previously the Ethiopian World Federation and the Twelve Tribes organizations had lead the Shashamanee initiative, now the House of Nyahbinghi seemed to be taking the initiative. In 1992 there were two international delegations from the United Kingdom which travelled to Ethiopia for this occasion. One of the Rastafari delegates from the House of Nyahbinghi in Jamaica, Ras Ivi Tafari, has published a moving account of this experience (Tafari, 1993).

These missions lead to renewed contact between the Rastafari settlers in Shashamanee and Rastafari in the diaspora. In the intervening time a Tabernacle Building Project program has been established by the Centenary Committee for Rastafari based in London. Its goal is to build a permanent Nyahbinghi Tabernacle at Shashamanee, on the same piece of land where the first Nyahbinghi Tabernacle in Ethiopia was erected temporarily for the centenary celebrations. The Committee hopes to hold opening ceremonies and an international conference there by July 1996.

In the same vein, another unique event took place in November 1993, to commemorate the coronation of Emperor Haile Selassie, which is another event celebrated annually by Rastafari. In Philadelphia a Rastafari-Ethiopia cultural celebration was held at International House, sponsored by the Folklife Centre and Ambassa, and organized primarily by a Rastafari couple, assisted by some of their children. This was the first time that the Rastafari community and the Ethiopian community had come together in this way. The purpose of the occasion was for both communities to learn more about each other. Delegates came from Canada and the eastern United States, including a substantial representation from Miami.[12]

Most recently, in May 1994, another International Rastafari Assembly was held in Miami, on the occasion of African Liberation Day, sponsored by several Rastafari communities in the eastern United States, and again one of the primary organizers was a Rastafari woman. While several themes were developed which provided continuity with earlier conferences, a major accomplishment of this "work" was the publication of a pamphlet called the *REDD Pages,* a lengthy compendium of Rastafari businesses and organizations. This Rastafari economic development directory is a substantial contribution to Rastafari economic self-sufficiency, and can be used as a guide to doing business and providing services within the Rastafari community itself.

In addition, the organizers were clearer and more formal in their expectations surrounding the logistics of the conference. An attempt was made to invite and sponsor official delegates to give reports from different regions. Dress codes were expressly stated, and both open and closed sessions were announced beforehand. The closing Nyahbinghi celebration was held on a Seminole First Nations Reservation near Miami. It is evident from both the organization and manifestation of this Assembly that the Rastafari community in the United States has further consolidated its energies towards the goals of Rastafari unity and repatriation.

CONCLUSIONS

While it is not possible in the present paper to analyze in more detail the social and political dynamics of the above events, several sensitive but important questions can be raised. These issues are even more pressing because of the increasing globalization of Rastafari.

It would seem that the House of Nyahbinghi has established itself as a major spiritual and organizational force in the globalization of Rastafari. First, being based in Jamaica, how will it accomodate the many manifestations of Rastafari which have arisen globally? In the past, even between Jamaican and the Eastern Caribbean Rastafari, there has been evidence of strain, let alone having to relate to Rastafari communities outside the region. Second, since Nyahbinghi represents the most orthodox of Rastafari traditions, with a male-dominated eldership, how will it come to terms with the increasingly active and high profile role that many Rastafari women are playing internationally? Third, how will the House of Nyahbinghi with its Afrocentric orientation respond to the increasing number of Rastafari of non-African descent? And finally, given the closer links between Rastafari and Ethiopia, what kind of role can Rastafari be expected to play politically in both Ethiopia and other African states?[13]

ENDNOTES

1. "Overstanding" is a Rastafari concept which refers to the fact that if a person comprehends something, it must be a progressive movement forward. Therefore, one cannot go "under," one must go "over" or be raised up by such knowing. It is a term coined in accordance with the principles that govern Rastafari word

formation and syntactical structures, resulting in Rastafari speech known as "I-ance" or "Dread Talk." For further expositions of these patterns, see Homiak, forthcoming "a"; and Pollard, 1985.

2. Horace Campbell was the first to apply Amilcar Cabral's idea that culture is a major aspect of resistance to foreign domination to an extensive analysis of the political history of Rastafari. (See Campbell, 1987) As fruitful as this framework may be for social scientists, Rastafari generally do not refer to themselves as a "culture of resistance." Their contention with labels is mostly focussed on whether or not Rastafari is a religion in the more narrow sense or a way of life. While part of the Rastafari stuggle for legitimacy has been to have their religious rights recognized by the State, such as the right to wear dreadlocks and head coverings in the school system, many resist being categorized as only one more religion in a multi-religious secular state. Rastafari has traditionally been theocratic in orientation, which implies a completely different conception of the relationship between "Church" and "State." Indeed, it would be part of their critique of "Babylon" (their term for the dominant society against which they struggle) that the separation of Church and State has lead to a moral decline in the decadent West. While Rastafari might have to argue within Babylon's legal system that they too have constitutionally protected religious rights, this does not mean they approve of the overall secular framework. In a theocratic model, Rastafari can be both a religion and a way of life in the holistic sense that its adherents defend.
3. A major exception is the Rastafari organization The Twelve Tribes of Israel, which developed in the early 1970s out of Local 15 of the Ethiopian World Federation in Jamaica. Twelve Tribes is organized along institutional lines, with a registered membership, which pays dues, and a hierarchical leadership. It is not as well researched as the rest of Rastafari, although it has been the focus of a paper by Frank Jan van Dijk, 1988.
4. See my paper "Rasta Mek A Trod" (Yawney, 1993), which discusses the impact of Rastafari globalization on the movement's symbolic expression. I make a point of refraining from using the term "universalization" to refer to this process, because it might be taken to suggest that Rastafari has "universalized" the humanistic content of its cultural system in order to appeal internationally to a greater cross-section of people. While undoubtedly universal values such as peace, love, truth, and justice are a core part of the Rastafari way of knowing, it has made its expansion abroad by focussing primarily on its Afrocentric, Black conscious appeal, which incorporates, but does not concentrate on, such universal values to the exclusion of the other aspects of its message. Frank Jan van Dijk has also addressed the impact of the international Rastafari assemblies, suggesting that while they have not done much to promote unity, they have greatly facilitated communication and emphasized the role of Jamaican elders (Van Dijk, 1993, p. 271).

5. Rastafari themselves will tell you that the term Nyahbinghi means "death to black and white oppressors." This is an orientation which developed in Jamaica in the late 1940s out of the House of the Youth Black Faith. See Chevannes, 1978; and Homiak, forthcoming "a," for a more detailed discussion of the history of Nyahbinghi. Nyahbinghi embodies a way of life or "livity" based mainly on Old Testament practices. Thus orthodox Nyahbinghi practitioners do not cut their hair or "locks," follow vegan nutritional guidelines, and generally live as natural or as "ital" as possible. Men are expected to keep their locks covered by a tam or "Crown" except when attending to religious duties, while women are to keep their heads covered at all times. Moreover, women are expected to follow a modest dress code and to avoid certain responsibilities, such as preparing food, when menstruating.
6. Homiak has also commented on this cultural reversal (Homiak, forthcoming "a," pp. 5-6).
7. When I serve in court as an expert witness on Rastafari, I myself find it most helpful to use the Nyahbinghi teachings and practices as the basic frame of reference for a more general discussion of Rastafari, and its various manifestations.
8. See Homiak, forthcoming "a," which specifically addresses variability in Rastafari.
9. See the collection of papers edited by Caroline Brettell called "When They read What We Write: The Politics of Ethnpography," which deals with the experience of several anthropologists in this regard (Brettell, 1993).
10. See also the account by Dawtas United, 1984, and JAHUG, 1992, for transcriptions of the contributions by several elders.
11. See report on this mission by Charmaine Montague and Carole Yawney, 1985.
12. A detailed account of this event by Ras E.S.P. MacPherson, along with a reprint of the address he made at it, can be found in the *Ethiopia Jamaica Society Newsletter,* a publication which he edits (MacPherson, 1994).
13. Campbell has raised this issue by suggesting that "Rastas cannot be against Babylon in the West and support reaction in Africa" (Campbell, 1987, p.229). These are crucial questions if any Rastafari are to be involved in lending support for the establishment of a Constitutional Monarchy in Ethiopia.

REFERENCES

Baku, Shango. (1984, April 6). Rastafari's story of struggle and triumph. *Trinidad Express,* p.8.

Brettell, C.B. (1993). *When they read what we write: The politics of ethnography.* Westport, CN: Bergin and Garvey.

Campbell, H. (1987). *Rasta and resistance.* Trenton, NJ: Africa World Press.

Chevannes, B. (1978). *Social origins of the Rastafari movement.* Kingston, Jamaica: Institute of Social and Economic Research.

Clifford, J. (1992). Traveling cultures. In L. Grossberg, C. Nelson, and P. Treichler (Eds.), *Cultural studies,* pp. 96-112. New York: Routledge.

Dawtas United (1984, March/April) Realistics. *Black on black,* pp.7-8, and pp.34-35.

Dijk, F.J. (1988). The twelve tribes of Israel: Rasta and the middle class. *New West Indian Guide,* 62, (1-2), pp.1-26.

———. (1993). *Jahmaica (sic): Rastafari and Jamaican society, 1930-1990.* Utrecht: I.S.O.R.

Homiak, J. (Forthcoming "a"). Dub history: Soundings on Rastafari livity and language. In B. Chevannes (Ed.), *Rastafari and other African-Caribbean worldviews.* NY: Macmillan.

———. (Forthcoming "b"). From yard to nation: Rastafari and the politics of eldership at home and abroad. In M. Kremser (Ed.), *Ay Bobo: Afro-Caribbean cults: Resistance and identity.* Vienna: Proceedings of the 2nd Interdisciplinary Congress of the Society for Caribbean Research.

JAHUG (1992). To mark the centenary of the birth of Tafari. *JAHUG.* London: Published by C. Gayle and Y. Gayle for Repatriation Productions.

Harris, V. (1982, Nov./Dec.). Rastafari: Issues and aspirations of the Toronto community. *Fuse,* pp.174-189.

Keita (1991). *Synchro vibes.* Tokyo: Japan.

MacPherson, E.S.P. (1994, 1:2). The first annual Rastafari/Ethiopian cultural celebration: An Ethio-Rastafari accord—Unity in diversity towards a working developmental relationship. *Ethiopian Jamaican Society Newsletter,* pp.18-21.

———. (1994, 1:2). Rastafari, the Ethio-diaspora and Ethiopia in this "age of transition": The makings of a Pan-Ethiopianist development march for progress, modernity and a programme-of-action towards the 21st century. *Ethiopiam Jamaican Society Newsletter,* pp.22 -30.

McDonald, M. (1982). *Credo: I, Rastafari.* Auckland: New Zealand Television.

Mansingh, A. and Mansingh, L. (1985). Hindu influences on Rastafarianism. *Caribbean Quarterly Monograph,* pp.96-115.

Montague, C. and Yawney, C. (1985). *Voice of thunder: Dialogue with Nyahbinghi elders.* Toronto: Masani Productions.

Pollard, V. (1985). Dread talk: the speech of the Rastafarian in Jamaica. *Caribbean Quarterly Monograph,* pp.32-41.

Post, K. (1970). The bible as ideology: Ethiopianism in Jamaica. In C. Allen and E. Johnson (Eds.), *African perspectives,* pp.185-206. Cambridge: Cambridge University Press.

RAS (1988). *Focus On Rastafari: Selected presentations for Rastafari focus '86.* London: Rastafarian Advisory Service.

International Rastafarian Conference Committee (No date). *International Rastafarian conference report.* Toronto: International Rastafarian Conference Committee.

Tafari, I. (1993). *Centenary trod to Ethiopia: 28th June to 3rd August 1992.* London: Levi House of Publications.

Turner, T.E. (1992). *Rastafari and the new society: Caribbean and East African feminist roots of a popular movement to reclaim the earthly commons.* New York: International Oil Working Group.

Warner-Lewis, M. (1993). African continuities in the Rastafari belief system. *Caribbean Quarterly,* (3-4), pp.108-123.

Yawney, C.D. (1993). Rasta Mek A Trod: Symbolic ambiguity in a globalizing religion. In U. Fleischmann and Bremer, T. (Eds.), *Alternative cultures in the Caribbean* pp.161-168. Frankfurt/Main: Vervuert Verlad.

DE LA MARGINALISATION À LA DÉTERRITORIALISATION DU RASTAFARI

Anny Dominique Curtius

Mouvement révolutionnaire mais surtout religion antillaise née de diverses conjonctures socio-historiques, le Rastafari a subi, dès son émergence en Jamaïque en 1930, une grande marginalisation avant d'acquérir une certaine popularité. Celle-ci se caractérise, toutefois, par une déterritorialisation-recontextualisation aussi bien dans les autres îles des Antilles qu'en Amérique du Nord, en Europe et ailleurs. Il s'agit de réexaminer le Rastafari dans deux contextes : d'une part il s'agit de revoir ses caractéristiques fondamentales y compris sa marginalité en Jamaïque; d'autre part il s'agit d'étudier sa réappropriation en Grande Bretagne et en Martinique où le Rastafari, ayant subi une forte érosion idéologique, est devenu surtout un mode et un phénomène social.

Rastafari appeared in 1930 in Jamaica as a revolutionary movement but more importantly as a Caribbean religion, the product of a variety of social and historical factors. In its early days, it remained relatively marginalized but gradually became more popular in the other islands of the Caribbean, in North America, in Europe and elsewhere. Its popularity has meant that it did not necessarily retain its religious aspects but rather has become deterritorialized and recontextualized. This article reconsiders Rastafari within two contexts: first, it deals with its basic characteristics as well as with its marginality in Jamaica; secondly it focusses on its reappropriation both in England and in Martinique where Rastafari has mainly become a fashion and a social phenomenon and has gone through a deep ideological erosion.

AFIN DE RETRACER les origines du Rastafari, et pour comprendre l'évolution de cette religion fondamentalement anti-colonialiste, il importe de remonter aux temps de l'esclavage. Il faudrait alors considérer d'une part, cette réticence des colons à permettre aux esclaves d'épouser la foi anglicane parce qu'elle était jugée trop sophistiquée pour ces derniers. D'autre part, ces mêmes colons craignaient que les enseignements religieux ne suscitent la révolte chez les esclaves. En outre, on ne peut passer sous silence cette puissante résistance anti-esclavagiste menée par les Marrons, qui, ajoutée aux éléments que nous venons de citer, ont favorisé en Jamaïque une tradition de résistance ainsi que le développement d'une large variété de religions dont les soubassements sont africains.

Lorsque le Rastafari naît vers 1930 en Jamaïque, il ne peut trouver un meilleur terrain d'acceuil que celui d'une classe sociale pauvre, désoeuvrée et profondément religieuse. Il devint alors la confession religieuse par excellence d'une population victime de l'oppression, de l'essouflement d'un système colonial. Le Rastafari émerge en réaction contre les religions chrétiennes qui ne correspondent pas, selon les Rastas, aux attentes de la population. À l'époque où le Rastafari émerge, la Jamaïque est toujours sous tutelle britannique; économie, conditions de vie décente et couleur de peau vont de pair, il n'est donc pas étonnant que le Rastafari, prônant la résistance contre les institutions coloniales, promettant le salut, la liberté, et l'espérance pour les opprimés, corresponde aux aspirations des Noirs pauvres des ghettos de Kingston.

Avant son départ pour les États-Unis en 1916, Marcus Garvey proclama: «Look to Africa for the crowning of a black king, he shall be the redeemer». Une telle prophétie fut déterminante dans l'émergence du Rastafari et a valu à Garvey une grande popularité et même une certaine vénération au sein du Rastafari. Mais c'est Hailé Sélassié, la figure la plus importante pour les Rastas. De son vrai nom, Ras Tafari, Ras étant un titre de noblesse en Éthiopie, et Tafari, son nom, signifiant créateur, il fut couronné Negus Negusta, empereur d'Éthiopie en 1930. Il prit le nom de Hailé Sélassié (Très Sainte Trinité) auquel il ajouta celui de Roi des Rois et Lion de la Tribu de Judée. Lors de son couronnement, nombre d'adeptes du Garveyisme se souvinrent de la prophétie de Marcus Garvey quelques années auparavant et virent alors Hailé Sélassié comme le messie de la rédemption africaine et l'Éthiopie comme le paradis, la terre promise pour tous les Noirs.

À cet effet, il est intéressant de remarquer que ce n'est pas un hasard si l'Éthiopie, qui n'a pu être véritablement colonisé par une puissance occidentale, et ce, malgré les tentatives des Italiens, est choisie comme la terre promise par les Rastas, farouches partisans de la décolonisation.

Le Rastafari est peut être encore considéré comme une source de dysfonctionnement en Jamaïque, puisqu'on lui attribue l'instabilité sociale du pays, mais il conviendrait de considérer son émergence, comme le produit du dysfonctionnement de la société jamaïquaine où il est né, mais aussi de certaines sociétés antillaises où il s'est propagé. Puisés dans les chansons de Bob Marley, les messages de paix, d'amour de justice pour les opprimés ont captivé un public jeune et lui ont permis, dans une certaine mesure, de se familiariser avec la doctrine rasta. Par contre, il est certain que le phénomène Marley a en grande partie contribué à une récupération esthétique du Rastafari aussi bien en Europe, que dans la Caraïbe, en Amérique du Nord et au Japon. Toutefois, la popularité du Rastafari ainsi que la déterritorialisation qu'il a subie, n'ont pas suffisament fait l'objet d'analyses, surtout dans le cas de son antillanisation. Nous ajoutons au terme déterritorialisation celui de recontextualisation, car les deux étapes sont complémentaires. À la mutation du Rastafari s'ajoute, comme nous l'analyserons plus loin, une réappropriation dans un nouveau contexte.

Lorsqu'on considère l'évolution du Rastafari dès sa naissance en Jamaïque, on se demande comment il a pu résister aux persécutions régulières de la police, à la peur qu'il suscitait dans la bourgeoisie jamaïquaine pour s'imposer en tant que religion à caractère révolutionnaire et anti-colonialiste. En outre, on est amené à s'interroger sur le contexte dans lequel il a pu être récupéré par la jeunesse antillaise, européenne, nord-américaine. Par ailleurs, il faudrait se demander comment les symboles de résistance, dont le Rastafari s'est doté, ont pu être récupérés à des fins «autres» pour aboutir à une érosion idéologique du mouvement.

De même que la grande majorité de religions antillaises, jugées païennes par une tradition religieuse canonique chrétienne, qui ont réadapté le Christianisme aux situations particulières des populations locales, créant ainsi ce que l'on a appelé la théologie noire (Erskine, 1981), les Rastas ont fondé leur salut et leur libération sur leurs origines ethnographiques et vivent dans l'attente perpétuelle d'un retour vers la Terre promise, l'Éthiopie. Par une relecture des écrits bibliques où le paradigme de l'exode, la recontextualisation de la notion du paradis et la revendication de Hailé Sélassié comme le Messie vivant constituent des symboles efficaces, le Rastafari a jeté les bases d'une idéologie de résistance, dont les composants constituent un syncrétisme problématique. Dans notre effort de comprendre la marginalisation du Rastafari ainsi que sa déterritorialisation—recontextualisation, nous analyserons certaines caractéristiques qui lui sont inhérentes, telles que le symbolisme des systèmes de force dont le mouvement s'est doté, les notions de rapatriement, d'espérance, la conception de la temporalité et la vision de Dieu. Ensuite, il s'agira de repenser la déterritorialisation-recontextualisation du Rastafari, en Angleterre et en Martinique.

Le potentiel d'espérance, qui constitue un élément fondamental dans l'idéologie rasta et qui possède un lien direct avec le rapatriement en Éthiopie, mérite une attention particulière. En effet, selon Henri Desroche dans *Sociologie de l'espérance,* il faut distinguer deux types d'espérance ou d'attente effervescente. Il existe tout d'abord selon lui

> l'attente exaltante, mobilisatrice, motivante, fomentatrice d'énergies, de sursauts, de résistances ... d'ébranlements et de mise en route pour des groupes sociaux, des nations ou des sectes qu'elle hisse au-dessus d'eux-mêmes dans une créativité culturelle inédite. Puis l'attente inhibitrice, démobilisatrice, peut multiplier par son virus anémiant les faiblesses d'une société anémiée. (Desroche, 1973, pp.33-34)

L'espérance d'un retour vers la terre promise pourrait être, à la fois exaltante et inhibitrice. Exaltante dans la mesure où leur croyance en un Messie vivant et le désir de refuge dans un paradis perdu leur a permis de se construire une identité et des stratégies de résistance contre le pouvoir colonial. Elle pourrait être également inhibitrice en ce sens que cette attente trop caractérisée par l'extériorité, par cette récupération en un ailleurs idéalisé, a déstabilisé nombre d'entre ceux à qui le Rastafari proposait des attentes trop abstraites qui n'apportaient aucune solution à leur misère.

Mais les points de vue divergent au sein de la communauté rasta en ce qui concerne la perception de ce rapatriement. Un certain nombre d'adeptes du Rastafari, que Leonard Barrett estime représenter la moitié de la communauté rasta de la Jamaïque, croient à un retour en Éthiopie, et ce par l'intervention du Messie vivant Hailé Sélassié. Par contre, ce n'est pas le cas pour d'autres adeptes plus jeunes qui ont réadapté leur conception du retour en fonction d'une vision plus politisée, inspirée du discours de Hailé Sélassié. En effet, lors de la visite de ce dernier en Jamaïque en 1966, s'exprimant sur le rapatriement des Rastas en Éthiopie, il a déclaré que le retour ne peut avoir lieu que si les Rastas oeuvrent d'abord pour leur propre libération en Jamaïque. Dès lors, le slogan "Liberation before Repatriation" a acquis toute sa signification et la citation qui suit en témoigne.

> We realize that Rastafarians over the years have been clamoring for repatriation and that is the spritual goal of all Rastafarians. But now we have come to the understanding that I and I cannot get repatriation under the present condition because we are not liberated .... Repatriation involves government-to government contact; we are not a part of government so we cannot exert ourselves on this matter. When we are truly liberated in power, then we shall be free to go as we please.[1]

De telles déclarations montrent que bien que certains Rastas reconnaissent la portée spirituelle du retour en Éthiopie, ils ne peuvent que l'insérer dans une perspective activiste et politique. La réorientation du rapatriement, nous invite à contextualiser cet élément fondamental de l'idéologie rasta, en fonction des notions de retour et de détour que Édouard Glissant a conceptualisé dans *Le Discours antillais.* Les réflexions de Glissant ne sont pas issues d'un contexte Rastafari, mais leur pertinence ici, réside dans le fait qu'elles se rapportent à une situation globale, de laquelle est né le Rastafari et que vit tout colonisé des Amériques, celle de la traite, de l'esclavage, de la colonisation et de la dépossession qui en résulte.

> La première pulsion d'une population transplantée, qui n'est pas sûre de maintenir au lieu de son transbord l'ancien ordre de ses valeurs, est le Retour ... et une population qui mettrait en acte la pulsion de Retour, et cela sans qu'elle se fût constituée en peuple, serait vouée aux amers resouvenirs d'un possible à jamais perdu. (Glissant, 1981, p.30)

Ces réflexions de Glissant viendraient déterminer les contours de la raison d'être du Rastafari ainsi que la réorientation que subit son idéologie. Aussi aimerions-nous associer cette idée de l'urgence du retour à celle du rapatriement en Éthiopie, et celle du détour, à la prise en compte, par une partie non négligeable de la communauté rasta, de la Jamaïque en tant que nouvel espace de reconfiguration d'une idéologie et d'une identité rastas.

Selon Glissant, le retour vers l'espace géo-matrifocal, l'Afrique, se manifeste en tant que pulsion, puisque ce retour s'avère concrètement impossible pour la diaspora noire des Amériques. Ainsi, la quête identitaire ne peut se réaliser que par le biais d'un détour qui est d'abord géographique, puisqu'il s'agit de consolider l'appartenance à la terre du transbordement, puis de concrétiser ce détour d'un point de vue culturel, linguistique, religieux, etc.

> Le détour n'est pas un refus systématique de voir. Non, ce n'est pas un mode de la cécité volontaire ni une pratique délibérée de fuite devant les réalités. Nous dirions plutôt qu'il

résulte, comme coutume, d'un enchevêtrement de négativités assumées comme telles. (Glissant, 1981, p.32)

La notion du retour qui demeure à l'état du rêve pour la diaspora noire des Amériques a été resituée dans un contexte spirituel et religieux par les Rasta. Il importe, cependant, de souligner que même si cette pulsion du retour s'est concrétisée chez les Rastas, dans une doctrine où le retour demeure le but ultime, le Rastafari n'échappe pas à ce cheminement que décrit Glissant ci-dessus—la quête identitaire de tout colonisé aux Antilles. La considération de la Jamaïque en tant qu'espace à reconquérir et à libérer de la domination coloniale semble constituer une orientation militantiste voire un détour politique pour le Rastafari, une étape dans la quête d'un but, un recours contre la marginalisation. Mais ce détour ne pourrait-il pas être aussi vu dans une perspective plus pragmatique, et ce compte tenu de la réalité du moment, c'est-à-dire, l'évidence de l'impossibilité d'un rapatriement imminent en Éthiopie?

Il importe maintenant de s'attarder sur les catégories de l'espace, du temps et la vision de Dieu qui sont rattachés à ces notions de retour et de détour. Une conception linéaire du temps selon un modèle occidental, c'est-à-dire un passé indéfini, un présent et un futur infini s'avère problématique dans l'idéologie rasta, dominée par une temporalité panchronique. En effet, la distinction entre l'espace et le temps y est absente, puisqu'il y a une nostalgie continuelle (la perte d'un paradis), une recréation du cosmos (le paradis perdu est à retrouver non pas au ciel mais sur la terre en Éthiopie), une recréation d'espaces rêvés et lointains et la recherche d'une consolation dans un temps fort reculé. L'espace se définit en fonction du temps et c'est par le temps que l'espace acquiert sa légitimité, éléments d'une métaphysique de la nostalgie selon Cioran. Cependant, nous ne dirons pas comme Cioran que la nostalgie ne coïncide avec aucun moment discret dans le temps, puisque les Rastas en se basant sur la Bible déclarent que les Noirs, véritables descendants des Israélites, ont été opprimés par les Blancs et réduits en esclavage. C'est plutôt la consolation, la guérison de cette nostalgie qui ne correspondent ni à un moment, ni à un espace précis (en effet s'agit-il de l'Éthiopie actuelle ou de l'Abyssinie?). Comme le déclare Cioran, la remontée à la source des temps, la consolation dans un passé reculé et immémorial, réfractaire aux siècles, et ce afin de retrouver le paradis véritable, est nécessaire pour les Rastas (Cioran, 1960, pp.113-114). Les catégories du temps et de l'espace dans l'idéologie Rastafari sont imbriquées dans une circularité constante où le temps répond à une double dimension, un très long passé et un présent intense. Quant au futur, on ne peut dire qu'il est aussi long que le passé. Il serait plutôt difficilement définissable dans la mesure où il n'existe que grâce à un espace regretté, l'Éthiopie, et se nourrit abondamment du passé. Il prend aussi appui dans le présent et la Jamaïque actuelle. C'est la nostalgie du paradis perdu qu'il faut retrouver dans un futur indéterminé qui crée une dialectique entre le présent et le passé.

La conception circulaire du temps d'un point de vue africain, à savoir un passé infini, un présent et l'absence du futur serait à considérer dans une perspective rasta. Toutefois, au lieu de parler d'une absence de futur, il conviendrait plutôt de souligner le rôle du futur en tant que catégorie temporelle légitimatrice du déroulement d'une temporalité à deux dimensions, et non en tant que catégorie participant activement au déroulement de cette temporalité. Autrement dit, les Rastas réaliseront leur retour en Éthiopie, parce qu'ils en sont originaires et c'est ce retour prochain en Afrique qui leur permet de faire face à l'oppression et à la marginalisation dont ils sont victimes dans le présent.

Dans cette foi en l'avenir chez les Rastas, ne retrouverait-on pas les éléments de toute idéologie qui cherche à transcender des moments négatifs dans l'histoire d'une communauté? Le caractère hybride du Rastafari se manifeste par sa temporalité panchronique qui incorpore des éléments propres à la temporalité de toutes religions. L'idéologie rasta aurait ses origines dans une pensée africaine en fonction de sa notion d'un temps et d'un espace inséparables, mais aussi, de sa conception de Dieu. Les Rastas croient en l'immortalité de Hailé Slassié, car Dieu, qu'il nomme Jah, est présent partout, en tout homme et ne peut être vénéré en tant qu'esprit. Son royaume est un environnement qui est familier à l'homme, et ne peut, par conséquent, être au ciel, mais sur la terre, l'Éthiopie. Dans ces réflexions de John Mbiti à propos de la conception africaine de Dieu, on peut dégager des similarités avec la pensée des Rastas au sujet de Jah.

> Nature in the broadest sense of the word is not an empty impersonal object or phenomenon: it is filled with religious significance. Man gives life even where natural objects and phenomena have no biolological life. God is seen in and behind these objects and phenomena: they are His creation, they manifest Him, they symbolise His being and presence.... The invisible world presses hard upon the visible: one speaks of the other, and African peoples "see" that invisible universe when they look at , hear or feel the visible and tangible world. (Mbiti, 1990, p.56)

> God is omnipresent and He is "reachable" at any time and any place. People worship Him where and whenever the "need" arises. (Mbiti, 1990, p.73)

En effet, l'appréciation d'une alimentation essentiellement naturelle connue sous le nom de I-tal, les rapports étroits avec la nature, l'utilisation de l'herbe sainte, la marijuana, ou ganja, favorisent la communication des Rastas avec Jah. Ces éléments rapprochent chaque Rasta à Jah, dans une quête identitaire au cours de laquelle le Rasta doit atteindre une communion parfaite avec Jah. Cette omniprésence de Dieu dans la vie quotidienne des Rastas se reflète bien dans leur fréquente utilisation de l'expression «I and I».

Si l'on considère les symboles utilisés par les Rastas, c'est par eux qu'ils se sont forgés une identité, ont résisté aux différents systèmes étatiques en place en Jamaïque et se sont manifestés par un apport culturel propre, tout en ébranlant la Jamaïque aux niveaux social, culturel, politique et même économique. Ces symboles sont certes des stratégies de résistance contre Babylon mais aussi des systèmes de «force», terme utilisé par Émile Durkheim et repris par Henri Desroche pour analyser le concept de l'espérance comme «idéation collective». L'on citera tout d'abord le symbolisme des couleurs, le rouge, le jaune, le vert et le noir utilisées dans les tenues vestimentaires. Le langage, dont le lexique fait référence à de nombreux termes bibliques, langage que l'on qualifie de «soul», «ghetto» ou «hallucinogenic language». L'emploi de «I and I» est important dans la mesure où il renferme une composante l'idéologie rasta, que l'on retrouve chez les Hindous ainsi que dans l'Église orthodoxe éthiopienne. «I and I» signifie que Jah est présent en chaque Rasta et qu'il appartient à chacun, par une pureté, et une sagesse de l'âme, de le chercher.

Selon Virginia Lee Jacobs,

> The First "I" refers to the divine, the second "I" to the man and together, the resulting union of "I and I" is the only way Rastafarians can talk about themselves and the world around them. The use of "I and I" is a constant reminder of the presence of Jah. (Jacobs, 1985, p.92)

Ce binarisme qui se fond tout de même dans une symbiose entre l'être divin et le Rasta, révèle qu'au sein de la religion, les Rastas n'effectueraient aucune distinction entre la quête d'identité collective et individuelle et que l'unité de tous est capitale. Rex Nettleford remarque à cet effet:

> The assertive individualism of Rastafarianism is therefore a silent challenge to the propensity of secular political movements to freeze their kind into such categories as the "masses", the "lumpen proletariat", the "sufferers", "quashie", small man" or "little people." For the Rastafarians each member of the "masses" or "the proletariat" has a personality, an individual and finite identity , a divine dimension with direct routing to the Creator, Jah, himself. (Nettleford, 1992, p.xv)

Quant aux dreadlocks, ils ont une double fonction. D'abord ils provoquent l'indignation, peut être même la peur pour ceux qui estiment qu'il y a rupture avec une «normalité esthétique». Ensuite, ils ont pour fonction de valoriser une négrité que Cashmore souligne.

> The appearance of locks celebrated blackness: made its quality and possession esteemed and positively valued. In no way was the growing of locks an element of black racialism, but a strenuous effort to cleanse the black man of white-defined self-images and to instil in himself confidence, pride and dignity in being black. Dreadlocks were a reformulation of the labels of the white world by "cleaning up one's own back garden" and determining the "true self." (Cashmore, 1979, p.159)

Il faut aussi noter que les Rastas utilisent des passages de l'Ancien Testament pour légitimer leur consommation de la marijuana, qu'ils appellent l'herbe sainte. Fumer de la ganja, c'est pour eux un acte spirituel d'une grande émotion, qui leur permet de communiquer avec Jah. Les passages suivants extraits de l'Apocalypse de St-Jean sont souvent cités par les Rastas : «Je vous donne toute herbe: cela vous servira de nourriture ..., il y a un arbre de vie qui donne du fruit douze fois par année. Les feuilles de l'arbre servent à la guérison des nations» (Apoc. 22, 2-3).

Le symbole du Lion, que l'on retrouve dans leur artisanat, dans leurs temples, leurs maisons, est aussi très significatif en ce sens qu'il représente, d'une part, Hailé Sélassié, et d'autre part la force, la résistance.

Mais puisqu'il n'est plus possible de négliger l'impact du Rastafari en Jamaïque, les systèmes de force dont il s'est doté peuvent être à la fois exaltants et inhibiteurs. Ils sont exaltants parce que certains ont permis aux Rastas de s'impliquer culturellement, politiquement et socialement, mais aussi économiquement grâce au développement de l'industrie du reggae. Du point de vue politique on ne peut passer sous silence la première participation d'un Rasta aux élections de 1961 en Jamaïque, Ras Sam Brown, qui batit sa campagne sur les *Twenty-One Points* (Barrett, 1977, pp.148-150), qui constituent les fondements de la religion.

Ces mêmes symboles sont ausi inhibiteurs parce que ce sont ces mêmes systèmes de force, les dreadlocks, la consommation de la ganja qui ont valu au Rastafari sa marginalisation dans la société jamaïquaine, marginalisation qui se reproduit lorsque le mouvement se mondialise.

LA DÉTERRITORIALISATION DU RASTAFARI

Il faudrait analyser le Rastafari en considérant son expansion à travers le monde, expansion paradoxale lorsqu'on sait que l'une de ses caractéristiques principales est précisément le repli vis-à-vis du monde extérieur. Mais son expansion se caractérise d'une part par une récupération de ses systèmes de force à d'autres fins, et d'autre part par une certaine érosion idéologique, due à la subversion et à l'effritement de sa base doctrinale. L'appropriation du Rastafari par des groupes marginaux en Angleterre et en Amérique du Nord est paradoxale dans la mesure où dans la perspective rasta, les courants de pensée occidentaux, de même que ses valeurs ont souvent été associés à Babylon. Ainsi, dans le contexte de cette expansion, le terme déterritorialisation que nous empruntons à Deleuze et Guattari[2] a le sens de mutation, de disjonction, de transfert. De prime abord on pourrait dire que les «marges» de la «périphérie» se voient récupérées par celles du «centre». C'est le cas dans notre contexte puisque la Jamaïque en tant que lieu de naissance du Rastafari est le centre. La Martinique représente cette périphérie où, même s'il existe une érosion idéologique du Rastafari, la quête identitaire qu'effectuent certains Rastas détermine l'existence d'un certain fondement philosophique en Martinique. L'Angleterre incarne aussi la périphérie, mais cette redéfinition de soi n'y est pas prédominante, puisque la seule marginalité du Rastafari est valorisée en tant que mode ou protestation contre les valeurs établies. Si les catégories «marge», «périphérie», «centre» devaient être utilisées dans un tel contexte, il faudrait tenir compte d'un fait: celui de la récupération des éléments marginaux propres à des cultures dites subalternes par des groupes vivant en marges de sociétés dites hégémoniques.

L'EUROPÉANISATION DU RASTAFARI

Les Rastas qui immigrèrent en Angleterre au début des années 1970, urbanisation et immigration que l'on pourrait considérer comme une forme de déterritorialisation interne du Rastafari, furent considérés comme des parias de la société britannique alors que ce ne fut pas le cas pour les Punks. Selon ceux-ci : "We're on the same side as the Rastas. People think they are as luny as us. But it's because they are their own people, projecting their own image." (Cashmore, 1979, p.197)

Une telle association s'explique par le fait que dans les sociétés occidentales, des groupes vivant en marges d'une culture établie, tels que les Punks ou les Rockers, récupèrent les éléments esthétiques appartenant à d'autres cultures pour manifester leurs ressentiments à l'égard d'une société qui ne répond plus à leurs besoins. Si le moyen le plus souvent utilisé par ces groupes marginaux est le style, c'est qu'à travers lui, toute une philosophie, une éthique, un mode de vie sont exprimés. De plus, le style devient une arme, une stratégie de résistance contre un ordre établi, que ces groupes ne cherchent pas nécessairement à détruire, mais à en subvertir la normalisation, à choquer, à provoquer la majorité, à défier l'ordre public pour détruire le mythe du consensus.

Dans une analyse de ces groupes marginaux, David Bollon souligne:

> Le Mal des Punks, c'est, pêle-mêle et dans la plus grande confusion le fascisme, le communisme, le sado-masochisme, les déviations sexuelles, la Grande Ville, et toutes les hyprocrisies que cachent la démocratie, la reine d'Angleterre. Bref, c'est la part obscure du social, tout ce qui se tapit et grouille sous l'écorce des apparences ... Ce n'est pas tant en fait le Laid ou le Mauvais que les Punks célèbrent: ils portent au pinacle de leur univers l'inverse du Beau et du Bon consacrés, afin que la société découvre, effarée dans le regard qu'elle porte sur eux, la fragilité dérisoire des frontières à priori, esthétiques et morales, qu'elle s'est données et que jamais elle ne met en question. (Bollon, 1990, pp.171-172)

Commentant les affinités entre Rastas et Punks, Dick Hebdige remarque:

> There is a tenuous but discernible bond forged between punks and Rastas, who were to become subjects of a moral panic in their own right at the end of 1977. The links strengthened as both groups became aware of similarities in their respective critical postures. One obvious ramification of this affinity was the adoption of the visual iconography of the black jamaican street style, as well as the introduction of reggae bands into punk clubs ... Through their familiarity with the music the punks were able to identify Babylon as another way of expressing contempt for the same social order that they were criticising. (Cashmore, 1979, p.199)

Ces similitudes auxquelles l'on fait allusion sont certes celles du rejet d'un système étatique ainsi que la révolte par le style. Mais il convient d'être prudent quand on effectue ce parallèle entre les Punks et les Rastas en ce qui concerne leur symbolique esthétique qui n'a pas certes la même pertinence. C'est à ce niveau que nous parlerons, de déterritorialisation externe puisque les agents de transformation et de réutilisation du Rastafari viennent de l'extérieur. À cet égard, il conviendrait de distinguer deux types d'agents. Il existe d'une part, ceux qui viennent des groupes marginaux, donc qui à priori dénoncent un système étatique en place et d'autre part ceux qui ne font pas partie de groupes marginaux et qui ne désirent utiliser la symbolique rasta qu'en tant que mode. On constate alors que l'esthétique rasta est utilisée à deux fins. On peut évoquer tout d'abord l'asocialisation ou la protestation contre des valeurs occidentales. On constate qu'au détriment de leur idéologie, tout ce que propose le Rastafari n'est compris que comme phénomènes singuliers et frappants, comme de nouveaux moyens, venus d'ailleurs pour permettre aux jeunes de souligner leur marginalité. D'autre part, Rasta devient aussi mode de socialisation. Par socialisation nous entendons l'unique participation à un habitus sociétal, la mode et dans ce cas, la mode rasta telle qu'elle fut adoptée en Europe, en Amérique du Nord. C'est sans doute, dans cette dernière catégorie qu'on retrouve la plus grande partie des «adeptes» européens ou nord-américains du Rastafari.

L'ANTILLANISATION DU RASTAFARI: LE CAS DE LA MARTINIQUE

Quoique généralisée, la propagation du Rastafari dans la Caraïbe, n'est pas uniforme, car le respect de la doctrine, l'importance de la ritualisation divergent d'une île à l'autre. Par exemple, les Rastas st-luciens n'envisagent pas un rapatriement en Afrique, car selon eux, l'Afrique en tant qu'espace géo-spirituel peut être recréé ailleurs.

Dans le cas de la Martinique, le Rastafari semble y avoir émergé, vers la fin des années 1970, à la fois en tant que mode et en réaction contre les valeurs, les courants de pensée du système colonial français. Toutefois, son adoption n'est pas le résultat d'une longue tradition de résistance. Il s'agit plutôt d'un repli sur soi, d'un refuge dans un ailleurs qui n'est pas nécessairement l'Afrique, et d'une récupération esthétique, d'un style de vie.

Une brève archéologie du phénomène religieux en Martinique est nécessaire afin de comprendre les caractéristiques de la recontextualisation martiniquaise du Rastafari. La Martinique est un département français d'outre mer et du fait même de cette situation de colonisation, les tentatives de résistance, ainsi que la pratique de religions d'origine africaine, n'ont pas bénéficié d'une appréciation positive, mais plutôt ambiguë, de la part de la population. Ainsi, ce syncrétisme entre religions africaines et chrétiennes que l'on peut observer par exemple à Cuba, avec la Santeria, en Haïti avec le Vodou, au Brésil avec le Candomblé, est présent en Martinique uniquement sous la forme du quimbois. Toutefois, même si l'environnement colonial a créé chez les Martiniquais des habitus, pour reprendre un terme propre à Bourdieu, c'est-à-dire des dispositions acquises pour une acceptation passive de l'homogénéité institutionnelle en place, il demeure que le quimbois, qui a été recomposée sous forme de traces, bénéficie auprès de la population d'une popularité que l'on peut qualifier de problématique.

Sa marginalité lui a été conférée par l'église catholique qui l'associe au mal. Même si les Martiniquais sont de fervents pratiquants de la religion catholique, ils consulteront toujours les quimboiseurs. Cependant, pour s'être adonnés à des pratiques religieuses jugées sauvages par l'Église, et puisqu'ils ont intériorisé cette marginalisation, ils subiront une double culpabilité, celle de leur entourage, mais aussi la leur. Ecoutons Glissant :

> Au long du peuplement, ont vocation de quimboiseurs, les marrons qui en Afrique remplissaient déjà des fonctions socio-culturelles: chargés de la vie religieuse, des soins de médecine, du rythme des travaux etc. A l'intérieur de cette contestation globale qu'est le marronnage, le quimboiseur est en quelque sorte l'idéologue, le prêtre, l'inspiré. C'est en principe le dépositaire d'une grande idée, celle du maintien de l'Afrique et par voie de conséquence, d'un grand espoir, celui du retour à l'Afrique. Mais au long de l'établissement sur la terre nouvelle, le quimboiseur dégénère, jusqu'à verser dans le charlatanisme le plus délirant (à la satisfaction des autorités civilisatrices, qui l'avaient toujours ainsi prédit). Dépossédé de ses fonctions culturelles, le quimboiseur n'a plus de raison d'être. L'évolution sociale a fait de lui ce qu'on avait dès le départ, pour combattre le danger qu'il représentait, voulu qu'il fût et annoncé qu'il était : un charlatan.
>
> La relation de la collectivité au quimboiseur s'apparente au rapport habituel qui naît du jeu des superstitions, mais cette relation est nouée aussi à un déséquilibre "en profondeur" de l'ensemble de la population. L'espoir raturé du retour à l'Afrique n'a pas été remplacé (une fois ce retour avéré impossible) par un enracinement déterminé dans la terre nouvelle, mais par un autre mirage (aussi "lointain"), celui de la francisation ... Mais le maintien de l'Afrique impossible se maintient au niveau de l'anormal: du pathologique, du traumatique. (Glissant, 1981, p.104)

La résistance permanente du Rastafari contre l'hégémonie occidentale, le rejet du système colonialiste, voire même la destruction de la culture dominante, et la valorisation de l'Afrique et de sa culture dans sa marginalisation, ont permis à de nombreux critiques de voir un parallèle entre le Rastafari et les différents groupes ou mouvements tels que les Mau Mau au Kenya, la Harlem Renaissance qui ont émergé en Afrique et au sein de la diaspora noire. L'autre parallèle que l'on aime noter est celui avec la négritude, qui en tant que Weltanschauung est né en réaction contre le colonialisme et le racisme et a refusé toute assimilation à l'Occident, sa culture, sa rationalité. Contrairement au Rastafari, la négritude n'a jamais prôné un retour concret en Afrique, mais (et c'est là que réside l'intérêt d'une comparaison possible) a plutôt cherché à revaloriser la culture africaine, à favoriser une quête de l'identité nègre au sein de la diaspora noire, à se constituer en tant que discours anti-colonialiste. Si Aimé Césaire considère que la révolution haïtienne (qui a d'ailleurs mené à la formation de la première république noire indépendante en 1804), est une forme de négritude en action, Édouard Glissant a tenté d'expliquer, dans *Le Discours Antillais* l'apparition du Rastafari en Martinique, comme un passage à l'acte favorisant le rééquilibrage des valeurs et consacrant l'oeuvre de la négritude.[3] Autrement dit, il serait une concrétisation de la négritude, dans la mesure où cette part africaine des Antillais, qui a souvent été niée, est sans cesse valorisée par les Rastas. Pour notre part, même si le Rastafari est pour une minorité de Rastas martiniquais, une forme de stratégie de résistance passive, c'est-à-dire le rejet de Babylon, la colonisation française, nous croyons plutôt que l'esthétique et le style de vie du Rastafari ont été récupérés par la jeunesse martiniquaise des classes défavorisées, des jeunes chômeurs, mais aussi par un nombre non négligeable de jeunes bourgeois désoeuvrés en quête d'autres idéaux et justement d'autres styles de vie. La ritualisation n'a pas beaucoup d'importance pour certains Rastas en Martinique et si les symboles sont réutilisés, ils ont une nouvelle fonction. La consommation de la marijuana a perdu le sens profond de spiritualité, de communion, de communication avec Jah. Le port des dreadlocks est une nouvelle façon de se coiffer, le végétarisme une nouvelle façon de manger, le reggae une nouvelle musique à danser. Par ailleurs, comme en Jamaïque, le Rastafari martiniquais s'est vite associé à la délinquance et aux actes illégaux perpétrés par ceux qui se disaient Rastas et qui ont ainsi aidé à le discréditer. Nous n'écartons pas l'idée que cette érosion idéologique existe ailleurs dans la Caraïbe, mais il va sans dire que le poids de la colonisation en Martinique et l'implantation d'une culture française y jouent probablement un rôle fondamental dans ce contexte. C'est d'ailleurs à partir de ces éléments que nous comprenons comment le Rastafari est passé de l'état de marginalisation à une certaine internationalisation mais surtout à une banalisation de ces symboles fondateurs.

Toutes ces réflexions indiquent qu'au cours de ce processus de déterritorialisation-recontextualisation, le Rastafari, que l'on pourrait considérer comme une forme contemporaine du marronnage des esclaves rebelles jamaïquains, est devenu progressivement un phénomène social aussi bien antillais, européen qu'américain. Selon Leonard Barrett :

> The message and visions of movements like Rastafarians point the way to new patterns of society.... As a dominant cultural force in its original context, the Rastafarians must be seen above all as the champions of social change on the island of Jamaica. (Barrett, 1977, p.206)

Tel n'est pas le cas en Martinique où l'on assiste déjà à une dimunition du nombre de Rastas. Alors qu'ils étaient très présents dans les rues commerciales de Fort-de-France au début des années 1980, ils ont tendance, aujourd'hui à s'installer à la campagne où ils vivent en communauté. On remarque aussi que certains des premiers adeptes ont délaissé le Rastafari pour épouser d'autres confessions religieuses principalement protestantes.

Sans être pour autant une construction utopique déçue, puisque le Rastafari a largement contribué, un peu malgré lui, à l'histoire de la Jamaïque et au développement de son patrimoine culturel, de son économie, on peut s'interroger sur une nouvelle et plus pertinente implication du Rastafari dans la sphère politique jamaïquaine. En ce qui concerne la Martinique, la question politique ne se pose pas puisque la structure coloniale y est solidement implantée.

Par ailleurs, en ce qui concerne la récupération du Rastafari par d'autres groupes marginaux en Europe, en Amérique du Nord ou ailleurs et des similarités que l'on croit trouver entre le Rastafari et les Punks par exemple, nous croyons qu'il est important de souligner que le malaise que dénoncent les Punks est dû à l'essoufflement d'une société européenne ou américaine qui ne répond plus à leurs besoins, alors que celui que combattent les Rastas a ses origines dans l'histoire de la traite, de l'esclavage, de la colonisation et du néo-colonialisme.

NOTES

1. Propos recueillis par Leonard Barrett auprès d' un membre du Rastafarian Movement Association, été 1975, in *The Rastafarians. The Dreadlocks of Jamaïca,* op. cit., p.179.
2. Voir Deleuze, Gilles, Guattari, Félix, Kafka. *Pour une littérature mineure,* Paris: Éditions de Minuit, 1975.
3. Glissant, Édouard, op. cit., pp.200-201.

RÉFÉRENCES

Barrett, L. (1977). *The Rastafarians. The dreadlocks of Jamaica.* Kingston: Sangster.

Bollon, D. (1990). *Morale du masque.* Paris: Seuil.

Cashmore, E. (1979). *Rastaman: The Rastafarian movement in England.* London: Allen & Unwin.

Cioran, E. (1960). *Histoire et Utopie.* Paris: Gallimard.

Deleuze, G., Guattari, F. (1975). *Kafka. Pour une littérature mineure.* Paris: Editions de Minuit.

Desroche, H. (1973). *Sociologie de l'espérance.* Paris: Calmann-Levy.

Erskine, N.L. (1981). *Decolonizing theology: A Caribbean perspective.* Marynoll, NY: Orbis Books.

Glissant, E. (1981). *Le Discours antillais.* Paris: Seuil.

Jacobs, V.L. (1985). *Roots of Rastafari.* San Diego: Avant Books.

Mbiti, J. (1990). *African religions and philosophy.* London: Heinemann

Nettleford, R. (1992). Introduction. In *O. Joseph Dread. The Rastafarians of Jamaica.* Kingston: Sangster.

CHAPTER II

WRITERS BETWEEN WORLDS

CARIBBEAN CANADIAN WRITERS: A LITERARY FORUM

These texts by Austin Clarke, Cyril Dabydeen, Cecil Foster and Dany Laferrière have been adapted from the transcript of a round table hosted by John Harewood at Carleton University during an evening of discussion and poetry reading with Caribbean and Canadian/Caribbean writers in the context of the annual meeting of the Canadian Association for Latin American and Caribbean Studies (1993). The writers were invited to discuss the particularities of writing in Canada.

Austin Clarke describes the genesis of his fiction and speaks of recreating the black immigrant experiences of the 1950s and 1960s by putting English-speaking West Indians face-to-face with the politics of skin colour. He mentions the influence of black American writers like Leroi Jones and James Baldwin and emphasizes the fact that "everything we write has got to be political and has got to be adversarial to the system."

Cyril Dabydeen talks as much about his writing as he does about his personal experiences and his evolving sense of identity as he moved from Guyana to Canada.

Cecil Foster notes the growing importance of Caribbean writers in Canada and calls for more recognition by the mainstream media and publishers.

Dany Laferrière, writing in English for the firt time, presents a comic dialogue with his mother, making fun of Candian bureaucracy, his reaction to what he perceives as the strange logic of organized Canadian society.

The final comments by Makeda Silvera, a writer and publisher in Toronto (Sister Vision), confirm Clarke's vision of the writer's adverserial position by emphasizing the fact that non-white women writers of Caribbean or other origins, given the racial and gender hierarchies which still function in Canadian society, must often take an especially firm stance in order to be recognized.

Les textes d'Austin Clarke, de Cyril Dabydeen, de Cecil Foster et de Dany Laferrière ont été retranscrits à partir d'un enregistrement réalisé pendant une table ronde, animée par John Harewood. Cette rencontre entre écrivains venus des Caraïbes et écrivains canadiens d'origine caraïbéenne a eu lieu à l'Université Carleton dans le cadre d'une soirée de discussion et de lectures de poésie. La rencontre faisait partie de la réunion annuelle de l'Association canadienne des études latino-américaines et caraïbes (ACELAC),les écrivains y étaient invités pour réfléchir sur leurs rapports avec la société canadienne.

Austin Clarke nous livre la genèse de sa fiction face aux expériences des immigrants noirs des années 1950 et 1960. Ecrire, pour lui, signifie rendre compte d'une confrontation continuelle entre les Antillais et le milieu canadien ambiant, confrontation exacerbée par l'existance d'une politique «épidermique» très active dans ce pays. L'auteur renvoie aux influences des écrivains noirs américains—Leroi Jones, James Baldwin entre autres—et insiste sur le fait que «tout ce que nous écrivons doit poser un défi au système».

Cyril Dabydeen parle de ses écrits, de ses expériences personnelles et de l'évolution de son sens d'identité depuis son départ de la Guyane.

Cecil Foster fait remarquer l'importance croissante des écrivains antillais au Canada et souhaite plus de reconnaissance pour eux de la part des média et les maisons d'édition qui représentent la culture dominante.

Dany Laferrière, qui publie son premier texte en anglais, présente un dialogue comique avec sa mère, une réaction personnelle face à la logique incompréhensible de la bureaucracie canadienne.

Les dernières remarques de Makeda Silvera, écrivaine et directrice d'une maison d'édition torontoise (Sister Vision), correspondent à la vision de Clarke au sujet de la nécessité de politiser ses rapports avec le milieu où elle vit. Elle confirme la notion d'une hiérarchie raciale et sexuelle bien ancrée dans les valeurs institutionnelles de la société canadienne qui s'adapte difficilement aux différences. Pour cette raison, les écrivaines non-blanches d'origines antillaises ou autres, doivent souvent s'affirmer d'une manière radicale pour être reconnues par ce milieu.

AUSTIN CLARKE

I FEEL THAT THE REPRESENTATION of Canada depends upon your experience in that it relates to the number of years you have lived in the country, assuming of course that you have decided that Canada is going to be the raw material for your fiction work.

I shall deal with these points: "historical/personal"; the "learned"—the experience in Canada; the "observed"; and the police and various institutions; and I shall deal with the stereotype. I shall deal with Canada so far as the Caribbean (writer) citizen is not accessible to the realms of power; and since I am Barbadian I shall deal with the Barbadian experience versus the Canadian experience which is the experience of the immigrant in a new country, and I shall relate these five points to the five works of mine.

So far as the "historical/personal" is concerned, I shall relate that to my book, *The Meeting Point.* I shall relate the "learned" to my collection of short stories, *When Women Rule;* the "observed," and the police shall be discussed in the context of my collection of short stories, *In This City.* I shall talk about the "stereotype" by referring to the novel *More,* which has not been published. My discussion about Canada, not being accessible to us writers, will bring me to the new book which is called *There Are No Elders.*

Let me say at the beginning that unlike all of our models who went to England, and in Dany Laferrière's case went to Paris, France, I did not come to this country to be a writer. I happened to be a writer. That may not be a good thing, but it may be a good thing. So that if I look back upon the first book I wrote, it had to be based on my historical comprehension of what Canada was and that had to be taken into consideration with my personal experience.

I chose the book *The Meeting Point,* because that is the first book I wrote that was based upon these two factors. The historical was that in the mid-1950s, the Canadian government invited Barbadians and Jamaicans and Trinidadians to be landed immigrants if they would accede to a certain domestic scheme in which they worked in the homes of wealthy persons for two years before being allowed to become landed immigrants. We thought this was acrimonious and an insult, because some of the women who came under the scheme from Jamaica and other countries in the Caribbean were not in fact and had not been domestics, but had been high school graduates.

So when I was writing my first book in a trilogy, *The Meeting Point,* I had to consider these things: What was the relationship between Canada and Barbados and the West Indies? And what in fact were my personal experiences?

In 1955, there were very few West Indians of my colour or complexion on the campus of the University of Toronto, and since it was understood that they were not going to remain in Canada we were treated like princes and princesses. So that my only experience at that time, 1957-

1967, had to be based on a very rough-hewn understanding of Canadian society. And I would say that as writers, everything that we write has got to be political and has got to be adversarial to the system.

It seems to me that when I read the works of all my colleagues, even if the work did not set out to be controversial and in opposition to the Canadian situation, I am able, in spite of the author, to see where the work is making a very critical point of the society; and even if the book was not set in a historical sense it seems to me that the personal experience of the author would give credence to his personal or oral history or sense of history and would have the same conclusion.

Now to go on to the second point. Our feelings about Canada may be learned. I remember that when I was writing my second novel I was very impressed by a novel published in America by James Baldwin called *Another Country.* This to me was the most important novel ever written. And it was this anger and this adversarial aspect towards the society: he was able to portray the black man as a tragic figure. When I looked around Toronto, I could not see that our experiences were equal to that grandeur of protest. So what I did, I invented the protest because we were not lynched in Toronto, and certainly if there was some aspect of racism it was not so immediate and so persistent and so insistent as was the case in America. So I then learned about the situation in America and took it as my own experience, with the result that if you read the second book in the trilogy, *Storm of Fortune,* you would see a very distinct aspect of invention. I am talking about the "learned experience" or the "learned protest."

One example I may give is Leroi Jones in his beautiful poem "We Need a Black World, Let the World Be Black." And I feel then that in Toronto in spite of the fact that we were involved in the NAACP civil rights activism and we had picketed, that the problem had not become so crystallized that as creative artists, we could use it with the same power as the Americans. Then comes a very serious philosophical and artistic point. Do you have to inject in your writing this degree of racialism in order to make it relevant? Now we have two important intellectuals who have warned us against doing this kind of thing. I shall mention the first one—whom I do not like—V.S. Naipaul who said: "After the Black American novelist has exploited racism in his work of fiction, there is very little more that he can do." The exceptions he gave were James Baldwin and Richard Wright.

The second authority for this warning or caution is the author of *Invisible Man,* but this quotation comes from *Shadow and Act.* I am referring to Ralph Ellison. And Ralph Ellison I think was much more expansive and much more serious and helpful perhaps in the position he made when he said:

> As black authors we have got to be very careful how we use racism in our work. If racism is used in the right way, it becomes part of the art. If it is used as a weapon and if it is the focal point, then in fact we may be expressing ourselves as not very good artists.

So I was faced in 1970 with this problem which is, were we young black writers in Canada relevant? How is it that we could not have produced *Another Country* (James Baldwin), *Dutchman* (Amiri Baraka formerly Leroi Jones), *Invisible Man* and things like that.

And I would say that so far as the creative writer is concerned, he does not stop only at writing, but he is influenced to a large extent by the theatre, in the origins of *Dutchman,* and by music. And if any of you were living at the time, then you would know that coincident with these books I am talking about, there was a renaissance of jazz, the featured artists of which were John Coltrane, Sonny Rollins, Miles Davis; the singers were Nina Simone, Aretha Franklin before she became so popular, and of course Abbey Lincoln.

Now from that experience I wrote the book called *When Women Rule,* in which I tried to show precisely the relationship between the learned protest, or the learned backlash or effect on racialism in America, and my own experience in Canada. I should say to you deliberately—to embarrass my so-called biographer (Stella Algoo-Baksh (1994). *Austin Clarke, a Biography.* ECW Publications.), that she figures that this book *When Women Rule* is something "ignominious." It is so big a word and so intellectual, but she seems to feel that this book is anti-woman.

I can't be anti-woman, because I was born from a woman.

Let us go now to the "observed" and the police.

May 4, 1992 a very important event took place in Toronto, derived precisely from Los Angeles. All of us saw in graphic detail the brutalization of a person, not a black person, a person.

It appalled me as an artist that during the trial the argument on the part of the defence of the police was that perhaps what you were seeing was a dream. In other words, we were asked to doubt that we were seeing. Against that I write our experience with the police. Now when I say our experience I am not suggesting that these very established successful, well-off writers necessarily have experiences with the police; but since by ethnicity, if not by colour, they must identify with the victims of police brutality, as artists then they must have some sensitive feeling towards this.

It occurred to me that I had to move from the esoteric and face the reality of my own living in Toronto, which sometimes could be a very brutal society. I shall give you the examples of that brutality. I am not saying that Toronto is a worse place to live than Ottawa is. I still consider Toronto to be the last place in the world where a black man can live with dignity, but for the argument that we are faced with.

There was a man in a rooming house in the so-called black area and he probably asked his wife to make love with him and she said no because she is a women's liberationist and she called the police and the police came in and shot him.

Then there was another man, whose wife was making peas n' rice and jerk chicken on a Sunday and the police came in and shot the man, and what I consider to be the most reprehensible image in my whole life is to see these bullets hitting the cover of the pot containing the peas n' rice and scattering these succulent pieces of jerk chicken, and the children were present to witness this horror. I shall never forget that image.

I tried to move away from the aspect of art for art's sake in my previous books. Even though the *Meeting Point* did contain certain aspects of the difficulties of West Indians who had to work as domestics, and even though *When Women Rule* deals with situations in which women in fact are in control of men so far as jobs, let's say the boss, the bank manager, the landlady, the wife, I felt that I had not faced the situation as it existed. So I was thinking that about what I as a writer had observed around me and had, because of my privileged position, taken a position of no comment. I felt that the time had come when I had to descend into the arena and take a position. So I wrote *In This City*, which deals with the problems of the police.

I do not know what your view of fiction writers is. I do not know if you subscribe to the prevailing opinion among academicians, which is to say that in every book of fiction you could find a significant if not the significant aspect of autobiography. I feel that the creative writer comes out of himself as a person different from himself, and takes on the characteristics, even if they are heinous and murderous, of the character. Because of his ability to fantasize and imagine, he is able to make these characters livable. It is therefore dangerous, to say the least, for the critic to feel that this man is so tied to his work that it may be termed autobiographical.

I then started to work on a novel, which I should tell you is a very brilliant novel. It was rejected 35 times by American publishers; that tells me something about their taste and tells me something about my own erudition.

Naipaul, for all the bad things we West Indians say about him, is a brilliant writer: his use of language, his use of structure, satire and his interest. And he is the only West Indian to have understood a foreign sensibility in such brilliant literary terms that he was able to write the novel *Mr. Stone and the Knights Companion,* which is the story of an old white man in England thinking about retirement and pension. And when I read this book, had I not known Naipaul, I would have said this book is written by an Englishman, certainly a white Englishman.

I am not going to discuss Naipaul vis-à-vis this book. I am going to discuss it in broad terms. To young writers who come to me foolishly asking me to help them to write because they think that they can only write from their experience, I say it doesn't mean if you want to write a story about a murderer you have to go out and kill somebody! But you have enough evidence in society from the newspaper that you ought to know with your modicum of imagination how to write about a murder. In my own case, it must be an aspect of my rejection of this society in which I have lived since 1955 that I have never been able to write a book or even a short story about Canadian characters. So I am saying then Naipaul's book is a tremendous victory of the ability of an artist to span the two cultures. I tried it in *More* and that is why, as I said, the book has been rejected by 35 American publishers. Of course, I could always say, as we used to say as a political tactic, "they reject my book because I'm black." But that doesn't make sense after serious consideration.

Ceci Foster recently said to me that the change in my point of view and the change in my language shows a change in my present stage of the representation of Canada in my fiction. It might be a result of my age, it might be the result of my greater wisdom, but I do not see the same immediacy of protest and urgency to say that something has happened because of race. I am trying now to see whether I could make the same point, with the same urgency and dramatic irony by pointing out or trying to see the heart and the moral fibre of the person that I am dealing with in the story.

And then finally, there is the question of the language we use, not meaning French or English, but the spirit in the language, the morality of the language. And I feel that if we are to succeed as authors from the part of the world from which we originate, we must pay particular attention to this question of the representation of Canada. It is obvious to those who have influence over what we write that we—and when I say we, I don't mean West Indians or Haitians only but we who in English and who are in the Establishment—are the new voices.

WORKS BY AUSTIN CLARKE

(1965) *Among Thistles and Thorns.* Markham, Ontario: McClelland and Stewart.

(1967) *The Meeting Point.* Toronto: McMillan of Canada.

(1971) *When he was Free and Young and He Used to Wear Silks.* Toronto: Anansi Press.

(1973) *Storm of Fortune.* Boston: Little Brown Press.

(1975) *The Bigger Light.* Boston: Little Brown Press

(1978) *The Prime Minister.* Markham, Ontario: Paper Jacks Press.

(1980) *Growing up Stupid Under the Union Jack: A Memoir.* Toronto: McClelland and Stewart.

(1985) *When Women Rule: Stories.* Toronto: McClelland and Stewart.

(1986) *Nine Men Who Laughed.* Markham,Ontario: Penguin Books of Canada.

(1986) *Proud Empires.* London: Gollancz Press.

CYRIL DABYDEEN

One's writing career and ideas usually develop over a lifetime: the presence and the sense of being in a struggle to discover one's self as a writer, all that occurs in the silent even awkward moments I sometimes refer to as the "ubiquitous unconscious (as said of Proust)."

Although I am known chiefly as a poet, underlined by the fact that I served as the Poet Laureate of Ottawa in the mid-1980s; but I also write fiction—now more than ever—and have published two novels, *The Wizard Swami* and *Dark Swirl.* My third, *Sometimes Hard,* is forthcoming shortly. Other shorter pieces of fiction have been appearing in the literary magazines in Canada, the United States and elsewhere. So my writing has been somewhat varied, straddling genres, (with essays, reviews, journalistic pieces) to reflect the writing life as fully as I possibly can.

It is significant for me to reflect on my beginnings in Canada, perhaps as a West Indian-Canadian (whatever these labels mean). I actually arrived in Canada in 1970, but the country was known to us in the Caribbean well before this and in a sense, it had been part of my psyche for a long time, an evolving consciousness more or less, which I alluded to earlier. The Maroons, for instance, were here very early in Canada's East Coast, establishing the basis for interconnectedness between the Caribbean and Canada, and influencing Caribbean immigrants here in defining the sense of roots in terms of identity. Now, whether seen as the "other," or in striving to become integrated in a changing, palpably Canadian immigrant society, it seems to me to be all part of what I have come to expect, living in Canada for almost 25 years now. Some of these feelings, or imaginative impulses and attitudes, are reflected in my concept of "here" and "there," which I touched on in the anthology *A Shapely Fire: Changing Literary Landscape.* My reason for undertaking this work was primarily to enhance this interconnectedness of peoples, as well as a desire to seek a better understanding of myself in a changing Canada.

My original South American-Caribbean source has also undergone change which continues to influence my apprehension of roots and heritage, all part of the process of coming to grips with one's self, as well as of constantly "becoming." And, indeed, I have been back to the region a few times over the years. In 1992 for instance, I participated in "Carifesta V" and was intrigued by what the head of CARICOM described as Caribbean peoples aspiring to "charisma and clarity." Then I quickly reminded myself of poet Derek Walcott describing the region, in metaphorical-cum-political terms, as the place with "drinks with umbrellas floating across the pool": that, in the metropolitan world's eyes, tourism is all the region is capable of, the end-all and be-all of Caribbean existence. Therefore, one's identity appears limited in terms of expectations or aspirations to go beyond being mere "waiters and waitresses." Novelist George Lamming of Barbados—one of the early influences on my imagination and sensibility—among others such as John Hearne, Edgar Mittelholzer, V.S. Naipaul, Vic Reid, Sylvia Wynter and Sam Selvon—no doubt challenged this concept of self and identity in his keynote speech during "Carifesta V" by asserting that "we are intellectual workers, but financially illiterate" as people.

Lamming went on to argue that exploitation is still with us, using the metaphor of the "donkey"—the ordinary people of the region—counterpointed with the image of the "horse"—no doubt the influential classes—which, bristling as he argued, always got the promotion! For Lamming, the Caribbean is a theatre of the class struggle, and no doubt his views are rooted in fundamental Marxism, an ideology I grew up with in Guyana as part of the struggle to get rid of colonialism and to reclaim the self, politically and imaginatively. You see, I lived in the region in the 1960s when one State after another was wresting its political independence, though not financial and economic.

But all that is changing now, I imagine, due not only to Cuba's decline, or to leftist ideologies being under attack. Ironically, in Trinidad, when I heard Lamming's address I hurried to Woodford Square in Port of Spain to listen to the reaction to his words being broadcast to the masses. But there was scant interest from the paltry, hodge-podge crowd, including derelicts in a state of ennui or desolation, as if they'd heard it all before. So you see, the intelligentsia, committed as they were, also experienced their own unique limitations. This is part of the ongoing crisis and dilemma affecting Caribbean development and the fulfilment of aspirations of the spirit of human imagination.

When I came to Canada as part of my personal quest and eveolving state of consciousness, I found myself not living in a large city but in Northern Ontario. Here, the sense of E.J. Pratt's vision of Canada reflected in the "twin bars of solitude and beauty," all that the vast landscape inspired, the somewhat tragic feeling of the place, did come home to me in a substantial way, especially as I sat close to Lake Superior and ruminated for hours on all the haunting qualities of time and place. Later, I worked in the forest seasonally as a tree planter (between 1970 and 1973), an experience which also helped me to redefine my sense of the spirit of the place, and enriched my understanding and appreciation of what I previously conceived Canada to be. Northrop Frye, besides identifying as a major theme the twin bars of beauty and solitude, saw another central dimension reflected in Canadian literature: one of "satire and exuberance" which I gradually also began to see around me in the day-to-day experience of intermingling with other Canadians. This came home to me more forcefully as I travelled from one end of the country to the other. During this time, I began to wrestle with an assortment of images in the context of the mythical and realistic elements that I had brought with me from the Caribbean and Guyana, as well as the veiled mystical vein particularly inspired by the landscape of Guyana (a part of the wide Amazon region). Some of this is reflected in my novel *Dark Swirl*, written while living in Ottawa, though its source is definitely my Guyanese years evoked through plumbing the so-called "bottomless pool of origins."

Gradually, too, I was starting to come to grips with what the late Jewish-Canadian writer Henry Kreissel called the strong undercurrent of passion and emotion that exists here, but which is often "hidden under a thick layer" of what he described as "reticent puritanism." As Kreissel, also foreign-born, adds: "To the man who comes here from abroad, this is not an easy country for him to know and write about"; this is one of the impulses that has remained with me in trying to adapt to my new surroundings. In this context, I admit to having difficulty writing authentically about Canada: to reflect in my being, the landscape as only "beauty and solitude," or the sense of the haunting spirit of the place as it should be. Maybe this is because I think writers do not simply sit down to write about a place or subject in any deliberate way, but only through the process of what is being formed and forming, the experience filtered through the imagination over a lifetime.

Creatively, things began to evolve slowly as I tried to make sense of what was and is around me, thereby exacting order, shape and form to those experiences that are significant, yet appear chaotic—but which ultimately would become solid or permanent as art. Indeed, it is a hit-or-miss process, I must admit.

Besides the post-colonialism that I reflect in my writing, let me say too, that Canada is now increasingly figured in the shaping of my consciousness. For instance, my early reading of Austin Clarke gave me a different sense of Canada which I might not have ordinarily understood, despite my knowledge of the Maroons in my sense of the farm labourers who were coming to Canada to live their transient lives and then to return back home.

I read Clarke's novels eagerly and became enthralled for a while by the vibrancy and overall passion of his writing: the way he used dialect, his verve, his vigour in depicting characters, especially those in his early trilogy describing the life of Caribbean domestic workers in Toronto. All of which has led me more forcefully to confront the question of identity, and indeed now I keep seeing myself as "the writer" in terms of a new nationality. Interestingly, the late Sam Selvon, who lived for many years in Calgary, would often say to me that he considered himself the only "Caribbean writer." The much younger Neil Bissoondath, also born in Trinidad, described himself unequivocally as "a Canadian writer," whereas Austin Clarke is simply "a writer." My own impulse in terms of identity is to see myself in the later category: I am not overly preoccupied with place because of what I have said previously about changing perspectives in one's consciousness. It is also a question of freedom of the imagination no doubt, or, overall, a form of liberation of the self that writing helps me to explore and achieve.

In my readings across the country, I have come to define my writing in terms of what the black activist Eldridge Cleaver said literature should be: "the combination of the alphabet with volatile elements of the soul." And that is what I wrestle with daily in my prose and poetry, the integrity stemming from it that goes along with being a writer or artist. And maybe this is the kind of responsibility that I see for all artists and writers everywhere, Caribbean-born, or those born in Canada. It is the concern for the human condition, uppermost which preoccupies my mind and spirit, combined with the shaping of experiences of the first 25 years when I lived in Guyana that is also significant as memory, and which still remains with me. No doubt, it is also a form of "jogging," reflection in "Jogging in Havana" (1992), an elaborate metaphor for the kind of painstaking process that the writer must undergo in trying to grapple with intricate experiences as a form of survival.

WORKS BY CYRIL DABYDEEN

(1977) *Goatsong.* Oakville, Ontario: Mosaic Press.
(1977) *Distances.* Vancouver: Fiddlehead Poetry Books.
(1979) *Heart's Frame.* Cornwall, Ontario: Vesta Publications.
(1979) *This Planet Earth.* Ottawa: Borealis Press.
(1980) *Still Close to the Island.* Ottawa: Commoner's Pub.
(1982) *Elephants Make Good Stepladders.* London: Third Eye.
(1985) *The Wizzard Swami.* Calcutta: Writer's Workshop.
(1986) *Islands Lovlier than a Vision.* Leeds, Yorkshire: Peepal Tree Press.
(1987) *A Shapely Fire, Changing the Literary Landscape.* C. Dabydeen (Ed.) Oakville, Ontario: Mosaic Press.
(1988) *To Monkey Jungle.* London, Ontario: Third Eye Press.

CECIL FOSTER

I do not think that we are as adequately represented in the mainstream media and in mainstream publishing as we should be, and I think of the struggle that people like Austin (Clarke) have had to endure over the last while, I don't want to say how long, you know, just to keep the flame out there. But I think that is about to change and I am confident that something is going to happen. I can think back to an article that I saw in the Montreal Gazette some time ago which said that, in fact, the people who are adding spice and new direction to Canadian literature are immigrants, and by and large the people they talked about were West Indians. This is not unusual because those of us who come from the Caribbean have come from an area that despite its geographical size and despite the fact that in terms of numbers we are perhaps no more than about six million, we have always been able to have a greater say beyond our relative size and that is why we have produced outstanding writers like Derek Walcott and others.

Last year when I was promoting my book in the United States, I found that there was almost a hunger there among people who wanted to share this West Indian experience and they also wanted to get some sense of how the West Indian and immigrant experience is a part of multiculturalism. As you know, multiculturalism is becoming a big issue or is the big issue in the United States, where they are beginning to move away from the notion of the melting pot to the notion of multiculturalism, which in itself creates opportunities for us.

In my case, I came into fiction writing probably riding the coattails of the fact that I was a journalist and certainly I had contacts in the industry which I was able to utilize. But at the same time, I know that I had to be following in the footsteps of a prolific writer like Austin Clarke. I think we need to recognize the work that other people have done before us.

WORKS BY CECIL FOSTER

(1992) *No Man in the House.* Toronto: Random House.
(1995) *Sleep on, My Beloved.* Toronto: Random House.

DANY LAFERRIÈRE

It's very terrible for anybody to use a language that he don't know especially for someone who would like to explain his sensibility and other such literary things. *C'est mon identité même qui est en quéstion. Je me demande toujours quelle sorte d'individu je suis. C'est parce que j'aimerais dire que je suis un écrivain haitien aujourd'hui parce que Haiti est dans une situation très difficile. D'ordinaire je ne me le dis jamais, je préfère croire que je suis peut-être un écrivain.* I would like to say that I am a Haitian writer today because my country is in pain and many times I say that I am only a writer and sometimes I think I wouldn't like to be a writer because when you are something, anything, you are dead. I am not in life to be something! I would like to do many, many things, maybe become an actor. I am the father of two daughters, make movies, have good friends in the life. I remember the first time someone called me a writer and I felt so cornered because you don't know when you are an adult exactly. A friend of a friend of mine talks about his daughter who has a very old boyfriend—40 years old—and he (the father) is very mad because he (the boyfriend) is FORTY YEARS! A very old man. And after, he's going to the toilet and he looks at himself in the mirror and he says, "I am FIFTY!" (he laughs). He forgets.

Sometimes you know about other persons. This is true you know. I know my age because now when I read in the newspaper I (see that) I am 40 years, and ten years ago I was only 30. Yes, it's true. Now I'm older than any policeman—yeah—they are younger than I. I am a middle-aged man—me—the son of my mother!

I said the son of my mother because my mother is so "tight" about her age. I remember when I went for the Canadian citizenship, and I called to my mother in Port au Prince (Haiti)—she is living now in Port au Prince.

I said: "Maman, I would like to know your age because of the government of Canada."

She said, "The government of Canada?"

"Yes!" I said,"Yes, the government of Canada would like to know your age."

She said, "But why does the government of Canada want my age?"

And I said, "The government of Canada is like that." And the government wants to know.

This is the knowledge, the BIG KNOWLEDGE!"

And she said, "You know that I was born in 1934?"

And I said "Maman! ... I said the Government OF CANADA!"

"Nineteen ... 1929!"

I said," MAMAN!"

She said, "O.K., O.K. Wait for me. I am going to get my real papers."

And I still don't know the age of my mother. We are like that in my family. We don't know many very important things—governmental things—it is maybe why I am so "tight" about what I am. It is so difficult for me to say "profession." What are you? Yeah, yeah, it is very "tight" in Canada about that.

I remember I am going to the telephone. I want to use the telephone.

She (the operator) says, "What's your name?"

"Laferrière."

"First name?"

"Dany."

"Your phone number?"

I said, "I am here to get a phone."

She said, " Yes, your phone number?"

I said, "This is my first phone number. I am from Haiti. I have just arrived here."

She said, "Yes, but there is a line (on the paper). I have to put something in this line. Phone number?"

And I think that was my first encounter in Canada. I thought that this was a really good country, a logical country! Yes! I prefer. Because in Haiti—Wow—Crazy country. When you don't have a phone nobody asks you your number phone. And yes, because people are so mad. They don't like to see you with a number phone. And in Canada no!

You are going to the supermarket to buy something. They ask you for your number phone. Yes! Now, when you try to say to anybody you don't have a card, MasterCard, credit card, they still ask me: "Your credit card?" "I said, I don't have a credit card." They look at me, not because they are mad that I don't have a credit card. They don't understand why I don't have a credit card. Yeah! But I have a good answer. I say that I am from Haiti. "You know there are many problems there now?" They say, Yes! Yes!

WORKS BY DANY LAFERRIÈRE

(1985) *Comment faire l'amour avec un nègre sans se fatiguer.* Montreal: VLB.

(1987) *Eroshima.* Montreal: VLB.

(1991) *L'odeur du café.* Montreal: VLB.

(1992) *Le goût des jeunes filles.* Montreal: VLB.

(1993) *Cette grenade dans la main du jeune Nègre, est-elle une arme ou un fruit?.* Montreal: VLB.

(1994) *Chronique d'une dérive douce.* Montreal: VLB.

DISCUSSION

Makeda Silvera: Perhaps this is not really a question, it is more of a statement. I've heard what Austin had to say and I think it is really quite wonderful what he had to say and also that I have read his works and I have always admired the kind of work that he has done in terms of Caribbean women in Canada, in terms of domestic workers.

What is actually quite disappointing to me is on this panel, is that I look around and they are all men and that there are no women. And that there are a lot of emerging women Caribbean writers within Canada, which is not reflected here. Please don't get me wrong and don't try to alienate yourself from me. I mean it is not a criticism toward any of you on the panel.

John Harewood: One interjection. I don't have the time to tell you the effort that we expended to get women to participate on this panel.

Makeda Silvera: I am the publisher of Sister Vision Press, which is the first and only black women and women of colour publishing house in Canada. We publish only women authors. We have many titles and they are all women. I don't wish to name names here because I'm not coming up here in a protest. I am just saying that there are lots of women out there and that we have been trying to make that connection. I am not an academic, but as academics and also as literary people you go for what you know. You don't take chances on people. There are a lot of new writers out there and there are a lot of new women. At Sister Vision Press we publish the new women.

Ewart Walters: Austin Clarke spoke about a manuscript that was rejected 35 times, which leads me to ask of the panelists to give us some sense of the difficulties of the mechanics really of having completed the work or even before you complete it, the mechanics of getting it published in Canada.

Cecil Foster: Let me say that to some degree I share what Makeda (Silvera) said earlier. And I think that's why we need to have greater access to major publishing houses. Getting published, I know, can be a very daunting thing. Very often you have your manuscript typed up and you send it off. You have to worry: do you need an agent before you send it off? And sometimes you cannot get an agent until you have already made an initial contact; you cannot get that initial contact until you have an agent to go and intercede for you; it becomes very difficult.

For me I was able to get through the system perhaps because I had a name in another area—in journalism—and I had an idea of how the industry works. I was able to cut through that.

Austin Clarke: And because you are good, so don't be too modest.

Cecil Foster: Well I hope that that is also true, but I think that in terms of the mechanics, there are many manuscripts out there that I think are also good that haven't been published.

Cyril Dabydeen: The question raised by Ewart is a very important one in my view. Many years back I had been publishing in the Caribbean of course, before coming to Canada. Somewhere I learned that you must get your work published in the small magazines, the so-called little magazines. It was felt that once you get a whole pile of things then a publisher would become interested in you, in your work, whether it is poetry or short fiction and then to bigger things. Even then it's an uphill task; but the more fundamental question or experience I have discovered is that most of the mainstream publishers tended not to understand fully the ethno-specific background from which our works or manuscripts are written.

I have had some extraordinary horror stories which I don't want to bore you with. But you will use words, which are familiar to any of us perhaps in the room here, but yet I have had an important publisher mark up my manuscript and a particular word as if it were a typo and it wasn't a typo. The word was "sitar" and they felt it was a typo, they didn't know the word "sitar."

There is another instance of a big American magazine. I sent a them a manuscript, a short story some years back. They praised the short story, but it was about a man who suddenly took off his clothes before an audience of school children. And she (the publisher) wrote to me and said: "Why is that such a strange thing, because people in the Caribbean do go around naked." That really threw me off because there again is a question of stereotyping in North America of those who are in the stranglehold of the mainstream publishing industry.

Within the last three, four, five years, I have personally seen a change in the attitude of some of the publishers, and some people like Sister Vision Press, of course, and other minority publishing houses have come to the fore; but nevertheless, to get your works published it seems the mainstream houses have a long distance to go.

WORKS BY MAKEDA SILVERA

(1983) *Silenced: Caribbean Domestic Workers Talk with Makeda Silvera.* Toronto: Sister Vision.

(1989) *Growing Up Black.* Toronto: Sister Vision.

(1991) Anthologized by M. Silvera, *Piece of my Heart. A Lesbian of Colour Anthology.* Toronto: Sister Vision.

(1991) *Remembering G. and Other Stories.* Toronto: Sister Vision.

(1993) M. Silvera (Ed.), *The Other Women. Women of Colour* in Canadian Literature, Toronto: Sister Vision.

(1993) Speaking of women's lives an imperialist economics: Two introductions from *Silenced, Returning the Gaze: Essays on Racism, Feminism and Politics.* H. Bannerji (Ed.). Toronto: Sister Vision.

(1994) *Her Head a Village and Other Stories.* Vancouver: Press Gang Publishers.

NOTES ON LATIN AMERICAN-CANADIAN LITERATURE

Jorge Etcheverry

Jorge Etcheverry focusses on certain characteristics and problems of Latin American literature in Canada, mainly its socio-cultural status in relation to the dominant literatures.

Jorge Etcheverry, cerne les caractéristiques et les problèmes de cette littérature latino-américaine au Canada, son statut socio-culturel ainsi que ses rapports avec les littératures dominantes.

*

LATIN AMERICAN-CANADIAN LITERATURE is currently undergoing rapid development. Practically nonexistent, until the second half of the 1970s except for the presence of certain writers, it is now laying claim to a well-defined space within the "Canadian mosaic." Symptomatic of this trend is the fact that publishing houses such as Coach House, Wallace, Québec Amérique, and others,[1] are publishing Canadian-Latin American authors in English and French translation. Apart from this activity, there are also publishing efforts in the Latin American ethno-cultural sphere itself, characterized by editorial criteria that vary from publisher to publisher; however, all these publishers give priority to the publication of exiled authors, namely those who were formed in their countries of origin, or those whose textual characteristics can be assimiliated to Latin American literature per se (for example, publishers such as Cordillera, Split Quotation, Omelic); while publishers such as El unicornio verde and La enana blanca are more interested in authors formed in Canada and linked to the Latin American community, with a focus on the local aspect. Girol, which focuses mainly on the academic Hispanic market, has begun to publish the occasional title by Latin American-Canadian (or Canadian-Latin American) authors.

National, regional and local magazines and newspapers publish texts, critical notes and interviews about this literature, produced by authors of Latin American (especially Chilean) origin,[2] and the authors read or present their work in different contexts at various institutional levels. There is a plethora of fora and of publications from the mainstream to the fringe. We define the mainstream media as a cultural vehicle in one of the official languages, within a framework socially sanctioned and perceived as "Canadian"or "Québécois."[3] Books published by the more marginal venues, such as some of the small publishing houses mentioned above, are sometimes reviewed in the established media, and sometimes receive some funding from various levels of official organizations. Some of the marginal cultural/literary events (that is, from the point of view of their management by an ethno-cultural minority group, in this case Latin American) are beginning to acquire a more institutional character, even if they continue to be perceived as particular, since they represent a non-hegemonic linguistic/cultural sector. Funding of these events depends on fulfilling two conditions: the partial or total use of the prefix denoting their Canadian character; and its inclusion in their presentation of an event or the title of a publication. The cultural events in this category occur mostly in regions where the cultural/social ambiance tends to trans-culturalism.[4] Apart from these activities, however, is the "pure" ethno-cultural (Latin American) cultural/literary/publishing activity that seems to be growing in recent years as a result of an increase in the Hispanic population and the work initiated by exiled Latin American groups during the 1970s and 1980s. The work of these latter groups has created an ambiance that fosters the existence of a real Latin American cultural space, which though limited, is nonetheless expanding. Collaboration—somehow implicitly discouraged in Canadian-North American society—between a perceived "elite" and the grass roots of the community, explains how a certain institutional or social stability is attained through these events, as well as a specific literary level (understood as the presence of specialized discursive and textual elements that imply the assumption of an historical development in literature and writing).

Why does this result from collaboration between classes? In terms of the society at large, Latin American literature produced in Canada can only expand within the space allowed by the dominant literatures, defined by the institutional and literary market framework. Without institutional support, most of this literature would not be developing as it is. Like most literary production/circulation/distribution, the subsidization of authors and publications constitutes the backbone of this cultural activity. This implies the presence of certain criteria for the allocation of funding. The receptivity of the public is based on its expectations, which are rooted in its presuppositions (in the sense given to the term by the Theory of Receptivity) and on more general determinants of what society expects from literature.

From this perspective, literature is primarily conceived as a reflection and testimony of the life, circumstances and idiosyncracies of the producer group, for which the author is considered a sort of spokesperson. The literary discourse conceived in this way tends to limit the so-called "poetic function" and the mediation peculiar to literary language, as it is to all aesthetic languages. One of the main defects of a literary text from this point of view is its lack of accessibility or of transparency that extends from the "formal" aspects to the "content," thus precluding ambiguity, parody and certain forms of humor, irony and the grotesque. There exists alongside a general conception of the genders in which "poetry" is basically the lyric expression of the self and in which prose implies a "plot" as its necessary and basic element.

All of this creates an ambivalent picture: on the one hand, literary expression is democratized through emphasis on its accessibility; on the other, its artistic sophistication tends to be eliminated, together with those elements that do not conform to prevalent, normative manifestations perceived as universal. Another equally ambiguous aspect arises from the location of Latin American-Canadian literature within the process of emergence of groups previously marginalized from the mainstream economic areas and from socio-political-decision-making. As in the case of other minority groups or so-called "special interest groups," literature as part of culture became a space for the expression of ethno-cultural or generic identity and vindication. It appears, and this is a very personal view, that in spite of the gradual disappearance of an alternative social order, the so-called "system" nevertheless allots space for a certain affirmation of the specificity and the revindication of the "marginal" groups, among them ethno-cultural ones. The cultural manifestations so produced reaffirm the right to existence of these communities without putting into question the socio-economic framework of society as a whole. In other words, it seems that regardless of their language, dress, beliefs or preferences, everybody wants to live in suburbia. Institutional support for political correctness more or less meshes with the movement that originates within the marginal communities, drawing them toward forms that do not alter the social system. It is worth noting that an alternative seems to have disappeared at the world level as well. The space assigned to minority cultural manifestations appears to be governed by two criteria: first, demographic, which assigns space to groups according to the demographic weight of their community and, second, the possession, or not, of a defined profile of the community (manifest or visible minority). Within this framework, Latin American-Canadian literature is ruled by the demographic alterations of the collective population it represents and by the acquisition of a defined profile in the sense of visible minority.

Canadian-Latin American (or Latin American-Canadian) literature and the determination of its consumption and production are shaped by the expectations and presuppositions about it. The 1970s and 1980s that saw Latin American immigration/exile acquire a relative presence also saw the shaping of a preconceived content for the literature that this community of mainly exiled writers began producing in Canada, its basic elements of content being exoticism, exile, political oppression and vitality, the latter appearing as just another variant of the *bon sauvage,* present in Western culture since the discovery and conquest by the West of the rest of the world.

In the beginning, these elements were not clearly delineated and were not prevalent in the publishing efforts by Latin American communities.[5] It was somewhat later, due to the intervention of mainstream Canadian and Québécois publishers and critics, that these elements became more prevalent, resulting in a certain demand for Latin American literature produced in Canada. These features were coupled with that most universally demanded of newcomer literatures, namely, a tale of acculturation. These characteristics sometimes lead to involuntary distortion, colouring the very biography of an author. A case in point is a reported interview in the media in which an author, in passing, had mentioned persecution. The journalist who had conducted the interview then made an issue of it to the point of explaining even the author's writing in terms of this experience.

In general terms, the phenomenon of demographic determination mentioned previously and of the acquisition of profile as being relevant to the assigning of a cultural space, is a feature of North America that tends to obliterate the universality which constituted one of the predominant traits of modernism (it may be that the whole of the new literature that tends to express by demand the perspective of a specific group in North America is post-modernist). Due to the importance of the population of Hispanics in the United States, it is not strange that there is in that country, an abundant literary Hispanic production in magazines and publishing houses and that it is the object of critique and academic study, phenomena that until recently did not exist in Canada. The Latin American Hispanic community in Canada will never become a major ethnic group; thus, the incidence of institutional studies of Hispanic or Latin American literature in Canada, at a university level, in Spanish departments for instance, will remain less than marginal. Generally however, most of the books of Latin American literature produced in Canada and published in English or French are reviewed in mainstream magazines and newspapers, but never in the specialized Candian Hispanic publications. However, relative accessibility has put self-publication within everyone's reach who is interested, resulting in texts that are often valuable sociological documents but seldom truly literary texts. In general, literary texts tend to have already received recognition and to be written by authors who have produced work in their country of origin.

For a number of exiled Latin American authors, literature is marked by universality, in which the level of expression is as important as the complexity of content; document and testimony are considered almost as second-class literary forms, even if their documentary quality is acknowledged and ideologically promoted and defended in some instances as a vehicle to show the Latin American reality and all its social contradictions. In spite of their being politically motivated, most of the exiled Latin American authors (the majority of whom are Chilean) who introduced Latin American literature produced in Canada in the 1970s and 1980s did not automatically produce committed or documentary writing.[6]

For most of these authors, who were former militants in politically progressive or revolutionary organizations in their countries of origin, there were always more practical vehicles for political action and influence: "the duty of the revolutionary is to make revolution" was the famous motto of Che Guevara. The social contradictions are so evident in Latin America that no special effort is needed to perceive them. Moreover, the formation of Latin American writers is important in other ways. Listening to the radio, reading, and engaging in readily available conversation, made the experience of reading and writing more mediated and more closely linked to their linguistic element. I have the impression that literature in North America, which has to compete with the sensorial bombardment of television, tends to minimize mediation and to place a value on the boldness and strength of immediate communication ("slight" and "strong" are not by accident critical criteria), at the expense of connotation and ambiguity. These are some of the problems that writers, formed in Latin America, have to face here, and yet they still make up the majority of active writers in the Latin American community.[7]

From this panorama arise certain tasks for Latin American producers of culture in Canada. Organizations must be created for the diffusion and communication of culture at a national level, a culture that is interdisciplinary and popular, linked with the community, without deleting the more specifically literary "elitist" elements. It is also essential to establish agreements with the media of the Latin American community in Canada to alot space for literature alongside sports and folklore, gastronomy, and social notes. The ongoing, though slow, development of a consumer public of literary books in Spanish produced in Canada has been coupled with the increase of books in English about Latin America which are not merely translations of the big names of the Latin American literary boom. This relatively new development of Latin American culture produced in Canada increases the responsibility of editors in the selection of works for publication, if the Latin American heritage is to evolve and not be turned into a sort of subculture. There is a tendency toward fragmentation as a side effect of the cultural manifestation of the different non-mainstream or para-mainstream groups and a tendency towards cultural regionalization. This general trend tends to lead Latin American-Canadian culture toward a niche market. In confronting the above, it also appears necessary to develop links with other ethno-cultural groups to generate intercultural activities and products, like the anthology *Symbiosis* (Girol, 1992), by the Ottawa-based poet of Chilean origin Luciano Díaz, who put together for the first time in book form the poetry of different ethnic communities of the Ottawa valley.

ENDNOTES

1. Coach House Press has published the work of Rafael Barreto-Rivera, the well-known experimental poet of Puerto Rican origin; Québec Amérique has published the work of Marilú Mallet, the Chilean-Québécoise prose writer and filmmaker; Cormorant Books, the Chileans Leandro Urbina and Naín Nómez, the latter now

living in Chile; Alfonso Quijada Urías, the Salvadorean poet and writer; and a number of texts by Latin Americans who live in Canada appear in the anthology *Compañeros,* mainly compiled by Hugh Hazelton. Humanitas/Nouvelle Optique has published the work of Alberto Kurapel, the Chilean Québécois playwright, the Salvadorean poet Salvador Torres, the Colombian-Québécois poet Yvonne Truque; VLB the work of Jorge Fajardo, the Chilean-Québécois prose writer and filmaker and the Argentinian-Canadian prose-writer Pablo Urbanyi.

2. The most significant has been the issue of *Canadian Fiction Magazine* devoted to Latin American writers in Canada, including the work of Ramón Sepúlveda, Raúl Gálvez, Marilú Mallet, Pablo Urbanyi, Luis Lama, Ludwig Zeller, Leandro Urbina, Renato Trujillo, Miguel Retamal, Alfredo Saavedra, Jorge Etcheverry, and David Mibashán. More limited in scope seems to be the selection of authors in the recent *Canadian Literature.* 142/143, Fall/Winter 1994, entitled "Hispanic-Canadian Connections," which includes work by Margarita Feliciano, Naïn Nómez and Jorge Etcheverry, plus some articles on particular authors. The only encompassing article, "Quebec Hispánico: Themes and Integration in the Writing of Latin Americans Living in Québec" by Hugh Hazelton refers to the "high proportion of Chileans (about half) within this group" (pp.120-121).
3. Harbour Front, Le salon du Livre de L'Outaouais, the Ottawa Valley Book Festival, and the Festival de poésie de Trois-Rivières, can be considered mainstream literary events.
4. The Celebración cultural del idioma español, which includes a literary section and that is held every year in Toronto with support from the community, universities and other institutions and organized mainly by professor and poet Margarita Feliciano, is the most important event of Latin American culture in the country.
5. At the time these efforts were being made by the Chilean publishing house, Cordillera, operating in Ottawa, and Oasis publications, based in Toronto, and directed by the surrealist poet of Chilean origin, Ludwig Zeller. Oasis has published (and still does) texts by Zeller as well as selections of surrealist writers, classic and new. Cordillera has published the testimonial and committed *Las Malas Juntas,* a book of short stories by Leandro Urbina which became a classic of the period in Chile and has been recently published again by Planeta. Between 1981 and 1985, it has also published among other titles, the individual books of poetry of the members living in Canada of the neo-avant-garde poetic group of the 1960s in Chile, The School of Santiago, plus the almost complete work of Gonzalo Millán, one of the most important Chilean poets of his generation who at the time lived in Canada. The importance given in these notes to writers and poets of Chilean origin arises from the special circumstances of their exile in the early 1970s; they constituted a more or less homogeneous group whose literary careers were already underway in

Chile and who also worked in different aspects of solidarity with Chile, including cultural practices that were organized and depended on the support of their basically exiled community. Accordingly, they began with certain advantages that resulted in a stronger presence and they tended at times to take the lead over other Latin-American communities in cultural matters. Nevertheless, I believe they share with other Latin American-Canadian writers certain general elements, to the point of being a representative example. The latest project of Cordillera in Canada in Spanish to date is the anthology *Enjambres: Poesía latinoamericana en el Québec,* co-edited by Jorge Etcheverry and Daniel Inostrosa and co-published with La Enana blanca y El gallo rojo. *Enjambres* was the first anthology of Latin American writing in Quebec to include the "experimental," the "lyric," the "documental" and the "committed."

6. As an example, the Salvadorean poet Salvador Torres Sasso writes committed poetry, poems that continues the modernistic Latin American tradition of Rubén Darío and poetry that incorporates elements of the Anti-Poetry of the Chilean contemporary author of the Artifacts, Nicanor Parra; Juan Ramón Mijango is a committed Salvadorean poet; and Alfonso Quijada Urías, the best known in Salvador, appears to be committed in his prose, though not in his poetry.
7. Almost all of of the Latin American writers in Canada who have been published in a 'professional' way, who are more or less known in their countries of origin, who have produced work recognizable for its individual traits, or who have achieved some measure of recognition in Canada are between their late 30s and early 50s, sometimes even older. Until now, a second generation of Latin American-Canadian or Hispanic writers is largely absent, with the exception of the odd case, such as that of Alejandra Bravo. The demographic factor mentioned previously of the Latin American community would not allow for the preservation of cultural skills that are greatly specialized and not easily marketable, such as Latin American literature produced in Canada, namely, a literature in a foreign language. That is not to say that more marketable and less sophisticated products, such as dancing, cooking and crafts, cannot survive; they may well proliferate and become consumer products without an organic link to their original communities.

LATIN AMERICAN WRITERS IN CANADA: INTEGRATION AND DISTANCE, WRITING AT THE CROSSROADS

Naïn Nomez

The author attempts to show "how the process of adaptation to the cultural context has been reproduced in the literary discourse." He also points out the situation of Latin American writers who, like himself, return to "the horror filled country which we never wanted to leave."

Naïn Nomez nous montre «la manière dont le processus d'adaptation à un contexte culturel se traduit en discours littéraire.» Il met en relief également la situation des écrivains de l'Amérique latine qui, comme lui, reviennnent «aux horreurs d'un pays qu'ils n'ont jamais voulu quitter.»

*

THE PHENOMENON of the massive transplantation of Latin American intellectuals to other areas of the world, particularly to more economically developed countries, that began in the 1970s has generated a varied literature dealing with the problems of transculturation, exile, and the symbolic relationships of the individual with these diverse societies. Due to its specific original matrix of an English domaine belatedly converted into an independent nation state, Canada has a porous way of absorbing ethnic groups of diverse genesis without completely destroying them. At the beginning, some of the typical cultural traits of these groups were retained, but with time, these traits became more and more superficial and stereotyped. In the specific case of writers, a more selective and articulate individual and collective memory grafted onto itself certain elements of the unfamiliar, day-to-day reflective experiences, until they formed a mosaic, a collage, a shoal of diverse elements creating a mix of languages and varied messages, shaping a literature of diaspora, which is itself a kind of graft onto the tissue of the dominant culture of this nation.

Exiled and immigrant writers search feverishly within the new cultural domain for a sublimation of the void left by their origins (whether or not they were happy then) and of other negativities which affect their lives in a world that alienates them from their language, the meaning of their lives, the geography of their neighbourhoods, their cities and their nation, their relatives, friends, their social values, and all the cultural coordinates of their individual origins.

The immigrants with fewer economic and intellectual resources attempt to balance their truncated social links, the loss of everyday cultural habitat and of their capacity to communicate, by dulling themselves through work and seeking compensation through consumerism and material well-being. The intellectual and the professional strive to integrate into the new environment while attempting to overcome the psychological stress that comes from living and working in a society very different from one's own, and sometimes hostile. To this end, the intellectual and professional attempt to transform the aggressor-stimuli—irritability, insomnia, anguish, depression, physical disease—into a postive stimulus by means of an awareness of both cultures, that of origin and that of exile.

In this sense, the Canadian context, with its mosaic of races, languages and customs, offers a specific symbiosis to the Latin American immigrant. The writers can even give an account of their experiences and lives in their own language, Spanish, issuing signals and messages for a limited, almost nonexistent public, which nevertheless makes the writers live the illusion of an historical and cultural continuity with their place of origin.

In the case of Chileans, most of whom emigrated in the aftermath of the military coup, the majority of them, for a certain time, chose as the main theme of their work the experiences of uprooting, frustration, cultural separation, nostalgia for the lost world, the repression there, loneliness and the differences between the two worlds, all of which produced a symbolic freezing of the memory and a denial of the acceptance of the present. In their literary work, the constant of exile crops up, a continuous process of integration and disintegration in which the appeal from both cultures acts both as motivating and schismatic forces.

In most writers, the process of cultural reappropriation is only partially achieved and, in many cases, it is not completed until at least two generations later. However, this has not been the Chilean case. Even if Canada's multicultural policies revitalize a series of minuscule subcultures articulated around ethnic publications, prizes and activities, this peculiar seal of approval seldom transforms itself into a dialogue which could enrich diversity and new cultural forms.

To come back to the experience of Chilean writers in Canada, an experience I have shared for the past 20 years, it would be necessary to show how the process of adaptation to the cultural context has been reproduced in the literary discourse. If we analyze such a process in its totality, we find it has three stages of development:

1. The fixation on the culture of the original country seen as a time of plenitude, broken by the social cataclysm that drives the subject writers out of their motherland.
2. The disintegration and fragmentation of this already non-existent past mixed with a hopeless and disillutioned attitude toward the future, which produces in the present a feeling of emptiness, loneliness and uprootedness.
3. The questioned integration that implies a reassessment of the relations of identity with the Canadian world and the place of origin. This reasessed integration is manifested as an attempt to balance the relationship with both cultures through the critical mediations provoking the assumption of the new social identity. This new identity would mean creative maturity; the attempt to assume the porosity of Canadian society, creating an art developed in the interstices and hollows of its cultural body, which would grow out of a critical relationship with its surroundings in order to resist both alienation and attachment. Thus, the writer becomes the owner of a double motherland, of an ever-changing and multifaceted identity, which identifies itself more with differences than with similarities, more with what is hybrid than with what is uniform. It maybe that this form of cultural reappropriation, which can generate writing that accepts itself as antagonistic, heterogeneous and diverse, implies the idea that what is ours, what characterizes us, is what is always beyond, and that signifies much more than motherland, nation or language.

And what happens to those who return?

Coming back is always difficult and never complete. "The horror-filled country which we never wanted to leave" is not the same. Neither are we. Strangers in all lands, those who left come back after the long voyage, hoping to find the niche they left and to fit in again. But everything has changed. New generations of writers have arrived who watch distrustfully those who return, who have learned to speak another language and who are full of exotic customs. The writer seeks to integrate the experience of exile with that of return, but the result is a pastiche made out of experiences that do not belong to either, because the writer has lost his or her natural public. Detached from here and there, the returning writer swings on a tightrope in perpetual movement that wants to keep being part of both cultures, to talk about them, to contrast them, to force them into a dialogue, to learn and to teach what others can tell us more wisely. But the writer seldom reaches the balance necessary to produce a discourse that would allow him or her to trespass the heavy screens of continental, national, regional and local identities. So, writer of nowhere, of everywhere, or at least, of two places, the returned writer attempts once and again to recover the best of the two worlds in a gesture that is basically symbolic, discursive, and imaginary, but which, like all rites, seeks to exorcise the break created and to escape the curse.

WRITING IN EXILE: WRITING NOWHERE FOR NOBODY?

José Leandro Urbina

The problem of cultural exile is the central motive of this text: "my personal mythologies have become hybrid, the narrative of Chile is still present, but Canada is also on my horizon."

Le problème de l'exil culturel est le motif central de l'intervention de José Leandro Urbina. Il affirme: «mes mythologies personnelles sont hybrides; le récit chilien est toujours présent mais dorénavant, le Canada fait partie de mes histoires.»

*

COMPELLED TO THINK about my particular state of life as a Chilean-Canadian writer who came to this country as an exile, I have been literally overwhelmed by the number of different angles and levels from which it is possible to review such an experience. One could in fact write several books just on the most obvious problems encountered when writing in exile.

If I had to define simply, for the purpose of analysis, what I thought a writer was, I would say that he or she is an individual who produces texts by working with a specific language and within a particular mythology, reproducing this mythology, or criticizing it, from the perspective of the social group or groups to which he or she belongs.

This definition is perhaps general, and certainly not very romantic, but it does allow me to touch on three points that I consider essential in order to grasp the problem of cultural exile: 1) the language issue; 2) the question of national or personal mythology (a question that also raises the problem of personal identity); and 3) the social condition and social position that defines one's perspective as a writer (moral values, taste, and the world one chooses to represent, etc.).

"Words, words, words" complained Hamlet to Polonius: authors (and, thus, their characters) have known for a long time that language can be manipulated, and that the ability to manipulate language is of supreme importance in the battles of life. Language can be used as a means to an end. That was discovered by the Greeks; they were the first to suspect language in its capacity to convey the truth. The initial development of writing and public speaking were closely linked to the development of politics and political power, and were therefore also closely linked to negotiation and persuasion, and (why not) coercion and deception; after all, the sophists were the most skillful rhetoricians.

Language is neither innocent nor disinterested. Language takes the place of reality, and can mask it; it can create beauty in a world of pain and, in doing so, can bury the truth. At the same time, language makes possible—to a significant extent—the development of our relationship with the world and with others, and it is an indispensable tool in the construction of identity. Language feeds memory and forgetting. We know that we can make sense of our lives as in a narrative, even when our lives are absurd. We are always telling ourselves and others stories about who and how we are, where we came from and what our position in the universe is, whether this universe is big or small.

Writers are professional storytellers. We have an uneasy relationship with language. ("Words, those little whores," Julio Cortázar used to say). We, of course, love them. They make us possible, but they can also destroy us. So you can imagine what silence means for a writer, and what it means to be expelled from the prison house of language—on parole. To abandon your language is to abandon your skin, because to move into another language is not like changing your clothes. Reason and emotion are constituted through language, creativity is part of the power of words. Indeed, in the beginning, was the Word.

Our fundamental mythologies are also expressed in language:

Chile fértil provincia y señalada	Chile, fertile province, famous
en la región antártica famosa	In the vast Antarctic region
de remotas naciones respetada	Known to far-flung mighty nations
por fuerte, principal y poderosa:	For her queenly grace and courage,
la gente que produce es tan granada,	Has produced a race so noble,
tan soberbia, gallarda y belicosa,	Dauntless, bellicous, and haughty

que no ha sido por rey jamás regida	That by King it ne'er was humble
ni a extranjero dominio sometida.	Nor to foreign sway submitted.1

(Alonso de Ercilla, 1550)

Language created Chile before it was a nation. The poet sang our first people as they were being taken by force. Our first poem is an epic of winners and losers, but, as a poem with no ending, history remains for us an open book.

The 19th century saw our struggle for independence, and our founding fathers used to say incredible things in the midst of battles. They say that, while trying to break a siege, O'Higgins said: "Either to live with honour or to die with glory, the brave ones follow me." And later, during the Pacific war against Perú and Bolivia, our mythical hero, Arturo Prat—captain of a small warship that was sunk—was said to have jumped overboard, sword in hand, and to have died on the deck of the ennemy battleship while making a wonderful speech about commitment to the Chilean flag. We might lose the battle, but, boy, are we courageous and brilliant speech-makers. So we absorb our mythological past and are defined by it. Our stories define our community and to a large extent our personal identity. Writers are fed by these stories and either they come to work within the script or they rebel against it. One way or another, our mythology is inescapable; it is one of the major elements to link us to our audience; it is what we know together.

So you can imagine what it means for writers to be severed from their mythology, to go to another culture where the references that constitute their identity are unknown, where the fictional worlds they create are nothing but shadows.

Finally, we grew up in a class society, where culture, art and literature were mostly, if not completely, monopolized by the upper classes; artists represented themselves and others within the cultural parameters dictated by their own privileged social position. Coming from such a tradition, many of us who didn't belong to the upper classes economically but nevertheless possessed a somewhat "upper class" education, struggled trying to find alternative representations. In the throes of this search we were forced to abandon, we arrived in a country whose class structure was flexible and where everybody considers himself or herself a part of the middle. How do we situate ourselves here? And when we have to assimilate the new cultural borders that divide the social space in an "either you're in or you're out" that sometimes ressembles "either you're up or you're down," where are we?

It has been a long battle for many of us writers to reconstitute ourselves, to be able to reconstruct our creative basis. Everyone has chosen a different alternative. Personally, I chose to stay with my first language in my creative writing. Trying to wrench from a language the qualities that make art possible is a task that is too difficult and an endeavour that is too long to just be thrown away. So I live most of the time in English, but I continue to write in Spanish. Sometimes I translate. My personal mythologies have become hybrid, the narrative of Chile is still present, but Canada is also on my horizon. Which Canada? As for where I am, where I write from, maybe I could say, like everybody does nowadays, that I write from the border, or from the crossroads of up-and-down in-and-out, in a language that has evolved far from its source. What I will continue to be able to produce under these circumstances, and for whom, I cannot say. The ghosts of fossilization and banality haunt us, irrelevancy sleeps under our pillows. Our quest for reality in a place that we'll never know well enough is a quest that is constant, and sometimes we long for a place that is no longer the same. So we become our own only stable territory; we fill our pens with our veins. I became the whole world. But at the same time, because of a ridiculous paradox, curiosity for the "others" increases. I have remained curious. I keep searching, learning, inventing, writing when I can, copying the shadows from the wall of the cave for who knows who. But I love it.

ENDNOTE

1. De Ercilla, A. (1945). *La Araucana.* C.M. Lancaster, P.T. Manchestor (Trans.) Nashville: Vanderbilt University Press.

MESSAGE FROM THE CROSSROADS

Alfonso Quijada Urías

Here, exile is seen as a universal experience for the writer: "in every writer there's an escape artist, a fugitive, an exile ... within his or her own country."

Alfonso Quijada Urías croit que l'exil est une expérience universelle pour l'écrivain: «dans chaque écrivain, il existe un artiste, un fugitif, un exilé à l'intérieur de son propre pays.»

*

THE NOTION OF "CROSSROADS," which in Spanish also has the figurative meaning of "dilemma" is associated with another closely related word, "labyrinth," which in present times implies a pathway through a literary universe where Kafka, Borges, Hawthorne and Octavio Paz, author of *The Labyrinth of Solitude,* all serve as guides. I believe that as writers and poets become aware of their vocation, they discover a different world—of words, of the imagination—and that this discovery makes them appear strange to other people. They are perceived as having failed to adjust to a reality that is too harsh or alien for their sensibilities; instead, they transform it, and in doing so free themselves from an overwhelming burden. Thus writers and poets, as in the ancient tale of the labryrinth of Crete, spend their days twining magic thread or searching for the master key that will let them find their way out of the labyrinth, or dilemma. It is the power of the word that allows us to escape the labyrinth because without the word we would be condemned to perish within it.

For Latin American writers, the labyrinth, or dilemma, is much more than a metaphor. From the moment we first become aware of this tortuous configuration we know that in our search for the way out we are bound to meet up with the monster. Like some animal from the Apocalypse, this beast has a multitude of heads and names: dictatorship, poverty, illiteracy, consumerism, advertising. The monster is not fond of mirrors; it does not like to look at itself in the waters of poetry; nor does it tolerate laughter, happiness, or any kind of spiritual understanding. That's why in every writer there's an escape-artist, a fugitive, an exile, perhaps even someone exiled within his or her own country. I think of Quevedo, of Dante. (How many sandals did he wear out traversing the twelve circles of exile?) I think of Darío and his *Wandering Song;* of Neruda fleeing General Videla, Neruda on horseback as if he were the reincarnation of Joaquín Murieta; of poor Vallejo going mad with sorrow in the rain in the suburbs of Paris. I think of all those poets, both famous and anonymous, who despite pain, banishment, mockery, and hunger, were able to leave us their finest legacy: laughter, celebration, hope.

Fleeing, like them, from our own local dilemmas, from the police-state labyrinths in which the rewards of physical and spiritual searching are death and madness, we are faced with a new and unknown reality: that of being strangers in a new land where English, French, and many other cultures and languages all converge. We are uprooted; we speak of identity because we feel guilty. We are terrified by the spiritual coldness around us—an outgrowth of consumerism—and by the ruthless market forces that transmit their diseases of selfishness, ugliness and evil. Fortunately, geographic proximity allows us to maintain ties with our countries of origin and fall back on the great Latin American family, daughter of the diaspora, a true cultural embrace that reproduces ancestral signs. It is with her that we dance to salsa, lambada, reggae, danzón: those slow movements with which we gradually carve out a new space within Canadian society that we then cross-culturally transform with our own Latin American characteristics.

Octavio Paz, in his essay on Hispanics living in the United States, said that Catholic Hispanic society was communal and that its nucleus was the family, a miniature solar system which revolves around a single sun: the mother. The cardinal importance of the image of the mother in Latin American society is certainly no accident: it is a symbol that combines ancient feminine deities of the Mediterranean with Christian virgins, pre-Columbian goddesses with those of Africa, Isis with Maria, Coatlicue with Yemayá. Axis of the world, wheel of time, centre of movement, magnet of reconciliation, the mother is the source of life and the repository of religious beliefs and traditional values.

One of the miracles of poetry comes through the gestation of the word in freedom. Through its loving imagination, poetry calls human beings together, unifies them, and makes them pass through the eye of the needle of the spirit. We must defend the right to use words in unrestrained liberty, without being harassed or dictated to by the tyranny of the mind or by intellectual shallowness and conformity. To write in freedom is to exorcize, our demons; it is to invoke the forces of life, occult powers that will keep us from falling into tedium and indifference, coldness and egotism. I say this because of the risk of being infected by the stupor that is typical of the inhabitants of the rich nations, of societies in which surfeit has led to sclerosis. In Latin America, as in any country in the Fourth World, poverty, hunger, and the nightstick have only made the flame of love of life burn with greater intensity. We continue to dream and believe in the power of love, of intelligence, and of human solidarity. Funerals in our villages are followed by celebration and carnival; sometimes the music is so good that even the dead person climbs out of the coffin and joins in the dancing. This is what leads to a meeting of the baroque and the straightforward in our literature, and why the magic of our writing grows out of an excess of reality. Realism and surrealism are words from the same source; they are also empty words that mean nothing in Mexico, Argentina (I'm thinking of Borges), Chile, Honduras, or El Salvador, precisely because they take in everything that has seemed natural to us since childhood, all that is part of our world, the universe of Juan Rulfo, the landscape of Salarrué.

The dilemma of being there and here, of being foreign, of speaking English or French and thinking in Spanish, is like a change of skin, an unending metamorphosis, for we never cease remembering the past or lose the desire to return to the motherland as to a source of life. But for every illness there is a cure: herbs that help us to heal our wounds, words and magic spells, poems that make us look ahead, like this poem by Mahmud Darvish, which reflects the whole of our longing:

> Seal me with your eyes;
> Take me away wherever you go ...
>
> Protect me with your eyes
> Carry me off like a relic of
> the house of pain ...
>
> Take me away like a toy, like a brick,
> so that our children never forget
> to return.

THE WRITER IN EXILE

Pablo Urbanyi

Exile is also the theme of Pablo Urbanyi's text where personal and social aspects of exile interweave as "periodic uprootings of people—slaves, artists, or philosophers—are deeply rooted in phonomena well documented in ancient times."

L'exil est le thème central du texte de Pablo Urbanyi, où des éléments personnels et sociaux s'entremêlent à la manière des «déracinements ponctuels des peuples—esclaves, artistes ou philosophes—des phénomènes bien documentés dans l'antiquité.»

*

FOR ANYONE, ARTIST OR NOT, the experience of exile is bound to be upsetting to their happiness and well-being (if such things really exist). It matters little whether such an uprooting is the result of voluntary emigration in search of a better world or forcible banishment from one's homeland. The loss of points of reference, of the feeling of belonging, combined with an abrupt break in the continuity and evolution of a person's life, are overwhelming and can lead to an acute sense of disorientation and chaos, especially if the person is a writer.

In order to clarify certain issues of scientific or academic methodology—or simply to put this paper itself into better perspective—it would be a good idea to specify what kind of emigration or exile we are talking about. Our discussion should also include points such as the person's age, where he or she came from, the dates of departure from the home country and arrival here, and the motives that caused the departure.

Despite the modern rush to examine and try to explain people's motivations for emigrating, as well as digging into the origins of their other sorrows and misfortunes—motivations that have been extensively discussed and studied elsewhere—I personally do not believe there is any real answer to the problem. I think that this paper—clearly a First World academic luxury—will in the end be nothing more than words. I will go on living and giving vent to personal bitterness somewhere else. The lucky ones will eventually be able to share their rancour with someone else like themselves, thus falling into a vicious circle of dangerous ruminations. Emigration and exile are, like cancer, incurable illnesses. And one recourse that comes up when looking for a cure, that of returning to one's native land (if the conditions are right) ironically often results in only making the illness worse.

In any case, let's leave out those who left their homeland voluntarily in search of golden dreams, which nowadays boil down to a colour TV and a new car. Regardless of whether or not emigrants fulfil their goals, they will end up paying the price of their ambitions as they grow older and begin to miss their home town, their native land, or their childhood (which probably wasn't as happy as they remember it). I say this because I believe that there are only two real reasons for emigrating: either to save one's life if it is threatened by hunger or some manifestation of power, or for the sake of love transformed into passion, a risk that fewer and fewer people are willing to take these days. The other motives, such as the TV set, the car, and other such gadgets—as well as simply getting rich—all leave me indifferent.

I would also leave aside children who are torn away from their parents. They say that children adapt better and more easily than adults to the sometimes bizarre worlds in which they find themselves. This accounts for their ability to learn foreign languages more quickly and for their greater flexibility of outlook. Such an adaptation seems probable, though I'm not sure it is really true.

But let's return to my central theme. With the possible exception of nomadic peoples, periodic uprootings of people—slaves, artists, or philosophers—are deeply rooted phenomena well documented in ancient times. I am always afraid to give specific examples because there are inevitably many other points that can be provided to support the exact opposite point of view. Nevertheless, I cannot go on without mentioning the name of Lucian of Samosata, a philosopher who travelled all over the world, or at least what was known of the world in the first and second centuries A.D. Perhaps on account of all of his travels, from the Black Sea to Gaul (I'm not sure if the phrase "travel enriches the soul" existed back then), we could accord him the title of Expert in Travel and Emigration.

One of his biographers, in spite of the little that is known about his life, says that he was motivated, even driven, by the desire for fame and glory. This seems quite probable; after all, who isn't? Even though all ambitions are dubious, some—such as the desire for immortality—are more dubious than others. It is also probable that Lucian failed: if he hadn't, how would he ever have been able to write his satires? Rage and anger can be the driving forces of creation just as much as love, the difference being that we don't know whether or not love has ever truly existed.

Why then do I use Lucian as an example when there were other great travellers in antiquity, such as Plato and Euclid? I do so because the other travellers roamed about for the purpose of study, and all of them either found a new place to settle or accomodated themselves to the old one: Plato in Athens and Euclid in Alexandria. Lucian, on the other hand, in spite of having lived 20 years in Athens, never seemed to have found either hearth or home. Ironically, it was in Athens that he wrote his finest work.

Lucian's travels, however, have raised a whole series of questions in my mind. In ancient times, when neither nations nor customs existed in their present form, was there greater mobility and ease in moving about and less yearning for lost homelands? The theme of nostalgia for one's native land does not appear in the works of Lucian or other writers of his time with anything like the frequency that it does in the work of emigré writers today.

I myself am not a scholarly academic struggling to discover, or even seriously trying to guess at what Cervantes was thinking, or what distracted him, when he got involved in that business about Sancho Panza's donkey. I have no idea what went through Lucian's mind, nor do I know his feelings. I am aware, as all of you probably are, that in those days condemnation to ostracism, separation from one's people or the loss of one's "roots" could be a fate worse than death.

Examples of loss and uprooting can be found from ancient through modern times, as can examples of what such experiences entail, ranging from despair, depression, and suicide to the creation of works of art that never would have been written if the person had stayed home. But enough of examples.

What about us?

Whatever happens in the future, whether a person commits suicide or writes a work of literature as a cathartic reaction to problems in his or her life, such answers are never more than partial. Whatever subject one may study, however much one may know about a given topic, even the most scholarly investigation will never be more than a diagnosis or description that may raise the readers' awareness or soothe their souls; it will never be completely able to orchestrate their reactions.

To be an emigrant or someone living in exile is to be condemned; it is a weight that is never lifted from one's shoulders and which will be forever accompanied by the shadow of bitterness.

It is in what we do with exile, how we bear its weight, how we accept it, that we will find the answers to our questions.

AQUÍ ESTAMOS: AN OVERVIEW OF LATIN AMERICAN WRITING IN QUEBEC TODAY

Hugh Hazelton

Writing from the translator's and critic's viewpoint, Hugh Hazelton provides a panorama of the new "latino-québécoise" literature that "has put down roots in Quebec during the last two decades and is now bearing abundant fruit."

Hugh Hazelton, écrivant du point de vue du traducteur et du critique, fournit un panorama de la nouvelle littérature latino-québécoise qui est «bien enracinée au Québec depuis vingt ans et qui maintentant porte des fruits.»

*

A NEW LITERATURE, *la latino-québécoise,* has put down roots in Quebec during the last two decades and is now bearing abundant fruit. Born from seeds transplanted from almost every part of Latin America, it is both an autonomous field of literary endeavour and a part of the worlds of Quebec and Canadian literatures. Over the last few years, it has increasingly appropriated its own space to grow and become part of the northern literary scene.

Much time has gone by since the first Latin American authors began to arrive in Canada among the refugees and immigrants who left their native lands at the beginning of the 1970s. The Chileans, Argentines, Uruguayans and others who settled in Quebec during that period have now spent several decades in their adopted country: in Chile, 20 years have elapsed since the coup d'état against Salvador Allende; in Argentina, the principal members of the military junta that seized power 17 years ago have already been arrested, imprisoned and set free again. In the meantime, other Latin American writers—from Peru, Colombia, Guatemala,

El Salvador and other countries—continue to arrive, due to the social, political and economic upheavals that still affect the area. The first wave of writers to come to Quebec remained isolated for many years both from the main literary currents of the province and from each other. Lately, however, Latino-Québécois writers have been able to draw together and establish their own space. There has been significant progress in the reception of their work in Quebec and in the growth of their importance within Quebec literature, both in French and in English. An increasing sense of self-confidence has been accompanied in some cases by key changes in the themes about which they write.

The event that inaugurated this stage of development was the organization of the first Spanish-language poetry reading in Quebec in a secondary school in Outremont in the fall of 1986, as part of a Latin American Week of cultural activities. For the first time Spanish-speaking writers of Montreal, who had worked in isolation until then, realized that they formed a new branch of literature, one which had never before existed in Quebec: they constituted not only a Latin American literature of the North, but also an entirely new branch of Quebec literature.

This realization led to many others. First, as Latin American writers, they would have to participate in Quebec society to make their presence felt; after all, they did share the sphere of Latin culture with the Québécois. Moreover, as members of a single linguistic group that included 19 different countries spread out over a continent and a half, Latin Americans now constituted one of the principal linguistic groups of Quebec.

While Spanish-speaking authors were beginning to enter the world of Québécois letters, Quebec itself was slowly opening up to foreign influences. After passage of the famous *Charte de la Langue Française* (Bill 101) by the Parti Québécois in 1977, Quebec began to try to actively assimilate the majority of immigrants into Francophone society rather than letting them integrate into the Anglophone sphere on their own, as had previously been the case. Until quite recently, the world of Quebec literature had always been, as critic Ronald Sutherland has said, "une affaire de famille" (Sutherland, 1989, p.1). Prior to the arrival of the Latin Americans, only two major groups of immigrant writers had been accepted into the mainstream of Quebec literature. The first was made up of emigrants from Francophone countries and people from other nations who had been educated in French. Examples include the large number of Haitian writers, such as Anthony Phelps, Emile Ollivier, Gérard Étienne and

Roland Morrisseau, who settled in Quebec after the first wave of Haitian emigration of the 1950s, Naim Kattan, of Iraq, and Anne-Marie Alonzo, of Egypt, both of whom began to publish during the 1970s. The second group was composed of Italian-Canadians, such as Antonio d'Alfonso and Marco Micone. Although some were the sons and daughters of immigrant parents and therefore already second-generation, many of them have written and published in two or three languages—French, Italian, and English—and thus have much in common, linguistically at least, with Latino-Québécois writers.

For the majority of Latin Americans writing in Quebec, translation has been the principal obstacle to recognition. Thus, when a second large-scale reading by Latin American authors was organized in 1989, it was held in both Spanish and French. This initiative was an enormous success: fifteen Hispanic authors read over three consecutive evenings, and the event was followed by the publication of the first anthology of Latin American authors to appear in French, *La Présence d'une autre Amérique* (1989). In *Lettres québécoises,* the critic Jean Jonaissant (himself of Haitian origin), praised the anthology and compared its vitality to the pallid material in another collection that came out that year, made up of the same Québécois authors as always, "repris sans cesse à tort ou à raison par tous et chacun, ici et là" (Jonaissant, 1991, p.36). In the next few years there was a boom in the publication of anthologies of Latino-Québécois writing in all three languages. Meanwhile, authors working in fields other than poetry and the short story proliferated, and l*a littérature latino-québécoise* soon included works in literary criticism, history, autobiography, essay, theatre and children's stories.

Since then, more Latin American writers in Quebec have been publishing in French and English, as well as in Spanish. During the 1970s the Chilean poet Francisco Viñuela produced two bilingual (Spanish/French) books of poetry; other poets, such as Alfredo Lavergne, of Chile, Yvonne Truque, of Colombia, and Salvador Torres, of El Salvador, brought out bilingual Spanish/French collections of poetry during the 1980s. The Chilean poet and playwright Alberto Kurapel has written six plays directly in both languages, with bilingual versions of each soliloquy and dialogue. Various writers have also begun to write directly in French and English. The Chilean poet Nelly Davis Vallejos was perhaps the pioneer in this field, with the publication of her unilingual French book of poems, *Ballade,* in 1984. As Latino-Québécois writers have begun to feel more comfortable in at least one of the official languages of the country, a few authors, such as Salvador Torres, have started writing in either French or Spanish and then translating their texts back into the other language.

Several writers have chosen to work almost exclusively in French or English, without losing their identity as Latin Americans. Gloria Escomel, for example, born in Uruguay to a French mother and a Catalan father and raised in several South American countries, arrived in Quebec in the mid-1970s and is now a well-known novelist and poet in French. The dominant theme throughout her work, however, continues to be that of exile and return to her homeland. Indeed, she could be considered a Francophone Latin American, although lately she has returned to writing in Spanish.

On the English-speaking side, Renato Trujillo, who came to Montreal from Chile at the end of the 1960s, works only in English and has integrated into the world of Anglophone writers of Quebec. His poetry is widely respected in English Canada, and he is no longer interested in publishing in Spanish.

Latin American writers are also beginning to break into the mainstream of Quebec publishing. Self-publication and limited distribution, which have been so characteristic of Latino-Québécois writing, continue to be the norm, especially for newly-arrived authors. Various small presses, such as CEDAH (Centre d'Études et de Diffusion des Amériques Hispanophones), la Naine Blanche, les Éditions Omélic, and El Unicornio Verde, are now publishing on a regular basis. In their struggle to achieve greater access to the French-speaking and English-speaking public, however, increasing numbers of Hispanic writers in Quebec are sending their texts directly to mainstream literary reviews and publishing houses. A list of writers published by large-scale concerns, most of which have financed translation into French or English, might begin with Chilean filmmaker Marilú Mallet, who brought out two books of short stories with Québec/Amérique in the early 1980s. The list would also include the half-dozen Latino-Canadian authors of the publisher VLB's Collection latino-américaine; the Mexican novelist Gilberto Flores Patiño, who has put out a novel and book of short stories with Boréal; Alberto Kurapel, who has published three books of plays and a memoir with Humanitas, as well as two books of poems with les Ecrits des Forges; Salvador Torres, the Salvadoran writer who won the Prix Humanitas, awarded by the publishing firm of the same name, in 1989; Alfredo Lavergne, who has brought out seven books of poetry with les Editions d'Orphée; Elias

Letelier, a Chilean poet whose two bilingual Spanish/English books have been published by The Muses' Company; and Salvadoran poet Juan Ramón Mijango Mármol, who brought out a semi-bilingual collection of poems with les Ecrits des Forges in 1992.

Next year, les Editions de l'Hexagone will publish a major bilingual anthology (French/Spanish) of poetry by Latin American writers of Quebec, and plans a corresponding anthology of fiction for 1996. On the Anglophone side, Gary Geddes and I have brought out the anthology *Compañeros* (1991), which includes writings on Latin America by 87 English-Canadian, Québécois, and Latino-Canadian writers.

A major factor in the higher profile that Latin American writing in Quebec has had recently has been the publication of the literary review *Ruptures: The Review of the Three Americas,* which was founded in Montreal in 1992 by the Haitian-Canadian writer Edgard Gousse. The goal of this quarterly journal is to define and work toward a Literature of the Americas by publishing authors from all over the Western Hemisphere (and beyond), from the Yukon to Tierra del Fuego. An important innovation is that the review translates and publishes most of the work accepted in the four principal languages of the New World: French, English, Spanish, and Portuguese. *Ruptures* has provided Latino-Québécois writers with an opportunity to showcase their writing, translation, and critical abilities. Several, such as Alfredo Lavergne and Salvador Torres, have now translated a number of Québécois authors into Spanish, not only for publication in *Ruptures,* but also in reviews in Latin America and Spain. Thus the wheel of translation and dissemination has come full circle, and Latin American writers in Quebec are now helping traditional Québécois authors achieve greater recognition in the Spanish-speaking world.

It is, therefore, undeniable that Latino-Québécois authors now feel much more at home in Quebec culture than they did in the 1970s or 1980s and that their writing is moving into the mainstream of both the Francophone and Anglophone spheres of Quebec literature. The extent of the current opening, however, should not be exaggerated. On the French side, there has been far greater interest in what is currently being written in Latin America and Spain than there has been in Spanish-language writing within Quebec. VLB's Collection latino-américaine, for example, has relatively few Hispanic writers from Quebec, and books by Latino-Québécois writers are rarely reviewed either in the press or in scholarly magazines. A recent special issue of *Lettres québécoises* (no.6, 1992), dedicated to immigrant authors, made no mention whatsoever of Latin

Americans, other than the Uruguayan literary critic Javier García Méndez, because they do not write regularly in French. Moreover, on the English side, in spite of the range of Latin American writers of Quebec, the anglophone literary world of Montreal has continued to keep publishing the same two or three authors, without looking for new talent. In general, then, advances in recognition and access to publication have only been made after long and difficult struggle.

From the thematic point of view, it should be noted that the new and greater degree of acceptance that Latin American writing in Quebec now enjoys has had surprisingly little effect. Over the years, the amount of time that a given author has spent in the North evidently has much less impact on his or her thematic penchants than do the writer's personal interests. Gilberto Flores Patiño, for example, has been in Quebec for over ten years, yet he is interested primarily in Mexican or philosophical themes, and has never written a word about Quebec. Similarly, Elias Letelier-Ruz has spent 15 years in Canada, but continues to write almost exclusively on the theme of political militancy, either in his native Chile or in Central America. Alberto Kurapel has written about the anguish of exile for over 12 years, finally converting the theme into a symbol which he has extended to cover a whole syndrome of psychological alienation.

Other authors, however, are now writing more frequently on the relatively new themes of adaptation and acceptance—though not necessarily assimilation—that arise from the fact that they have settled permanently in Quebec, and they often use the relationship between the immigrant parent and child as a symbol for the immigrant's feelings toward Quebec society. In the short stories of Hernán Barrios, published in Chile under the title *Landed Immigrant,* Quebec is seen almost exclusively through the eyes of characters from the South. "Las noctilucas" (The Phosphorescence) (Barrios, 1990, pp.37-43), for example, deals with a Latin American father who laments the lack of magic and wonder in the new environment in which he is now raising his children, but later realizes that North America also has its share of surreal surprises. Similarly, the poetry of Maeve López often reflects a profound distrust of the developed world, perhaps as a result of the repression that it has inflicted on the South. For the Colombian poet Yvonne América Truque, the relationship between mother and daughter has strong parallels with that between the familiar world which the immigrant has left behind and the uncertain future she has chosen for herself.

The Latin American authors who have settled in Quebec have left the mark of their psychological as well as physical presence. Whether they speak of solitude or exile, of political struggle or adaptation, these authors have taken firm root in the Quebec literary world.

REFERENCES

Barrios, H. (1990). *Landed immigrant.* Santiago, Chile: Documentas.

Davis Vallejo, N. (1984). *Ballade.* Montreal: Self-published.

Hazelton, H., Geddes G. (Eds.). (1991). *Compañeros: An anthology of writings on Latin America.* Montreal: Cormorant Press.

Jonaissant, J. (1991). Des poésies québécoises actuelles. *Lettres québécoises,* 62 (36).

La Présence d'une autre Amérique. (1989). Montreal: Naine blanche.

López, M. (1992). El niño me amenaza.... *Antología de la poesía femenina latinoamericana en Canadá.* Montreal: El Unicornio Verde.

Sutherland, R. (1989). *No longer a family affair: Ethnic writers of French Canada.* Unpublished manuscript.

Truque, Y.A. (1991). *Portraits d'ombres et profils in achevés / Retratos de sombras y perfiles inconclusos.* Montreal: Ediciones CEDAH.

LE THÉÂTRE DE L'ATÉRITÉ DANS LA COMPAGNIE DES ARTS EXILIO

Alberto Kurapel
Le guanaco Gaucho

The Company of Arts Exilio, the first Latin American company of theatre-performance was founded in 1981 as a scenic expression of exile, integrating the place of its birth, North America, into the multiple Latin American roots of its practitioners.

The result is an interdisciplinary form of theatre-performance which integrates different media: film, video, texts, dance, slides, electro-acoustic music, as it experiments with postmodern strategies of staging Otherness, always understood within the special circumstances of these exiled creators.

La Compagnie des Arts Exilio, la première compagnie de théâtre-performance latino-américaine, a été fondée en 1981 en tant qu'expression scénique de l'exil; par cela, elle est devenue un espace d'intégration dans son lieu de naissance, l'Amérique du Nord.

Il en résulte une forme interdisciplinaire de théâtre-performance qui a recours aux différents média : film, vidéo, danse, textes, musique électroacoustique. Dans cette expérimentation avec les codes scéniques de la Performance post-moderne, l'Altérité devient un des signes distinctifs de cette Compagnie.

A TRAVERS LA CRÉATION scénique, les images de chacun des composants du théâtre, configurent un univers qui relève exlusivement de la spectacularité théâtrale performative, où chacun des icônes correspond à une réalité propre, associée évidemment à la participation d'autres disciplines, le tout constituant un produit spécifique ouvert sur un cosmos inconnu.

Je me réfère à des qualités particulières du théâtre-performance qui n'imitent pas la vie, même si à l'évidence elles en dérivent. Cette série d'icônes qui crée un langage théâtral performatif, fait face à l'inconnu, à l'imprévisible, à l'inimaginable, à l'imprésentable. Ces caractéristiques pourraient configurer l'Altérité.

En 1981, alors que j'en étais à ma septième année d'exil—période qui m'a permis de cerner plusieurs réalités qui s'agitaient dans ma trajectoire théâtrale—j'ai fondé à Montréal la Compagnie des Arts Exilio.

A partir de ce moment, il fallait énoncer les objectifs d'un théâtre d'exil; c'est-à-dire présenter une proposition esthétique/éthique développée, fondée sur une terre étrangère dont j'allais extraire les caractéristiques propres aux situations surgies de l'exil. Pour cela, il fallait analyser les obstacles spécifiques qui se présentaient et qui étaient l'essence de l'exil en Amérique du Nord.

On parle beaucoup du phénomème de l'«Exil»; certains en parlent pour s'y submerger, d'autres pour s'y retrancher.

> L'«Exil» et la «Mémoire» sont indivisibles.
>
> L'Homme détient dans la «Mémoire» sa plate-forme de création/lutte. Il retrouve dans l'«Exil» une grande plate-forme de douleur.
>
> Nous «La Compagnie des Arts Exilio» en Exil cultivons, recherchons, et créons une relation de deux pôles fondamentaux entre lesquels notre groupe s'est formé.
>
> | Exil | Mémoire |
> |---|---|
>
> Mettre sur pied des activités culturelles en Exil ne signifie absolument pas faire un «Art d'Exil», comme se plaisent à le faire croire certains opportunistes culturels.(Kurapel, 1987, p.XXI)

Une des premières frontières qui se dresse dans la plupart des cas, c'est la langue. Dans notre cas, il fallait créer dans un pays dont l'idiome était différent du nôtre. Nous devions faire face à travers le langage scénique aux problèmes qui en découlaient, comme la perte graduelle d'identité, l'isolement, l'incommunicabilité, la perte de la langue maternelle, la marginalisation, en somme, il fallait traverser et additionner les différences culturelles. Dans ma conception :

> Les spectacles devaient être bilingues, soit en espagnol et en français. Cette nécessité m'a amené à explorer la Voix comme étant un véhicule transmetteur de textures sonores, plus que comme porteuse de textes. De plus, il était indispensable, de montrer la difficulté de communiquer dans une langue apprise à vingt-six-ans par rapport à celle apprise à travers le processus normal de l'enfant depuis ses premières années. En transmettant un texte en espagnol, puis, immédiatement, sans aucune transition, en français, il était difficile d'arriver à une correspondance des deux langues. L'image créée lorsqu'on dit le mot «table» en espagnol n'est pas la même que lorsqu'on le dit en français. Les tables du continent latino-américain, même si elles sont différentes entre-elles, ont certaines caractéristiques immuables qui dessinent une image plus ou moins commune. Par contre, le mot «table» dit en français produira chez le spectateur une autre image qui s'appuiera logiquement sur les références particulières de la communauté francophone. A cela s'ajoute le fait que les images que j'ai avant de prononcer le mot «table» sont nombreuses et qu'elles appartiennent toutes à des tables que j'ai vues, que j'ai eues, avec lesquelles j'ai vécu plus de vingt ans, et, incluent entre autres, quelques tables québécoises. (Kurapel, 1993, p.29)

Jamais nous n'avons tenté de cacher et encore moins d'effacer l'accent que nous avons en parlant français ou anglais. Au contraire, nous l'avons souligné sachant qu'ainsi nous ajoutions un autre signifiant précieux à l'expression scénique: rejeter la pensée du colonisateur en refusant de recréer son accent. Il n'y a pas d'acteur/performeur qui n'ait pas d'accent individuel qui l'amème à s'exprimer d'une façon particulière et fascinante. Ces couleurs de la richesse dans la différence sont la lumière et l'ombre de l'Altérité. La dimension cosmique de l'Altérité.

Nos créations doivent symboliser notre marginalité par l'utilisation de tous les langages scéniques pour pouvoir exprimer notre inconscient collectif : de nouvelles relations de textes, de langues, de gestes, de signes pour modifier et briser les barrières qui se dressent contre l'expression de l'Autre. La séparation, l'inhabituel, la spécificité créent une relation scénique qui approfondit la perception et qui nous situe loin des points de référence familiers. Nous sommes toujours en train de créer au carrefour des cultures différentes. Notre contexte culturel est le point de départ de notre déchirement. Nous devons partir de cette réalité et créer avec les droits et les incertitudes, car notre création doit apprendre à établir des liens avec cette incertitude que l'homme a essayé de nier tant de fois, en construisant des dogmes qui à travers les temps ont montré leur inéfficacité. Aujourd'hui cette évidence se présente à nous impitoyablement et c'est pour cela que nos signes scéniques ne peuvent plus être les mêmes qu'avant la bombe d'Hiroshima, la guerre du Viêt-nam, la guerre du Golfe, l'implantation institutionnelle des dictatures en Amérique latine, la tombée du mur de Berlin, la désintégration de l'URSS, la crise d'Oka au Québec et l'accord signé entre l'OLP et Israël, ou l'assassinat systématique des Bosniaques musulmans. Partir de ces réalités créant une expression théâtrale imprégnée et conductrice d'autres sens modelés à travers la mémoire : l'éloignement, la fragmentation, le présent, la naissance de l'éternel, la mort, telle a été la trajectoire que nous avons développée dès le départ.

LA COMÉDIEN DE L'ALTÉRITÉ

Notre acteur doit être préparé pour transpercer avec son corps chacun des obstacles colonisateurs qui se dressent, pour bloquer le phénomène créateur. Son corps doit être le signe producteur de tous les sentiments générés par la **matière de l'exil** et c'est dans la mémoire qu'il doit trouver les voies et les sources de son expression.

L'exil est le segment le plus difficile à jouer.

Cette Performance Théâtrale que je PRÉSENTE est la distance qui semblerait exister entre les personnages et les performeurs. Distance où s'enracine toute la présence de l'expression. (Kurapel, 1989, p.40)

Jusqu'ici j'ai parlé **d'acteur/performeur.** Je l'ai fait comme des fonctions opposées qui cohabitent dans l'action de notre texte scénique. Nous avons choisi pour nous exprimer le théâtre-performance parce qu'il nous semble être le moyen le plus approprié de mettre en action notre vision. Ces deux expressions antagoniques se développent à travers notre action scénique et expriment les contradictions, les rites, l'interdisciplinarité, la déconstruction que nous habitons et qui nous habitent.

Le comédien n'est qu'un des signes du phénomène théâtral, mais c'est à travers, par et dans le comédien que nous réussissons l'accomplissement du rituel théâtral. L'acteur avec son corps et sa complexité est le Shaman de notre monde.

> S'appartenir à soi-même pour ensuite se rejeter et marcher en marquant chaque pas avec tout le poids de nos doutes; et dans ce frisson terrestre, convulsionner nos recherches qui sont la découverte de nos chutes.(Kurapel, 1993, p.140)

Dans notre cas, c'est comme des **créateurs-comédiens-exilés** que nous avons tissé notre réalité scénique et aussi comme des **performeurs** qui la possèdent comme une vision du monde.

Le théâtre d'exil exige comme condition inéluctable une connaissance profonde de la part du comédien de **tout** le phénomène théâtral, pour ainsi pouvoir l'affronter d'une façon adéquate et répondre aux nouvelles exigences techniques afin de créer à l'intérieur des sociétés technologiquement sur-développées. Nous présentant comme des comédiens/performeurs, comme des **comédiens du rejet,** créant avec et dans le rejet reçus dans une terre étrangère, nous pourrons être des **comédiens d'exil en exil.** Assumant notre altérité dans nos oeuvres, parce que dans celles-ci nous sommes aussi des étrangers, en présentant cette attitude, nous pourrons éveiller chez le public, une vision du «phénomène exil», que d'une façon ou d'une autre tout créateur éprouve.

LES LIEUX SCÉNIQUES

Bannis de nos édifices théâtraux, pour nous exprimer, nous ne pouvions pas aller chercher des constructions semblables dans d'autres géographies. Faire du théâtre dans un lieu qui n'a pas cette vocation, équivaut à transposer sur l'espace scénique la situation de l'exil; le phénomène scénique sera lui aussi étranger dans cet espace et en cherchant son essence nous trouverons une expression «autre».

D'autre part, les conditions générales de production et la situation économique des créateurs ne permettaient pas l'usage des édifices théâtraux, cette condition ne devait à aucun moment être un empêchement. N'importe quel espace peut se constituer en un lieu d'accueil pour un **théâtre d'exil.** La rue, les entrepôts, les dépotoirs, les édifices abandonnés font partie de notre existence et doivent être présents dans nos créations; de cette façon, nous ferons jaillir des signes avec des référents multiples.

Si nous créons dans un lieu autre que l'édifice théâtral, nous reproduirons dans cet espace une **situation artificielle** où les acteurs et les spectateurs se sentiront dans un «no man's land»; c'est-à-dire que nous insérons, grâce au lieu, les conditions de l'exil dans le texte scénique. Nous percevrons de cette façon une relation parfaite entre l'acteur/performeur et l'espace scénique.

Nous savons qu'aucun travail ne se réalise ni ne assume la dignité créatrice sans conséquence.

Il est indispensable de proposer une option scénique différente, déliée du manichéisme, liée à la polyvalence du désir inemployé, désorienté qui à l'heure actuelle dissipe ses impulsions dans des réalisations insignifiantes, dans des univers de dissolution instantanée.

La volonté de persévérer n'est que la vocation ancestrale réincarnée dans une tâche incessante dans la sphère de la CONNAISSANCE et de la RECHERCHE.

Contre la destruction et l'oubli, nous devons exécuter un saut périlleux pour qu'une rennaissance permanente et la construction d'un port où mille bateaux fantômes, sans destination, nous unissent par timon atavique pour nous mener vers l'embouchure de l'avenir. Nous nous occuperons du présent en préparant la pensée scénique du siècle nouveau, sans savoir si nous y parviendrons. (Kurapel, 1994, p.145)

Les acteurs/performeurs, grâce à la relation intime qu'ils établissent avec l'espace, sont ceux qui lui accordent une vie autonome dans le langage scénique.

Un espace ingrat peut être converti en signifiant et signifié de l'exil, espace où les acteurs et les spectateurs seront étroitement liés dans le rite théâtral et où le spectateur trouvera à l'intérieur de la problématique scénique les référents qui lui permettront d'expérimenter des émotions provocatrices qui le pousseront vers une recherche plutôt qu'à une contemplation dans le va et vient de ces territoires nouveaux.

La scénographie, comme constituant de l'espace scénique, détermine le lieu social de l'oeuvre. Dans notre cas, l'espace de l'exil demeure géographiquement indéfini. Nos scénographies ont toujours été conçues comme **des installations sculpturelles,** un autre facteur qui nous rapproche de l'«expression performance».

Il existe toujours une relation intime entre le lieu, le costume et le maquillage. Le costume inachevé du comédien l'amènera à préciser son langage, à remplir de sens l'espace, s'unissant au maquillage conçu constamment comme un masque mobile qui renferme l'univers du performeur et de l'espace scénique, pour manifester une **cérémonie du sens occulte.** La poussière, la terre colorée, la boue sont des éléments signifiants.

Nos costumes ne sont pas immortels, ils ne réfèrent ni à Arlequin ni à Pantalon; ce sont les costumes de l'inconnu, des icônes de l'étranger. Le modèle ne peut être transmis parce que nous ne le possédons pas. Il n'y a pas de distance entre le performeur/comédien et son costume; tout en lui est inachevé, en voie constante d'achèvement. Le trajet scénique est le prix qu'il doit payer pour acquérir un langage et les systèmes signifiants qui lui correspondent.

Je ne prétends pas mettre en scène un homme abstrait; tout au contraire. Ce caractère indéterminé est son attribut comme «corps d'exil» et le Costume doit privilégier son parcellement. Il doit être écran d'un exil incrusté dans tous les signifiants et signifiés du système scénique. Le costume affirme la différence, trace les frontières des comédiens/performeurs. N'importe quel tissu peut habiller nos acteurs; ceci permet la rencontre du comédien-personnage aux limites d'une désintégration vestimentaire qui rend le sens. Le costume peut être aussi un signe de **pouvoir;** les guenilles sont les signifiants de la désolation. Toutes les relations sociales peuvent se présenter par cette absence apparente d'indices d'où nous déterrons nos icones d'exil.

LE THÉÂTRE DE L'ALTÉRITÉ

Le théâtre d'exil est le lieu de rencontre de la mémoire collective avec les techniques de la transculturation. C'est à travers le risque, réitération transcendentale que le comédien accomplit sa fonction supra-sociale.

C'est dans l'imaginaire où doivent apparaître les signifiés de l'exil. Cette notion n'apparaît pas comme signifiant dans le texte, mais c'est à partir de différents composants et signes que celui-là atteint le spectateur, non d'une façon directe, mais à travers l'interférence, la surcodification ou la transformation des systèmes signifiants. C'est le cas des costumes, qui ne donnant pas de précisions, nous permet une lecture ouverte guidée par le signifié d'exil que nous y avons incorporé. Les guenilles qui couvrent un comédien/performeur sont des éléments signifiants d'un costume inachevé ou délabré, avec des faufilures, des indices de la confection qui se présentent comme des empreintes qui guident vers un autre univers le regard du spectateur. Cet univers autre, lointain, est un complément inconnu, une fraction de son identité dans le chaos qui cherche à s'ordonner. C'est l'**Altérité.**

L'exil est aussi une situation d'images accélérées, tronquées. Le cinéma, image en mouvement devient son signifiant scénique. La vidéo annule la fiction, amène «sa» notion de réalité: commotion des espaces, des images signifiantes «réelles», crise du réseau, exil virtuel. Cette image médiatisée est un élément connotatif parce qu'à travers elle, la réalité devient étrangère et concrétise la notion d'exil dans l'espace scénique.

La signification la plus profonde de l'exil est sa **fragmentation,** que nous introduisons, encore une fois, par l'intégration des **médias** à l'intérieur du système spectaculaire. Avec eux, nous nous sommes proposés comme besoin expresssif la reconnection des images et des circuits déconnectés. Le montage, caractéristique de tous ces langages, se réalise à l'intérieur de chacun d'eux et aussi dans le langage scénique. Chacun de ces **Médias** possède des caractéristiques qui lui sont propres, qui se conservent et s'accentuent à travers l'inter-action avec les performeurs à l'intérieur d'une unité spaciale. Cette dialectique de matériaux, de formes et de circuits s'étend à travers des décombres, des lieux alternatifs, des maquillages crasseux, toujours des éléments dissonants de contamination avec **le réseau médiatisé** et avec la **fiction dans d'autres espaces :** ouverture envers le monde, jeu d'opposition entre la chaleur de la présence scénique et la mécanique de la technologie concrète que je **présente de façon évidente.** Des éléments déstabilisants qui, incorporés au langage scénique, créent d'autres relations et questionnement chez le spectateur. Discontinuité, recherche du hasard et du désordre comme résultat de la **vie scénique artificielle.** Exil de la théâtralité.

Avec l'usage des **médias** nous avons accentué la notion «d'encadrement» à deux niveaux qui diffèrent fondamentalement. Le cinéma, la vidéo, les diapositives apportent «de gros plans» en grossissant l'objet à la vision du spectateur; rapprochement artificiel, rupture spaciale. D'autre part, l'espace scénique, la scène tridimensionnelle offre au spectateur de multiples encadrements et possibilités de choix.

C'est la dichotomie scène-image médiatisée, qui devient génératrice des images exilées à l'intérieur du système spectaculaire.

Je ne crois pas ceux qui disent que le théâtre ne peut exister sans «texte» s'appuyant sur la parole écrit. Je crois, tout au contraire, que cette dramaturgie serait véritablement enrichie si elle prenait en compte les autres signes théâtraux comme des entités différentes et non seulement comme des éléments illustratifs, subordonnés à ce que "disent" les personnages.

De cette façon, le comédien deviendrait un émetteur plus représentatif de ce qu'il est actuellement. Le texte a déjà trop servi pour donner une progression dramatique à l'oeuvre à l'intérieur des antagonismes, des conflits, de l'ampleur des objectifs défendus par des forces opposées et antagonistes plus ou moins puissantes. Mais, nous savons qu'au delà de tout ceci, l'action dramatique se développe à travers d'autres trames qui surpassent la parole, produisant ainsi une dialectique théâtrale, et par cela je veux dire une collision de signes dans le but de communiquer l'incommunicable, de présenter l'imprésentable.

Nous retrouvons des traces de cette proposition en Amérique Latine, surtout chez des jeunes qui encore aujourd'hui, sont arrêtés, paralysés par une institution théâtrale fossile, qui hiérarchise aussi les diverses étapes créatrices, les isolant à l'intérieur des dictas orthodoxes: dramaturge-metteur en scène-acteur-scénographe-éclairagiste-maquilleur etc.

Il est nécessaire que la théorie et la pratique théâtrale transvasent leurs langages dans toute la portée du processus de création, de façon à donner une extension maximale à chaque signe scénique. Il y a une carence de connaissance théorique et de théorisation des pratiques de la part des dramaturges, des metteurs en scène, des comédiens, des théoriciens. Conflit éternel qui subsiste et qui aujourd'hui plus que jamais doit être réglé en Amérique Latine. De là naîtra ce que j'appelle **auteur scénique,** lequel en écrivant, en mettant en scène, en éclairant sera en train de composer des particules scéniques fragmentatrices et fragmentées ou les arts majeurs et mineurs s'uniront, créant ainsi une expression scénique qui sera non seulement en accord avec l'époque où nous vivons mais aussi en avance des temps que nous avons réussi à survivre.

Éliminer le «patron» dramaturge, le «patron» comédien, le «patron» éclairagiste, avant que ceux-ci nous éliminent conplètement.

A l'intérieur du chaos de l'acte créateur, le créateur rompt sans le vouloir les «patrons» même si inconsciemment il les utilise pour pouvoir être dans l'instant où il crée et pouvoir ainsi continuer et passer à une autre oeuvre. La forme qui le tue pourra seulement le rattraper après sa mort.

Le concept d'**auteur scénique** m'apparaît irrésistiblement segmenté, parodique, rituel, millénaire et contemporain, et me donne la possibilité de connaître et de créer dans la crise de toute identité dans le théâtre-performance, se manifestant d'une façon atypique et par l'écoute du langage de lieux infinis qui existent en Amérique Latine et qui resignifient l'expression scénique.

La dramaturgie et le théâtre, naissant des lieux scéniques Latino-Américains qui pour être Latino-Américains sont universels, seront éternellement une forme inachevée.

A l'intérieur d'un texte spectaculaire, la vitesse des événements scéniques dans le déroulement ou ligne dramatique évolue au delà de la transgression. Alors, il existe une réalité-matière-scénique renfermée dans le corps de chaque comédien et de chaque signe scénique qui précipite des mouvements, des émotions et des sensations vers un univers de réalisation artificiellement temporel, où tout est permis. Avec la tendance du texte dramatique à imiter une parlure-comportement quotidien (syntaxe-émotion-modulation-articulation) on contrarie le tempo scénique dans son essence, le forçant à être univoque, le précipitant dans la didactique. Cette pratique n'est pas innoçente, tout au contraire. Afin de maintenir une hégémonie et un pouvoir on impose des lois maladroites, des pressions et des censures qui avec le temps deviennent partie du corps scénique. Ceci commence avec la dramaturgie, figurant ainsi une vision d'irréversibilité ou de despotisme, qui commence dans le quotidien et qui se glisse et se répand sur la scène théâtrale vers une société des spectateurs qui à la fois exercent leur *dogme* vers d'autres manifestations culturelles, laissant ainsi tous les domaines avec une carence totale des capacités analytiques, et avec pour seule préoccupation de dévier ses intérêts de survie vers le théâtre et vers la consommation culturelle. Ainsi, on détruit souvent l'initiative créatrice dans les centres périfériques qui ne possèdent même pas les moyens minimaux pour réaliser des projets créateurs.

A toutes les époques chaque intervention créatrice a été considérée comme un chaos malsain dans un paradigme donné et programmé; mais ce chaos a ré-ordonné les éléments oubliés, niant ce qui conformait un ordre identifié, une stabilité. Tout chaos surgit avec des caractéristiques nouvelles, la représentation devra se présenter comme l'origine d'une nouvelle relation de changement. Aujourd'hui au Chili, cette nouvelle relation se concrétise à partir d'une revalorisation du public et du comédien comme les éléments de nouveaux codes théâtraux, de nouvelles communications. Au départ, de gestuelles dissemblables, de langages visuels et sonores appartenant à des époques différentes et à des ethnies qui jour après jour se «révèlent». Matérialité scénique qui est Corpus-pensée. C'est là où les articulations actuelles pas encore retrouvées se «mettront en action» face à une identité, non perdue mais fragmentée. Métissage assumé, ré-unissant trois, quatre, cinq cultures pour faire du monde un état de représentation du moi qui permettra d'être-agir scéniquement.

Dans cette matérialisation, l'acteur/performeur ne peut qu'explorer de nouveaux chemins de l'expressivité scénique prenant en considération la signification de l'étranger, de «l'Altérité» où il se reflète.(Kurapel, 1993, p.73)

Tout créateur est d'une certaine façon un exilé. Le créateur explore toujours des propositions exilées, il cherche l'étranger. La scène est le lieu où on se met partiellement à nu, du strip-tease éternel qui ne se termine jamais. L' **Altérité** dans ce lieu est un amas de fragments mnémoniques qui par l'artifice de son rôle nous mène au **déchirement spectaculaire.**

Le visage est le lieu de l'amour, le corps est le lieu de la séduction. L'Altérité n'a pas de visage.

RÉFÉRENCES

Kurapel, A. (1987). «Premier Manifeste. La Compagnie des arts exilio», *3 Performances théâtrales.* Montréal: Editions Humanitas/Nouvelle Optique.

———. (1989). *Prométhée enchaîné selon Alberto Kurapel.* Montréal: Editions Humanitas/Nouvelle optique.

———. (1993). *Station artificielle.* Montréal: Editions Humanitas/Nouvelle optique.

———. (1993). The first instalment of a trilogy. *Canadian Theatre Review,* 75, p.73

———. (1994). *Colmenas en la Sombra ou l'espoir de l'arrière garde.* Second manifeste. Montréal: Editions Humanitas.

CHAPTER III

CRITICAL PERSPECTIVES ON CONTEMPORARY WRITERS

REDEFINING THE CENTRE: AUSTIN CLARKE AND OTHER WEST INDIAN CANADIAN WRITERS

Stella Algoo-Baksh

This paper argues that West Indian Canadian Writers have contributed significantly to a redefinition of the *centre.* Such writers have moved black characters from the periphery to centre stage, exploring the black experience from the inside rather than from a Eurocentric vantage point. Questioning the "hegemony of the centre," they often examine the problems of their societies from a fresh perspective. In the process, they expose the insidious effects of colonialism on the colonized, who ultimately lose sight of their own history, heritage and at times even their identity. The author emphasizes the work of Austin Clarke, the pioneer among West Indian Canadian writers. She shows how he has foregrounded the fortunes of the marginalized black immigrant in Canada to demonstrate how marginalization, whether in the Caribbean or in Canada, tends to rob men of their dignity and identity, thus inducing frustration and despair.

Les écrivains Canadiens d'origine antillaise ont contribué, de manière significative, à la redéfinition du *centre.* Grâce à ces auteurs qui ont écrit du point de vue de l'intérieur plutôt que d'une perspective eurocentrique, les personnages noirs ont été déplacés de la périphérie au centre de l'action. Cette remise en question de «l'hégémonie du centre» aboutit à une analyse des problèmes sociaux d'une perspective renouvellée d'où on examine les effets insidieux du colonialisme sur le colonisé, celui qui, finalement, perd de vue sa propre histoire, son héritage et même son identité. L'auteur ancre sa réflexion dans les oeuvres d'Austin Clarke, un pionier parmi les écrivians canadiens d'origine antillaise anglophone. Selon Algoo-Baksh, Clarke met en relief le portrait de l'immigrant noir au Canada pour démontrer que la marginalisation, qu'elle ait lieu au Canada ou dans la Caraïbe, crée des êtres désespérés en leur enlevant leur identité et leur dignité.

POST-COLONIAL LITERATURES challenge the hegemony of the centre, for artistic and literary decolonization involves "a radical dis/mantling of European codes and a post-colonial subversion and appropriation of the dominant discourses" (Tiffin, 1988, p.17). One of the vital thrusts of such literatures is their depiction of the everyday realities confronted by long-marginalized peoples; the literatures subvert the Eurocentric perspective on decolonizing societies by their insistence that life in the latter be examined "from the inside, as it is experienced by those who live there" (Harris, 1992, p.9). West Indian writing has long been animated by such concerns. As Kenneth Ramchand (1983, p.4) notes, post-war West Indian writers "apply themselves with unusual urgency and unanimity to an analysis and interpretation of their society's ills." Black characters are no longer "restricted to being peripheral or background figures" (Ramchand, 1983, p.5). The centre has in effect been redefined. It ceases to represent the preoccupations of the Eurocentric world view. Its focus is now the black experience, with West Indian writers offering a "different and necessary perspective" on that experience (Harris, 1992, p.13). And West Indian Canadian writers, it might be argued, have helped to nurture that new growth.

Neil Bissoondath is a case in point. The centre in *A Casual Brutality* is Trinidadian society, particularly its East Indian element, and, in dwelling on the moral degeneration that accompanied the oil boom of the 1980s, Bissoondath offers a harsh indictment of the community at a specific point in its history. The novel is a terrifying portrayal of power without justice or pity, of wealth without wisdom, of nationalism without vigour in leadership, and of crass materialism. As in Austin Clarke's *The Prime Minister,* the returning native, though driven by high expectations regarding a new life in the land of his birth, is so repelled by the corruption, the violence and the brutality that he witnesses and so troubled by a rejection by his own people that he withdraws to start afresh in a foreign land. In *Black Light,* Ishmael Baksh, too, explores life in the native element of that society, though he writes from a vantage point that allows him to regard it with greater sympathy. He presents an insider's view of the insidious effects of colonialism as it imbues the young Nazrul Khan with the values and outlook of the European master, but he demonstrates as well how the subtle racism and political immorality of Canadian university life induce an awakening in an older Khan that leads him to a redefinition of his sense of identity.

But Bissoondath and Baksh are not alone among West Indian Canadian writers in attempting to hold at bay the world view of a dominant white society. Claire Harris, for instance, probes the enduring effects of colonialism on its black subjects. In her poem "Mask," Harris (1985, pp.86-88) mourns the loss of the black inheritance and black history, while in "Sun Ripened Fruit" (1984, p.32) she laments the psychological colonization of young native girls by Eurocentric nuns, native girls "vivid with expectation of fulness/gleaming in sensuous innocence." And the black experience is by no means confined to that of the Caribbean. West Indian Canadian writers counter the perceptions of blacks emanating from white Canadian society by interpreting the black experience in Canada from the "inside." Among them is Dionne Brand. In her poem "Winter Epigrams," for example, Brand (1985, p.15) devalorizes the beauty of winter, employing the season as a metaphor for Toronto's frigid response to black immigrants, who persist in "rooting in their gardens/looking for green leaves." Again, Brand highlights the black female protagonist who finds herself "in enemy territory," whether as a partner in domestic life with its male-female violence, as a lover of other women in a frowning heterosexual society, or as a black woman in a white society. In her short story "At Lisbon Plate" (1990, pp.744-55), she suggests that the source of the black woman's immense strength, her ancestors, is female and black, that the fount of her fortitude is the legacy left by female African elders of the past. Cyril Dabydeen (1992), too, ventures intermittently into an account of the West Indian immigrants' Canadian experience. "The Rink" (pp.117-125) deals with the ambitions of a black man who is determined to fit into his new country, symbolized by his ambition to learn to skate, and who is intent on transmitting any skill he might acquire to his expected child. "All the King's Men" (pp.126-140) demonstrates that, while the attainment of an education is highly desirable for the black immigrant, it is somewhat pointless if unaccompanied by wisdom and the accessibility of jobs. "A Plan Is a Plan" (pp.108-116) ponders the black male-white female relationship intimating that, while some blacks view intermarriage as a route to harmony, the colonial mentality that induces a valorization of the whites actually makes many black men vulnerable to exploitation by white females.

As insightful and penetrating as such writers are, Austin Clarke remains the unrivalled pioneer of West Indian Canadian literature, the West Indian Canadian writer who has contributed most to foregrounding the black experience in the Caribbean and Canada. In his fiction set in the Caribbean, Clarke delves with striking authenticity into the world of blacks in a colonial society. In the process he undermines the perspective of the centre, shattering the image of the benevolent Mother Country that the imperial power has attempted to perpetuate. He exposes, instead, the inhumanity of a colonial system that fosters the oppression of the weak by the strong. One of the evils of this system is the emergence of a social structure that is highly resistant to change. The Barbados that Clarke describes in *The Survivors of the Crossing* possesses the essential elements of the transitional society delineated by Fanon (1968, pp.150-163), a society in which a new, largely black, political leadership is powerless to challenge the entrenched economic might of a white elite. In *The Survivors of the Crossing,* the looming plantation house, which "rose out of the dawn like a monster" and survives intact though the sugarcane fields about it are engulfed by flames (pp.191-192), signifies the impregnability of the white plantocracy. From Clarke's perspective, constitutional change in Barbados has produced no significant reforms in the society; the black masses are doomed to a depressing poverty. It is a destiny nicely symbolized by Rufus' experience:

> For so many years, his world has been the cane field, and now that he is fleeing from his world, he finds himself back in the cane field. And the cane fields lead him one way only, right back to the plantation. (p.191)

Shunned by the new political elite, which appears content with the mere trappings of authority and with the social prominence attached to election to the House of Assembly, the poor are numbed by a sense of powerlessness and a consuming despair. Such despair, such frustration, is manifested by Rufus when he attacks the plantation soil as though it were an enemy:

> But he raised the four-pronged agricultural fork high above his head and plunged it into the passive earth, and with a choking bitterness in his heart grunted, 'Yahh!' Again and again he raised the fork in the air, and each time the explosiveness within him choked the word from his mouth, as if he were breaking his heart. (p.3)

The black masses manage a bare existence in a nightmarish world that reduces them almost to chattels.

But there are other ways, Clarke's novel suggests, in which colonialism ravages the society. Certainly, it engenders social as well as psychological distortion among the blacks. To begin with, the power of the plantocracy drives the workers apart; many worry about losing their jobs or about being blackmailed by the planter because of involvement in a strike. The temptation exists, too, to betray another black simply to court the favour of a powerful white. From this perspective, the actions of Biscombe, who betrays Rufus as the latter attempts to organize a strike among the plantation workers, is not difficult to comprehend. Disunity among the black masses is but one concomitant of colonialism. Gullibility is another. Deprived of an adequate education, they are easily misled, as Rufus is when he accepts a friend's word that Canada is a virtual utopia (p.24), and they are incapable of effective political action. On the contrary, they are prone to emotion and irrationality, as Rufus discovers when he tries to lead them: "All he had intended was a peaceful talk with the overseer or the manager. But now he saw that the tide of emotion was taking the whole business out of his hands" (p.42). The workers' simple-minded attitude and conduct stand in stark contrast to the cool, calculated planning of the better-educated manager. Given the urgency of the problem of survival, vacillating loyalty, opportunism and living for the moment become a way of life for many. Boysie and Mango, for example, have no real vision of the future and are engrossed in the satisfaction of immediate needs. And the apparent immorality to which Stella, Rufus' wife, succumbs is simply what she has been coerced into by the unrelenting structure of the society; she is impelled by her destitution to exploit her wits and her sexual charms to salvage her own life and to rescue her children from a dismal fate.

Clarke heaps scorn on institutions he views as buttressing the status quo and privileging the culture and world view of the centre. In *The Survivors of the Crossing,* he implicates the school and the church in the oppression of the blacks. Whippetts, the schoolmaster, who is supposedly in charge of the education of the young is in fact a white man in a black skin, serving in essence primarily the purposes of his white masters. Imitating the dress, the speech and the habits of his white superiors, he presents a ridiculous figure who has no sympathy with the real needs of the people. The school system, as Clarke shows with greater vibrancy in *Growing Up Stupid Under the Union Jack,* accomplishes little but distorts the development of the young through its immersion in colonial forms of education which induce a worship of all that is white and a consequent belittlement of the black self. This is a theme that recurs in Clarke's work. In *Amongst Thistles and Thorns* (1965, pp.12-13, 165, 172-176), for instance, Clarke depicts the brutality and ignorance of a subservient and self-serving schoolmaster, the detachment and insensitivity of a white inspector who consumes his delicious lunch in the presence of starving schoolboys, the absurdity of the school syllabus and accompanying textbooks far removed from the requirements of local life, and the incessant glorification through the educational system of all things British and white.

In *The Survivors of the Crossing,* the church, too, is painted as deficient, for it is shown to be largely indifferent to the problems of the black masses. The Anglican minister, McKinley, who is a foreign white, has little comprehension of the people around him. Even when he tries to persuade the plantation manager and overseer that the workers' desire to improve their lot does not imply that "they are plotting to overthrow the plantation" (p.41), he does not persevere in his efforts. The traditional alliance of the Anglican Church with the Barbadian higher classes is evident in McKinley's notion that "it was not ordained by God for the people to rise up against their leaders, whether spiritual or temporal" (p.29). The church, the novel hints, has too long been an instrument of the elite and has consequently lulled the poor into an uncritical compliance with a social order that prolongs their repression.

Clarke is interested, also, in how the workings of a colonial society impinge upon blacks for whom social ascent is increasingly feasible. He is drawn in particular to the character of black involvement in the political arena, and he attaches blame to the colonial heritage for the imperfections of political life. *Proud Empires,* which is set in the period immediately preceding the achievement of political independence, becomes a vehicle for disentangling the ramifications of the colonial heritage in the political life of Barbadian society. Education, in Clarke's view, is of paramount significance in shaping the nature and outcomes of political activity. For one thing, the scarcity of opportunity in an elitist system of education produces an inflated and unquestioning regard for those who are educated. The ordinary person is seduced into admiration for people like Boy simply because they are educated. There is, furthermore, a reverence for "big" men, and, since few can attain the educational levels to achieve social prominence, "bigness" comes to be defined in terms of other attributes as well. Wealth, authority and power, as well as physical strength, brutality and sexual prowess, are acceptable qualifications for "bigness," and despicable men like Sarge and Seabert can command respect in the community. It is therefore possible not only for the educated but also for unscrupulous men to achieve positions of political power, and blackmail, terrorist tactics, murder, nepotism, and moral decrepitude in a variety of forms are all accepted elements of political life. When the prevailing norms tolerate such corruption, social reform becomes a virtual impossibility.

Deficiencies relating to education may take another destructive form. Schooling, whether formal or informal, is not designed to foster a critical social consciousness; rather, it serves largely to reinforce compliance with the imperatives of a British cultural heritage. Thus, Boy's mother instils in him a pride in and awareness of his Scottish ancestry but ignores his African heritage, and Boy's formal education solidifies within him a faith in white cultural and racial superiority, persuading him to devalue the black. As late as his last year at Harrison College, Boy "had never heard of the Middle Passage. And even if he had been taught about it at College . . . he was not eager to bear any ties of family with *those* men. African or slaves" (p.22). When Boy returns from Canada, his uncle attempts to enlighten him about his full racial identity and goes so far as to depict imperialist heroes like Columbus, Codrington and Harris as foes of the blacks, but he has been shaped so inexorably by his education in Barbados and Canada that he is in all likelihood incapable of change. Indeed, he is already entering the folds of the elite, symbolized by his arrival before the Thorne family home (p.224). The class consciousness that comes with social ascent and the overzealous identification with white society and the culture of the centre helps to drive a wedge between the new rulers and the masses, and distances politics from the needs and concerns of the poor.

In enlarging on such themes, Clarke's work is quite in keeping with the tendencies of much post-colonial literature. Such writing, like post-colonial culture generally, is driven in part by an "impulse to create or recreate an independent local identity" (Ashcroft, Griffiths, and Tiffin, 1989, p.195), a purpose that implicitly informs a great deal of Clarke's work. Arguably, the achievement of a new local identity by the colonized presupposes an understanding of themselves and of the forces that have made them what they are. Only then are they well prepared to proceed to a redefinition of the self. Clarke offers a demonstration of this process in *Amongst Thistles and Thorns.* To comprehend who he is, the young Milton must grasp the nature of the society that has moulded him, and he makes gains in this regard. Revealing a ripening sensitivity to the physical and social world about him, he begins to question the racial inequities in Barbados. He is puzzled that an idle white woman enjoys a comfortable existence while his mother toils all day just to survive (p.171). He makes connections between the structure of the society and the behaviour of the blacks, recognizing that his mother's harshness toward him is rooted in the debasing treatment meted out to her by her white employer and by life as a whole. Of course, mere recognition of the forces that press upon blacks is not enough for fundamental self-renewal; alternatives to the norms of the centre are crucial. For young Milton, Harlem symbolises an alternative constellation of imperatives. The young boy has gained a knowledge of Harlem from Willy-Willy, who has himself discovered fulfilment in black America and has returned to inform his people about unconstrained black possibilities. The Harlem of which Milton dreams valorizes the black world. It is alive with racial consciousness, racial pride, and significant racial independence. It is a world in which the dominant truths emanate from the blacks themselves and in which the values and standards meet the needs of blacks in their quest for material, cultural and psychological gain. What Clarke attempts to do, then, is precisely what post-colonial writing in general seeks to accomplish. He tries to encourage a critical social awareness and he reminds blacks of the need to reject both "the consolation of civilisation" offered by the centre and "the notion that colonial societies exist in a historical void" (Bhaba, 1979, p.110).

Clarke's preoccupation with the black experience is not restricted to colonial times, however, for his novel *The Prime Minister* exposes what he sees as the failings of the black elite in a politically sovereign territory still caught in the aftermath of colonialism. Returning to his native land after 20 years in Canada, John Moore assumes the prestigious position of Director of National Culture in which he plans to foster both the local culture and a sense of national identity. From early in his stay, however, he begins to sense his alienation from the local society. He grasps, for example, that despite being black he is perceived by the local people as an outsider (pp.22-23). In addition to such lack of credibility, other obstacles block his integration into the community. He has lost the capacity to assess carefully "each action and word" (pp.26-27) and he cannot comprehend the meanings beneath the subtle nuances of local speech, so that he is unable to unravel the likely repercussions of what is said. Such deficiencies marginalize him and render him incapable of effective communication with the people he wishes to serve.

Contributing most to Moore's alienation, however, is a marked clash of values. Such divergence is evident in relation to sentiments about the tourist industry. Given the desperate economic conditions inherited from colonialism, the government and often the man in the street view tourism as an indispensable source of national income, a perception that has led to a symbiotic relationship in which the tourists have their every whim and fancy satisfied while wealthy and powerful locals derive riches from their presence. As Moore learns, for example, several prominent nationals own apartments or houses which they rent to the tourists, sometimes supplying the latter with men or women for their sexual gratification (p.79). In Moore's view, though, tourists "are not good for the development of a free country" (p.22), for their presence encourages a permanent dependency on foreign elements. Furthermore, tourism leads to a devaluation of the worth of the black population, since blacks become essentially instruments for the satisfaction of the white visitors' needs. In addition, blacks are reduced to second-class citizens in their own country because their rights are minimized in order that the society might ingratiate itself with the foreign whites. It is a facet of local life captured in the reference to a popular calypso, "The Rate of Exchange," which comments on the abnormally harsh penalty imposed by the court on a young beach-boy for theft from a female tourist to whom he has sold his sexual services. The tourist industry, Moore feels, contributes little to solving the economic and social problems of the society, but this is a stance which brings him into conflict with the ruling group (p.78).

The ruling group itself proves the most formidable barrier to Moore as he attempts to raise the status of the local culture and create a sense of national identity. The blacks in power retain the values of the former colonizer, a phenomenon symbolized by the fact that the prime minister likes "European women best of all his women" (p.90). The sad truth is, as Moore discovers, that in certain other politically independent islands "people were talking about black power, and other versions of black nationalism" (p.30), while he has to curb himself and not utter statements in praise of blackness since such sentiments were not in favour in local political circles (p.32). Equally unfortunate is the tendency of the government to perpetuate a class system not dissimilar to that of colonial times. There are very few blacks at parties given by members of the ruling group, but whites from abroad—including, significantly, a South African—are treated with obscene generosity, with the destitution of the black masses all the while ignored (p.72). Moore soon comes to realize that the governing black elite is composed mainly of philistines whose interest in culture is strictly utilitarian, since they have invited "all the best artistic brains" simply to create a facade of "sophistication and culture and style to the new country" (p.36). Their primary objective is to exploit the current situation to their own advantage, fully prepared to escape to another country with their ill-gotten gains should circumstances ever necessitate such action.

There is yet another sense in which Clarke redefines the centre. In choosing in much of his work to grant a strong voice to lower-class blacks, he questions the tendency of the literature of the centre to stress the experience and perspective of the middle and upper classes. He is one of many West Indian novelists who have, as Lamming (1960, pp.38-39) puts it, "restored the West Indian peasant to his true and original status of personality." In exploring the world of the black "peasant," Clarke does not attempt a literal rendering of the dialect, but has captured the rhythm, the colour and the raciness of local Barbadian speech. He achieves this effect in part through periodic suspensions of the grammatical rules of standard English, a limited vocabulary, simple syntactical structure, Barbadian idiom and slang, and spelling based on local pronunciation. Sarge's speech in *Proud Empires* is illustrative:

> I telling you now, that if in them days, I was a man, if I had-already-make a man of myself, I would have propose, yes, man, I would have propose marriage to Ella. If you know what I mean? But in them days, Nathan, as you know, I was a man without a job. The same Guvvament we have-in now, we had-in, then. Was no blasted good for black people like me and you. And now that I is a sergeant of police, on the Force, if you know what I mean? Now, Nathan, look at life, eh. (p.73)

Where it suits his purpose, Clarke has refrained from privileging standard English, which has long reinforced a structure of power in which the centre reigns supreme. His work evidences to a large degree the "appropriation of language and writing for new and distinctive usages" so common among post-colonial writers (Ashcroft et al., 1989, p.6). It revels in a language that serves as an instrument for rejecting European metaphysics and furnishing a new truth about the black experience, a truth that permits blacks the possibility of self-renewal and dignity.

Clarke extends his exploration of the black experience to the North American, mainly Canadian, setting, and he examines in depth the world of the black West Indian immigrant. The traditional subject of Canadian immigrant writing has been white and European. Examples of this trend are not difficult to find. In *Roughing It in the Bush,* Susanna Moodie tells the story of an English woman from a genteel family background who has to adapt to a new environment and new peoples as she attempts to make a home in the wilds of Canada. In *The History of Emily Montague,* Frances

Brooke provides an account of an English garrison community in Quebec, pointing out contrasts between the new world and England in terms of religion, politics, dress, manners and other aspects of social life. Again, Frederick Philip Grove is a spokesman for white immigrants outside the Anglo-Saxon group, and such novels as *Settlers of the Marsh* and *Fruits of the Earth* are peopled with characters from a wide range of European backgrounds, so much so that they offer a portrait of Canada as little more than a white society. Canadian literature generally has tended to focus on whites and to depict the world from a white perspective. In his novels and short stories set in Canada, Clarke redefines the centre. He directs his attention to the fate of a marginalized group, and, armed with his own experience as an immigrant who had struggled at the lower rungs of the society as well as with a knowledge of black immigrant life acquired through his long association with the Canadian black community, he gives an account of the black experience in Canada from the inside. In the process, he counters the perceptions of blacks and the interpretations of black behaviour rampant in the dominant society and challenges powerful myths—that it adheres to Christian values, that it is free of racism—which that society has complacently perpetuated about itself.

As a group, Clarke's novels *The Meeting Point, Storm of Fortune* and *The Bigger Light,* frequently referred to as his Toronto trilogy, furnish the first comprehensive depiction of the lives of black West Indian immigrants in Canada, but his short stories also highlight important dimensions of the experience of the immigrants. The picture that Clarke paints is a depressing one. The black West Indians migrate to Canada in search of financial betterment and human dignity, but discover both to be beyond easy reach; the immigrants learn instead that they have merely exchanged one form of imprisonment for another. Bernice, in *The Meeting Point,* soon grasps that she is regarded by whites as belonging to an inferior species of humanity. She is described by whites as "nasty" and "not fit" to live among whites (p.20). Her inferiority is made manifest through the type of work she is required to do; she is a "twentieth-century slave" (p.5) who is compelled to perform an unreasonable amount of domestic work. She is dehumanized, an object to be exploited by the family that has employed her. She achieves a modicum of financial security but it has little value for her, for while she can afford new clothes her social opportunities are virtually non-existent. Racism bars her from social intercourse with the white population at large. Not only is she psychologically scarred, but she is also trapped and isolated, even as are her conterparts in Barbados. Again, all the stories in *In This City,* with the exception of "A Short Drive," foreground the trials and tribulations of the blacks from the insider's point of view. "Gift Wrapped" (pp.1-24), "I'm Running for My Life" (pp.75-96) and "Trying to Kill Herself" (pp.97-126) tell of the marginalized black female, domestic, single woman, or mother who finds herself in a hostile country, alienated, isolated, and even unhappier than she has been in the West Indies. Those who cannot escape from "the belly of hell" (p.125) to more desirable conditions of life often try to extricate themselves in other ways—through suicide, as the protagonist does with alcohol and pills (pp.125-126), or by compromising their morals despite having to live subsequently in disgust with themselves.

The theme of racism threads its way through Clarke's writing as a major element of the black experience, and Clarke challenges the image white Canada has attempted to preserve of itself as a non-racist society. He asserts that blacks face injustice even at the hands of the police and even while still children. It is observed in "Sometimes A Motherless Child" (Clarke, 1992, p.208) that BJ "had spent four hours in this same police station, in another cell, alone and not knowing really why he had been locked up, not having had a charge laid against him, not having had a policeman enter the warm cell and interrogate him about the alleged theft of a kid's bicycle that afternoon in August." Racist stereotypes are shown to lead to the wrongful arrest of the 16-year-old BJ and to his death at the hands of the police. The horror and violence bred by unchecked racism are captured in the scene in which BJ's mother catches her first glimpse of his body:

> And she saw the head, and it was out of shape from something that had hit it. Disfigured. And the blood was covering the face. And the stretcher was covered in thick blood. And the black clothes the youth was dressed in, were red now, more than black.... It looked as if a cannon had struck the head, and the head had exploded and had been cut into pieces, like a watermelon that had slipped out of the hand. To her, it seemed as if the brains of the young man were coming out through his mouth, as if his eyes were lost against the impact of the bullet. To her, it looked like a watermelon that was smashed by the wheels of a car. (1992, p.213)

And no black is safe from the evils of racism. Discrimination occurs even in academia. In "The Letter of the Law of Black," a black student receives a B for a paper while the same paper submitted by a white student is given an A (1992, p.71). It is possible that blacks, no matter how wealthy or educated they are, will not be treated the same as whites. They are always forced into humbling themselves before whites regardless of the latter's status. As a black woman notes in "If the Bough Breaks":

> Back home we'd be ruling the roost. We'd be women with men and husbands that make decisions and run things. But here ... if it is not some woman in the Eaton Centre, and don't mention Holt Renfrew or some o' them places in Yorkville Village, if it is not some damn racist cop, if it isn't some woman in a beat-up Toyota, while you ... are driving a BMW, or I behind the wheel of my husband's Benz, anything, any-blasted-body, we always have to explain some thing to them. Explain ourselves. Explain. (1993, p.60)

The requirement that they continually explain who they are or what they are doing frustrates and debilitates blacks, undermining their efforts to maintain a sense of personal worth.

Racism is evil, too, because it sustains stereotypes that produce unjustifiable fears, serving to widen the gap between blacks and whites. In the story "In An Elevator," Susan Cole finds herself alone with a black in an elevator. The young man is only delivering a parcel, but because her upbringing and her racism lead her to see black men as potential rapists, Susan is fearful of the black:

> She knew she could pick him out **like that** from any lineup in a police station, even if he left his dark glasses at home to hide the fact. And she knew that never again, not ever, would she be found **dead** in an elevator with a black man. She'd get off first! And wait until a white man came in! (1993, p.60)

After a friendly remark by the black, Susan overcomes somewhat "the terror of his company" (p.61) but she is still unable to shake off her racist orientation. The conditions of life faced by black immigrants in Canada are in some ways especially destructive for males. A powerful sense of eroded masculinity may overwhelm the male who is financially dependent on the female. This is evident in *The Meeting Point* when Boysie confides in Boysie about his feelings about his relationship with Dots:

> You want to know something? I come into this country, as you might say, through the back door, meaning I come in only in the behalfs of swearing out an oath that I was going to marry that stupid woman, Dots, in a specified time. Not that I had no ... in the matter. I had as much choice as a rat in a burning canefield.... It pains my arse to think o' myself, as a man sponsored, and sponsored, gorblummuh, by a woman at that! (pp.83-84)

The stigma of dependence on a woman is worsened when the male learns, as he so often does, that his hopes of success in Canada are not easily realized. In this connection, Boysie discovers that after eight months of seeking employment he is still without a job and remains indebted to Dots for support. He declares he is not "a idle man" but has nevertheless not managed to "get any lot o' money outta this country" (pp.213-14). The result of such misfortune is a recurrence of the psychological mutilation of the black male previously associated first with slavery and later with with colonialism, when economic conditions denied the black the resources to discharge effectively the conventional role of breadwinner for his family.

In portraying the world of the black immigrants, also, Clarke counters stereotypical labels that white society is sometimes tempted to attach to blacks. The black immigrant, Clarke suggests, is not inherently idle or lazy; he may sometimes appear to be such because he has been deprived of opportunity. Similarly, blacks are not inevitably promiscuous; external factors may force them into relationships they would normally avoid. It is clear from *The Meeting Point,* for instance, that isolation and emotional starvation may cause some women to accept even temporary escape from their unhappiness. Thus, a lonely Bernice seizes a chance to engage in an affair with Michael when she can supply some of his financial needs, though the young man abandons her for a white woman as soon as the opportunity arises (p.124). And it is at least in part because the colonial heritage impresses upon blacks the notion of the superiority of whiteness that black men in Canada freqently gravitate toward white women. In *The Meeting Point,* both Boysie and Henry evidence such an inclination. Boysie regards his wife Dots as "a stupid woman" (p.83) and enters into a liaison with another black while having an affair with Brigitte, a German maid. For his part, Henry observes that though he is a "one woman man" there is no question that "that woman have to be white!" (p.83). Ironically, while Henry is perceptive enough to view Boysie's absorption in Brigitte as an indication of surrender to the myth of white superiority, he fails to see his own fascination with the white Agatha in a similar light (p.237). It is an awareness of this male blindness that induces Carmeeta Sweet, a black immigrant, to declare resignedly that black women in Canada appear doomed to watch their men "dance with white women, take out white women, and spend their money on white women" (p.69).

White racism itself may often be among the external explanations of black behaviour. It may arouse a deep sense of anger that so transforms its victims that they engage in thought and action quite foreign to their everyday dispositions. In *Storm of Fortune,* for instance, Henry is so infuriated at the prospect of unfair treatment at the hands of the law that he feels like "walking down Yonge Street and smashing every goddam store window there" (pp.51-52). And, as he hunts for an apartment, an encounter with racism so angers him that he spits in a proprietress's face as she is about to close her door on him. A similar encounter with another landlord leads him to seize the other man by the neck, and his wife has to restrain him (p.282). As he intimates, "racism does some funny things to a man's mind" (p.282). Clarke's proposition, once more, is that the actions of blacks may well be due to factors beyond their control, that blacks are not by nature over-emotional or violent—as white society often stereotypes them to be—but may be made so by the predispositions of Canadian society itself.

Clarke, however, does not interest himself solely in the relationship between blacks and the society they have entered; he examines as well the impact that liaisons which whites have on blacks. Surfacing once more is the familiar phenomenon of the psychological mutilation of blacks. The relationship between Henry and the white Agatha in *Storm of Fortune* is illustrative of the predicament in which blacks find themselves when they establish intimate connections with whites. Henry is in desperate financial straits, for he is unemployed and, in spite of his efforts, cannot find a job. His complete financial dependence on Agatha parallels and emphasizes the black male's indebtedness to his black mate in both the past and the present. The relationship produces in Henry the inevitable sense of inferiority and a consciousness of being "a goddam failure" (p.55). The effect of the conditions of his existence on his behaviour is striking but understandable. Desperate to salvage some pride and dignity in a culture that forces upon him obligations he cannot meet, he is driven to lie to his wife and to create an imaginary world in which he gains at least minimal success. As he says to his friend:

> Goddamn, Boysie, a man don't admit he is a failure to his wife. He does lie, he lies like hell. And she does have to find out for sheself. He tells her he's working, that he's drawing money every week from some job; goddamn, sometimes, if he is a real failure, he even invents a job and tells her every two months that he got a raise. That kind o' man is me. (pp.54-55)

His sense of masculinity threatened, he tries to impress Boysie with his manliness by exaggerating the number of policemen required to overpower him in an incident in which he has been beaten up by only two. And his psychological well-being is further threatened when his wife, in describing his racial attributes as having "beauty," in reality gives him an inferiority complex (p.277). The black man's association with a white woman, Clarke implies, does not necessarily bring him the social and psychological upliftment it promises. In Henry's case, the effect on the spirit is so damaging that suicide appears the only hope of escape from despair. The effects of interracial connections may be no less destructive for black females. In her affair with Sam Burrmann, Estelle must come to grips with a situation that is not fundamentally different from her grandmother's on the plantation; while Burrmann increasingly sees her as attractive, his response to her fluctuates wildly as her blackness reminds him of her "inferiority," and in the end Estelle becomes little more than an object for his sexual gratification (Clarke, 1967, p.187).

Not surprisingly, Clarke is fascinated by the question of the blacks' quest for identity in a society in which they tread a path strewn with social and psychological hazards. *In The Meeting Point,* Bernice's initial response is self-hate and a denial of her commonality with blacks. She despises those blacks who, through their civil rights marches and demands for equality, pose a threat to her relatively comfortable existence in the sheltered world she has created for herself. She disgustedly denounces the protestors as "a lot o' stupid black people marching 'bout the place" and it irritates her to "see what this blasted world o' black people is coming to" (p.220). Despite her contact with racism, she naively tries to divorce herself from the blacks of America, since she has grown up "in a place, the West Indies, where nobody don't worry over things like colour" (p.220). This submergence of one's true identity, Clarke is hinting, is a form of self-deception and self-denigration. In *Storm of Fortune,* though, Bernice eventually grasps the reality of her situation. She realizes that, her years of toil in the Burrmann household notwithstanding, Rachel Burrmann still perceives her not as a full person but as just another black woman. Thrown on her own resources, she grows psychologically as she employs her wits and courage to find a new job and begin life anew. In all this, she is helped by her black friends, who provide her with physical and moral support and nurture within her a pride in her race, and she shortly begins to experience a sense of community and kinship with her black counterparts. For the first time since her arrival in Canada she can be her true self, liberated from her inner tensions and psychological disfigurements (pp.239-240).

Such certainty of redemption eludes Boysie in *The Bigger Light.* Boysie is now reasonably prosperous but feelings of inferiority to whites still trouble him. The solution for this problem, he begins to think, is to deny his blackness. He therefore severs his connection with black West Indians, casts aside whatever reminds him of his West Indian roots and blinds himself to the difficulties confronted by his fellow immigrants. But the result is simply confusion. He is less than consistent in the position he takes on diverse matters; he is uncertain in his attitude toward West Indians, and he wavers in his feelings for his wife, Dots. In the process of his drive for acceptance by white Canada, he becomes alienated from Dots and in the end, still unfulfilled and still uncertain about what he ought to be, he transfers his possessions to his wife and leaves for Harlem in a quest for salvation. His attempt to achieve a new identity by abandoning his roots and his true self has clearly not been fruitful.

Clarke and other Canadian West Indian writers have contributed to a striking redefinition of the centre in both the Caribbean and Canada. In their work set in the Caribbean, they have brought to centre stage elements of the population that have long been treated as peripheral, making the social world and experience of such people central themes in art. In the process, the writers have dispelled myths, long cherished by the imperial centre, about the nature of the association between the colonizer and the colonized, depicting as well the aftermath of that relationship.In their work set in Canada, also, Clarke and other Canadian West Indian writers have foregrounded the experience of groups that have enjoyed little more than marginal status in the society. At the same time, the writers often paint pictures of life in Canada that are at odds with the self-congratulatory "truths" held dear among dominant groups about the character of Canadian society.

REFERENCES

Ashcroft, B., Griffiths, G., & Tiffin, H. (1989). *The empire writes back.* London: Routledge.

Baksh, I.J. (1988). *Black light.* St. John's: Jesperson.

Bhabha, H.K. (1979). Some problems in nationalist criticism. *Literature and History 5,* 109-115.

Bissoondath, N. (1985). *A casual brutality.* Toronto: Macmillan of Canada.

Brand, D. (1985). Winter epigrams. In Lorris Elliot (Ed.), *Other voices* (p.15). Toronto: Williams-Wallace.

Brand, D. (1990). At Lisbon Plate. In R. Brown, D. Bennett, & N. Cook (Eds.), *An Anthology of Canadian Literature* (pp.744-755). (Revised and Abridged Edition). Toronto: Oxford.

Brooke, F. (1961). *The history of Emily Montague.* Toronto: McClelland and Stewart.

Clarke, A. (1964). *The survivors of the crossing.* London: Heinemann.

———. (1965). *Amongst thistles and thorns.* Toronto: McClelland and Stewart.

———. (1967). *The meeting point.* London: Heinemann.

———. (1973). *Storm of fortune.* Boston: Little, Brown.

———. (1975). *The bigger light.* Boston: Little, Brown.

———. (1977). *The prime minister.* Don Mills, Ontario: General Publishing.

———. (1980). *Growing up stupid under the Union Jack.* Toronto: McClelland and Stewart.

———. (1986). *Proud empires.* London: Victor Gollancz.

———. (1992). *In this city.* Toronto: Exile Editions.

———. (1993). *There are no elders.* Toronto: Exile Editions.

Dabydeen, C. (1992). *Jogging in Havana.* Oakville, Ontario: Mosaic.

Fanon, F. (1968). *The wretched of the earth.* New York: Grove.

Grove, F.P. (1966). *Settlers of the marsh.* Toronto: McClelland and Stewart.

———. (1983). *Fruits of the earth.* Toronto: McClelland and Stewart.

Harris, C. (1984). *Fables from the women's quarters.* Toronto: Williams-Wallace.

———. (1985). Mask. In Lorris Elliot (Ed.), *Other voices* (pp.86-88). Toronto: Williams-Wallace.

Harris, M. (1992). *Outsiders and insiders.* New York: Peter Lang.

Lamming, G. (1960). *The pleasures of exile.* London: Michael Joseph.

Moodie, S. (1962). *Roughing it in the bush.* Toronto: McClelland and Stewart.

Ramchand, K. (1983). *The West Indian novel and its background.* (2nd ed.). London: Heinemann Educational Books.

Tiffin, H. (1988). Post-colonial literatures and counter-discourse. *Kunapipi,* 9, 17-34.

NARRATIVE QUILTING IN *BANANA BOTTOM* AND *VOYAGE IN THE DARK*

Carolyn Allen

Banana Bottom and *Voyage in the Dark* tell the stories of female protagonists faced with the challenge of reconciling two worlds, two cultures. In spite of the differences in race and class, both heroines identify themselves with a Caribbean space incomprehensible to the "master" culture, even as they are seduced by the beauty and power of the narratives of that culture. The result is a cross-cultural sensitivity. In these works by Jamaican born Claude McKay and Dominican born Jean Rhys, this cultural creolization is figured in the patchwork design of the narratives, which brings together a variety of texts and voices, dominant and subordinated, central and marginal. The article explores the dynamics of the heroines' cultural *créolité* and the narrative strategies it evokes from the writers.

Banana Bottom et *Voyage in the Dark* sont deux récits dont les protagonistes féminins doivent reconcilier deux mondes et deux cultures. Malgré les différences ethniques et sociales, les deux héroines s'identifient à l'espace caraïbéen. Impénétrable selon la culture du «maître», il séduit par la beauté et le pouvoir des récits de cette culture. Il en résulte une sensibilité trans-culturelle. Dans les oeuvres de Claude McKay, né en Jamaïque, et de Jean Rhys, née en Dominique, cette créolisation culturelle est représentée par une structure en "patchwork." Ce sont des récits qui regroupent une variété de textes et de voix à la fois dominantes et subordonnées, venues du centre et de la périphérie. L'article explore la dynamque particulière de la créolité culturelle de ces héroïnes telle qu'elle est évoquée par les stratégies narratives de l'écrivain.

The notion of Creolism is fundamental in all that has to do with the knowledge, interpretation and understanding of historical phenomena in the Caribbean. (René Depestre)

*

EVER SINCE THE FIRST NATIONALIST stirrings in the Caribbean back in the 19th century, our intellectuals have been engaged in efforts to elaborate a model of identity. The deterministic European model proved problematic. It would demand a degree of intellectual sleight of hand to construct a persuasive argument of origins in a region where the indigenous population was all but eradicated. The solution? Creole. A cross-cultural definition which distinguished persons of Old World lineage, but New World birth and breeding. The term was used for first generation descendants in several colonial zones, but it is in the Americas, and particularly in the Caribbean, that it has had a lasting and dynamic career, being subsequently applied both to persons of mixed blood (the new native breed championed by Betances, Hostos and Martí) and regional languages. Today, a growing interest in the creative manifestations of cross-cultural contact has brought the term into literary discourse. Creolism is indeed a concept with which we must come to terms in any attempt to know and describe ourselves.

Without presuming to sketch the history of this idea across the region, it is interesting to note that in each language area it has been taken up at different times as the basis for elaborating a cultural theory or poetics: from the Spanish American preoccupation with *lo criollo;* to Walcott and Brathwaite in the Anglophone Caribbean; followed by Glissant, whose work inspired the Bernabé, Chamoiseau, Confiant manifesto *Eloge de la Créolité (In Praise of Creoleness).* Most recently, Antonio Benitez-Rojo has approached the challenge of describing the culture of Caribbean creole societies through the principles of postmodernism and chaos theory. In *The Repeating Island,* the region is imaged as a Milky Way, a galaxy "where we detect dynamic regularities—not results—within the (dis)order that exists beyond the world of predictable pathways" (Benitez-Rojo, 1992, p.36). He offers this as a reading distinct from, but not negating or opposing other descriptions of the region: the unifying, which privileges the similar, or the "entirely severalized," which emphasizes differences. Despite its broken and tempest-tossed movement from enclave to enclave, certain constants remain with each redefinition of "creole": the resistance of monolithic models; an interest in accounting for an acknowledged and willingly embraced cultural heterogeneity; and a desire for integration.

I propose here to take a speculative step into this arena of discourses on creolization, to examine, in two prose fiction texts, a narrative strategy which makes evident the West Indian writer's characteristic act of negotiating between worlds, between the infamous great tradition and its opposite, the metropole and the outpost, the scribal and the oral; the familiar list of binary opposites goes on. I have chosen two works which are, themselves, in some ways on opposite sides of these distinctions. It is tempting, in fact, to read these texts as exposure and negative. Claude McKay's heroine is black. Jean Rhys' is white. The former (perhaps an unexpected twist), the daughter of a landowner; the latter, without hope of inheritance, though her father was once a man of property. *Banana Bottom* (1933) is set in rural Jamaica; *Voyage in the Dark* (1934) in London, for the greater part, England throughout. The fecundity and natural exuberance of McKay's rural, tropical setting is in stark contrast to the unredeemed, grey monotony of Anne's rooms. The world to which Bita has returned after her education in England, is the one from which Anne is torn away. Neither is willing to completely abandon, reject or disregard the world left behind. The challenge of reconciling the two becomes central in the novels. The shape of the image is very much the same, with light and dark reversed.

This similarity derives, at least in part, from the writers' own experiences of living between worlds. Both were born in the Caribbean, but departed definitively in their youth. In these texts they are exploiting their memory of a community shaped by the history of the plantation, that very special circumstance of multi-cultural co-existence, the crucible of Caribbean creole culture. The texts concern themselves with the protagonists' relationship to a post-emancipation, colonial world, still living heavily in the shadow of the plantation. In McKay, the symbolic, white "planter's helmet" of the mulatto descendant is enough to evoke the legacy.

> It rested upon the head of busha and planter like a halo of protection. Under it slave-owners and slave-drivers had goaded the black herds to toil. And under it in spite of changing times they still remained the lords of the tropics. (McKay, 1961, p.264).

It is within the protagonist that we see the dramatic tension of the creolization process at work. Bita must come through the repressive regime of protestant English propriety (represented by Mrs. Craig), the curse of the landed mulatto (condemning her forever to "nigger" smallness), and the threat of being totally consumed by the powerful spiritual forces of her African ancestry. She comes through all this, and more, to arrive at a place where neither mind nor body need be denied. As complements to each other, they work together in harmony, and in this self the achievement of cross-cultural integration is posited. This reconciliation of two worlds proves unattainable for Rhys' protagonist, Anne Morgan. A psychic disintegration is underway as she is unable to conceive of both worlds simultaneously, to experience them both as real: "Sometimes it was as if I were back there and as if England were a dream. At other times England was the real thing and out there was the dream, but I could never fit them together" (1969, pp.7-8). Yet her primary identity, like Bita's, is intimately linked to the Caribbean space. Anne's vivid memory of bathing in the pool at Morgan's Rest (1969, pp.77-78), is as intense as Bita's renewal of the childhood pleasure of Martha's Basin (McKay, 1961, p.117).

This feeling for place which extends into an affection for those most deeply rooted in the land, meets with disapproval, in both cases, from the female figure who has (taken) charge of the young protagonist and who sees only Europe's civilization as valid. In Bita's case, the missionary, Mrs. Craig, conceives a plan to redeem her of the stigma and consequences of being raped by the village idiot/genius Crazy Bow. The plan includes her education in England as preparation for a life of religious service as the wife of the intended successor to the mission, Herald Newton Day. Mrs. Craig's attitude to the locals, and especially to their Africa-derived cultural practices, is antipathetic and disdainful. Similarly Hester Morgan, Anne's stepmother in *Voyage in the Dark,* finds the girl's affinity to local culture objectionable. The desired identification with motherland is frustrated as Bita and Anne are steered toward the colonial Mother Country. The issue of emotional bonding and identification becomes central. The natural mother is absent. The father, though present, is distant or peripheral. The second most influential figure in their lives becomes an older English male. The nature of this relationships seals their fate.

Anne seeks in Walter Jeffries a love which will give her life meaning. In harsh terms she becomes a slave to his sexual desires. There is no physical cruelty, but by her own surrender of will, Anne confers on him the status of master, and is haunted by the memory of the name of an 18-year-old slave girl. Yet, for all her efforts, she is unable to find fulfillment within his view of the world, for it allows no room for the reality of that other place with which she identifies. By contrast Bita finds in Squire Gensir a mentor who encourages her to value her own culture as much as she admires Europe (McKay, 1961, p.125). His comments on art "Everybody borrows or steals and recreates in art" (p.124) suggest a creole reading of cross-cultural contact. The Squire furnishes Bita with a philosophy which allows for the co-existence, if not necessarily integration, of entities formerly experienced as antagonistic. This, Anne's master cannot offer, and so her failed relationship with Walter, exacerbates her condition of being torn between two worlds. Increasingly her memories, her feeling of being in a dream, become dominated by nightmarish imaginings, culminating with the jeering carnival mask and the bolting horse.

In the depiction of the heroines' moment of ultimate cultural (dis)integration, the writers exploit the realm of local, secular ritual. Carnival, the moment when identity is mutable, when Anne if allowed, could play out her desire to be black, comes back as a mocking gesture, locking off the possibility of co-identification as she aborts the child conceived of her implicit trade, father unknown. Bita's ultimate insertion into the world of Banana Bottom is celebrated at the Tea Meeting, a distinctly creole social ritual of song, dance and stylized courting at which she is queen and her favour is bought by her husband-to-be.

It is useful to consider these moments in relation to Benitez-Rojo's description of Caribbean culture. Going back to the comments of Pere Jean-Baptiste Labat—among the earliest to posit the existence of a common Caribbean culture—he picks up on the phrase: "It is no accident that the sea which separates your lands makes no difference to the rhythms of your body" (Benitez-Rojo, 1992, p.75). Rhythm is taken as the definitive element, demonstrable through a variety of performances, among them the dance and percussion central to events like Carnival and Tea Meeting, to which the texts allude.

Yet another of Benitez-Rojo's performance examples appears as an important evocation in McKay and Rhys: the market. The description of 19th century Santiago de Cuba (Benitez-Rojo, 1992, pp.78-79) is uncannily, though not surprisingly, similar to McKay's (1961, pp.40-41): the buzz and swarm of activity, the mode of dress, the movement of the women (especially), the "babble" of creole speech, the centrality of rhythm. Bita's response is informed by her experience of Europe, the source of Hauranne's perspective.

> The noises of the market were sweeter in her ears than a symphony. Accents and rhythms, movements and colours, nuances that might have passed unnoticed if she had never gone away, were now revealed to her in all their striking detail. (McKay, 1961, p.41)

Here is a scene of polyrhythms, visual and aural, appealing to smell, taste and touch. It is hardly coincidental that Anne's most vivid and persistent memory of home is also of Market Street (Rhys, 1969, p.7), emphasizing smells and recalling the women and their cries. It captures the essence of Caribbean creoleness. Referring to Hauranne's market place, Benitez-Rojo concludes:

> It is not a "mulatto" mixture, if that term is meant to convey a kind of "unity"; it is a polyrhythmic space that is Cuban, Caribbean, African, and European at once, and even Asian and Indoamerican, where there has been a contrapuntal and intermingled meeting.... Within this chaos of differences and repetitions, of combinations and permutations, there are regular dynamics that co-exist. (Benitez-Rojo, 1992, p.81)

Without venturing into the realm of chaos theory, we can pull from this description the notions of polyrhythm, coexisting distinct entities, intermingled meeting and repetition, and propose the simple, visual metaphor of the quilt, in which we can find these principles at work in a fixed relationship. The model is not original. Carole Boyce Davies and Elaine Savory Fido, in *Out of the Kumbla: Caribbean Women and Literature,* substitute it for what was previously described as the fragmented form of several women's texts engaged in experiments in narrative strategies (1990, p.6).

Here, the quilt is invoked as objective correlative of a specific structural feature in *Banana Bottom* and *Voyage in the Dark,* a feature which presents the creole imagination at work in the juxtaposition, or articulation, of a variety of discrete fragments of text against/in contact with each other, to create the new whole which is the body of the novel. "Narrative quilting" refers to the construction of a (new) text by means of seaming together selected bits of narrative—song, conversation, slogan, proverb, canonical text. This fabrication images as it narrates the heroines' very necessary construction of self, a construction which leads Bita to integration, Anne to disintegration.

Perhaps the most obvious object for the kind of narrative juxtaposition of modes under investigation is language. The complexity of the

Caribbean situation is evident in both texts. Stepmother Hester shows obvious distate for Anne's creole speech:

> I tried to teach you to talk like a lady and behave like a lady and not like a nigger and of course I couldn't do it. Impossible to get you away from the servants. That awful sing-song voice you had! Exactly like a nigger you talked—and still do. Exactly like that dreadful girl Francine. When you were jabbering away together in the pantry I never could tell which of you was speaking. (Rhys, 1969, p.56)

As I noted earlier, Hester's intentions for Anne are similar to Mrs. Craig's ambitions for Bita. Both are persuaded that a European training would accomplish the task. It is interesting to note McKay's description of Bita's voice "firm round creole" on the occassion of the Sunday School prize giving "pronouncing every syllable clearly as she had learned to speak English" (McKay, 1962, p.62).

Though both heroines are at home in the world of island creole or patois, as the market scenes suggest, creole speech is conspicuous by its absence in the Rhys text. It appears only once, as Anne recalls her participation in the story-telling ritual, using Francine's language: "'Timm, Timm,' and I had to answer, 'Bois sèche.'" (1969, p.61). It is in McKay that a variety of speech patterns are presented, several stages along the creole continuum being shown as distinct from the standard English of the narrative and its (England) educated characters, by attempts at orthographic simulation of the sounds produced: "Youse fast to butt in in thisya. An' ah'll break you' big bammy face wid this bottle ef you fools wimme" (1962, p.69). It should be remembered that McKay was the first to put this voice into verse, under the influence of his mentor Walter Jekyll, immortalized through the novel in the figure of Squire Gensir. The text incorporates sermons, Obeah chant and the "speechifying" of Tea Meeting and country wedding, all celebrating creole rhetoric in performance.

The novels also give way to other voices through the reproduction of letters, which take over the narrative. This written text is accompanied by telegram, advertisements, captions under paintings, and printed invitations, with quotations from real and imagined sources expanding the range of language use and sign systems at play in the text. While McKay shows confidence in the word, as in books, Rhys seems to question the truth-bearing capacity of language, the authority and trustworthiness of the written word: "What is purity? For thirty-five years the answer has been Bourne's Cocoa" (1969, p.50). Language is an agent of power, depicting, even as it dictates, social status. Should we read Laurie's penchant for the long word—she substitutes "lugubrious" for Anne's "gloomy" (1969, pp.104-105)—as a way of masking her impotence and vulnerability in that society? Certainly, Anne's failure to master the chorus girl slang is a failure to arm herself against the contempt of proper society.

It is not surprising then, that we search in vain for any overt reference to canonical texts in *Voyage in the Dark.* Rhys' protagonist is a skeptic. Early in the story we find her reading a novel entitled *Nana,* which prefigures the kind of life she herself will lead in London, as a "tart." Her fellow chorus girl is disgusted and dismisses the authority of the text.

> I bet you a man writing a book about a tart tells a lot of lies one way and another. Besides, all books are like that—just somebody stuffing you up. (1969, p.9)

But Anne remains impressionable, and must refuse to read in order not to succumb to the power of the written word, for it is from books that she has taken her romantic view of life (1969, p.64).

By contrast, McKay presents a heroine who, far from being alienated or overwhelmed by her encounter with the scribal, exploits the canon in her own self-affirmation. In addition to her conversation with Gensir discussing the ideas of various philosophers and writers, we see Bita in intense private contemplation. The texts on which she meditates become part of the narrative. At the end, her successful integration, what we might call her cultural creolization, is imaged in her easy movement from the philosophical French of Pascal to the domestic creole of Aunty Nommy.

Music is also a pervasive presence in these novels. They beg to be heard. The range is sweeping, from high culture classical pieces to bawdy folk humour and music hall. Again we find the effect of the film negative at work. Bita is the accomplished pianist, Anne the musician manqué. The most impressive performance, for its sheer talent and range, from oratorio through spirituals to picnic jigs, is undoubtedly Crazy Bow's: "How bewitching was his playing!" (McKay, 1962, pp.257-258). This in contrast to Anne's reliance on a limited selection of records (Rhys, 1969, p.137). There is no Bach (whatever the title) and as she plays the same song over and over again, the monotonous cycle of her life is evoked. In this mechanical and pre-ordained plastic performance there is no possibility of improvisation, no contact between performer and audience, essential elements of performance in the dynamic oral community of which she is deprived. In fact, the repeated song "Connais-tu le pays?" poses a haunting question for Anne (Do you know the country?), triggering a memory which makes this sense of loss, distance and difference explicit (Rhys, 1969, pp.138-140).

Music translates a sense of the world inhabited by the protagonists. In addition to the high/low culture dynamic, music is also important for its personal impact. In her moment of defiance of Mrs. Craig's prohibitions, Bita is bolstered by the memory of a dance tune endorsing individual will: "Just going to do the thing I want, No matter who don't like it" (McKay, 1962, p.219). In a similar way, Anne exercises her will to make her own definitions by rewriting the songs she sings, appropriating them to her own uses (Rhys, 1969, p.90), whatever the "correct" lyrics should be: "I'll sing it how I like it" (1969, p.132). In spite of this effort, she is not a conquerer. Her memories of tunes from the Caribbean recall a deep sense of anguish at her inability to be assimilated into the world to which she is emotionally drawn. She wants to be black, but she is merely a "brown girl" caught in a downward spiral, haunted by images of the past.

> There were three musicians at the head a man with a concertina and another with a triangle and another with a chak-chak playing There's a Brown Girl in a Ring (Rhys, 1969, p.156, italicized in the original).

Anne's hallucination at the end of the novel evokes an event which occurs repeatedly in McKay—the troop of balladiers, making commentary on local happenings. Bita herself has been the object of their art. A mocking ballad was written about her rape by Crazy Bow, but ridicule turned to envy when she returned a "lady" from England. Nonetheless, it is a tune which has haunted her, the refrain taken up again and again in the early chapters of the text.

> You may wrap her up on silk,
> You may trim her up with gold,
> And the prince may come after
> To ask for your daughter
> But Crazy Bow was first. (McKay, 1962, p.14)

The ballads, like calypsoes, are expressions of the community sensibility. These song writers are the news reporters and analysts, the chroniclers of experience. McKay in recording, or simulating the lyrics, is once again inserting into the public and legitimate world of the scribal what had hitherto belonged exclusively to the private and oral sphere. There is an ethnographic thrust to the text. McKay writes as a fictional anthropologist accounting for almost every aspect of the community's life. In addition to the ballad lyrics, he records hymn verses, revival choruses and songs, Tea Meeting selections, jamma work songs and other ditties. (In life Walter Jekyll had a great interest in folk music and published scores and lyrics.)

We may see this structural juxtaposition at play in the writers' treatment of many other areas of experience, religion among them. But, in the end, the ultimate expression of the "quilting" strategy is the very appearance of the text on the page. The flow of margin to margin prose lines is interrupted by the insertion of fragments. Various markers are used to indicate the border between narrative and insert: capital letters in titles, quotation marks, italics, hyphens, parentheses and suspension dots, so that the reader receives a visual signal of the transition.

Rhys' use of these indicators is clearly deliberate. Anne's thoughts as she attempts to adjust to life in London are presented as parenthetical, internal commentary on external action. The textual marker enacts her separation. In the early section of the novel, this difficulty of integrating into her new world is signalled visually in the alternation between roman and italic type, the latter containing her efforts to adjust psychologically: *"This is England, and I'm in a nice, clean English room with all the dirt swept under the bed"* (italics in original, Rhys, 1969, p.27). The principle is applied once more, with greater dramatic effect in the final pages of the novel. During her abortion, Anne hallucinates, recalling scenes from the Caribbean as well as her more recent past. The moments in her mind are made visually distinct by the use of italics, and the appearance comes closest to the image of a quilt's symmetrical units set against each other. Throughout the body of the text, the protagonist's intermittent returns to the place of her birth in memory are marked by suspension dots at opening and closing. Within these passages the use of conventional punctuation marks is suspended. Phrase and sentence breaks are irregular, and where they are made a hyphen is used. The effect is to alter not only the appearance of the text on the page, but the rhythm in which the passage moves. Cultural distinction becomes textual performance. Thoughts of the creole space appropriate the rhythms of that space.

McKay's use of these markers' distinguishing inserts is more conventional, but frequent enough for the visual appearance of the text on the page to become similar to Rhys's text. We must also consider the use of spatial divisions, setting narrative modes apart from each other. These breaks appear frequently in *Banana Bottom,* where we encounter islands of verse, song lyrics set apart from the narrative, surrounded by a small sea of space. And so, playing a little on the quilting metaphor, one might speak of the narrative fabric of these works as being made up of *text/iles.*

Literature is one of the most exhibitionist expressions in the world. This is because it is a stream of texts and there are few things as exhibitionist as a text. (Benitez-Rojo, 1992, pp.22-23)

Though *Banana Bottom* and *Voyage in the Dark* were intentionally selected as works pre-dating the era of a self-conscious exploitation of these kinds of disruptions, the fragmentation of text for the production of multiple meanings and the destabilizing of the word, the novels are clearly multiple in their incorporation of various bodies of language, their drawing on several systems. The source of this, I am suggesting, is the cross-cultural, creole experience and perspective of the writers. The result is the construction of a syncretic narrative giving a textual, visual and implicitly aural presence to their position, and that of their protagonists. Each fragment gets its meaning in its articulation against other fragments, as part of a whole, but not as synthesis.

The literature of the Caribbean can be read as a mestizo text, but also as a stream of texts in flight, in intense differentiation among themselves and within whose complex coexistence there are vague regularities, usually paradoxical ... projects that communicate their own turbulence. (Benitez-Rojo, 1992, p.27)

If one is permitted to make a large claim based on the analysis of a single feature, I would say that the quilted narrative structure of *Banana Bottom* and *Voyage in the Dark* is one example of the "daring improvisations" which Benitez-Rojo proposes as a characteristic of the creole Caribbean text:

The Caribbean text shows the specific features of the supersyncretic culture from which it emerges. It is, without a doubt, a consummate performer, with recourse to the most daring improvisations to keep from being trapped within its own textuality. (Benitez-Rojo, 1992, p.29)

REFERENCES

Benitez-Rojo, Antonio (1992). *The repeating island: The Caribbean and the postmodern perspective.* (James E. Maraniss, Trans.). Durham and London: Duke University Press.

Boyce Davies, Carole and Savory Fido, Elaine (Eds.). (1990). *Out of the Kumbla: Caribbean women and literature.* Trenton, NJ: Africa World Press.

McKay, Claude (1933). *Banana bottom.* Reprint. New York: Harcourt Brace Jovanovich, 1961, Harper & Row.

Rhys, Jean (1969). *Voyage in the dark.* London: Penguin. Twentieth Century Classics.

NATURE AND IMAGINATION: THE BESTIARY OF DULCE MARÍA LOYNAZ

Nara Araújo

The principal aim of this article is to explain the poetics of Cuban writer Dulce Maria Loynaz. Winner of the Cervantes Prize in 1992, her work is still almost unknown outside the Spanish-speaking world. This text outlines her literary and intellectual career and her silence after the 1950s. The author emphasizes the *Bestiarium,* her first book of poetry, written in 1919 but not published until 1985. Although this is a text of her youth, it already reveals the main trends of her poetics: solitude, spiritualism, love of nature. Comparing her text with those of Jorge Luis Borges and Nicolas Guillen, the author shows that Loynaz creates a "private" space as opposed to the masculine writer's "public" space, a vehicule for the expression of the feminine/masculine tension: nature versus civilization, liberty versus authority, imagination versus classification.

L'auteur veut faire connaître la poétique de Dulce Maria Loynaz, écrivaine cubaine née à la fin du XIXe siècle. Titulaire du Prix Cervantes de 1992, elle est toujours mal connue en dehors du monde hispanophone. Ce texte trace son parcours littéraire et intellectuel ainsi que son silence après les années 1950. Son premier texte poétique *Bestiarium,* écrit en 1919 mais publiée seulement en 1985, est une oeuvre de jeunesse importante puisqu'elle annonce les tendances dominantes de sa poétique : la solitude, le spiritualisme, le goût de la nature. Une comparaison entre l'oeuvre de Loynaz et celle de J.L. Borges et de N. Guillen permet de cerner la spécificité de cette écriture. Elle crée un espace «privé» de la femme où s'exprime la tension entre le masculin et le feminin, c'est-à-dire des conflits entre nature/civilisation, liberté/autorité, imagination/classification.

IN 1992, THREE CARIBBEAN WRITERS were honoured with important literary prizes: Dereck Walcott with the Nobel, Dulce María Loynaz with the Cervantes, and Patrick Chamoiseau with the Goncourt. This seems a delightful coincidence in a year in which, between debates and festivities, the encounter between Europe and the so-called Americas was remembered.

The simultaneous recognition of artists from three linguistic areas of the Caribbean seems more than a fateful coincidence and might be explained by other causes. The Nobel and the Cervantes are awarded to a whole body of work, and the Goncourt, in accordance with the statutes of the Academy of the same name, "to the best volume of imagination in prose." Nevertheless, the awarding of these honours could be determined under similar circumstances by the purely aesthetic quality of the work as a *sine qua non* condition.

These prizes of '92, might be seen as part of the honourable transactions of the *cuota alternativa* that often play a role in these conclaves, creating a space in the mainstream for those who are at the margins, and all the more so because of the fifth centennial of the discovery of the Americas. Or perhaps this literary phenomenon is due to a gradual widening of the cultural space in which the world's yet dependent writing is beginning to co-exist with and perhaps even surpass that of longer lived traditions. The hierarchical stratification of the centre and the margins, which has not changed with respect to economic relations, seems to be in a process of modification in favour of a space where ideas are exchanged, and where emergent literatures offer a renewing energy.

These prizes sanctioned the entry that Loynaz, Walcott and Chamoiseau had made earlier in another "centrist" institution: the prestigious publishing houses. Acceptance by these institutions is indispensable for writers who want to make their way to the other side of national borders, especially in countries with less developed publishing industries. It would be utopian to disregard the role of these publishing institutions in the establishment of the literary canons and the corresponding dissemination that they provide through the cultural market—publishing, distribution and promotion. The entry into the sanctified spaces is decisive for those where are seeking global awareness of their work, which, despite its merits, has obtained only a partial response.

Another Nobel, Josef Brodski, the poet of Russian origin, has complained of the ignorance of European readers with respect to the great works of Walcott, due to the confinement of these works in the English-speaking world. The prize of the Swedish Academy immediately widened the horizon of reception for the writer of small Saint Lucia.

The Goncourt, faithful to its tradition of distinguishing publishers who are used to winning literary prizes, gave its prize to the novel *Texaco* by the Martinican Patrick Chamoiseau, more than half a century after Rene Maran, another Caribbean writer obtained this valued prize. With *Texaco,* critics in France affirm that, Creole writing has entered "literary history," appearing alongside *chef d'oeuvres* such as *A l'Ombre des jeunes filles en fleur* by Proust or *La Condition humaine* by Malraux.

The Cervantes brought Loynaz' work to an apotheosis in the same year in which the Cuban writer reached her ninth decade of life. The prize rescued a forgotten name in the Spanish-speaking world and renewed the importance of this writer by inspiring the re-editing all of her books, journalistic chronicles and essays, as well as unpublished texts. While Walcott and Chamoiseau are authors at their peaks of creativity, Loynaz had ceased to create in the 1950s. The prize has given her new legitimacy in spite of her 30 years of silence.

How and when did the spiritual adventure of this Cuban writer, born with the century, begin? The creative cycle of Dulce Maria Loynaz began in the 1920s, when at the age of 20, the daughter of General Enrique Loynaz del Castillo, who distinguished himself in of the War of Independence, published her first poems in the Cuban press. Daughter of a mambi[1] unoz Sanudo, a wealthy family, Dulce Maria spent her childhood in a secluded environment. Along with her brothers and sister Enrique, Carlos Manuel and Flor, she received her first schooling at home. She herself has told how, as a result of a tragic event, the children were confined to the family home.

Literary precedents in the family circle were not abundant, but the mother had studied painting and her dramatic voice expressed itself through singing while she accompanied herself on the piano like a professional. Dulce Maria and her brothers and sister mastered several instruments, and in their free time in the studio, they would entertain themselves with their small orchestra. Due to the strict obligations of mourning at the death of their parents, the children had to abandon music and seek refuge in poetry. In this fireside environment, the daughter of the General composed her first verses (Simon,1991, pp.31-33).

The poems published in the Cuban press during the 1920s and 30s allowed her to be included in the anthologies of Cuban poetry.[2] In 1938 she published her first book, *Versos, 1920-1938.* In this work, Dulce

Maria builds a spiritual universe in which a tendency for the impossible, for silence, for solitude and for nature, feeds the voice of the lyric subject.

This existential preoccupation would return in *Juegos de agua* (1947), a poetic volume in which water—river and ocean, rain and pond—constitutes an ideal metaphor of human existence due to its unrestrained and constantly flowing nature. The originality of Dulce Maria's poetry, so very different from that of other Latin American women poets of her generation (the tragic poetry of Delmira Agostini, the passionate poetry of Juana de Ibarbourou, the melancholic poetry of Gabriela Mistral or the mystical poetry of Clara Silva), was already clearly defined.

Juan Ramon Jimenez, who would visit the home of the writer in Havana—as would Federico Garcia Lorca and Gabriela Mistral—wrote a biographical sketch of Dulce Maria following the encounter, seizing the nascent spirit of the Loynaz family:

> The large crystal glass, on the floor, from which Federico Garcia Lorca drank lemonade, with stalactites and stalagmites and spiders caught at once. (Oh, yes then I knew suddenly wherefrom all the latest ravings of Lorca's writing came!) Dulce Maria disappeared and reappeared from strange crevices in the form of rays of light and shadow.
> (Jiménez,1937)

I would like to retain from this very revealing text the words "strange crevices" and "rays of light and shadow." I do not doubt that the actual physical presence of the poet may have caused this impression, but I suspect it was her verses that provoked this imagery in the poet from Moguer. Juan Ramon himself had written the prologue to the anthology *La Poesia cubana en 1936,* in which Dulce Maria had been included. When the poet received him in the famous mansion by the sea, she seemed elusive and tenuous ("crevices"), indefinable ("strange"), contrasting ("rays of light and shadow"). These were the very characteristics of her poetic universe, a universe outlined not only in verse and stanza, but also in prose. The novel *Jardin* (1951), the passionate *Carta de amor a Tut-Ank-Amen* (1953), the paradigmatic *Poemas sin nombre* (1953), the peculiar voyage chronicle *Un verano en Tenerife* (1958), although they are prose texts, belong also to the realm of poetry with their lyrical emphasis and use of symbols. All written during the 1950s, they complemented the cycle which began with the first two books of verse.

During this decade more works were published and interest for her work increased. Public life was intense: conferences, awards and homages in Cuba and abroad. But by the end of that decade and particularly in the next, surprisingly, silence fell.

When asked about the nature of poetic creativity, Dulce Maria says that poetry belongs to youth. It is perhaps for that reason—at the end of the 1950s—that her abandonment began. A series of events added to this process of creative withdrawal. Problems with her habitual Spanish editors and family preoccupations with the thunderous arrival of 1959: the husband's, family members', and friends' parting. Dulce Maria returns to the domestic cloister, a space cherished by her brothers and sister—poets of exceptional and eccentric tendencies.

A cloud then covered Dulce Maria's universe: her books were ignored, critics became silent. Meanwhile, she remained quiet at her mansion in Vedado between hand-held fans and ivory statuettes, Meissen shepherds and biscuit ornaments, accompanied by headless statues and the bronze eagle that observed her movements from the entrance while her faithful dogs guarded her in the now empty corridors.

The living myth of the Cuban who was born to renowned forefathers and who resisted abandoning her native land, as well as the emptiness surrounding scant and rare works that circulated amongst novices and mystic apprentices of the literary profession, enlarged the legend. The legend became reality in the early 1980s, when those who revered her saw their wish fulfilled of seeing her texts published. They also saw her reappear outside the ancient walls. It was like the raising of a shipwreck.

The demand for unedited texts led her, at that period, to submit for publication a notebook that had survived the onslaught of time. She remembered how some of her famous professors had found in her work something more than straightforward factual writing, and so she submitted the notebook crammed with fables, and with it, fragments of recollections that she had written as a young girl. These poems illuminated the beginning stages of her creative cycle.

Dulce Maria has told how while in secondary school, she showed up for an exam on the subject then called Natural History. It was during the early 1920s. The young student answered the examiners' questions correctly. But she had not been warned about a complementary requisite: the submission of notebooks with her description of 20 species of the animal kingdom, 20 plants, and 20 minerals. Profoundly humiliated by what would represent the only failure in her secondary studies, she decided to write a book of fables and submit it in joking vengeance. A teacher-friend, afraid of the possible consequences of her act being misinterpreted, made a timely rescue of the fable book. Time had its way with the manuscripts, and only the book of the animal kingdom was saved from the moths.

Writing in a genre of such ancient origin, the secondary school student revealed her interest in literary tradition. She found the form of the fable book a way of challenging academic strictness. When I spoke to her regarding these poems, she answered me with a smile: "It was only a joke." More than the joke, however, the surviving notebook holds a moral lesson and anticipates some of the fundamental elements of her future poetry. At the age of 17, the future Cervantes prize winner, was already building—without meaning to—the basis for a firmly-rooted and sustained poetry, an inheritor of traditions but impossible to classify as belonging to schools or movements.

Literature has at least educational value, but this function can reach a higher level depending on social factors. The Middle Ages was one of the periods in which the evaluating function was developed from ethical and didactic perspectives. The new society, product of the fusion between Germanic peoples and those of the old Roman Empire with their Greco-Latin culture, sought new literary forms which, in the name of Christianity, would transmit educational and moral values.

In this context, the fable book became popular and was modelled on the Greek *Physiologus.* The origin of this anonymous text is believed to be the second century A.D. It consists of a series of stories based on scientific facts, established according to the good judgement of the so-called Physiologus or naturalist. According to *The Encyclopaedia Britannica,* it was made up of 48 sections in which animals, plants or minerals were described. The presence of elephants and unicorns—of East Indian origin—revealed the multicultural link. But the first known fable book of Western culture had a close relation to the doctrines of early Christianity, as transmitted through biblical principles.

In the early Middle Ages, the *Physiologus* was widely translated from Greek to Latin and other languages. It inspired the many medieval fable books that circulated in vernacular versions. The educational function of these texts was basic and overpowered the aesthetic function. The description of an animal, a plant or a mineral was combined with the allusions to Christian doctrine: fear of death and of final judgement.

Some of the values praised were abstinence and chastity; the sin most attacked was heresy. The cognitive function was subordinate to the educational function. It mattered little whether the fox appeared as an animal that simulates death in order to seduce its prey, the deer kills its enemy the serpent in its den, or the mongoose enters the mouth of the crocodile in order to eat his entrails. What mattered was to transmit a good lesson. The fable books showed mythical images such as that of the bird Phoenix that could be born again from its own ashes; they showed heraldic emblems; they enriched symbolic visual language; and they discovered the symbols relevant to the teaching of Christianity. When the needs of a society led by the spirit and bent on the perception of conduct and a vision of the world disappeared, the fable remained as part of the arsenal of literary forms; only the order of its functions changed. From then onward the aesthetic function or gnoseology could dominate, or both could interrelate in such a way that the creation of a book of fables with fantastic animals—created by the human mind—could help in understanding what Jung called the collective unconsciousness, victim of memory and myth. But the prime, educational function, in the aesthetic and didactic sense, was preserved.

The popularity of these books originated in the Middle Ages but they always reappeared—in verse or in prose—because they were the description of the animal world; an artistic way to encounter human problems. The modern development of the genre no doubt led to *Animal Farm* by George Orwell. Other great writers such as Guillaume Apollinaire and Ramon del Valle Inclán, Jorge Luis Borges and Nicolás Guillén made use of the fable book; each used this model of ancient origin to express a different poetic world.

Guillen produced a book of fables after having written his principal books. *El gran zoo* (1967) is a compendium of his previous work. As its title indicates, the broadening of the limits of the genre indicates the strong will of the writer. The inclusion of the "animal-like" KKK as well as the *Tonton Macoute,*[3]—to cite only two examples—implies a new "animalization," although the original significance of fable book is preserved. These "animals" illustrate the renewing of the genre and at the same time the typical social character of Guillén's poetry.

Dulce Maria Loynaz' fable book, on the other hand, is a dawning text. It reveals the intimate and philosophical inclination of her future work. As the title *Bestiarium* indicates, there exists no will to depart from the generic norms, but rather to conserve a similarity to the original rules of the genre. The title *Bestiarium* and the name in Latin which—in parenthesis—accompanies the name of each animal entry, imitate the jargon of biologists. At the same time, they evoke the language of the first fable books. Each of the poems is conceived as a lesson and takes its title from the described animal. The scientific name produces an academic tone, and the precision with respect to nomenclature seems to allude to the desire to express objective knowledge.

In the last verse of the First Lesson, dedicated to the common spider, the poet establishes unusual links. The spider "love and death with its threads ties" and the material that it sews is like a net laid out "to the sea motionless of air." What is commonplace is magnified with appeal to sublime topics—love, death—and to natural elements of vast dimension—sea, air. The imagination exalts the insignificant spider in order to reveal sympathy towards the animal kingdom. But some of the constants are also expressed in Loynaz' poetry: Eros, Thanatos and Nature.

In the lessons that follow, the variety of items of reference produces diversity with respect to semantics. The nightingale is the "roving flute"; the firefly, "lamp with neither oil nor beacon"; the rhinoceros, "carries a black moon on its nose"; the bee is "honey in process and gold in living nugget"; the flies, "black stitches that sew one day to the next"; the serpent is a "Sign of Infinity."

The image moves towards nature itself (sea, air, gold, moon), human activity (flute, lamp, beacon), or the abstractions built with elements of distinct orders (black stitches that sew one day to the next; honey in process), that may reach philosophic generalization (Sign of Infinity).

This exercise of the imagination which tries to capture real essence, brings with it a reflection which is in itself educational. More than the "humorous lesson" that Dulce Maria wanted to teach her strict teachers, her *Bestiarium* is a search which has as its prime objective—as did medieval fable books—the animal kingdom. Its final goal: the human species.

The time when fable books served to frighten is long past; they promised cruel punishment for sinners. Nothing is further from Dulce Maria's fable book than religious terror and the occult. In it we find feelings such as impotence, loneliness and a certain nonconformity with humans, their weaknesses and limitations. However her educational influence is not as important as she might have desired.

The contrast between what is most insignificant and what is vast produces a series of images and relationships based on volumes. In the Second Lesson, the simplicity of the animal described—emphasized by the strophic form of a single tercet—contrasts with the magnitude of an existential question:

What will the caterpillar do
with so many feet
and so short a trip?

In the Fifth Lesson, dedicated to the common fly, the contrasts are numerous:

Flies, black stitches
that go sewing one day to the next ...
Flies settled on the large cake
of fifteen small candles ...
Flies, Sun.
To tie the tedium, furtive pinch
in the scarce sweetness man.

The contrast between what passes briefly—flies, black stitches, furtive pinch—and what lasts—one day to the next, sun, tedium, scarce sweetness of man—accentuates and magnifies. The contrast underlined by the sharp brevity of the fifth line, "Flies. Sun" creates a distance; but it also magnifies. The contrasting relationship between what is concrete—flies, large cake of 15 small candles—and what is abstract—one day to the next, tedium, scarce sweetness of man—emphasizes what is habitual and basic in human existence. There is no exaggerated eloquence. This would become another essential characteristic of Dulce Maria Loynaz' poetry.

Bestiarium includes other examples of small poetic form: the toad and the spider, the bee and the caterpillar, the firefly and the mosquito, the butterfly and the nightingale, belong to the domain of family life. The other animals are those of the Sunday zoo and the circus: the serpent and the rhinoceros, the camel, the elephant, the brown bear and the lion. In a sense, it is an extension of family life. There are neither fantastic nor mythical animals as in Borges; nor human characters—as in Guillén—made into animals. The seahorse, the silkworm and the bat complete this simple inventory. The ordinary is boosted by image. As in other poetic texts of Loynaz, a desire for spirituality emanates from her attachment to a natural and immediate universe.

The animals serve as an excuse to judge the cruelty of humans exercised against the small—the butterfly, the silkworm, and the large—the bear and the lion. To take their side reveals the tendency of Dulce Maria's poetry toward nature, the essential complement to human beings. In her poetic universe, nature is a constant reference, a point of comparison.

In order to define her concept of poetry, Dulce Maria has established an analogy: like a tree, poetry must be born favoured by vertical impulse. Both are born of the earth and of the earth they will make use, but with the instinct of height.[4] In defining her lyric personality, Dulce María has accepted being compared to water that flows, and leaves (Simóon,1991, p.46). Water is her poetry, symbol of explicit poetics and implicit poetics yet to be discovered.

Her appeal to nature may be interpreted—more than as a romantic undercurrent—as a subliminal association with the paradigms of what is feminine: what is liquid, what is fluid, what is unrestrained. Water as a protective element of the maternal body. From the binary contrast of culture/nature, nature seems to be taken as liberty (what is feminine) and not culture, such as authority (what is masculine), which sets order, classifies and subjects. In fact, the reaction of the student who wrote a poetic zoology notebook was a protest of the imagination as nature in the presence of culture as an institution.

To opt for nature does not mean ignorance with respect to the progress of knowledge. There is no idealization, for what is harmful stays as such. In an analogy which indicates the inserting of what is modern, the mosquito is:

> Minute airplane in which
> Yellow Fever travels.

To opt for nature is not a rejection of accumulated experience, of the cultural continuum. The choice of a literary model of an origin which is popular while sanctified by academic tradition reveals this. In her fable book the elephant is a descendant of the last mammoth, the bear dances a foxtrot, the serpent is made of Saturn rings and recalls an enchanted garden. The nightingale is that of Juliet.

To opt for nature as imagination is, rather, to set free the desire to escape from the norm that restricts and ties. The desire for freedom and the right to dream flow through this book of poems. The lyric subject wishes to ride the seahorse, "to the trot of a dream to be dreamt" and be "as light as a dream." It attributes to the camel "the minimal dream of green and the promised water." The bat is admired, the exceptional union of two glories—wings and chest—in a single body.

The desire to conceive the impossible as a way of possibly exorcising a liberating wish or reaching it through language is another of the constants of Loynaz' poetics. Her poetry, of a simple nature, closer to formal style than innovative experiment, is filled with that "high instinct," which Dulce Maria defined as an essential characteristic.

Her early *Bestiarium* transmits a restlessness about the existence of humans and their relationships with nature. The relevance of the model—branded since its founding by the educational function—contributes to reflecting upon the human condition and to emphasizing the desire for spiritual awakening. The manuscript, of lettering as fine and fragile as the body of its author, has remained as a defence of liberty through imagination. This precept holds up all of Loynaz' poetry.

Since her first book *Versos,* liberty remained explicitly associated with imagination. In the poem "En mi verso soy libre" not only is the vital content of liberation poetics through language—old desire of the old avant-garde—announced from the very title, but also announced is a position in the world, that her own life would confirm and still does:

In my verse I am free: it is my sea.
My sea wide and naked of horizons ...
In my verse I walk upon the sea,
I walk upon unfolded waves
of other waves and of other waves ... I walk
in my verse; I breathe, live, grow
in my verse, and in it my feet have
way and my way direction and my
hands something to hold and my hope
something to wait for and my life its meaning.
I am free in my verse and it is free
as I. We love one another. We have one another.
Outside it I am small and I kneel down
before the work of my hands, the
delicate mud moulded between my fingers ...
Inside it, I raise myself and I am myself.

ENDNOTES

1. Mambi: Cuban soldier in the War of Independance against Spain
2. For example, *Poetas jóvenes cubanos,* Barcelona, 1922; *La poesia moderna en Cuba,* Madrid, 1926; *La poesia cubana en 1936,* La Habana, 1937.
3. The Klu Klux Klan created terror in the Southern United States just as Duvalier's hated private police force (the Tonton Macoute) did in Haiti.
4. In 1950 Dulce María Loynaz gave an address "Mi poesia: autocritica", which can be considered her *Ars poetica.* (See *Valoracion Multiple. Dulce Maria Loynaz.* (Ed. Pedro Simón), La Habana , Casa de las Americas, 1991, pp.79-97.

REFERENCES

Jimenez, J.R. (1937). Estado poético prologo, *La poesía cubana en 1936.* La Habana, Institution Hispanocubana de Cultura.

Loynaz, D.M. (1938). *Versos 1920-1938.* La Habana: Imp. Vcar.

———. (1947). *Juegos de Agua.* Madrid: Editora Nacional.

———. (1951). *Jardín.* Madrid: Aguilar.

———. (1953). *Carta de Amor de Reu Tut-Ank-Amen.* Madrid: Nueva Imprenta Radio.

———. (1953). *Poemas sin nombre.* Madrid: Aguilar.

———. (1958). *Un verano en Tenerife.* Madrid: Aguilar.

———. (1992). *Bestiarium.* La Habana: José Marti.

———. (1991-92) *Bestiarium,* (in brail) La Habana: José Marti.

Plasencia, A. Bestiarium: testimonio inapreciable de oficio poético, Valoración Multiple Dulce Maria Loynaz, *Granma Internacional,* 1/IX/1991.

Simón, P. (1991). Conversacion con Dulce Maria Loynaz, *Valoración Multiple. Dulce Maria Loynaz.* La Habana.

Yañez, M. (1991). Didascalico y poético, *Valoración Multiple. Dulce Maria Loynaz.* P. Simón (Ed.). La Habana.

POETIC DISCOURSE IN BABYLON: THE POETRY OF DIONNE BRAND

Frederick Ivor Case

There is a striking stylistic and thematic versatility in the poetic works of Dionne Brand. She brings to Canadian poetry a deep ideological concern with the effects of oppression on individuals and on societies. A serious study of her work reveals the aesthetic processes of enunciation that give expression to a committed ideological discourse. This discourse is rich in the semantic and semiotic devices that Brand uses with the skill of a poet who is sensitive to the exigencies of a culture in evolution. Despite the general lack of optimism in her work, there is no despair and her verse itself is a testimony to her celebration of life.

L'oeuvre poétique de Dionne Brand est marquée par une grande diversité d'éléments stylistques et thématiques. Elle apporte à la poésie canadienne une réflexion sur l'oppression et ses conséquences sur l'individu et sur la société en général. Une étude en profondeur de son oeuvre révèle un processus esthétique qui exprime un engagement idéologique certain. Ce discours s'organise selons divers procédés langagiers et sémiotiques que la poète manie avec le talent d'une écrivaine à l'écoute d'une culture en pleine évolution. Manquant, certes, d'optimisme, l'auteur n'est pourtant jamais désespéré, au contraire, ses vers chantent la vie.

*

THOUGH DIONNE BRAND is not a member of the Rastafari, her published collections of poetry[1] display characteristics of one who has lived the alienation of Babylon and has had to confront it with the arms at her disposal. While her poetry is essentially about the right to define and to determine one's own being, it would be misleading to speak of the universal appeal of her work, since there are many who would react sharply to her unambiguous ideological perspectives.[2]

It is essential to emphasize the thematic aspects of Brand's ontological enterprise, and it is equally important to bear in mind the poet's social purpose.[3] However, Brand's collections of poetry reveal an experimentation with various aesthetic forms and the perfection of certain devices which enhance the process of enunciation. When the processes of structuration are closely examined,[4] we discover that there is a general absence of striving for effect, an avoidance of hermetism and a great effort to produce a coherent and intelligible body of work. Brand has brought to Canadian poetry a sustained anger, a consistent pathos and an exposition of alienation, which are expressed in dynamic and varied forms.

My analysis of the poetic discourse in Brand's work consists of a discussion of the aesthetic processes of enunciation that give expression to the ideological discourse. In the references to literary critics and to other poets, I am attempting to arrive at a deeper appreciation of Brand's work, and I therefore do not apply critical theories to the analysis of her poetry. I simply refer to ideas on poetic discourse that are pertinent to the work of Dionne Brand.

In this context, discourse analysis[5] consists of the study of words and thoughts used in the poetry, and also of the structures which convey those words and thoughts. Though we may study these two notions separately, they are closely interdependent.

In this discussion of the expression of content, I am concerned with those surface structure elements which convey a message to us. I am concerned with what has been written and its sense implications and therefore tend to look for coherence and incoherence, consistency and inconsistency of ideological perspective. I look for meaning, understanding and aesthetic appreciation. There is also a certain preoccupation with the poetic narrative as it progressively reveals the theme of the poem.

In the case of the poetic structures[6] that convey the substance of the poetic discourse, I examine the stylistic methods of arriving at meaning and aesthetic expression. I therefore analyze the structure of the poems, the semantic devices and the semiotic principles that give them their final form. It is from the aesthetic structure[7] of the poem that we derive both emotional and intellectual appreciation of the poem.

SOCIAL COMMENT AND POETIC STRUCTURES

Dionne Brand's poetry is primarily an ideological discourse in which the social messages are explicitly conveyed. Throughout her work there is a preoccupation with those who have been systematically subjected to institutions beyond their control but who manage to maintain some degree of hope or optimism.[8] Her work is an intellectual exploration of oppression in which she analyzes the micro-cosmic and macro-cosmic aspects of socio-economic and political exploitation. There are consistent attempts to adapt the poetic expression to the narrative voice[9] and it is here that one sees the versatility of Brand's work.

The naïve stylistic simplicity of "Eleven Years Old" in *Earth Magic* is deceptive. The first stanza reads as follows:

> I'm old enough
> to work in the fields,
> my grandmother says:
> your limbs are young
> and strong,
> your mind won't rust,
> we need the extra hands
> to tend the crop
> and feed the goats
> and till this ungrateful land.

One does not know whether the declaration of the first two lines is the direct speech of the 11-year-old girl or the reported speech of the grandmother. The punctuation deliberately leads us into the ambiguity and to the realization that over the three generations represented there is a commonality of labour. The implicitly missing generation also produces a questioning in the mind of the reader, who is no further advanced by the end of the poem. However, the circumstances of the poetic discourse lead to the conclusion that the missing generation must also have fallen victim to deprivation. The rest of the stanza is devoted to the words of the grandmother. The focus of the grandmother moves from the affirmation of the potential for physical labour to a negative qualification concerning the mind and returns to the physical attributes of the girl symbolized by her hands.

The image of "the extra hands" is at the same time metaphoric and direct in its realism, but what is most striking is the use of the definite article which depersonalizes the owner of these limbs. This is in sharp contrast to the use of "your limbs" and "your mind." Furthermore, in lines 7, 8 and 9 "the" becomes an internal anaphora, and it is significant that the objects indicated are:

> ... the extra hands
> ... the crop
> ... the goats

If we are guided by the anaphoric structure, "... the extra hands" are equated with the crop and the goats, but in another sense the hands perform a function since they "... tend the crop" and "feed the goats." In this manner Brand has produced two levels of meaning, the first being a metaphoric understanding of the process of labour. However, the fact is never far from our consciousness that we are listening to the discourse of a child of 11 years.

The infinitive "to tend" at the beginning of line 8 recalls the infinitive "to work" at the beginning of line 2, and the two lines are almost identical in meaning. However, the infinitive of line 8 has its prolongation in the conjunction "and" at the beginning of the two succeeding lines. This repetition serves to underline the accumulation of duties of the young girl. But the progression of the personal pronouns also leads to this culmination. The "I" of line 1 is the same as the person referred to in the adjectives "my" then objectified in "your." The person thus designated is excluded from the "we" of line 7, "we need the extra hands." The young girl is thus reduced to her labour potential and valued for her contribution to the opposing "we." But the "we" could also be inclusive of the initial "I" and the unnamed 11-year-old girl becomes even further subsumed in a relentless process of integration into what one can only surmise is a cycle of poverty and frustrating labour.

The language of the second stanza introduces an entirely different tone and content which contrast sharply with the harsh realities of the first. However, an analysis of the stylistic structure demonstrates the extent to which the entire poem is driven forward by the same social imperative.[10]

> 11 Maybe
> I'll go to school
> when the crop is in,

when we take the few yams
from the soil,
then I'll wear a new dress,
and leave when it's early day,
for it's only one mile to the school.

The sole, isolated word "Maybe" of the first line of the second stanza expresses hope in its normal semantic context but here emphasizes the hopelessness of the girl's situation. The hypotheses introduced by the first person singular pronouns of lines 12 and 16 contrast sharply with the affirmation associated with the use of this pronoun in line 1 of the poem. The extension of the uncertainty expressed by "Maybe" is sustained by the repetition of the word "when" in lines 13 and 14, which introduces notions based on facts that are fully possible. Paradoxically, the seemingly assertive and conclusive use of "then" announces the most hypothetical factor in the poem since this adverb is dependent on the uncertainty of the adverb "Maybe." The rapid succession of adverbs underscores the uncertainty of the child's existence. The only certainties are those telluric elements (lines 13, 14 and 17) that punctuate and limit her life.

Furthermore, our meta-textual information makes us wonder if the girl will ever go to school. This serious doubt is underscored by line 6 of the first stanza since the assertion that "your mind wont rust" could well imply the contrary.

The sense of motherlessness and isolation of this early poem is found in a much later one in which the content is different but the sentiments expressed are quite similar. In "I am not a refugee," we read:

I am not a refugee,
I have my papers,
I was born in the Caribbean,
practically in the sea,
fifteen degrees above the equator,
I have a Canadian passport,
I have lived here all my adult life,
I am stateless anyway.

In "Eleven years old" we listen to the words of a young person; we evaluate her situation and arrive at our conclusions. In "I am not a refugee," we are faced with the conclusions of an adult. The facts are irrefutable, and there is not even the vain hope presented by the earlier poem. However, in both cases the future is equally pessimistic and closed to positive development, unless one believes in miracles and indulges in hope.

"I am not a refugee" derives its poetic significance from a careful symmetry which is immediately obvious in the pattern of repetition of "I."

The first and the last lines both begin with "I am," but this identification of the being, of the self, is in both cases a negation. The first negation provokes the question concerning the identity of the "I" and this question is answered in the last line by the second negation. The self-assurance of "I am ..." and "I have ..." give the impression of a person defining the self, but the final negation "I am stateless ..." reveals a self that is defined and determined by others. This final negation is emphasized by the adverb "anyway" which expresses a certain degree of resignation and despair. The preceding six lines give information that seems irrelevant and even superfluous once the information of the last line is given. But the seemingly irrelevant information is essential for the play of opposition and contrasts in the poem. In this crisis of national identity, there is no search for ancestral roots, there are no allusions to parents, there is no stable point of reference. It is in this context that we are to understand the following lines of "Old Pictures of the New World" in *Chronicles of the Hostile Sun:*

> now I am frightened
> to be alone,
> not because of strangers,
> not thieves or psychopaths
> but, the state.

Here the poet confronts us with the apparent paradox of a social order which should provide security of mind and body and produce in us an integrated wholeness and well-being, but engenders only fear and total alienation.

In *Earth Magic,* the poem "Old Woman" presents us with a comparable pathetic landscape. The social commentary is unambiguous but the stylistic qualities of the poem are not sufficiently disciplined, and the lines are merely the expression of a series of observations ending in a banal reflection. In their article "La construction du poème," Molino and Tamine write that poetic specificities may disappear in the interests of argumentation.[11] Unfortunately, argumentation is absent from "Old

Woman." The poetic subtleties of style are also lacking and there is an awkwardness in the use of language rarely seen in Brand's work. Brand has given ample proof that she is capable of using the language of everyday life in a poetic mode. In "Old Woman," it is therefore not the commitment to the theme but the means of poetic communication that has to be carefully examined.

The poem consists of five distinct grammatical and semantic groups. Each one begins with the anaphora "She." But, whereas the first and the last groups follow a regular sentence structure, the three intervening groups are each divided into two parts between which there is a grammatical and semantic rupture of varying degrees. The first part consists of a proposition followed by a clause or phrase that is the elaboration of the initial proposition. It is particularly at the juncture of the two parts that the poetic structure is lacking and could be seen as striving for poetic effect. This weakness culminates in the final sentence, which is banal in the thought expressed and devoid of any poetic effect:

> She is
> too old
> to live
> like this
> I think.

Apart from the use of the anaphora, there is insufficient stylistic or linguistic structure to produce a coherent poetic unity. The two-syllable lines quoted above depend on the spill-over effect of the single word anaphora for their structural unity with what has preceded. We have been presented with a series of socially consistent images which are unambiguous in their focus. Brand has successfully expressed destitution without infusing her words with the necessary internal poetic devices: rhythm or cadence; symmetry or deliberately structured dissymmetry; symbolic, semiotic or other elements which produce coherence of expression through consistency or deliberately structured inconsistency, and so on.

But Dionne Brand has demonstrated abundantly that she is capable of producing poetry of a highly sophisticated order whilst sustaining the sincerity of her social commitment. "Old Woman" is an important aesthetic failure because it obliges us to concentrate on what is inadequate and provides us with more or less precise notions of what we are looking for in poetry. The poem forces us to define our criteria of judgement.

There is little doubt that one of the most striking of Brand's poems is "La Souffrière" in the collection *Chronicles of the Hostile Sun.* The poem is divided into five stanzas of unequal length. The first three stanzas comprise more than half of the poem and give us a background of local colour in the Caribbean. The prevailing impressions are those of the sky, the sea and the darkness in which is inserted the haunting image of a "little girl." The fourth stanza marks the thematic and aesthetic rupture with the first three and introduces us to the realities of race, class, sexuality and the inhuman exploitation of the hardworking poor by the vain and idle rich. Though the topographical details strongly suggest that the poem is situated in Saint Vincent, it really does not matter since the general focus of Brand's poetry is on the oppressed wherever they may be. The explicit and implicit contextual details of the poem make of it a true social event as defined by the linguist Michael Gregory.[12]

The thematic opposition of Freddie Oliviere and "his vanload of henchmen" to the "eight old upstarts" he is threatening recalls the "six generations of estate workers" and the relationship of the master and the slave. The familiarity of the form of the Christian name of the only person named in the poem, this affectionate diminutive form of the Christian name, contrasts with the surname. The Portuguese resonance of the surname evokes the presence of the *conquistador,* the ancestral predator and indigenous master. It is significant that Freddie Oliviere is the only person named though five place names are given whilst 13 other persons and an undetermined number of "henchmen" are referred to. Freddie Oliviere is named three times in exactly the same manner, underlining the various social, historical and economic aspects of his identity. There is a significant progression in the context in which he is seen. The subject of the verb is transformed as the aged workers challenge Freddie Oliviere and as the poem progresses to its conclusion:

(1) Freddie Oliviere fondled his gun
and threatened ...
sitting in his expensive jeep
he threatened ...

(2) Freddie Oliviere jumped out of his expensive
japanese jeep,

(3) Freddie Oliviere talked as if ...

In (1) the affectionate character of the Christian name, Freddie, is prolonged in the verb "fondled" and in the alliteration in "f" whilst the surname is complemented by the predicate "gun." At the same time the association of "fondled" and "gun" reiterates the device of contrast used in the name. The repetition of the verb "threatened" underlines the meaning and implications of the word, but serves also to emphasize the courage of the response.

In (2), the reaction to the initial challenge is menacing action; it is also intended to bring to our attention the prestige of the imported jeep in which Freddie Oliviere is first seated. The expensive jeep has obviously replaced the stature and strength of the horse, but the gun still has its traditional role in the process of communication between the classes. But the imported jeep is as much a sign of social and economic strength as the horse was. Whilst Freddie Oliviere is in the jeep the spatial dimension of his opposition to the old peasants is emphasized by the economic power that ownership of the vehicle represents. The jeep also suggests great mobility and Freddie Oliviere's physical force transformed into mechanical power. But he borrows some of his essence from the various forms of power that the jeep represents. As he jumps from the security of the jeep he becomes less powerful and we realize that his dependence on the vehicle is a metaphor. Despite his behaviour he is reduced once again to the empty verbal threat.

Finally in (3) he merely talks "as if" and the force of the earlier threats has almost completely disappeared before the persistent challenge from the eight old workers. Unlike his predecessors Freddie Oliviere cannot whip them. He cannot shoot them without having to face serious consequences, and his armed threats backed up by his paid lackeys turn out to be empty. He is the one who is described as "livid and wounded by their new tone" as these once voiceless people begin to speak up for themselves.

Thus, from the forcefulnes of the initial physically threatening behaviour, Freddie Oliviere is reduced to confidence in the mere manifestations of his power. The final fondling of the gun is an empty nostalgic action.

The very title of the poem conjures up the image of the latent volcano waiting for its moment to erupt, and the responses of the "eight old upstarts" to the threats of Freddie Oliviere appear to be the beginnings of the social eruption so long awaited. He is incapable of reading the social and psychological signs around him and is faced with the unexpected.

In "La Souffrière" as in "Eleven years old" there is the juxtaposition of the young and the old, the young girl and the old woman. Once again the absence of the intervening generation creates a gap that is as much a social and economic reality as it is a poetic one. Are the members of this generation simply lost, sold or so completely deprived that they remain invisible in these particular poems?

THE ANAPHORA

We have already referred to the use of anaphoras in Brand's poetry, and it is important to indicate some of the diverse methods of their aesthetic application. Indeed, one has the impression that this aesthetic device is the most consistently explored by the poet. Her work demonstrates a progressive perfection in the use of anaphoras of phonemes, words, syntactic groups and syntagmes.[13] We will examine some of these applications in an attempt to show the process of deliberate structuring of Brand's poetry.

The examples of phonemic anaphoras are rare in Brand's work. The most convincing application of this type of anaphora is in "Epigrams to Ernesto Cardenal in defense of Claudia" in the collection *Winter Epigrams.* But even here the anaphora could be other than simply phonemic and may be said to have a definite semantic quality:

> poorest Claudia
> to the love of a poet
> to the singing of a madrigal
> to the dictators american shoes
> to the wall
> to the afternoon blossoms
> to the escape across unknown borders
> to the perfume of a freedom

The formula preposition plus definite article contains semantic meaning in its two components, but the preposition makes no semantic contribution to the syntagma of each line. In the context of the poem, and of this particular stanza, it is not possible to make an immediate grammatical or poetic connection between "poorest Claudia" and the preposition, or between the preposition and what follows. We can therefore conclude that the preposition is used for phonetic and therefore rythmic effect. In this way the word "to" loses its semantic and grammatical functions to become the phonemes "t" and "o" exploited exclusively for their phonetic qualities.

"Blues Spiritual for Mammy Porter" appears in the collection *No Language is Neutral.* The poem is a perfect example of the use of syntagmic anaphoras to convey a body of subjective meanings:

> she waited for ... to turn
> she waited until ... to take a photograph
> to take a photograph and to put those eyes in it
> she waited until ...
> to make sure ...
> to make sure ... would lose
> would lose ... her eyes ... her hands
> she knew the patience ...
> she knew that if she had the patience,
> to avoid ...
> ...
> she waited until ...
> to take this photograph and to put those eyes in it.

Brand infuses a power of will into Mammy Porter that is communicated through the precision of the poetic devices used. The meaning of the verb is emphasized by grammatical structure which culminates in the active form of the infinitive. Mammy Porter does not have a photograph taken, she takes a photograph. Furthermore, "she waited" in order "to make sure" because "she knew." This particular poem conveys a striking degree of certainty, purposefulness and confidence in the subject who has defined and determined her being as it is portrayed in the photograph as it is described to us.

This particular use of vertical and horizontal anaphoras as phonemic and semantic aesthetic elements tranforms waiting and patience into a dignified act of will and self-esteem. But even in producing this highly sophisticated and touching poem Brand does not overburden the enunciation with superfluous elements. The poem is also a fine example of economy of style.

In *Earth Magic,* the poem "Wind" relies primarily on the function of the vertical anaphora "I" as the first phoneme of each main clause and is positioned with only two exceptions at the beginning of a line. In this case the phoneme is a word employed with the fullness of its semantic charateristics. In the context of the poem the reiteration of the first person singular pronoun produces the impression of the power to do, to conquer and to transform. The experience is superhuman and given poetic authenticity through the person of the narrative voice.

In the same collection the poem "Rain" consists of 11 lines:

> It finally came,
> it beat on the house
> it bounced on the flowers
> it banged the tin roof
> it rolled in the gutters
> it made the street muddy
> it spilled on the village
> it licked all the windows
> it jumped on the hill.
> It stayed for two days
> and then it left.

The first ten lines are all introduced by the anaphora "it." In line 11 the anaphora "it" and the verb are in the final position. In line 1, the impersonal "it" is separated from the verb by an adverb, and in line 11, the transformation of the stylistic formula that precedes announces and produces the end of the poem. If we analyze the entire poem we see the following:

> anaphora + adverb + active verb
> anaphora + active verb + adverbial phrase
> “ “ “ “ “
> anaphora + active verb + direct object
> anaphora + active verb + adverbial phrase
> anaphora + active verb + direct object
> anaphora + active verb + adverbial phrase
> anaphora + active verb + direct object
> anaphora + active verb + adverbial phrase
> “ “ “
> conjunction + adverb + anaphora + active verb

This produces a stylistic pattern that is as follows:

a bb c b c b c bb d

Except for line 11, which marks the rupture with the sequence of events, the poem is based on lines of five or six syllables. The poem is clearly a deliberately structured work depending for its rhythm on grammatical devices as well as on syllabic consistency.

Various anaphoras are dispersed throughout the 14 cantos of *Primitive Offensive.* There is considerable diversity in their application and in their contexts, but in this case they are used for very evident ideological purposes. In Canto II, for example, we have the following litany:

ancestor dirt
ancestor snake
ancestor lice
ancestor whip
ancestor fish
ancestor slime
ancestor sea
ancestor stick
ancestor iron
ancestor bush
ancestor ship
ancestor old woman, old bead

In the same canto, the vertical anaphora "ancestor" is used again elsewhere in addition to others. Of the fourteen cantos, Canto II is the only one that begins with the prolonged usage of the anaphora. The repetition of the anaphoric metaphor "ancestor" serves to emphasize the semantic quality of the word but also undelines its polysemic dimensions through the metaphors that follow it. Each of the complements is in fact a synonym with its own polysemic ramifications, and each one is underscored by the anaphoric device that has produced it. The semantic quality of the anaphora changes constantly and at the same time each meaning of "ancestor" comprises all of the others. In this way each of the lines quoted above is an entire chapter in the history of African peoples of the Americas. Some of the associations are quite evident (lines 3, 4, 7, 8, 9, 10, 11 and 12); others are obscure (line 2); whilst others are possibly hermetic (lines 1, 5 and 6). This is, indeed, poetry for the initiated.

The allusions are sufficiently specific to require a precise historical knowledge and social awareness. In *Primitive Offensive,* there is an intensity in the use of language which is unequalled in Brand's other collections.

The breadth of linguistic diversity and the depth of allusions recall Edouard Glissant's words:[14]

> Toute parole est une terre
> Il est de fouiller son sous-sol
> Où un espace meuble est gardé
> Brûlant, pour ce que l'arbre dit

This poetic definition of polysemy is most appropriate to Brand's work since Glissant is describing an analogous socio-historic and aesthetic path. Glissant's poetry, despite its frequent hermetism,[15] often concerned with very specific Caribbean and Third World preoccupations, and these are the principal themes of *Primitive Offensive.* This particular form of the anaphora characterizes some of the most memorable lines of such poets as Aimé Césaire and Edward Brathwaite.[16]

Eventually, the chanting tone of the anaphoras at the beginning of Canto II gives way to the urgency of the search for the original African name. The urgency of the quest is expressed by a precipitation of questions in a series of relatively short lines. This contrasts considerably with Canto I in which the anaphoras are more evenly interspersed in a series of relatively long and ponderous lines. In the succeeding cantos the lines are short, but there are relatively few anaphoras and they are concentrated on the personal pronouns "you" and "I." However, nowhere else in *Primitive Offensive* is there a similar intensity of aesthetic structure and meaning in the use of anaphoras.

Brand uses this device regularly throughout her other works, and it is in the second part of *Chronicles of the Hostile Sun* where we see a similar intensity of anaphoras. This is the part of the collection that deals with the invasion of Grenada in 1983. At that time Dionne Brand was living in Grenada, and the experience has left an indelible mark on her work.

In the poem "October 25th, 1983" Brand uses a series of diverse anaphoras. The poem consists of six stanzas of unequal length. Stanzas 1 and 2 consist of six lines each, stanzas 4 and 6 consist of one line each, whilst stanzas 3 and 5 are much longer than the others. It is in these latter two stanzas that we find the anaphoras.

The first series of anaphoras is announced after the cesura of stanza 3, line 3 where we read "... you cannot fight" followed by a series of substantives indicating machines of war, people and institutions. The list continues for another three lines of the stanza, and it is in line 7 of the stanza that the grammatical anaphora is used a second time but at the beginning of the line. From line 8 to line 15 the grammatical anaphora, still at the beginning of each line, is extended by two syllables to become a syntagmic anaphora: "you cannot fight it with ..." The anaphora reappears in line 17 but not at the beginning of the line. Each of the anaphoras from line 7 onwards is followed by a positive aspect of the Grenada revolution through the use of metaphors. Finally, an echo of the anaphora is found in the last line of the poem, which is rendered even more devastating in its meaning and ideological implications by the anaphoric processes that have led to this conclusion.

In stanza 5, the composition is much more complex. Of the 25 lines, 23 contain vertical and horizontal anaphoras. Though the vertical anaphoras predominate at the beginning of the lines, there are several to be found in other positions. The major concentration is on the grammatical anaphora "you must," the anaphoras of words "you," "your," and the syntagmic anaphora "they will say." The polarization indicated by the choice of pronoun is particularly significant in this very bitter poem dealing with a most unpleasant subject-betrayal by ordinary people "... because they want to eat." A careful reading of the poem reveals that it is a work of considerable ideological and aesthetic sophistication. The key to the poem is found in stanza 5 in which the diversification of the anaphoric structure reflects the anguish caused by the subject of betrayal:

> ... you must run into the street
> you must crawl into a ditch
> and you must wait there and watch
> your family,
> your mother, your sister, your little brother,
> your husband, your wife,
> you must watch them
> because they will become hungry,
> and they will give you to the americans,

In this poem a great deal depends on the intonation of "you must." If the intonation corresponds to a particular Caribbean form then the meaning is that "you should" or "you are advised to." It is also possible that "you must" might correspond to the Standard English intonation and meaning. Of course, the ambiguity heightens the tension of the poem and serves to reveal, even further, the anguish of the Grenadian people.

The progression from the "you must," plus verb formula, gives way to the rapid precipitation of the series of "your" introducing those who are closest in relationship. There is then a return to "you must" before the introduction of a new and the most frequently used anaphora of the stanza "they will."

The shifting anaphora produces its own disturbing rhythm in the poem since there is a seeming inconsistency within the coherence of structure. That seeming inconsistency reflects, in an apt manner, the very unsettling social situation. It is perhaps significant that the horizontal anaphora is used for the expression of the most abject betrayal.

The poem ends on a note of complete ideological and social failure because it seems in the end that the fight is not only against the war machine of the United States but also against one's own people: "And finally you can only fight it with the silence of your dead body."

This is, of course, the ultimate degradation of Babylon, the betrayal by one's kith and kin for the sake of a crust of bread. Brand's belief in the Grenadian revolution, and her belief in the people, do not prevent her from seeing the realities around her and documenting them in a poem of considerable aesthetic accomplishment. The bitter sentiments of this moral failure are reiterated elsewhere in the collection and particularly in the short poem "After ..." Zegoua Nokan has written:[17]

> L'art doit être optimiste.
> Oublions le marécage, la boue.
> Chantons notre courage, nos victoires.

For Dionne Brand the experience of the rapid and sordid demise of the Grenada revolution is such that the words of Nokan strike no chord in *Chronicles of the Hostile Sun.* It is evident that at times the experience of Babylon is too bitter, too deeply humiliating for optimism, and the poet sets about expressing her individual perception and that of many others. However, the very act of producing this ideologically determined work is a continuation of the fight against the political and socio-economic constraints of Babylon.

Despite the absence of optimism in much of Brand's ideologically inspired work there is no confusion or despair. Her work is characterized by a sustained commitment to revolt against the fundamental ideological, political and social bases on which exploitative capitalist society is founded.

ENDNOTES

1. Dionne Brand, *'Fore Day Morning,* Toronto, Khoisan Artists, 1978; *Earth Magic,* Toronto. Kids Can Press, 1979; *Primitive Offensive,* Toronto, Williams-Wallace, 1982; *Winter Epigrams & Epigrams to Ernesto Cardenal in Defense of Claudia,* Toronto, Williams-Wallace, 1983; *Chronicles of the Hostile Sun,* Toronto, Williams-Wallace, 1984; *No Language is Neutral,* Toronto, Coach House Press, 1990.
2. See, for example "For Stuart" and "four hours on a bus ..." in *Chronicles of the Hostile Sun.* In these two poems Brand reveals some of the reactions to herself and to her poetry. "For Stuart" concerns an incident still spoken of in Sudbury.
3. 3. See H. Nigel Thomas, "A Commentary on the Poetry of Dionne Brand," *KOLA,* Vol. 1, No. 1, February, 1987, pp.51-61. Thomas' words on the social purpose of poetry recall the writings of the Ivoirian poet/essayist/dramatist Zegoua Nokan in his foreword to *Les malheurs de Tchakô,* Honfleur, P.J. Oswald, 1968: "L'écrivain, partie intégrante du peuple, doit exprimer les peines, les joies de ce dernier, son combat pour l'amélioration de sa condition ... La substance d'un poème ne réside pas dans la musique des mots et la profusion d'images. Il existe des situations poétiques. J'ai tenté, ici, d'en appréhender quelques-uns."
4. For a discussion of the close interdependence of ideology and aesthetics in Caribbean writing, see F.I. Case, "Idéologie du discours esthétique césairien," in *Aimé Césaire ou l'athanor d'un alchimiste,* Paris, Editions caribéennes/A.C.C.T., 1987, pp. 337-346.
5. Despite the general tendencies of literary criticism the notion of discourse analysis should not be limited to prose. In so far as there is human communication there is discourse. Molino and Tamine have written: "Mais la poésie est aussi discours et, comme le discours, s'organise autour d'un axe, d'une progression qui constitue le fil du discours. Cet axe peut prendre deux formes: il y a d'un côté la progression narrative, qui est celle des événements d'une intrigue et de l'autre la progression d'un raisonnement plus ou moins cohérent." Jean Molino et Joëlle Tamine, "La Construction du poème," *Recherches sémiotiques/Semiotic Inquiry,* Vol. 1, No. 4, 1981, p.360.
6. In referring to poetic structures we mean those elements—phonological, lexical, grammatical and graphological—that give coherence and consistency to the form and substance of the poem.
7. By aesthetic structures we refer to the interrelation of elements listed in the preceding footnote, together with the various semantic and semiotic factors taking into account the explicit and implicit literary and social contexts.

8. In this work hope and optimism are defined in the following manner. Hope is a positive perception of the future based on ideological or socio-psychological mystification and often leads to resignation to the present context. Optimism is a positive perception of the present and future based on the socio-economic realities and potentialities of the present context and precedes action to modify that context.
9. In so far as the poem is discourse there is a narrative voice.
10. In this poem the two stanzas are apparently independent units, each having its specific structural characteristics and each having its own tone, the unifying theme is entirely implicit. Each of the two stanzas is organized around its own explicit axis. Molino and Tamine write (art. cit. p.364): "La strophe organise l'argumentation puisque chacune est une étape dans la progression du texte et se déroule autour d'un lieu central."
11. Molino and Tamine, art. cit., p.364: "La spécificité poétique, c'est-à-dire le couplage avec le vers et surtout la strophe, peut d'ailleurs disparaître au profit de la seule argumentation."
12. See Michael Gregory, "Marvell's 'To his coy mistress': the poem as a linguistic and social event," *Poetics,* No. 7, 1978. p.351.
13. For a succint and precise discussion of the anaphora see: Renée Baligand, *Les Poèmes de Raymond Queneau: Etude phonostylistique,* Montréal, Didier, 1972, pp.37-49.
14. Edouard Glissant, *Un champ d'îles* in *Les Indes,* Seuil, 1965, p.20.
15. For a discussion of Glissant's poetry see F.I. Case, "L'esthétique poétique d'Edouard Glissant," *Tijdschrift voor Poezie/Revue de Poésie,* Vol. 5, Nos. 1-2, May 1986, pp.88-100.
16. I am referring specifically to Aimé Césaire's *Cahier d'un retour au pays natal* and Edward Brathwaite's trilogy, *Rights of Passage, Masks and Islands.*
17. Zegoua Nokan, *Les petites rivières,* Abidjan, CEDA, 1983. pp.98-99.

REFERENCES

Baligand, R. (1972). *Les Poèmes de Raymond Queneau: Etude phonostylistique.* Montréal: Didier.

Brand, D. (1978). *'Fore day morning.* Toronto: Khoisan Artists.

———. (1979). *Earth magic.* Toronto: Kids Can Press.

———. (1982). *Primitive offensive.* Toronto: Williams-Wallace.

———. (1983). *Winter epigrams & epigrams to Ernesto Cardenal in defense of Claudia.* Toronto: Williams-Wallace.

———. (1984). *Chronicles of the hostile sun.* Toronto: Williams-Wallace.

———. (1990). *No language is neutral.* Toronto: Coach House Press.

Brathwaite, E.K. (1967). *Rights of passage.* London: Oxford University Press.

———. (1968). *Masks.* London: Oxford University Press.

———. (1969). *Islands.* London: Oxford University Press.

Case, F.I. (1986). L'esthétique poétique d'Edouard Glissant. *Tijdschrift voor Poezie/Revue de Poésie 5* (1-2). pp.88-100.

———. (1987). Idéologie du discours esthétique césairien. In *Aimé Césaire ou l'athanor d'un alchimiste* (pp.337-346) Paris: Editions caribéennes/A.C.C.T.

Césaire, A. (1971). *Cahier d'un Retour au Pays natal.* Paris: Présence Africaine.

Glissant, E. (1965). *Un champ d'îles* in *Les Indes.* Paris: Seuil.

Gregory, M. (1978). Marvell's 'To his coy mistress': the poem as a linguistic and social event. *Poetics 7.*

Molino, J. & Tamine, J. (1981). La Construction du poème. *Recherches sémiotiques/ Semiotic Inquiry.* 1 (4), pp.343-392.

Nokan, Z. (1968). *Les malheurs de Tchakô.* Honfleur: P.J. Oswald.

———. (1983). *Les petites rivières.* Abidjan: CEDA.

Thomas, N (1987). A Commentary on the Poetry of Dionne Brand. *KOLA.* 1 (1), pp.51-61.

MAÎTRE OU MENTOR: L'OMBRE DE GLISSANT DANS *TEXACO* DE PATRICK CHAMOISEAU

Marie-José N'Zengou-Tayo

Après avoir reçu le Prix Goncourt pour son roman *Texaco,* Chamoiseau avoue, dans plusieurs entrevues, que Glissant est son maître littéraire. L'article retrace cette influence à travers le roman, telle qu'elle est articulée dans la relation binaire Mentor/Maître. Cette distinction a des implications importantes pour Glissant et son statut dans la société et la culture martiniquaises. L'étude porte notamment sur les textes de Glissant qui ont un rapport avec le roman de Chamoiseau, tels que *Le Quatrième Siècle* and *Le Discours antillais* afin de tracer l'organisation de cette relation intertextuelle à partir des catégories d'histoire, d'espace, de temps et de langague. La conclusion rend compte de la réaction de Glissant face au mouvement culturel de la *Créolité.*

In various interviews following the awarding of the Prix Goncourt to his novel *Texaco,* Patrick Chamoiseau acknowledged Glissant as his literary master. This paper retraces this influence in *Texaco,* as it is articulated in terms of the binary distinction mentor/master which has important implications for Glissant's status in Martinican society and culture. The paper identifies, the texts by Glissant which are more obviously related to *Texaco,* such as *Le Quatrième Siècle,* and *Le Discours antillais,* and how the intertextual relations are organized within the categories of history, space, time and language. The article concludes by asssessing Glissant's response to the cultural movement of *Créolité.*

DANS LES INTERVIEWS accordés à la presse, lors de l'obtention du Prix Goncourt 1992 pour son roman *Texaco,* Patrick Chamoiseau reconnaissait le rôle déterminant joué par Edouard Glissant dans sa vie d'écrivain et d'homme antillais. Le romancier donnait ainsi acte de l'influence de Glissant sur *Texaco* comme sur ses oeuvres précédentes. Cependant, cette reconnaissance, déjà présente dans divers textes ayant précédé *Texaco* (*Eloge de la Créolité,* articles publiés dans *Antilla* et enfin la dédicace et les exergues de *Texaco* même), nous invite à nous interroger sur la véritable nature de la relation Glissant-Chamoiseau et à essayer de repérer/identifier les traces de l'influence de Glissant dans *Texaco.* Autrement dit, «maître» ou «mentor», quelle place Glissant occupe-t-il dans *Texaco*?

Pourquoi poser cette relation en ces termes pourra-t-on nous objecter? A cela nous répondrons par l'évidence de l'écart d'âge. Les questions auxquelles nous voulons tenter de répondre, dans cet article, s'articulent autour d'une relation entre des écrivains de deux classes d'âge différentes (1928, 1953), appartenant à deux générations qui ont eu des expériences historiques différentes mais qui se rejoignent sur d'autres plans. Tous deux s'interrogent sur les questions du statut colonial, de la Négritude, de la dissidence (l'Amiral Robert), de la départementalisation, de l'autonomie régionale et de l'indépendantisme, même si Chamoiseau s'est fait connaître dans les années 1980 alors que Glissant est déjà un écrivain reconnu depuis les années 1950. Cette réalité chronologique incontournable nous invite à lire la relation Glissant-Chamoiseau selon ce rapport. Cependant nous avons voulu envisager deux facettes possibles de cette relation où, en raison de la différence d'âge, Glissant occupe la position d'aîné/initiateur potentiel et Chamoiseau celle de cadet/initié éventuel. Avant d'aller plus loin, indiquons que nous avons volontairement évité d'appréhender cette relation selon la perspective d'une relation père/fils en raison des implications psychoanalytiques d'une telle approche, ce qui nous entraînerait trop loin de notre projet d'étude. En organisant notre réflexion sur un mode binaire nous voulons rendre compte de deux modes relationnels : l'un de type très scolaire, vertical, qui serait une relation de maître à élève et l'autre, transversal ou horizontal, où «l'initiateur» occuperait une position de retrait. Il nous faut donc maintenant préciser les deux termes autour desquels s'articulera notre propos.

Qu'entendons-nous par «Maître»? Que signifie «Mentor»? Pour ce qui est du premier terme, nous nous plaçons dans une structure hiérarchique, celle de celui qui «sait», qui contrôle un savoir et qui envisage de le transmettre dans le contexte d'une structure de pouvoir bien implantée.

Il est évident que malgré tous les progrès de la pédagogie moderne, nous utilisons volontairement ici ce terme avec toutes ses connotations passées (la férule du maître, le maître qui sait tout ...). En effet, quand nous parlons ici de «maître» nous voulons interroger la relation Glissant-Chamoiseau dans la perspective d'une influence avouée mais en plus «dirigiste» où Glissant, détenteur d'un «projet» esthétique/littéraire, se serait placé dans la position de celui qui «enseigne» l'art d'écrire à un Chamoiseau, lui-même installé dans la position «d'élève»/«apprenti», revoyant sa copie. Cette description de la relation Glissant-Chamoiseau peut paraître caricaturale mais il s'agit d'une relation fort semblable à celle ayant existé par exemple au XIXe siècle entre Flaubert et Maupassant, où Flaubert manifeste un souci de faire acquérir ses techniques d'écriture à Maupassant, l'invitant à corriger et re-corriger ses textes.[1] Cette figure du «Maître» telle que nous la décrivons ci-dessus est, en fait, présente dans *Texaco* à travers le personnage de Ti-Cirique, l'Haïtien, que la narratrice décrit en notant qu'à son arrivée, il avait «une tête d'instituteur hagard» (p.354). Dès le début du roman, nous le voyons réprimander l'auteur dans une «épître» (Cf. Exergue, p.19) et la hiérachie est marquée par Chamoiseau dans les adjectifs qui proclament son humilité d'apprenti, «honteux», «réponse du lamentable». Le «Maître» en Ti-Cirique se déploie cependant pleinement dans ses rapports avec la narratrice Marie-Sophie quand il découvre qu'elle tient des cahiers. Il les lit d'abord «sursautant du fait de l'orthographe et des phrases emmêlées» (p.355) de la narratrice, puis il prend l'habitude de s'asseoir avec elle pour «lire [ses] cahiers, corriger [ses] horreurs, donner sens à [ses] phrases ...» (p.356), éveillant en elle «le goût des mots précis» (p.357) dont pourtant elle n'atteindra pas la maîtrise.

Comment situons-nous le «Mentor» de ce point de vue? Si nous nous référons au *Petit Robert,* le mentor serait un guide, un conseiller sage et expérimenté. Plus effacé/discret que le «maître», le mentor chercherait selon nous à obtenir le meilleur de son protégé mais sans autoritarisme apparent, lui donnant—et c'est notre interprétation personnelle du "mentor" aux fins de cet article—l'impression de la liberté de choix et de l'autonomie. Signalons que la figure du mentor apparaît pour la première fois dans le *Télémaque* de Fénelon, à travers le personnage du même nom qui aide le fils d'Ulysse à acquérir sa propre personnalité, et que cet ouvrage avait été écrit pour la formation du Dauphin de France. Cependant c'est dans le roman de Chamoiseau, que nous avons trouvé le personnage du «mentô» (Mentor) qui illustrait bien l'idée que nous nous en faisions. En effet, Esternome au cours de ses errances rencontre un «mentô» ainsi défini :

Il faut savoir qu'avec les hommes de force (l'Histoire les appelle quimboiseurs, séanciers ou sorciers), surgissait parfois *la* Force, et c'était s'il te plaît, Le Mentô. [...] Un Mentô dit la parole, n'a jamais souffert du fouette ou du cachot; à l'heure des fers et de la barre on les oubliait net; les envies méchantes de qui que ce soit ne s'exerçaient jamais contre eux. Et c'était là (s'il fallait savoir les trouver) l'insigne même des Mentô. Ils vivent parmi les hommes sans bruit et sans odeur. (*Texaco,* 62, 63)

Pourtant, si le «Mentô» antillais se veut invisible parmi les humains (nègres antillais et békés), il devient, au dire de la narratrice, celui qui leur insuffle le vouloir-être dans ce pays où ils ont été implantés malgré eux:

Cette parole [la parole du Mentô] [...] insuffla dans son coeur le coeur même de partir. Elle érigea aussi le Mentô à la source de notre difficultueuse conquête du pays. (p.65)

Le «Mentô» lance la Parole, libre à celui qui l'entend de la recueillir et de l'inscrire dans sa vie comme l'indique l'épisode raconté un peu plus loin de la rencontre des nouveaux libres et des quatre mentors (pp.109-112).

Le Mentô lui [une vieille négresse Ibo, oubliée] parla dans une langue sans veut-dire, ou inaudible, ou bien mal prononcée, en tout cas déférente. [..] Le Mentô lui tint une tirade brève, s'inclinant gentiment et rejoignit les autres. [...] (p.111)

Interrogée, la vieille négresse «traduit» la Parole du mentor

– Yo di zot libètè pa ponm kannel an bout branch! Fok zot désann raché'y, raché'y, raché'y! ... (Liberté, n'est pas pomme-cannelle en bout de branche! Il vous faut l'arracher ...) (p.111)

Cette Parole mystérieuse va cependant donner un sens à la vie de plusieurs d'entre eux :

Tous l'avaient perçue comme par-derrière les mots. Tous, c'est à croire se sentirent travaillés par cette Parole en des endroits divers, et tous se trouvèrent délivrés en eux-mèmes. [...] Elle devait gonfler de partout, levée au même allant, comme si dans chaque coin de cette misère, les quatre messagers avaient rappelé qu'une liberté s'arrache et ne doit pas s'offrir—ni se donner jamais. (p.112)

Le commentaire de la narratrice signale un au-delà du langage et développe la métaphore de la pâte à pain pétrie et mise à lever. Notons également que ces «Mentô» âgés ne manifestent à aucun moment le désir de diriger, d'orienter leurs jeunes congénères. Après ces rencontres décisives, Esternome, père de la narratrice, passe sa vie en quête d'un «mentô» au sein de l'En-ville, les recherchant à un moment au niveau de la classe politique (il s'en va écouter les discours électoraux) mais pour en revenir déçu à chaque fois.

> ... alors que la rumeur signalait l'existence du petit nègre magique, mon Esternome, s'appuyant sur mon épaule était parti pour écouter Césaire. [...] Il avançait en murmurant *Ça doit être un Mentô, ça doit être un Mentô,* et ces mots lui baillaient un allant qui neutralisait la raideur de ses genoux. [...] Il avait toujours voulu retrouver un Mentô afin de savoir comment aborder cette conquête de l'En-ville. D'entendre un nègre provoquer un tel engouement à la manière des mulâtres politiciens, avait sans doute amené mon Esternome à le prendre pour un Mentô. Et là, ce jour-là, il allait pour le voir, pour l'entendre, lui parler, l'écouter, savoir les nouveaux ordres et sans doute me les transmettre. (p.277)

Il est très significatif qu'Esternome ne se laisse pas impressionner par Césaire, ce qui lui permet de prophétiser de façon lapidaire son échec politique (en tant que chantre de la négritude).

> Les haut-parleurs nous transmettaient de loin le discours de Césaire, son français, ses mots, sa voix, sa ferveur. Mon Esternome s'était arrêté, avait écouté, puis ses griffes s'étaient enfoncées dans mon épaule : *Annou Sofi ma fi, an nou viré bo kay,* Sophie ma fille retournons à la maison ... [...] Au bout de quelques pas, il me dit dans un souffle [...]
> —C'est un mulâtre ... (p.277)

Puisque nous parlons de Césaire, il nous semble intéressant de noter que celui-ci contrairement à Glissant, est un personnage de *Texaco,* avec une double présence politique (député et maire de Fort-de-France) et littéraire puisque *Le Cahier...* est mentionné comme un livre-phare par la narratrice, bien qu'elle soit une autodidacte semi-lettrée (lecture du *Cahier...*, p.401). Glissant n'apparaît qu'à un détour du texte, lorsque Marie-Sophie Laborieux fait part de son expérience de l'écriture et de ses difficultés à la figure anagrammatique de l'auteur (Oiseau de Cham, Petit Cham),[2] celui-ci la rassure en retour en donnant Glissant comme exemple de la même expérience, mais cette référence à Glissant est introduite à la manière d'une citation, donc comme un para-texte, impliquant l'impossibilité de faire de Glissant un personnage romanesque :

(...) Je connais cette épouvante. Edouard Glissant l'affronte : son oeuvre fonctionne comme ça avec un grand bonheur.

708e lettre du Marqueur de paroles
à l'Informatrice
Chemise XXXI
1988. Bibliothèque Schoelcher. (*Texaco,* p.354)

L'absence de Glissant comme personnage de Texaco s'explique puisque celui-ci a refusé tout engagement dans la vie politique de la Martinique, se consacrant à son oeuvre. Pourtant, il a tenté par son enseignement (l'Institut d'Etudes Martiniquaises—1972-1979) et la revue *Acoma* de contribuer à un changement de la mentalité martiniquaise. Par ailleurs, nous pensons que le Mentô de *Texaco* renvoie à Glissant lui-même et à ce rôle de mentor qu'il s'est choisi dans la société martiniquaise avec sa production littéraire (surtout avec ses essais, *Le Discours antillais* plus que tous les autres). De ce fait, la relation Glissant-Chamoiseau semble se jouer sur deux plans. D'une part, au niveau d'un hors-texte, où Chamoiseau n'arrête pas de se référer à Glissant : dédicace (apocryphe peut-être ou inspirée du *Quatrième siècle*) et épigraphes citant *Le Discours antillais* (p.133/*Texaco,* p.421); et aussi articles et conférences (Cf. *Antilla*). D'autre part la relation se noue au niveau d'un en-texte, celui de sa fiction romanesque. Dans ce contexte, la référence à Glissant est implicite et se situe au niveau du projet d'écriture lui-même : dire l'histoire (chaotique) du peuple de l'En-ville martiniquais en conservant sa diversité et son oralité (cf. *Texaco,* pp.410 etc.). Deux références à Glissant s'imposent ici : tout d'abord un texte de fiction, *Le Quatrième siècle,* en raison de la similitude des démarches : interrogation des témoins/acteurs de l'histoire non-officielle de la Martinique; et les personnages du couple Mathieu/Papa Longoué, reproduits par Chamoiseau au niveau du couple Informatrice/marqueur de paroles.

Le second point commun entre *Le Quatrième siècle* et *Texaco* semble se situer au niveau de la démarche: quête de la mémoire, remontée dans les traces des mornes (*Quatrième siècle*), quand Mathieu, l'historien, s'informe auprès de Papa Longoué, le descendant des nègres marrons; remontée dans le lacis des "passages" de *Texaco,* alors que l'urbaniste (Christ) et le marqueur de parole (Cham) recueillent la parole de Marie-Sophie Laborieux, retraçant la conquête de l'En-ville, par les marginaux de l'Emancipation et de la départementalisation.

Cependant, parallélisme et recoupement des démarches signifient-ils similitude des projets? Vingt-deux ans après Glissant, Chamoiseau se remet-il dans les pas de son aîné? Ce n'est pas tout à fait le cas. Alors que les personnages de Glissant quittaient la ville pour explorer le morne et y rechercher l'espoir d'une dé-colonisation, les personnages de Chamoiseau, après une brève tentative d'occupation des mornes, reviennent s'enraciner dans l'En-ville, forçant celle-ci à reconnaître leur présence (raccordement au réseau d'électricité, à l'eau courante et, finalement, décision municipale de réhabiliter le bidonville), signe de leur ré-appropriation de l'espace. Pourtant, paradoxalement, Chamoiseau réalise ainsi le projet suggéré par Glissant dans *Le Discours antillais* : l'appropriation d'un lieu vécu comme multiple, mouvant, diffus et divers. Chamoiseau, (*Antilla* 557, p.27), reprend à Glissant la notion de l'errance pour l'appliquer à l'En-ville comme lieu privilégié de son actualisation:

> La pensée de l'errance que définit Edouard Glissant se concrétise dans la culture créole par le phénomène de la Drive. [...] une des caractéristique de la Drive était de se réaliser en ville. [...] L'En-ville désigne ainsi, non pas une dimension urbaine bien repérable, distincte de la campagne, mais essentiellement un contenu, donc [...] une sorte de projet. (*Antilla* 473, p.29-30)

Dans cet article, Chamoiseau donne acte à Glissant de lui fournir un cadre conceptuel de référence pour appréhender l'univers martiniquais. «A la lumière des propositions de Glissant», Chamoiseau peut «tenter d'imaginer la pensée» des marginaux de l'En-ville. Ces propositions d'Edouard Glissant lui apportent donc le support nécessaire pour décoder le «monologue occidental sectaire» et il cite alors Glissant parlant de «l'exil intérieur» et de «l'errance» de ceux qui ne se sont pas encore constitués en «communauté» capable d'avoir un «rapport à son entour» (p.32).

On se rend donc compte que *Texaco* retrace cet effort en vue de se constituer en communauté. Ainsi dans le roman, Ti-Cirique, l'Haïtien, apprendra à Marie-Sophie qu'ils sont une communauté (p.30). Chamoiseau illustre donc, dans le cadre de la fiction, les réflexions du *Discours Antillais,* c'est sans doute par ce biais que nous pouvons dire que l'ombre de Glissant plane sur chaque étape du récit de Marie-Sophie et dans son organisation en «Temps» centrés sur les matériaux ayant servi à construire l'En-ville. La trame chronologique se base, non pas sur le calendrier (même si les dates sont indiquées en sous-titres), mais sur l'évolution des matériaux de construction. Cette datation du récit renvoie sans doute à

Malemort, mais également au *Discours antillais* où Glissant constate que le temps antillais ne respecte pas la datation de la chronologie occidentale, mais plutôt celle d'événements exceptionnels marquant/brisant le rythme de la vie quotidienne.

A ce point que l'histoire obscurcie s'est souvent réduite pour nous au calendrier des événements naturels, avec leurs seules significations affectives «éclatées». (p.131)

L'art de Chamoiseau est donc d'assumer ce rapport au Temps et à le façonner de sorte qu'il garde à la fois l'incohérence multiple de «l'a-chronisme» antillais et établisse une succession évolutive, faisant passer les générations de noirs martiniquais de l'esclavage à la départementalisation, du temps des carbets à celui du béton. Le temps antillais se constitue alors selon une spirale,[3] dans la mesure où sa «circularité» routinière se voit propulsée dans un plan différent, en raison du contact inévitable avec la technologie occidentale introduite dans l'espace martiniquais par la «mère-patrie». Je me garderai d'orienter cette spirale selon un axe de «progrès» technologique ascendant, car les relations de la Martinique à la Métropole, telles qu'elles sont analysées par Glissant et Chamoiseau, sont loin d'être positives et quant au devenir de la culture martiniquaise, cette spirale pourrait même être descendante.

Enfin, l'influence de Glissant peut se repérer dans l'utilisation de la langue créole par Chamoiseau. Il faudrait dans un travail ultérieur analyser en détail l'utilisation complexe que fait ce dernier de la langue créole dans *Texaco,* cependant, nous y retrouvons la réalisation des commentaires de Glissant au sujet de cette dernière. Tantôt, le romancier joue sur la diglossie martiniquaise par le passage indifférencié du Créole au Français.

Esternome mon papa disait à Bonbon: *Ou pé pran'y! Fok nou pran'y, se la tij manyok-la yé ...! (Tu peux la prendre, il faut la prendre, c'est ici que tout se décide ...)* (p.94)

Tantôt, la langue créole prend possession du texte français, faisant éclater sa syntaxe, notamment dans les séquences d'action (prendre-courir : «Tout le monde y prit-courir» [p.110]) ou à l'intérieur même de la phrase, sous le voile de l'orthographe française : Mon papa Esternome les voyait *se gourmer* pour une couleur d'étoffe, [...]. (p.94)

Texaco respire cette présence fantômatique du texte de Glissant, ce qui a permis à Jacques Coursil de l'Université Antilles-Guyane de présenter ce dernier comme un «troisième personnage implicite» de *Texaco* et il la définit en ces termes:

> Dans mon propos d'analyse, *Discours antillais* est tout à la fois (et tour à tour) le titre d'un livre, le nom d'un discours et enfin le nom de toute une nouvelle génération littéraire. (*Antilla,* 561, p.29)

Il parait évident que Coursil fait allusion à Bernabé, Confiant et Chamoiseau et à leur mouvement de la Créolité. Signalons pour conclure que la relation Glissant-Chamoiseau est orientée de Chamoiseau vers Glissant. Ce dernier est d'ailleurs assez discret sur ses relations à ces jeunes écrivains. Une chose est sûre : Glissant admire leur «énergie de production inouïe avec une stratégie presque militaire de l'occupation du terrain» (Interview accordée à Patrice Delbourg dans *L'Evénement du Jeudi* du 2.12.93 et reproduit dans *Antilla,* 563, p.34). Il refuse cependant la place «d'un sage dans un rôle paternel» (*Antilla,* 563, p.34) et prend ses distances vis-à-vis du mouvement de la créolité, en établissant une distinction entre «créolité» comme concept figé, et «créolisation» comme concept toujours en cours. Ces différences sont précisées dans une interview accordée à Gilles Anquetil du *Nouvel Observateur* à l'occasion de la parution de son dernier livre *Tout-Monde* et après l'attribution du prix Goncourt à Chamoiseau).

> Mes amis Raphaël Confiant et Patrick Chamoiseau se sont un peu trop hâtés de leur *«Eloge de la créolité»* : la créolité, ça ne marche pas ailleurs qu'aux Antilles. La créolisation, elle, n'est pas une essence, mais un processus universel. (...) Prendre véritablement conscience du métissage, c'est la valeur ajourée de la créolisation. (...) C'est pour cela que je suis hostile à la créolité, qui est une prison, comme la latinité, la francité ou la négritude. (*Antilla,* 563, p.36-37)

De ce fait, Glissant me semble occuper dans l'espace culturel martiniquais la position du «Mentô», offrant (la sagesse/la «Force» de) sa parole (ses écrits) mais ne se préoccupant pas de ce qu'en font ceux qui la recueille. Il me semble ainsi refuser, tout comme les «Mentô» de *Texaco,* la position du «Maître» telle qu'on voudrait la lui faire assumer.

NOTES

1. Cf. biographie de Maupassant, A. Lanoux. (1967) *Maupassant, le bel ami.* Paris: Le Livre de poche, 1979.
2. Oiseau de Cham comme anagramme de Chamoiseau, abrégé familièrement en Petit Cham. Rappelons que Glissant avait indiqué dans *Le Quatrième siècle* l'origine de son nom comme version anagrammatique de Senglis, nom du maître. *Texaco,* p.352-357; 394-395.
3. La Narratrice de *Texaco* exprime cette intuition en s'interrogeant sur la possibilité d'une écriture qui pourrait rendre compte de la circularité de la vie en gardant son dynamisme. (p.356)

RÉFÉRENCES

Bernabe, J. (1993). De la Négritude à la Créolité: éléments pour une approche comparée. (3 parties). *Antilla,* 552 (24.9), pp.26-29, 553 (1.10), pp.32-33, 554 (8.10), pp.27-29.

Bernabe, J., Chamoiseau, P. et Confiant, R. (1989). *Eloge de la Créolité.* Paris: Gallimard.

Chamoiseau, P. (1992). Nègres Marrons de l'En-ville: à propos du driveur. *Antilla 473* (27.2), pp.29, 30.

———. (1993). Contre la Mémoire et l'Histoire. *Antilla,* 557 (29. 10), pp.25-31.

Coursil, J. (1993). La Muette qui parle: esquisse de personnages dans *Texaco. Antilla,* 561 (26.11), pp.29-32.

Glissant, E. (1958). *La Lézarde.* Paris: Seuil—Coll. Points-Roman, 1984.

———. (1964). *Le Quatrième siècle.* Paris: Gallimard.

———. (1975). *Malemort.* Paris: Seuil.

———. (1981). *Le Discours antillais.* Paris: Seuil.

Glissant, E., Anquetil, G. (1993). Interview. *Nouvel Observateur* du 2.12.93. Reproduit dans *Antilla, 563* (10.12), pp.35-37.

Glissant, E., Delbourg, P. (1993). Interview. *L'Evénement du jeudi,* 2.12.93. Reproduit dans *Antilla, 563* (10.12), pp.33-34.

BANISHED BETWEEN TWO WORLDS: EXILES IN CHILEAN CANADIAN LITERATURE

Sylvie Perron

The theme of exile is traced through the prose of two Canadian/Chilean writers, José Leandro Urbina and Hernán Barrios. The concepts of remembering and nostalgia are inherent in all exile literature while spatial and temporal distance experienced by the exiled writers enable them to take a reflective stance with respect to their own social history. By focussing on the protagonists in this fiction, we come to understand how these writers shift through their lives in an attempt to recover their identity by reconciling their past with their present experience.

Le thème de l'exil est examiné à travers la prose de deux écrivians canadiens/chiliens : José Leandro Urbina et Hernán Barrios. Les notions fondamentales de nostalgie et de mémoire se retrouvent dans toute littérature de l'exil; dans ce cas-ci cependant, la distance spaciale et temporelle vécue par les écrivains exilés, leur permet une réflexion critique sur l'histoire sociale de leur propre pays d'origine. En examinant les protagonistes de cette fiction, nous comprenons la démarche de ces écrivains qui passent en revue leur vie, afin de saisir le sens d'une identité qui reconcilie le passé et le présent.

*

THE STUDY OF LATIN AMERICAN literature written outside the country of origin leads inevitably to the theme of exile. First treated during the Middle Ages, the problem of exile lends itself in various ways to literary study. One such way is provided by the exiled character him or herself, a source of insight into a wide sphere of social issues. Appearing periodically in

Latin American literature to illustrate the various sociopolitical upheavals of history, the exile in our own time figures prominently in Chilean writing in Canada, where writers are currently reworking this theme, each in their own style. Of particular interest are two works written in Canada and published in Chile: José Leandro Urbina's novel *Cobro Revertido* (1992) and the short story by Hernán Barrios *El discurso de la Macarena* (1990), both of which unfold around the exiled protagonist.

The concepts of remembering and nostalgia are inherent in all exile literature. The spatial and temporal distance experienced by exiled writers enable them to take a reflective stance with respect to their own social history which leads inevitably to a critical revision of the past, a stage that is essential to the eventual reintegration of this past by the author. Rejected by their country and in permanent conflict with a world in which they no longer play their former role or occupy their former place, exiles tirelessly sift through their past in an attempt to recover their identity. During this process, the exile must reconcile two different realities: the past that belongs to the country of origin and the present as lived in the new country. The object of my work is, in fact, to represent these two worlds, the past and the present, as seen through the eyes of the main characters in *Cobro revertido* and *El discurso de la Macarena.* More precisely, I will attempt to focus on the perception of the past as rebuilt in the characters' memories, and then extend my observations to the views they currently hold with respect to their new country, in this case, Canada. My main purpose is to determine where the exiled protagonist situates him or herself in relation to the two worlds and the extent to which entering a new society has had a positive effect on his or her life.

In José Leandro Urbina's novel *Cobro revertido,* a phone call from Chile informs the "hero" of his mother's death. This news, followed by the character's promise to return to his country to attend his mother's funeral, together spark the unravelling of his memory. The central figure, who remains unnamed in the novel and is referred to only by his nickname "the sociologist," re-collects his past, not only his Chilean past, but also his immediate Canadian past. These recollections are inspired by images surrounding the various affective relationships which the protagonist has had with different women at different times of his life: María, his mother; Magdalena, his Chilean lover; Meg, his Anglo-Canadian wife, and Marcia, his current Québécois girlfriend. Among these women, the dominant figure, and the most significant one, is the mother, not only because of the concrete role she plays in the narrative, but because of the way she is reconstructed in the character's memory, gradually becoming, in the eyes of the reader, a metaphor of the other mother: the Motherland. In this novel, it is through the metaphor of the mother that the reality of the country of origin will take shape. As an authoritarian figure, a social climber and a repressive force in the life of the protagonist, the mother apparently represents the Chilean military dictatorship. The parallel between the mother and the regime is in fact suggested several times throughout the novel; even her laughter is described in such a way as to evoke the most dramatic moments of the coup d'état. The protagonist recalls that "Every time my mother let loose one of her famous laughs the windows would shake, as if tanks were going by outside" (Urbina, 1992, p.29).

What is discovered then is a mother who meddles with every detail of a boy's life, even the most intimate, in order to watch over and repress him. She is omniscient; the protagonist recalls that, during his schooldays, his teachers "kept her informed of the slightest of my movements" (Urbina, 1992, p.26).

She is dictatorial, a mother that decides everything, especially her son's future: "You will be a lawyer," she says, "a brilliant lawyer." Finally, she is a mother that will not accept the slightest opposition.

However, the mother is not only a metaphor of the dictatorship, a metaphor of the Motherland; in this novel, this character also functions contiguously as a metonym of the past. Far removed from an idealized past as seen through the eyes of the exiled character, the reader witnesses the process of its metonymical demystification. The process becomes all the more acute when the protagonist's memories of his mother are contrasted with, for instance, the hallowing words of Dona Sarita, a compatriot of the sociologist, spoken during a speech delivered in the midst of a drunken fervour:

> She was a brave woman, one who you realized at first glance had the firm foundation that constituted the best of Chilean women who don't bow their heads and who confront the greatest adversities with a stout heart. She was a loving mother, who will kill on behalf of her children, who dreams of leading them to the best in life claiming no more than a little love in return. (Urbina, 1992, p.63)

This novel is not a mere retelling of the "lost paradise" myth, recreated with the aid of the falsifying mechanism furnished by the protagonist's memory, such as can be seen in many novels about exile. Here, the past is represented for what it was, no more, no less. Here, "paradise" shows its other face, namely, "hell." The mother and the past are simultaneously needed and rejected. The ambiguity with respect to both the Motherland and the past, as well as their demystification, constitute, in my view, the central axis of this work.

It might seem that exile, as opposed to either suffering or punishment, represents liberation for the character, his escape from the oppressive mother as well as from the repressive Motherland. But the idea of liberation would surely imply a more optimistic view of the future, the possibility of a transformation as a result of which the character becomes aware of his new existence in a different socio-cultural milieu. This, however, will not happen here. Our "hero" will not be changed by his exiled circumstances at all, but will continue to be the same spineless being he always was: someone will buy clothes for him, lead him to and enroll him in a university program. Women and friends determine his decisions: he poses as a revolutionary because his Chilean girlfriend likes him that way; he studies law to please his mother and sociology to please his Canadian wife; and just as his going into exile meant abandoning his career as a lawyer, so too does his separation from Meg put an end to his sociology studies. So he goes from being an "almost lawyer" to an "almost sociologist." Paralyzed into an embryonic state, "the sociologist" seeks refuge from his precarious existence in the world of women, in the rhetoric of exile, and in alcohol. Thus, the only real contact between the protagonist and the Canadian world surrounding him occurs solely at the sensory level. In fact the "almost-sociologist" lives, as the narrator points out, "in a society where he will always miss the nuances ... exiled from another one he thought he knew but from which he only retains the doubts" (Urbina, 1992, p.146).

There are other characters who will convey, at times sarcastically, a vision of our Canadian society or, more precisely, of Montréalais society. Over the carnivalesque background of Carifête, the Caribbean festival held in Montreal, the reader will discover a preeminently multi-ethnic city where immigrants do not establish much contact with the natives and where they work as merchants or have menial jobs like "office cleaning engineer" (Urbina, 1992, p.41).

In spite of all this, the Chilean exiles, in the novel, think of themselves as people with a mission: to defend and uphold their image as revolutionaries in the progressive and heteroclite world of Montreal, full of a "caterwaul of leftists with a hippie past, anglo liberals, francophone nationalists, stalinists, social democrats, and progressive homosexuals" (Urbina, 1992, p.86). The world to which they have come does not offer them many opportunities. In the end, it would seem that they have arrived in a world where, as Josefo the Spanish immigrant would say, "the best thing is for one to forget he ever had a country and bring out whatever there is left of his family, because here if you put your nose to the grindstone, at least you can have a somewhat comfortable life" (Urbina, 1992, p.110).

The "hero" of *Cobro revertido* will never leave the intermediate space between past and present; he will continue to be a wanderer looking for sensations and for refuge, until he arrives at his final destination, the only possible end to his drifting and exile: death.

Another work I would like to comment on is a short story written in Montreal which also represents a view of the past and a demystification of exile. I am referring to *El discurso de la Macarena* by the Chilean Hernan Barrios.

The whole short story is a monologue by Macarena, the female protagonist, who has gone into exile with her husband. At the time of her speech, which is addressed to an interlocutor which the reader assumes to be her husband, Macarena has already made a critical assessment of her past. She followed her partner into exile and now she is leaving him. Macarena's speech is a farewell speech, a cry of liberation. She believes that her decision to leave her husband "before the stage of an imaginary sierra where half of the banana trees would shout: we will win, and all the parrots would be called Manuel" (Barrios, 1990, p.14), will mark the beginning of a better future before which she feels "scared shitless of losing her earrings, her bluejeans, and her left nipple" (1990, p.10).

Macarena decides, not to go back to her country of origin, but to throw herself fully into the new geographical and cultural space that surrounds her. Macarena crosses the limits of that middle zone mentioned earlier. She identifies this break clearly and in her own way: "We totter in the space that separates one step from the next and we try to maintain our sense of balance" (1990, p.9). Because the exile of Macarena is of a different nature, she can put an end to it by going back to her country. Her exile occurs at another level, at the level of her own identity. As a result, she wants to break the mold she was forced into by her husband, a false mold that is in open contradiction with her bourgeois origins and built with left-wing rhetoric and intellectual clichés. Then Macarena announces her disappearance: "My vanishing from this chair ... from this universe of pencils, Hungarian cook books, IRA manifestos, Portuguese wine bottles, seashells from Isla Negra and socks from Chiloé" (1990, p.10). Macarena is in fact asserting her right to return to her social class, to recover her identity as a "woman" and to vindicate her sexuality.

Here the geographical exile is perceived as an opening to the outside world. Her encounter with another reality allows Macarena to raise her self-awareness and to unmask her husband and, thus, her past with him. This is what will finalize her decision and decisively transform her character. "So much pot-washing, watching the days go by, smoking American cigarettes, drinking a dozen coffees per day and reading English, French and Mexican newspapers, has made me become kind of heterogeneous" (Barrios, 1990, p.10), she tells us in an attempt to explain her new self, a self that tries to affirm her role as a woman who is free to express herself without shame. In the story by Hernan Barrios, we meet a character freed and transformed by her transplantation into another world.

These two works by Chilean writers in Canada add nuance to the possibilities of living between two worlds. Both attempt to simultaneously demystify the past and exile. Both attempt to unmask the rhetoric of exile. I would like to conclude by underlying the originality of the self-critical view presented in these narratives of Canadian exiles: these works indeed compel the reader to adopt a new view of exile literature in general.

REFERENCES

Barrios, H. (1990). *El discruso de la Macarena. Landed immigrant.* Santiago: Documentas, 9-21.

Urbina, J.L. (1992). *Cobro Revertido.* Santago: Planeta.

WOMEN'S WORD: FROM RESISTANCE TO CHALLENGING THE PATRIARCHAL CULTURE[1]

Lady Rojas-Trempe

Feminist and nonfeminist writers have opened a breach in the patriarchal culture of Latin America which has allowed critics to establish epistemological bases for a kind of knowledge that moves beyond Manichean stereotypes, sexist generalizations and macho discourse. Through the works of Mexican women writers, Sor Juana Inés de la Cruz, Rosario Castellanos, Ulalume González de León, Elena Milán, Patricia Median and Rosmaría Roffiel, the author brings to light a cultural critique of images of women in patriarchal literature.

Ecrivains féministes et non-féministes ont ouvert une brèche dans la culture partriarchale de l'Amérique latine pour permettre à la critique de jeter les bases épistémologiques d'une forme de connaissance qui dépasse les stéréotypes manichéens, les généralisations sexistes et les discours machistes. A partir des oeuvres des écrivaines Mexicaines : Sor Juana Inés de la Cruz, Rosario Castellanos, Ulalume González de Léón, Elena Milán, Patricia Median et Rosmaría Roffiel, l'auteur examine leur entreprise de remise en question des images culturelles de la femme dans la littérature patriarchale.

*

CONTEMPORARY LATIN AMERICAN literature in the past two decades—the 1970s and 1980's—reliably proves that the written word of women has contributed to the outlining and definition of a culture which challenges male hegemony as well as androcentric power relations and knowledge.[2] The breach that certain feminist and nonfeminist writers opened in the patriarchal culture allowed them, as a point of departure, to underline the fact that they were different from men. At the same time, they emphasized the historical cost of marginalization and took up the struggle for fair treatment.[3] Soon after, they established certain epistemological bases for a kind of knowledge which would move beyond Manichean stereotypes, sexist generalizations, and macho discourse.[4]

Through the works of Mexican poets Sor Juana Inés de la Cruz, Rosario Castellanos, Ulalume González de León, Elena Milán, Patricia Medina, and the novelist Rosamaría Roffiel, we will examine the critical literary expression concerning the cultural images of women and women's relationships with men. Their contribution consisted in conceiving a culture which would include not only women but also all marginal sectors of society. The literature of resistance, after yielding to the law of the Father, as we shall see, went from radical rebellion to the search for a symmetrical and complementary system that would not exclude the Other. The operative poetic strategies range from the voice of ironic protest, the decisive gesture of appropriating the word, humour, and the affirmation of sexual pleasure.

We have chosen the area of poetry (still ignored by the critics) because, as Rosario Castellanos (1925-1974)—a major voice in women's literature in the 20th century—affirms in an interview to Emmanuel Carballo (1986, p.520): "The words of poetry constitute the only way to reach what is permanent in this world." To this lyrical quality of timelessness, we may add those of transgressing fixed norms, truths, and reason. The works of Sor Juana Inés de la Cruz (1648-1695), which reach their heights of expression towards the end of the 17th century, synthesize such values.[5] The figure of Sor Juana as a lucid intellectual endures as the pre-modern paradigm of a writer who assumes her professional responsibility despite the Inquisition and the religious authorities' censorship of all writing not conforming to social and divine laws. Franco (1989, p.xv) explains, "the importance of Sor Juana is that she defended the rationality of women and was able to do so because the slippage between her devalued status as a woman and her empowerment by writing led her to understand gender difference as a social construction, and interpretation as a rationalization of male interest."

The voice of Sor Juana proclaims women's right to education, knowledge, and to dignified treatment by men. In her poetic discourse written in quatrains or ten-line stanzas, Sor Juana expounds her damning testimony against male hypocrisy and warns women of the dangers incurred in a submissive relationship with a man. In one of her most famous poems, "She demonstrates the inconsistency of men's wishes in blaming women for what they themselves have caused," the lyric voice states:

Silly, you men-so very adept
at wrongly faulting womankind,
not seeing you're alone to blame
for faults you plan in woman's mind.

After you've won by urgent plea
the right to tarnish her good name,
you still expect her to behave-
you, that coaxed her into shame.

You batter her resistance down
and then, all righteousness, proclaim
the feminine frivolity,
not your persistence, is to blame. (1988, p.111)

In her dirges,—as "In which, with deep feeling, she foresees the pain of separation"—and sonnets, Sor Juana presents her notion of love as a profound, gnoseological test of her passion and desire:

Behold my loving flesh
surrendering when racked:
in all else but a corpse;
in suffering, body still. (1988, p.69)

Almost three centuries later, Rosario Castellanos (1984b, p.17) considers herself to be ideologically and artistically indebted to Sor Juana Inés de la Cruz,[6] of whom she says, in "Asedio a Sor Juana" included in *Juicios Sumarios I:* "She listens, criticizes, reflects, and mocks." According to Castellanos these excellent intellectual qualities were not enough to save Sor Juana from silence or from her own emptiness. Rather, we can state that such an attitude allowed Sor Juana to protect her identity as a woman writer. When we read "Meditation on the Threshold," (*Poetry Thou Art Not,* 1948-1971), by Castellanos we see how she recaptures the cruel history and tragic end of Sor Juana and other women or female characters, and how she rebels against feminine passivity and encourages readers to seek change:

No, it's no solution
to throw yourself under the wheels of a train
like Tolstoy's Anna
nor to down the poisoned cup of Madame Bovary
nor to wait on the high plains of Avila
for the visit of an angel armed with a javelin
before tying your robe around your head
and starting to act.

Nor to review the laws of geometry
while counting the beams of your punishment cell
like Sor Juana Inés. Nor is the solution
to write in the Austen living room
while the guests are arriving,
nor to close yourself up in an attic
of a New England home
and to dream with the Dickinson family Bible
beneath your virgin's pillow.

There must be some other way that is not
called Sappho or Messalina or Mary
of Egypt or Magdalena or Clemencia Isaura.

Another way of being, free and human.

Another manner of being. (1988, p.49)

It would not be until the 1960s that the change in the feminine condition, so longed for by Sor Juana and Castellanos, would begin its "free and human" journey through the efforts of other women. According to Castoriadis (1988), feminism arises as a "cultural movement" that propounds the necessity of systematically revolutionizing relationships of domination in all spheres of existence. We use the term "cultural movement" because feminism's first goal was to fight against the stigmatized image of "the feminine" and to attack mental and patriarchal oppression, as well as socio-economic institutions that maintained the division of labour and control over women's reproductive systems for the glory and benefit of male supremacy. One of the fundamental achievements of feminism consisted, according to Belluci (1992), in defining, in an epistemological manner, other forms of meaning which would portray gender as a symbolic, cultural construction rather than as an inescapable biological destiny.

A decade before the feminist movement, Mexican literature had already expressed both a social malaise and the necessity of global renovation in the narrative, poetry, essays, and dramas of Rosario Castellanos. Castellanos criticizes a society in which all privileges are bestowed upon men in the name of the patriarchy and of capitalism, much to the detriment of marginalized and exploited groups among which we continue to find women, native people, and children.

For this paper I have chosen works written in the 1970s and 1980s because at that decisive moment women's literature confronts androcentric power, asserts its discursive cultural role as an agent of change, and incorporates a semantics of bodily enjoyment into its language. The feminine experience in Mexican poetry is rich in themes and styles and tones.[7] In this critical investigation I propose to highlight the poetic contribution of Castellanos and the literature of authors who identify themselves with feminism, such as Patricia Medina, Elena Milán, and Rosamaría Roffiel. At this historical moment, feminism constituted the collective aim of what can be called feminine culture. This collective movement was reinforced even by writers who rejected the label "feminism" as such political labels.[8]

The first Mexican novel which addresses the subject of lesbianism, *Amora,* by Rosamaría Roffiel (1989) synthesizes, in the following lines, the giant strides that the feminist movement had made since its beginnings up to the eve of the 1990s:

> Millions and millions of women being born to a new identity, searching within and outside ourselves, eager to attempt new ways of being, anxious for a more dignified and equitable relationship with a man or with another woman, knowing ourselves for the first time in our lives. The panorama of possibilities open to us has startled us, we can't believe our eyes. Some of us are perhaps terrified. But it is too late to stop.The process has begun and there's no going back. It becomes clearer every day: we are the force of the future, the engine driving our coming history, and men know it and tremble. Many men will share our dawn. The rest will resort to desperate measures that will only hasten their downfall. Those willing to renounce their privileges will build the new society by our sides. (1993, p.216)

The combatant optimism which novelist and poet Roffiel expresses about the feminine condition is one of the milestones of a long journey, which, as we will see, had to unleash its force through the unmasking of the discourses of the dominant culture. Castellanos would be the first to question in her poetry the patriarchal symbolism based on the myths surrounding the universal and abstract woman. In this sense we understand her open opposition to the myths of the eternal feminine in "Poetry Thou Art Not," as well as to myths of romantic love and erotic passion, because these simply confirm the social legitimization of hegemonic discursive practices.[9] Castellanos (1984c, p.21) unhesitatingly denounces the complicity of women who conform to the dominant ideology, while she exalts in *Juicios Sumarios II*: "another breed of women: the strong, the stubborn, those who challenge what is preached to them, those who shake off the yoke that brutalizes them, the ones who are free."

In "Narcissus 70" the poetic voice asserts her feminine existence through the power which poetry confers on her, and in "Interview" (1988, p.127) she rejects "the indifferent adjective\behind which was hidden my person, my book,\my latest lecture" which labels her. Through the task of purifying the language the speaker reclaims her real identity and in "Small Chronicle," after sarcastically scorning the resources of amorous discourse, she discovers that she must start over on the job of poetic construction from the beginning:

> Between us there was
> what at times occurs between lovers:
> blood of a torn hymen. (Can you imagine?
> A virgin at thirty—and a poetess! Damn it.)
>
> The monthly haemorrhage or that in which
> a child says yes, says no to life.
>
> And the vein
> —mine or another's, what's the difference?—
> into which the suicidal edge plunges
> perhaps deeply enough to turn
> one into a death notice.
>
> There were, perhaps, other humors:
> the sweat of work, that of pleasure,
> anger's green secretion,
> semen, saliva, tears.

In short, nothing a good bath
won't erase. And I wonder
with what, then, will I write our story?
With ink? Ah, but ink comes to us
from such distant sources. (1988, p.129)

Castellanos took on the arduous task of creating material—ink—and poetic devices as her own distinct form which dismantled sexual stereotypes and fought feminine submissiveness. Another text, "Dialogues with the most honourable men" that appears in *Bella dama sin piedad y otros poemas,* (1984a, pp.133-138), is a long, intertextual poem with the most widely read poets of Spanish America and Spain, including Porfirio Barba Jacob, Pablo Neruda, Miguel Hernández, Juan Ramón Jiménez, Ramón López Velarde, Rubén Darío, and Federico García Lorca. The use of this demystifying feminine discourse as a counterpoint to the poems of the major literary authority figures of the moment gives us an idea of the heated debate in which women became embroiled in order to dismantle Christian ethical suppositions and paternal values concerning God, love, woman, and the cosmos, which had been considered to be immutable.

Another assumption which had to be undermined was the myth of woman as wife and mother, self-sacrificing and tender. In the six poems which make up the called text "Kinsey Report," Castellanos (1988, p.151) ironically analyzes the contradictions which married women live between resistance to marital and family demands and the age-old custom of obedience: "I always resist, for decorum's sake.\ But, too, I always submit. Out of obedience." She immediately goes on to destroy the prototypes of women based on marital and sexual status: the unmarried whore, the divorcee, the nymphomaniac, the lesbian, and the young nubile *señorita.* While most of the female voices in these poems mock social expectations and subvert them through the fulfilment of erotic desire—experiencing afterwards, however, the sting of guilt—the *señorita* continues to follow the traditional phallocentric pattern.

Castellanos seems to ask how it can be that a social minority continues to cling obsessively to the ideology of finding economic security, social respect, and motherhood in a heterosexual marriage. We are well aware that although economic structures have been modified so as to allow women a certain financial autonomy, the legendary patriarchal ideology is still weighted against change. At the same time, it is interesting to observe that the radical modification of male-female relationships which the protagonists experience is fundamentally due to the ideological revolution achieved by the feminist movement.

Certain female characters of the "Kinsey Report" dissociate femininity from motherhood, control partially or completely the needs of their bodies, and are aware that they can assume the right to conception, contraception, divorce, and artificial insemination. Such transformations in social practices, private as well as public, weakened the traditional view of the feminine and fragile nature of women. A young generation of Mexican poets who take the illuminating work of Castellanos as their point of departure rightly criticizes and ridicules the aggressive male culture and advocates more human values.

In her book *Plagiarism* (1973), Ulalume González de León builds on Castellanos' poetic discourse in "Domestic economy," "Self portrait" and "Valium 10" to construct her own mode of expression in such poems as "Inventory," "The marvellous exercise of awakening," and "Changes of skin." González' poetry is more in keeping with its urban, technocratic context, from which springs a poetic voice, using a surprisingly simple versification in the process of self contemplation and tracing the succession of life's vital steps:

> I do not think
> I raise myself up upon my legs
>   I realize
> I dress
>   I comb my hair
> I organize a few words for the day. (1973, p.49)

Femininity is transformed into metaphor and follows an apparently more serene, less realistic course than in Castellanos. The poem "Changes of skin" describes the predicament of a woman who, in putting on makeup each day, multiplies the possibilities of her own fragmentation:

> Each day
> I change face and throw away the one
> that is hardly a day old
> But each new face gets progressively older
> It hardly lasts out the day
> I fear
>   that sometimes
> it could break before nightfall. (1973, p.50)

The system of old-new, and day-night dichotomies sets González' poetry squarely in the tradition of her precursor, though we also catch certain glimpses of a departure from it. The dislocation implicit in the free verse and the hesitating tempo of "But ..." and "I fear /that sometimes" speak of the inner intensity and originality of the poetic voice of *Plagiarism.*

Elena Milán's poem, (1979) "The extremely complicated problem of how to rape a man," taken from her book, *Circuit Loves and Annexes* destroys the concept of women as passive beings but also questions the resignification of women for a type of feminism which demands equality at all cost. According to Milán the feminism of equality proposes equity for women in a male world.

The six stanzas of Milán's poem read like the recital of a recipe in which the speaker addresses women and through the instructions urges them to work towards the result announced in the title. However the discursive remedy of a certain type of literature may cheapen the text of "How to rape a man," it is humorous because it intertwines incongruous codes recognized by the female reader as masculine semantic fields. In the first stanza, "Preinstruction: / Learn to flourish the lasso / Shoot with a rifle and shotgun / Work with ether and chloroform / And a little bit of judo and karate" (1979, p.17) one is invited, in effect, to learn skills that originate in male activities historically consecrated as cattle farming, hunting, chemistry, and martial arts. If the instructions underline the need for technical knowledge and the acts of the stanzas entitled "First, second and third trial" guide us, these lines cast doubt upon the act of learning and emphasize the tricks and skills used to conquer the prey. The right to romantic conquest and to violence, which cultural systems have awarded to men as a sign of their superiority, in this way becomes a culinary catalogue to which anyone has access.

The last verse, "And a little bit of judo and karate," however, also points to the irony of the power that has been granted to "feminine" seduction, which is associated with the image of woman-object moulded by the capitalist system so that she consumes its material products. Milán traces the ironic history of the female body, condemned to suffer because it was first perceived as the domain of weakness and sickness; then as the exalted symbol of the fantasies of a voyeuristic society which continues to reduce women to the role of conquering prostitute. In this sense, the parody of sexual assault of a man by a woman is, in the final analysis, incongruent in that the antagonistic and polarized schemes of male-female relationships produce only alienation and the desire for conquest of one human group by another.

In another poem, "Inquiry," Milán warns us that feminism which seeks only sexual equality, and shares aggressive masculine values, can lead to failure:

> It is possible:
> to be the Amazon with breast amputated to facilitate
> the use of the shield,
> the throwing of the discus, the contest of archery.
> Explore, investigate:
> perhaps you will discover that the victory was not worth the pain. (1979, p.23).

Another poetic discourse which has recourse to the liberating effects of Castellanos' work is that of Patricia Medina (1987), who, in "From now on despite my mother" from the book *Trajectory of the Human Being* expresses her decision to break away from the Christian ideology of her oppressive and judgemental mother in order to set out on her own path:

> From today onwards despite my mother
> In prayer I will not say
> I a sinner, I hope, I punish
> I in full view of all
> hope not to kill, tell necessary lies,
> fornicate.
> I declare myself a thief, but exempt
> from that voice which chastizes me in the name of the father.
> I have decided not to love without scourges,
> feeling the pulse,
> to sanctify the man who renounces his language
> if he resembles my son.
> I renounce my baptism
> over flesh in flames.
> I swear today to don desire
> as an arm and testament,
> I am obstinate in hope
> I allow myself as woman. (1987, p.39)

Medina's poem clearly envisages the historical moment of demarcation between the past of female submission to the patriarchy and the poetic present of ideological, discursive, and active subversion. The "I" of the speaker cuts the umbilical cord which ties her to her mother's ideology, and consequently, she also breaks from the strict religious mentality which conditions human behaviour through fear, punishment, and sexual hypocrisy. The act of assertion by which she becomes herself compels her to erase the footprints of a history that tied her to a discourse which defined her as a weak and passive being, and to a borrowed and limiting form of language; at the same time her discourse confronts and challenges male prohibitions that categorize her according to her sex.

Learning how to be free begins for the female voice with the distinction between her maternal origin, that is the principle which reproduces the code of indoctrination, and the pattern of sexual repression. She continues her revolutionary venture when she renounces the patriarchal images of God and his priests, the father and the husband to which her mother and the mother of women have yielded for centuries.

The reinsertion of the "I" which testifies and wants to repair historical injustices, constructs itself through rejection of verbal isotope of conquest and asserts itself with the conviction that the rebellious word can open unexplored horizons. The semantic play with Christian rhetoric destabilizes the code of faith, succeeds in showing a deformed reality, and sets out to change it.

When the speaker appropriates male discourse she inverts its imaginary symbolic force giving it a dynamic no longer of resistance as did that of Castellanos but rather of open challenge. The human nature of woman is urgently proclaimed, as a free subject with her own private-public history, who, without renouncing either motherhood or her complementary union with the Other can realize her vital human mission. In this programme of dialogic opening, the "son" finds himself on the side of change, of desire and hope expressed in the language of affirmation which yearns to avoid the first and necessary confrontation with patriarchal ideology, in the hope of overcoming binary dichotomies: reason-intuition, masculine-feminine, oppressor-oppressed, that still govern reality and literature.

The author Roffiel (1993, p.215) goes further in this feminine search which leads her to affirm "We are women and enjoy being women." Her poem "Gioconda" which she dedicates "to women" is a joyous, erotic celebration of her sexuality. As the poetic voice accepts her sexual body and the biological transformations taking place within it, she feels the amorous potential that knowing, touching, speaking to it brings. As never before we sense in these lines the glorification of fully 20th-century womanhood:

My vulva is a flower
she's a shell
a fig
velvet
she is full of scents flavors and corners
she's the color of a rose
soft
intimate
fleshy

When I was twelve she sprouted down
a cloud of cotton between my thighs
she feels vibrates bleeds gets angry gets wet throbs
she talks to me

Jealously between her folds
she guards the exact center of my cosmos
tiny moon that bursts into flames
wave that leads to another universe

Every twenty five days she turns red
explodes
screams
then I squeeze her between my hands
I whisper words of love to her

She is my second mouth
she's naughty
she frolics
spouts
she drenches me

She likes tongues that think they're butterflies
solidary penises
the pulp of woman's plum
or simply
my own caresses

She's a panther
a gazelle
a rabbit
she plays the coquette if you spoil her
she's my accomplice
she's my friend
the eternal smile of the pleasured woman. (1993, pp.213-214)

As we have seen, Roffiel approaches the topic of sexuality from a new perspective because she has overcome the taboos surrounding genitalia. Her playful, metaphorical, enumerative style confirms her daring frankness and freshness. No traces remain of the victimization of women as depicted by Sor Juana or Castellanos, nor of the dauntless struggle against military and sexual violence present in the poems of Milán, nor of the religious, patriarchal intolerance which is a topic of Medina's verse. Roffiel's eroticism of the self gives a sense of well-being because it presupposes the possibility of bodily stimulation and enjoyment as natural valuers which allow us to become freer and better.

To conclude, I may say that the poetic course followed by certain Mexican women writers engaged in the evolving struggle of women allows us to trace the evolution of female discourse. In its initial phase, female discourse constitutes a semiotic response and challenge to the ideological and discursive barriers of the patriarchal system which relegate woman to an inferior status. In this respect, we may speak of resistance to the dominant culture, to the stereotype images of women in dependent relationships with men. In a second phase, female discourse becomes an independent and defiant semiotic, proclaiming its own system of images through which the feminine subject wishes to overcome every kind of oppression and repression, in order to achieve a fair and complementary basis for relationships with men. In the roots of this discourse we still see preserved Castellanos' dialogic approach to the Other in "Poetry Thou Art Not":

Because if you existed
my existence also were assured. And that is a lie.

There is nothing more than the two of us: the couple,
the two sexes reconciled in a child,
one head beside the other, but not contemplating one another

(let no be a mirror)
but looking straight ahead, toward the other.

The other: mediator, judge, opposites
in equilibrium, witness,
knot which ties what had been torn.

The other, muteness that asks for voice
from its possessor
and demand hearing of him who listens.

The other. With the other
humanity, dialogue, poetry begin. (1988, p.149).

ENDNOTES

1. I would like to express my gratitude to those who have encouraged and supported me. The translation of my own article owes much to Rodney Williamson's thoughtful reading and insights. My deepest appreciation is due my contributing librarian, Lorraine Albert.
2. Caridad Silva-Velásquez and Nora Erro-Orthman (1986) made a historical introduction to pioneering work on Latin-American writers and literary critics in *Puerta abierta, la nueva escritora latinoamericana,* pp.7-11. For an extensive discussion of Mexican women writers and culture, see Jean Franco (1989), *Plotting Women. Gender and Representation in Mexico,* pp.XI-XXIV.
3. The book by Mora G. and Hooft, K. (1982) *Theory and Practice of Feminist Criticism* is fundamental to this subject.
4. Rose Minc (1985) refers to the question of radical change in "Nota particular" to the issue *Escritoras de la América Latina* in *Revista Iberoamericana,* 51, pp.132-133.
5. For a new literary account of this great writer, see Stephanie Merrim, (Ed.), (1991), *Feminist Perspectives on Sor Juana Inés de la Cruz.*
6. In 1962 Castellanos said to Carballo (1986, p.526) that she identified with the poetry of José Gorostiza and of Sor Juana Inés de la Cruz. Castellanos (1984) wrote in *Juicios Sumarios I* on the Mexican nun-poet: "Asedio a Sor Juana," pp.15-21 "Otra vez Sor Juana," pp.22-26.
7. Worthy of mention in the same generation as Castellanos is the mythical pen of Enriqueta Ochoa (1928). In the following generation the main writers are Thelma Nava (1931), and the winner of the Premio Nacional Villaurrutia in 1938, Carmen Alardín (1933), and in 1977, Isabel Fraire (1934). Later, we can mention Elva

Macías (1944) with her oriental touch, and Elsa Cross (1946) with her spiritual and mystical note.

8. The debate on the definition of feminist culture has not reached its conclusion. The reader may consult the following three texts: Naturaleza, cultura, posición social by Rossanda, R. (1981), in Sobre la cuestión de la cultura femenina, *Débats* 7, pp.1-29; Marcus, G., and Clifford, J. (1986). *Writing Culture, the Poetics and Politics;* and, Lerner, G. (1981). The Challenge of Women's History, in *The Majority Finds its Past, Placing Woman in History.*
9. In her theatrical work entitled *El eterno femenino* we can feel the real feminism of Castellanos (1975) that will unmask both men and women who take pleasure in remaining in the patriarchal system.

REFERENCES

Belluci, M. (1992). De los estudios de la mujer a los estudios de género: han recorrido un gran camino". In A.M. Fernández, (Ed.), *Las mujeres en la imaginación colectiva, una historia de discriminación y resistencias,* pp.27-50. Buenos Aires: Paidós.

Carballo, E. (1986). Rosario Castellanos 1925-1974. *Protagonistas de la literatura mexicana,* pp.519-533. México: Secretaría de Educación Pública, Lecturas Mexicanas 48.

Castellanos, R. (1975). *El eterno femenino.* México: Fondo de Cultura Económica.

———. (1984a). *Bella dama sin piedad y otros poemas.* México: Fondo de Cultura Económica, Lecturas Mexicanas 49.

———. (1984b). *Juicios Sumarios I.* México: Fondo de Cultura Económica.

———. (1984c). *Juicios Sumarios II.* México: Fondo de Cultura Económica.

———. (1988). *Meditation on The Threshold.* J. Palley (Trans.) Tempe AZ: Bilingual Press.

Castoriadis, C. (1988). *Los demonios del hombre: Las encrucijadas del laberinto.* Barcelona: Gedisa.

De la Cruz, S.J.I. (1988). *A Sor Juana Anthology.* A.S. Trueblood (Trans.). Cambridge MA and London: Harvard University Press.

Franco, J. (1989). *Plotting women: Gender and representation in Mexico.* New York: Columbia University Press.

González de León, U. (1973). *Plagio.* México: Joaquín Mortiz.

Lerner, G. (1981). The challenge of women's history. *The Majority Finds its Past, Placing Woman in History.* New York: Oxford University Press.

Marcus, G., & Clifford, J. (1986). *Writing culture, the Poetics and Politics.* Los Angeles: University of California Press.

Medina, P. (1987). *Trayectoria del ser.* Guadalajara: Universidad de Guadalajara.

Merrim, S. (Ed.), (1991). *Feminist perspectives on Sor Juana Inés de la Cruz.* Detroit MI: Wayne State University Press.

Minc, R. (1985, July-December). Nota particular. In *Escritoras de la América Latina, Revista Iberoamericana, 51,* pp.132-133.

Mora, G. and Hooft, K. (1982). *Theory and practice of feminist criticism.* Ypsilanti: Bilingual Press.

Roffiel, R. Excerpt from *Amora.* Trans., Paravisini-Gebert, L. And Gioconda. Trans., Lovelady, S. In Fernández Olmos, M. and Paravisini-Gebert, L. (Ed., 1993). *Pleasure in the Word.* New York: White Pine Press.

Rossanda, R. (1981). Naturaleza, cultura, posición social. In Sobre la cuestión de la cultura femenina. *Débats,* 7, pp.1-29.

Silva-Velásquez, C. & Erro-Orthman, N. (1986). *Puerta abierta, la nueva escritora latinoamericana.* México: Joaquín Mortiz.

"L'AMÉRIQUE C'EST MOI": DANY LAFERRIÈRE AND THE BORDERLESS TEXT

Alvina Ruprecht

The geographical image of the *border* (elaborated by E. Hicks) and the concepts embedded in this notion of territorial limits become the departure point for an analysis of some of the literary mechanisms used by Haitian-Canadian writer Dany Laferrière in his three North American novels. Translating the border dynamics by means of ironic images of transgressive sexual behaviour as well as parodic reappropriations of French, North American and Caribbean literary canons, Laferrière produces a provocative literary performance that aims at subverting stereotypical thinking about blackness.

L'image géographique de la *frontière* (élaborée par E. Hicks) et les concepts inscrits dans cette notion qui jouent sur les limites territoriales, deviennent le point de départ d'une analyse des méchanismes littéraires qui se retrouvent dans les trois romans «américains» de l'écrivain haitien-canadien Dany Laferrière. Une ironie, ancrée dans un comportement sexuel transgressif ainsi que dans la réappropriation des traces textuelles des littératures canoniques françaises, nord-américaines et antillaises, permet à l'auteur de produire une performance littéraire provocatrice qui subvertit les stéréotypes associées à la notion d'une identité noire.

*

THE WRITINGS OF DANY LAFERRIÈRE, and more specifically his three North American novels[1] centered on the adventures of a sexually insatiable black man, are examples of textual hybridity, characteristic of "Border Writing," as defined, among others, by Emily Hicks (1991). This notion, inscribed in a geographical metaphor, is the nucleus of a multidisciplinary network of categories useful to the understanding of a writer like Laferrière, whose work paradoxically defies and encompasses borders of all kinds.

The border as metaphor, evokes, among other things, a space securely partitioned by physical limits but where the different areas defined by those limits must inevitably co-exist (Hicks 1991, p.xxiii). This space produces a de-territorialized gaze which encompasses everything appearing on both sides of the boundary and also registers instability, movement, incessant leaving, arriving or crossing over. In this space, composed of a confluence of traditions where subjects pass through leaving traces that impact upon the status quo, notions of origin and authenticity are necessarily put into question. Border space, the point where one leaves one's place of origin, historicizes origins. It shapes them as a sequence of moments subjected to new arrivals and new influences, a space which is constantly becoming and therefore un-rooted and disconnected from its past.

Just as important is the way in which the border metaphor evokes a play of literary and linguistic mechanisms and strategies. In the case of Laferrière, these intertextual relations rely on parody, on a fragmented narrative held together by a single narrating voice, on an intertwining of oral and scribal boundaries, and on a multiplicity of encounters between high literary tradition and what Bakhtine calls "le corps grotesque," the low body of popular culture (Bakhtine, 1990, p.35).

Most striking, however, is the way in which the redefining of literary territories as a co-existence of boundaries that are respected, transgressed, displaced, but always interdependent, takes place as highly problematic sites in these three novel, within the representation of racialized relations. Laferrière sees North America as a space where tenuous borders exist in a constant flow and intermingling of ethnic groups; this has resulted in or is inevitably bound up with racial confrontation: "La guerre fait rage au Nouveau Monde ... la confrontation Blanc/Noir ... il n'y a que ça qui m'intéresse en Amérique" (Laferrière, 1993, p.13). Using the three novels, which constitute a trilogy because they all involve the same narrator moving across the Northern continent, the author represents this confrontation by waging his own "war" against racial stereotyping. Operating on the terrain of language where he confirms Henry Louis Gates' notion of race which distinguishes between the physical (biological) reality of dark skin and the various meanings produced by the notion of blackness functioning as "a dangerous trope" (Gates, 1986, p.5), Laferrière inscribes his principal character, Nègre, in the paradigm of constructed difference. He rewrites Simone de Beauvoir's statement, "On ne naît pas Nègre, on le devient" (Laferrière, 1985, p.153) and makes it the postface of his first novel. Henceforth, race has replaced gender and Laferrière's battlelines are clearly drawn.[2]

Laferrière, who lends his own voice to the narrator in these three novels, thus blurring the distinction between the central character and the author, cannot help but inspire a certain curiosity about his own life experience as a possible source of clues to his texts. We learn, not surprisingly, that the author is a border subject himself. His life has been a constant defiance of territorial limits. Born in Haiti, where he wrote controversial commentary for a local paper, he arrived in Montreal in 1976 where he continued his journalistic activity, publishing in the *Haiti Observer* of New York.[3] His first novel appeared in 1985 in Montreal and he has since published five more works, one of which won the Grand Prix Carbet (1991).[4] In 1990, he left Montreal to settle in Miami. Although he lives in Florida now, he continues publishing in French in Montreal and appears regularly on Quebec television as a literary and social critic. One of his recent works, *Cette grenade dans la main du jeune nègre, est-elle une arme ou un fruit,* is part novel, part film scenario, part journalistic account of a real and symbolic voyage across the United States, where the narrator comes into contact with issues currently erupting in that country. Thus the crossing of geographical, socio-political, linguistic, cultural and ideological borders constitutes the author's real life experience. Nevertheless, it is Laferrière's inscription into a predominantly white North American society as a Haitian (i.e., black French-speaking male from the Caribbean) that underlies the whole of this lived experience. From his multidimensional and highly unstable border space has emerged a vast network of multilayered linguistic and textual strategies through which he confronts discourses about blackness and the relation between his "colour" and racist perceptions of interhuman activity, based on colour differences. How then does this border writer, who is uncomfortable within boundaries, represent the deconstruction of racial stereotyping, and show, with Gates that this "war" is ultimately the product of and constituting factor of a "pernicious act of language" (Gates, 1986, p.5).

Verbal provocation becomes the first weapon. The title of Laferrière's first novel, *Comment faire l'amour avec un nègre sans se fatiguer,* was meant to provoke the Quebec public and it did. Non-black Québécois saw it as an insult; non-white Québécois said the author seemed to be condoning stereotypes. Especially revealing, however, was the reaction of certain Haitians in Montreal who also appeared uncomfortable with this book for other reasons. According to them, this author "does not write like a Haitian: from his novel, you can't even tell he is a Haitian."[5] Expectations about writing "like a Haitian" pose the whole question of boundaries. They imply that somehow, Laferrière's writing is not legitimate, precisely because he has not respected his particular origins. The author provides a laconic quip in a more recent work, almost as though he had foreseen the objection: "Toujours la même connerie. Les gens doivent écrire sur leur coin d'origine. J'écris sur ce qui se passe aujourd'hui là où je vis" (Laferrière, 1993, p.15).

It is obvious from Laferrière's other novels[6] that he does not reject his origins as a Haitian, but his representation of his place of origin is imbedded in the multiple histories of the past. His writing does not reflect a lived experience which stops at the border of Haiti, a country he left 17 years earlier. Rejecting the "salvage paradigm" discussed by James Clifford,[7] the body of Laferrière's work rejects stereotypes of exotic Haitianness by refusing to reduce origins to homogeneous definitions frozen in time. Since Laferrière insists he can write only from the present, he cannot avoid the layers of lived experience as well as material and discursive practices that act on his own particular consciousness. Characteristically, in a recent interview about his latest book, the author stated: "Chacun est susceptible de dire l'Amérique c'est moi" (Chartier,1993), and he constantly refers to America as a "tout" (Laferrière, 1985, p.29), something he wants to grasp in its totality with all its differences. By referring to each American as incarnating a totality composed of a sum of differences, he suggests the ironic play which is fundamental to his literary production. As a statement, *L'Amérique c'est moi* becomes a parody of two texts that refer to the cultural background of the author as an inhabitant of a former French colony, as the offspring of African slaves and as a Haitian growing up on what was formerly the Island of Hispaniola where the contacts between the Spanish (Cuba, the Dominican Republic) and the French colonies all contributed to the construction of this "moi Américain." This statement *L'Amérique c'est moi* evokes Laferrière's French colonial education as it becomes a rewording of the declaration by the French King Louis XIV, *L'état c'est moi,* a laconic summing up of the political theory of the divine right of kings who incarnate the State and, more relevantly, justify metropolitan power over the colonies. Laferrière, looking back to his slave ancestry, reverses the roles of power by suggesting that he is himself the incarnation of the continent; in so doing, he thumbs his nose at the French State and blithely rewrites French history while paradoxically acknowledging his own French colonial background—part of his Haitian past he cannot erase.

However, this statement also echoes the notion of José Marti's *nuestra América mestiza* (Martí, 1974, p.25). This fundamental concept which structures the thinking of the Cuban writer, philosopher and spiritual father of the revolution, sums up the nature of the new American individual as a mixture of cultures and races, characteristic of the Caribbean and of Latin American populations, as opposed to the white Eurocentered individual of North America. Thus by stating L'Amérique c'est moi, Laferrière borrows discourses from two geographical locations and several cultural sources representing two opposing ideological positions, but he conciliates them by binding them in a multi-layered syncretic context. Similar strategies can be traced throughout all his writing where he links not only two opposing sources, but sometimes four or five, subjecting them to a constant flow of provocative associations until all hope of a unique or authentic origin is rendered impossible; the borders are constantly blurred and redefined until the verbal play-acting, the textual performance itself becomes the dominant reality. But that is, of course, the focus of these works.

Laferrière rejects any kind of unique origin either in terms of his own lived experience or in terms of his aesthetic and linguistic production; and so we might say that Laferrière's writing produces an extremely insecure and borderless space symbolized by the way language inevitably calls everything into question, especially the identity of the protagonist Nègre. Uneasy definitions of identity, of blackness and whiteness as well as of interracial relations, and how these relations are constituted as problematized sites through language, are the very foundation of his creative effort. More unsettling still, in his first novels, the writer confronts the unsuspecting Québécois and Canadian reader with all these questions by filtering them through provocative discourses on sex.

—La question raciale reste très importante pour moi.

—De quelle manière?

—Du point de vue sexuel. Je ne connais pas un seul Blanc que le sujet de la baise interraciale ne fasse pas saliver. (Laferrière, 1993, p.14)

Of course, when Laferrière talks about sex, he means the sexual act, ritual fucking (l*a baise*), no seduction, no emotional or sentimental play; the author is interested in the workings of the genitals, the hips, the pelvis, the stomach and all the "lower body functions" that constitute the bakhtinian vulgar *popular* body.[8] Obviously, writing about sex in such mechanical street terms and locating this "popular oriented" language within such a literary framework, transforms these acts and their accompanying verbal patter into a highly subversive force; the novel becomes precisely the weapon of the third title *Cette grenade* ..., a means of disturbing the reader by unexpectedly confronting him or her with all that polite Canadian society dare not say aloud. This becomes then the perfect weapon, the best means to explode white supremist racial stereotyping. All the women in these novels— the majority are liberal Montreal anglophones—that have relations with the narrator, are white, because it is this black/white mixture which produces the most violent racially related negative reactions from the hostile segment of the population. However, apart from the fear and abhorrence of these sexual relations felt by those who wield the stereotypes the author wants to destroy,[9] fantasy and obsession stalk the black narrator. The perpetrator of this unmentionable sexual frenzy, recognizes himself as the target of the European/colonial fascination with the dark body of the "primitive" other, erased from the history of European/American populations. Laferrière parodies this colonial relationship, linking the movements of this vulgar popular body with high Metropolitan culture, more specifically, "Le déjeuner sur l'herbe,"—Manet's (1862) scandalous painting that changed the course of modern art history. Within the logic of gender discourse, the naked lady sitting in the forest with two clothed males was considered morally transgressive by bourgeois Metropolitan French society; similarly, within the logic of racialized discourse, two black males cut off from the outside world of metropolitan Montreal, contemplating interracial sexual relations implies equally scandalous behaviour.

> Deux Nègres dans un appartement crasseux de la rue Saint-Denis ... C'est le *DEJEUNER DES PRIMITIFS.* Le thé bout. On n'a pas de radio, pas de télé, pas de téléphone, pas de journal. Rien qui nous relie à cette foutue planète. L'Histoire ne s'intéresse pas à nous et nous, on ne s'intéresse pas à l'Histoire. C'est le kif kif ... (Laferrière, 1985, p.33)

Laferrière's textual performances on fucking function more effectively than anything else as strategies of demythification. The colonial stereotype of the dark other as closest to the "primitive," transforms sexual relations between the black male and the white female into the ultimate transgression because they occur precisely as an act of ironic ontological destruction, bringing the white human being closest to the "animal," a rejection of the Christian duality which values the mind and the spirit over the flesh. In *Eroshima,* delving into Gates' "pernicious act of language," the author uses the image of the atomic bomb as a humorously exaggerated symbolization of the profoundly destructive effect of interracial fucking: "Si vous voulez un aperçu de la guerre nucléaire, mettez un Nègre et une Blanche dans un lit" (Laferrière, 1985, p.19). And there you have it—the end of our basic Judeo-Christian values, and all the societies that have flourished around them.

In his second novel *Eroshima,* Laferrière locates his images (Eros-Hiroshima) in Freudian theories of Eros (instinct of pleasure and survival) and Thanatos (the attraction to death), two opposing but closely related human impulses, which Freud tells us are interdependent. Here, such associations naturalize the "dangerous" attraction of racially different couples, confirm their normality, inevitably heighten the provocation and set the scene for a whole series of playful encounters intended to make the interracially unconverted's hair stand on end.

In all these works, the author proposes a single narrating voice called Nègre.[10] Although the voice does have a specific address in Montreal, and therefore can be located in an identifiable reality, the only concrete characteristics of the voice are its gender, its "black" skin, its language and its identification with the author—this French-speaking male voice is also a writer/journalist in the process of writing the book and/or producing a series of articles. These are all, therefore, metafictional texts in which the narrator, while discussing the writing of fiction, the form of the American novel and his own aesthetic choices, writes himself into the texts as he proceeds.

> —T'écris, Vieux?
> —Qu'est-ce que c'est?
> —Un roman.
> —Dis pas ... un roman! Un vrai roman?
> —Ben ... un court roman. Pas vraiment un roman, plutôt des phantasmes.
> —Raconte ça.
> —C'est simple, c'est un type, un Nègre, qui vit avec un copain qui passe son temps couché sur un Divan à ne rien faire sinon à méditer, à lire le Coran, à écouter du jazz et à baiser quand ça vient.
> —Hé, Vieux, ça me plaît. J'aime l'idée du type qui ne fout rien.
> —Normal, puisque j'ai utilisé tes traits.

> —Ah! ces écrivains, tous des salauds, rien que des salauds.
>
> ... Le saxe de Hawkins joue "Body and Soul"(1939). (Laferrière, 1985, p.55)

"Nègre" is, therefore, on the one hand, a non-essentialist literary creation, a linguistically constructed voice inscribed into North American literary traditions, and legitimated by Laferrière who layers his text with countless literary allusions and parodies. On the other hand, "Nègre" is the parody of the colonial "primitive," this ambivalent stereotype produced as a fixed unchanging reality, the site of phobia but also of fetich, just as Said's "oriental," the site of "dreams, images, fantasies, myths obsessions" (Bhabha, 1986, pp.159-161). Nègre parodies his role as primitive man by playing out the "vengeance of the oppressed according to those terrifying stereotypical images of savagery, cannibalism, lust and anarchy ... the scenes of fear and desire in colonial texts" (Bhabha, 1986, p.159).

In the first novel, Nègre's roommate, the other black French-speaking male called Bouba spends his time reading the Koran, reflecting on non-Western philosophy and sleeping. His is the passive, feminized, "meditative" voice of the East (also a product of Western clichés), while Nègre actively assumes the male function as the subversive fantasy playing out these stereotypes in his encounters with white women. With much howling, screaming, dramatic noisemaking and intermittent discussion, a lively succession of white female fantasies, which are just as much the product of Nègre's fantasy as he is the product of the white racist fantasy, parade through his Montreal apartment and into his bed, with stops in his kitchen and bathroom to accomplish all the other lower body functions. The women, like Nègre, have no individual identity, but represent specific classes, as well as cultural and social groups. There is the white female intellectual from McGill University (Miz Littérature); the white female upper middle class (Miz Snob); and the white female lower middle class (Miz Punk, Miz Suicide). In *Eroshima,* there is even self-parody of the narrator's own cliché-ridden images of Japanese women who appear as mysterious creatures partaking in special sexual behaviour which mirrors Nègre's own secret desires and erotic fantasies. There is too, for this stereotypical black voice, the ultimate sexual fantasy of the black man—as assumed by the white male population—the unattainable North-American blond, the unique construction of white American pop culture which has, confesses the narrator—echoing the stereotype—conquered the non-white males of the Third world. This reworking of already existing stereotypes produces a *mise en abyme,* an infinite mirroring of images which absorbs the narrator into its own momentum, reducing these notions to arbitrary acts of language and eliminating any possibility of authentic identities.

In this deconstruction of prejudice and racism by a parodic playing with the discourses that produce these ideas, sex is only an enticing starting point. Moving from the lower body, Bakhtine's "*corps grotesque*" more closely related to oral forms of language (orature) (Cooper, 1993, p.9), Laferrière moves over to scribal traditions, to high cultural sources—parodies of racial stereotyping inspired by various literary sources. The author talks about "Négriture" (Laferrière, 1985, p.17), his own parodic binding of "Littérature" and "Négritude," his way of confirming Gates' "dangerous trope," since, according to our author, writing based on the notion of "blackness," can only function in as much as it subjects those criteria to an ironic deconstruction.

Ultimately then, Laferrière's "Black writing" starts its process of demythification with discourses on sex that dissolve into a multiplicity of literary strategies, which appear disruptive but in fact echo the mirroring produced by the sexual relations portrayed so energetically by the author. For example, in *Comment faire l'amour ...* the enclosed cocoon-like world of Bouba and Nègre, perfumed with incense and threatened by the thunderous Beezelbub, a noisy neighbour living directly above. This chaotic sanctuary and stifling microcosm, where Bouba chants and reads the Koran and where Nègre carries out his strenuously multicoloured and carnavalesque activity, parodies the American counter-culture of the 1960s as foretold by the American Beat writers and specifically by the works of Jack Kerouac. In *Cette grenade ...*, the writer refers to the structure of the American novel, an obvious allusion to the text which the narrator is in the process of writing, as well as those he has already written: "une collection de textes brefs, reliés entre eux par un fil souple et solide" (Laferrière, 1993, p.27).

Maintaining the literary references, Laferrière transforms Nègre's roommate, Bouba, into a parody of the counter-culture guru and its obsession with oriental philosophy, essential to all Beat writing: "affalé sur le Divan dans sa pose habituelle (couché sur le côté gauche, face à la Mecque) à siroter du thé de Shangaï tout en feuilletant un bouquin de Freud" (Laferrière, 1985, p.13). The descriptions of his (in)activity become reworded excerpts from the Koran as well as direct quotes from the book.

> Son sommeil est, parfois aussi aigu que la trompette de Miles Davis. Bouba est alors ramassé sur lui-même, le visage fermé, les genoux repliés sous le Menton.(...) Le Coran dans sa pleine magnanimité dit: "tu fais succéder la nuit au jour et le jour à la nuit, tu fais sortir la vie de la mort et la mort de la vie. Tu accordes la nourriture à qui du veux sans compte ni mesure". (sourate, III, 26). Bouba espère ainsi gagner sa place aux côtés d'Allah (que son saint nom soit béni). (Laferrière, 1985, pp.12-13)

Through his linguistic choices and ordering of the text, Laferrière rewrites the American road novel in which he appropriates the jazz rhythms characteristic of Kerouac, Ginsberg and the Beat poets. This jazz-related phenomenon is analyzed in detail by Regina Weinreich (1990). The "spontaneous bop prosody" (Weinreich, 1990, p.8), the "free prose ... a deliberate attempt to dissect and analyze the sources and the patterns of the music itself" (Weinrich, 1990, p.22). Among Kerouac's literary structures inspired by the jazz riffs is "the brief musical phrase that is repeated, sometimes with a very subtle variation ... improvisation ... the control of cadence" (Weinreich, 1990, pp.8-9), while cutting, mixing and integrating various fragments on related themes, in repetitious rhythms and sound patterns. All these are literary adaptations of the techniques of improvisation related to jazz composition. In this way, parts of Laferrière's texts become musical scores:

> On attend avec impatience, en haleine, la fin du monde. L'Apocalypse privée. Sur mesure. SILENCE. Puis ce cri tendu, en contre-ut, aigu, soutenu, inhumain, tantôt allegro, tantôt andante, tantôt pianissimo, cri interminable, inconsolable, électronique, asexué, sur fond de saxe Parker; unique, chant de cette aube.(Laferrière, 1985, p.15)

Of course, these sources have their beginnings in black American culture, but Laferrière picks up the literary adaptations through the Beat writer's appropriation of the music. Eventually, though, he carries them much further, producing texts that are explicitly angry and polemical.

His short literary pastiches which resound like improvised variations on anti-racist themes, borrow from the writings of Franz Fanon, among others. His parody of Fanon's *Peau noire, masque blanc,* especially chapter 3, "L'homme de couleur et la Blanche," produces a pseudo-philosophical, sociological and psychological patter, spotted with learned vocabulary, smatterings of popular slang, with a final ironic return to the naif universe of French painter Matisse where the representation of living beings rejects all stereotypical typology. Everything is seen through a completely new prism.

C'est ça le drame, dans les relations sexuelles du Nègre et de la Blanche (...) C'est que dans l'échelle des valeurs occidentales, la Blanche est inférieure au Blanc et supérieure au Nègre. C'est pourquoi elle n'est capable de prendre véritablement son pied qu'avec le Nègre (...) Il n'y a de véritable relation sexuelle qu'inégale. LA BLANCHE DOIT FAIRE JOUIR LE BLANC, ET LE NEGRE, LA BLANCHE. D'où le mythe du Nègre grand baiseur. Bon baiseur, oui. Mais pas avec la Négresse. C'est à la Négresse à faire jouir le Nègre (...) ET VOILA MIZ LITTERATURE QUI ME FAIT UNE DE CES PIPES (...) En tant que Noir, je n'ai pas assez de recul par rapport au Nègre. Le Nègre est-il ce cochon sensuel? Le Blanc, ce cochon transparent? Le Jaune, ce cochon raffiné? Le Rouge, ce cochon saignant? Seul le Porc est Porc. Je ne sais pourquoi j'ai toujours imaginé l'univers comme cette toile de Matisse. (Laferrière, 1985, pp.43-44)

In language terms, portions of the text become accumulations of clichés, popular slogans, ironic associations and word games, to create playful circular movement like a jazz riff. The longs lists of images and repeated sounds produce analogies and isolated clumps of meaning through a global process of association. Typical is this brief historical overview of *Le Nègre* in America, as depicted by this list of anti-black clichés, references to the relationship between racism and economics anchored in current discourses about Haitian refugees, and ironic shifts of vocabulary, as told by our generic narrator Nègre. The author's musical ear organizes sound associations so that the text produces the discordant screech of the improvising saxaphone along with the fine tuned harmony of layer upon layer of literary sources all converging in an angry monologue:

Ca va terriblement mal ces temps-ci pour un dragueur nègre consciencieux et professionnel. On dirait la période de la NEGRITURE terminée, has been, caput, finito, rayée, Nègre, out. Go home Nigger. La Grande Passe Nègre, finie! Hasta la vista, Negro. Last call, Coloured. Retourne à la brousse, p'tit Nègre. Faites-vous hara-kiri là où vous savez. Regarde, maman, dit la Jeune Blanche, regarde le Nègre Coupé. Un bon Negre, lui répond le père est un Nègre sans couilles. Bon, bref, telle est la situation en ce début des années '80 marquées d'une pierre noire dans l'histoire de la Civilisation Nègre. A la bourse des valeurs occidentales, le bois d'ébène a encore chuté. si, au moins le Nègre éjaculait du pétrole. L'or Noir. TRISTE, LE SPERME DU NEGRE EST BLANC. (Laferrière, 1985, p.17)

In *Eroshima,* there are constant references to the *Kama-Sutra,* providing a literary pretext for his voyeuristic relationships as Nègre observes sado-masochistic and lesbian encounters with Hoki, Keiko, Reiko and Kéro, his Japanese roommates more counter-parody of his own stereotypical vision of the world which he continues to explode by seeking out more racial and ethnic permutations and combinations. These appear as a variety of sexual encounters with women from Berlin, Rome, Port au Prince, San Juan, Manhattan, Montreal, and the Hassidic community of Brooklyn. In this gallery filled with an array of female bodies and voices, each choice represents the ironic twisting of a stereotype through the subversive fantasy world of our omnipotent and sexually ravenous narrator/voyeur "qui bande à faire sauter le voltmètre" (Laferrière, 1987, p.89). One of the most interesting literary transpositions of this appetite is entitled "Un paysage du Douanier Rousseau retouché par V.S. Naipaul." Here, Laferrière, referring to the works of the French naif artist, which have been associated with forms of contemporary Haitian painting, reconstitutes a new naif paradise: a cartoon-like, gaudy and vulgar American pop-culture influenced and sexually explicit urban landscape which could be Florida, but which turns out to be Port au Prince (Haiti). V.S. Naipaul, the Trinidadian writer, becomes the voyeur, observing the seductive rituals of courting, cleansing and flirting as carried out by familiar laferriéresque fantasies: a group of young, beautiful, scantily clad and sexually aggressive Haitian women.

In the third novel, *Cette grenade* ..., Nègre travels across the United States, documenting all the discourses that constitute a great variety of cultural and racial relations in that country. One of his aims seems to be to dispel any illusions of a homogeneous black culture and to show the multiple borders and cultural crossings by confronting "high literary" and "popular" cultural icons. An imaginary interview with James Baldwin, the homosexual writer and one of the canons of 20th century American writing is set off against a particular vision of super-model Naomi Campbell, an icon of American fashion and black American feminine beauty. Nobel prize winner Derek Walcott, whose literary production is itself a fusion of a vast multiplicity of cultural influences, meets Rodney King, the star of amature video and the focus of recent racial/political activism in the United States. Miles Davis, who isn't interested in all that "tradition shit" greets Nègre with "fuck you," while a discussion with rapper Ice Cube, becomes a dialogue that turns into a prodding and poking match over the singer's racial politics with strong suggestions that Laferrière does not appreciate the reasoning of the Reverend Farrakhan. Laferrière's writing echoes not only literary works but eventually the daily news and tabloid journalism.

Ultimately, Laferrière confirms the thinking of Uruguayan poet Eduardo Galleano who says in a filmed interview (*L'Etre américain*, Société Radio-Canada, 1992) that we are living in societies "infected with racial democracy" because we live in "Bobalia, the land of the great stupidity.... Racism is a crime against the intelligence. It blinds us to what is best about ourselves. It deafens us to our own voices." Nègre then circulates through all these texts, trying to see and hear clearly, by banishing the stupidity through humour and subversive associations.

He inserts his literary voices not only into North American, European and Caribbean traditions but he draws also on non-Western canons, the *Koran*, *Kama-Sutra*. *Eroshima* is also indebted to popular Japanese poetry, specifically the Haiku in its original form, the Haikai.[11] The result is a writing that mixes and transgresses all borders, suggesting what Benedict Anderson calls *imagined communities* (1983), what Edouard Glissant calls *Tout-monde* (1993), what Benitez-Rojo calls, perhaps more problematically, *the culture of the Archipelago* (1992) and even what Bernabé, Confiant and Chamoiseau call *Créolité* (1989). These notions do not refer to the same cultural dynamic, but they all signify, in some way, the necessary questioning of arbitrary geo-political boundaries, in an attempt to understand the way identities are represented and constructed.

It is significant, however, that in spite of the literary framework and textual allusions, Laferrière refers to his texts as a series of "spasmes" (Chartier, 1993), therefore primarily a kinetic activity, free of intellectual or psychological intrusion, a form of creation centered on the body and its performance. He would seem to illustrate Paul Gilroy's remarks in relation to music, but which apply directly to certain forms of linguistic-based texts:

> The distinctive kinesis of the postslave populations ... ought to contribute directly to the understanding of the traditions of performance that continue to characterize the production and reception of African diaspora musics. This orientation to the specific dynamics of performance has a wider significance in the analysis of Black cultural forms than has so far been supposed. Its strengths are evident when it is contrasted with approaches to Black culture that have been premised on textuality and narrative rather than, say, on dramaturgy, enunciation and gesture—pre- and anti-discursive constituents of black metacommunication.... All of them are marked by their compound and multiple origins in the mediation of the African and other cultural forms that are sometimes referred to as "creolization." (Gilroy, 1991, p.114)

Obviously, when Laferrière has Nègre wear the mask of the black male stereotype (perhaps also in reference to Genet's play *Les Nègres*) and when he talks about kinetic creation, he is thinking in terms of performance, corporeal theatre and one of its instruments, the human voice. In fact, Laferrière's texts are highly theatrical. The speaking voice is dealt with primarily as part of the body—it is located in vocal chords, sounds, rhythms, movement, energy and prosodic effects, presented through the text in performance modes: musical scores, dramatic monologues, dialogues, soliloquies, interruptions, participatory voyeuristic descriptions, journalistic accounts of the observer in the middle of the action and stand up comic gags, smart one-liners and double meanings, all seen as verbal confrontation between the voices in the text or between the performer and his imaginary audience, the reader. He adopts the performance strategies of an actor, his provocation, his seduction, his titillation, his poking and prodding echo the comic routines of black American pop culture sources, the split second sense of humour and the flippant and angry one liners like those of Eddy Murphy and Arsenio Hall. However, they also go back to the strategies used by the American performance companies of the 1960s counter-culture, to transform passive audiences into activists and protesters. Just as the Living Theatre wanted to create anti-war protest, perhaps Dany Laferrière is trying to produce anti-racist activists. But whether his texts function as provocative rituals of transformation intended to produce real life change or whether they are read as literary parodies intended to subvert North American and European canonic texts, the notion of "border" with its multiple, contradictory, overlapping, heterogeneous and hybrid categories provides a perfect framework for the reading of this writer whose corrosive humour cannot be contained by or inserted into precise definitions of any kind.

ENDNOTES

1. (1985) *Comment faire l'amour avec un nègre sans se fatiguer.* VLB; (1987) *Eroshima.* VLB; (1993) *Cette grenade dans la main du jeune nègre est-elle une arme ou un fruit?* VLB. Since I began this article, the author has published a fourth book in his North American series. It deals with his first years in Montreal and is located in time just before that of the first novel: (1994) *Chronique d'une dérive douce.* VLB.
2. The notion of race and its treatment in English-Canadian fiction has been explored from a sociological point of view by Terrence Craig (1985); *Racial Attitudes in English-Canadian Fiction 1905-1980.* Waterloo: Wilfrid Laurier University Press.

3. Much autobiographical detail of his own life in Haiti is revealed in his Haitian cycle of novels and in (1994) *Chronique d'une dérive douce.* VLB.
4. (1991) *L'Odeur des jeunes filles.* Montréal: VLB.
5. Remarks noted during informal conversations with Haitians in Montreal.
6. (1991) *L'Odeur du café.* VLB; (1992) *Le Goût des jeunes filles.* VLB.
7. The "salvage paradigm" is a geopolitical and historical paradigm that has organized Western practices of 'art-and culture-collecting' reflecting a desire to "rescue authenticity out of destructive historical change.... In western taxonomy and memory, the various non-Western 'ethnographic presents' are ... always about to undergo the impact of disruptive changes associated with the influence of trade, media, missionaries, commodities, ethnographers, tourists, the exotic art market, the world system ... a deluge of corruption transformation, modernization.... A good country is perpetually ruined and lamented by each successive period, producing an unbroken chain of losses leading back ultimately to ... Eden" (Clifford, 1987, p.121-122).
8. A la différence des canons modernes, le corps grotesque ... franchit ses propres limites. L'accent est mis sur les parties du corps où ... le monde pénètre en lui ou en sort ... c'est-à-dire aux orifices, aux protubérances, à toutes les ramifications et excroissances : bouche bée, organes génitaux, seins, phallus, gros ventre, nez. Le corps ne révèle son essence, ... que dans des actes tels que l'accouplement, la grossesse, l'accouchement, l'agonie, le manger, le boire, la satisfaction des besoins naturels (Bakhtine, 1990, p.35).
9. Homi Bhabha, referring to F. Fanon and E. Said analyzes the ambivalence of the colonial stereotype and shows how, crucial to the range of differences and discriminations that inform the practices of racial and cultural hierarchization, the racialized body is inscribed in an economy of pleasure and an economy of power as much as in an economy of fear (Bhabha,1986, pp.150-155).
10. In a recent article, James Arnold analyzes *créolité* in the light of what he calls an Erotics of Colonialism. According to this male dominated dynamic, the role delegated by Dany Laferrière to his predatory narrator Nègre corresponds to the gendered master narrator, le "conteur," the dominant male voice, replacing the super-male figure of the Maroon who never made his place in the Francophone literature of the West Indies, in what James Arnold and gender theorists see as the voice of the erotics of colonialism inscribed in the male-centered notion of *Créolité.* This analysis is of course interesting but Laferrière does not take this male narrator at his face value—he is constantly subverting him, and unmasking him as a colonial construction.
11. The Haikai, an autonomous genre, admits popular and vulgar expressions and does not require any particular education to understand. In the 17th century, it became a fashionable popular pastime within all the social milieux. Thanks to the poet Basho, it transcended, at the end of the 17th century, the limits of burlesque

poetry, and was transformed into a more refined form of expression, the Haiku. Haikai was revitalised by Massaoka Shiki at the end of the 19th century. Haiku, the japanese poem of 17 syllables, was the result of a breaking away from the Haikai form of which it retained the first three lines. (1983). Haikai. *Grand dictionnaire encylopédique Larousse,* Editions Larousse, 5, p.5118.

REFERENCES

Anderson, B. (1983). *Imagined communities: Reflections on the origin and spread of nationalism.* London: Verso.

Arnold, J. (1994). The Erotics of colonialism in contemporary French West Indian literary culture. *New West Indian Guide,* 68, pp.5-22.

Bakhtine, M. (1990). *L'Oeuvre de François Rabelais et la culture populaire au moyen âge sous la Renaissance.* Paris: Gallimard.

Benítez-Rojo, A. (1992). *The Repeating island* (J. E. Maraniss, Trans.) London: Duke University Press.

Bernabé, J., Chamoiseau, P., & Confiant, R. (1989). *Eloge de la créolité.* Paris: Gallimard.

Bhabha, H.K. (1976). The other question: Difference, discrimination and the discourse of colonialism. *Literature, politics and theory, papers from the Essex conference* (pp.148-172). London: Methuen.

Bordeleau, F. (1994, Printemps). Dany Laferrière sans arme et dangereux; entrevue. *Lettres québécoises,* 73, (pp.9-10).

Chartier, J. (1993, Septembre). Laferrière dégoupille. *Le Devoir,* 21, p.D2.

Clifford, J. (1987). Of other peoples: Beyond the "Salvage Paradigm." In Hal Foster (Ed.), *Discussions in contemporary culture* (pp.121-130). Seattle WA: Bay Press.

Cooper, C. (1993). *Noises in the blood: Orality, gender and the "vulgar" body of Jamaican popular culture.* London: MacMillan Press.

Craig T. (1985). *Racial attitudes in English-Canadian fiction 1905-1980.* Waterloo: Wilfrid Laurier University Press.

Fanon, F. (1952). *Peau noire masque blanc.* Paris: Editions du Seuil.

Gates, H.L. (1986). Editor's Introduction: Writing "race" and the difference it makes. *Race, writing and difference* (pp.1-20). Chicago: University of Chicago Press.

Gilroy, P. (1991). Sounds authentic: black music, ethnicity, and the challenge of the changing same. *Black Music Research Journal,* 2, pp.111-136.

Glissant, E. (1993). *Tout-monde.* Paris: Gallimard.

Guay, H. (1983). Haikai. *Grand dictionnaire encyclopédique.* Larousse. Editions Larousse, 5, p.5118.

Guay, H. (1994, 11 septembre). L'écrivain qui se dessinait un visage. *Le Devoir,* p.D10.

Hicks, E. (1991). *Border writing, the multidimensional text.* Minneapolis: University of Minnesota Press.

Hall, S. (1992). What is this "black" in black popular culture? In G. Dent (Ed.) *Black popular culture* (pp.21-33). Seattle: Bay Press

Hutcheon, L. (1985). *A theory of parody.* New York: Methuen.

JanMohamed, A. (1986). The Economy of manichean allegory: the function of racial difference in colonialist literature. In H.L. Gates (Ed.) *"Race", writing and difference* (pp.78-106). Chicago: University of Chicago Press.

Laferrière, D. (1985). *Comment faire l'amour avec un nègre sans se fatiguer.* Montreal: VLB Editeur.

Laferrière, D. (1987). *Eroshima.* Montreal: VLB Editeur.

Laferrière, D. (1993). *Cette grenade dans la main du jeune nègre est-elle une arme ou un fruit?* Montreal: VLB Editeur.

Martí, J. (1974). *José Martí nuestra América.* La Habana: Casa de las Americas.

Pelletier, J. (1994, Printemps). Toutes couleurs réunies. *Lettres québécoises,* 73, pp.11-12.

Weinreich, Regina (1990). *The Spontaneous poetics of Jack Kerouac.* New York: Paragon House.

CHAPTER IV

INDIGENOUS CULTURES: CREATIVE ENCOUNTERS

CULTURE AND EDUCATION IN POST-COLONIAL DEVELOPMENT: A SOUTHERN ANDEAN STUDY

Maria-Inés Arratia

This article hopes to contribute to a clarification of the dynamic aspects of culture in order to help social scientists and development workers deal with minority cultures in post-colonial situations.

Recent research on native education in Northern Chile, shows a continued pattern of cultural domination which devalues local knowledge, fosters migration and produces a negative impact on community development.

The present case study is an analysis of the situation in one rural administrative district in the Chilean altiplano. A post-colonial pattern of resistance and accommodation and the presence of diverse external agents contribute to the problems and dilemmas faced by a greatly reduced native population which wants to survive and to foster development in its communities, in spite of the penetration of a market economy and the allure of modernity.

Il s'agit de contribuer à la clarification des aspects dynamiques du concept de «culture» afin d'aider les spécialistes en sciences sociales et les travailleurs sur le terrain, à mieux interagir avec des minorités culturelles en situation post-coloniale.

Des recherches récentes dans le domaine de l'éducation des autochtones au Nord du Chili, montre une tendance vers la mise en avant d'une forme d'expression culturelle qui dévalorise la connaissance locale, qui provoque l'immigration et qui, de manière générale, a un impact négatif sur le développement communautaire.

Cette étude repose sur l'analyse d'une situation dans une circonscription administrative rurale du haut plateau chilien. Un modèle de résistance et d'accomodation post-coloniale et la présence de divers agents externes, contribuent aux problèmes que doivent affronter une population indigène qui veut survivre et qui veut promouvoir le développement de ses communautés malgré la pénétration d'une économie de marché et ses promesses de modernité.

*

THIS PAPER DEALS PRIMARILY with the need to integrate local cultural dynamics into all activities related to community development, including education. It also deals with a particular positioning for social scientists committed to the defence of native cultures and to the promotion of a pluralistic and democratic attitude towards local development through the use of participatory methodologies (Fals Borda, 1979, 1980, 1987). Based on my field experience and understanding of development as cultural action, I am questioning previous categories of analysis and constructed theoretical positions affecting the various processes involved in community development.

In this paper I focus on development processes as they are situated within the interface between the Aymara communities and a series of external agents. Although relevant and significant, I do not address internal village dynamics such as gender and age differentials. This is meant as emphasis; it is not an oversight. My intent is to concentrate on one of the main features of cultural penetration into otherwise remote highland localities in the region of Tarapaca in northern Chile and to show the relevance of culture in education and in community development.

I begin with an historical overview of the regional context, to establish how issues in national development directly relate to the issues of penetration into the highlands and to cultural change. I then focus primarily on the role of education in the promotion of a particular kind of "modernity," and the negative impact this has played on local social organization. Finally, I make an argument for local development as the basis for an increased regional viability and the construction of a culturally pluralistic and democratic society. But first, a definition of culture is required.

Culture has been the domain of inquiry for anthropologists since the birth of the discipline. While culture tends to be generally defined as the arts (i.e., world philosophy, literature and the fine arts), the anthropological definition is much broader in scope. It entails "a bounded universe of shared ideas and customs" (Keesing, 1990, p.46) or, in a classic version, "that complex whole which includes knowledge, belief, art, morals, law, custom, and any other capabilities and habilities acquired by man [sic] as a member of society" (Tylor, 1871, p.1). More succinctly, it is "the way of life of a people" (Hatch, 1985, p.178). But the definitions are many, varying in nuances perhaps, but not in their holistic substance.

Integral to this holistic quality of culture is the process of its reproduction. Education in its broadest sense has been understood as the means for cultural transmission (Singleton, 1974), an important element in the process of enculturating the young. Thus culture and education are, supposedly, both part of the same way of life. What occurs in reality is somewhat different, given the development of formal educational patterns based on European concepts and visions. Education imposed on subordinated cultural groups in colonial and post-colonial situations is part of the cultural domination pattern.

CULTURAL CHANGE IN HISTORICAL PERSPECTIVE

Since the northern territories of Chile were annexed to the young nation-state at the end of the War of the Pacific (1883), a war fought over the rights to exploit nitrate, the central government had a particular concern regarding the "chileanization" of this territory. This region became a colonization zone for Chile. But its distance from the central zone and multicultural population has contributed to maintaining a specific "northerner" identity. For someone raised in the central zone of Chile, like myself, however, the *Norte Grande* appears heavily militarized and its way of life involves a great many militaristic rituals meant to glorify the birth of the Nation and the heroic feats of the "forefathers," even in the remote highland rural areas, where the population is Aymara, distinctly pastoral-agricultural with its own history, language and culture. Perhaps the imposition over the Aymara is stronger, since they are generally perceived as "Bolivian."

The highland Aymara are herders of llama and alpaca and as such have a dispersed settlement pattern throughout the area.[1] There are some nucleated villages in the highlands where elementary schools were built for Aymara children by the Chilean government. Despite the high rate of depopulation, some of these schools continue to operate. The Aymara also live in the agricultural canyons and valleys, in semi-urban settlements and in the cities of the north, where access to complete schooling is less of a problem, but where Aymara distinctiveness fosters discrimination.

With the opening of the roads from the coastal Chile to inland Bolivia, there is a penetration of "modernity" into the rural areas. As a result of this cultural process, urban migrations have increased and the young have acquired a taste for consumption. Their interest in their own community activities has waned considerably. The presence of the Chilean State in education and in the imposition of the national draft have been instrumental in these processes.

The military draft takes male youths away from their villages and into the barracks for at least one year (it used to be two years during the years of the military dictatorship). Even before young males reach the drafting age, male and female children have been socialized within the schools to adhere to the State with all its national symbols, including the colonial language, at the expense of their own cultural background.

EDUCATION: A MODERN INVASION

Primary schools in the low-lying rural areas began to appear at the turn of this century. In the highlands, the situation was markedly different because of the remoteness of the area. Literacy and basic math instruction were initially imparted by policemen stationed in the region and the first schools were opened only in the late 1950s.[2] And school buildings followed the standards for rural schools elsewhere.

National schools are visually, socially and culturally an intrusion in all rural villages, but the impact of their presence is perhaps felt more strongly in the life of highland villages, where the way of life is camel herding in wide open spaces, and where the population density is extremely low.

Schooling has disrupted the previous patterns of socialization of the younger generations oriented towards a pastoral or agricultural subsistence pattern, or both; it has placed children in chilly classrooms and constrained them into desk spaces that bear no connection with their pastoral activities out in the fields (Foucault, 1979); it has forced children to concentrate on written forms of communication which have no connection with the language of their homes or with their oral tradition, filled with stories dealing with the ethics of reciprocity and a holistic view of nature, the "cosmology" that guides their daily experiences. Instead, their reading books tell them (in Spanish) about buses, streets, shopping centres and the subway, all of which are quite relevant in the capital city, Santiago, but certainly not in the rural areas of the country. School then becomes an agent of modernization in its agenda to "civilize" Aymara children into Chilean ways. In short, education is a means of imposing what Pierre Bourdieu has called "symbolic violence" over a minority population (Bourdieu, 1972).

Further, the expense of having to conform to school rules, which include buying a uniform, books and other school items places a yearly economic burden on the parents to produce marketable items to cover these costs to the household. Within the household, education is seen both as a necessity and as a problem. All parents feel that children need to be educated so that they "will become better than us." They know that knowledge and power go together, and they have come to believe in the modern myth that an education will ensure a "better" future for their offspring. This is a hope shared by most parents anywhere. But what happens to the majority of highland youths is indeed quite remote from this possibility.

The national education program is completely urban-oriented and modernizing in the sense that it shapes a consumer population; it dislocates the young Aymara from their own surroundings, from their socialization within the kin group, and it delivers them deficiently trained into a discriminating, competitive society that refuses to even accept them as "Chilean," given their visible distinctiveness. The stories of the many pains of discrimination endured by young students arriving in the city are legion among the urban-Aymara. The general attitude observed both in Arica and Iquique substantiate these narratives.

Local reaction to the external nature of national schooling and of the cultural changes it has imposed, the patterns observed in the highland regions, are a mixture of accommodation and resistance. As various authors have indicated (Bourdieu, 1972 and 1984; Giddens, 1984), the insidious effects of long-term domination are internalized and reproduced through cultural practices that eventually become incorporated into the cultural system. These complex processes sometimes result in a "mirroring" of the dominating culture, while other times the outcome is a protective barrier.

ACCOMMODATION AND RESISTANCE

Accommodation is manifested in the hopes for a brighter future expressed by parents who have acquired a belief in the promise offered by the system. This is a well-established myth that can be traced back to the 1952 revolution in Bolivia, where the communities were able to gain important political rights. The situation in Bolivia developed along quite different paths, given its political, demographic and environmental conditions.[3] But the idea appealed to the Chilean Aymara, and the elders who played instrumental roles in pressuring the authorities for the provision of rural schoolteachers are proud of their contribution, despite the failure of the system to fulfill its promise.

Resistance is generally passive and silent. It becomes evident in the rifts between parents and teachers, in the ongoing litany of complaints that frustrated parents make of their children's abilities (or lack of) and in the insistence that children not abandon their household chores. Before or after their school period and during holiday times they are generally expected to uphold their share within the household. But this becomes increasingly complicated with the pressures to do homework for school. The parents know something is very wrong. Their children do not respect them as they should, nor do they show the expected interest in household activities. But they find no alternative solution to what they clearly identify as a problem. To a growing number of families the solution has been to send the children to the city where they are at least *assured* a proper education. Some parents hope that these youths might bring back new ideas to address their situation.

While sending children to the city might appear as a reasonable household solution, this alternative not only increases the vulnerability of the already disrupted community, it works against the possibility of strengthening it. It entails the loss of younger members and the potential loss of the household. In sending a child away, the family unit will be closer linked with an urban centre and incorporate this possibility into its subsistence strategies. If everything else fails, there is now the choice to move down (i.e., migrate). The reaction of children to this distance from the family unit varies by gender. In the majority of cases, distance creates a rather negative impact which appears to be worse on girls than boys.[4]

The pervasiveness of these patterns is evident in the steady urban migration flow and the increasing number of Aymara youths in boarding schools in semi-urban centres and localities closer to the cities and in the cities of Arica and Iquique.

These are some of the consequences of cultural domination and the imposition of an educational system that has no regard whatsoever for local identity, local knowledge, local cycles and more important, local sociocultural dynamics. The more recent political changes in Chile have allowed for a degree of acknowledgement of these problems, and this is indeed hopeful.

DEMOCRATIZATION AND EDUCATION

Since the inception of a democratically elected government in 1990, there have been some attempts to alter this pattern of domination and to restore the legitimacy of cultural distinctiveness as a first step in support of all native communities throughout Chile, the Aymara included. This effort has taken shape as the negotiations for a Native Law (passed in October, 1993) have fostered a new awareness about cultural diversity in Chile. In practice, it has meant a greater number of scholarships for native children so they can pursue higher levels of education.[5] During the electoral process in 1989, native groups met with the (then) candidate Aylwin and presented to him and the *concertación* (coalition of parties supporting his candidacy) a list of claims among which educational improvements and cultural rights were a high priority. The promise made by the Aylwin government of an education with quality and equality for all children has meant that educators have needed to reflect on what it is they have been doing and just how they have been "educating." The barrier to culturally sensitive education has been that the patternings within the institution of education have their own history, which is colonial in its fundamental tenets.

Teachers see themselves as dutifully carrying out their mission. And they are right. It is the mission that has been wrongly founded and wrongly aimed. They are under attack for committing a number of cultural blunders, yet cannot fully comprehend why they are being blamed. Teachers have been trained to deliver specific national (urban oriented) programs packaged by the Ministry of Education based in Santiago. The majority have not been encouraged nor trained to innovate. They expect certain results from applying the pedagogical techniques learned at university and in their frustration at the poor results obtained in national tests applied in their settings (the highland villages), they try to find new ways within their repertoire for these children to learn. But when they do so, they are not thinking of the dynamics of Aymara culture; they are pressuring the children to conform with the expectations of the system. They are "civilizing (i.e., modernizing) agents." There is little, if any, recognition of local cultural patterns, let alone the effects of long-term culture contact and the insidious effects of cultural domination.

The Ministry of Education has been well aware of the many problems in education, particularly since the reforms introduced by the military regime. Under the Aylwin government the ministry has attempted to promote curricular innovations through educational projects. Local school teachers everywhere have been encouraged to present proposals for project funding. While the initiative has potential and merit, it has not worked out as expected. Even when projects have been approved and started, the teachers have not had the necesarry skills to carry them out. This has required the hiring of support professionals, which in turn has meant a higher cost to a program with very limited funding.[6]

After a short trial period in 1992, the situation improved somewhat in 1993 through a ministerial program supported with international funding devoted to provide specific skills to the rural school population in the so-called "Concentration Schools" (grades 1-8).[7] In this latter case, however, the issue of "culture" has not been taken into account either. Rather, the predominant criterion has been to provide the students with specific skills to enter the job market.[8] This kind of training, although useful, does not resolve the dislocation problem for the youths, nor for the community.

DIRECTIONS FOR CHANGE: A PILOT PROJECT IN INTERCULTURAL EDUCATION

The negative effects of a nationally imposed educational system have been documented by social scientists in various studies (Gundermann, 1986-1992; González, 1990). Unfortunately, since the planning is national (while the administration is local), nothing major had changed up to 1993. And there are a number of reasons for this, including a healthy degree of caution on the part of educational innovators. This caution is based on the attempts during the Allende years to overhaul Chilean education. The proposal for one universal system of education (ENU) for all Chilean children was perceived as "the straw that broke the camel's back" (Farrell, 1986). It turns out Chileans are very conservative when it comes to their two-tiered (public-private) educational system, which fits well with their class structure and ensures the reproduction of an educated elite (Bourdieu and Passeron, 1977).

In the I Region, there have been some developments initiated by the non-governmental (NGO), thus "private" sector, however. First, the Methodist Corporation of Chile, developed the idea of an agricultural High School for Andean youths (male and female), and brought it to fruition in March of 1992.[9] Second, an NGO based in Iquique obtained funding to develop a special training programme for Andean school teachers at the university of Iquique and this programme was inaugurated in April, 1993.

At the regional government level, a Regional Educational Commission (CRECI) has been operating since 1991, and several conferences have been held on the subject of "intercultural education," with the participation of Ecuadorian, Peruvian and Bolivian educators (Mena y González, 1992). But in the face of a crisis situation such as exists in the highlands, nothing significant has been proposed to deal with it.

In August of 1992, another NGO, Taller de Estudios Andinos, TEA of Arica, decided to support my own initiative and became involved in a pilot project with school teachers of the most remote and poorest of highland areas in Chile. The request to "do something for the rural teachers" came from the schools' superintendent for the district, and the planning involved myself and one of TEA's educators (Arratia, 1993, 1994).

Most of the local schools in this administrative district are rather small (5 - 25 students). Most village schools are run by one single teacher, trained to impart the national curriculum to Aymara children. The pilot project was aimed toward sensitizing these rural teachers to cultural issues as a means to promote an attitudinal change and motivate innovations in practice and curriculum to improve the situation. The programme consisted in the development and use of distance education modules, complemented with monthly field visits to each of the rural schools for the purposes of professional support in the form of special training in the anthropological aspects of education.

The educational modules were organized around a collection of instructional texts published by UNESCO, based on experiences in various Latin American countries, for the support of bilingual, intercultural educators (UNESCO, 1989).

Once a month, an educator from TEA and an anthropologist (myself) visited each one of the highland schoolteachers to provide support and discuss the readings in light of their daily practical experiences. At the end of each month, when the teachers were on leave in the city of Arica, a workshop-seminar was held to further encourage the learning process with the use of videos and participatory (Freirian-style) methods.[10]

The experience was a participatory research opportunity for myself and a consciousness-raising process for the school teachers. Its consequences were thus varied. For some, the readings and discussions enriched their perspectives and clarified a number of grey areas already perceived, albeit unclearly, in their practices. For others, it allowed them the possibility to prepare projects that would bring the school closer to the communities and begin the process of integrating education into community development. Yet for others, the perception that their role as educators was being questioned became a matter of concern and defensiveness. It was the beginning of a longer-term process which will produce unforeseen changes.

One of the most important issues dealt with in the training process were the dynamic aspects of culture. These included communication patterns, interactional patterns, participatory initiatives, community leadership styles. The teachers were able to come to terms with the fact that they were dealing with a different cultural system. How to deal with this, however, is something they have to discover and negotiate through their daily experiences as they begin to incorporate cultural elements into their educational practices and change the previous dominating patterns. The change of attitude produces a change in positioning of the teacher vis-à-vis the community and this in turn generates other changes. This is only the beginning of the process to make the school an integral part of the community.

CULTURE AND SOCIAL ACTION IN DEVELOPMENT

While the schools orient the young toward the city, they do not actually prepare them for that setting. The persistence of an identity linked to the land and the development of a sense of "ethnicity" in urban settings are important issues in the understandings we bring to grassroots and local community development. I perceive these processes as an indication of the positioning that people take under different circumstances. There are indeed multiple identities which become operational in specific contexts. The analysis of these processes allows us to focus on the dynamic aspects of "culture."

Social scientists working in development would have to experientially grasp the dynamics of cultural patterns, and for this purpose the fieldwork experience is perhaps the only effective method of gaining this level of understanding. I think of the example of the rural school teachers with whom I worked. Most of them had been living in the villages for some time, but their positions as external authorities marginalized them from the internal processes of community living. Once they were made aware of the cultural repercussions of their attitude and of their work, they had to reconsider their position in the face of their students and of the community. This is a task that requires awareness of the pervasive asymmetries, the willingness to make changes, and the time and patience to implement them.

The interactional patterns in development are, of course, asymmetrical. North/South cooperation is perceived as First/Third World interactions. The North is the "successful" party teaching or applying certain techniques to the "less successful." That is the "model" to be replicated. And decade after decade, this recursive pattern has become accepted by all of the parties involved. At one point, it was called "dependency" and criticized for its negative impact. My point is that large asymmetries have existed since the so-called "Age of Discovery," and argue though we may about their forms and variations, they not only continue to exist, they have become entrenched. I would say we have created a post-colonial culture of development, complete with language, myths, beliefs, knowledge, rituals, experts, social organization, patterns of control, etc. We are still on the modernization treadmill (whether we acknowledge it or not), particularly when we deal with native populations with a distinct worldview. And, as intellectuals, we carry on the cultural hegemonic tradition: the European colonizing tradition, within our models, within our interpretive schemes, within our analytical toolkit.

I suggest that in order to break this recursive pattern we need to: a) become aware of this pattern and its implications (the consciousness-raising process); and b) consciously change our models, our theories and our research techniques. This may appear a simple matter-of-fact prescription. But of course it is not.

CULTURE IN DEVELOPMENT PRACTICES

A comparison might help. Some years ago, social scientists discovered the absence and silence of women in development. Initially, the thought was to "add women," that is to say, to gather information specifically on women and attach to previous analyses of the situation. The results were that new approaches had to be created and as a result most social sciences were greatly enriched by whole new areas of research opening up, such as the "informal sector," household activities linked with the market, previously not recorded as significant, and the important issue of gender as a structuring device in most (perhaps all) societies (Moore, 1988).

In a similar manner, we are now coming to terms with the absence of cultural understandings in development. But to correct this situation the point is not to simply "add" culture to our analyses. We need to draw out cultural elements already incorporated into the patterns in place which combine both elements of resistance and elements of accommodation to domination. While we continue to search for conceptual clarity (precisely so as not to reproduce the recursive pattern), we cannot delay in dealing with the urgent issues of incorporating a cultural dimension into development practices.

One approach thought to bring culture into social action has been used by non-governmental organizations (NGOs) throughout Latin America since the 1970s. This has been the introduction of participatory methods into development projects (Arratia, 1991). In fact, we now have at least a decade of experiences in the use of popular education (Freire's term) and participatory research (Fals Borda's term) in a number of countries in most regions of the world, carried out primarily (but not exclusively) by NGOs.

The goal of participatory development practices is twofold: first, to foster self-generated, self-sustained development; and second, to train people for increasing autonomy in the execution of development projects. In a way, it is a road out of the dependency previously built into development practices.

Not only are participatory practices perceived favourably by international cooperation agencies, in Chile they are now also promoted and used in government social programmes. But judging from my own knowledge of these experiences, it appears that they became the "thing to do" during the past decade. Thus, the emphasis on the part of the "practitioners" of development has been to apply participatory methods as a prescription for remedial action, rather than become fully aware of the dynamic aspects of the interactions. The issue is rather to find ways to transform the previously set patterns of interaction. As a result of the pragmatic approach used, we now see a reification of the method minus its original intent.

To reiterate, the initial thrust of participatory methods in development has been to raise the levels of consciousness about the patterns of domination and to produce knowledge *for* the people involved. Freire calls this "cultural action" (1985). They are not simply methods to be used, but rather a means towards a different kind of interaction, toward establishing a dialogue of equals, toward the acknowledgement of alternative knowledge systems and the value of cultural identities.

In the case in question, for instance, the controlling factor in participatory programmes has remained external to the Aymara communities.

Although new local organizations have been successfully struck within some communities, the need for varying degrees of external support continues. The process of developing autonomy depends a great deal on the amount of information people have about the contexts within which they will need to negotiate that autonomy (i.e., local government, political parties, social agencies, etc.).

The inherent goal to transform the one-way instructional mode used in the imposition of development programmes into a dialogue with the "beneficiaries" of the programme demands that social scientists or technicians, or both, promoting social action, engage in the discussion of their input to the programme. This means that its goals and aims and the ways of implementing would be shared with the participants, who are generally less formally educated and structurally subordinated social groups, such as workers, peasants, natives. This does not mean to say that the degree of social asymmetry has to be ignored. Rather, the goal is to consciously bridge the gap and reach a synthesis of the "two sides" of the asymmetry.

But we must not forget the longstanding and persistent recursive patterns that have characterized these interactions throughout time. They have a history and they involve processes of accommodation and resistance with which people have become comfortable. These patterns are part of the culture of colonialism in its various forms. Whatever new kinds of actions are instituted, they need to be sustained through a period of time for these patterns to be altered, so that a new pattern can emerge. Naturally, the manner in which this begins to occur will vary depending on local conditions, the preparedness of the parties involved and the degree of success obtained as each step is taken.

To be fair, there has been a degree of improvement brought about by the training of leaders in participatory activities in the case in question. Yet the process of developing longer-term interactional patterns that will enable the rural Aymara, now in greatly reduced numbers, to bring new life to their demographically and economically impoverished communities requires costly field support. Few funding agencies realize this; government offices expect rapid changes impossible to produce in the short term, yet necessary for their political aims.

I think all of us who have been involved in social action appreciate the fact that to change the course of previously established patterns is not only a difficult but also slow process. Here, the barriers also appear to be twofold: a) the lack of understanding regarding the nature of cultural barriers; and b) the longstanding, recursive nature of social interactions.

LOCAL KNOWLEDGE, CULTURAL IDENTITY AND MODERNITY

My experience has shown me that local knowledge and local social patterns are important assets in the decision-making processes and implementation of development measures. With Fals Borda I agree that we need to "de-colonize" knowledge (1979). It is in this area that the penetration of modernity has made its greatest impact. Local knowledge is no longer valued by those who possess it, save a few exceptions. At least on the Chilean side of the border, Aymara knowledge is greatly de-structured. It is virtually impossible to link the available pieces together. Normally, the Aymara look to Bolivia for expertise in various areas of their own "tradition."

Yet, once the consciousness-raising process begins, we have found that the participants themselves become more open about their practices and about local knowledge in use and begin to acknowledge their shortcomings, suggesting possible avenues for recovering their "traditional lore" or to introduce new knowledge where they see that it is needed.

The Aymara have had to learn to live "in-between" two worlds as changes have affected them. Their subsistence needs have made it necessary to learn to work in various environments, to do various kinds of paid labour. The preference for highland people has been to hire out seasonally for agricultural activities in lower-lying areas, in the border salt mines, or even accross the border in Bolivia. In these cases they are still within their highland cultural environment, albeit with local variations. Yet others have chosen to sell some animals, purchase a vehicle and carry freight between Chile and Bolivia or else from the urban markets into the highland fairs. In the measure that these activities begin to replace local subsistence patterns, dependency on market activities increases and with it, external knowledge begins to predominate. This is the "other world," ruled by different norms, which have to be acquired.

Local knowledge includes issues such as those related to herding and the proper care of the animals, natural (herbal) medicine, climate observation to protect the crops from frost, quality of soils, etc. So that when we talk about the expected "synthesis" of knowledge we envision a recovery of local knowledge and an integration with the systematicity and perhaps some techniques that external knowledge can bring. The recording of local knowledge is typically the work that anthropologists have done in various parts of the world where they have worked. This work has barely begun in northern Chile, due to the political and economic circumstances under which social scientists have worked.

In the case of the Chilean-Aymara, local knowledge has been in competition with urban knowledge for some time, given migration, national education and increased market contacts. Once a household becomes dependant on the money economy, then the need to integrate into "modern" (urban) patterns becomes greater and urban knowledge becomes increasingly more relevant to everyday life, thus rendering the compulsory assimilation process less reversible.

There are various things to be done in this respect which fit in rather well with the pilot project with the school teachers. As part the programme, the teachers were given various "research guides" (included in the UNESCO texts) which they could integrate into community projects to be carried out as part of integrating the school into community development.

Remote rural areas (all of the rural areas in the I Region of Chile) are deficiently serviced in terms of basic needs such as health, sanitation and social and technical services, due to the high cost to the government (cost per capita). Therefore, for example, systematic research into herbal practices would not only be convenient for local conditions, but a highly economic measure. Since the evidence of natural healing effectiveness is already well known this would be a logical answer to the problem of provision of health services. Some research was done in the early 1980s, but the information obtained was never utilized to ensure that access would be available in all villages.

Some Aymara urban organizations have been considering the possibility of recovering ancient knowledge and have carried out small workshops of herbalists to gather this kind of information. But again the lack of resources to carry out a sustained and systematic programme has meant that nothing further has been done. There is a need to incorporate internal and external sources in the effort. But there are two main barriers to this processes: one is the issue of funding; the other is the lack of appropriate organizational systems to make possible such a process of integration. Although there are Aymara organizations in the urban centres which might assist in this effort, the rural/urban communication is always difficult.

THE POLITICS OF NATIVE ORGANIZATION IN CHILE

Native organizations at the national level are another "modern" innovation in Chile. As already indicated, native organizations for ethnic rights rose during the last decade.

The activities of these organizations show the great deal of work to be done in the integration of urban and rural Aymara, a process also affected by the lack of resources. An asymmetry has arisen between those in the cities and those on the "land," primarily due to the modernizing influences of education but also through the experiences of living in a different milieu. The distance between rural and urban Aymara is considerable and the gap is not closing, despite interactions related to community projects. If asked, many of the urban Aymara will say they would rather not live in the rural area, but they would support community development efforts. There is a need to bridge this gap so that those who are defending Aymara rights in the face of the regional and national authorities and who are at the same time attempting to maintain a cultural space for themselves and their families in the city will bear with them the product of a closer participation with rural dwellers.

In this respect, we must acknowledge the negative influence of the national political parties. It has been advantageous for urban leaders to become involved in the regional political process, which provides a means of participation in the national political system and has allowed them to participate in the drafting of the first Native Law for Chile. But since this kind of participation is based on clientelism, it is doubtful whether it will do much to change the dynamics between the dominant and subordinate groups, i.e., the Aymara will be given only a small, peripheral space within those "structures." Further, the vacuum between urban leaders and the grassroots is bound to grow as a result of the leaders' integration into the bureacratic system. In a way, what is developing is yet another version of the culturally dominant pattern. The urban Aymara are subordinated to the (non-Aymara) national political organization and in turn the Aymara grassroots are subordinated to their urban leadership. There is still a great deal of work to be done in this area, to build the bridges that allow for a full representation of the rural communities in urban Aymara organizations.

CONCLUSIONS

The process of incorporating "culture" into development continues. And it is complex, for it also involves an incorporation of diversity into the self-image of the nation-state (Arratia, in press). As a social scientist working in the local context, I feel it is important to learn local patterns and to listen more in order to improve communications among the various groups involved. It is also necessary to incorporate new relevant elements into the dialogue. A sustained involvement in support of native projects and an open attitude through time can bring us closer to finding ways to break the recursive patterns of domination, colonialism and the pervasive influence of a particular conception of modernity, and to begin to set culturally sensitive interactions in which we cease to impose external criteria and become mediators or facilitators of self-generated and sustainable community development.

Through my work in formal education and adult training I have been able to experience the close connections between these two sets of activities and other aspects of development. This localized experience has provided me with information on the political process, the demographic problem (migration and de-population) and the reproduction of hegemonic practices, all of which have broad consequences in development issues and practices.

I suggest that to include "culture" in our definitions and analyses of development has to lead to new approaches. These require that we: a) analyze the historical background of present conditions to identify the dynamics of power asymmetries, the ways in which they are reproduced in practice and the way people have survived domination; b) work to change the institutions that carry on reproductive functions which erode the local knowledge base and social identity; c) identify how local knowledge and identity are embedded in everyday actions; d) establish the local knowledge base still existing amidst culturally distinct populations and find the place reserved for "traditional" ways within their pattern of accommodation and resistance to domination and e) propose new integrations of local patterns of knowledge, of social interaction, of organization, etc. with information emerging from social scientific analyses, so that new expertise can be incorporated through culturally appropriate channels.

ACKNOWLEDGEMENT

This research was made possible by a post-doctoral fellowship from the Social Sciences and Humanities Research Council of Canada. This assistance is gratefully ackowledged. I also gratefully acknowledge the support and assistance of Taller de Estudios Andinos with my research and action project.

ENDNOTES

1. The Aymara population has been estimated to be 40,000 in the entire I Region of Chile. The highland population is estimated at about 3,500, and the lowland valley and canyon population is estimated at 17,000, according to statistics gathered by Taller de Estudios Andinos of Arica. The majority of the Aymara population lives in the cities of Iquique and Arica. Results of the 1992 census are not yet available for a more precise and updated figure.
2. Until 1967 primary schooling consisted of six grades. After the School Reform of the Christian Democratic Government, elementary education was increased to eight years.
3. Highland areas in the Bolivian plateau receive more rainfall than those on the Chilean side of the border. The communities are more densely populated and can make a living from agriculture and various kinds of husbandry. On the Chilean side, the herders are limited to llama, alpaca and sheep.
4. I had the opportunity to interview 31 highschool students (15 females and 16 males) and found the issue of personal security to be an important factor in their views about city life and city schools.
5. The special commission for native peoples (CEPI) was able to increase the number of scholarships and in 1993 there were about 90 awards to Aymara children and youths in various levels of schooling.
6. The monies for these projects came through a taxation reform and the hiring of support professionals came under scrutiny. Since the funds were earmarked for educational projects it was difficult to justify the addition of professional staff.
7. These institutions were a creation of the military regime. They are residential schools covering grades 1 to 8 and are meant to replace the local village schools. They are in the highlands but distant from the villages where the children's families live.
8. The EEC has donated complete "shops" in mechanics, carpentry and electricity to be installed in the "Highland Concentration Schools." These institutions have a complete elementary program from Grade 1 to Grade 8.

9. This is the social action division of the Methodist Church of Chile, which has an extensive trajectory in the south of Chile in schooling for Mapuche youths.
10. Paulo Freire's popular education methods have been extensively used in a variety of adult training situations throughout Latin America and other parts of the world. In this specific case, the idea was to develop a sense of consciousness on the part of the teachers regarding the cultural implications of their practices (Freire, 1968, 1985).

REFERENCES

Arratia, M. (1994). Una Experiencia Piloto de Educaciön Intercultural. *Revista Educaciön.* Santiago, Chile.

———. (1993). Una Experiencia Piloto en Educacion Intercultural en la I Region de Chile. *Pueblos Indigenas y Educacion.* Vol. 27/28.

———. (1991). *Cultural action and cultural synthesis? Participatory methodologies and the Aymara of Northern Chile.* Ph.D Thesis.

Bourdieu, P. (1984). *Distinction. A social critique of the judgement of taste.* Translation by Richard Nice. Cambridge MA: Harvard University Press.

———. (1972). *Outline of a theory of practice.* Translated by Richard Nice. Cambridge: Cambridge University Press.

Bourdieu, P. and Passeron, J. (1977) *Reproduction in education, society and culture.* Translated by Richard Nice. London: SAGE.

Fals Borda, O. (1979). Investigating Reality in order to transform it: The Colombian experience. *Dialectical Anthropology.* Vol. 1:35-55.

———. (1980). Reflections on the meaning and role of science in people's participation: Theoretical aspects of participatory research. Yugoslavia: Symposium on Participatory Research.

———. (1987). *Ciencia Propia y Colonialismo Intelectual.* Bogotá: Carlos Valencia, editors.

Farrell, J. (1986). *The National unified school in Allende's Chile. The role of education in the destruction of a revolution.* Vancouver: University of British Columbia Press.

Foucault, M. (1979). *Discipline and punishment: The birth of the prison.* Part III. New York: Vintage Books.

Freire, P. (1968). *Pedagogy for the oppressed.* Translated by Myra Ramos. New York: Continuum.

———. (1985). *The Politics of education.* South Hadley, MA: Bergin and Garvey, Publishers.

Giddens, A. (1984). *The Constitution of Society.* Berkeley: University of California Press.

González, S. and Mena, F. (Eds.). (1992). *Actas del "Primer Seminario Internacional de Educaciön Intercutlural, Provincia de Iquique—Chile".* Iquique: TER/UNAP.

González, S. (1990). *El Aymara de la Provincia de Iquique—Chile y la Educación Nacional.* Iquique: TER/PEBI

Gundermann, H. (1985-1992). *Proyecto de Investigación del Instituto de Antropología y Arqueología de la Universidad de Tarapacá.* Unpublished Reports. Arica: UTA.

Hatch, E. (1985). Culture in: *The Social science encyclopedia.* Adam Kuper and Jessica Kuper, (Eds.). p.178. London: Routledge and Kegan Paul.

Keesing, R. (1990). Theories of culture revisited. *Camberra Anthropology.* Vol 13, No. 2, October.

Moore. H.(1988). *Feminism and anthropology.* Minneapolis: University of Minnesota Press.

Singleton, J. (1974). Implications of education as cultural transmission in *Education and Cultural Process. Toward an Anthropology of Education.* New York: Holt, Reinhart and Winston.

Tylor, E. (1871). *Origins of culture.* New York: Harper & Row.

UNESCO (1989). *Materiales para la Formación Docente Bilingüe Intercultural.* 5 Vols. Santiago: UNESCO.

YEKMASEUALKOPAN : Y-A-T-IL UNE MANIÈRE MODERNE D'ÊTRE NAHUA?[1]

Pierre Beaucage

On ne peut donner à la Modernité, concept issu du contexte historique propre de l'Occident, un contenu unique, valable pour toutes les cultures, qu'en l'assimilant arbitrairement, à son antithèse, la Tradition. Toutefois, en tentant d'éviter le piège inverse d'un «ethnisme» qui enferme chaque culture dans une essence immuable et incommunicable, cet article veut considérer les sociétés amérindiennes actuelles comme porteuses d'identités specifiques (dont les marqueurs sont culturels) et impliquées dans une interrelation historique multiforme avec les sociétés nationales. A partir d'une recherche de longue durée (1963-1993) dans une région autochtone du Mexique, l'auteur montre qu'un processus de modernisation en profondeur a lieu, sans être globalisant ni linéaire. Ses formes concrètes dépendent d'une dialectique complexe entre des facteurs démographiques et economiques d'une part, et des capacités d'hégémonie et d'organisation entre groupe dominant et groupes dominés d'autre part.

The notion of modernity, a concept which originates in the historically specific context of the Western world, can be applied arbitrarily to all cultures, if that notion is associated antithetically, with the idea of tradition. In order to avoid the inverse trap of "ethnism," which encloses each culture into its unchangeable essence, it would be interesting to consider present day Amerindian societies as bearers of specific identities (designated by certain cultural markers), defined by their historical interelations with national societies. Based on a long-term research project (1963-1993) in an indigenous region of Mexico, an attempt is made to show that an in-depth process of modernization is taking place which excludes globalizing or linear structured phenomena. This dynamics depends on a complex dialectics between demographic and economic factors on the one hand, and the capacities for control and organization by the leading and subordinate groups, on the other.

COMME LE SOULIGNE BAUDRILLART, on ne peut donner à la notion de modernité un contenu précis, valable pour tous les lieux et toutes les époques : couvrant un champ aussi vaste que flou, elle recoupe les domaines de l'histoire et de l'idéologie, de l'économique et de l'éthique, de l'esthétique et de la politique. Elle est à la fois «catégorie générale et impératif culturel [...] Mouvante dans ses formes, dans ses contenus, dans le temps et dans l'espace, elle n'est stable que comme système de valeurs» (1985 : 424). Selon le même auteur, ses principaux traits sont : la sécularisation de la pensée et de la science, la valorisation du changement-progrès suivant un temps historique linéaire, un productivisme économique visant une reproduction sans cesse élargie, une conception abstraite du pouvoir et de l'Etat, de l'espace et du temps, et l'émergence de l'individu, tant comme sujet de libertés économiques et politiques, que comme subjectivité aspirant au bonheur individuel et cherchant dans le privé une personnalisation disparue des rapports publics (*ibid.*).

Compte tenu de l'ampleur de son contenu, on ne peut essayer de définir la modernité que par opposition : c'est «un mode de civilisation caractéristique, qui s'oppose au mode de la tradition» (*ibid.*). Cette opposition s'est inscrite dans une trame historique. L'avènement de la modernité, que l'on situe en Occident au XVIe siècle, a impliqué une rupture progressive par rapport à un type de société tendant à sa reproduction simple, pourrions-nous dire, en empruntant l'expression à Marx : la société médiévale européenne se représentait l'univers sous la forme d'une hiérarchie englobant les humains et la nature, ainsi qu'un monde immatériel transcendant. La vie sociale était régie par les cycles immuables des saisons, de la vie humaine. Seule une intervention divine pouvait introduire un avant et un après, l'ébauche d'une linéarité : la naissance du Christ donnait son sens à une histoire qui réalisait le grand projet divin. La Renaissance, par sa revalorisation du monde antique païen, introduira des critères alternatifs de mise en ordre de l'histoire, le Classicisme approfondira le changement de perspectives en prônant la supériorité des Modernes sur les Anciens tandis que le Siècle des Lumières se posera lui-même comme la rupture essentielle par rapport à l'«obscurantisme».

Quelle que soit la définition que l'on donne de la modernité, c'est toujours par rapport à cette tradition occidentale qu'on la définit. Cependant, malgré ses racines particulières, on confère au concept une validité universelle, que l'on fonde sur un double postulat, d'ordre politique et cognitif. Au plan politique, la modernité «irradie mondialement à partir de l'Occident», certains y voyant la preuve de la supériorité intrinsèque de ce mode d'être, d'autres en faisant le simple résultat d'une contrainte politico-économique qui s'est exercée depuis cinq siècles par les pays d'Europe de l'Ouest puis d'Amérique du Nord. Il s'ensuit qu'au plan cognitif, les autres sociétés sont assimilées à la Tradition, se voyant attribuer des caractéristiques similaires à celles de l'Europe d'avant la rupture : personnalisation des rapports sociaux, cyclicité du temps, transcendance du surnaturel. Quel que soit leur point de départ, leur inscription dans l'histoire (c'est-à-dire la conquête et la colonisation) signifie pour les autres sociétés le début d'un processus d'acculturation devant les mener tôt ou tard à un état de société et de culture voisin de celui de l'Occident (le «développement»). La volonté de certains groupes d'interrompre le processus ou de l'orienter autrement (appelée «retribalisation» ou «contre-acculturation») apparaît d'emblée voué à l'échec (Bastide 1971 : 57-58). Une acceptation non critique du concept de modernité et de ses corrélats implicites aboutit alors à une reprise de l'évolutionnisme linéaire qui caractérisa les sciences humaines au XIXe siècle.

Face à cet universalisme assimilateur, et à ses multiples variantes, s'est développée en anthropologie une perspective particularisante (souvent appelée «ethniste»), qui met l'accent sur l'irréductibilité de la différence et de la persistance culturelles. Ses tenants les moins critiques, renouant avec le culturalisme allemand qui fut aux origines mêmes de la discipline, avancent l'hypothèse de la permanence absolue de la culture, de l'immuabilité des valeurs profondes des peuples, l'histoire ne faisant que les manifester sous des formes multiples. Dans cette perspective, les changements qui ont affecté les sociétés amérindiennes depuis un demi-millénaire ont laissé intacte l'«âme indienne».[2] Dans le cadre des mouvements de «droit à la différence», certains auteurs et certaines organisations indiennes et leurs porte-parole défendent des points de vue similaires.[3] Du point de vue qui nous intéresse, les termes de l'équation (tradition et modernité) demeurent alors inchangés par rapport à la position précédente : seul est modifié le jugement de valeur à leur endroit.

Un autre courant, au sein duquel je me range, s'efforce de comprendre les sociétés amérindiennes actuelles comme étant à la fois porteuses d'une identité spécifique (dont les marqueurs sont sociaux et culturels) et impliquées dans une interrelation dynamique aux plans économique, politique et culturel avec les non-Indiens. Cette dynamique a pour cadre historique les diverses sociétés nationales, et a bien sûr un impact direct sur la définition de l'identité des uns et des autres (Bonfil Batalla, 1981; Beaucage 1987, 1994).

A partir d'une recherche de longue durée (1969-1994) dans une région autochtone du Mexique, j'essaierai de démontrer ici que :

a) Contrairement à ce qu'affirme l'approche ethniste «dure», un processus de modernisation, qui affecte en profondeur les sociétés autochtones, a bel et bien lieu. Cependant, ce processus n'est pas aussi globalisant ni linéaire que les «modernistes» l'assument généralement. Il touche à des rythmes différents divers niveaux de la vie sociale et peut prendre des directions opposées, à certains moments différents.

b) Le processus historique concret de modernisation implique une dialectique entre des facteurs objectifs (démographiques, économiques, écologiques), d'une part, et les capacités hégémoniques et organisationnelles du groupe dominant et des groupes dominés, d'autre part. A chaque étape, l'état de fait résultant de la situation antérieure intervient comme une nouvelle donnée du problème, tandis que s'ouvrent et se ferment des options.

MODERNITÉ ET IDENTITÉ DANS LA SIERRA NORTE DE PUEBLA.

Le thème de la modernité est présentement l'objet d'âpres débats au Mexique, comme dans beaucoup d'autres pays du tiers-monde. Face à l'épuisement du modèle hérité de la Révolution de 1910-1917, le gouvernement Salinas (1988-1994) a fait d'une modernisation conçue en termes néo-libéraux l'axe principal des réformes économiques, politiques et éducatives qu'il a entreprises depuis 1988. A l'intervention de l'Etat dans l'économie (par ses politiques d'investissement, de prix et de redistribution des revenus) on veut substituer les forces du marché, pour impulser l'industrialisation et régulariser la croissance; au lieu du système politique corporatiste qui intègre les syndicats ouvriers et les organisations paysannes et indigènes dans le Parti Révolutionnaire Institutionnel (PRI), (automatiquement reconduit au pouvoir depuis un demi-siècle) on dit vouloir mettre en place une démocratie multipartite à l'occidentale; enfin, au lieu d'une culture traditionnelle, autochtone ou métisse, et d'un nationalisme populiste, on charge l'école et les média de former une culture moderne, cosmopolite et tournée vers l'avenir.[4]

Dans les régions à forte majorité autochtone, on trouve une autre version de cette opposition tradition-modernité, version véhiculée par les modèles spontanés qu'élaborent les divers acteurs sociaux. Dans la Sierra Norte de Puebla, la terminologie adoptée par chacun des deux groupes ethniques en témoigne. Les non-Indiens, Métis ou descendants d'immigrants européens, s'auto-désignent *gente de razón,* («gens de raison») face aux *indios, inditos, mejicaneros* (Nahuas), pioncitos , naquitos (Totonaques). Ils détiennent depuis plus d'un siècle le pouvoir économique et politique et considèrent qu'ils ont apporté «le progrès» dans la région, en introduisant à la fin du siècle dernier les cultures du café et de la canne à sucre, l'élevage des bovins, et en effectuant d'importants travaux d'urbanisation dans les chefs-lieux où ils se sont établis. La tradition métisse rapporte :

> Le premier maire de Cuetzalan fut un Indien, nommé Palagosti. Il construisit la mairie et la couvrit de paille, car il ne connaissait rien d'autre. Imaginez : une mairie de paille! (*¡ un palacio de zacate!*) Ensuite on a eu des maires *de razón* et ils ont fait construire le bel édifice de pierre [...]. On a même eu l'électricité avec un barrage qu'ils avaient construit sur la rivière Apulco. C'est pour celà qu'on a baptisé notre ville Cuetzalan del Progreso.

Pour la *gente de razón,* leur catégorie identitaire est donc ouverte et inclut toute la société urbaine moderne du Mexique et de l'extérieur, dont ils constituent un détachement local, face à la tradition représentée par les autochtones. Cette conception dualiste et hiérarchisée se manifeste quotidiennement au niveau du discours. Par exemple, lors des élections de novembre 1992, il y eu une dispute au sein du PRI local concernant le candidat que Puebla voulait imposer, un instituteur originaire de l'extérieur. «Il nous faut quelqu'un d'ici!» argumentait l'une des factions lors d'une réunion. Ce à quoi un ancien maire, également né à l'extérieur, répliqua : «Le progrès, c'est nous, les étrangers (*los forasteros*) qui l'avons apporté. Autrement, bien sûr il y aurait eu aussi des maires. Mais il se seraient appelés Juan Cuamait» ... (patronyme nahuat).

La ritualisation majeure de la conception métisse apparaît lors de la *Feria del Huipil y del Café,* qui, fait significatif, se tient parallèlement à la fête religieuse de saint François (patron de Cuetzalan), soit le 4 octobre. Voici comment la fête s'est déroulée en 1991. Sur la place face à l'hôtel de ville, dans la soirée, a eu lieu le couronnement de la «reine du café». L'heureuse élue, étrennant une robe du soir achetée dans la capitale, apparut au bras du prince consort (*chambelán*), lui aussi tiré à quatre épingles, sous les applaudissements et les éclairs des appareils-photos, et avança majestueusement au son d'une musique d'orchestre diffusée par des haut-parleurs, jusqu'à une estrade ornée de draperies. A la table d'honneur, siégeaient les députés et les maires de la région, ainsi qu'une ex-Miss Puebla et une ex-Miss Sierra Norte. Plus tôt dans la journée, sur le parvis de l'église, en contre-bas, on avait choisi la «reine du huipil»,[5] parmi huit jeunes Amérindiennes en costume traditionnel. Les autorités locales y avaient fait une brève apparition, et la femme du député avait lu—laborieusement—un discours de circonstances ... en nahuat! Trois musiciens autochtones avaient interprété des airs de *xochipitsaua;*[6] l'estrade sur laquelle se tiennent les participantes était ornée de palmes et de fougères.

L'événement nocturne, directement inspiré des plus récents *shows* télévisés, constituait donc le point culminant d'un rituel à deux temps dans lequel l'identité autochtone apparaissait comme un point de départ, mais qui aurait survécu, dans une position latérale et subordonnée. Si les *cuetzaltecos* exaltent à l'occasion les traditions indiennes en ce qu'elles ont de pittoresque et de «typique» (*típico*), c'est essentiellement comme attrait touristique, tout comme les ruines préhispaniques de Yohualichan, situées sur le territoire du municipe de Cuetzalan. Par ailleurs, les Métis soulignent volontiers aux étrangers que les Indiens d'aujourd'hui ne possèdent plus la «vraie culture indienne» : les jeunes hommes ont abandonné le costume traditionnel en cotonnade blanche pour les vêtements manufacturés, les radio-cassettes ont remplacé le *xochipitsaua* et la langue nahuat elle-même est—disent-ils—bourrée d'hispanismes!

La conception autochtone de l'identité est à la fois complémentaire à celle des Métis, et en rupture avec elle. Les Amérindiens considèrent aussi comme des «étrangers» les non-Indiens, même ceux qui habitent depuis des générations dans la région : toutefois, le terme *koyot* qui les désigne (qui peut se traduire aussi bien par *mestizo,* «métis», que par *catrín,* «de la ville» ou *forastero,* «étranger») n'a rien d'élogieux.[7] Le discours autochtone concernant les non-Indiens souligne constamment la non-légitimité de leur présence. La tradition orale insiste sur les luttes menées contre tous les envahisseurs étrangers : les Espagnols d'abord, les Français ensuite, puis une faction métisse de la région, pendant la révolution (Taller de Tradición Oral 1994; Beaucage, 1994 : 173-176). On invoque la toponymie et les récits des anciens pour démontrer que partout (même sur le site du chef-lieu actuel) l'occupation indienne du territoire est antérieure à celle des Métis, qui ont parfois utilisé la fraude pour acquérir des terres (Taller *ibid.* : 130-132, 271-272).

Concernant les marqueurs de l'identité amérindienne, les autochtones en donnent une description souvent ambiguë. Ils mentionnent les traits distinctifs traditionnels (la langue, le vêtement, la nourriture, la musique —Beaucage, 1987 : 29-35), en soulignant qu'«on ne devient pas Indien» : il y a une «vraie manière indienne» (*yekmaseualkopan*) de parler et de se comporter qu'un non-Indien n'acquerra jamais, quel que soit le nombre d'années passées dans un village. Il est important de noter qu'au plan de la structure agraire, rien ne distingue les Amérindiens des non-Indiens : alors que dans d'autres régions, les autochtones ont préservé ou récupéré la propriété communale du sol, dans la Sierra, les paysans ont enregistré privément leurs parcelles après l'abolition des titres communautaires par le gouvernement libéral, en 1856.[8] Malgré les nombreuses similitudes culturelles des deux groupes (nourriture, agriculture, religion) les autochtones partagent avec les non-Indiens la conception qu'ils forment deux identités ethniques distinctes et opposées, que leur identité propre est fermée par rapport à l'autre qu'ils considèrent ouverte. Le passage d'une identité à l'autre est possible, mais dans un sens seulement. On peut *devenir* non-Indien : il y a même un terme (humoristique, mais vexant) pour celui qui abandonne les marqueurs extérieurs de l'appartenance amérindienne pour ceux de l'identité «mexicaine moderne» : on sera *arrazonadillo,* pour les Métis, *xalkoyot* pour les Indiens. Par contre, il est clair qu'on naît Indien ou qu'on ne l'est pas.[9]

Si les deux entités, indienne et non indienne, demeurent distinctes, il n'en demeure pas moins que la culture indienne change. Par rapport au processus de modernisation des villages, les conceptions autant que les attitudes concrètes des autochtones sont marquées par l'ambiguïté. D'un côté, ils concèdent volontiers la perte récente de nombreux aspects de la culture traditionnelle : à mes questions concernant les *quelites* (herbes comestibles, sauvages et cultivées), un jeune homme répondra ironiquement : «Qui mange encore des *quelites*? Aujourd'hui, les gens ne veulent que la nourriture qu'on achète dans les boutiques». A l'occasion, on verra cette perte comme négative : «La terre d'ici produit tout ce dont on a besoin, à condition de travailler», commentera une aïeule. «Mais personne ne veut plus aller aux champs. On ne plante que du café». Pour la majorité, cependant, les changements survenus depuis une génération sont dans l'ensemble extrêmement positifs : la construction des routes, l'électrification, l'adduction d'eau, un meilleur accès à l'éducation et aux services de santé, des revenus monétaires accrus. Peut-on alors affirmer, avec un auteur mexicain récent, que «les traditions prennent congé» et que :

> Les membres des ethnies sont dans les meilleures dispositions pour collaborer avec les «ethnocidaires», ils veulent se défaire d'usages et de coutumes millénaires, peut-être par la faute des radios-transistors, de l'enseignement des instituteurs et des efforts de fabricants de coca-cola pour cocacoliser des Indiens. (González y González 1986 : 12)

Je ne le crois pas et j'en veux pour preuve le renforcement de l'appartenance ethnique qui a accompagné, après 1975, le processus accéléré de modernisation de la région. Pour comprendre ce phénomène, en apparence paradoxal j'examinerai rapidement les principales caractéristiques et l'impact du mouvement paysan indigène qui se cristallisa dans la création de la Coopérative Régionale *Tosépan Titataniské* (Ensemble nous vaincrons).

LA MODERNISATION STRUCTURELLE DANS LA SIERRA (1970-1993) : DES «CHEMINS DE MAIN-D'OEUVRE» À LA TOSÉPAN TITATANISKÉ

Lorsque j'ai commencé mes recherches dans la Sierra en 1969, la région, tant en haute qu'en basse montagne, présentait les principales caractéristiques de tant de «régions de refuge» autochtones : un réseau routier très limité et une agriculture paysanne mixte combinant la production pour l'auto-subsistance (maïs, haricots, légumes) et le commerce (café, canne à sucre, arbres fruitiers). Au plan socio-culturel, des centaines de communautés amérindiennes, nahuas et totonaques, dépendaient économiquement et politiquement de quelques chefs-lieux (Zacapoaxtla, Cuetzalan, Huehuetla ...) dominés par une bourgeoisie non indienne, forte de son avoir foncier et surtout, de son contrôle du commerce régional. Au plan politique, le *cacique,* par son pouvoir personnel diffus mais omniprésent, contrôlait les autorités des chefs-lieux et des communautés, et constituait le point d'articulation entre le pouvoir local et régional et le sytème national du parti unique (Paré, 1975a). La région n'avait pas connu de mobilisation sociale importante depuis les années trente, mais, en 1970, une lutte contre la réforme de l'impôt foncier s'amorçait : elle déboucha, en haute montagne, sur un mouvement agraire radical qui connut son sommet au milieu de la décennie (Beaucage et al., 1982).

Le président Echeverría (1970-1976) fut confronté, dès le début de son mandat, à l'usure du modèle de substitution des importations qui avait permis au Mexique de connaître une croissance soutenue depuis 1940. Le secteur agricole destiné au marché national (oublié par une révolution verte qui avait profité à l'agro-industrie—Hewitt 1980) fut le premier à entrer en crise : l'insuffisance des livraisons de céréales et légumineuses de base, avec l'inflation subséquente, attirèrent l'attention sur la paysannerie, qui devenait tout au long de la décennie l'acteur le plus turbulent sur la scène sociale mexicaine. De nombreux programmes virent le jour, pour accroître la production et «ramener la paix à la campagne». Pour occuper pendant la morte saison les ouvriers agricoles et les paysans appauvris, l'Etat fit ouvrir des pistes dans les régions éloignées comme la Sierra : les *caminos de mano de obra,* dont certains deviendront par la suite de véritables routes, tandis que d'autres seront emportés par les pluies ou envahis à nouveau par la végétation. On intensifia aussi dans les campagnes l'effort d'alphabétisation, qui n'atteignait qu'une faible partie de la population d'âge scolaire.

Cependant, l'initiative qui aura le plus d'impact fut la mise sur pied, en 1974, du Plan Zacapoaxtla. Comme le Plan Puebla dont il était la réplique (Paré, 1975b), il visait à étendre à la paysannerie, en l'adaptant, le modèle de technicisation de l'agriculture qui avait connu un succès indéniable auprès des moyens et grands producteurs. Des équipes de conseillers (*asesores*) (agronomes, éducateurs, comptables), récemment diplômés d'un milieu universitaire en pleine crise de conscience sociale et politique, s'attaquèrent aux tâches suivantes : a) identifier les éléments techniques et économiques susceptibles de hausser rapidement la productivité agricole, et b) regrouper les paysans dans les structures adéquates pour leur donner la formation requise; acheminer efficacement vers eux les crédits et les intrants (engrais, pesticides, semences améliorées); et concentrer, pour la mettre en marché, la production des petites exploitations (Aguilar Ayón, 1986; Mora Aguilera, 1985). Une telle entreprise impliquait, sinon la marginalisation, du moins la refonctionnalisation de la structure économique en place depuis un siècle, où une bourgeoisie d'intermédiaires assurait le lien entre le marché capitaliste et des unités de production régies par des rapports de parenté et de voisinage. Au plan politique, elle impliquait pour l'Etat une nouvelle forme d'encadrement et de participation de la population, confirmant la désuétude du système des caciques.

Les structures du Plan Zacapoaxtla, modifiées sous les sexennats ultérieurs, fournirent le cadre légal à l'intérieur duquel put se développer un mouvement coopératif autochtone. Mise sur pied en 1976, la Coopérative régionale Tosépan Titataniské comptait en 1984 plus de 8000 membres, appartenant à une cinquantaine de villages indigènes, particulièrement dans la région de Cuetzalan (Sanchez, 1985). C'est l'approvisionnement de la région en denrées de base (maïs, haricots, sucre, savon ...), obtenues à prix subventionné des agences d'Etat (CONA-SUPO-COPLAMAR, puis DICONSA) qui constitua sans contredit l'activité la plus réussie : un réseau de boutiques coopératives, occupa rapidement plus de la moitié du marché, déterminant le niveau général des prix. En ce qui concerne la production, la Tosepan put commercialiser le poivre (*Pimienta dioica*) et la sapotille (*Pouteria sapota*) mais ne put s'attaquer au principal produit d'exportation, le café, que se partageaient le secteur privé et une puissante institution gouvernementale, l'Instituto Mexicano del Café (INMECAFE). La Tosépan constitua néanmoins rapidement une organisation capable de rejoindre et de mobiliser plus de gens que le parti unique (PRI) et les institutions qui lui sont inféodées (CNC, CTM), faiblement implantées dans la région. Elle devint donc l'interlocuteur privilégié des diverses agences gouvernementales en milieu rural (ministères de l'Agriculture, de la Santé, de l'Education, etc.) (Martínez Borrego, 1991). La bourgeoisie régionale et les caciques, voyant court-circuiter leur rôle d'intermédiaires économiques et politiques, livrèrent une lutte acharnée à la coopérative naissante. Mais la détermination des *compañeros,* et les appuis qu'ils surent obtenir au niveau de l'Etat central l'emportèrent, et la Tosépan Titataniské devint une force politique avec laquelle les politiciens locaux et même nationaux durent composer.

LA MODERNISATION DE L'IMAGINAIRE

Le changement ne se limita pas aux structures. La population paysanne autochtone des villages (*pueblos, xolalmej*), désormais définie comme appartenant à des *comunidades,* («communautés») était appelée à «s'organiser» et à «participer» activement et démocratiquement au processus, avec l'aide de ses conseillers, qui appartenaient à des agences gouvernementales ou des ONG. Cette «participation» démocratique, censée *refléter* les «valeurs communautaires», constituaient en fait une *innovation.* Leur fonctionnement politique traditionnel obéissait à un modèle hiérarchisé-électif, dont le cadre de base (la double hiérarchie civile et religieuse) fut hérité de la colonisation espagnole et modifié à plusieurs reprises par les divers régimes qui se sont succédés depuis l'indépendance. Officiellement, les autorités civiles (*tayekanani*), maire, conseillers, juge de paix, étaient «élues par le peuple». En réalité, ils étaient généralement désignés par le cacique régional parmi les familles de notables indiens, et étroitement contrôlés par des fonctionnaires non indiens (le secrétaire—souvent un instituteur métis—l'agent du ministère public, etc.—Durand 1975). Quand aux responsables religieux, il étaient et sont encore désignés par leurs prédécesseurs, sous réserve de l'approbation du maire. Pour l'élite politique régionale, la fonction des *tayekanani* était de veiller à ce que les impôts soient perçus, l'ordre public maintenu, les menus différends réglés à l'amiable et les corvées effectuées.

En même temps, les autochtones définissent les postes comme des «charges» (*cargos*) que le titulaire doit remplir pour le village, sans en tirer d'avantages personnels. Les autorités locales étaient et sont encore vues comme «nos autorités» (*totayekanka*) et les villageois considèrent que leur fonction principale est de les représenter face aux «étrangers» (*koyomej*) des niveaux supérieurs. Les élus des villages occupent donc des fonctions essentiellement contradictoires, selon le point de vue où l'on se place, et il leur incombe de gérer cette contradiction, dans la certitude de ne pouvoir satisfaire tout le monde.

Les premiers responsables des coopératives locales (*comisionados*) et les représentants régionaux furent également choisis parmi les mêmes familles de notables, trait important à une étape où leur principale fonction était de recruter des membres. A la différence des *autoridades* d'antan, cependant, ces responsables avaient désormais des contacts directs avec l'appareil d'Etat central, contacts facilités par les conseillers qui provenaient des régions urbaines. Les *comisionados* durent bientôt préparer des ordres du jour et des budgets, participer à des négociations compliquées, solliciter du crédit. A la génération des notables bénévoles succéda bientôt celle d'autochtones plus jeunes et plus scolarisés, rémunérés, et plus à l'aise dans l'univers non indien du chef-lieu régional, où ils devaient désormais passer le plus clair de leur temps; avec des voyages fréquents à Puebla et à Mexico.

Ils héritèrent, comme les notables, de l'ambiguïté attachée à la fonction d'*autoridad.* Pour le gouvernement mexicain et ses agences, une coopérative comme la Tosépan constituait un mécanisme de modernisation économique et sociale de la région. Les grandes lignes de son fonctionnement étaient décidées à Mexico, depuis les modèles concernant le déroulement des réunions jusqu'au prix des denrées vendues par les coopératives locales. Pour les membres de ces dernières, cependant, et pour leurs représentants aux assemblées générales hebdomadaires, la coopérative était un organisme à eux, destiné à acheminer leurs requêtes et réclamations vers le centre et à canaliser vers les villages l'aide économique du gouvernement. Dans ce rôle, la coopérative était perçue comme une manière de court-circuiter la bourgeoisie *koyot* des chefs-lieux qui, pensait-on, avait toujours détourné à son profit les largesses des instances supérieures.

Les représentants régionaux devaient donc désormais dominer non seulement deux langues, mais deux langages. Il leur fallait en effet traduire en termes bureaucratiques les demandes des membres, pour les rendre politiquement acceptables aux fonctionnaires. En même temps, ils devaient pouvoir faire accepter à la base les directives des instances supérieures, qu'il s'agisse des hausses périodiques des prix à la consommation (surtout après 1984) ou des campagnes d'alphabétisation, de vaccination, de rénovation des plantations, etc. L'affirmation de l'identité à travers une organisation indienne et paysanne entraîna donc paradoxalement une intégation plus poussée à la société non indienne. Au plan linguistique, le phénomène le plus frappant de la période fut l'adoption rapide par les *cooperativistas* de la terminologie bureaucratique, du niveau régional (où les réunions se tenaient en espagnol) jusqu'aux assemblées locales, où l'on parlait nahuat ou totonaque. Dans ces dernières, le langage devient parfois truffé d'hispanismes au point que même quelqu'un qui ne possède qu'imparfaitement la langue nahuat (comme moi) pouvait suivre les débats sans trop de peine.[10] L'adoption d'hispanismes n'était que la manifestation d'un processus plus large de changement culturel : on vit se répandre rapidement le port des vêtements urbains (pour les hommes, le pantalon, la chemise et les souliers à la mode, au lieu des vêtements de coton blanc et des *huaraches*); le stylo, le bracelet-montre et la calculatrice de poche devinrent des accessoires quasi indispensables pour les *comisionados,* ainsi que l'usage d'expressions savantes (*paréceme*), et même ... la poignée de mains soixante-huitarde (introduite par les certains *asesores*).

L'adoption de modèles extérieurs se doublait cependant d'un processus d'*appropriation* des formes culturelles et institutionnelles nouvelles par les autochtones. Ainsi, on fixa les réunions régionales au dimanche, jour où les paysans se rendent au chef-lieu pour assister à la messe, vendre et acheter au marché et bavarder avec les amis. Nonobstant les règles formelles, ces réunions se déroulèrent comme des assemblées traditionnelles : sur chaque point, se succédaient de longues interventions, souvent répétitives, qui témoignaient autant des consensus que des oppositions tenaces des représentants des soixante communautés, de sorte que la durée moyenne était de quatre à six heures. Alors que l'Etat cherchait, par son encadrement, à stimuler la production, la réunion la plus courue, à chaque mois, fut toujours celle de l'approvisionnement (*abasto*), signe de l'acuité des problèmes à ce niveau et de l'avantage que les paysans trouvaient au réseau alternatif. Par ailleurs, les thèmes traités débordaient toujours largement l'ordre du jour, puisque la *junta* hebdomadaire devint le forum général où étaient débattues les questions touchant la politique, l'éducation et même la moralité publique.

Au plan de l'espace régional, la Tosépan Titataniské adopta le modèle hiérarchisé préexistant : on établit le siège dans le chef-lieu métis, Cuetzalan, et les branches locales, dans les villages indiens. (Signalons que toute autre option spatiale aurait impliqué des coûts considérables en temps, puisque le réseau des pistes converge vers le chef-lieu). On acceptait de la sorte la subordination traditionnelle des villages au chef-lieu. Cependant, les autochtones disposaient désormais dans le chef-lieu (qu'ils considéraient toujours comme leur appartenant de droit) d'une place à eux où ils pouvaient entrer avec leurs famille et demeurer aussi longtemps qu'ils le voulaient.

En même temps, les nouvelles institutions modifiaient les paramètres spatio-temporels locaux. Dans les villages, naguère dépourvus de commerces de détail—à l'exception de quelques débits de boisson où les hommes consomment debout, sous un auvent—la boutique coopérative constitua un espace social nouveau tout comme le moulin de *nixtamal* (pâte de maïs) mu à l'électricité.[11] L'assemblée de la coopérative locale que l'on tint le soir pour ne pas concurrencer la régionale, contredisait le mode traditionnel d'emploi du temps qui veut qu'on traite des affaires importantes à l'aube, qu'on travaille le jour, qu'on passe la soirée chez soi et qu'on se couche tôt. Les hommes se plaignaient de devoir «veiller tard parce que certains n'en finissent pas de parler» (*semi se tayoua por in seki amo keman tamij tajtoskej*). Au niveau des rapports sociaux eux-mêmes, le principe fondamental de la vie coopérative, la participation régulière de tous aux discussions et aux décisions, trouva son modèle dans les assemblées villageoises extraordinaires des moments de crise. C'est pourquoi, alors qu'on s'y rendait, au début, pour entendre parler «les ingénieurs» elles se transformèrent progressivement en un vaste forum où l'on présentait les réclamations de toute sorte : contre un *cacique* qui menaçait les membres de tel village, contre DICONSA, l'agence gouvernementale, qui livrait du maïs de mauvaise qualité et en quantité insuffisante par rapport aux besoins, contre INMECAFE dont les prix au producteur étaient invariablement plus bas que promis.[12] Débordant le rôle strictement socio-économique que lui attribuait l'Etat, la coopérative en vint à occuper une place importante dans la politique régionale, le tout culminant avec la présentation de son propre candidat à la mairie de Cuetzalan, lors des élections de 1986 (Aguilar Ayón et Mora Aguilera, 1991).

Même les rapports hommes-femmes en furent affectés. Leur redéfinition—partielle—s'avéra une question délicate, dans une société ou «se parler» (*monojnotsa*) entre non-parents, c'est se faire la cour. Les femmes ou bien refusaient d'assister aux réunions, ou bien se plaignaient, en public ou en privé du comportement des hommes.[13] Néanmoins, elles s'intégrèrent progressivement à l'organisation, en occupant des emplois comme vendeuses dans les boutiques coopératives, *promotoras* de santé, puis en fondant leur propres organisations de commerce et d'artisanat.[14] Elles demeurent cependant très minoritaires dans les postes électifs, ce qui traduit les difficultés qu'elles éprouvent à combiner le travail à l'extérieur et leurs tâches traditionnelles, qui n'ont pas été modifiées (Bucher, 1993).

CONTRADICTIONS NOUVELLES ET PERSPECTIVES

L'apparition d'un mouvement paysan autochtone en basse montagne, dans les années 70, mouvement qui se transforma plus tard en organisation coopérative, a permis que la modernisation entreprise par l'Etat mexicain ne débouche pas sur une perte de l'identité amérindienne, mais plutôt sur un renforcement de cette dernière. En même temps, les paysans indiens vivaient cette acculturation-modernisation comme une appropriation d'éléments positifs dont ils avaient été trop longtemps exclus. Ce qui ne veut pas dire que le processus fut exempt de contradictions, bien au contraire. En effet, les luttes de factions ne cessèrent pas en 1981, lorsque la bourgeoisie régionale décida d'abandonner sa guerre économique et politique contre la coopérative. A partir de 1985, des secteurs de la population villageoise (incluant des bien nantis autant que des paysans sans terre, qui retiraient peu de l'organisation) se regroupèrent dans une opposition aux candidats de la coopérative lors des élections locales. Si le candidat de la Tosépan gagna celles de 1986 (malgré la cabale des *koyomej*), il perdit en 1989, et les élections de 1992 entraînèrent une crise politique qui dura des mois.

Au sein même de la Tosépan, un clivage s'approfondit entre les deux niveaux de l'organisation. Le niveau local, que les villageois appellent simplement *la cooperativa,* en vint après quelques années à être considéré par certains comme le seul vrai niveau où pouvait s'exercer une prise de décision démocratique, tandis que beaucoup considéraient que le niveau régional (*la Tosepan*) était dirigé par des bureaucrates amérindiens ayant peu à voir avec les réclamations et les besoins locaux. L'introduction du salariat et d'autres avantages matériels (voyages, bourses d'études, etc.) et les contacts fréquents avec la bureaucratie gouvernementale ont en effet apporté dans les années 80 un changement important au statut social des *comisionados,* ce qui leur attira la méfiance populaire. Pour certains, l'élection à un poste de responsabilité vint à être considérée comme une rupture avec l'indianité, identifiée à la paysannerie, et la porte d'entrée à la petite bourgeoisie régionale. L'intégration véritable au sein de cette dernière demeura cependant impossible, car l'élite régionale restait fermée à ces indios à qui elle ne pardonnait pas de l'avoir partiellement supplantée. L'ascension sociale des comisionados demeura tronquée, d'où la crise d'identité qui en affecta plusieurs.[15]

Les paysans nahuas et totonaques des communautés de basse montagne avaient adhéré avec enthousiasme à un mouvement à la fois ethnique et économique, au cours des années 70. Contrairement à leurs voisins nahuas des hautes terres, qui prenaient l'option révolutionnaire (Beaucage *et al.,* 1982), ils avaient choisi une voie «légale et pacifique» pour améliorer leur sort. Jusqu'en 1982, le niveau élevé du prix international du café (conjoncturel) et la manne des subventions gouvernementales liées au programme de modernisation rurale de López Portillo (soutenu par l'essor pétrolier) semblèrent leur donner raison. Mais la crise financière de 1982 amena les présidents De la Madrid (1982-1988) et Salinas de Gortari (1988-1994) à réorienter leur politique selon les critères du néolibéralisme dictés par les grands bailleurs de fonds internationaux. La modernisation passait désormais par la suprématie du marché. On vit donc s'effriter, au fil des ans, l'appui matériel que l'Etat apportait à la paysannerie et aux groupes autochtones : les subsides aux denrées de base s'amenuisèrent jusqu'à disparaître, l'Etat mexicain supprima l'agence INMECAFE qui achetait le café à un prix garanti (et ce, en même temps que les cours mondiaux s'effondraient), et on mit un terme aux programmes d'appui à la scolarisation en langue autochtone. La gelée qui détruisit les caféteraies de la Sierra Madre Oriental à l'hiver 1989 ne fut que le coup de grâce à une économie agricole en déclin. Pour acheter un kilo de maïs, il fallait en 1973 deux kilos de café—si on trouvait preneur. Les jeunes autochtones qui, il y a dix ans, s'établissaient dans les villages et comptaient «vivre à notre manière indienne» (*tipanoske maseualkopan*) en combinant l'agriculture et diverses activités de marché, partent aujourd'hui pour Mexico, où ils espèrent trouver de l'embauche comme aide-maçons. Dans l'intervalle, leurs compagnes tentent de faire survivre les enfants en vendant des «broderies typiques» sur un marché d'artisanat saturé.

Cette nouvelle voie de la modernisation-avec-exclusion laisse un goût amer dans la bouche des paysans qui ont vécu l'espoir d'un développement régional autonome, où il y aurait place à la fois pour un mieux-être matériel et pour le droit à la différence. Seront-ils tentés par une autre voie vers la modernité, voie pour laquelle ont opté les autochtones des montagnes du Chiapas quand ils se sont vus coincés dans la même impasse?

NOTES

1. Les données de base ont été recueillies dans la Sierra Norte de Puebla, au Mexique, où je poursuis, depuis 1969, des recherches (financées, à diverses reprises, par le Conseil de recherches en sciences humaines du Canada). Depuis 1984, j'ai entrepris, en collaboration avec le Taller de Tradición Oral, une organisation culturelle autochtone, l'étude de divers aspects de la culture et de l'identité des Nahuas de basse montagne. Conformément à l'usage établi par le Taller, j'utilise le terme «Nahua» pour désigner les autochtones eux-mêmes, et «nahuat», pour la variante lingüistique locale.
2. Ainsi, Roger Renaud parle de «l'inébranlable volonté de [l'Indien] de rester ce qu'il est et a toujours été.» (1972 : 34) comme si les autochtones avaient pu, depuis cinq cents ans, demeurer en marge de l'histoire. Robert Jaulin, pour sa part, oppose à notre civilisation «cannibale» un monde indien idéal, gouverné par «la loi de l'«autre» [...] la discrétion, la compatibilité [...] la non-extension de soi» (1970 : 15-16).
3. Voir par exemple la thèse de l'«éternel retour du Tawantinsuyu», qu'expose Virgilio Roel Pineda (1981); dans le contexte canadien, voir Lyons (1984). Au niveau des organisations, le *Movimiento Indio Peruano* défend des thèses similaires (1981). Au Mexique, cependant, la majorité des organisations autochtones ont davantage mis de l'avant le droit à l'égalité, en insistant sur les revendications de type universaliste (terre, éducation, démocratie ...) (Bonfil Batalla, dir., 1981 : 390-412).
4. Doit-on souligner que le soulèvement récent au Chiapas (janvier 1994) est venu rappeler aux Mexicains, et au monde, l'écart qui existe entre le discours et la réalité. Au plan politique, le Parti Révolutionnaire Institutionnel n'a jamais accepté une alternance véritable : si l'opposition, de droite ou de gauche, peut occuper des sièges au Congrès, tous les moyens sont bons (coercition, fraude) pour l'empêcher d'accéder au pouvoir exécutif, non seulement au niveau national, mais encore à celui des états (à deux exceptions près) et même des municipalités. La réduction des subsides à l'agriculture et la révocation de l'inaliénabilité des terres autochtones, mesures prises au nom de l'ALENA, ont frappé durement les populations paysannes et autochtones, surtout dans le centre et le sud du pays. Visiblement, libéralisation, justice sociale et démocratisation ne vont pas de pair pour le gouvernement, qui, s'il est prêt à considérer certaines compensations pour les secteurs les plus

vulnérables (comme le Programme *Solidaridad*), n'admet qu'aucune autre force ne lui dispute l'hégémonie politique, à quelque niveau que ce soit (Voir Castañeda 1993).

5. Le *huipil* ou *quechquemitl* est une pièce de tissu rectangulaire, de gaze légère, portée par dessus la blouse brodée.
6. Le *xochipitsaua* est une danse traditionnelle autochtone qu'on retrouve dans plusieurs régions du centre et de l'est du Mexique, entre autres chez les Nahuas et Totonaques de la Sierra Norte de Puebla (Voir Taller de Tradición Oral 1984; Beaucage 1985; Chávez Tomás 1992). Jadis exécutée lors des mariages et souvent accompagnée de chants, elle est maintenant de plus en plus réservée aux manifestations officielles de l'indianité (les Amérindiens, surtout les plus jeunes, lui préférant les musiques modernes).
7. Le terme péjoratif *koyot* (coyote, *Canis latrans*) semble se rapporter à leur activité d'intermédiaires commerciaux, jugée parasitaire par rapport aux producteurs paysans comme celle du coyote voleur de poules (Beaucage 1987 : 39).
8. L'analyse des archives régionales et locales a révélé les détails et le contexte de cette importante mutation foncière. Il apparaît qu'à la fin de la Guerre d'Intervention française (1862-1867) à laquelle ils participèrent activement, les autochtones de la Sierra, sans doute encouragés par leurs leaders Juan Francisco Lucas et Palagosti Dieguillo, optèrent finalement pour la fragmentation des terres communales, dans un contexte d'affrontements avec des non-Indiens qui les convoitaient (Thompson 1991; Ramírez, Jaimez et Valderrama 1992).
9. Comme je plaisantais sur mon «indianisation» après plusieurs mois de résidence dans le village, un ami amérindien me répondit très sérieusement : «Tu sais, l'institutrice est ici depuis dix ans. Elle s'habite à l'indienne et parle très bien nahuat. Et pourtant, elle n'est pas encore à moitié indienne. Alors, imagine, toi!»
10. Ainsi il n'était pas rare d'entendre des phrases comme la suivante : *Moneki tinombrarosque* se *presidente de debates, uan se secretario para kitajkuilos in acta* («Il faut nommer un président des débats, et un secrétaire pour qu'il rédige le procès-verbal»).
11. Comme me le disait une paysanne : «Autrefois, on échangeait des nouvelles à la fontaine; depuis au'il y a l'électricité et l'eau courante, on se rend toutes à sept heures au moulin de *nixtamal*, pour commérer un peu».
12. Un ancien leader de la Coopérative régionale me racontait : «Au début, quand on convoquait une réunion, les gens avaient peur d'entrer dans la salle; il fallait leur dire : *¡Xiuiki, tokniuan!*) («Entrez, frères!»). Ensuite, ils venaient, mais ils ne disaient rien; il fallait leur dire : *¡Xitajtokan, tokniuan!* («Parlez, frères!»). Maintenant, ils veulent tous parler en même temps et il faut dire : *Por favor, ¡ orden!* («S'il vous plait, à l'ordre»).
13. Dans un village, une femme protesta ainsi, en pleine assemblée : «Je vis seule avec mon enfant. On me dit d'assister aux réunions sinon on va m'empêcher d'acheter à

la boutique. La dernière fois, en rentrant chez moi, je me suis fait attaquer parce que les hommes de mon quartier avaient filé en douce, de peur des ragots, me laissant seule». Les ragots (*cholopijyot*) pleuvent en effet sur celle qui s'absente du foyer, même pour aller rencontrer d'autres femmes; à plus forte raison, sur celle qui doit sortir le soir et entrer en rapport avec des hommes (Bucher 1993). Leurs maris feront aussi l'objet de lourdes plaisanteries.

14. A San Miguel Tzinacapan, un groupe de jeunes femmes fondèrent, il y a sept ans, une mercerie (baptisée *Yankuik siuat,* «Femme nouvelle») pour y vendre «les choses dont nous avons besoin, comme du fil, du ruban, des vêtements, que les hommes ne veulent pas vendre au magasin de la coopérative». Au niveau régional, des artisanes fondèrent en 1990 une coopérative de mise en marché de l'artisanat. Cette association s'impliqua rapidement dans d'autres dossiers, comme celui de la violence faite aux femmes. Après des débats houleux, ses membres optèrent pour l'indépendance par rapport à la Tosépan Titataniské (voir Pastrana Moreno 1993; Martínez Corona et Mejía Flores 1993).
15. L'humour populaire nahua ne manqua pas de souligner le phénomène : «Quand quelqu'un va à la Tosépan, il peut se passer trois choises. D'abord, il grossit, parce qu'il mange mieux et ne va plus aux champs. Ensuite, il prend une deuxième femme, parce qu'il ne revient plus dormir au village. Finalement, il se met à boire; c'est là que ça devient sérieux».

RÉFÉRENCES

Aguilar Ayon, A. (1985). *La comercialización de la pimienta gorda a través de la* CARTT *en la Sierra Norte de Puebla.* Xalisco : Universidad de Nayarit.

Aguilar Ayon, A., et Mora, S. (1991) : *Participación de la Cooperativa Agropecuaria Regional Tosepan Titataniske en la estructura regional de poder y su influencia en el desarrollo rural.* Mexico : Universidad Autónoma Metropolitana-Xochimilco (Mémoire de maîtrise en développement rural).

Bastide, R. (1971). *Anthropologie appliquée.* Paris : Payot.

Baudrillart, J. (1985) : «Modernité» *Encyclopedia Universalis* 12 : 424-426.

Beaucage, P. (1985) : «La jeune fille, les fleurs et l'orphelin. Notes sur la poésie amoureuse nahuat de la Sierra Norte de Puebla» *Recherches amérindiennes au Québec,* 15 (4) :79-90.

———. (1987): «Les identités indiennes : folklore ou facteur de transformation» in *Construction/destruction sociale des idées : Alternances, récurrences, nouveautés* (B. Dumas et D. Winslow, dir.) Montréal, ACSALF :23-42.

Beaucage, P. (1994). «The Opossum and the Coyote : Ethnic Identity and Ethnohistory in the Sierra Norte de Puebla» in *Latin American Identity and the Construction of Difference* (A. Chanady, dir.). Minneapolis, Univ. of Minnesota Press :149-186.

Beaucage, P., Gobeil, M., Montejo, M.E. et Vitye, F. (1982). «Développement rural et idéologie paysanne. Ce qui se passe au village» *Anthropologie et sociétés,* 6 (1) :131-174.

Bonfil Batalla, G. (1981): «Utopia y revolución» in Bonfil Batalla, dir. 1981 : 11-53.

———. (dir.) (1981): *Utopía y revolución. El pensamiento político contemporáneo de los indios de América latina* Mexico : Nueva Imagen.

Bucher, D. (1993). *Gender status and the division of labor by gender. A case study in the Sierra Norte de Puebla.* Montréal : Université de Montréal, (Mémoire de maîtrise en sociologie).

Castañeda, J.G. (1993). *La casa por la ventana. México y América Latina después de la Guerra Fría.* Mexico : Cal y Arena.

Chavez Tomas, I. (1992). «Xochipitsaua o la historia poética de la relación hombremujer desde el cortejo hasta el matrimomio» in *Voces de Tzinacapan.* I. Chávez et al.), Montréal : Groupe de recherches sur l'Amérique latine (GRAL) :15-23.

Durand, P. (1975). : *Nanacatlan. Société paysanne et luttes de classes au Mexique.* Montréal : Presses de l'Université de Montréal.

Gonzalez y Gonzalez, L. (1986). «Las tradiciones se despiden» *México mañana* (H. Aguilar Camín et al.) Mexico, Oceano-Nexos 1986 :9-18.

Hewitt de Alcantara, C. (1980). *La modernización de la agricultura mexicana 1940-1970.* Mexico : Siglo XXI.

Jaulin, R. (1970): *La paix blanche. Introduction à l'ethnocide.* Paris : Seuil.

Lyons, O. (1984): «Spirituality, Equality and the Natural Law» in *Pathways to Self-Determination. Canadians Indians and the Canadian State* (L. LittleBear, M. Boldt, J.A. Long ed.) Toronto : University of Toronto Press :5-13.

Martinez Borrego, E. (1991): *Organización de productores y movimiento campesino.* Mexico : Siglo XXI.

Martinez Corona, B., et Mejia Flores, S., (1993): *La satisfaccción de necesidades básicas, estrategia en una organización de mujeres rurales indígenas.* Communication présentée au XIIIe Congrès international des sciences anthropologiques et ethnologiques, Mexico, juillet-août.

Mora Aguilera, S., (1985). *La Cooperativa Agropecuaria Regional Tosepan Titataniske en el proceso de desarrollo rural : el caso de la región de Cuetzalan.* Chapingo, Tesis de Licienciatura.

Movimiento Indio Peruano, (1981). «Manifiesto» in Bonfil Batalla, dir.1981 : 265-274.

Pare, L. (1975a). «Caciquismo y estructura de poder en la Sierra Norte de Puebla» in *Caciquismo y poder político en el México rural* (R. Bartra, dir.), Mexico : Siglo XXI : 31-61.

Pare, L. (1975b). *El plan Puebla : una revolución verde que está muy verde.* Chapingo : Universidad Autónoma de Chapingo.

Pastrana Moreno, O. (1993). *Un programa de género en la organización de mujeres artesanas.* Communication présentée au XIII Congrès international des sciences anthropologiques et ethnologiques, Mexico, juillet-août.

Ramirez, C., Jaimez, G. et Valderrama, P. (1992). *Tejuan titalnamikij ... Nosotros recordamos el pasado.* Puebla, Gobierno del Estado de Puebla, Secretaría de Cultura.

Renaud, R. «Introduction. On n'a jamais découvert l'Amérique, on l'a niée» in *De l'ethnocide* (coll.) Paris : Union Générale d'Editions :7-35.

Roel Pineda, V. (1981). «Raiz y vigencia de la indianidad» in Bonfil Batalla (dir.) 1981 : 127-136.

Sanchez, M.E. (1985). *Une communauté mexicaine en développement synergique.* Paris : Ecole des Hautes Etudes en Sciences sociales (Thèse de doctorat).

Taller de Tradicion Oral del CEPEC (1984). *Xochipitsaua. Sones indígenas de Cuetzalan, Puebla.* San Miguel Tzinacapan, Cuetzalan, Centro De Promoción Educativa Para el Campo (CEPEC).

———. (1994). *Tejuan tikinintenkakiltiayaj toueyitatajuan / Les oíamos contar a nuestros abuelitos. Etnohistoria de San Miguel Tzinacapan.* Mexico : Instituto Nacional de Antropología e Historia.

Thompson, G.P.C. (1991). «Agrarian Conflict in the Municipality of Cuetzalan Sierra de Puebla) : The Rise and Fall of 'Pala' Agustin Dieguillo, 1861-1894» *Hispanic American Historical Review* 71 (2) :205-258.

ART AS A FORMATIVE FORCE IN LATIN AMERICA: THE RECLAMATION OF THE INDIGENOUS AND POPULAR PAST IN THE ART OF NICARAGUA

David Craven

During the 1980s, the Nicaraguan revolution sponsored a remarkable process of cultural transformation based on a concept of art as a formative force in society as a whole. Accordingly, the arts in Nicaragua were not only made more publicly visible, but also more publicly accessible owing to the way in which there was an innovative socialization of the means of artistic production through various new cultural programs, such as the national network of Centros Populares de Cultura and Talleres de Poesia. As part of this process of cultural self-determination, there was a construction of a new sense of national, ethnic, and popular identity. This historically-constructed identity drew on both the past, as in the pre-Colombian cultural forms featured in the paintings of Santos Medina, and on the present, as with the new vision of gender parity in the paintings of Maria Gallo.

Pendant les années 1980, la révolution au Nicaragua a mis en marche un processus remarquable de transformation culturelle basée sur le concept de l'art pris au sens d'une force agissant au sein même de la société qui en ressent l'impact formateur. Selon ce modèle, les arts étaient, non seulement, plus souvent exposés au public, mais aussi mis davantage à la disposition du public par la socialisation innovatrice des moyens de production artistiques à travers un ensemble de nouveaux programmes culturels, tels que le réseau national de Centros Populares de Cultura, et les Talleres de Poesía. Une partie de ce processus d'autodétermination culturelle comportait la construction d'un nouveau sens d'identité populaire basé sur des sentiments nationaux et ethniques. Cette construction identitaire a puisé aussi bien dans le passé—surtout dans les formes pré-colombiennes mises en évidence dans les tableaux de Santos

Medina—que dans le présent, par exemple, à travers les représentations des relations basées sur l'égalité des sexes, caractéristiques des tableaux de Maria Gallo.

*

IN HIS BOOK OF 1983 entitled *Nicaragua tan violentamente dulce,* the writer Julio Cortazar observed the following: "The fact is this, hardly had I arrived in Nicaragua, on the 19th of July of course, when the word 'culture' began to echo in my ears and to form part of an extremely varied thematic and sweeping program ... [Nicaraguan] culture did not appear to me to be an isolated component of social sustenance nor did it seem to be the salt or sugar that were added as mere flavor or seasoning to a plate of food" (Cortázar, 1983).

With this observation, Cortázar emphasized a position earlier articulated by Bertolt Brecht that art is not a mere reflection of reality, but rather is a hammer for constructing reality. According to this interpretation, which was central to the revolutionary process in Nicaragua during the 1980s, art is more productive than reproductive, so that it is seen as a fundamental force for advancing the self-determination of a people.

Far from simply increasing the distribution of artworks, the Sandinista National Liberation Front and the Union of Visual Artists directly addressed the issues of by whom and for whom art is produced. Much of the acclaim conferred on the revolution relates to how it altered the modes of cultural production.[1] Not only did the new Nicaragua dramatically increase the level of literacy from 50 per cent to almost 90 per cent,[2] but it also notably advanced the aesthetic literacy of its population and expanded the cultural resources of the nation as a whole. Here it should be added that the level of literacy in Nicaragua has sharply declined to only around 70 per cent since the electoral victory of the United Nicaragua Opposition (UNO) in February of 1990. Perhaps not surprisingly, in an infantile act that has been internationally condemned, the ultra-rightwing mayor of Managua, Arnoldo Alemán, was responsible for the destruction of several important mural paintings, including the remarkable work in Velásquez Park by Alejandro Canales, along with several assistants, such as María Gallo, which celebrated the noteworthy successes of the National Literacy Crusade in 1980.[3]

The advances throughout the 1980s both in education and in the arts by the Sandinista-led revolution were realized by means of what Paolo Freire has called the "dialogical method" for cultural progression. This dialogical method breaks with the traditional conception of culture as a static entity that is transmitted to passive people (Freire, 1981). Instead, the dialogical method was conceived to promote an active participation on the part of the various social sectors, popular organizations, and ethnic groups, in order to enrich as well as extend the existing nature of art and body of knowledge to which the process was heir. As such, both Nicaraguan culture in general and its art in particular came to signify something more intellectually complex in addition to being something more intelligible, two things which are, after all, generally antithetical in a non-revolutionary society.

In a certain sense, prior to the Sandinista-led insurrection and successful revolution of 1979, the people of Nicaragua were not unlike the inhabitants of Macondo in the novel *Cien Años de Soledad* by Gabriel García Márquez, the Colombian novelist. In part, they were unable to advance the project of self-determination in the present because they had lost their place in the past. In this paper, I will discuss the critical reclamation in the Nicaraguan visual arts of indigenous traditions and popular cultural forms as a means of artistic self-determination during the decade of the 1980s. This new synthesis in art through a dialogical convergence of distinctly different cultural languages in turn formed the basis for social formations that at the same time assumed major importance for the structural transformation of society as a whole.[4]

Accordingly, I am going to analyze several works of art to underscore the role of art as part of the general reconstitution of identity and as a preamble to new social and political configurations. The first example is a well-known painting by Santos Medina entitled "The Revolutionary Unity of Indoamericans," which won prizes at the 1982 *Certamen Nacional de Nicaragua* (or Annual National Exhibition of the Artist's Union) and also at the *Bienal be la Habana.* A salient aspect of this painting is the way that it features a complex interchange between Western avant-garde art and the pre-colonial art of Central America. This painting in oil, which is a technique that was invented in the 15th century by what is termed "high culture" in the West, has an obvious link with the Cubism of Georges Braque and Pablo Picasso, particularly as it has been reworked by Diego Rivera of Mexico in his Cubist paintings, by Carlos Mérida of Guatemala in his murals, and by Joaquín Torres-Garcia of Uruguay in his pictographic paintings.

Revealingly, this connection with European vanguard artists such as Gauguin and Picasso, among many others, reminds us that the avant-garde used non-Western art as part of a critique to reconstitute Western art even as official Europe attempted to dominate the rest of the world through a colonial system that operated under the ideology of the purported "superiority" of official European culture, which after all was the adversary of and foil for avant-garde art. As Meyer Schapiro has observed of this contradictory situation:

> By a remarkable process the arts of subjugated peoples, 'discovered' by Europeans in conquering the world, became norms to those who renounced this conquest. The imperialist expansion was accompanied at home by a profound cultural pessimism in which the arts of the colonial victims were elevated above the traditions of Europe. The colonies became places to flee to as well as to exploit (Schapiro, 1988, p.173).

If we consider the painting by Santos Medina from an even broader vantage point, we are lead to recognize that there exists a formal affinity that is as much related to pre-Columbian art as it is to European art. Contrary to the Cubist works by Braque or Picasso or even Rivera, in which there is a distinctive fragmentation of forms in alliance with a disjunctive spatial dynamism, the painting by Santos Medina features a quite divergent pictorial logic because it is at once more precise and less fluid owing to the tight imbrication of the fragments that constitute its composition. Consequently, the notable density and the particular intertwinement of the composition by Santos Medina does not have the same fugitive effect as do the Cubist works from Europe. In fact, these formal attributes of the artwork by Medina noted above were based primarily on the related traits to be found in the Luna Ware that dates from around 1200 A.D. in precolonial Nicaragua.

Similarly, Santos Medina combined these pre-Columbian conventions for constructing pictorial space with a distinctive type of incised line derived from the tradition of polychrome ceramic that was produced on the Nicoya peninsula of the Nicaraguan Pacific coastline around 800 A.D. There also appear in Medina's painting allusive figurative elements that are reminiscent of the glyphs that were used on Ceramic Nicoya. In order to extend farther this inter-image dialogue with ancient Indoamerican culture, Santos Medina executed his painting in a mixture of oil paint and sand, with the resulting texture resembling much more the surface of pre-Columbian ceramics than that of Western paintings.

In addition, the earthy colors (burnt orange, burnt sienna, and burnt umber) that were used by Santos Medina are those of the Nicaraguan countryside, and they were linked during this period to the references to nature that were so significant not only in the visual arts but also in literature, as for example in the "geographical poetry" of Father Ernesto Cardenal (such as the famous poem entitled "Las Tortugas") or in the justifiably acclaimed *testimonio* by Omar Cabezas, *Una Montaña es algo más que una inmensa estapa verde*.[5] In Santos Medina's work as well as in this Nicaraguan literature, the allusions and references to nature as an unbridled force in alliance with the movement on behalf of self-determination were signifiers for national liberation in the face of United States intervention in the area.

The use of this discursive and dialogical language, which is more or less abstract, or rather largely non-figurative, has been explained by the Nicaraguan art critics Raúl Quintanilla and Luis Morales as follows: "The passion for an abstract language, as a means for communicating more open sensations and as a mode for advancing spectator participation, that is, as an art without a conclusive narrative, has been a tendency emerging [in Nicaraguan art] for a long time" (Morales Alonso, 1986).

The reclamation of cultural elements at once indigenous and popular has not been done without a critical reconstitution of these elements themselves. A 1986 painting by María Gallo entitled "Mujer Vendedora," or Woman Street Vendor, served both as a site of convergence for different visual languages and as critique of traditional gender relations. (Here it should be noted, though, that machismo is in many respects yet another legacy of colonialism, as Eleanor Burke Leacock has shown in her anthropological studies.)[6] There is a very clear dialogue between her painting and a famous one by Paul Gauguin entitled "Tahitian Women with Mangoes of 1898." María Gallo, in working from a feminist perspective, gives to her painting an air of intimacy quite at odds with the undue familiarity of the work by Gauguin, so that her work is marked by an attendant sensibility of relaxed sensuality as opposed to the more calculated eroticism in Gauguin's work. Here as elsewhere, María Gallo made a noteworthy attempt to embrace the experiences of the popular classes while also continuing to engage critically the major art from elsewhere, particularly the West.

In addition, Gallo made dialogical references in her heavily impastoed (or richly textured) painting to the popular tradition of marmolina sculpture (which is characteristic of the area around Esteli at San Juan de Limay) that is as simple as it is elegant, as elemental as it is sophisticated. Significantly, this sculptural tradition, which goes back to the pre-Columbian period, was revived by the Ministry of Culture during the Sandinista-led years of the 1980s. It was at this time that María Gallo was the national coordinator for the painting instruction program for the national network of Centros Populares de Cultura, within which the tradition of marmolina sculpture was revived.

In the case of the audience for the paintings by Santos Medina and María Gallo, as in the case of the paintings by the *campesina primitivista* school from Cardenal's parish commune in Solentiname, reception theory is right to claim that a visual language "selects" its audience. Such a "selection" occurs through the construction of a lexicon of class-based, or at least class-mediated, signs that are aimed at determinate sectors of society. Nonetheless, *Rezeptiongeschichte* in the West generally presupposes two things at odds with a cultural process that is as dynamic and as transgressive as the one that took place in Nicaragua during the 1980s, namely, unchanging spectators and conclusive artworks. Contrary to what is assumed by reception theory, the dialogical process of artistic production within the Nicaraguan Revolution was responsible for helping to change the spectator, along with the conventional terms of spectatorship. This change occurred through the use of an open-ended signification via the abstract languages, which nonetheless presupposed shared cultural experiences that were in the process of being altered.

Instead of communicating along standard lines with a presumably non-changing audience, the Nicaraguan art of dialogue and *mestizaje* (or hybrid mixture) in the 1980s served as a stimulus for reconstituting the audience of the visual arts in more advanced terms. At the same time this art by Medina and Gallo, among many others, was reaffirming certain shared public experiences in aesthetics, this same art was also producing new cultural experiences owing to the novel combination of earlier forms. The interchange that this dialogical art generated was both old and new simultaneously, so that it was at once a reaffirmation and a reconstitution. Consequently, the distinctive convergence of these various visual languages (and without language there is neither collective labor nor shared public experience) was a fundamental aspect of a process of cultural transformation that was as important as the economic and political changes in Nicaragua during the 1980s.

The dialogical concept of art manifested in Nicaragua in the decade of the 80s, which acted as a deeply formative force within society, was aptly summarized by Father Ernesto Cardenal, the Minister of Culture in Nicaragua during this period:

After the triumph of the Revolution, culture ... has become democratized. The people are no longer simply consumers of culture; the people themselves are now the producers of it. [Yet] we are not seeking a low level of culture for everyone but rather an elevated culture that is really accessible to all....We seek an integration of popular culture and high culture, of indigenous culture and international culture. (1985, p.43)

ENDNOTES

1. For an extended treatment of this issue, see: Craven, D. (1989). *The New Concept of Art and Popular Culture in Nicaragua Since the Revolution in 1979.* Lewiston, New York: Edwin Mellen Press.
2. Cardenal, F. and Miller, V. (1981). "Nicaragua 1980: The Battle of the ABCs," *Harvard Educational Review,* 51, No. 1, 1-26.
3. Rosenberger, J. (July 1993). "Nicaragua's Vanishing Sandinista Murals," *Art in America,* 27.
4. For a discussion of these structural changes, see: Vilas, C. (1986). *The Sandinista Revolution.* Translated by Judy Butler. New York: Monthly Review Press.
5. For a sustained discussion of these "geographical" references in the arts, see Craven, D. *op.cit.* (pp.140-155).
6. Leacock, E. and Etienne, M. (Ed.), (1981). *Women and Colonization.* New York: Praeger Books.

REFERENCES

Cardenal, E. and Murillo, R. (1985). A new culture. In P. Zwerling (Ed.) *Nicaragua: A New Kind of Revolution,* (p.43). Westport: Lawrence Hill, 1985.

Cortázar, J. (1983). *Nicaragua, tan violentemente dulce* (p.53). Barcelona: Muchnik Editores.

Freire, P. (1981). *Pedagogy of the oppressed.* Translated by M.B. Ramos. New York: Contiuum.

Morales Alonso, L. (1986) Arte Nicaraguense. *La Segunda Bienal* (pp.420-421). Havana: Ministry of Culture.

Schapiro, M. (1988). The Nature of abstract art. *Modern Art: Selected Papers* (p.173). New York: Braziller.

BEYOND DEVELOPMENT AND MODERNITY: REGENERATING THE ART OF LIVING

Gustavo Esteva

Rejecting the Western understanding of *development* and its counterpart *underdevelopment* as concepts of rupture and historical discontinuity that pushed four-fifths of the peoples of the world into a humiliating and undignified condition, the author affirms the emergence of an era "beyond development," where one cultural activity among many, namely the art of story-telling, offers clues to the reclaiming of an indigenous past as a means of acquiring alternative ways of knowing and developing, rooted in cultures that have been erased by the official culture of Mexico.

La notion de *développement* et sa contre-partie le *sous-développement,* issues d'une dynamique de rupture et de discontinuité historique, doivent leur origine à des sociétés industrialisées de l'Occident. Cette dynamique a occasionné pour la plupart des peuples du monde, des conditions de vie à la fois humiliante et indigne à tout point de vue. Cependant, selon l'auteur, nous assistons actuellement, par exemple au Mexique, à l'émergence d'une nouvelle époque «au-delà du développement». Dans ce contexte, un acteur culture—le conteur populaire—peut fournir des possibilités permettant de revaloriser le passé indigène et ce afin de mettre à la disposition de certaines couches de la population mexicaine, des moyens de connaissance et de développement autres, ancrés dans des cultures effacées par la culture officielle du pays.

IF THE HOUR HAS COME for rethinking modernity, it is time to make very explicit the irrenconcilable opposition between culture and development. An analogous opposition would seem to be a good starting point for my argument. "Genetic endowment and cultural heritage evolve according to opposite laws.... Biological evolution sprouts new branches that do not cross-fertilize, branches that never again unite once they have become solid. Culture evolves along another route: its forms are anastomosis; like a river, its waters divide, meander and reunite. Biological evolution remains ungraved while culture implies the memory of things past, which survive only in myth or history or custom"(Illich, 1982, p.140).

Vernacular cultures are like a dance. One always leads and the other follows, sometimes with a nod, sometimes with a change. There is no identity, repetition, imitation; it is a response. Each cultural creation manifests the initiating gender, the responses of the other gender and the specific subjects of history who assume them: the "*gens,*" the "*lares,*" the "*ejidos.*" These subjects are commons[1] which designate the ambiguous and asymmetric match of a self-limiting set of women and men." (Illich, 1982, p.174) These commons express, in their symbols and practices, traits and cultural creations shaped by previous generations.

Development produces the transmogrification of the subjects of history. It can be expressed as a social Darwinism because its design resembles genetic programming and natural selection. It generates a new type of instinct, which takes the shape of history's new subjects: genderless, ideological constructs, like classes, nations, corporations, partnerly couples. Development poses an impossible imitation, a grotesque repetition. Rather than syncretisms, it produces dissonances. Dedicated to the modernization of poverty, it transforms the present into an always postponed future. Focused on rupture, in historical discontinuity, it transmogrifies skills into lacks, hopes into expectations, destiny into illusion, transcendence into mirage. All that is solid melts into thin air.

My intention is not to dwell on the cultures that died. Nine out of every ten people died because of hunger or small pox, those astonishing collective suicides. If their gods died, how could they still continue living? What could be the meaning of their lives after the death of their gods? When nine of every ten die, the survivors cannot sur-vive them. Over the survivors thus falls a double stigma: the ignominious mark of being what they are, in a society denying them the right to be themselves, and also the mark of being still what they are, of not having had the dignity of dying.

Therefore, instead of talking about what is dead, let us discuss what is fully alive, the cultural creations of those denied civilizations, those which crossed with dignity through colonization and development and reacted with sociological imagination in the time of crisis. These people are now advancing, steadfastly, in the taks of regenerating their dreams and their art of living and dying; how they are dedicating themselves with unusual vigour, to the creation of their new commons, generating new myths and confronting new challenges.

Here, I can neither speak in my own language, to shape my words, in the appropriate vernacular expression; nor can I employ the formal categories that are no longer capable of grasping the novelty of what is happening. I am therefore constrained to tell new stories or retell old ones; stories that evoke images. This means I must entrust myself to your imagination.

I was only 13 years old when I got underdevelopment, that illusion, that kind of sickness. It is an unspeakable condition that has no resemblance to any misery of the past; it is more profound and complete than any other undignified condition. No slave in history suffered anything of this kind. Notwithstanding, underdevelopment is assumed with fervour and enthusiasim, as an opportunity for liberation.

My father died a little after I got underdevelopment. This era was not for him. He was not able to witness the end of my confusion, when I found an option to the constant doubts I had previously had about which road to follow. I fully immersed myself into making the new promise a reality. Bravely, I became the first generation of students with a profession that was something like business administration. Following such a career, I was told, I will have the privilege of occupying myself with giving the proper remuneration to investors, satisfactory conditions to workers, and honest services to the community. I would be a pioneer of my country's struggle to develop itself. The dream was already dreamt. The route was already designated. To do what or to go where were questions already answered. There was no point in looking back.

Thirty years later, in 1985, at the conference of the Society for International Development, I dared to suggest that the future of studies about development was to be found in archeology. Only an archeological gaze could give us proper accounts of the ruins left by development. It was clear to me then that the era of development was coming to an end. In spite of the many attempts to resurrect it, the possibility of the new era "beyond development" was emerging (Esteva, 1985).

My story starts with such a change of spirit; with identifying two moments of rupture, of awareness, to allude to three different mentalities, three distinct mental topologies: the one I had in the first years of my life; the one I acquired when I got underdevelopment; and the one now emerging as I heal myself from my underdevelopment.

The first rupture has a precise date and place: January 20, 1949, Washington, D.C. On that day, President Truman substantially changed the implications of world development by introducing its counterpart: underdevelopment. At that precise moment, from one day to the next, four fifths of the peoples of the world were pushed into a humiliating and undignified condition. For them, for us, development meant having to start transporting ourselves, like cattle, on a road that others know better; to launch ourselves towards a goal that others have reached; to race up a one-way street.

Development, in this contemporary connotation, exclusive to the postwar era, was born as aid, as caring, as sharing, to help the underdeveloped to be like the developed. At the same time, it was born in the context of the Cold War. Truman was looking for the predominance of the American way of life. He saw himself as proposing a democratic and equalitarian ideal overcoming the communist threat by closing the gap between industrial and "underdeveloped" countries.

Thus, the emblem was born as a reaction to the initiatives of the colonized world, which were challenging again Western domination. The "others," the social majorities of the Earth, were looking to put an end to a history of marginalization and submission, which transmogrified them into "barbarians," less than men: for the Greeks—infidels and pagans, a threat to faith, for Christian Europe—savages, a threat to civilization; for Englightened Europe—self-sufficient natives, a threat to economic expansion for industrialized and capitalist Europe. By the middle of this century, the "natives" were finally awakening. They seemed determined to change the nature of their resistance to evangelization, civilization and education in the needs of the market, imposed on them for almost 500 years. Instead of awakening, a new colonizing tool entered the world scene—underdevelopment. Truman succeeded in what was impossible for Churchill—prolonging the colonial yoke; Socialit Nehru became his main ally; he transformed Gandhi into an impractical mahatma, unbeatable as the father of the nation but too underdeveloped to help this new nation in its modern construction. Thanks to the myth of development, "natives" everywhere were transformed into "underdeveloped" persons to be modernized and transformed by professional educators, social engineers and man-power planners. The culturally diverse imaginations and dreams of different peoples, full of energy only a few years before, were progressively dismantled and reduced to the illusion of soon possessing, with development aid, the American way of life.

This was the first rupture, the so called "lost decade for development" of the 1980s when the real nature of the developers' myth became evident. The social majorities, for whom development has always been a threat, spoke it louder for the first time. Their resistance was no longer easy to dismiss as traditional fanaticism or mere resistance to change. It became clear that underdevelopment is not a naturally occurring human condition, but a creation of the development enterprise itself. Only by rejecting the enterprise will its effects be removed. And the enterprise appeared in all its nakedness—a malignent myth whose pursuit causes the continual destruction of environments and cultures; a world experiment which failed miserably for the world's majorities.

We finally discovered a solid, well-founded, brilliantly articulated discourse; one which clearly anticipated our experiences with development. We found lucid voices to say what we wanted to say. Expert establishments documented what we already knew. The new missionaries, trying to cover the stench of development with popular participation, holism, self-help, sustainability and other deodorants, are unable to get enough clients for their new Church. We are ready to bury the corpse of development, from which every pest still contaminates the world.

Now, let me speak about the three topologies of the mind defined by these two moments of rupture. Three different stories will try to illustrate the differential condition of each of them.

As a child who was not yet underdeveloped, I had a tradition and the dream of enriching it. I had a place in the world and concrete customs. These gave me a precise orientation in my daily life: how to address adults, how to pray, what to do in the case of birth or death.

My home was built in a new, middle-class section of Mexico City. From time to time, a drover of walking turkeys crossed through my street. I was the one privileged to choose the turkey that my mother would feed for the next few months on the roof of our house, fattening it for our Christmas cooking. Every year, on holiday, I was taken to my grandmother Dolores, "Lolo," in Oaxaca, a magnificent Indian and colonial city in the South of Mexico. Her family tended a stall in Oaxaca's traditional market. I played around the market place with the other children, enjoying a freedom already impossible in Mexico City. Since I was a well-mannered child, I could not ask my grandmother to buy me a lovely knife displayed at the market. One morning, she said to me: "I will buy you your knife." She took me by the hand to exactly the place, and started a long conversation in Zapoteco with the stall-keeper. Then we just left. Of course, I could not say anything. The next morning, after another long conversation with the man, now in Spanish, she said: "My grandson wants his knife." "Good," he answered, as he placed my cherished knife on a table by his right. Once again we left without the knife. Morning after morning, during that holiday, my grandmother chatted with the man, but I did not get my knife.

One year later, on my second holiday in Oaxaca, my grandmother took me by the hand exactly to the same place and told the stall-keeper: "My grandson has now come for his knife." The man took the knife from the table where it had remained for one year, my grandmother paid the price apparently settled the year before, and finally I got my knife. My four-year-old son now has it.

Everything became déjâ vu and at the same time was entirely new. My dreams became tinted by fantastic images of prosperity I saw at the movies made in Hollywood. I still remember my fascination with the first mall, created by Sears & Roebuck a few blocks from my middle class home. The old department stores, established by the French, a century before, were left immediately obsolete. Our *tianquis* and traditional markets became dirty, incoherent, chaotic. The market of Oaxaca suddenly became a folkloric curiosity. I still respected and loved the world of my grandmother. But clearly, I did not want it for myself or my offspring, nor for my country. My nation and people desperately needed to be "developed," and I wanted to be part of that epic adventure.

For that purpose, I could not appeal to my customs, to my experiences, to my traditions. Only "experts'" advice, education and professional handbooks could help. I came under a system of permanent education. Everything I was learning in the school or in my jobs was rapidly becoming obsolete. If I wanted to keep the pace of development, fulfill my duty to myself, my family and country, I should learn as fast as possible. Every day, the next lesson must be mastered.

The turkey drovers became an extinct species, together with the shoe-repair man, who used to sit at our door step, chatting with us and drinking the lemon water my mother offered him while he performed his craft with our shoes. In 1937, a year after I was born, a National Cogress of

Architects was organized. All architects love to make projections into the future. After long deliberation, they submitted an urgent plea to the President of Mexico: if he did not follow their proposals immediately, our beautiful "City of Palaces," already overcrowded with one million people, would become, in 50 years, an urban monster of 2 million people! Later, in 1951, just two years after Truman's speech, this same group of architects advised the President on how to accelerate the growth of our city, and explained how they would manage a glorious capital of 5 million people. During the 50 years of their imagination, the reality of development has transformed it into a city of 20 million.

In half a century, development and the cities created by it, have transmogrified the very definition of human nature, the mode of being in the world. But I can no longer speak about it without some hesitation. It invariably makes me dizzy. I can neither use formal, cold categories, like those of social science, nor can I have the blindness of the development struggle. My gaze beyond develpment is difficult to articulate but always tells me about the painful losses we have suffered, about the terrible sufferings development imposed on my people. The following story is precisely one of loss, the story of real, living men and women who became, through the experience of development, uprooted living dead.

Last month, we confronted a tragic event in the place where I live, in a small village near the city of Oaxaca. A young woman, who recently became our friend and neighbour, lost the child she was expecting. Just 15 days before the due date they discovered that the foetus was dead.

The horror I witnessed was not the death itself, something sad, but part and parcel of our human lot. It is something almost unspeakable. To tell this story, allow me to start with something like a clinical record.

The woman is 30 years old, born in Mexico City, from a middle-class family. She has lived there most of her life. I will call her Anna. She is a competent producer of TV programs. After disappointing experiences with her job and her involvment with the leftist opposition and feminist movements, she came to our place one day, to visit a friend and liked it very much. She convinced her husband to move here but we had some doubts about accepting them. After the ups and downs of her doubts about our way of life and our confidence in their capacity to belong, they finally built a house and moved in last December.

A year ago, Anna discovered she was pregnant, a pregnancy that ended in a miscarriage. The doctors took care of the problem and recommended a treatment. Shortly after that, an ultrasound told her that she was pregnant again. Month after month, she had tests describing the evolution of the foetus. Amniocentesis informed her about its sex and a few months later, Anna made a video of it.

Shortly after these tests, the institution where whe worked erupted into an acute labour conflict. Instensely involved in the conflict, she lost her job after the institution closed. In the meantime, her husband got a good job, professionally and economically speaking, and was happy to become the provider of the house but Anna seemed to find the situation of being unemployed and staying home, particularly humiliating.

Two months ago we learned her ambivalence about her situation and future prospects. It was on the occasion of the first birth in our land. With the help of a local midwife and all the women in our community, a beautiful boy was born to Anna's friend and neighbour in the farm. Anna followed this natural labour with admiration, but with a lot of fear. She could not hide her increasing anxiety about the prospect of giving birth outside the hospital.

A month later, she reported a terrible headache. A clinical exploration revealed no heartbeat. She was rushed to a doctor who informed her, after the ultrasound, that the foetus was dead. At the moment of birth, they realized that the foetus had been dead for two days.

After recovering from the anesthesia, she entered into a state of panic. She refused to abandon the foetus to the hospital or to call the funeral parlour. After a lot of persuasion, she accepted the burial of the child in a small cemetary of our village. Our friends helped us perform the burial. They knew exactly what was to be done. They helped us dig the hole; cover the small coffin with earth; place flowers around a small rustic, wooden cross made by one of them; give mezcal and tamales to everyone, following the local tradition. But they knew nothing at all about matters like "proper feelings," to help the woman out of her confusion.

The burial started out very beautifully. In a cemetery with simple graves, no fences, a kind of semi-wilderness, no clear paths. There we were, around an open hole. The peasants helped the father put the small coffin in the hole. As an elder, I placed the first handful of earth while others followed. However, Anna's husband, her family, her mother and friends stood petrified, immobile, and silent. She did not move either. Marcela, a pesant woman, broke the embarrassing situation by stepping forward with a beautiful bouquet of wild, colourful flowers she had just picked on her way to the cemetery. She knelt and with the help of another woman, arranged the flowers next to the small wooden cross. Then, another pot of wildflowers appeared; followed by a broken plastic bucket. Very soon, the grave was strewn with flowers from the fields. Once this ceremony was completed, the villagers waited patiently for the next step: a short prayer. Nothing happened. They waited to hug and to comfort her—nothing happened. Suddenly the father pronounced an embarrassingly formal phrase of urban thanks, rapidly turned around, and with Anna and her family, ran towards their car. Without any other words, all of them hurried into the car and drove off, forgetting that the mezcal was in the trunk. We had no mezcal left. Then, we also left, with a feeling of sadness and shame. In the cold abruptness of their departure, they seemed to our small community of peasants and us, more dead than the buried child. Theirs is the dead of those who continue living in the absence of tradition, history and customs, to orient them in the arts of dying, suffering or celebrating.

Anna is now trying to recover from that experience. When she speaks about coming back to her professional life, perhaps in Mexico City, I perceive a kind of relief in her face. While she thinks about her final decision, she occupies herself for hours with images brought to her by the dish antenna she purchased a few months ago. Her education has taught her very well how to entrust herself, her body or her mind to the hands of professionals. That is why her conduct with the doctors or the nurses at the hospital was so impeccable. But in Oaxaca, considered the most underdeveloped state of Mexico, there are several developed people, like Anna, without enough developed services for providing the standard therapies, modern peoples are convinced they need. For example, there are no bereavement counsellors as they have in the United States; experts educated to advise and train people who have either forgotten or never learned how to behave in the case of death of some other severe personal loss. This leaves developed people like Anna without that kind of professional "treatment" they learn to "need." Her "basic needs" unmet by trained professionals, totally lacking any cultural capacity or memory of her own traditions, she is, like millions, left neither here nor there, but caught somewhere in between: lost, desolate, deprived, disinherited. Her's is the story of what happens to people after development detroys communities and cultures.

Did Anna ever know what quickening is? Ultrasounds, cameras and other mechanical devices monitored her whole pregnancy. She constantly read printed materials on foetal develpment and motherhood. A predefined official due date established for her the different stages of foetal growth. The village women expressed their surprise about Anna's expectations. For, unlike her, these women refrain from all reference to the child, their eyes quietly smiling the hopes they have for their own growing wombs. Yet, they never mention an infant; it is considered bad luck for humans to declare that they know what the future will bring, something the gods alone can foresee. They expect nothing, they only have their hopes. If a mother or an aunt of a pregnant woman are asked for whom they are knitting and weaving, they usually answer "I don't know. Some little one may come to our house."

Trapped by technology and professional intermediaries, Anna never seemed to be able to form a real relationship with the living being moving inside her. How could she relate to the shadow she was clinically presented in TV monitors? When she was suddenly confronted with the death of that shadow she did not know what or how to mourn. Here, no ultrasound could give her guidance to direct her about what to do with a foetus that no longer blinks. How to perform a vigil with candles and flowers, with friends, tamales and mazcal? Perhaps she considered it outrageous or ridiculous to grieve. She obviously felt the failure of her own and the physician's expectations about her work. She had not produced what the doctors call "the product." Why should she show this to everyone? Was it not better to hide the whole thing and to suffer in the privacy of the nuclear family unit? Anna was unable to identify her loss or to give it a real shape. She cried of course, but confusion and ignorance prevented her from grieving.

But now, let me move on. Allow me to talk a little about this peculiar condition in which more and more of us find ourselves today. We have not, as yet, the proper words to describe our gaze, our ways of seeing and experiencing. We can be there, beyond development, but unable to speak our thoughts. Formal categories are useless, or even ordinary words. We are once again seeing with our own eyes. But our eyes do not speak. And we have not yet created the new postmodern discourse, to describe what our postmodern gaze discerns.

For use, underdevelopment is not the opposite of development. It is a pejorative disqualification, based on the simplistic assumption of some unilinear evolution of societies. The opposite of development is hospitality; to accept with respect that the others exist, that their existence, in their own days, theirs gods and hopes should be respected. Keeping our traditional hospitality, in spite of bad past experiences, we are now walking along our own paths, trying to regenerate our own dreams, and attempting to rebuild our new commons as the world seems to fall apart and the old paradigms collapse. Was it not Nietzsche who said, in 1886, "Development does not look for happiness but only for development and nothing else."

To go beyond development does not mean a further step in the same sequence. It leaves behind the mere movement of resistance, the antidevelopment struggle. It goes straight to the heart of the matter, dissolving the very essence of the development entreprise, the postulate of a unique ideal of life, inside economic societies. By acknowledging that there is totally fundamental and irreconcilable cultural relativity among peoples on Earth, after development people can propose their own redefinitions of the good life. This does not mean a new paradigm, another universal ideal to offer an ideological substitute for development. Instead, it opens a thousand different forms in which people may conceive ideals of life and of social organization.

After Paul Streeten and the Basic Needs Approach, most social strategies and programs are conceived to fulfill the needs of those supposedly deprived. It is not easy to challenge such a well rooted premise of the modern mind. Only a few have preceived the historicity of the present notion of needs, the way development transformed the perception of human nature, in the last 50 years, to transmogrify "homo sapiens" into "needy man" and to transform the limitation of the human condition into dependence and the market and addiction to specific goods and services into "needs."

Fifty years ago, when I was a child, the word "needs" was only used, in ordinary language, when my mother gave me instructions to ask where I could "satisfy" them while visiting a strange house. Nobody would have considered a school, a health centre or a telephone as a "need."

Twenty years ago, I had the opportunity to attend the Public Assemblies of Investment organized by a presidential candidate throughout Mexico to promote his nomination. In a remote village of Central Mexico, I saw the officials of almost every agency promoting all the goods and services they had to satisfy "basic needs"—potable water, credits, roads, schools, jobs, etc. The Assembly had almost come to an end when Don Chuy spoke for one of the communities. "We are so poor," he said, "that we don't have any of the needs mentioned by our *compañeros*. We only want to continue living. But now they are preventing us from even that." Almost everyone laughed, attributing to him poverty of language and typical peasant ignorance. But in conversation with Don Chuy later, I heard the colourful vocabulary he used to describe his people's success in preventing the pollution of development from invading their perception. In Don Chuy's town, people did not have "needs"; they were busy enough with living, fully aware of the restrictions imposed on the human condition. They looked for supports that allowed them to florish and endure in their own terms. Unfortunately, no institution responded to their initiatives. No institution focused on development was prepared to give them assistance.

"Needs," as moderns understand them, emerged with capitalism and the enclosure of the commons. Simultaneously, scarcity was established as the organizing principle of social life. The economy was disembedded from culture, and instituted as an autonomous sphere at the center of politics and ethics.

The pursuit of development in the postwar era brought "needs" to the center of Western political discours; it became appropriate "to designate the moral relations between strangers in a dream world made up of well-fare states"(Illich, 1991, pp.88-101). It provided managers with a philanthropic rationale for the destruction of cultures. It is now being replaced by the new emblem of "basic requirements," under which the new goal "survival of the earth" can be justified (Illich, 1991, p.98).

By claiming respect for the autonomy of our new commons, we are attempting to go beyond development, to regenerate our own notion of a good life. We perceive this to be, once again, a cultural expression, alive and changing; the expression of a community well rooted in its tradition and soil. It represents a new search for freedom, justice and radical pluralism. Based on the assumption of cultural relativity,[2] it claims, for the peoples constituting the majority of the earth's population, what they have been denied for the last 500 years: autonomous paths for their unique, locally rooted lifestyles, to flourish and endure.

While scholars, NGOs and governments are still looking for development alternatives, we have begun looking for and materializing alternatives to development. The question is no longer to find alternative ways to come to the same point. The time has come to say no to the point of development. We will never be like the peoples of the North. We don't wish to "develop." This awareness is neither driving us to the cynical acceptance of injustice nor to the desperate search of alternative means. It is giving us the occasion for celebration. For in our cultural terms, it means abandoning the project for the Westernization of the world.

For the people on the margins, dismantling economic forms of interaction inside their modes of living is frequently no more than giving up dangerous illusions:

a) Illusions that equate education with diplomas. By accepting the economic definition of learning, we embraced scarcities of teachers and schools. By re-embedding learning in our cultures, we have begun to enjoy the affluence of constantly enriched knowledge. And with a little help from friends outside our tradition, we are further enriching our experiences and remedies, which allows us to give up education in the hour of its crisis.

b) Illusions that equate health with dependence on medical services. As "marginal," we lacked doctors, health centres, hospitals, drugs. Now, after recognizing health again as the autonomous ability to cope with the aggressions of the environment, we are regenerating our healing capabilities. We benefit from the traditional wisdom of our healers and from the curative capacity of our environments. We are thus healing from the medicalization of our society.

c) Illusions that equate eating with the technical activities of production and consumption. Dependent on the mediation of the market or the State, we lacked income and suffered scarcity of food. By regenerating and enriching our relationships among ourselves and with the environment, we are learning once again to nourish both our lives and our lands. We are learning to cope with the shortages that still affect us. For example, we are stepping out of commercial crops or giving up the addiction to credit or industrial outputs. A return to intercropping is helping us regenerate both land and culture and improve nutrition as well. We are re-embedding food in agriculture.

d) Illusions that equate dwelling with housing and public services. Seventy percent of Mexico's houses have been built by the dwellers themselves. This tradition, badly damaged by development and its housing projects, is now regenerating. Methods like dry-sanitation bring low-cost, immediate improvement in our living conditions; delinking our stomach from any centralized bureaucracy also gives us lessons in political autonomy. We are learning to dwell again in our own spaces. We no longer have "needs" of food, health, education and housing. In a thousand different forms we are regenerating our art of living and dying, and finding again, in spite of severe personal and collective restrictions, new opportunities of delight and integrity.

I want to conclude by retelling one story that, misunderstood, would be conterproductive to my intentions. For it is a terrible story, but a very important one. Instead of hopelessness in the face of the destruction caused by development, it demonstrates all the possibilities for regeneration. When my people can remember their traditions, when they have a living memory of community, then they can find community even in the midst of sordid urban ghettos, like those of Tepito in Mexico City.

One day, as we returned from a visit to one of the post-earthquake constructions neighboring Tepito, we were surprised by a general state of excitement. That same morning, a four-year-old girl had been raped by one of the neighbours of the *vecindad.* The doctor found no physical damage at all, but there was no doubt that the attempt had been made and the act had been discovered in the making. The entire *vecindad* was discussing what to do.

One of our companions reacted violently, expressing her middle-class rage:

To jail with him, she demanded peremptorily.

The neighbours gazed at her calmly.

Why, they asked, so they can turn him into a criminal?

At least send him to a psychiatrist, she demanded.

Why, they insisted, so that they can make him crazy?

They continued discussing for a long time. Some suggested that it was necessary to kick him out of the community. Others argued that this man had fought alongside with them for the past 20 years and had worked hard as the most dedicated for the new homes. Someone suggested that he be sent at least to a different *vecindad.* That would also be unfair ran the counterargument.

Here at least we know him, we know how he is, we can take care of him and of ourselves. Who knows what he would do in another *vecindad.*

They continued discussing. Finally they decided to let him stay but only if the child's mother accepted. The mother agreed. The man still lives there. I am told he is a model of cooperation and solidarity. He no longer lives alone as he used to since he found a young woman to live with him despite his 50 years of age. He seems content.

I still cannot escape from my perplexity; I do not know what to make of such a matter nor how to handle it. To tell this story implies risking its distortion. Some listeners distort by reading into it reactionary idealization of the life in the *barrios*: dignity, autonomy and conviviality of the *barrio* that culminates in this brutal, unbearable raping of a child. I know that the reaction of my companion is widely shared. I have often been told that acts of this kind should be left in the hands of experts and their institutions—in jails or psychiatric hospitals.

But I also think that this story illustrates other alternatives to the problems that surround us today. Problems of what to do with the unwanted, or the unneeded, of wasted humans as much as of our human waste. With the water closet we get our excrements out of our sight and thus come to believe that we have solved the predicament of handling our own shit. Sending it to the sewage we wash our hands of it. Similarly, when we send a neighbor or a relative to jail or to the hospital we believe we have found the appropriate solution for the problem that their conditions create for us. We wash our hands of it, satisfied. We celebrate or calmly accept our dependency on experts and their centralized bureaucracy.

In attempting to go beyond development, we are clearly engaged in transforming our relationship with the world, with our surroundings. This new relationship begins with accepting concrete responsibilities for our rapists and our other shit. We recognize that it is no longer enough to pull on a handle to wash away our excrements. With our composting latrines and ecological toilets, with and through our communal relationships, we can take care directly, socially, of our troubles and our troubled ones, of those who fall into unacceptable behaviour in our spaces. It implies accepting serious, real responsibilities—not always pleasant, and for which we will never feel prepared. For many modern people, this is the equivalent of accepting a regression, a step back in history. Many consider sewage, the Alzheimer and psychiatric clinics to be irreversible and unquestionable conquests of civilization and progress. To us, they now appear as degrading technologies and institutions, conducive to the dissolution of the social fabric, increasing the disability of men and women to live their lives on their own terms, in their own communities and cultural spaces. Such technologies apply the law under the prejudice of equality, sacrificing ethical principles, basic feelings and emotions on the altar of modern institutions.

The emerging judicial inflation and litigation explosion are clear threats to our lives, but judicial deflation is no rose garden. It demands taking life into our hands once again. It assumes that creativity and autonomy, in a community context, always imply responsibility. It accepts that the art of living is always also the art of suffering, that pain cannot be excluded from the unbeatable joy of consciously giving birth or of consciously dying when the time for it has come. I am not sure if our passive, anaesthetized societies are now ready to live again, if for that they must pay the price of suffering. Many mothers share with their doctors the responsibility for unnecessary C-sections, so that they can avoid the suffering of giving birth, thereby denying themselves wakefulness at the time of their child's emergence from the womb. The cold and cruel agony of the scientific medicine of the elders seems better to many modern men and women than the natural, demedicalized, traditional forms of passing away.

I am not sure if our passive societies are redy to recover freedom in exchange for accepting responsibility.

I don't know if they would ever opt for effective and radical justice in exchange for the injustice of the judicial, economic and political mechanism created in the name of the equalitarian dream.

Of course, our community ways are not royal roads. Nor do they take us to a promised land. To count our blessings, those that we still have in spite of colonization, development and the very hostile forces surrounding us, does not imply closing our eyes to our setbacks and handicaps. We hope that others may listen to our arguments, thus finding with us opportunities for living peacefully, flourishing and enduring inside spaces where being outlawed amounts to a kind of privilege.

ENDNOTES

1. The Commons is a term which designates a common piece of land related to agricultural practices in pre-industrialized England. It refers to land cultivated for the benefit of the community as a whole according to preestablished rules. The *Ejido,* which dates back to indigenous practices in Mexico, also refers to common land cultivated by the whole community according to pre-established rules.
2. Cultural relativity is the opposite of excluding universalism and cultural relativism. It assumes pluralism of reality, beyond ideologies and modes of perception. This notion has been elaborated by Raimon Panikkar. See in particular, "Alternative à la culture moderne," *Interculture.* Montreal: Intercultural Institute of Montreal 1982. "Religious Pluralism: The Metaphysical Challenge," *Religious Pluralism.* Boston V. 1984. "The Pluralism of Truth," *World Faiths Insight,* New York and London 26, October 1990.

REFERENCES

Dumont, L. (1977). *From Mandeville to Marx: The genesis and triumph of economic ideology.* Chicago: University Chicago Press.

Esteva, G. (1985). Development: Metaphor, myth, threat, *Development 3.*

———. (1991). Preventing green redevelopment, *Development 2.*

———. (1991). Development. W. Sachs (Ed.) *The Development Dictionary, a Guide to Knowledge as Power.* London: Zed Books.

Illich, I. (1982). *Gender,* New York: Pantheon Books.

———. (1991). Needs. W. Sachs (Ed.) *The Development Dictionary.* London: Zed Books.

Polyani, K. (1944). *The Great Transformation.* New York: Rinehart and Co.

Sahlins, M. (1972). *Stone Age Economics.* New York: Aldine.

CHAPTER V

POPULAR CULTURE IN THE HOOD

HAITIAN MUSIC IN THE GLOBAL SYSTEM[1]

Gage Averill

This paper examines the repercussions of globalization for Haitian music and musicians, and, by extension, for cultural artists from the "periphery" of the global system. Using interviews with (and texts generated by) Haitian musicians and culture industry personnel, I critique common frameworks for understanding the status of globally-circulating musics of post-colonial societies. I argue against an analysis of globalized musics as thoroughly deterritorialized and incapable of representing identities. Rather, these new musics better represent identities that are both local and supra-local (national, diasporic, transnational).

The agency evident in the approach of Haitian musicians to global markets raises questions about "cultural imperialism" and appropriation of models, supporting a treatment of theses musics as a post-colonial discourse. World beat markets allow their visibility (or audibility) in global markets to provide an important critique from the margins of the global system.

Le phénomène de mondialisation a des répercussions évidentes sur la musique et les musiciens haïtiens, et par extension, sur l'artiste de la «périphérie» du système mondial. En partant des entrevues et des textes produits par des musiciens haïtiens et par le personnel de l'industrie culturelle, cet article propose une critique des grilles d'analyse à partir desquelles les chercheurs cernent les musiques des sociétés post-coloniales qui circulent actuellement à l'échelle mondiale. Cette critique rejette toute représentation de ces musiques commes phénomènes déterritorialisés. L'auteur montre, au contraire, que ces nouvelles musiques représentent, mieux que tout autre production artistique, des identités qui sont à la fois locales et supra-locales, soit nationales, diasporiques et transnationales.

Par ailleurs, le fait que les musiciens haïtiens contrôlent pleinement leur activité dans le marché mondial, remet en question l'étiquette d'«impérialisme culturel» et la notion de l'appropriation des modèles, qui justifieraient la catégorie de discours post-colonial pour ces musiques. En effet, le marché du «World beat» donne une visibilité (ou une audibilité) à cette musique et permet une critique importante du système mondial, à partir de la marge.

Lendi nou kouche	Monday we lie down
Ak yon tèt mal	With a headache
Rezon miltinasyonal	Of multinational causes

"Move Nouvèl" (Zèklè, 1984, side 1, track 2)

*

FEW ISSUES HAVE GENERATED as much academic interest across disciplines in recent years as the process of globalization. The world's economic, political, demographic, and socio-cultural geography has radically metamorphosed under the impact of technologies and media that shrink time and space in the quest for rapid turnover of capital (Giddens, 1990). Although the long-term effects of globalization on nation states, futures markets, and the drug trade, etc. are unclear at best, none of these approaches the complexities and the problematic status of cultural identity in the globalizing environment.

This paper examines the repercussions of globalization for Haitian music and musicians, and, by extension, for cultural artists from the "periphery" of the global system. Haitian musicians have participated to a limited degree in the expanding transnational markets for world musics and have evolved complex strategies for these interactions. In this paper, I attempt to outline a framework for these changes from interviews with (and texts generated by) Haitian musicians.

HAITI IN THE GLOBAL SYSTEM

Chak jou ki jou Ayiti pedi yon pyebwa	Every day, Haiti loses trees
Se lamizè, grangou, ak lamalsite ki fè sa	Poverty, hunger and sickness do it
Pouki gwo msyè vle touye yon piti ...	Why do the powerful want to kill the weak
Depi 1804 yap kenbe Ayiti anba dlo	Since 1804 they've kept Haiti under water
1992 yo kenbe nou sou Anbago	In 1992, they keep us under an embargo

"Anbago" (Papa Jube, 1993, track 2)

In October of 1993, United States President Bill Clinton made a strategic retreat on his Somalia policy after American troops were killed there. One day later, in Haiti, pro-military protesters blocked the waterfront in Port-au-Prince to keep American troops from landing; their immediate objective was to create the appearance of "another Somalia." As a result, journalists around the world cited the Haitian case to demonstrate how small the world had become, making Haiti an instant media example of globalization.[2]

The French colony that rebelled to form Haiti in 1804 was, of course, global from the outset, a product of the earlier global project of European colonialism and the African slave trade. Haiti's enduring peripheral and dependent status vis-à-vis Europe and the United States is mirrored in the social structure of the nation, in which a Europhile import-export elite, in collusion with foreign economic interests, severely oppresses the peasantry and proletariat to extract enormous profits. Haitian musicians, and indeed most Haitians, show that they are well acquainted with Haiti's disadvantaged position in the international system and with the history of colonialism and imperialism that is in part responsible for Haiti's present predicament. As a result, a surprising number of popular songs demonstrate a keen, if cynical, sense of global dynamics. The cultural troupe associated with the peasant organization Mouvman Peyizan Papaye (MPP) linked the machinations of international monetary organizations and the United States government with poverty and despair on the island:

> The Americans don't respect our country
> Their toxic waste is for us
> The plot to kill our pigs is for us
> The relief food full of worms is for us ...
> In October, the school doors will open
> But the IMF keeps all the students seated
> Big shots borrowed money to run their businesses
> Now it's the Haitian people who have to pay it back
> (Anonymous, 1990, Kreyòl text not available, personal communication, David Korb)

For the same reason, political troubadour Manno Charlemagne entitled his 1988 album "Nou Nan Malè ak Oganizasyon Mondyal" (We're Impoverished with the Global System, Charlemagne, M., 1988). Many popular songs attribute Haiti's plight to the vengeance of colonial powers intent on undermining hard-won Haitian independence. The following text uses a nightmare to place current events in a larger context:

Nou tout nan touman vre	We're all truly in anguish
Gan blan ap jwe jon	The White man is twirling a baton
Ap mare yon peyi	He's tying up the country
Pou li fè nou zonbi ...	To make us all into zombies ...
Se lan domi m te ye	I saw this in a dream
Yap elimine n	They're eliminating us
Yap efase n ...	They're erasing us ...
Piniszyon san rezon adje	Punishment without cause

"Adje" (Zèklè, 1993, track 1)

Scores of such examples could be easily culled from commercial and non-commercial Haitian music in recent decades, testifying to the pervasive global consciousness of a people on the margins of a global political economy, and very much at its mercy. I stress this global outlook in order to dispel any notions that Haitian musicians enter global markets as naive dupes of transnational corporations.

A POLITICAL ECONOMY OF THE HAITIAN MUSIC INDUSTRY

Vendredi, "Drive-in Rendezvous"	Friday, Drive-in Rendezvous
Samedi, ton "Hit Parèd"	Saturday, Your Hit Parade
Branchès sur le compte à rebours	Working your way through the countdown
Chacun attend son tour	Everyone waiting their turn
Number One	Number one

"Tambour battant" (Zèklè, 1984, side 1, track 1)

In the lyrics above to "Tambour battant" (Beating drum), a song by the group Zèklè about a 1970s Port-au-Prince radio disk jockey, the pointed reference to foreign terms and names dramatizes the extent of foreign ideological penetration through the imported media. Because the character of the music industry (especially its dependent nature and under-capitalization), has had a major impact on the efforts of musicians to globalize, I will describe and analyze its structure and history.

Globalized media, industries, and capitalist economy form a framework and interconnected system within which local music systems develop.

The worldwide export from the developed capitalist countries of what Sklair calls the "culture-ideology of consumerism," has been "the fuel that powers the motor of global capitalism" (1991, p.42). Various types of local and undercapitalized culture industries have evolved in dependent relation to the global system; the Haitian commercial music industry provides a particularly vivid example of a culture industry in the periphery.

Haiti had a small elite, a negligible middle class, and an impoverished rural peasantry; thus, its narrow base for consumption never inspired major investments in its recording industry, even during the American occupation. Trailing far behind the industrialized countries in access to recording technology, Haiti wasn't typical of the Caribbean or even of many developing regions. Recording projects began in India in 1902, and 14,000 records had been recorded for Gramophone in Asia and North Africa before 1910 (Gronow, 1983). In Cuba, the first recordings were made soon after 1910, and by the mid-1920s, American and British companies had a substantial catalogue of Cuban recordings.

In 1937, German-Swiss immigrant Ricardo Widmaïer recorded Jazz Guignard at his radio station HH3W. Widmaier produced a small number of 78 rpm recordings as gifts for friends, but the recordings were never released commercially. Using a field cylinder recorder, anthropologist Harold Courlander preserved peasant folk and liturgical music from the 1930s until the 1950s and recorded a series of non-commercial albums for Folkways Records, including one of parlour méringues[3] by the Duroseau family chamber group in 1951. But these recordings had a negligible distribution in Haiti and cannot be considered as part of a local recording industry.

With the advent of magnetic tape in the early 1950s, recording costs plummeted and Haitian entrepreneurs could afford to produce 78 rpm recordings. The Ensemble Aux Calebasses, under Nemours Jean-Baptiste, recorded its first commercial release around 1956. Nemours received about $200 for each of the early recordings and paid musicians about $5 per side (Interview: Denis, 1988). Most of the recordings in the 1950s and 1960s, in the early days of band leader Nemours Jean-Baptiste's konpa-dirèk (in French: compas-direct),[4] were done by Herby Widmaïer at his father Ricardo's station, Radio d'Haïti. Joe Anson, Haiti's first record magnate produced the records using his shop on Avenue Jean-Jacques Dessalines as the base for his Ibo Records label. After a falling out with Duvalier in the late 1950s, Anson moved to New York, giving the incipient music industry a transnational structure in its earliest years.

In the mid-1960s, Marc Duverger, a beauty parlour operator in New York City, decided to open up a record store in Brooklyn for the Haitian expatriate market. He, like Joe Anson before him and producer Fred Paul after him, exported raw musical materials (tracks and mixes) from Haiti for pressing and distribution in the United States and back to Haiti. Duverger found the market minuscule:

> It's too bad at the time there was not much money in Haitian music. Sometimes we sell 500 records, 1,000 records. This was not too many years ago! You could sell maybe 5,000, 6,000, maximum 10,000. The problem is clear: not too many people working in Haiti. I would fly [to Haiti] each time, do my recording, pay the studio and come home. (Interview: Duverger, 1987)

In the 1980s and 1990s (25 years later!) musicians still speak of the "5,000 who own stereos" as the upper limit for legitimate album sales in the country.

The underdevelopment of the Haitian music industry is partly a function of the dependent nature of the economy as a whole within the global political economy and of the peculiar features of Haitian capitalism. Much Haitian economic activity revolves around the import-export trade and achte-revann (buying goods and reselling them at a slight profit to others who turn around and do the same thing). These practices require minimum investment and produce a quick, if only incremental, return. An economy of scarce and shrinking resources encourages intense interpersonal competition, sometimes characterized by the metaphor of krab nan panye (or crabs in a basket, each one pulling the others down with the result that none make it out of the basket). Haitian music businesses have not emphasized marketing, distribution, resource development, and capital reinvestment.

The political economy of record production was, and still is, dominated by strategies of risk reduction. Musicians complain that producers "don't push the music" (that they don't pay for sufficient time in the studios to produce a quality product and that they fail to promote and distribute albums widely). According to trumpeter Anderson Cameau,

> These people they see the music just like a grocery store business. They buy this and they want to sell it and make one dollar or 25 cents on each record and that's it. Let's say we go to a producer and he tells us he's going to give us $5,000 to make an album, and he pays for the recording, pressing, album cover and put that album out. And after

that, he doesn't owe you no money. Even if you sell 20,000 or one million, he doesn't care about you. Not even a gift or a pair of shoes! (Interview: Cameau, 1987)

Producer Fred Paul provided a window on the transactions among businesspeople in commercial music, in describing his dealings with producer Joe Anson:

I had the same customers that Anson had. At the time, Anson was playing tough. With this business, you can't distribute one record. You need to have a lot of things selling. Otherwise the guys will order from the other guy who has a lot of records, because it's better to make the koupaj (major deal). So I was selling Anson the records at, let's say, $2, and he was selling me his at $2.50, but I had no choice ... and one day I got to be—well, not a gwo neg (big shot) but I got a little bigger—and I came down with a big order, 1,000 records or so, two or three different numbers, and I told him: "I want to pay for your records at the same price I sell you mine." He said "no." I had already unloaded, and I loaded back up and I left. And two weeks later, Mrs. Anson called me and we made arrangement! It wasn't easy, because I didn't have the money these people had. (Interview: Paul, 1992)

Many of the major producers started out with a store from which they developed their business. There are also many minor producers, for whom the store is still the primary business and record production only a sideline. One finds among store owners/music producers a mentality described by producer Jeff Wainwright as a boutikyè (shop owner) mentality:

... meaning that they have a boutique, and they make records to barter for other records and all kinds of other stuff.... You don't have a lot of companies that act like real labels, paying their bills and promoting their artists. They [Haitian producers] are always looking to stab you somewhere. If I ask them for money from my albums that they sold, there is nothing. So I have to wait. So basically my money is financing their project. When their project comes out, they're still not going to pay me. They're going to put me in a bind where I'll have to take a certain amount of their product and sell it to pay me back what they owe me. Four or five months go by and still no money. And I have to pay the artists. Until it changes, there will be a lot of debts and bad receivables, and things like that. (Interview: Wainwright, 1992)

Haitian bands recorded, and generally still record, for lump-sum fees, signing away their royalties to the album's producer. Many performers have come to regard the lump-sum fee as a hedge against exploitation, assuming that producers will under-report record sales anyway and that some will go bankrupt before paying their accounts. The lump-sum payment is clean and risk free, and yet it introduces a heightened alienation of the artists from the musical product. Whereas royalties imply a continuing ownership interest in intellectual and artistic product, the lump-sum system cuts the tie after the band leaves the studio.

The Haitian audience expects bands to produce one or two albums per year, often seasonally: one for vakans (summer vacation season, during which many bands tour the countryside) and the other for the Christmas and kanaval (carnival) season. Should a band avoid producing an album for a period of more than a year, audiences and the media question whether the band is "going down." This demanding schedule of annual or semi-annual seasonal production, combined with the practice of selling albums to producers for flat fees, encourages an assembly-line approach to aesthetic production that is certainly not unique in the world's commercial music (it may be the rule), but which exacerbates intrinsic "culinary" tendencies.

As an alternative, some bands have formed their own production companies to produce, promote, manage, and keep books. These "vanity" labels have included: Shleu-Shleu Records, Tabou Combo Records and Tapes, Ti-Da Records (Magnum Band), Pas De Shah (Skah Shah), Superstar Records (D.P. Express) and Machiavel Productions (System Band). Although musicians achieve control of the production of their music, the problems of under-capitalization, spotty distribution, meager markets, and lack of promotion aren't significantly redressed by this solution.

There are currently no grounds for enforcement of intellectual property rights in Haiti. The Haitian government has not signed any of the relevant international agreements protecting the rights of authors and composers, including the Berne Convention, the Universal Copyright Convention, and the Rome Convention. Even were Haiti to sign some of these agreements, the experience in states like Thailand indicates that there is a large gulf between acceding to international conventions and enforcing them.

> There's no rights; there's no security. It's not like here in the States where you make a record and if the record is doing very good, you make money on it, or in France where if your music is playing on the radio, you get paid for it. In Haiti, they don't pay you—shit, you have to pay them to play your music! (Interview: Martino, 1988)

Along with the absence of specific legislative remedies, Haitian artists have no organization representing their legal, economic, and creative interests. Most Haitian performers who sell records and tour in the French Antilles join the Syndicat des Auteurs, Compositeurs, et Editeurs de Musique (SACEM) to reap the benefits of at least this portion of their total market. Musicians have initiated discussions with SACEM about extending SACEM's purview to Haiti. Haitian performers active in the United States increasingly register their songs with the American Society of Composers, Authors and Publishers (ASCAP). The lack of copyright protection in Haiti, however, and the rampant piracy that results, is a disincentive to invest the time and money required to match international standards of recording.

The informal or unofficial sector of the Haitian music industry—which includes piracy (unauthorized copying) and bootlegging (unauthorized recording)—dwarfs the legitimate industry in the insular market by a factor of perhaps four to one. Pirated and bootlegged tapes are available in stores and from street vendors in all municipalities of Haiti at well below half the cost of long-playing records or compact discs.

> There are some people who buy a record of the band; they record the songs on a cassette, and then they sell the cassette on the streets or in the stores. As for live recordings, anyone can come with their cassette machine, record the music we're playing, and then make a copy and sell it before the music is released on an album. There are no laws against this in Haiti. (Interview: Pierre, 1988)

Many of the cassettes have hand-written covers and make no pretense at authorization or legitimacy. More recently, the ease of digital piracy has resulted in a rash of high quality pirate compact discs for the diasporic and foreign markets which simulate (and are sold as) legitimate recordings. Legitimate producers have never produced much in the way of cassettes for insular consumption, assuming that the cassette market is saturated with the cheap pirated versions. The pirate industry, then, is left as the only sector satisfying the large demand for cheap musical commodities under conditions of intense poverty.

Haitian music producers, then, can be divided into the four categories I've mentioned: pirates, boutikyè producers, vanity labels, and the more professional domestic entrepreneurs. None owns production facilities; nearly all work with independent pressing plants in Canada or the

United States. There are also few direct linkages to transnational music corporations. Such are the institutional, market, and political constraints faced by commercial musicians in Haitian music.

CROSSOVER DREAMS AND SCREAMS

Responding to the conditions of the Haitian music industry, many musicians turned toward external markets to survive and prosper. The term "crossover," a border crossing from geographically and demographically limited markets to more lucrative and deterritorialized ones was called "mainstreaming" before the mainstream disappeared into global cultural confluences.

Haitian musicians look to three cognitively distinct market types: diasporic, linguistic (French and Kreyòl), and global (world beat), the latter possessing national submarkets (Japanese, American, etc.). The critical factor is that Haitian musicians see each of these markets as confronting them with peculiar marketing problems that place contradictory demands on performers. Musical commodities that are intended for wide circulation throughout these markets are often compromise texts; the musicians, along with their promoters, labels, and producers, have "read" the aesthetics of markets and have positioned their creations for success to the extent possible given their resources, abilities, and creative sensibilities. I want to stress that for Haitian musicians, the "world beat" market is one of many possible markets (albeit with convincing rewards for the successful).

The same conditions that motivate Haitian artists to seek expanded markets may also be partly responsible for the inability of artists to break into expanding global music markets, even while Third World musics achieve unprecedented exposure and circulation. There are innumerable anecdotes about the culture conflicts that have arisen in the tentative crossover projects to date. Strategies aimed at opening up international markets would seem to be in the best economic interests of all players—a classic "win-win" situation for both performers and for local producers, who can receive lump-sum payments for signing rights to existing recordings to transnational companies—yet some producers have refused to cut these kinds of deals and lose control of their product; in the meantime, they "strand" their artists in local markets. Some magazines and agents now refuse to deal with Haitian music business personnel after experiences with unpaid bills, and some clubs and festivals have thrown up their hands when confronted with no-shows and cancellations. One festival got skittish when a Haitian political organization threatened a demonstration against a particular Haitian band that the festival had booked. And in one case, a band gave away all the promotional albums their new American label had advanced to them for concert sales. In each case, elements of the culture of origin have intervened in potentially deleterious fashion to limit access to global or crossover markets.

The interest of musicians in transnational markets was countered by the vivid historical memory of slights and oppression by foreign countries; thus musicians tend to be wary of foreigners with contracts, and the track record on interactions has been spotty. The first major Haitian hit in French markets (Tabou Combo's "New York City") had been owned by a Haitian producer who consigned the rights to a French businessperson, who, in turn, licensed it to a French-based transnational corporation. When profits rolled in, none of them made their way to Haiti, and the band was incensed. A member of the band Zèklè, spoke about a different kind of problem with a French label:

> We were with Warner in France, but I realized that it was just a FISC [he is referring to a tax scheme] so they could have compensation for the next album they were making after ours. They just declare ours bankrupt, a loss, so the next one that comes doesn't pay taxes. They're just using it. They make the money that they spend on you by producing 10,000 albums. But this is not their interest. They want to make 400,000 of the next LP without paying taxes. A lot of little groups have been drained out because of this. Right now, they can't mess around with me because I know the business too well. Automatically, you're not interesting [to them] anymore because you know too much. But that's the only way not to get swallowed up by the jaws, especially when you're coming from a little country like Haiti. (Interview: Widmaïer, 1988)

Still, the effort by musicians to cross over is embedded in much of their work and has a deeper time-frame than is generally understood. The first major commercial success in Haiti, the Ensemble Nemours Jean-Baptiste developed the dance music they called konpa-dirèk in the mid-1950s. It was already the most popular genre in Haiti when they bragged openly on their record album liner notes of the ensemble's appeal overseas:

> Thus, this humor, this poetry, intelligently orchestrated, harmonized, gives to Haitian music its great originality. It is in hearing the Super Ensemble de Nemours Jean Baptiste that the foreign connoisseur truly understands this. Nemours Jean-Baptiste, creator or

the Compas Direct [Creole: konpa-dirèk] rhythm, has definitely launched Haitian music toward the conquest of the continents, because this rhythm ... makes a sensation wherever it is heard, in the Americas as well as in Europe. (Nemours Jean-Baptiste et son Super Ensemble, Ibo Records, —catalogue no. ILP 1278)

In a song called "Compas mondial" ("World beat"), Nemours Jean-Baptiste wrote of the group's international markets:

Toupatou kontan pase	Everywhere they're more than happy
Yon sèl pawòl k yap pale	They're talking about a single word
Se konpa yo rekalme, Ayiti a letranje	They ask for konpa in Haiti and abroad
Sa son nesesite. Se li tout moun admire	It's a necessity. It's what everyone admires

"Compas mondial" (Super Ensemble Nemours Jean-Baptiste, 1966, side 2, track 3)

Foreign tours by Haitian bands are often the occasion for laudatory newspaper articles: "Bon Voyage System Band," "Paris Couronne le Machiavel [System Band]," "Heureux Retour de System Band" (selected titles from *Haïti-Observateur* 1988-1990) and for bals adieus (going-away parties). Foreign validation is a recurrent theme in Haitian popular music, and Haitian commentary on this subject often implies that it is a matter of national honour and prestige that Haitian music compete favorably with musics of other developing nations in global markets. Demonstrating the peculiar contradiction between nationalist pride and desire for foreign validation, Prestige Beer (the principal local brand) ran a television commercial in Haiti in the late 1980s that extolled the natif natal (native born) beer to Heineken, the imported brand, stressing its national roots. The commercial closed, however, with Americans at a poolside table as one calls out stiffly "Garçon, another Prestige, s'il vous plaît!"; the voice-over explained that foreigners prefer Prestige (and, therefore, so should Haitians!).

The most natural major market for Haitian bands is the Creole-speaking French West-Indian market, primarily the Overseas Departments of France that included Martinique and Guadeloupe (Guilbault with Averill, Benoit, & Rabess, 1993). Haitian bands experienced a lucrative period of popularity in the French West Indies, and at the same time, Martiniquans and Guadeloupeans living in Paris provided a staging ground for Haitian bands in France itself. Some Haitian musicians were also tantalized by North American markets, and for much of the 1970s, they attempted to find points of entrée, exploring linkages to

Afro-American funk and soul groups such as the Commodores, Parliament, Earth Wind and Fire, and Tower of Power.

In the mid-to-late 1980s, having failed to win over a substantial African American audience, and with French Antillean sales eroded by the popularity of a new Antillean dance music (derived in part from konpa) called zouk, Haitian musicians were confronted instead by a growing Euro-American and Japanese taste for "exotic" dance music—a market called world beat or ethnopop. The emergence of a market for world music, now assumed to be about five per cent of the total American market has reconfigured Haitian music, enabling border crossings in new directions.

THE CRITIQUE OF WORLD BEAT

Idealistic and technocratic explanations of the "global village" and "global supermarket" explain only the potential for the circulation of musical commodities, not the flow or the shape of these materials and transactions; "world beat" is created at the intersection of technology, political economy, and ideology. Much of the literature on world beat has focused on Western border crossers—Paul Simon, Peter Gabriel, Mickey Hart, David Byrne, and Brian Eno—because of their personal renown and market draw; in world beat, they bring name brand recognition to previously unmarketable musical products. The other category of border crossers includes performers from developing countries who cross borders, serve as contract laborers (or in the worst case scenario as unremunerated and uncredited sources), collaborate with Western musicians, signing with global labels, or licensing their locally produced recordings for global distribution. It is by taking into account perspectives that arise from this sector that I have arrived at the ethical and critical point of view that motivates this article. All musicians hoping to cross over encounter new sets of reception aesthetics, what Hans Robert Jauss calls "horizons of expectations" (1982, p.22) that constrain the artist and that engage intertextually with his or her work.

World beat aesthetics arise initially, I argue, from the condition Lucaks calls "transcendental homelessness," the secular, ironically distanced, individualized, fragmented, technologically dependent condition of individuals in the modern West in search of immanent totality, physicality and metaphysicality.[5] There are many contradictions built into this set of desires. World beat audiences seek authenticity in the relationship of the music to real communities (this, I believe, is an extension of the old authenticity quest in rock and roll), yet crossover threatens this perceived organic relationship of music and community and disrupts claims to authenticity. Seekers of immanent totality presume a set of musics to be natural, communitarian, and ancient; they presume these musics exist somewhere; that they are locatable in exotic spaces and in pristine unmediated, uncommodified states. Thus, at the very moment the music is dislocated on the level of consumption, its production needs more desperately to be located in "authentic" spaces. For this reason, world beat recordings, in their sound structure, packaging, and promotion, privilege the marks of difference and authenticity and signifiers of exotic locales. Promoters of world beat typically derive ancient histories for what are essentially contemporary musics. Naturalness and extinction are interwoven as themes. Recordings are often posited by the industry as rescue efforts within an aesthetics of disappearance. The emergent world beat market demands the "grain of the locale."

Variations on great escape, extreme identification, or even transference, are balms for transcendental homelessness. Globalization has made it possible for the "transcendentally homeless" to purchase the experience while increasing its use value. Touristic settings highlight and isolate those markers of exoticism and difference that attract tourists. Emphasis is on discovery, on "virginal" beaches and deserted paradises. But to participate in these is to render them inauthentic, the sites are used up; the experienced travellers leave for new virginal sites as the naive tourists arrive. Since the advent of fads for Latin American musics in the early decades of the 20th century, weekend musical tourism centers on clubs, restaurants, and dance halls specializing in exotic musics. Advertising, decor, entertainment, cuisine, refreshments, and apparel in these establishments reiterate the markers of the touristic experience, for example, the ubiquitous potted palms. In dance settings, the music provides invigorating encounters with the self outside the frame of daily convention; like tourism, they allow the participants to experience other identities for limited periods of time. The moment of discovery is important in all of this. In exotic club culture, fads are used up quickly; the original, exploratory audiences leave, replaced by suburban latecomers. World music is currently consumed by an audience that considers itself a border crossing vanguard (listen to the names of labels: Discovery Series, Earthworks, Globestyle, Island). One label advertises "We bring the world's music to you." As with tourism, popularity can negate the conditions that led to interest in discovery. The text can become over-consumed, over accessible, and spoiled by an excess of access.

World beat has been subjected to a variety of popular and academic critiques which resonate with the cultural studies perspective above. These critiques can be distilled as follows: The circulation and consumption of world beat is imprisoned in racist and colonialist historical discourses, structured by asymmetries of power and authority (Feld, 1988, p.37). Many see the interest in world beat as an expression of faddism, a means of feeding the insatiable appetite of the Western fashion mill for style turnover, disposability, systematized obsolescence ... in Stuart Ewan's term, "aestheticized waste" (1988, pp.233-258). Music critic Jon Pareles wrote, "The darker possibility is that the star [Western border crossers] could strip-mine a musical culture, reducing time-etched styles to pop novelties and then move on" (1988, p.16).

David Harvey claims that the global mobility of modern capital has resulted in "the active production of places with special qualities ... variegated spaces within the increasing homogeneity of international exchange" (1989, p.295). In other words, locales need to advertize their uniqueness as a competitive edge to attract international capital. A corollary within popular music would be that the music industry stresses local content in order to compete within a global music market that privileges such semiotic markers, even while their music and its commodity nature adopt many or most of the conventions of international musical exchange.

Ethnomusicologist Veit Erlmann[6] argues that Third World popular musics are incapable of representing or engaging meaningfully with the locale and population of origin; instead, he insists, all of this music become the "acoustic correlate of a whole new, geographically decentered system of ... late capitalism, information society, postmodernism" (1992, p.10). Erlmann used Niklas Luhmann's systems theory to describe world music in the context of universal commodity exchange: "Each subsystem therefore becomes a copy of the whole system in the special form of the difference between the subsystem and its environment" (p.10). Elsewhere, Erlmann refers to these examples of systemic metonomy with the term "instantiations." His numbingly pessimistic view is summed up in Erlmann's concluding sentence, "we now sing our difference as part of a system that condemns us to seek the signets of difference in the images it produces from within itself" (1992, p.23). Quoting Beaudrillard, Erlmann claims world commercial musics have become "'the hell of the identical' amidst the orgy of differences" (1992, p.2). This is a very persuasive critique, whose key points I have chosen as a basis to explore Haitian perspectives. Although Erlmann is willing to acknowledge that the system he imagines is not "fully entrenched," his appreciation for the asymmetries of power between the West and the "Rest" allows him to write out of the equation any role for the agency of musicians on the periphery of the system while he considers the "conceptual alternative that world music does not articulate any experience whatsoever" (1992, p.19).

THE PAUL SIMON CARGO CULT

Japonè yo mande	The Japanese asked
Kisa k ape jwe la	What we were playing
Depi mizik la frape	As soon as we struck up the music
Tout moun se leve kanpe	Everybody was on their feet

"Konpa Shelbe" (Tabou Combo, 1991, track 7)

Haitian musicians, witnessing the global access accorded to performers (e.g., Ladysmith Black Mambazo, Olodun, Youssou N'Dour) who had worked with various Western border crossers, looked to someone to do the same for konpa, catapulting Haitian music back into prominence in international markets. Eager to break down what they called the barye (the barrier between them and other markets), Haitian musicians had few reservations about participating in crossover projects that came their way. Haitians were not passive victims of global cultural strip mining in this endeavor: they were, and are, active and aggressive participants.

Lately, they've been looking for some African kind of rhythms, Paul Simon and Lionel Ritchie and others. On "All Night Long" you get that kind of flavor. So that means they're looking for new things ... and we've got new things! We need somebody that will say, "Oh man, look at this!" and take it and go with it. (Interview: Pasquet, 1988)

Have you heard that Paul Simon is going to work with Tabou Combo? [I confessed that I had, but that the members of Tabou Combo knew nothing about it]. They don't know about it? Ha! They're still waiting! The American business is very interested in music from some minorities, because they're trying to renew, to refresh the American music with what they can take from other peoples, and I think maybe they will come to some Caribbean music. (Interview: Robert Denis, 1988)

The recurring Paul Simon refrain in this period prompted me to coin the phrase, "the Paul Simon Cargo Cult," using the anthropological term for millenarian cults based on the fervent belief that outsiders will return bearing cargo.[7]

An early crossover experience for a handful of Haitian musicians was a recording project arranged by American band leader Kip Hanrahan using Tabou Combo's guitarist Elysée Pyronneau, Ambassadeurs' guitarist Ricardo "Ti-Plume" Franck and others. For Franck, the project was an experience in cultural validation:

> When I start playing with Kip Hanrahan, that was a big thing for me. It was my first taste of show business. I went to Europe with an American band.... So I came to New York in 1985 and we start to practice, and they say, "You go," and I was trying to please them by playing some jazz lines, and they say "No, You play Haitian!".... So we went to Europe, he paid me good, and we had fun. I'm not ready to forget what that trip did for my ego. It was my biggest souvenir [memory], a Haitian was playing jazz. I was very proud of myself.... Now they're going to see that Haitians are not just AIDS carriers; they're going to see that Haitians are good guitar players too. That's why I'm not going to forget that trip. (Interview: Franck, 1993)

Musicians tend to be particularly suspicious that the barye has something to do with foreign prejudice towards Haitians, and thus bands will adopt descriptive labels such as "French Caribbean" in order to market themselves in crossover venues. Other strategies to achieve crossover include extensive linguistic code-switching. This strategy is based on the questionable assumption that reggae has succeeded in England and in the United States because it is in English and that the small number of Kreyòl speakers in world markets limits the potential of Kreyòl music. There are also lingering middle-class Haitian prejudices against Kreyòl as an unsophisticated or ugly language ("broken French" is a common description). "Listen to this," one band leader told me as he inserted a compact disc of music sung in Lingala, "That's a beautiful language. Maybe Kreyòl is an ugly language! I don't know that we can make music like that in Kreyòl." (Interview: Anonymous, 1989)

The first album produced in this period of an individual Haitian group by a transnational label featured Boukman Eksperyans, a mizik rasin (roots music) group, on the Mango label owned by the British company Island Records. The rubric "mizik rasin" covers the various hybrids of contemporary popular music with traditional Afro-Haitian religious and processional music. By 1992, there had been six major (non-compilation) cross-over recordings of Haitian artists, and four of them were drawn from the ranks of mizik rasin movements. This bore little relationship to production figures in the Haitian system (where, by 1992, with 50 to 80 albums produced a year, only Boukman Eksperyans's 1990 album in Haiti, Nou La, was devoted to mizik rasin).

Foreign interest in the genre resulted in the formation of mizik rasin bands by Swedes (the group Simbi) and by North Americans (the group Noo Voodoo led by drummer Jimmy Daniels). More recent albums by Ram, Boukan Ginen and others have also targeted global markets, and a selection from the first Ram recording was featured in Jonathan Demme's film Philadelphia.

The dominant attention of world music markets to mizik rasin at the expense of other Haitian genres shows that there is an independent aesthetic of reception operating in world beat; world beat is not just culling the best from local markets, but is preferentially stimulating the growth of selected genres.

CONCLUSION: TOWARD A GROUNDED FRAMEWORK FOR WORLD BEAT

By understanding that so-called "local" musics actually embody multiple historical layers of global cultural flows, we may avoid the more essentialist and particularist notions of local musical practice. Does this mean that the music produced by generations of Haitian musicians, commercial and otherwise, have no residual or resistant local content and specificity, corresponding rather to Erlmann's mere "instantiations" of the global system, the singular in the plural? I maintain that this is not a fully realized project (and that its realization is more open-ended and messy than may be imagined). Musical production is a site at which the global system meets individual praxis, and the resulting product might better be envisioned as a kind of boundary flow turbulence. In other words, global systems are in an ongoing relationship with local systems, which are neither independent of the global systems nor fully incorporated in them. Local music systems are created and recreated by aggregates of individual decisions and behavior, and thus individuals cannot be written out of the equation, nor can they be presumed to be perfectly subservient to the systems in which they are located. To understand the operation of systems, we need to consider the desires, activities, and views of actors within the systems; we need to ground theory in these realms.

Popular music in the Haitian diaspora is intimately involved (as music is everywhere) with processes of individual and collective identity maintenance, formation, and construction. Uneven domestication of global musical influences, creative and original works, a continued bond between the musicians and local communities, and ideological projects that resist the world system through music (while employing aspects of it) all testify to this turbulence, employing elements of chaotic systems, at least up close, in contrast to the tight self-reproducing metonymy of Luhmann's system.

Erlmann's vision of world music as thoroughly deterritorialized simply doesn't correspond with lived experience. The border crossing passports that musicians carry are not one-way tickets to the West (to paraphrase Jon Pareles). There are real reasons why musicians return, why they continue to engage their music and their lives in local markets, politics, and cultures. But when they return, they return with their voices amplified and validated by success in expanded markets. They return more economically independent, freer, and with greater power to address critical social issues at home. They also return as exemplars of identities-in-transition, identities emerging in a world where so many humans are in motion across boundaries. The global circulation of expressive culture doesn't render it incapable of addressing identities, nor does it assign all the signifiers to the category of pseudo-difference. Rather, these cultural symbols better represent identities that are at once both local and supra-local.

Third World music circulating in the West forms a post-colonial discourse—a musical literature, albeit one mediated by a Western culture industry—that does not warrant the thoroughly pessimistic treatment it has received from some critics. I don't propose that we substitute an essentialized view of these voices as a "source of difference per se" (Erlmann, p.5, critiquing Iain Chambers "Travelling Sounds," 1992, p.8), nor do I want to reinscribe a discourse of authenticity. I do want to suggest that global flows are continually domesticated, reinterpreted, and reconstructed locally and that these are intimately related to emergent identity formations. I also propose that these texts (understood not just as the lyrics but the totality of a musical product) be interpreted as voices of these emergent identities in the developing world.

World beat provides a window of opportunity for Third World musicians to cross into expanded markets and be heard; I believe that this unfolding dialogue has aspects of an important critique from the margins of the global system. In the Haitian case study, musicians are eager to jump into the fray, to obtain access to channels previously denied them. In the words of singer Angelique Kidjo from Benin, "I think that the kind of music that I'm making is the only way for the Third World to talk to other people" (Ayre, 1992). The new markets are providing them with incrementally improved bargaining positions to record on their own terms.

The universality of consumerism and commodification has undercut previously vital local expressive traditions; it would be tragic indeed if the West were to deny—through theory—the right of the arts that flourish in place of those very traditions to speak to or for audiences. I believe that it is socially dangerous to assume that the global system and its "common meta-culture of social modernity" (Tomlinson 1991, p. 55) has erased difference or that cultural production, because it circulates in expanded markets, is necessarily flung free from any and all cultural reference. Haitian identities are at once spatial and non-spatial phenomena: local, diasporic, global, national and transnational, and Haitian popular music has come to symbolize that complex state of being. The increasingly global references in Haitian popular music correlate with Haiti's increasingly integrated status in the global system (the 1992-94 embargo not withstanding), and an increasing desire to take part in global discourse.

I have been critical of the ideologies inherent in the Western consumption of world beat, including Haitian music, to date. The circulation of the world's music—on the cultural terrain and on the socio-cultural terms of the West—will continue to be interpreted in relation to other discourses about the non-Western world and subject to the same tropes and stereotypes. Yet I also recognize that I am critiquing an emergent phenomenon. I suggest that the musical texts generated by the Third World are being more critically consumed by the West, that their status as novelty items is being negated by the self-reproducing niche they are carving for themselves in Western markets, and that this process is being affected by the discourses generated by musicians in developing countries. The categories are subdividing, becoming more elaborate and nuanced, proliferating audiences as they are proliferated by audiences.

Globalization is a process far from fully realized, and it is a process that produces a great deal of friction and turbulence in its implementation. Music from the periphery of this system embodies all of the contradictions of this turbulent process, and in doing so, it speaks directly to the contradictions of identity being experienced worldwide. They are voices of people acting in, around, and sometimes even against this system, not mere "instantiations" of it.

ENDNOTES

1. This paper is based, in part, on a lecture delivered in December of 1992 while a resident of the Wesleyan University Centre for the Humanities. I would like to thank my students at the Centre, the other Centre fellows, Mark Slobin, and Dick Ohmann, Centre Director, for their support and critique. The paper was revised for the Canadian Association of Latin American Studies Conference in November 1993, and I am indebted to my colleague, Jocelyne Guibault, for including me on the stimulating panel she organized. My wife, Giovanna Perot-Averill, was my main sounding board and editor, and, as usual, I am deeply in her debt. C.C. Smith and Gerard Tacite Lamothe kindly allowed me to use transcript of interviews they had recorded.
2. The American troops were on their way to participate in a joint Organization of American States and United Nations mission to restore the legitimate government of president Jean-Bertrand Aristide; one of a number of such global "New World Order" efforts to police local affairs. This global effort stalled in Haiti due to the friction between the global and the local. The Haitian military and their supporters had marshalled nationalist and xenophobic sentiment in the name of Haitian sovereignty to rally a sector of the public to oppose global efforts. The Haitian Army, created by the American Marines during an earlier global policing effort, was the historical guarantor of the rights of the comprador bourgeoisie (the segment of the elite whose survival depends on their linkages to the transnational capitalist class and corporations) to do business with the world. Following the ouster of Aristide, however, the Army donned the mantle of "saviours of national sovereignty" and cast the president, a lifelong anti-imperialist, as a puppet of foreign powers bent on enslaving Haiti. The labels "foreign" and "national" are, as always in Haiti, weapons wielded in a fierce class struggle (Averill, 1989).
3. The *méringue* is a syncretic music and dance genre that achieved the status of a "national" dance in the late 19th and early 20th centuries. One of its many varieties, the *méringue-lente* or slow meringue, was typically performed for intimate parlour and salon concerts.
4. This genre, in its many variations, remained dominant in Haitian markets for 35 years. For a stylistic history, see Averill, 1993. It has been profiled in numerous articles in the music magazine, *The Beat* (formerly *The Reggae and African Beat*), first in a series of articles by C.C. Smith and Gerard Tacite Lamothe (1987,

vol. 6(5), pp. 14-18, and 1988, vol. 7(2), pp.30-37) and later in the column "Haitian Fascination" by this author (1988-1994).

5. I am indebted here to Marianna Torgovnik, who, in her work, *Gone Primitive* (1990, p. 188), applies Lucaks' concept of "transcendental homelessness" from his *Theory of the Novel.*
6. The unpublished article by Erlmann to which I refer, "The Production of Difference: Toward an Aesthetics of World Music" served as a sketch for a later published work, "The Politics and Aesthetics of World Music," an introductory essay to Volume 35(2) of *The World of Music* (1993) which was co-edited by Erlmann. I use the earlier version because the argument is more detailed than in the latter.
7. Paul Simon became a leitmotif of sorts during a period of my work in Haiti. At one point, Simon was rumoured to be working with the Vodou drummers from a well-known temple called Lake Souvenans. The grapevine then had him interested in working with the dance band Tabou Combo. I was, on occasion, asked if I was working for Simon. In 1990, I received a call from a Miami music journalist asking for recommendations of Haitian musicians to collaborate with Simon. Finally, in Haiti in 1991, a musician friend told me I should stay an extra week in the country as they were going to have a party on the next weekend with Simon. Having heard one too many Simon rumours, I looked at him incredulously and declined. The next week, Simon arrived in Haiti for the party.

REFERENCES

Anonymous. (n.d.). Liner notes to Super Ensemble Nemours Jean-Baptiste. *Les trois dangers.* Ibo Records ILP 127.

Averill, G. (1989). Haitian dance bands, 1915-1970: Class, race, and authenticity. *Latin American Music Review* 10(2), pp.203-235.

Appadurai, A. (1990). Disjuncture and difference in the global cultural economy. *Public Culture* 2(2), pp.1-24.

Ayre, B. (1992). African Pop in the '90s: A musician's roundtable. *Afropop Worldwide Listener's Guide.* Brooklyn: World Music Productions.

Erlmann, V. (1992). *The production of difference: Toward an aesthetics of world music.* Unpublished manuscript.

———. (1993). The politics and aesthetics of world music. *The World of Music* 35(3), pp.3-15.

Ewen, S. (1988). *All consuming images: The politics in contemporary culture.* New York: Basic Books.

Feld, S. (1988). Notes on world beat. *Public Culture Bulletin* 1(1), pp.31-37.

Giddens, A. (1990). *The consequences of modernity.* Stanford: Stanford University Press.

Gronow, P. (1983). The recording industry: The growth of a mass medium. *Popular Music 3: Producers and Markets,* pp.53-76.

Guilbault, J. with Averill, G., & Rabess, G. (1993). *Zouk: World Music in the West Indies.* Chicago: The University of Chicago Press.

Harvey, D. (1989). *The condition of postmodernity: An enquiry into the origins of cultural change.* Cambridge, MA and Oxford, UK: Blackwell.

Jauss, H.R. (1982). *Toward an aesthetic of reception.* Minneapolis: University of Minnesota Press.

Pareles, J. (1988, Sunday, August 28). Pop passports at a price. *New York Times,* pp. H16-17.

Sklair, L. (1991). *Sociology of the global system.* Baltimore: The Johns Hopkins University Press.

Smith, C.C. & Lamothe, G.T. (1987). Legends of Haitian music, Part 1: locking horns. *The Reggae and African Beat* 5(2), pp.14-18.

———. (1988). Legends of Haitian music, part II: Compas! *The Reggae and African Beat* 7(2), pp.30-37

Torgovnik, M. (1990). *Gone primitive: Savage intellects, modern lives.* Chicago: The University of Chicago Press

DISCOGRAPHY

Charlemagne, M. (1988). *Nan Malè ak Oganizasyon Mondyal* [1p]. Boston: Kako Productions.

Jean-Baptiste, N. et son Super Ensemble (1966). *Nemours-New-Sound* [1p]. Port-au-Prince: Anson Music Center.

Papa Jube (1993). *Liberasyon* [cd]. Miami: Melodie Makers Inc.

Tabou Combo (1991). *Zap-Zap* [cd]. Teaneck, NJ: Zafem Records.

Zèklè (1984). *Stop* [1p]. Port-au-Prince: Zèklè Records.

———. (1993). *San Mele* [cd]. Brooklyn: Nouvel Jenerasyon Records.

INTERVIEWS CITED

*Anderson Cameau, Miami, 1987

Anonymous, Brooklyn, 1989

Robert Denis, Port-au-Prince, 1988

*Marc Duverger, Brooklyn, 1987

Ricardo "Ti-Plume" Franck, Brooklyn, 1993

Robert Martino, Miami, 1988

André "Dadou" Pasquet, Miami, 1988

Fred Paul, Long Island, 1992
Jean-Baptiste "Baba" Pierre, Port-au-Prince, 1988
Jeff Wainwright, Miami, 1992
Mushy Widmaïer, Port-au-Prince, 1988

*Interviews conducted by C. C. Smith and Gerard Tacit Lamothe

CARIBBEAN POPULAR MUSIC AND CIVIL SOCIETY: THE CALYPSO ARENA AS VOICE OF THE PEOPLE

Embert Charles

Caribbean popular music has, for centuries, articulated the questions of communities which have not been able to make their views known through the formal education system or the mass media. Locating his arguments in concepts of class struggle, empowerment and Gramsci's three sets of relations which constitute a capitalist society, Charles shows how the Calypso as an art form and an oranizational structure has contributed to the creation of a space where opinions and ideas are contested. Specific reference is made to the growth of Calypso in Saint Lucia, to the involvement of non-governmental organizations and to corresponding situations in the Eastern Caribbean.

Depuis des siècles, la musique populaire de la Caraïbe a été la voix des communautés qui n'ont pu se faire entendre ni à travers le système d'éducation ni à travers les média. En situant ses arguments dans un contexte à la fois marxiste et gramscien—surtout en ce qui concerne les trois ensembles de relations qui constituent la société capitaliste—l'auteur montre que le Calypso, en tant que forme artistique et structure organisationnelle, a contribué à la création d'un espace où les opinions et les idées sont remis en question. Le texte examine plus particulièrement la croissance de cette musique à Sainte Lucie, et l'existence des situations parallèles dans la Caraïbe orientale ainsi que l'engagement des organismes non-gouvernementaux.

CARIBBEAN POPULAR MUSIC HAS, for centuries, articulated the opinions, the grumblings and the questions of many communities in the Caribbean region which have not been able to make their views known through the formal education system or the mass media. The Flower societies of Saint Lucia in the emancipation and post-emancipation eras, the calypso and reggae in the period of colonization, and the Antillean zouk and kadans in the post-independence era are forms of music rooted in cultural expression, political experience and indigenous languages. These forms have survived political and economic obstacles because of their relevance to the growth of civil society in the Caribbean.

The calypso as an art form and an organizational structure has many distinct features which contribute to the creation of a space where opinions and ideas are contested. This space, which includes tents[1], associations and competitions, is not found in other forms of Caribbean popular music.

To explore the particular nature of the role of calypso, one must first examine such concepts as civil society and empowerment and their various manifestations in the Caribbean. For the purposes of this analysis, reference will be made to the growth of calypso in Saint Lucia and the involvement of non-governmental organizations (NGO's) with this form of music. We will also refer to similar situations in other states in the Eastern Caribbean. Above all, calypso will not be examined as a purely musical and artistic manifestation, but also as a vehicle for the articulation of concerns of the many interest groups within civil society.

CIVIL SOCIETY AND EMPOWERMENT

The two concepts of civil society and empowerment could lead to some disagreement if they are not understood the same way by the reader and the author. This is undoubtedly because they are based on assumptions rooted in class struggle and issues of hegemony, which in themselves are very complex. The concept of class in the Caribbean is loosely defined through the parameters of income levels, family relationships and opportunities to benefit from and enjoy economic, political and social power and dominance. Since the Caribbean has a tradition of ownership at different levels it is difficult to conceptualize class in the classic Marxist sense as being directly related to the relations of production.

Because of these peculiarities in the Caribbean, hegemony will be defined in such a way as to help us understand alliances in society which lead to the dominance or controlling influence of a class. It is within civil society that these alliances are born and nourished.

Antonio Gramsci notes that a capitalist society is made up of three sets of relations: (a) the basic relations between labour and capital in the area of production; (b) the relations which characterize the state and include elements of coercion such as laws and institutions; (c) all other social relations in the wider society. It is this final category which is described as civil society.

> It is the sphere where capitalists workers and others engage in political and ideological struggles and where political parties, trade unions, religious bodies and a great variety of other organisations come into existence. (Simon, 1982, p.69)

It is the sphere or arena of popular democratic struggles which arise out of groups of people defined by sex, age, race, locality, nationality, occupation, and other narrow interests. Thus the emergence of non-governmental organizations with broad mandates for community development or specific missions of advocacy on behalf of youth, women and disabled and ethnic groups, are part of the dynamics of civil society.

By extension, popular forms of expression such as music, dance and visual arts belong to that sphere of relations called civil society. Calypso, reggae and Antillean creole music have gained popularity because they are rooted in expressions and language understood by the majority of people within civil society; their verbal and musical content is immediately relevant to the life of these people.

Popular music is one of the forms of popular expression used by groups in civil society to articulate their concerns. Other forms include demonstrations, involvement in community building projects and mass media where popular access is guaranteed. These activities are all part of the continuing struggle for the creation of a democratic society.

A key element in the operation and organization of civil society is the peoples' participation. Defined here as their conscious and critical involvement, peoples' participation is important because it verifies the relevance of the form and content of any popular activity within civil society. Participation is predicated on and leads to the building of the economic, political and social power of the people.

In the Caribbean context, peoples' power means the relationship between people and their economic, social and political resources. For instance, in the social context, the fact that people have full control over their language as it is used to articulate their concerns to the wider society is viewed as having gained power. But power also depends on the appreciation, understanding and use by the society of this peoples' language. So power in this context has to be gained, since the peoples' language is one of many existing resources in the wider society over which dominance is sought. Gaining power then, means control of resources.

In order to understand power in this context, one must assume that capital in the capitalist production process, has a "human" component. Human beings, through households and organizations become a major resource for development, thus giving civil society a more prominent and significant role in national development (Duncan, 1990; Henry-Wilson, 1990).

Empowerment, therefore, refers to gaining power through struggle and advocacy and cannot be synonymous with the granting of power such as political independence or the donation of gifts to communities. Empowerment through peoples' participation is a learning process, since people search and discover and use social, political and economic resources in the society. Non-government organisations in the Caribbean operate on the assumption that no one can give anyone else power.

The numerous activities implemented by NGOs to empower groups, have been lessons which help the wider society understand why some groups have been kept powerless. The growth of cultural studies and youth movement are cases. The new emphasis on gender issues is one of the lessons. (Baker, 1988).

POPULAR MUSIC IN THE CARIBBEAN

The Caribbean region is made up of a large number of individual islands all of which have a legacy of colonialism. Unlike some other geographically similar regions in the world, there were myriad colonial influences ranging from language and culture to patterns of economic activity. Generally the political system was based on the European system of democratic government. Different colonial powers brought different languages the main ones being Spanish, English, French, Dutch. The main religious influence was Christianity. Economic activity was based on the plantation system of production where the labour force was culturally and ethnically different from the owners of capital and treated with less respect. The two most important cultural factors in the evolution of the Caribbean people were the exploitative behavior of the European colonizers and the continuous resistance of the workforce made up largely of Africans and Asians.

Out of the synthesis of these opposing cultures was the growth of some elements of socio-economic and political life which has come to characterize the Caribbean region. At the political level, thus, resistance manifested itself in Anancyism (the practice of trickery as a survival strategy) and maroonage[2] (the symbiotic relationship between socio-political resistance and the preservation of African traditions). From an economic point of view, the workforce built a tradition of petty trading and micro-enterprise. At the cultural and social levels "nation languages" have emerged and indigenous African and Asian cultural and religious practices have adapted to the Caribbean situation as both spiritual refuge and expression. Caribbean historian and poet Edward Kamau Brathwaite describes "nation language" as the combination of verbal and non-verbal cues in the communication patterns of Caribbean peoples:

> The noise and sounds that the maker makes are responded to by the audience and are returned to him. Hence we have the creation of a continuum where meaning truly resides. And this total expression comes about because people be in the open air, because they come from a historical experience where they had to rely on their very breath rather than on paraphernalia like books and museums and machines. They had to depend on immanence, the power within themselves, rather than the technology outside themselves. (Brathwaite, 1984, pp.18-19)

It is worth noting that the location of the Caribbean region near the continent of North America has led to various forms of cultural synchronization with the values and mores of the United States. Some writers have argued that the cultural imperialism of North America is part of a wider process of cultural exchanges and has positive effects on popular musics in developing countries, leading to the development of variations in popular genres (Robinson et al. 1990). We must add however that the responses of peoples to their changing environment, and the inner desire for exploration, are equally responsible for variations in established forms.

Popular music in the Caribbean has been born out of and continues to be influenced by the synthesis of dialectical, social, economic and political situations. Popular songs are sung in the languages of English, French, Spanish, Dutch and a large number of "nation languages" and local languages. Some of these "nation languages" include kweyol in the creolophone countries, Jamaican Patwa, Bajan, Trini, Sranan Tongo and Papiamentu.

In the English-speaking Caribbean, however, the three types of popular music which are predominant are reggae, calypso and zouk or kadans. All these genres have their variations. Reggae music has its origins in the blues tradition of the United States and the response of black people in Jamaica to colonialist efforts to eliminate their African heritage. Writers on reggae music have always highlighted its function as a dance form in the tradition of swing and big band music. But reggae, from its roots in ska[3] and rock steady[4] to its contemporary variations of dub,[5] also called dancehall, has been the vehicle for black resistance and redemption.

Jamaican ethnomusicologist Olive Lewin argues that despite the relatively little attention paid to it, mento[6] is the indigenous dance music of Jamaica. Lewin goes on to acknowledge however:

> Since 1962, popular dance music and songs containing much social commentary have flourished. The music has evolved through ska and rock steady to now internationally accepted and popular reggae, having originally emerged from Jamaican religous ceremonial music. Rastafarian philosophies and musical styles have in recent times exerted considerable and increasing influence on both words and music. (Lewin, 1983, p.43)

The rapid growth of reggae as a popular political expression of the urban poor in Jamaica in the period leading up to political independence grew out of prevailing ideological waves. (Witmer, 1989) Bob Marley is perhaps the leading representation of reggae's potential as a tool of political empowerment.

Reggae music has had a long and rich tradition of recording and distribution and is perhaps the most widely distributed music from post-colonial societies. The growth of the social movement of Rastafari and its characteristics of liberation colours, religious practices and political ideology has assisted the popularity of reggae music.

Antillean music comes from the creolophone Caribbean—Martinique, Dominica, Guadeloupe, Saint Lucia and Haiti. The music of the creole countries is the combination of the use of traditional African drums, percussion and other string instruments used in folk music. The rhythms range from slow ballads to up-tempo dance music. The lyrical content is largely about celebration of life and culture; songs are sung in the creole language. Like all other Caribbean popular musics, kadans and zouk articulate the feelings of exploitation and political oppression of some sections of the society. The different strains of Antillean contemporary popular music are kadans[7], konmpa and zouk.[8] Zouk is the most popular and is a leading dance music in the Caribbean today and has among other things encouraged a return to the creole language. According to Guilbault, "Much of zouk's strength in the four islands is the result of it being sung in Creole—and this for at least two reasons. First, the language is generally understood by everyone." The second reason is that "zouk touches a sensitive chord because it endorses a language that has been totally rejected or at best ignored for generations" (Guilbault, 1993, p.11).

Calypso and its main offshoot soca is the popular music of Trinidad and the Eastern Caribbean, but has grown in influence in other parts of the region. Calypso has grown out of the African storytelling tradition and unlike reggae and Antillean music does not require lots of instrumentation to enhance its appeal. Because of the focus on strong and incisive lyrics, the calypsonian has been dubbed social commentator who uses wit and double entendre as a tool of analysis and criticism. Calypso has grown as the guardian of carnival, its own cultural arena. Numerous accounts of discrimination and attempts to impose legal bans on calypso are part of the history of the Caribbean (Rohlehr, 1990; Hippolyte and Charles, 1990; Marshall, 1986; Omarde, 1986). Contrary to the other popular forms examined, calypso depends on audience and audience structures such as calypso tents and public competitions for its growth and success.

Some of these characteristics have been viewed as factors hampering the global distribution of the calypso. These factors have also helped in the development of the calypso "arena."

The calypso "arena" can best be described as that physical and institutional space for the calypsonian to operate. Generally this arena is a combination of the calypso tents, the various rounds of competition, other calypso shows and to a lesser extent recordings for distribution. Some of the main features of this arena are: (a) the absence of gags—this allows for inter-calypsonian and inter-tent debates which prey on faux pas; (b) a critical sometimes crude informal judging by the audience through well established cues, including jeers, boos and encores all with their own usage of metaphors and double entendre. This situation has created in the St. Lucian context a category of hecklers called "pinez" (bugs) (Hippolyte, 1992, p.6); (c) representation of all races, social groups and classes; (d) Physical space which allows for interaction and the free movement of the audience to and from the stage. Venues are not fixed but assume some permanence due to usage over time. These venues vary from cinemas and community halls in the smaller territories to large halls which have been customized in Trinidad and Tobago. Trinidad has been able over the past six years to have a venue[9] readily available for calypso performances throughout the year; (e) the venues are usually the least equipped of all venues used by different exponents of popular culture. Abandoned cinemas are usually poorly lit with delapidated seating and inadequate ventilation; and (f) the predominant use of popular language and idiom.

CALYPSO AND EMPOWERMENT: THE ENHANCING FACTORS

Numerous popular uprisings have occured in the Caribbean since the 1970s, which have been triggered by deteriorating economic conditions. The legitimacy and impact of these events have in most cases been directly related to their favourable treatment by the mass media. However, further popularization of these events through music, particularly calypso, has resulted in greater public debate. Lord Kitchener's "No Freedom" was one of the many calypsoes which commented on the black power disturbances in Trinidad and Tobago in the early 1970s. The revolutionary change-over of government in Grenada in 1979 has provided inspiration for many regional calypsonians. Among them was the eight-time Antiguan monarch Lord Short Shirt who in his unique style echoed "Viva Grenada" in 1979. An aborted political uprising in Union Island was the theme of Vincentian calypsonian Lord Help Me's work in 1980. Trinidadian Cro Cro[10] sang a prayer for Abu Bakr,[11] after an unsuccessful yet significant revolt in Trinidad and Tobago in 1990.

There is a general disenchantment with the Westminster system of government which in the Caribbean context does not force political leaders to be accountable to the electorate. Generally, the region's populations have not controlled the political decision-making processes. Organizations within civil society, such as trade unions and the church, have become allies of the State and the owners of the means of production.

The emergence of non-governmental organizations in the past two decades was an attempt to rekindle the element of struggle within civil society. This element of struggle became necessary due largely to the homogenization of political opinion in civil society and the state, on the one hand, and the use of market forces to distribute social, political and economic power, on the other.

Traditional tools of empowerment, such as trade union demonstrations and community councils, have become ineffective, due to manipulation by politcal parties or their agents. Besides, membership organizations which are significant political forces in civil society have extreme difficulty staying alive. The mass media has opened up to some public participation through call-in programmes on radio and wider television coverage. However, the interests of the owners of media systems still dictate the content of mass media. While NGO's have attempted through grassroots programmes to empower communities and interest groups, these organizations, with some minor exceptions, still employ approaches to community development, which do not use indigenous cultural resources and popular forms of expression.

It is against this background that calypso has become a powerful tool of empowerment. There are six broad characteristics which help in understanding this role of calypso.

The first is the organizational structure for the performance of calypso. These performances in the Caribbean context are held through tents and competitions. The tent is a show which allows for public participation through chorus and other forms of critical analysis such as jeering at songs which are lyrically and musically weak, and call for the encore of songs which provide potential to represent the voices of the people. Calypso tents help the calypsonian shape his or her product and provide ideas for the dramatic presentation of theme at the calypso finals. The tent also allows for the shaping of the song both lyrically and musically.

In the last decade, the competitions from quarter finals to the finals have increased in importance as a result of more attractive cash prizes. However, these shows have become the showcase of artist-audience dynamics where sections of large audiences support in very dramatic ways performers who articulate their concerns. These shows have also provided the opportunities for the ultimate expression of the calypso—the performance. Calypsos are most effective and best understood as social forces when they are presented and performed (Pierre, 1992; Samuel, 1993)

The second characteristic is the use of popular language. Calypsos are sung by performers steeped in the rhythm of nation languages, their nuances, and traditional and contemporary vocabulary. Perceived common errors of use have been turned around and used as strong points of articulation of issues. In spite of prevailing views on the need to make calypso universal by making it understood globally, the calypsos which are popular and also become classics are those which are considered serious by the audience. "Serious" in this context means a lyrically strong, slow-paced song that makes a strong, critical analysis of prevailing social, economic and political conditions. It must be noted that a serious calypso is not at variance with use of nation language.

The third factor which makes the calypso a strong tool of empowerment is its thematic and geographical focus. Where the calypsonian makes sweeping commentaries on contemporary situations, the song is focussed on a particular locality. The audience is best able to relate to the various illustrations and feels part of the situation.

Four, the calypsonian deals with issues relevant to civil society. The calypsonian's agenda is dictated by socio-political and economic issues. Historically, the calypso movement emerged out of the need by lower income and poor people in society to speak out about their concerns, in the absence of access to private or state owned mass media systems. Issues of political, economic and social victimization, respect of culture and national environment and more recently gender, are all part of the debates in civil society brought into the arena of calypso. In a somewhat modest declaration which could be applied to any Caribbean territory, Chalkdust[12] notes that: "If all the calypsoes of our nation that have been sung, were brought to the notice of our children, the social political and economic history of our nation can be easily obtained" (Chalkdust, 1988, p.75). These issues are addressed in popular form which is both entertaining and reflective. The calypsonian is able to point to contradiction in the role of political parties as the voice of the people. Saint Lucian calypsonian Ashanti notes:

> While they making big roro
> arguing about things like casino
> Lucia getting low low low.

In this song which looks at the population problem Ashanti prophesizes that the population problem will continue to have a detrimental impact on the society because the politician lacks the credibility to speak to the population on the issue.

The fifth factor is the seasonal nature of calypso. This seasonality has been viewed as detrimental to the development of calypso as a marketable product. However, seasonality is a feature of Caribbean culture and allows for preparation and reflection. The gaps between seasons provide the scenarios for the calypsonians, and there are some interesting coincidental factors in relation to seasons. One is that these calypso seasons end before the commencement of the Lenten season in the Caribbean Christian communities. The calypso season thus represents a conscious articulation of concerns dealing with the ills in the society before this intense period of Christian reflection, which, in turn, provides a rest for the artist. The second coincidence is that a full financial year for most governments would have elapsed, and thus the calypsonian is able to provide commentary on promises not kept as well as incomplete and completed government programmes. Seasonality encompasses ritual, which provides the rites of passage for the calypsonian on an annual basis.

The final factor is the organisation of calypso music within the season, which provides two streams of calypsos: socio-political commentary, on the one hand, and party music, on the other. This practice has been perfected to the extent that it determines audience treatment of some calypsonians. Road march and party calypsos have become institutionalized and have a particular function in the use and development of the calypso. Caribbean calypsonians have altered tempo and lyrics of local calypso to suit the taste of Caribbean nationals resident in the United Kingdom, United States and Canada. This feature provides a certain amount of insulation for the "serious" calypso from such critical comments as irrelevance in the global marketplace, lack of creativity and political insularity. The evolution of this streamlining has been documented and discussed (Warner, 1982; Williams and Harvey, 1986). This situation has challenged the calypsonian to make the calypso relevant in this context. Lord Short Shirt of Antigua, with 1976 recordings like "When," and "Tourist Leggo," is part of this response.

CALYPSO AND EMPOWERMENT: THE INHIBITING FACTORS

Like other influential opinion-makers within civil society, the calypsonian is censored in subtle and overt ways. One of the main inhibiting factors is the appeal to the calypsonian to consider the national interest which encompasses the main national economic sectors, political conservatism and the homogenization of local culture in accordance with North American values.

The traditional methods for enforcing this national interest are the banning of songs on State and privately owned electronic media, threatening libel suits against calypsonians, and restricting the use of public halls as venues for shows.

In less overt ways, narrow political and economic interests have been luring calypsonians to articulate their point of view through mass rallies and singing "safe" songs in return for sponsorship.

This recent phenomenon of paying calypsonians handsome fees to perform at party political rallies has the potential to affect negatively the credibility of the calypsonian. Chalkdust notes that "social commentary has been such a weapon in the calypsonians armoury, and it has helped to forge such a free society that no politician, no government authority dare interfere in the 1980s with the freedom of speech in Trinidad and Tobago, and to a large extent in the Caribbean (Liverpool, 1990).

Another recent phenomenon is the national or independence competitions in which criteria for participation include adherence to themes of nationalism and patriotism. These competitions have the potential for critical examination of these themes. However, they usually degenerate into rhetoric on nationalism.

Perhaps the greatest inhibiting factor is the need for the calypsonian to earn income from this chosen profession. Professionalism has become synonymous with commercialization. In its current manifestation, commercialization means unlocking the songs from their preoccupation with local politics and addressing universal themes and global issues without the double entendre, all the while ensuring that musical arrangements allow for dancing. There have been several approaches to this dilemma created by the seduction of commercialization and the desire for independence. Some calypsonians yield to the new reality, some utilize certain cosmetic features, such as enhanced electronic instrumentation, and others prepare different songs for different audiences. Some calypsonians, however, have remained true to the role as social commentators.

STRENGTHENING THE BASE OF CALYPSO

It must be recognized that while calypso, in its form as social and political comment, has potential to assist in the growth of popular expression in civil society, there are issues which need to be resolved. The first is the protection of the arena in which this form has developed. The calypso tent has been threatened by relayed television recordings and the discomfort of patrons due to poor venues and boisterous behaviour of some calypso fans. The tents are also affected by low levels of financial sponsorship and in some cases the absence of venues. The lack of venues has also threatened major competitions. Attempts by calypsonians to hold tents off-season have also been affected by these factors.

The second issue is the protection of the investment of the calypsonian. The intellectual property of the artist must be protected by copyright legislation. Such laws exist in many islands in the Caribbean but lack the mechanisms for implementation. The Copyright Association of Trinidad and Tobago is the only one of its kind in the region, but like many other international bodies it is understaffed.

The third issue is education programmes for the calypsonians to help them improve the skills of the craft as well as to develop management training. The formal education system does not provide the opportunity for the study of one of the region's best forms of popular expression. Calypso research and education projects have been initiated by the University of the West Indies (UWI), Institute of Social and Economic Research in Trinidad and Folk Research Centre, Saint Lucia, and are only the beginnings of what should be very large, established programmes. Recently the UWI (Barbados) initiated a teaching programme on cricket, which, according to historian Professor Hilary Beckles, "unlike any other aspect of popular social expression has assumed hegemonic proportions within West Indian culture" (Beckles, 1993). All forms of popular expression, including music in the Caribbean, must become the subjects of advanced study.

The resolution of these issues lies in the formation of strong calypso associations in the region. Each territory has a history of abortive attempts in this regard. Recently some associations have stabilized and provided institutional support for the growth of calypso. In some territories like Saint Lucia, Dominica, Antigua and Saint Vincent and the Grenadines, the Associations collaborate with local NGOs on organizational and educational activities.

The Folk Research Centre and the Saint Lucia Calypsonians Association have collaborated for the past five years, and the results have been a number of specific achievements:

- the publication of an annual magazine which discusses issues of calypso;
- the implementation of training activities in the craft;
- the establishment of an annual review mechanism through a calypso symposium;
- development of systems and criteria for judging;
- institutional and organizational support to the Association.

All these factors have led to strengthening the Association, enhancing its management of tents and competitions and its ability to attract sponsorship. This Association has also been a strong advocate for proper performing conditions for the calypsonians.

Above all, strong collective action through an association will ensure that the calypsonian remains a tool for the articulation of the concerns of civil society. While the associations throughout the Caribbean struggle as membership organizations to remain alive, the calypsonian remains committed to the task of articulating peoples concerns:

> I won't stop singing calypso
> Until the wrong is right all over
> Until there's no fault I can see
> In the regime representing we. (Robbie)[13]

ENDNOTES

1. Tents: the place where calypso shows and other outdoor Carnival activities are held; a yard covered with a tarpaulin or bamboo fronds, a hall or a theatre. [Definition from Donald R. Hill (1993). *Calypso: Early Carnival in Trinidad.* Gainesville: University of Florida.]
2. The Maroons were the escaped slaves who lived as free individuals by setting up parallel societies in circumscribed spaces on the different islands.
3. Ska: from Jamaica; earlier form of reggae in the 1960s characterized by choppy rythms and upbeat tempo, and the presence of the trombone. Ska, like reggae, uses an off-beat rhythmic guitar pattern.
4. Rock steady: dance form around the late 1960s and 1970s that comes after ska and just before reggae; slower tempo than ska; soloist instruments, such as the saxaphone, are incorporated; the use of the trombone in ska is replaced by a brass section.
5. Dub: also called "dancehall"; corresponds to the talk-over of a disc jockey or singer over the rhythmic section of a typical reggae characteristic rhythm.
6. Mento: Jamaican folk music at the origin of reggae; includes traditionally the following instruments: guitar, a four-string banjo, a rumba-box (bass sanza), a repeater (drum) and maracas. The banjo "filler," the guitar accompaniment and the bass rhythm can be traced through ska and rock steady.
7. Kadans refers to cadence rampa, a term that, according to Gage Averill (1993) is used interchangeably with compas direct—a dance music hardly differentiated from kadans. It is a dance music from Haiti that emerged around the mid-1950s and became the dominant music in Martinique and Guadeloupe from the 1960s to the early 1980s. Through the two French Departments, kadans also became popular in Dominica and St. Lucia (Guilbault, 1993). It is sung in French-based creole.

8. Zouk: dance music from the French West Indies that emerged in the early 1980s. Sung in French-based Creole.
9. Venues refers to particular locations, a term much more general than tents. Venues may take many forms (open field, theatre, nightclub etc.).
10. Cro cro: name of a calypsonian.
11. Abu Bakr: the person who staged the attempted coup in Trinidad in 1990.
12. Chalkdust: the name of a popular calypsonian in Trinidad; several years ago he was called Calypso Monarch.
13. Robbie is a St. Lucian calypsonian.

REFERENCES

Baker, P.A. (1988). An Analytical synthesis of themes in recent discussions about strategies for alternative development: The NGO perspective (Unpublished).

Beckles, H. (1993, January-June). West Indies cricket at UWI. Caricom Perspectives.

Brathwaite, E.K. (1984). *History of the voice.* New Beacon Books.

Campbell-Robinson *et al.* (1991). *Music at the margins: Popular music and global cultural diversity.* Sage.

Duncan, N. (1990, January-June). True development in the anglophone Caribbean and the role of non-governmental organisations. *Folk Research Centre Bulletin,* 1(1).

Guilbault, J. (1991, July-December). On Interpreting popular music—Zouk in the West Indies. *Folk Research Centre Bulletin,* 2(2).

———. (1993). *Zouk: World music in the West Indies.* The University of Chicago Press.

Henry-Wilson, M. (1990). Community empowerment. *Integration and participatory development.* FES/ACE.

Hippolyte, K. and Charles, E. (1990). Calypso through the years. *Lucian Kaiso* (FRC) 1.

Jn. Pierre, K. (1992) That is Calypso—Towards a basic appreciation of the art form. *Lucian Kaiso* (FRC) 3.

Lewin, O. (1983, March). Traditional music in Jamaica. *Caribbean Quarterly* 29, (1).

Liverpool, H. (1990). Kaiso and society. Juba Publications.

———. (1990). *Culture and education: Carnival in Trinidad and Tobago.* Karia Press.

Marshall, T.G. (1986). Notes on the history and evolution of Calypso in Barbados, presented at ISER/UWI Calypso Seminar, Trinidad.

Omarde, D. (1986). Calypso in Antigua, presented at ISER/UWI Calypso Seminar, Trinidad.

Rohlehr, G. (1990). *Calypso and society in pre-independence Trinidad,* Gordon Rohlehr.

Samuel, K. (1993). Presentation in the Calypso competition. *Lucian Kaiso* (FRC) 4.

Simon , R. (1982). *Gramsci's political thought—An introduction.* Lawrence and Wishart.

Warner, K.Q. (1982). *The Trinidad Calypso.* Heineman.

Williams, G. and Harvey, C. (1986). Tent management in Trinidad and Tobago, presented at ISER/UWI Calypso Seminar, Trinidad.

Witmer, R. (1989, February-April). Kingston's popular music culture—Neo-colonialism to nationalism. *Jamaica Journal* 22(1).

COME TO JAMAICA AND FEEL ALL RIGHT: TOURISM, COLONIAL DISCOURSE AND CULTURAL RESISTANCE

Honor Ford-Smith

The argument is made here that representational practices within tourism adapt and transmit old images of colonial domination and heterosexual relations to reproduce news forms of institutional and cultural racism. The author deconstructs several tourist brochures advertising holidays in Jamaica to show how the images of welcoming plantations, friendly "natives," lush scenery, and "hotblooded" brownskinned women, recycle colonial messages of the pleasurable nature of domination.

Des pratiques à la base de l'industrie touristique adaptent et transmettent de vieilles images de domination coloniale et de rapports hétérosexuels pour reproduire des formes de racisme resituées dans des contextes institutionnels et culturels. L'auteur déconstruit plusieurs brochures touristiques qui annoncent des vacances en Jamaïque pour montrer comment les images de plantations accueillantes, d'indigènes aimables, de paysages luxuriants et de femmes «chaudes» à la peau foncée, recyclent des messages coloniaux au sujet de la nature agréable de la domination.

*

THE UNITED NATIONS World Tourism Organization forecasts that by the year 2000, tourism will be the single most important global economic activity (Enloe, 1989, p.20.). Internationally, tourism employs more people than the oil industry. In the Caribbean, the hotel, the blue skies and the beach have replaced the great house and the sugar plantation as major foreign exchange earners. Mass tourism is transforming population patterns, the physical environment, aspects of sexuality and sexual relations, speech habits, education and forms of representation of the region.

I want to argue that representational practices within tourism recycle and adapt old images of colonial domination and heterosexual relations to reproduce new forms of institutional and cultural racism. As a significant part of the global reorganization of capital and the expansion of multinational corporations, the tourist industry works to undermine notions of the nation state. The coastal margins of the islands on which the tourist finds himself or herself are the borders between Euro-American cultures and Caribbean cultures, hitherto boundaried within the nation state. Relationships on the beach and in the hotel become a microcosm for the racialized relations of domination and subordination between the white world and its "others." The Euro-tourist is both a consumer and a creator since the impressions formed on short visits will mediate how she or he processes information about the people and the place she or he visits later on. The images of tour brochures alongside those of fund-raising campaigns to "save" the victims of famine and natural disaster, the inevitable reporting of violence, drug cartels, disasters, souvenirs and fragments of memory are the materials from which the tourist distils a picture of the Caribbean and its citizens, images which may then be re-deployed in relationships with people of colour living in Europe and North America. Since the holiday exists as a social space within which one can experience the temporarily utopic, and the enactment of fantasy existence, these images work not merely to represent what exists in a world of skewed power relations, but also to establish how raced and gendered subjects in a utopic or dreamlike space might resolve old social conflicts. Strategies of resistance to the colonizing forms which the industry takes in the region need to confront the specific ways in which tourism reconfigures sexuality, racism and nationhood and to find anti-racist strategies which both reveal and explode these recycled messages of the pleasurable nature of domination.

TOURISM AND COLONIAL DISCOURSE

For the Northerner, travel is one of the rewards of living in the relative affluence of pockets of the North and a sign of the increased access to leisure in that society. Tourism is a popular cultural practice which offers "the commodification of otherness ... as a new delight, more intense, more satisfying than normal ways of doing and feeling" (Hooks, 1992, p.21).

The brochures I refer to in this paper have been collected from travel agencies and the Jamaica Tourist Board, but they could have been made for any country in the Caribbean. They are the first site of commodification of the Caribbean and they offer very specific locations which tourist and "native" must take up in the narrative of the visit to a tropical island.

Karen Atkinson in her installation "Tales of Desire" superimposes images of Taino Arawaks drawn by the early European colonizers on tourist posters. In her introduction to the installation she illustrates the ways in which tropical nature is re-made in language evoking the female and the erotic. She traces the origins of this in early travel writing arguing that there is a strong similarity between the language of Caribbean tourist brochures and the language of the first Spanish colonizers:

> What started to interest me in this scenario was that the language used to sell these exotic hideaways and virgin territories, was so similar to the descriptions I'd been reading about a certain adventure that took place five centuries ago.... As we all know Cristobal Colon (Columbus) managed in 1492 to make it to a number of islands in the Caribbean ... the language used to describe these events is rather enlightening. Most of the language of discovery is couched in terms of a woman's body, and the fact that language similar to this is still being used today is rather frightening. (Atkinson, 1992, p.5)

She distinguishes between ancient (European) notions of travel pointing out that travel in the past was construed as a male quest for confirmation of a hero's stature, a test of strength and courage which revealed the traveller's identity. Atkinson argues that:

> Tourism is still predominantly addressed to the male traveller. Geography and real estate are still described like women's bodies. Women writers, tourist agents and tour guides are still using such language to describe the lands to be toured, explored, and exploited as if they didn't understand their implications. (Atkinson, 1992, p.8)

I propose that those who dream up the marketing strategies do understand their implications. Within the gendered messages lies a pedagogy of race. The tourist brochures deploy images of domination precisely because it is in the implications of domination that the sense of privilege, superiority and pleasure associated with tropical tourism lies. The messages carried by the brochures deny any suggestion of violent domination while simultaneously drawing on discourses of colonialism so as to make domination seem a natural part of the feminized landscape. Brochure after brochure echo this fantasy of superiority and privilege in combination with heterosexual delight. In hotels, with names like Swept Away, Couples, or a more excessively libidinous experiment at another resort Hedonism II, a language of seduction offers paradise, a feast for the senses, secrecy, escape and an opportunity to savour your (most secret) fantasies (Jamaica Tourist Board Brochure, 1992). The brochures are in marked contrast to those featuring Europe. There, the emphasis is on absorbing "high culture" and the richness of Western civilization, whether these be embodied in Buckingham Palace or the Sistine Chapel. Caribbean tourist brochures read as one strategy for constituting "the idea of European identity as a superior one in comparison with all the non-European peoples and cultures" (Said, 1979, p.7).

That the Caribbean tour offers a site for this comparison is an old one. It has been argued that the origin of the hospitality industry in the Caribbean has antecedents in the hospitality that white planters offered European travellers who visited the plantation enclaves (Husbands, 1983). In this welcoming society, governors and colonial assemblies lavishly welcomed and entertained newcomers and distinguished guests, anxious to create links with white society and to show that though they lived on the boundaries of European society they maintained and even enhanced its graces. The exaggeration of hospitality rites against the background of the plantation provided a spectacle of superiority for the "other" and deepened the visitor's appreciation of what European civilization was meant to be all about. In the tourist brochure, the images of welcoming plantations peopled with friendly "natives" in uniforms are manipulated to convey the idea of adventure and excitement in a context which is at once primitive, safe and compliant. One magazine, for instance, is called *Conquest.* (There is also *Sunquest,* a wordplay on the same trope.) The language of the brochure and the images forge the link between the welcoming society past and present, between white male sexual desire and power over nature and the "other."

But while the tourist trade draws on an old tradition of plantation hospitality and colonial encounter, it also transforms this history both in the specific social relations it creates and in its product. Both sugar and tourism require Caribbean societies to organize themselves to meet the needs of more powerful outsiders, but the industries differ in one important way. Plantation labour produced a commodity which was shipped away for consumption. Tourism, however, is an industry which creates an intangible product—pleasure—which is consumed on the spot by a market of temporary residents flown in from abroad. This industry, presaged as a harbinger of development, represents a significant shift away from an older paradigm, which constituted colonization as the expropriation of economic resources in return for the civilizing practices of Christianity and Western government. In tourism, the cultural exchange has nothing to do with religion or government. The values stressed are service and leisure, and the only exchange is bodily pleasure for money.

I want now to look at three images in detail and examine how they work. The images I have selected are fairly representative; they reoccur with shift of emphasis in travel magazines and brochures on the region almost regardless of the island they advertise.

Image number one might be called "Lovers on the Beach." "JAMAICA" is lettered over a long blue sky framed by an arc of two coconut palms. The blue sky gives way to blue sea and a sliver of white sandy beach. A small white heterosexual couple walk hand-in-hand at the edge of the water in bathing suits. The palms arc over their heads. The man leads slightly. No one else is in the picture. Under them, against the empty white beach is written:

> Come to romance.
> Come to excitement
> Come to Jamaica
> and feel alright.

The words of the song appropriate the chorus from Bob Marley's "One Love," a song identified in the 1970s with the cultural resistance of the Rastafari movement. This use of Rastafari is echoed in the televised advertisement for Jamaica. Here, footage of tourists frolicking in luxurious accommodation against the background of lush scenery intercuts with images of a dread walking along the beach playing with children to the tune of Bob Marley's "One Love," a song originally intended as a call to opposing factions to unite in the love of Rastafari. Here, though, the focus on the dreadlocked male contentedly enjoying nature to the exclusion of other images of Jamaicans, signals to the viewer that this is one of the representative images of Jamaica, an embodiment of the culture.

How does one read the appropriation of Marley's work? As an example of black oppositional imagery interrupting the conventional shots of lush scenery and luxurious accommodation? Is the image of the black Rastaman with children on the beach a sign of the "noble savage" domesticated? Is he no more than a figure in proud costume as "exotic other" available for sexy adventures and scathingly described by Jamaicans as a "Rent-a-dread"? Or is this image intended to counter the conventional one of irresponsible black paternity? By making "Come to Jamaica and Feel Alright" the theme of the campaign, the brochures subtly indicate that Reggae and Rastafari, once signifiers of protest and oppositional identity, are now part of a hegemonic alliance in support of the friendly apparatus of tourism. They too exist under a white gaze, complicit with the interpretations of reality and the locations they offer viewers of the brochures.

The focus in our image, however, is the white couple hand-in-hand on the beach, the man leading. The brochure is, after all, intended to market Jamaica, the tourist product, not the country. The image offers a guide to what a pleasurable fantasy ought to be, rather than an experience of a nation with a history and diverse, complex people involved in daily struggles to earn a living and to make meaning of their lives. As Arun Mukherjee and Ngugi Wa Thiongo have pointed out in relation to the films about the third world (in particular Out of Africa and A Passage to India),

> They do not propagate racism openly. In fact they are so seductive as depictions of lost paradises that they tend to disarm an unwary viewer. After all, what can be more apolitical than a man and a woman falling in or out of love. (Mukherjee, 1991, p.157)

The country is only a backdrop for an erotic fantasy of white people. In the context of this enactment the colonized have no reality or society of their own, but come to life when a white gaze is turned on them. They exist solely for the subjects of the brochure, the tourist, to serve up the conditions of pleasure and fantasy. Other variations on this image position the couple as explorers against a background of lush forrest metaphorically drawing on the tradition of Livingston and Mungo Park. The notion of travel as a confrontation with danger and as a search for identity combines with the idea of the pleasure to be gained from danger overcome, and through domination of these forces.

Image number two might be titled "The Myth of the Exotic Mulatta Incarnate." A woman of mixed race, (she could be African and Asian or European and African) with long black hair and an hibiscus behind one ear, reclines on the sand. She rests on her elbow, her legs slightly apart. She is smiling. Her bathing suit, made from the Jamaican flag is black, green and gold. Behind her a river breaks into waterfalls. The caption underneath her says: "Jamaica is more than a part of the Caribbean, it's the heart of the Caribbean." The island nation waits for discovery perhaps, prone like a passive woman defined as part of the scenery, inviting the active heterosexual man to penetrate her mysteries, experience her nature, passionate as the roar of the waterfall. The hibiscus evokes the lure of Gauguin's representation of the Polynesian. Perhaps here men can find such a woman and feel free to have an erotic adventure in a place where the restraints and the sexual taboos of the North can be rolled back and forgotten. Here perhaps one can experience the "other" in oneself, become more animal, like the inscrutable primitive who lives outside the hotel compound.

This image has a long history in the Caribbean and elsewhere. The long dark hair is particularly significant for it conjures up the image of the woman of mixed race, the exotic mulatta. Stereotypical images of the "hotblooded" brownskinned woman in Orientalist literature and art and in representations of mixed-race women in literature blend the supposed animal sexuality of the black African woman with the supposed offer of delicacy, docility and beauty of the Orientalist or European woman. As all women of colour are imagined to do, she offers sex without guilt since her own lascivious nature and desire to serve demand it. She promises sexual excess while making no demands.

Bell Hooks has drawn attention to the fact that "mass culture is the contemporary location that both publicly declares and perpetuates the idea that there is pleasure to be found in the acknowledgement and enjoyment of racial difference" (Hooks 1992, p.21).

She argues that for young white men the hope is that through a sexual encounter with the "Other," through "exploration into the world of difference, into the body of the "Other" they will reenter their own world no longer the same" (Hooks, 1992, p.25). This heightened experience of the "Other" is the sexual challenge equivalent to the physical adventure of exploring untamed nature. This adventure offers a chance to reenter one's everyday world somehow more authentic having reconnected with the primitive which "civilization" is believed to repress.

Most brochures do not picture a sexual fantasy for white women, but the televised advertisement for Jamaica hints at it in the form of the handsome smiling dread. A visit to any beach will reveal more than a few young black men, offering companionship for the female tourist and sometimes for the male tourist too. The fantasy of the noble primitive combines with the proverbial colonial image of the oversexed, athletic black man to produce a tour guide skilled in adventures of the flesh.

Image number three might be titled "Colonial Elegance Lives." It is a foldout of a colonial mansion—white with jalousie windows, royal palms. A garden of bright hibiscus in bloom. The Jamaican flag (off to one side) and a pool with a fountain made of little white (clothed) statues of children in the centre. Inset into the waters of the pool is a square of a white woman hugging a brown one. Behind them are a lot of straw hats. The brown woman wears a peasant blouse and a yellow head tie. She and the white woman hold a hat which says "Jamaica" in raffia. The caption reads: "Here at Devon House, you can buy a piece of Jamaica. This beautifully restored colonial estate is now the home of Things Jamaica. It's a showplace of the unique arts and crafts and fashions of the island." Here, as another brochure puts it, is the evidence that Jamaica blends all the flavours of the Caribbean: "The exotic enchantment of Africa. some of the enchantment of Spain and of course much of the British Colonial traditions, manners and civilized charm, that have been part of Jamaica for centuries" (Jamaica Tourist Board Brochure, 1992, p.2.).

Like the tour of Rose Hall, a restored Great House once a notorious slave plantation, Devon House is placed to stand in for colonial grandeur. The nastiness of the history of imperialism is ignored. The slave quarters, implements of torture, the resistance to slavery and what was created from that are all excluded. Slavery becomes what Jamaica Kincaid has called a harmless "pageant full of large ships" (Kincaid, 1988, p.54). At most, it is a sombre, but progressive necessity underlying the production of elegance. The violence of the past is reduced to a charming background for shopping. And hugging, smiling black and white sisters suggest that interracial familial intimacy is possible, even easy. Everything's all alright. No problem man.

RETHINKING TOURISM AND RESISTANCE

In the 1980s the government of Jamaica telecast a campaign encouraging Jamaicans to regard the tourist industry positively and above all not to "harass the tourists." The jingle warned "If yuh harass di touris yuh know, tourism a go get a blow." This government campaign made it clear that tourism is an industry which is tolerated, rather than enthusiastically accepted. It also exposed the myth that all Jamaicans benefit from the industry. If this were so, clearly harassment would be unnecessary. In spite of the fact that Caribbean people are actively discouraged from censuring the tourist industry publicly, there is widespread criticism of it. Indeed, in

December 1992 the industry was so enthusiastically "accepted" in Jamaica that the government installed soldiers on the streets in some tourist resorts—not to protect nationals, but to protect the invading pleasure seekers. Jean Holder, Secretary General of the Caribbean Tourism Association, described his view of the conflict this way:

> It (the Caribbean) is forced to chose between an industry it "deep down" does not really want, and the economic fruits of that industry which it needs and which it seems, more and more only tourism will provide. This conflict explains why Caribbean people "intellectually" understand that tourism is economically important but act out, perhaps involuntarily, social attitudes hostile to the industry. The economic considerations will, however force the Caribbean into more and more tourism. (Holder, 1990, p.74)

It is in what the brochures render invisible/silent that they become artifacts of a cultural imperialism which accompanies these economic considerations. Out of frame are those images which illustrate the price paid by the country and its people for the creation of this industry. The brochures do not show the policeman in plainclothes arresting "hustlers" on the beach, just as they exclude the ecological damage done by the industry to the environment—the sewage from the luxury hotel, for example clouding the blue waters of the idyllic beach. They do not show the inadequate housing provisions for the workers and craftspeople, who often have nowhere to sleep in a town full of hotels.

Tourism has developed in a context of tremendous unemployment against the backdrop of rapidly falling standards of living. Canadian economist Kari Levitt has estimated that the standard of living of the average Jamaican in 1990 was about half what it was in the 1960s. The contrasts between the luxury facilities for predominantly white tourists and the living conditions of the majority of the predominantly black residents have become increasingly shocking. As well, since Jamaica's image is tarnished by North American press presentations of "Jamaican posses" as inherently and criminally violent and the Americans have placed a travel advisory on the country, strategies to make Jamaica safe have become increasingly diverse. They range from the deployment of special police and soldiers to keep Jamaicans off beaches, which are legally public but actually private, to the building of high walls topped with barbed wire around resorts and beaches. Economic rewards from tourism clearly have not "trickled down." Attempts on the part of ordinary people to squeeze some rewards from the industry, have resulted in hoteliers inventing all kinds of strategies to separate them from the tourist. The most popular of these is the "all inclusive vacation," an apartheid-style tourism in which the Tourist never ventures outside the high walls of the hotel-plantation, unless it is in an airtight bus. Interaction with local culture is narrowed down to a small dot.

The commentary on race, national sovereignty, sexuality and culture produced by tourism is disconnected from theories of Caribbean political economy and its relationship to culture. Anti-colonial nationalism and resistance to neo-colonialism have tended to be based on demands for national sovereignty, ownership of production, and the creation of national state structures (often managed by local elites). They have focused on settled populations, the social separations of plantation and factory, the rigidly codified relations based on occupational categorizations, and the techniques for reappropriation of the value inherent in a commodity. Much discussion of popular cultural resistance to the plantation and the industrial model has emphasized reclaiming traditions developed in the hills and values connected to creolized Caribbean religions. Studies on coffee, sugar, manufacturing, and export processing abound, but research linking the economic to the qualitative effect of tourism and the cultural relations it engenders are hard to find.

Though Caribbean citizens often protest differential treatment at hotels and exclusion from beaches, the habit of seeing the industry within the sphere of economic development means that there remains much work to be done on thinking through alternatives to the present form the industry takes and its relationship to the history of anti-colonial thought. The post-independence state, which was supposed to deliver the rewards of anti-colonial struggle, actively condones an industry which relies on political conservatism and high mobility of capital in the interests of this so called development. Yet notions of economic underdevelopment are in themselves colonizing discourses, emphasizing the submission of all peoples to a unified economic track, using the American capitalist model as a yardstick. Western notions of linear progress, scientific modernization and technological systematization, buttressed by financial institutions like the International Monetary Fund and the World Bank have produced a battalion of experts, who determine targets, priorities and projects, which complement the search for markets. The apparent acceptance of these terms in the interests of "better" shuts down the space for a full consideration of alternatives within an industry based on the commodification of pleasure of the dominant group. Meanwhile the industry is busy creating relations which reshape subjectivities, identities and sites of struggle not only nationally, but also internationally.

In the language of development, the Caribbean is an inferior decaying imitative society in need of modernization and progress. It is presented as a place which can only emerge from "underdevelopment" through further integration into the transnational organization of production accompanying the new technological revolution. This representation is less about invoking a panacea to poverty than it is about shaping the desires of Caribbean peoples, the parameters of how we come to know ourselves as well as what we know about ourselves and the way we make sense of ourselves in our society. The emphasis on the economic obscures and indeed leads to the acceptance of the notion of progress bound and mediated through the meaning-making practices of the Euro-dominated media.

In spite of this, it is in the cultural sphere at everyday and symbolic levels that resistance to the colonizing narratives of tourism grows. This implies a refocussing of notions of resistance and social change around the social interconnections created by industries of pleasure and cultural production in this period of capital reorganization. If we conceptualize transformation within the frame of the Eurocentric discourse on "development," within androcentric discourses on nation state, labour and nature, it will be difficult to take up the challenges presented by the reorganization of capital. Theories of social change and education which ignore the struggles embodied in the symbolic forms discussed above and at the level of the everyday, risk misunderstanding the place of subjectivity and desire in organization and shut down the pedagogical possibilities for collectivizing the vocabulary implicit in practices of everyday resistance.

I want to conclude by pointing to three kinds of resistance which may contain important lessons for rethinking tourism and education. First, it is important to discuss the production of resistance which is carried on everyday by individuals working in the industry itself. Industry workers, whether they are receptionists, cleaners, prostitutes or lifeguards are not simply victims of a giant structure. They think about the industry and their potential agency within it. Second, there is the important place of those who can relate to both Euro-American and Caribbean culture, often themselves "hyphenated citizens," individuals who have been shaped by recent waves of Third World migration and who occupy a new place in history. Marginalized by the dominant narratives of the industry and the points of entry offered them, these people have an important part to play in responding to travel writing and promotion in the North. Third, there are the cultural workers who specifically work on the shows in the hotels, restaurants and night clubs who create the music, dance, art and craft for the tourist market. At each of these levels, the pedagical importance of discussing the racism inherent in the industry and of identifying the possibilities and limitations of individual resistance can be identified.

Trevor Rhone's play, *Smile Orange,* examines one example of individual resistance. Here, the tourist industry can be read as a metaphor for relations between the black and white worlds. From a male perspective, the industry is a metaphor for the neo-colonial condition of the small nation state. Ringo, the trickster figure, is a part-time waiter/gigolo who hustles white women to support his family in the hills. He models a form of covert opposition, which is simultaneously a system of accommodation to the empirical fact of the industry. In Ringo's scheme of things you kiss arse to kick arse, you play fool to catch wise. By inhabiting the stereotypical part which Euro-Americans expect of you—the fawning subservient sambo and the black buck, you exploit the exploiter who takes the mask for reality and never knows who you really are. In theory your "real self" is kept safe. You exploit the exploiter at his own game. After all, white male-dominated production may own and disseminate the meanings made of black masculinity, but it cannot control the subversive uses to which those stereotypes can be put. Ringo takes the white man's game and plays it while simultaneously using it against him. In so doing, he is able to survive, to create a breathing space, to wheel and come again.

The trouble is, as Rhone indicates, you can become the part you play, especially if you never leave the stage. The part ends up playing you, not you the part. The self which is partly relational is itself unsafe in this context. Ringo, for example, is always in role and can only undermine whiteness by targeting the inequalities in white society. He relates to the white women he picks up as if they are one dimensional stereotypes of sexual frustration who, unable to get it good from their own men, are hungry for the black you-know-what. The body in which Ringo resides has become the site which simultaneously accommodates and resists the violence of stereotypical images of black male sexuality.

Smile Orange represents a stage of resistance in which survival is the central value. Resistance here is not confrontational. To confront overtly is to lose. The battle is constituted in an elaborate struggle between the official version of reality and the informal one. The power relations become ambiguous in the re-enactment of the Hegelian master/slave relationship. The light-skinned manager of the hotel only thinks he controls, but Anancy the trickster survivor is really at the control producing a roller coaster of misfired adventures. Rhone's play illustrates the kind of resistance possible when the odds are completely stacked against you, a form of resistance through which you appear to collude in order undermine. As the Jamaican proverb says "Teef from teef, God laugh." (If you steal from a thief God will laugh.) In the end, the double mask cannot be maintained and diaster strikes. While Ringo escapes the consequences of his actions, others have to pay. The play asks: what kind of ethics underlies this unstable form of subjectivity? How does it affect other forms of difference in relationships between the oppressed? For example, how do these strategies affect inequities in gender relations, and relationships between people of different sexualities?

Female equivalents of Ringo also exist and are perhaps most visible in the living imagery of dance halls or in the rites which accompany ragga. Dance halls have become associated with tourism as more and more younger tourists come to the island in search of Jamaican music. The phenomenon of Jamaican music entering the American pop scene in a way that no other music from the Third World has yet done means that the music and the forms of entertainment associated with it take place at one level under a white gaze and at another under a black gaze. Here is a site in which women dance back to the fantasy of "Otherness" represented in image number three, for the majority of Jamaican women do not look like the image represented here and certainly do not behave as passively. Here is another instance of inhibiting a disfigured image to overturn it and to critique its opposite. The erotic play in dance hall involves the flaunting of black female sexuality in the face of the chanting of some of the most sexist lyrics. The opposition between the oral attempt of the deejay to impose male heterosexual "control" on the women is contradicted by the women's open flaunting of their own bodies and the acting out of autoeroticism in dance. The greater the attempt at control becomes, the stronger the challenge enacted by the women in dance. This has often been interpreted as women's collusion with male abuse. Carolyn Cooper, However, argues:

> Though the denigration of "slackness" seems to determine the concomitant denigration of female sexuality, this feminisation of slackness in the dance hall can also be read in a radically different way as an innocently transgressive celebration of freedom from sin and law. Liberated from the repressive respectability of a conservative gender ideology

> of female property and property and propriety, these women lay proper claim to the control of their own bodies. (Cooper, 1993, p.11)

Certainly, upcoming women deejays make clear in their lyrics that women are defiantly autonomous, that the "girlie-girlie": desires and activities of men are not threatening to women but rather are the achilles heel of masculine sexuality, which women collectively find rather foolish. If any sexual exchange with men is to take place, it is necessary that it be accompanied by money. The open discussion of heterosexual sex in relation to money may be an indication of many things, but one thing is clear, from the lyrics—it is not seen negatively by these women; on the contrary, it is seen as a fair exchange.

A second level of resistance within the cultural sphere turns on the subversion of the tropical travelogue. Jamaica Kincaid, writing an alternative travelogue, in *A Small Place,* subverts the voyeuristic colonial aspects of travel writing. Kincaid mocks the ignorance and hollow superiority of the tourist, to reveal the unsettling, violent and squalid underside of the hidden history of the region. She unmasks the pettiness of the desire to control and dominate by revealing the emptiness it conceals.

Kincaid is herself an Antiguan who lives in the United States. *A Small Place* both recalls and inverts Aimé Césaire's negritudinist poem Return to my Native Land. She is simultaneously both insider and outsider because of the act of migration to the United States. She is able because of this to undermine the binary oppositions of black/white, colonized/civilized, and exotic/banal which underlie the language of tropical travel writing. Her own shifting social location enables her to be both "tourist" and "native." She repeatedly makes public, and mocks, the contemptuous private thoughts which underpin the tourist persona. From her special positioning she is able to stress the differences between the white tourist and "the Antiguan black returning to Antigua from Europe or North America with cardboard boxes of much needed clothes and food for relatives" (Kincaid, 1988, p.4). Imitating the tone of self-hatred Naipaul is often accused of, Kincaid points to the worst of Europe in the Caribbean (the corruption, the robbery, the violence). She accuses Antiguan leaders of having learned corruption at the knees of the white pirates, and Antiguan citizens of provincial collusion in their own exploitation. (The book is banned in Antigua.)

> Then they speak of emancipation itself as if it happened just the other day, not over one hundred and fifty years ago. The word "emancipation" is used so frequently, it is as if it, emancipation, were a contemporary occurrence, something everybody is familiar with. And perhaps there is something in that, for an institution that is often celebrated in Antigua is the Hotel Training School, a school that teaches Antiguans how to be good servants, how to be a good nobody, which is what a servant is. In Antigua, people cannot see a relationship between their obsession with slavery and emancipation and their celebration of the Hotel Training School (graduation ceremonies are broadcast on radio and television); people cannot see a relationship between obsession with slavery and emancipation and the fact that they are governed by corrupt men, or that these corrupt men have given their country away to corrupt foreigners. (Kincaid, 1988, p.55.)

Kincaid's prose is accusatory, infused with anger and a sense of betrayal. The work holds a mirror up the the emptiness of the relations which underlie the industry. Kincaid's location and her subversive use of the travelogue form indicate that the apparent unity of North is itself a myth and that the migrant populations there have as important a role to play, making critical changes as the populations at home.

Finally, there is the potential for resistance in the work of the cultural producers who work within the industry. Battalions of dancers and singers work in hotels and restaurants. Artists and craftspeople also serve tourists. Often these products simply reinforce images which the brochures have created. Cultural workers within the industry can themselves create work which undermines these messages in spite of the fact that they are performing to audiences ignorant of their history. Just as Marley made his career by working with different levels of community, locally and internationally, so the cultural worker in the tourist trade can begin to explore the different communities she or he can work with. There are those who feel that Caribbean performers need to build local audiences and that to concentrate on the tourist spectator would somehow undermine this. It seems to me important to accept the split and do both. It is in the struggle between the different version of reality which the industry sets up that critical resistance to its colonizing narrative can begin.

REFERENCES

Alexander, M.J. Not just (Any) body can be a citizen: The politics of law, sexuality and postcoloniality in Trinidad and Tobago and the Bahamas, *Feminist Review* 48.

Atkinson, K. (1992). *Tales of Desire.* Details unknown.

Atkinson, K. and Liss, A. (1992). *Remapping tales of desire: Writing across the abyss.* Santa Monica CA: Side Street Press.

Brantlinger, P. (1990). *Crusoe's footprints.* London: Routledge.

Bennett, T. (1986. Introduction: Popular culture and the turn to Gramsci, in Tony Bennett, Colin Mercer and Janet Wollacott, *Popular culture and social relations.* Milton Keynes: Open University Press.

Cooper, C. (1993). *Noises in the blood: The vulgar body of Jamaican popular culture.* London: Macmillan.

Enloe, C. (1989). *Bananas, beaches and bases: Making feminist sense of international politics.* London: Pandora.

Giroux, H. & Simon, R. (1992). Pedagogy and the critical practice of photography, in *Afterimage* 20, (4).

Giroux, H. & Simon, R. (1989). *Schooling and popular culture.* Toronto: OISE Press.

Gordon, C. (Ed.). *Michel Foucault: Power/knowledge: Selected interviews and other writings 1972-1977.* Brighton UK: The Harvester Press.

Holder, J. (1990, July/August). The Caribbean: Far greater dependence on tourism likely, in *The Courier* 122.

Hooks, B. (1992). *Black looks: Race and representation.* Toronto: Between the Lines.

Husbands, W. (1983). The genesis of tourism in Barbados: Further notes on the welcoming society, in *Caribbean Geography* 1(2).

Kincaid, J. (1988). *A small place,* New York: Farrar Strauss and Giroux.

Levitt, K. (1990). The origins and consequences of Jamaica's debt crisis. Mona, Jamaica: Consortium Graduate School of Social Sciences.

Lindsay, K. (1992). *Dance hall music: Political subversion and the rise of the ghetto.* Amherst, Unpublished bachelor's thesis, Amherst College, Amherst, MA.

Mercer, K. & Julien, I. (1988). Race, sexual politics and black masculinity: A dossier, in Rowena Chapman and Jonathan Rutherford *Male Order: Unwrapping Masculinity.* London: Lawrence and Wishart.

Mukherjee, A. (1991). The third world in the dominant western Cinema: Responses of A third world viewer, in Ormond McKague (Ed.)., *Racism in Canada.* Saskatoon SA: Fifth House.

Gottfritt, L. (1992). *Dancing back in the jazz age: Discourses of danger and possibilities of pleasure.* Master's thesis: OISE, Toronto.

Rhone, T. (1981). *Old story time and other plays.* Burnt Mill UK: Longman.

Sachs, W. (1992). Development: A guide to the ruins, in *New Internationalist* 232.

Said, E. (1979). *Orientalism.* New York: Vintage.

Scholle, D. (1990). Resistance: Pinning down a wandering concept in cultural studies discourse, in *Journal of Urban and Cultural Studies* 1.

Taylor, P. (1986). Myth and reality in Caribbean narrative: Derek Walcott's pantomime, in *World Literature in English* 26, (1), pp.169-177.

Verhelst, T. (1991). *No life without roots.* London: Zed.

CONSTRUCTING CARIBBEAN CULTURE IN TORONTO: THE REPRESENTATION OF CARIBANA

Annemarie Gallaugher

This paper focusses on representations of Caribana (Toronto's annual Trinidad Carnival-based festival) and, by extension, representations of Caribbean community identity, as they have been articulated by recent mainstream Toronto press coverage of the event. A predominant image in these representations is that of the barricade, whether in direct reference to physical barriers or more subtle or implied references, separating the Caribbean community from the dominant Toronto culture. The barricade image raises important questions about the politics of representation in relation to contexts such as official Canadian multiculturalism.

Les represéntations de Caribana (le festival annuel à Toronto basé sur le carnaval de Trinidad) et, par extension, les représentations de l'identité de la communauté antillaise par les média torontois qui couvrent cet événement, mettent en évidence l'image de la barricade. Qu'on revoie directement à des barrières physiques réelles ou à des interprétations plus imagées et subtiles de la barriére, ce qui domine est une référence constante à la séparation de la communauté antillaise du reste de la culture dominate à Toronto. La récurrence de cette image souléve d'importantes questions concernant la poltique de la représentation dans le contexte du multiculturalisme tel que prôné par l'état canadien.

CARIBANA, BEGUN IN 1967 as the Caribbean community's contribution to Canada's centennial celebrations, has become a major annual summer event in Toronto, attracting some one million people. Inspired primarily by Trinidad's annual pre-Lenten Carnival, this two-week festival of the arts reflects the diverse expressive traditions of the Caribbean, bringing together a wide range of indigenous songs, dances, masquerade and oral traditions, and also various foods and folkways of the region.

In an August 1, 1993 front-page article in the *Toronto Star* reporting on the 26th annual Caribana festival, Mark Zwolinski wrote the following:

> Metro police Inspector Ernie Beale said barriers erected along the entire parade route this year was the key to the trouble-free atmosphere. "The barricades are working great and the crowd has been real good." (Zwolinske, 1993, p.A1)

As an attendant at Caribana 1993, I and a small group of friends experienced directly the brunt of Inspector Beale's barricades. We did not find that they were "working great." We found rather that the barricades—maintaining strict divisions between spectators and participants, preventing the crowds from jumping up and having a good time behind the calypso music band trucks, cordoning off sections of the parade area into overlabelled and overorganized spaces for eating and drinking, standing and dancing, and rigidly controlling access to the street—had effectively put an end to the imaginatively socially conscious, lively and creative participation that we believed Caribana had come to stand for.[1]

Having regularly attended Caribana and its considerably less restrained and contained parent, Trinidad Carnival, for over five years now, I cannot help but be struck by the force, and the irony, with which barricades have become a prominent and oppositional image in the context of a Caribbean cultural expressive form meant to symbolize a long struggle for freedom and equality. What is striking is that the barricades controlling Caribana are not just physical ones; they occur discursively in various texts used to represent the festival; for example, letters of greeting placed in Caribana literature by government and corporate sponsors, government speeches at Caribana events, and even everyday references by the dominant Toronto culture at large.

In this paper, I examine the ways in which barricades to Caribana and the calypso music upon which it moves are constructed in what, I believe, is currently the most influential and widespread textual representation of them, the mainstream Toronto press. Through discourse analysis, I aim to identify the component parts of these representational barriers, and the textual and contextual relations between them, in order to better understand the processes by which white group dominance is maintained and social and racial inequalities perpetuated in Toronto, a major centre in the Caribbean diaspora which, at an official level at least, prides itself as being one of the most multicultural, tolerant and non-racist cities in the world.

As recent work out of the University of Amsterdam by Teun van Dijk (1993a, 1993b, 1992) has indicated, the power of the press in maintaining official, dominant ideologies in the face of very opposing realities is particularly strong in situations where citizens have little alternative information. While alternative representations of Caribana are available to Torontonians to some degree through radio and television (both mainstream and community), and through more liberal community tabloids and black community newspapers, and while there is some differentiation in the type of reporting on Caribana presented in the mainstream newspapers themselves, I believe that the overall strategy of the mainstream press—which van Dijk analyzes as one designed to maintain, legitimate, and reproduce ethnic inequality (often by denying it)—supersedes these alternatives. It is largely through following such a dominant strategy that the mainstream press, in tandem with Police Inspector Ernie Beale quoted earlier, erects barricades, not only to Caribana, but to the larger Caribbean community in Toronto as well.

The first part of my analysis is centred on newspaper discourse at the autonomous or immanent level, i.e., features inherent in "the newspaper" itself, such as topic selection, organization, style and quotation patterns. The second part of the analysis considers the need for researching the link between the discourse of newspapers and one other source of mainstream power, official Canadian multicultural policy. The data on which my observations are based derive mainly from newspaper articles which appeared during July and August 1993 in the *Toronto Star* and *The Globe and Mail.* For purposes of comparison, I also refer to contemporary pieces written in the black community newspaper, *Share,* and to an earlier piece which appeared some years ago in the *Toronto Star.*

Before I begin, I would like to acknowledge the influence in the preparation of this paper of the work of British social geographer, Peter Jackson, whose 1992 article, "The politics of the streets: A geography of Caribana," complements much of the analysis I have undertaken. I would like to just briefly point out, however, a couple of ways in which I see my own work depart from his.

Central to Jackson's paper is the idea that "control of space is central to the politics of Carnival" (Jackson, 1992, p.139). He is concerned to show that, during Caribana, the Toronto city streets upon which the festival parade proceeds become an important public domain—albeit a highly regulated one, and often with the approval of the Caribana organizers themselves—in which a range of political issues can be actively contested and in which possible sites of resistance to the dominant order can be opened up. He cites the routing and frequent re-routing of the Caribana parade as evidence of the primacy of spatial conflict in Caribana's politics.[2]

While I think that control of street space is certainly important in the way that the politics of Caribana are played out. I believe that to posit this issue as central, as Jackson does, is not altogether accurate. It seems to me that even if the struggle for control of street space during Caribana were won, an even larger struggle, one involving the representation—or misrepresentation—of Caribana, both to and by agents (i.e., readers and writers) of the dominant culture, would still remain. I am interested, therefore, in what the mainstream newspapers report about the event, given that they are an important and regularly recurring document of the dominant representation of Caribana. Through these newspaper representations, the dominant culture in Toronto finds a main mechanism for the construction of its particular version of "the Caribbean other" and, in the process, reaffirms its own dominance.

Peter Jackson's work draws on a large number of newspaper articles as well. In contrast to the approach I am taking here, he quotes mainly from articles which have appeared in Toronto's two major black community newspapers, *Contrast* and *Share.* What I find rather unfortunate, however, is that his citations (which date back to the late 1960s and early 1970s when Caribana was first being established) are chosen to support his focus on "underlying tensions" (p.133) within Caribana itself, tensions which eventually led to an "irreparable rift" (p.133) in the mid 1970s. Certainly tensions were present historically within the Caribana organization; they are still present today. However, to focus as Jackson does on *inner* conflicts, without paying sufficient attention either to what constitutes conflict and differing conceptions of it, or to the dominant social and cultural milieu in which conflict is framed—here I am thinking of the restructuring of Caribbean society through the process of cultural transplantation—is to suggest that these conflicts *originate* from within and to thus perpetuate some long-lingering stereotypes.

The following review from a 1966 edition of the *Toronto Star* of a calypso concert at Massey Hall featuring two prominent Trinidadian calypsonians, Lord Kitchener and Lord Bryner, gives some idea of the milieu that existed in Toronto around the time-period in which Caribana began:

> There were a few good moments during last night's Calypso Fiesta ... but only for those who delight in dirty songs. The rest was a bore. It convinced me, for one, that once you've heard one calypso song and steel band number and seen one dance you've seen them all.... This show was supposed to show Torontonians what authentic calypso music with authentic calypsonians from Trinidad is all about. The calypsonians might have came from Trinidad all right, but give me supposedly "unauthentic" calypso singers such as Harry Belafonte any day. (Thomas, 1966, p.18)

What stands out in this piece is the overall tone of condescension, the reductionism and simplification, the allusions to deviant or "dirty" behaviour, the dismissal of the music as boring and repetitive, the fact that the writer is not Caribbean himself, and the writer's desire for "authenticity" on the part of "the other." It is now almost 30 years since this review appeared, and yet if we examine recent newspaper articles, we find strikingly similar patterns of discourse—patterns which set up barriers and boundaries designed to promote a positive treatment of the dominant "us" and a negative representation of the subordinate "them." As examples, I will cite three short excerpts from press coverage of Caribana 1993.

On July 30, the day before the Caribana parade, *The Globe and Mail* ran this headline in its front section: "Police prepare for weekend festival: Olympic Island security plan to provide quick response to unruly behaviour"(Abbate, 1993, p.A10).[3]

The accompanying article to these headlines was written by Gay Abbate who is identified as the Regional Police Reporter. It begins this way: "Police will be in large numbers at this weekend's Caribana festivities, but do not expect problems like those that marred last year's parade" (Abbate, 1993, p.A10). The logic of this statement is curious: if problems are not expected, why will the police be out in large numbers?

The "problems" which are only alluded to in *The Globe and Mail*—a shooting which occurred along the parade route in 1992—are actually identified and given a somewhat different treatment in the *Toronto Star* of the same day: "[Staff Sergeant John] Sillaots said the shooting "unfairly" reflected on Caribana since it was an unrelated domestic dispute" (Turnbull, 1993, p.A6). Again, although there is perhaps a more "liberal" spirit behind the *Star's* approach, the logic is questionable. If the 1992 shooting was "unrelated" to Caribana, why is it even necessary to bring it up? More generally, why is the police presence so predominant, not only in the parade, but in the press as well?

Two days after the 1993 parade, Moira Welsh, in the *Toronto Star* writes: "you could almost imagine the palm branches swaying, Olympic Island took on the atmosphere of the sultry Caribbean yesterday as Caribana festivities crossed Toronto harbour for a rollicking musical island picnic" (Welsh, 1993, p.A6).

The Globe and Mail on the same day reports: "Caribana '93 winds down today after Metro Toronto's biggest carnival drew more than a million people and injected more than $200-million into the city's economy" (Kyvrikosaios and Powell, 1993, p.A7).

As the above quotes serve to indicate, Caribana is regularly reduced to what seems to have become a set standard of journalistic essentials in coverage of the event: the policing and control of the crowd, the potential for violence, the weather, island images, the size of the crowd, the city economy and, most recently, the great potential benefit for the provincial tourist industry.

To punctuate the process of representation of Caribbean cultural forms in Toronto as touristic commodities, I will quote what an Arts and Entertainment editor at the *Toronto Star* said to me in 1989 when I inquired about writing a piece on calypso and Trinidad Carnival: "Well, quite frankly, what more is it really than just a bunch of people jumping up in the streets? There are no real artists or arts value there. Why don't you try the Tourism Section?"[4]

In my interpretation, the types of reductionist practices that the mainstream press uses in its representations of Caribana and calypso music are, in effect, a barricade to any deeper meaning or understanding of it. The history and the identities of the people who make it and for whom it is—in their words—"a way of life" are largely prevented from reaching Toronto's dominant culture which relies principally on "what the papers say" to shape their views of the local Caribbean community.

By comparison, the representation provided by a local weekly black community newspaper, *Share,* although it does share some of the same themes and images as noted above, frames and supplements these in ways that are quite significantly different. One of these is the sheer quantity of column inches. In the weeks leading up to Caribana, full editorials and letters to the editor on the subject can be found; a complete *Special*

Caribana Issue is also published at this time. Major articles profiling calypsonians and masquerade bands are frequent and are framed by numerous advertisements announcing events and festivities. The following statement made in a July 19, 1993 Share article by current Caribana Chair Lennox Farrell provides an idea of the different quality of discourse;

> Born of Carnival native to the countries of the Lesser Antilles in general—and to Trinidad and Tobago in particular—Caribana has survived against all odds, and is still here. It is a metaphor of survival and magnanimity, much like the peoples from whose sorrows and determination it is born and grown. (Farrell, 1993b, p.6)

Here we see evidence of what the mainstream papers appear to be lacking: a sense of history, seriousness, and respect. To return for a moment to the Zwolinski article I quoted at the opening of this paper. It begins: "What a party! What a parade! Caribana's parade joyfully frolicked along Metro's lakeshore yesterday, bringing a spell-binding taste of the Caribbean to a crowd estimated at about one million people. The brilliant sunshine lent a dreamy glow as 44 mas'bands, complete with wildly costumed masqueraders and adjoining musicians on tractor trailers, snaked along the parade route from the CNE [Canadian National Exhibition grounds] along Lakeshore Blvd. W. 'This is my culture, my life, this is my everything,' said Althea Pierre, a Trinidad native." (Zwolinski, 1993, p.A1)

What one might have wished for here is a fuller quote from Althea Pierre, someone who obviously "knows" Caribana intimately and directly. Instead, within a few short words Zwolinski crosses over from what seems to be a positive side of the fence, to invoke a very different set of images: "Spectators, police, and politicians praised organizers for staging the 12-hour event, which was free of the shooting incidents and violence last year that prompted police to end the party early" (Zwolinski, 1993, p.A1).

The actual makers of the culture are quickly silenced, "barricaded" from any further voicing of their views. And in that space of silence, graphically symbolized as a space between paragraphs, a boundary line is created and a strange, distancing ambiguity of opposition set up. On the one hand, Caribana is seen as "joyful," "spell-binding," and "dreamy"; on the other, it raises images of fear. This collocation of desire and dread, which recurs regularly throughout the articles I have examined, constructs an ambivalent, opposing set of relationships for the reader, and thus, I would suggest, acts as another type of barrier, a sort of representational confusion which makes it extremely difficult for white dominant culture to decode and understand what Caribana really is about.

Adding to this difficulty is a tendency for the press to highlight specifically non-Caribbean elements of Caribana (the participation in the parade of a largely white-dominated masquerade band operating from Toronto Island is one example), thus creating an imbalance in coverage and constructing a message rife with implications for critical issues, such as relations of dominance and subordination, cultural appropriation and identity politics.

How can these mainstream press representations of Caribbean cultural expression and identity—with their very selective and essentialist thematic focus, their strange juxtapositions of images of desire with images of fear, and their rather skewed emphases on non-Caribbean aspects—be interpreted?

An important context for interpretation is the relationship between the press and other mainstream power groups or elites, such as institutions in politics and government, academia, and corporate business. The work of van Dijk to which I referred earlier, posits the link between them in this way: "the press tends to sustain the ethnically relevant activities and the attitudes of the dominant elites" (1992, p.33); and, further: "the elites of politics and the press nowadays live in a virtual symbiosis when ... ethnic affairs are concerned" (1992, p.9). It would be interesting in this regard, therefore, to examine the nature of the symbiosis between press representations of Caribana and the politics of multiculturalism at various government levels.

Peter Jackson argues that Canadian multicultural policy, "defines the terms and sets the limits of the political potential of Caribana which its participants constantly threaten to transgress" (1992, p.130). He outlines the development of multicultural policy broadly since 1971 as a movement from "the celebration of cultural diversity" stage to the "recognition of equality rights" (1992, p.142) and suggests that the chronic lack of state funding for Caribana, coupled with a government discourse which speaks of "the lively traditions and heritage" (1992, p.143) found in Caribana, or, its "colourful demonstration of our thriving multiculturalism" (1992, p.143) indicate that Caribana is still being held in check at the earlier, less threatening, "celebration of diversity" stage of multiculturalism where it is still regarded as something of a traditional "museum piece" (1992, p.143).

In a speech delivered at the Caribana 1993 opening ceremonies, Ontario Premier Bob Rae—whose Ministry of Citizenship provided $105,000 to the Caribbean Cultural Committee—suggested that a somewhat more progressive attitude to Caribana may be developing. Alluding to a "deeper seriousness of purpose"—beyond music, dance and costume—that Caribana represents, he spoke openly of the racism and inequalities perpetuated against Toronto's Caribbean community. Not insignificantly, however, Rae's speech was reported in *Share,* not in the *Toronto Star* and not in *The Globe and Mail.* Further, while Rae's comments may seem to be a sign of a more liberal elite view of multiculturalism, their progressive thrust towards "deeper seriousness" is minimized when juxtaposed against the reality of his government's more prominent emphasis on Caribana's potential for expanding the tourist economy.

Thus within elite institutional multiculturalism, there resides a great paradox. In the case of Caribana in particular, the dominant strategy seems to be to minimize, contain, or even deny the "deeper seriousness" of the Caribbean aspects of the event and at the same time to show it off as having multicultural value. Multicultural value is often evidenced, however, not as coming from within the Caribbean community itself, but as a projection of white, dominant culture onto Caribbean culture. The appearance of members of the white, dominant culture in the parade, or newspaper accounts which perpetuate stereotypical associations of Caribbean culture with touristic "exotica," and the close attention paid to crime and violence are all clear examples of this type of projection. A barricade is thus erected, and a more "subjective" knowledge of Caribbean identity prevented.

One of the reasons for this paradox, I believe, is that while official multicultural policy may, in some interpretations, have moved towards a more openly political agenda involving equality rights, the multiculturalism promoted though mainstream newspapers seems to be stuck at the "celebration of cultural heritage" phase. Added to the celebratory aspects, is the stereotypical and culturally empty imagery of crime and violence on the one hand, and tourism on the other. And it is through these very distorted and paradoxical pictures that the general reading is taught to interpret Caribana, and, by extension, Caribbean culture as a whole. Thus the preferred meanings and definitions of Caribana conveyed by the press contribute to the reproduction of social and racial inequalities which the dominant culture is still very apparently trying to deny.

ENDNOTES

1. It should be noted here that, although many people who attended Caribana objected to the barricades as I did, they were nevertheless erected with the approval of the Caribbean Cultural Committee, the organization which mounts the Caribana festival. (See Farrell 1993a.)
2. It is important to indicate here that whereas the Caribana parade used to travel down a main city artery, with all the symbolism that such a politically prominent space invokes, it has recently been relocated, some would say "marginalized," to a boulevard along the city's lakeshore.
3. Olympic Island is the site of a consecutive two-day Caribbean music concert which follows the parade day.
4. Personal communication.

REFERENCES

Abbate, G. (1993, July 30). Police prepared for weekend festival. *The Globe and Mail,* p.A10.

Clifford, J. (1988). *The Predicament of culture: Twentieth century ethnography, literature an art.* Cambridge, MA: Harvard University Press.

Farrell, L. (1993a, August 3). Caribana head defends barricade use. *The Globe and Mail,* p.A10.

———. (1993b, July 19). Welcome to this magnificent festival [Special Caribana Issue]. *Share,* p.6.

Jackson, P.(1992). The politics of the streets: A geography of Caribana. *Political Geography* 2, pp.130-151.

Kyvrikosaios, D. and Powell, M. (1993, August 2). Caribana more than Carnival to city. *The Globe and Mail,* p. A7.

Manning, F. (1983). Cosmos and chaos: celebration in the modern world. In F. Manning (Ed.), *The Celebration of Society: Perspectives on Contemporary Cultural Performance* (pp.3-30). London, Canada: University of Western Ontario, Congress of Social and Humanistic Studies.

Nunley, J.W. and Bettelheim, J. (1988). *Caribbean festival arts: Each and every bit of difference.* Seattle: The Saint Louis Art Museum and the University of Washington Press.

Thomas, R. (1966, November 21). Calypso fiesta O.K.—if you like dirty jokes. *Toronto Star,* p.18.

Turner, V. (1987). *The Anthropology of performance.* New York: PAJ Publications.

van Dijk, T. (1993a). Analyzing racism through discourse analysis: Some methodological reflections. In J.H. Stanfield II and D.M. Rutledge (Eds.), *Race and Ethnicity in Research Methods* (pp. 92-134). Newbury Park, CA: Sage.

———. (1993b, May). Political discourse and racism: Describing other in western parliaments. Paper presented at the International conference on "Others" in Discourse, Toronto.

———. (1992, August). Elites, racism and the press. Paper presented at the Congress of the International Association of Mass Communication Research (IAMCR), Brazil.

Welsh, M. (1993, August 2). It's like being in the islands. *Toronto Star*, p.A6.

Zwolinski, M. (1993, August 1). A million revellers soak up Caribbean beat. *Toronto Star*, p.A1.

CARTOONING AND DEVELOPMENT IN THE CARIBBEAN

John A. Lent

This article is a reflection on the journalistic activity of those graphic artists, political cartoonists, who contribute to socio-cultural issues. Based on personal interviews, the author presents a brief survey of cartoonists working in Cuba and the English-speaking Caribbean to show how these artists, through humour, critique serious social and political issues in such a way that the masses can understand them. He concludes by stating that these artists, especially those working in the Caribbean must constantly be aware of the fine line that separates development journalism and propaganda, the right to help the public through critical information and the misuse of that right, especially in Caribbean societies where authoritarianism has abounded and where small populations can lead to exacerbated sensitivities.

Cet article examine une activité à la fois journalistique et artistique peu reconnue dans le domaine des relations socio-culturelles : la caricature politique. A partir des entrevues personnelles, l'auteur présente un bilan sommaire des caricaturistes oeuvrant à Cuba et dans la Caraïbe anglophone pour montrer comment ces créateurs d'images se servent de l'humour pour stimuler la réflexion critique et pour mettre l'actualité sociale et politique à la portée des masses. Il conclut en précisant qu'un danger guette néanmoins, ces artistes: c'est d'abuser de leur statut de journaliste, car il est toujours possible de transgresser la frontière très mince entre information critique et propagande.

Ce danger existe surtout dans les sociétés de la Caraïbe qui tendent vers un certain autoritairisme. Avec une population peu nombreuse, la possibilité de froisser les sensibilités est très réelle.

AS A NUMBER OF US PONDERED an ideal role for journalists at the first Philippine Press Institute seminars and workshops in 1964-65, and thus, established the foundation for development journalism, it did not occur to us to broaden the definition of journalists to include graphic artists. In a series of sessions held in Manila, topics ranged from provincial journalists to crime reporting and women's pages.

Throughout the 1960s, the Philippine Press Institute and, later the Press Foundation of Asia, worked out what they thought should be the responsibilities of journalists in developing countries. In short, they defined development journalism as the relaying in simple language of news and information that is beneficial and relevant to uplifting the masses, bringing about social change, and enhancing national development.

Right in front of our eyes—especially in the Philippines in the 1960s—were some very effective journalists who had been carrying out these tasks for years. They were the cartoonists. We were just too word-oriented to take notice of them.

Indeed, it is curious that cartoonists and other illustrators have not been termed development journalists earlier. Obviously, Jacques-Louis David sought to promote social change, emphasizing simple and relevant messages in his scathing and scatalogical cartoons against the monarchy during the French Revolution; William Hogarth used similar techniques to point out social ills in England, as did Thomas Nast in his depictions of the corrupt New York City political machine.

Throughout the world today, cartoonists tackle social and political problems such as government corruption, economic squeezing of the middle class, poverty, corporate greed, pollution, and the environment. Usually, they lambaste the individuals and agencies they hold responsible for these problems; at other times, they illustrate strips, comic books, and animation that serve developmental purposes, providing the public with information on nutrition, sanitation, health, or family planning.

DEVELOPMENT CARTOONISTS AND THE CUBAN REVOLUTION

Cuban cartoonists performed important roles as critics of society and government long before the 1959 Revolution. As early as 1848, a handbill by Cirilo Villaverde that appeared in the Tacón Theatre, featured a reformist editor singing the goodness of his ideas to Doña Isla, the symbol of Cuba (Tamayo, Blas, Juan & Hurtado, 1984). In the 1860s and later, periodicals such as the humor weekly, *El moro muza,* (*the Arab musulman*), pointed critically to Spain's presence in Cuba, and *La política cómica* (comical politics) parodied Cuba's heavy dependence upon the United States in the early 20th century.

By 1929, *La semana* (*The Week*) used many satirical cartoons, especially Eduardo Abela's "El bobo" (the fool), an extremely harsh portrayal of the excesses of the Machado dictatorship. "El loquito" (the nut), a character of René de la Nuez, played a similar role during the last part of the Batista regime (Tamayo & Blas, 1984).

Other cartoonists, including Conrado W. Massaguer, Adigio Benítez, Virgilio Martínez, and Santiago Armada (Chago), mocked the social life of the bourgeoisie, attacked Batista, or promoted the alternative of socialism.

Developmental messages have permeated the works of many cartoonists since Fidel Castro came to power. Gag panels, animation, comic strips, and comic books have saluted youthful workers, sugar cane harvesters, and Soviet friendship; promoted literacy and *poder popular* (people power), and denounced discrimination, the Vietnam War, and the United States as a fascist state.

Some cartoon characters were designed with a sole developmental purpose in mind. Such was the case of Francisco Blanco (Blanquito) and his "Matilde," a cow featured in 1970s comic books that promoted agriculture; others, such as "Tequita azuquita," dealt with sugar production (Interview: Polito, 1991).

Humanistic and developmental themes saturate all aspects of Cuban cartooning, including the humour magazines, *Palante* and *Dedeté,* and the International Humor Biennial, held in San Antonio de los Baños. The latter, inaugurated in 1978, exhibits works from dozens of countries, based on themes that promote peace, environmental, humanistic, and other worthy causes, while avoiding the degradation of the human condition.

Individual cartoonists attach a great deal of importance to working for international and national development campaigns. Foremost among them is René de la Nuez, called the country's "most brilliant satirical editorialist" (Armada, 1985, p.7). His strip, "El loquito" (1957), ridiculed Batista with the use of a special code understood by the people (Sarusky, 1983, p.6). As noted in an interview, Nuez takes pride in serving the public cause:

> There's nothing more beautiful than seeing the idea you've always fought for finally triumph. I drew 'El Loquito' for years and he finally saw Cuba liberated. For years I

drew cartoons supporting the cause of Vietnam and finally I saw Vietnam liberated. The same thing happened with Nicaragua. (Sarusky, 1983, p.6).

Nuez's objective has remained consistent: to make people think and to denounce grave dangers, such as modern technology and United States media imperialism.

Ernesto Padrón, who also excels in different cartooning genres, including animation, strips and gag cartoons, has used his drawing skills to promote national development, as has Tomy (Tomás Rodríguez Zayas). Tomy felt there are marked differences between cartoonists from capitalist and socialist countries, the latter having a keener sense of aesthetics, ethics, and "above all, humanism" (Tamayo, 1986, p.7).

Bettering society is at the top of the list of priorities for Manuel (Manuel Hernández), whose objectives are:

to be a sort of chronicler of the problems of the day. As a cartoonist, I try to do my job well, to fulfill my role in society. I draw cartoons as close to reality, to people, to contribute to an understanding of the times through my drawings. (Fariñas Rodríguez, 1989, p.12)

Another famous cartoonist, Carlucho (Carlos Villar Aleman), who, for years, was editor of *Dedeté,* has devoted much of his energy to attacking pollution and war. Concerning the latter, Carlucho said he not only draws about the possibility of nuclear war, but also the diversion of government funds to military buildups and away from the needs of the people. "Looking at myself in the mirror," Carlucho added, "I decided that as long as there are weapons and the threat of war, I would dedicate part of my life to this struggle" (Guerra, 1987, p.7). Carlucho characters are often desolate, weak, and expressionless.

Appealing to the human conscience is also a goal of two other cartoonists, Ajubel (Alberto Morales) and Angel Boligán. Winner of many international and national prizes for his cartoons, Ajubel is very clear on the function of humorous art—"educate, call attention to things, make people think. The purpose of humor isn't to make someone giggle but to appeal to man's conscience" (Castañeda, 1987, p.8).

The very young Boligán already has adopted a humanistic approach to cartooning. Describing what he does as a "style of ideas," Boligán said:

> At the moment, I am doing more national work. I believe that in Cuba and the world, there are many problems that no one should forget. It is very important to be inside (aware) of the troubles. Things like contamination, war, nature. (Interview: Boligán, 1991)

Boligán has been largely responsible for maintaining a unique cartoon form in his native San Antonio de los Baños. Since 1983, he and fellow cartoonists "bring out" a monthly mural newspaper, *El cartun,* devoted to cartoons and displayed in an optical store window in the center of town. "We deal with topical issues such as transport, shopping, favoritism toward the United States dollars, etc.," he explained (Interview: Boligán, 1991).

Economic hard times have hindered cartoonists in recent years; the results are that some have moved over to painting or out of the country, or sought an international audience. Despite the handicaps, many have retained their development-oriented and humanism-oriented approaches.

CARTOONING IN THE COMMONWEALTH CARIBBEAN

A barometer of national development is the degree to which media contents, in this case cartoons and comics, are indigenized. For years, the only strips and most editorial cartoons in newspapers of Trinidad, Bahamas, and Jamaica, were imported from the United States or England, but recently changes have occurred.

In 1975, Mahase Calpu created a Trinidad Express strip, "Sweetbread," based on rural life in that country, and local strips have since been tried in Jamaica. In the late 1970s and early 1980s, Leon Hines drew a woman character with martial arts skills, "Janny Jason," for the *Gleaner,* as well as a police strip; in 1989, Clovis Brown had a fact-based strip, "The Catch," in the tabloid *Star,* which a year later, carried another strip, "Squeeze" (Interviews: Brown, 1990, 1993).

Of the three dailies, the *Star* still leads in the use of strips, usually carrying six foreign and one local. Las May draws the Jamaican cartoons, including the one-panel, "De Connection," Monday through Wednesday; "Laugh with Us, Featuring Nuff Agony," a three-panel, full-page strip used on Thursdays, and "Story Tella." "Laugh with Us" has two main characters; a father and his son who usually outwits him (Interview: Mas, 1993).

Regular cartoon features commenting on local social and political issues are more prevalent. Besides "De Connection," other Jamaican cartoons of this type are those by Leon Hines in the *Herald* and Clovis Brown in the *Gleaner.* In Trinidad, Dunstan E. Williams draws "Dat's Dat" for the *Trinidad Guardian* and "So Dey Say" for the *Evening News,* while Calpu does "Grab-a-Grin" in the *Express.* All are daily features. Two daily cartoon columns appear in the Bahamas: Stanley Burnside's "Sideburns" in the *Nassau Tribune* and Samuel Williams' "Sip Sip" in the *Nassau Guardian.*

Most of these cartoonists promote the developmental goals of their countries, whenever they exist, but when those objectives tread on political affairs, they back off. Sensitivities are very near the surface in such small countries where everyone knows the cartoonist, as well as everyone else. In Trinidad, Williams and Calpu both try to stay out of politics because of this reason and the sensitivities of the leaders (Interviews: Williams & Calpu, 1990). Calpu said cartoonists must be careful because of the smallness of the society where "it is easy for people to get the wrong impression." He sidesteps potential difficulties by not attacking anyone, thus pleasing his editors immensely. As Calpu said:

> The editors are scared of publishing the "heavy" political cartoon. The ones that criticize or poke fun at the politician are not going to be published. The editors seem to think it is a recipe for the libel courts, although they have not told me so. Whenever I did those types of cartoons in the early days of "Grab-a-Grin," they were not used. (Interview: Calpu, 1990)

The situation is not better in Jamaica where *Gleaner* cartoonist Clovis Brown's role as critic is hampered by a number of off limits topics that are political. He said:

> Most cartoonists have been afraid to draw about certain fellows in our society. I'm not afraid of any politician, but the editor sometimes gives me a warning not to be too strong. I should leave that alone. I have to think whether to deal with it or not. Sometimes I just play around the whole thing. (Interview: Brown, 1990)

Some topics related to national development are among those Brown does not depict in his cartoons; these include the project sector organizations, the National Housing Trust, and building contractors. As is the case in many countries, development projects oftentimes are linked closely to politics and government because of the nature of funding, and thus, are off limits for criticism.

One cartoonist who uses development topics to his advantage is Stanley Burnside in the Bahamas. His six-day-a-week strip, "Side-burns," carries a number of development themes, which Burnside said, cuts through the "froth and zeroes in on the heart of issues such as politics, sports, religion, business, etc." (Interview: Burnside, 1990).

His social conscience is most evident in efforts to lead the public in self-help programs such as the Heart Foundation, vaccination program, or stop drunk driving campaign. Describing his style as "poking fun at local political events and characters," Burnside said he feels no political limitations, "absolutely not." Like his Trinidad colleagues, he mentioned the smallness of his country as a potential constraint, but unlike them, did not succumb to the threat. "It is very easy for someone with a forum to be the target of a political party," Burnside said, "but as long as I have both sides complaining about what I'm doing, I'm doing okay" (Interview: Burnside, 1990).

CONCLUSION

A fine line separates development journalism and propaganda, the right to help the public through news and information and the misuse of that right in the name of "government-say-so journalism." That line is extremely thin in parts of the Caribbean, where authoritarianism has abounded, as well as a rather personal type of leadership, and where the smallness of the populations have resulted in sensitivities.

For cartooning to have developed as much as it has during the past generation is laudatory given these restrictions.

REFERENCES

Armada, C. (1985, July 14). Nuez, his mastery and his latest book. *Granma Weekly Review*, p.7.

Castañeda, M. (1987, September 3). Ajubel: The laughing man. *Granma Weekly Review*, p.8.

Fariñas Rodríguez, G. (1989, September 24). Street chronicler. *Granma Weekly Review*, p.12.

Guerra, F. (1987, July 5). Humor without borders. *Granma Weekly Review*, p.7.

Sarusky, J. (1983, June 19). René de la Nuez: A cartoonist who heralds victory. *Granma Weekly Review*, p.6.

Tamayo, E. (1986, November 2). Tomy: A humorist for the year 2000. *Granma Weekly Review,* p.7.

Tamayo, E. and Blas, J. (1984). *Más de Cien Años de Humor Político,* Tomo 2. Santiago de Cuba: Editorial Oriente.

Tamayo, E., Blas, J. and Hurtado, O. (1984). *Más de Cien Años de Humor Político,* Tomo 1. Santiago de Cuba: Editorial Oriente.

INTERVIEWS

Boligán, Angel, cartoonist, San Antonio de los Banos, Cuba, May 24, 1991.

Brown, Clovis, cartoonist, *Gleaner,* Kingston, Jamaica, July 23, 1990 and May 26, 1993.

Burnside, Stanley, cartoonist, *Nassau Tribune,* Nassau, Bahamas, May 5, 1990.

Calpu, Mahase, cartoonist, *Express,* Port of Spain, Trinidad, May 24, 1990.

May, Las, cartoonist, *Star,* Kingston, Jamaica, May 26, 1993.

Polito (Jose Emilio Polo Madero), cartoonist, Havana, Cuba, May 22, 1991.

Williams, Dunstan E., cartoonist, *Trinidad Guardian,* Port of Spain, Trinidad, May 24, 1990.

EDUCATION AND POPULAR CULTURE IN THE CARIBBEAN: YOUTH RESISTANCE IN A PERIOD OF ECONOMIC UNCERTAINTY

Pedro A. Noguera

This article examines the role of education in political socialization and the construction of national identity, as well as the relationship between education and popular culture. In the post-emancipation period, eduction served as a vehicle for cultural colonization. However, the patterns of non-conformity and resistance to this are evident in the way Caribbean youth expresses itself in the popular culture. An analysis of this youth resistance also shows the ways schools are responding to the emergence of a rebellious youth culture.

L'éducation joue un rôle certain dans la socialisation politique et la construction d'une identité nationale surtout par rapport à la culture populaire. Dans la période post-esclavagiste, l'éducation était un moyen de véhiculer une colonisation culturelle. Cependant, des tendances à l'encontre de cette forme de colonisation sont de plus en plus évidentes dans les expressions actuelles de la culture populaire, issues de la jeunesse caraïbéenne. Une analyse de cette résistance des jeunes montre également que les écoles ont leurs propres réponses à l'émergence d'une culture de ces jeunes révoltés.

WHILE THE ROLE OF EDUCATION in political socialization and the construction of national identity in the Caribbean has been recognized and studied by several scholars (Bell, 1967; Fagen, 1969; Jansen, 1991; Torres, 1991; Miller, 1991), its relationship to popular culture has received considerably less attention. In part, this is due to the tendency of Caribbean scholars to conceive of educational institutions primarily as instruments of the state to propagate and reinforce the hegemony exerted by domestic and foreign elites over political and economic institutions (Carnoy and Samoff, 1989; Henry and Stone, 1983; Miller, 1989).[1] Curriculum content, student assessment and placement, and the recruitment of training of teachers, have been viewed as the primary means through which social reproduction and the dissemination of the dominant ideology are carried out.

This paper explores the relationship between education and the dynamic popular culture among Caribbean youth. Paget Henry (1983) points out that in the post-emancipation period, education has served as a vehicle for cultural colonization, holding out the possibility of social mobility for those able to acquire the most highly valued cultural capital—a European cultural orientation and identity. With some important modifications, primary and secondary educational institutions throughout the Caribbean have continued to serve as transmitters of a foreign, Anglo-American cultural hegemony, even during the decolonization period. However, the transmission and embracement of a foreign culture is never complete or absolute. Patterns of non-conformity and resistance are clearly evident among Caribbean youth, especially within the popular culture. Drawing upon the work of scholars such as Giroux (1992), Willis (1977) and Ogbu (1978), this paper analyzes youth resistance and the ways in which schools are responding to the emergence of a rebellious youth culture. This is considered in light of recent changes in the political economy of Caribbean nations brought about by neo-liberalism and structural adjustment policies, which influence the social and political context in which youth culture reacts and is shaped.

This paper is an exploration of the ways in which current economic and political developments in the Caribbean have influenced the relationship between education and youth culture. I will be moving across two distinct theoretical traditions within the sociology of education. The first pertains to how the character of educational institutions is shaped and influenced by the social structure of Caribbean societies. The second, concerning the role of education in cultural reproduction processes, draws upon the theoretical framework developed by scholars such as Carnoy and Levin (1985), and Morrow and Torres (1994) which recognizes the existence of parallel connections between social structure and education. Such a distinction allows for greater openness to the possibility that education, like the State, occupies a position of relative autonomy in relation to forces of economic power, and therefore creates room for agency and resistance as forms of social action which can actually influence social practice and public policy.

DECOLONIZATION AND CULTURE IN THE CARIBBEAN

In the post-colonial period, a central feature of decolonization is the reconstruction of a national culture and identity. This is generally a difficult and complicated task because most political, economic and social institutions have been created in the image of the colonizing power. Completely remaking these so that they begin to reflect and embody indigenous sensibilities and aspirations is no simple matter, for those who typically inherit positions of leadership in the post-colonial period are the individuals who were most closely identified with the culture of the foreign power. According to Cabral, the only way to overcome this separation is through a "reconversion or 're-Africanization' accomplished through daily contact with the popular masses in the communion of sacrifice required by the struggle" (1973, p.43).

Such a process was initiated during the 1960s and '70s in most parts of the Caribbean. Coinciding with the rise of middle class political leaders who assumed control of the State following independence, a more general affirmation and ascendence of the once repressed Afro-Creole culture took place. Throughout this period, nationalist expressions which affirmed these cultural traditions were combined with support for contemporary expressions of popular culture which were rooted in the reality and experience of the lower classes. The new leaders enlisted the support of the lower classes to neutralize members of the elite planter-merchant class that sought to combine its economic power with political power in the wake of colonial rule. This alliance was achieved primarily through two strategies: 1) the adoption of social democratic policies characterized by import substitution, social welfare and public ownership of numerous enterprises (Riviere, 1990); and 2) the promotion of cultural symbols associated with the lower class Afro-Creole population (Henry and Stone, 1983). The rise of nationalist consciousness in politics was matched by an outpouring of nationalist expressions in literature, music and the arts. Though still in its early stages, decolonization throughout the 1970s appeared to be building momentum, as many of the symbols that were associated with foreign control were replaced by symbols that were Caribbean in form and content.

In contrast, the 1980s and '90s have been characterized by a decline in nationalist tendencies and a strengthening of neo-colonial attachments. Though efforts to facilitate the construction of an authentic Caribbean identity have continued to be central to the work of numerous Caribbean scholars and artists, the deepening structural dependence of the region's economy has mitigated against its emergence. Most forms of production in the region are based upon foreign control and reproduce patterns of dominance and subordination which have existed since colonialism and slavery. This is especially true in tourism, where "service with a smile" in exchange for low wages, assures the continuation of master-slave relations, albeit in new forms. Finally, the control and penetration of Caribbean markets by western media via telecommunications has become yet another formidable obstruction to decolonization in the cultural sphere.[2]

Even within this climate of unconditional surrender to foreign interests, pockets of resistance are evident, particularly among Caribbean youth. Increasingly, youth culture in the region is characterized by a rejection of passivity and a desire to resist a fate of hopelessness and despair. Though the form through which resistance is manifest differs sharply from past expressions of nationalism, and may more often appear self-destructive and anti-social, it is through the attitudes and behaviour of large numbers of disillusioned youth that cultural hegemony is being contested.

POPULAR CULTURE AND THE EMERGENCE OF PATTERNS OF RESISTANCE AMONG CARIBBEAN YOUTH

In examining possibilities for resistance to hegemonic forces, a focus on popular culture is logical because it constitutes one of the few social arenas in which contestation occurs. In this paper, the treatment of popular culture focuses on the forms which fall outside the domain of corporate control and are produced by the local population. Such a focus is problematic in that it assumes the relative autonomy of more indigenous and authentic cultural forms, when in fact the production of these forms never occurs in isolation. In this respect, Giroux's point regarding the nature of popular culture as necessarily a hybrid product of multiple influences is important. He writes that "there is no popular culture outside of the interlocking process of meaning, power and desire that characterize the force of cultural relations at work at a given time and place in history" (1992, p.188). However, to the extent that popular culture serves as a source of distinction between dominant and subordinate classes, investigations of these forms have the potential to draw attention to differences with respect to the political, economic and social interests of the two groups, and the ways in which social consciousness is shaped by virtue of class position.

The work of Antonio Gramsci is useful here, because implicit within his conceptualization of hegemony is a recognition that hegemony is based upon a constant struggle to win the consent of subordinate groups to the existing social order. According to Gramsci, ruling elites can prevail in the struggle for consent only if they are able to appropriate and articulate some of the values and interests of these groups. Education, plays an important role here for as Gramsci points out "every relationship of 'hegemony' is necessarily an educational relationship ... between the various forces of which the nation is composed." (1971, p. 350).

Stuart Hall points out that "cultural hegemony is never about pure victory or pure domination; it is never a zero-sum cultural game; it is always about changing the dispositions and the configurations of cultural power, not getting out of it" (1992, p.21). The malleable, dynamic and shifting nature of popular culture enables it to serve as a site for strategic defense against the complete control of the dominant classes. Though its survival and authenticity are constantly challenged by processes aimed at commodifying, appropriating and co-opting the forms which are produced, its potential as a source of resistance is not negated. Commenting on the potential of popular culture as a source of hegemonic resistance, Giroux points out that "the key structuring principle of popular culture does not consist in the content of particular cultural forms" (1992, p.187).

Hence, although the artifacts and expressions of popular culture are historically situated around prevailing meanings and practices, and therefore always vulnerable to commodification, the medium through which audiences interact with these operate primarily at the affective and visceral level of consciousness. Popular culture is rooted in the pain and pleasure, joy and suffering, hope and desperation of the people. Its strength is derived from the existential aspects of its meaning and the connection it creates among those who receive and respond to it. Its potential as a source of hegemonic resistance is derived from both its production, which often falls outside the control of the dominant classes, and its content. For this reason, whether it takes the form of counter-narrative sung through calypso, or whether it is little more than a word or phrase rooted in the vernacular of common folk, popular culture serves as a means through which the aspirations, sensibilities and experiences of those who have been marginalized can be affirmed.

Affirmations of humanity and dignity by the poor and powerless, however should not necessarily be taken as signs of resistance. For example, though the widely acclaimed artwork and music produced by Haitian artists serve as evidence that the spirit of the Haitian people has not been broken by years of brutal repression, such expressions of the popular culture have not constituted a threat to political control exercised by the Douvaliers or the military leaders who have succeeded them. Such affirmations can, however, be extremely important to the survival and dignity of the oppressed, and may prove instrumental to the "language of possibilities" (Giroux, p. 80) which have become essential to democratic social movements which have emerged since the fall of the Douvalier regime.

Describing the importance of popular culture as a means of countering the de-humanizing effects of racism experienced by African Americans, Stuart Hall writes:

> However deformed, incorporated, and inauthentic are the forms in which black people and black communities and traditions appear and are represented in popular culture, we continue to see, in the figures and repertoires on which popular culture draws, the experiences that stand behind them. In its expressivity, its musicality, its orality, in its rich, deep, and varied attention to speech, in its inflections toward the vernacular and the local, and above all, in its metaphorical use of the musical vocabulary, black popular culture has enabled the surfacing of elements of a discourse that is different—other forms of life, other traditions of representation (1992, p.33).

It is important to note however, that even when elements of popular culture undermine or challenge the social practices which are used to inscribe and signify the distinctions between the dominant and subordinate classes, these practices can quickly and easily be appropriated and distorted. Hence, their potency as a source of resistance is almost always limited.

Therefore, to look for the potential for resistance within the popular culture we must look for more than mere affirmations of humanity. Resistance implies agency, the ability to take action aimed at shaping or controlling the social context (Grinberg, 1994, p.124). Within the realm of popular culture there are openings and possibilities for agency. These may be manifest through language, music, religion, dance and creative artistic expressions. Other forms which may represent more direct challenges to the dominant culture are possible as well.

During the late 1960s and '70s the Rastafarian movement constituted such an expression.[3] Though unorganized, informal and non-hierarchical, the movement spread rapidly throughout the Caribbean and beyond. Prior to being embraced by record companies and the Jamaican tourist industry, Rastafari was equated with the lower class and was despised as an expression that was antithetical to the Europhilic tendencies of the Jamaican middle class (Campbell, 1987, pp.103-105). Based upon a total rejection of Babylon, Christendom, materialism and most aspects of western culture, the simple assertion of Rastafarian values and ideas evoked repulsion and disdain.

Much of the contempt toward the Rastas focused originally upon their appearance. In the eyes of the Caribbean middle class, dreadlocks signified more than a hairdo; it represented a rejection of their way of life, and an ideological posture that was in opposition to their neocolonial sympathies. Though the movement lacked a unifying dogma or criteria for membership, those identified with it were widely seen as rebels and a threat to the social order, and were subjected to various forms of repression and harassment throughout the Caribbean.[4] Nonetheless, as proof of its ability to absorb even those elements which appear most opposed to it, elements of Rastafari have eventually been appropriated by the dominant culture and denuded of much of its subversive character.

Though the potential is there, the rebelliousness associated with much of the youth culture in the contemporary Caribbean has not yet met a similar fate. While the fashion and music industries scurry to find ways to absorb and appropriate forms and styles associated with the youth culture, politicians and civic leaders have generally been too preoccupied with the criminal elements associated with these trends to contemplate strategies for co-opting. Increasingly, young people in the Caribbean are receiving the lion's share of blame for the rise in drug trafficking, drug usage and the violence associated with it.[5] Despite substantial evidence showing that it is adults who are primarily responsible for the flow of weapons and arms in urban areas, these are largely seen as youth problems, and young people are disproportionately targeted for police action.

Beyond the fear of crime, however, there is considerable consternation over a more generalized sense of rebelliousness, irreverence and insolence among growing segments of Caribbean youth. Particularly in urban areas, youth culture is identified with black nationalism and contempt for the bourgeois values and lifestyle that gained prominence among economic elites during the 1980s. A strain of dancehall reggae music identified with performers such as Buju Banton, Terror Fabulous, Redd Foxx, Super Cat and Ninja Man, and infamous for its sexually explicit language, is seen as emblematic of this youth culture. More typically this trend is described as an attitude or mentality once believed to be endemic to the ghettos of New York City, but now firmly rooted in the youth culture of the Caribbean. The upsurge in the popularity of basketball as compared to more traditional sports such as soccer and cricket, is yet another manifestation of the change. Its emergence is now widely recognized as a break with Caribbean traditions and much more than just a passing fad. As one commentator from a regional publication, *Caribbean Contact* put it:

> Its manifestations are all around us: on the street corners, in the prisons, in the drug related offences, in our psychiatric hospitals. Poor passes at CXC and similar examinations are followed by a high drop-out rate in secondary school and declining enrollment in our regional university. In the home, increasing absence and in some cases a discounting of men's traditional role is leading to a situation where growing numbers of women prefer not to entertain any serious relationship with them....We do not know who or what we are up against! Society is undergoing fundamental change. (1993, September)

While such views seem to echo the concerns about nihilism raised by Cornell West (1993) in an essay on African American youth, another interpretation is possible. Rather than focus on the extent to which Caribbean youth culture undermines traditional family values, it may be possible to see its potential as a source of resistance to domination by considering its forms and expressions in light of current conditions in the region.

EDUCATION, SOCIAL CONTROL AND STRUCTURAL ADJUSTMENT

In past years the educational system of the Commonwealth Caribbean played such a dominant role in the socialization of young people that the kind of developments described above would have seemed unthinkable. Developed in the image of the British system of public education, the educational system placed heavy emphasis upon memorization, regimentation and discipline. Often managed by religious denominations with public subsidies, Caribbean schools served as a model of stability. With the power and prerogative to utilize corporal punishment, school masters and teachers commanded absolute authority in most Caribbean schools. More often than not, this power was reinforced in the home. The youngster who received "licks" for some misdeed at school could count on more of the same at home should his or her parents find out. School, family and community were bounded together in an interlocking set of mutually reinforcing relationships which provided a powerful source of cohesion for society. Each child knew his or her place because there was a wide array of adults to be encountered each day who would not hesitate to remind those who forgot.[6]

The educational system of the English-speaking Caribbean is unusual for several reasons. First, with the exception of the advanced industrialized societies, few countries have primary school enrollments that compare with the high levels found in the region (Miller, 1992, p.23). Second, the public educational system was established in the 19th century and predates the formation of an independent nation-state by almost one hundred years (Gordon, 1963, p.72). Finally, the mass character of public education, at the primary, secondary and university levels, contrasts dramatically with the more stratified systems found in most developing countries (Benavot and Riddle, 1988).

There are two important historical considerations that help to explain why the educational system developed in this way. First, following emancipation in 1838, the British feared the unleashing of African resentment, such as occurred in Haiti, and offered primary schooling "as an inducement to ex-slaves not to seek revenge.... In providing mass education, the colonial powers hoped to ensure that the subordinate groups in their Caribbean colonies remained loyal subjects" (Miller, 1992, p.25). Secondly, the expansion of access to education became a central feature of the social democratic state after independence. Education was promoted throughout the region as an essential aspect of development, and prior to the economic crisis of the 1970s, expenditures for education increased steadily (Miller, p.35).

Underlying these factors was also the ever-present reality that education served as an effective instrument of social control for the British, as well as the political elites who succeeded them. As a formal socialization activity controlled by the State, education has served as a vehicle for the transmission of a Eurocentric, neo-colonial ideology which fostered dependency and inferiority through its negation of African Creole culture

(Henry, 1984, p.103; Miller, 1989, pp.132-139). According to educational historian Shirley Gordon, efficiency rather than learning was the highest priority of the educational system during the colonial period. Elementary schools were managed through a "payment by results" system,[7] which distributed funds to schools on the basis of student performance on exams, student attendance and "teacher efficiency in management and discipline" (Gordon, 1963, p.79). Social control achieved through a disciplining of the mind and body was a major preoccupation for the educational system.

During the period immediately following independence, significant efforts were made to improve the quality and accessibility of the educational system in the region (Miller, 1992, pp.28-30). However, the economic crisis brought on by the rise in oil prices in the 1970s, and the subsequent mushrooming of debt which continued through the 1980s, resulted in a dramatic curtailment in educational expenditures. For example, the People's National Party (PNP) government headed by Michael Manley in Jamaica was forced to implement austerity measures in education after turning to the International Monetary Fund (IMF) and World Bank in 1977 for debt relief. This was a government that had previously made substantial progress in expanding access to education at all levels (Barry, Wood and Preusch, 1984, pp.341-351). Under Manley, subsidies for poor families were eliminated; teacher-training services were reduced substantially; and school facilities that had been scheduled for upgrade and rehabilitation were neglected (Miller, 1992, pp.32-34). There were similar developments in Trinidad, Guyana and the eastern Caribbean. As more severe structural adjustment programs have been enacted at the behest of the foreign lending agencies in more recent years, public disinvestment in education has progressed even further.[8]

ECONOMIC CRISIS AND YOUTH RESISTANCE

As could be expected, retrenchment in education has weakened the influence that schools are able to exert over the lives of children. As more and more children are "pushed out" or denied access to school, the social control function of schooling has diminished. Moreover, the shrinkage of the public sector has drastically reduced the number of jobs available to school leavers and graduates. Consequently, the possibility of achieving upward mobility through education has become increasingly remote and the facade of meritocracy, which once served as an important source of solidarity in the alliance between middle class political leaders and their lower class constituents, has been severely weakened.

As a result of these developments, schools are not only less able to respond to the needs of youth, but their decline, combined with the overall dismantling of significant components of the social infrastructure, has helped to produce a crisis among Caribbean youth. Characterized by high rates of unemployment, underemployment, poverty and crime, the youth crisis has affected all countries in the region (Miller, 1992, pp.35-39). Young people are certainly not alone in experiencing the hardships which have accompanied the austerity measures adopted by Caribbean governments, however they have, thus far, been more likely than other segments of the population to exhibit signs of resistance. Though generally not expressed in an organized form, signs of resistance are increasingly evident within youth popular culture.

Faced with the reality that hard work in school provides no guarantee of future employment, the appeal of education as an avenue to upward mobility has begun to wane. As they mature, more and more adolescents are coming to the realization that their future presents them with two options: emigration, usually to the United States, Canada or Britain, in search of opportunity, or resignation to a life of poverty in low paying and unfulfilling jobs. While many youth end up accepting these choices, more and more are demanding alternatives. For a growing number, crime, particularly in the form of drug trafficking, has become a viable third option. The proliferation of cocaine and its derivatives which swept the region since the mid-1980s (Thomas, 1988, pp.170,171) has in many cases filled the economic void created by the decline in economic growth and opportunity. Particularly in urban areas, drug trafficking has now become a central feature of the "informal sector" of the economy; a sector which traditionally has provided employment and a marketplace for goods that are otherwise hard to obtain (Mintz, 1989, pp.216-224). Describing the growth of this sector and its importance to a growing segment of the population in the region, Clive Thomas writes that:

> The prevalence of the "black market," "informal," "underground" sector in some of the region's economies has reached a stage where in at least two territories (Guyana and Jamaica) it accounts for a substantial share of employment, importation of basic goods, ownership of financial assets, "illegal" exports and earnings of foreign exchange. It includes the well-known marijuana trade and the not-so-well-known illegal export of precious metals from Guyana. Despite the importance of this sector, in neither of these

territories has there been a serious and sustained attempt to collect and order the available data for use in public policy (1988, pp.369-370).

The proliferation of drugs has contributed to the deterioration of social conditions in the Caribbean and eroded the quality of life for many. More often than not, young people have been its primary victims, as both consumers and low level distributors. Within the context of economic decline and shrinking employment opportunities, a number of young people have turned to the drug trade, despite its illegality, as an alternative to accepting a life of hopelessness and despair. The potential for quick and easy access to cash, and the thrill derived from participating in a trade in which violence and glamour characterize the lifestyles of those who are most successful, have made drug dealing one of the most visible manifestations of this new rebellious and defiant youth culture. Despite its self-destructive and socially malevolent consequences, these illicit activities are being construed as a viable means for "beating a system" that is increasingly perceived as negligent and unresponsive to the needs of Caribbean youth.[9]

Though drug use and drug dealing are an increasingly prominent feature in Caribbean youth culture, however, there are other non-criminal manifestations which more clearly reveal signs of youth resistance. In addition to a more general change in the attitudes and demeanor of young people which one commentator decried as a "phenomenon that threatens to dislodge the stilts on which our already fragile societies are perched,"[10] forms of resistance can also be seen in music, poetry and the journalism produced by young people in the region.

One example of this comes from *Youth Voice* magazine published by the St. James Youth Center in Trinidad. Organized by young people in Port of Spain and Diego Martin, the magazine was launched to serve as a vehicle for the articulation of concerns pertinent to the condition of youth in Trinidad and Tobago. Much of the magazine's focus is devoted to sports, entertainment, music and cultural events of interest to young people. However, the magazine has also served as a medium for poetry and essays which offer political and social commentary. Consistently, these expressions convey dissatisfaction with the direction taken by political leaders to address economic and social problems in the country, and boldly put forward the need for new priorities. For example, the government's implementation of a new value added tax (VAT) on goods and services drew the following criticism:

> We wish to state that we are not satisfied that other alternatives were sufficiently explored before VAT was implemented. We are not satisfied that enough compassion for the people was demonstrated, and we are not satisfied that VAT will in the long term contribute to the qualitative economic development of our country (Vol. 3, no. 12, 1992).

Similar themes are conveyed through *New Vision,* a newspaper published in Barbados. Though officially the organ of the Pan African Movement of Barbados, the publication has also served as an outlet for articles and poetry written by young people. In an issue devoted to biting criticisms of the government headed by Erskine Sandiford and IMF structural adjustment programs, an article entitled "Barbados Is My South Africa" written by a 17-year old Barbadian, put forth the following denunciation of police practices:

> The armed forces of contemporary Barbados are now openly doing what people used to associate only with South Africa, the United States South and other prominent areas of black oppression. Illegal searching of the black person on the streets by the police is now common place. No stopping and searching of whites, Indians, Syrians or Jews—only blacks. No raiding of plantation houses or business people's homes, just those of the poor and defenseless. They ask us for identification cards and work permits like the South African Security. They must realize that we are human beings and not baboons." (March 1992, p.9)

In music, opposition to the policies and priorities of governments in the region have become increasingly common in both calypso and reggae. Both genres have long histories of being used as outlets for political criticism, however the pursuit of crossover marketability led to a substantial reduction in political satire and commentary during the 1980s. However, as more well-known performers concentrated on penetrating foreign markets, a new wave of calypso and dancehall reggae has grown in popularity among Caribbean youth. Calypsonians such as Black Stalin in Trinidad, Ajamu in Grenada, and Gabby in Barbados, revived the practice of intermingling political criticism and social commentary with calypso songs. Rather than reaching for a broader appeal, such artists have concentrated their talents on the local market, focusing on themes that are often meaningless to outsiders but which resonate profoundly among locals. The appeal of music of this kind has helped to revive interest in calypso among young people and to counter the trend toward Americanization in the music that is most popular among Caribbean youth.

Similar developments have occurred in dancehall reggae, though the commentary contained in this new form of reggae generally falls well short of the standards set in previous decades. Characterized by lyrics that are often sexually explicit, and a raucous, bass-laden beat, dancehall reggae has surpassed most other forms of popular music as the preferred selection of Caribbean youth. In keeping with earlier forms of reggae, the political content of dancehall music focuses upon the plight of the poor and powerless. The following excerpt from "The Good, The Bad and The Ugly" by the well known Jamaican reggae artists, Yellowman, is a typical example of how such themes are conveyed.

> Me born as a poor man's pikney
> I say me born as a poor man's pikney
> Why dem does fight me down so
> Why dem does fight me down so
> Me born in the ghetto and me grow up in the street
> Me born in the ghetto and grow up in the street
> Sufferation is all that I meet
> Life in the ghetto it not sweet
> You can't get nuff food to eat
> Its the good, the bad, and the ugly

Surprisingly, despite its often illicit content and irreverent social commentary, dancehall music has in some cases been more successful at crossing over into foreign markets than some mainstream versions of calypso and reggae sung by more well known artists. In part, this is due to the similarities between dancehall and rap music, both of which rely upon electronically produced sound and the rhythmical rapping of the artists. Such music has also found tremendous appeal among youth in the Caribbean communities of New York City, Miami, London and Toronto.

YOUTH RESISTANCE: MORE THAN JUST A PASSING FAD?

Given the ability of the dominant culture to mollify and render impotent forms of popular culture which might otherwise draw attention to distinctions in interests between classes, it might seem reasonable to conclude that even the most subversive aspects of Caribbean youth culture will eventually meet a similar fate. If past patterns of commodification and appropriation are upheld, one might expect dancehall performers to tone down their lyrics, or at least limit their commentary to sex, as they more aggressively pursue access to foreign markets. Likewise, youth publications that hope to stay in print may be forced to de-politicize their message in order to obtain financial backing from local businesses.

While such developments could very well occur, at present there is no sign that there will be any improvement in the conditions which have given rise to the spirit of defiance that is now prevalent among Caribbean youth. Throughout the region, the uncritical acceptance of liberalization and structural adjustment policies, has contributed to a swelling of the ranks of the poor and marginalized and a withering of social welfare programs. With no signs of a reversal in the economic performance of the region evident in the near future, further deterioration of social and economic conditions appears likely. Young people will disproportionately bear the brunt of these hardships.

However, youth resistance is more than a reaction to a particular set of policies. Though there is evidence that many young people are aware of how structural adjustment policies are affecting their own opportunities, it would be a mistake to reduce the connection between structural adjustment policies and the emergence of this rebellious youth culture to a cause and effect relationship. Rather than characterizing it as a response to particular policies, youth resistance must be seen as a more general dissatisfaction with the trend toward homogenization of cultural experiences and the steady decline in material conditions. Whether the frustration of youth will lead to more organized forms of resistance, however, is a question that can not as yet be answered. While publications such as *Youth Voice* and *New Visions* demonstrate a higher level of resolve and a greater commitment to action than other more subtle forms of defiance, neither publication has indicated an interest, or demonstrated ability in mobilizing youth into a social movement. Moreover, the success of both publications has been contingent to a large extent upon the assistance of adults who have provided financial and logistical support. Such cross-generational alliances may in fact be precisely what is needed if youth frustration is to be harnessed into endeavours which actually have an influence upon the policy and direction of Caribbean states.

Perhaps more than any other group, teachers could potentially have the most to gain from an alliance with youth. With their salaries in a steady state of decline, and conditions within schools deteriorating as a result of austerity measures, teachers have a tremendous need for political support (Miller, 1992). Rather than looking exclusively to other labor unions, many of which have also been weakened by economic crisis and disinvestment in the public sector, teachers could look to the youth for political support. For such an alliance to work, however, teachers would need to adopt a more critical stance toward the role they play as agents of social control within schools. Instead of passively accepting their roles as gatekeepers and guardians of a social system that has become increasingly less responsive to the needs of working people, teachers would have to adopt a more critical perspective toward the educational process and the roles that they are preparing youth to fill in society.[11]

Whether or not teachers or any other adults will be able to develop meaningful links with youth will undoubtedly also be based upon how they relate to the rebelliousness within youth culture. Most adults, especially teachers, find the irreverence and defiance among youth to be so offensive that they can imagine no way of responding that does not include an attempt at putting them in their place. Despite the futility of such efforts many adults can imagine no other response given that so many aspects of youth popular culture represent such a fundamental break with well-established Caribbean traditions (i.e., courtesy toward elders, rigidity of gender roles, respect for authority, etc.).

The social cleavage along generational lines that is becoming more pronounced with the advent of this change in youth culture and the typical adult response to it represents more than just a generation gap. Generational conflicts based upon challenges to existing norms and mores have happened before, and Caribbean societies have coped with these without experiencing severe fragmentation. However, the current situation is different. Youth rebelliousness is one of the manifestations of the deterioration in social and economic conditions in the region. As disparities between social classes widen, and the institutions that once served as a source of stability and social cohesion are weakened, challenges to the legitimacy of the established political order will undoubtedly increase. How adults respond to the forms of resistance exhibited by Caribbean youth will undoubtedly determine whether or not young people will grow more alienated or become participants in a broader effort aimed at improving conditions for all.

ENDNOTES

1. Due in part to the lack of research conducted in the evolution of educational systems in the Caribbean, the field has not been subject to the kinds of debates relat-

ed to cultural reproduction and structural correspondence that have characterized the sociology of education in North America and Western Europe. Errol Miller's work has helped to make the connections between British colonialism and the character of Caribbean education systems explicit; however, a theoretical framework linking changes in the political economy of the region to institutional policies and practices in education remains largely undeveloped.

2. See "The Politics of Telecommunications Reform in Developing Countries" by Ben A. Petrazzini (Honolulu: Pacific Telecommunications Council, 1993).
3. For a discussion of the ideological and historical roots of the Rastafarian movement see *The Rastafarians* by Leonard Barrett (Boston: Beacon Press, 1977).
4. Although for very different reasons, Rastafarians have been targeted for harassment by both left-wing and right-wing governments in the Caribbean. In Grenada, although Rastafarians were instrumental in the overthrow of Eric Gairy in 1979, many were later detained by the People's Revolutionary after being accused of counterrevolutionary activity. See Sunshine pp.59-60 and *Rasta and Resistance* by Horace Campbell (Trenton NJ: Africa World Press, 1987) pp.153-174.
5. For an example of how this issue has been depicted in the Caribbean press see "Young Male Offenders Increasing in Trinidad and Tobago" by Maureen Benjamin in the September 1993 issue of the *Caribbean Contact* (Vol. 19, No.9).
6. For an historical discussion on the role of education in providing social stability to Caribbean societies see "Education and Society in St. Kitts and Nevis" in *Education and Society in the Commonwealth Caribbean* edited by Errol Miller (Mona, Jamaica: Institute of Economic and Social Research, 1991) pp.30-33.
7. The payment by results systems was started in England in 1861. The system was first introduced in Barbados in 1866 and later implemented in other parts of the West Indies. Under this system, funding for schools and teacher salaries were tied to student performance and attendance. The lack of compulsory education laws made this a difficult system to maintain. See *A Century of West Indian Education* by Shirley Gordon (London: Longman's, 1963) pp.79-92.
8. For a discussion on how structural adjustment policies have affected expenditures in education in the Caribbean see *Storm Signals: Structural Adjustment and Development Alternatives in the Caribbean* by Kathy McAfee (Boston: Southend Press, 1991) pp. 139-145.
9. Rationalization about drug dealing expressed by young people often point to the lack of viable alternatives. In one youth publication, a young author, Livingston Ferguson, posed the following question: "Is there hope for youth in the streets?" His response: "Each day they beg for a living and when they do get work, which is not often, the people who take them sometimes don't pay them. Some turn to rugs because that is the only life they know. You can't expect them to just go hungry

and not do anything about it." Taken from *Youth Voice* (Port of Spain, Trinidad: Published by St. James Youth Center, Vol. 111, No. 12).

10. Commenting on the crisis facing Afro-Caribbean male youth, Maureen Benjamin writes that "Our young men between the approximate ages of 17-35 are increasingly being sidelined and excluded from playing any meaningful role in society. Faced with attitudes ranging from sheer indifference to a debilitating sense of self-pity, society is being deprived of full utilization of its young people at the most productive time of their lives." *Caribbean Contact,* Vol. 19, No. 9, September 1993.
11. For a discussion on how teachers can change their relations with students such that their role as agents of social reproduction and social control is transformed, see *Teachers As Intellectuals* by Henry Giroux (New York: Bergin and Garvey, 1988) pp. 121-128.

REFERENCES

Abbot, E. (1988). *Haiti, An insiders history of the rise and fall of the Douvaliers.* New York: Touchstone Books.

Barrett, L. (1977). *The Rastafarians.* Boston, MA: Beacon Press.

Barry, T., Wood, B. Preusch, D. (1984). *The other side of paradise.* New York: Grove Press.

Bell, W. (1967). *The democratic revolution in the West Indies.* Cambridge MA: Schenkman Publishing Co.

Benavot, A. and Riddle, P. (1988). The expansion of primary education, 1870-1940: trends and issues. *Sociology of Education* 61, (July).

Cabral, A. (1973). *Return to the source.* New York: Africa Information Service.

Campbell, H. (1987). *Rasta and resistance.* Trenton, NJ: Africa World Press.

Caribbean Contact (1993) 19, No. 9.

Carnoy, M. and Samoff, J. (1990). *Education and social transition in the third world.* Princeton NJ: Princeton University Press.

Carnoy, M. and Levin, H. (1985). *Schooling and work in the democratic state.* Stanford CA: Stanford University Press.

Fagen, R. (1969). *The transformation of political culture in Cuba.* Stanford CA: Stanford University Press.

Ferguson, J. (1984). *Grenada: revolution in reverse.* London: Latin American Bureau.

Giroux, H. (1992). *Border crossings.* New York: Routledge.

Gordon, S. (1963). *A century of West Indian education.* New York: Longmans.

Gramsci, A. (1971). *The prison notebooks.* New York: International Publishers.

Grinberg, J. (1994). From the margin to the center: teacher's emerging voices through inquiry. In R. Martusewicz and W. Reynolds (Eds.), *Inside out.* (pp. 107-123). New York: St. Martin's Press.

Hall, S. (1992). What is this "black" in black popular culture. In G. Dent (Ed.), *Black popular culture* (pp. 34-68). Seattle WA: Bay Press.

Henry, P. and Stone, C. (1983). *The newer Caribbean—Decolonization, democracy and development.* Philadelphia PA: Institute for the Study of Human Issues.

Hintzen, P. (1992). Ethnicity and class in post-colonial Caribbean Politics. In A. Serbin (Ed.), *El Caribe hacia el ano 2000.* San Juan, Puerto Rico: ILDIS.

Jansen, J. (1991). The state and curriculum in the transition to socialism: The Zimbabwean experience. *Comparative Education Review* 35, No. 1.

Mazuri, A. (1978). Political values and the educated class in Africa. Berkeley CA: University of California Press.

McAfee, C. (1991). *Storm signals.* Boston MA: Southend Press

Miller, E. (1989). Post-Emancipation Education. *Caribbean Affairs,* July-September, 2, No. 3.

———. (1991). *Education and society in the commonwealth Caribbean.* Mona, Jamaica: Institute for Economic and Social Research.

———. (1992). *Education for all: Caribbean perspectives and imperatives.* Washington, DC: Inter-American Development Bank.

Mintz, S. (1989). *Caribbean transformations.* New York: Columbia University Press.

Morrow, R. & Torres, C. (1994). Education and the reproduction of class, gender, and race: Responding to the postmodern challenge. *Educational Theory,* 44, No. 1.

New vision. (1992, March). Bridgetown, Barbados: The Pan African Publishing Co.

Petrazzini, B. (1993). *The politics of telecommunications reform in developing countries.* Honolulu: Pacific Telecommunications Council.

Riviere, B. (1990). *The state systems in the eastern Caribbean.* Mona, Jamaica: Institute of Economic and Social Research.

Searle, C. (1984). *Words unchained.* London: Zed Books.

Sunshine, C. (1982). *Grenada the peaceful revolution.* Washington, DC: EPICA Task Force.

Thomas, C. (1988). *The poor and the powerless.* New York: Monthly Review Press.

Torres, C.A. (1991). The State, nonformal education, and socialism in Cuba, Nicaragua, and Grenada. *Comparative Education Review,* February, 35, No.1.

Wa Thiong'O, N. (1986). *Decolonizing the mind: the politics of language in African literature.* London and Nairobi: Heineman.

West, C. (1993). *Race matters.* Boston MA: Beacon Press.

Yellowman, (1993). *The Good, the bad and the ugly.* On *Zunggizung.* (CD) London: Sanchi Records.

Youth voice (1992), 111:12. Port of Spain, Trinidad: St. James Youth Center.

MYTH AND SIGNIFICATION IN PERRY HENZELL'S *THE HARDER THEY COME*

Gladstone L. Yearwood

The narrative development of the hero, in the film *The Harder They Come,* who transgresses proscribed social positions in his struggle against the established order and must be punished for it, raises questions about realist models of film language and their effectiveness in the formulation of an alternative cinema that foregrounds the experiences and aspirations of marginalized peoples. This article posits that film is capable of altering social consciousness and of helping to construct new social meanings. It also suggests, however, that the task facing the Caribbean filmmaker is not the reproduction of images of society by means of an illusory realism that merely confirms the harsh realities of colonial and post-colonial structures. It is rather the use of the signifying languages of the cinema as a means of producing knowledge of that reality as a force in the transformation of society.

L'évolution du héro transgressif dans le film *The Harder They Come,* qui lutte contre l'ordre établi et en subit les conséquences, soulève des questions concernant l'efficacité des modèles réalistes de langage cinématographique pour mettre en relief les expériences et les aspirations des peuples marginalisés. Si le cinéma peut transformer la conscience sociale et construire des significations sociales nouvelles, ce n'est pas nécessairement en reproduisant les images de cette société d'une manière mimétique. Reproduire la réalité ne fait que confirmer l'existence des structures coloniales et post-coloniales. Voici la tâche qui confronte le cinéaste caraïbéen. Il faudrait plutôt élaborer un langage filmique qui permet au cinéma de produire un savoir qui deviendrait une force de transformation de la société.

THE HARDER THEY COME (1971) is a chant of black dreams and frustrations. It is the story of a betrayal, the loss of innocence and the intrusion of foreign values and technologies into the contemporary Caribbean. Writers Perry Henzell and Trevor Rhone craft a narrative about a mid-20th century Jamaican folk hero Ivanhoe 'Rhygin' Martin, whose mythic fight against the established order parallels the day-to-day struggle of society's disenfranchised. In the film, Ivan is trapped between two worlds—the persistent poverty of Jamaica's suffering underclass and an alluring metropolitan North American lifestyle. Eventually he dies because of this forced interface.

The signification of the hero in *The Harder They Come,* his narrative development and narrative destiny, raise serious questions about the capabilities of realist models of film language to formulate new possibilities for emerging forms of cinema. Within the ideological system of the film's narrative, the hero transgresses proscribed social positions in his struggle against the established order and consequently must be punished for it. *The Harder They Come* provides an opportunity to observe the way the system of filmic signification prevalent in traditional cinema is inadequate as an expressive language for the development of an alternative cinema that foregrounds the experiences and aspirations of marginalized peoples. Narrative realism lies at the heart of the traditional Hollywood film, which is so obsessed with guaranteeing our sense of realism—in an Aristotelean paradigm—that it overlooks the fact that its realism is the consequence of a social construction. Despite the fact that filmmaker Perry Henzell is able to push *The Harder They Come* to the limits of narrative realism as an expressive form, the ideological baggage of narrative realist signification creates a dead weight that serves to limit the narrative power of the hero, the narrative functioning of the female in the film and the film's ability to go beyond what it perceives as social reality.

Film is capable of dialectically altering social consciousness and can be instrumental in helping to construct new social meanings. In fiction, the way the hero surmounts his or her narrative obstacles, or is overcome by the superior power of the established social order, plays a key role in harnessing or liberating the potential for social change. As myth, film is intricately related to our sense of social possibility and social change. The system of filmic signification that we develop in our cinematic expression also is related to our conceptions of social power and its seeming mutability or immutability. The task facing the Caribbean filmmaker is not the reproduction of society in all its imagined beauty and illusory realism or as documentary empiricism, which merely confirms the harsh reality of colonial and post-colonial structures, but it is the use of the signifying languages of the cinema as a means of producing knowledge of that reality as a force in the transformation of society.

HEROISM AS A FORM OF RESISTANCE

Ivan is a hero from a different time who inevitably comes into conflict with society's enforcers because he refuses to live out his prescribed social role and seeks to develop his potential outside his powerless social position. Immediately, Ivan's narrative desire seeks to violate the laws of his social existence. His heroism contains the seeds of his revolutionary development, but the filmic vehicle within which his narrative is played out sabotages this potential. His is a quest for freedom; but it is the freedom of the matinee hero-adventurer. Ivan identifies with the cowboy heroes of the Old American West. He lives out the oppressive individualism of the Western hero, but society has grown more complex. Gone are the mythical days of the "lone star" hero, the fearless cowboy whose invincibility and courage surmount all in the end. Ivan's eventual downfall occurs precisely because he seeks his freedom in a mythological system that has sought to guarantee his subordination. He uses a reactionary celluloid illusion and foreign popular cultural paradigms as the model for his struggle. However, schooled in the entertainment genres of the Hollywood cinema, we know that the cowboy lives a dangerous life, on the edge, on the fringes of society.

Ivan's narrative fate is tragic because there can be no symphony orchestrating the expressed hopes and struggles of the oppressed and society's refusal to allow a significant challenge to its social order and concomitant social change. This system of narrative realism, based on Aristotle's model of tragedy, requires that the hero must die. The happy ending is not allowed, for the Aristotelean system of poetics generates a socially reinforcing and equilibrating function for the tragic hero and for a culture-bound, gender-specific spectator who develops an empathic relationship with him. Augusto Boal observes that this system of narrative "is designed to bridle the individual, to adjust him to what pre-exists. If this is what we want, the Aristotelean system serves the purpose better than any other; if on the contrary, we want to stimulate the spectator to transform his society, to engage in revolutionary action, in that case we will have to seek another poetics" (1979).

The film does thematize the anarchy of "cowboy days"—a recent era in Jamaica's political history—but without contextualizing the social conditions that surround this violence. Given his fixation with the movies on the one hand, Ivan lives out the demeanor of the cowboy, and on the other, he lives out the real life circumstances against which he rebels in Jamaican society.

The Harder They Come is loosely based on the activities of the post-Second World War Jamaican rebel Rhygin Martin, who was a real-life obscure petty criminal catapulted to national attention because of his daring escapades. On the morning of Thursday, September 2, 1948, the *Daily Gleaner* published banner headlines:

> Police Hunt Desperado after Running Gun Battle ...
> 2 killed, 4 shot by
> Escaped convict
> Shoots way out of Police Cordon
> Slays woman

Rhygin was the first media created superstar in Jamaica's cultural history and his story rarely left the front pages in the 42 days between his emergence in the media and his eventual termination at the hands of the police (Thelwell, 1992).

In the narrative, we cannot dispute the fact that particular historical events did occur; however, we may question the established historical canon, initiate an alternative reading and create new approaches to film narrative without capitulating to the tautological exigencies of the original historical event and the subsidiary contrived realism of popular film. The film within the film and Ivan's fixation on the Old West play an important role in his narrative motivation. When these are coupled with the intertextual references to the urban outlaw Rhygin, the narrative signifies a double failure for the hero: in so far as he seeks out and utilizes the cultural models of the oppressor without transforming them, he reinforces his own oppression; and furthermore, in so far as the film relates even distantly to a real-life urban Jamaican cowboy, only a revolutionary filmic signification can creatively penetrate the realism of the popular image. But the system of narrative realism tends to glorify the hero, and a rebellious hero who seeks to alter the scheme of social relations in opposition to the reproduction of traditional social positions cannot be fulfilled within narrative realism.

In Ivan's transformation from poor country boy to slick city hustler, instead of gaining the control over his future and the freedom he yearns, he loses both progressively. In the course of the narrative, Ivan neither has the personal freedom that marks a revolutionary character, nor the freedom of mobility in society characteristic of traditional heroes. The filmmaker skilfully builds a structure of visual images that poignantly clarifies political and economic contradictions in Jamaican society; and within the film language he uses, grasps several important insights concerning the plight of the poor and the constitution of power in society. Henzell's thematization of the country boy hero and Ivan's subsequent downfall within the jungle of the city does not devalue the strength and character of rural life, but critiques the brutal and immoral vicissitudes of urban existence. Without a doubt, the filmmaker deplores the massive flow of humanity from the rural areas into the degradation of the city. This motivating premise of the narrative is crucial to the film's signification as evidenced by Ivan's arrival in town. All hell breaks loose in the city, and the hero is placed in an alien environment, which he does not understand and cannot control.

As the bus arrives in the city, visual signifiers emphasize the modernity of the city. Billboard advertisements claim: "Talk with Phillip Waite for a Better Life." The motion of moving from the country to the city is now complete as the overloaded bus disgorges its load. Ivan, carrying his possessions on the street, encounters a push-cart vendor.

Vendor: Hey, country boy ... Get out of my way. Move out the way.
Ivan: Wait a minute man, yuh know de way to Milk Lane?
Vendor: Yuh have money? If yuh have money, yuh go anyway, yuh know ...
If yuh don't have money, yuh fart ... Yuh better stay home.

The push-cart vendor sends Ivan to collect a debt from a man who owes him money, but the vendor absconds with the possessions Ivan brought with him from the country. In contrast to the city slicker, the country man is a noble character. On the bus to the city, Ivan displays a mango. A male passenger asks him whether he has more. Ivan tells the man it is the last one, and it's for his mother. "Put it up," the man replies. In the city, this kind of compassion does not exist, for Ivan is given a rude welcome. As soon as he arrives, he is impoverished further when the push-cart vendor cons him out of his possessions.

Ivan is a dreamer. He dreams not of spiritual fulfilment in the search for God, but of a crude material gain. The nature of his dreams is just as idealistic as the "pie-in-the-sky" variety he condemns so vehemently. The narrative presents a view of religion as having a socially equilibrating and cathartic function in contrast to Ivan, who conceives of the Church as waiting patiently for some future utopian promise that he views as a useless undertaking. Ivan wants his future now, in today's life and at this moment. However, the structure of his desire and his struggle to fulfil it turn out to be, ironically, of the same variety as that which he condemns. This is a major flaw in the structural possibilities of narrative realist signification, which is the expression of a bourgeois world-view that posits the notion of an essentialist individual. It makes no distinctions between concretely different historical circumstances, but merely informs us that the actions and desires of the individual will remain essentially the same, because human desire and actions reflect certain core truths that, more or less, prove intractable through historical time. This view of the world implies that members of various social classes have essentially the same interests; for example, to attain social advancement or the good life, and they will abuse power and incur social corruption in the same manner as social elites. A dialectical reading of history avers a different understanding. The poor do not have dreams of this sort, for these are a middle-class luxury. The poor have forthright realities to fulfil. Yes, the poor do have dreams, but the system of narrative realism refuses to differentiate between the dreams of the powerful and those of the powerless.

His first night in town, Ivan wants to go to the Rialto cinema. In the framed film narrative that features a Western being screened at the Rialto, a lone gunman is besieged by a score of hostile masked men. As they approach menacingly, the audience cringes in fear for the lone man's life. The odds are against him. But Jose, who brought Ivan to the cinema shouts out: "You think de hero can die till the last reel." In what appears to be his final moment, the lone gunman grabs a Gatlin gun and mows down his enemies. In this film within the film, the hero does not die; but in the framing film, Ivan's fate is sealed within the system of narrative realism so long as he opts for the outlaw lawlessness of the Western outlaw.

Within this variety of narrative, the hero's motivation, his desire and the structure of his quest are related more to the cosmopolitan aspiration of Jamaica's middle classes because the poor are not the point of production of these views in *The Harder They Come.* The system of narrative realism claims implicitly to be a neutral articulation of various voices in social discourse. It appears to speak for all social classes folding their consciousness into its own and masking the fact that there is a dominant perspective from which the narrative speaks, a perspective that is concealed or repressed to generate a facade of democratic discourse. The articulation of poverty and the struggle that the hero undertakes against it all emanate from the position of society's advantaged classes, which guarantees its expression in the cinema through the system of narrative realism. The sensitivity with which Henzell handles his filmic material should not be devalued, but it is constrained by his mode of expression. His filmic language plays tricks on him: it unilaterally determines the structure of desire of his hero and subsequently, his hero's destiny.

Ivan's heroism is rendered futile within the filmic signification of narrative realism. The connections between the lives of the poor, their need for survival and their inevitable transgression of the law as a means of rectifying their powerless social position are carefully elided from the space of the narrative. The film does present the cultivation of ganja (marijuana) as a means of survival, and characteristically points out the nature of foreign and local exploitation of the trade. Most of the profits elude the farmers, those who produce it and take the risk in the first place. When Ivan challenges this system, he is isolated and must be put in his place. He becomes a man on the run. His eventual capture hinges on an increasing isolation through a deepening of the economic crisis the farmers are experiencing: They cannot earn a living because the police have put a halt to the trade until Ivan is caught. Surely, the cultivators of the crop will suffer; but the narrative carefully avoids the question of the effects of the ban on the local elites and international distributors, for so long as the trade is halted, the international connections also experience the drought.

All this leads us to question the speaking voice of the narrative, for it is necessary to interrogate the system of biases it incorporates and the ideological interests it seeks to protect. Narrative realist signification suggests that individual characters speak from their individual and social class interests. But this understanding only masks the fact that the filmic world in the traditional cinema is constructed by dominant social forces and speaks to their concerns. Out of necessity, the voice of the poor resonates in opposition to that of those dominant social groups. Thus, although Ivan's dream of removing himself from the yoke of exploitation and poverty is concrete and necessary, the manner in which he pursues this dream through the glorified life of the star and the illusory fame of the entertainment world is more the creation of the speaking voice of the narrative than of the poor. Within the narrative, Ivan is transformed from a pre-revolutionary peasant-type into an urban street hustler, whose revolution centres on the acquisition of a cosmopolitan lifestyle and consumption of North American consumer goods. Here, we witness the way the genre contains the revolutionary potential of the film. As a result, when Ivan begins to live out his dream, he loses touch with the social realities of his life. Ivan appears to be a crazy man, driven into a stupor of insatiable insanity. Hence, the narrative creates a space for Ivan's rebellion, but it develops the revolutionary potential within the context of a fantasy, a world within which the hero is destined to die. This kind of rebellious hero, who challenges the system must die within the system of narrative realism of traditional cinema, because his winning puts the dominant system of values and meanings into crisis.

NARRATIVE REALISM AND FILMIC SIGNIFICATION IN *THE HARDER THEY COME*

In the narrative, although Ivan appears to have acquired the trappings of power, such as guns, money and mobility, the filmic signification does not confirm their traditional meanings; rather it contradicts them. When juxtaposed with Ivan's flamboyant clothing and conspicuous urban manner, the concept of lack anchors these signifiers. Ivan acquires the form without the substance. There is the acquisition of material goods, but he does not control the power that society associates with having such possessions. Ivan is thereby an increasingly vulnerable and dangerous figure within the system of social signification, for the development of his character seems a fullness where in fact there is absence. Ivan's narrative transformation from country boy to city slicker is constructed intertextually upon a filmic signification developed in the Hollywood cinema that stereotyped the urban North American black male in popular culture as a Zip Coon-type character. Within this delineation, the Zip Coon signifier is marked by castration and powerlessness especially in its low-comic zeal. Based on the symbolic codes of our culture, the flamboyant coquettish attire of the street hustler signifies an absence, the lack of power. In *The Harder They Come,* Ivan is transformed from square country boy to city slicker who wears fancy, colorful hats, jeans, suede outfits, wet-look vests, leopard-patterned shirt and dark glasses. Ivan is transformed into the Johnny-Too-Bad signifier from a song used in the film's soundtrack. In the Johnny-Too-Bad scene, Ivan turns on the radio and the song "Johnny-Too-Bad" provides a backdrop to this encounter in the preacher's workshop.

Longo:	Hey, pretty boy ..., pretty hat. Johnny-Too-Bad, bring me the hammer.
Ivan:	What happen, yuh can't get it yuhself?
Longo:	No man, you bring it for me.
Ivan:	Bring the hammer!
Longo:	You have on pretty hat this morning.
Ivan:	Yuh like it?
Longo:	You really look like Johnny-Too-Bad. You only need to have a gun to look like Johnny. But before you get a gun, get the broom and go sweep out de shop.

The signifier of Johnny-Too-Bad is already loaded with a question mark. The lyrics of the original song signify the "rude-boy" culture in the song "Johnny-Too-Bad." He is the urban gangster predator "walking down the road with a pistol in the waist," who is looting and shooting while his victims are wailing. The song informs us that his judgment day will come, and there will be no running, no hiding place for Johnny. The misreading of Ivan's rebelliousness in terms of the Johnny-Too-Bad signifier compromises the filmic signification of the narrative. As the lyrics of the song indicate, this is a strident critique of the glorification of gangster elements in contemporary urban Jamaican culture:

> Walking down the road with a pistol in your waist,
> Johnny you're too bad;
> Walking down the road with a ratchet in your waist,
> Johnny you're too bad;
> You're just robbing and stabbing and looting and shooting ...

But whereas the sound image undertakes a sophisticated critique of a social problem, its juxtaposition with the visual image of Ivan wanting to break out of his poverty and oppression engenders new meanings. Apparently the narrative is unable to separate righteous rebellion from gangsterism. It presents us with a loaded signifier: a hero with whom we can empathize, whose act of resistance we invest in emotionally, but whose rebellion is linked with signifieds of urban gangster terrorists who prey on their own community. What we glean here is that a reformulated hero cannot be developed within traditional narrative signification, for the ideological baggage of narrative realism tends to support conservative cultural models more than give shape to the narrative potential of a reformulated heroic tradition.

Henzell's narrative presents a sophisticated paradigm of social change coded in the form of transportation technology, which is used to propel the narrative. Ivan is in control when dealing with forms of transportation that he has integrated into his social existence. As the newly arrived country boy, he harnesses and masters the technology of the bicycle. He actually builds the bicycle from bits and pieces retrieved from the rubbish heap. The bicycle is also the vehicle for his romantic encounter with Elsa. Later in the narrative, he even manages to escape on a bicycle from the soldiers who close in on him. When Longo claims the bicycle after Preacher orders Ivan off the church premises, there is a moment of uninhibited violence and bloodletting. Given the structure of the incident, Ivan's choices are limited because the one moment when he is about to have control over his life is being snatched away from him. He must strike out violently, and he does. Regarding the phenomenon of violence by the oppressed, Frantz Fanon writes: "He of whom they have never stopped saying that the only language he understands is that of force, decides to give utterance to force" (1968).

Ivan plays out a Fanonian theme of violence as purgative for the oppressed. His swift and spontaneous anger against Longo is not the result of the narrative's claim of a suitor's rivalry over Elsa between the two men, but the result of Longo's attempt to deprive Ivan of the creative moment when he has mastered his environment and constructed the bicycle. In a garish, exhibitionistic display of violence, Ivan mutilates the man's face. This incident propels Ivan into a life of crime in which his ambitions to become a famous singer preoccupy the major interest of the narrative. But a more important reading locates these events within a vantage point of the paradigm of power relations within the narrative. Ivan's swift response to Longo's attempt to seize his bicycle is his most important stand in the course of the narrative. By building the bicycle from the rubbish heap, Ivan has engendered some modicum of control over his life. One cannot simply take this away from him without a serious fight on his part. Ivan's punishment is just as violent. He receives eight strokes of the tamarind switch. The legally constituted violence of the system is brutal in its execution. It sheds its humanistic ideals in order to maintain the legal order. The liberal humanist ideology characteristic of narrative realism avers that violence in all its forms begets only violence. There is an apparent condemnation of all forms of violence through the genre's structuring of crime and punishment, and the futility of resorting to violence is underscored given that the forces of the law control and exercise more overpowering means of violence. The ideology of this system of narrative suggests that to struggle against the dominant order leads only to futility.

The filmmaker fashions his narrative around the encounter of the individual with technology. Using the form of a riddle, Henzell codifies the problems of Third World development in relation to the acquisition and utilization of forms of technology. This theme is developed in the Jamaican context through the metaphor of forms of transportation technology that the hero engages in struggling for his survival. The technological option he chooses, given the state of social development of his environment, contains the seeds of his survival or his narrative death. Ivan's encounter with various forms of transportation technology fuels the complications of the narrative. The more advanced forms of transportation technology—the motorcycle and the motor car—lead eventually to the hero's downfall and are linked narratively with various kinds of lawlessness. A discarded automobile is where Ivan sleeps. Preacher finds in it various signifiers of death and decadence: space-age toy gun, *Two-Gun Kid* comic book, *Playboy* magazine and pin-up posters of nude women. The motorcycle is the means for transporting ganja; it even becomes an accessory to the murder of a policeman.

Throughout the film, Ivan yearns for the freedom signified by the automobile. As the film opens, we see him as the outsider inside the bus looking longingly and excitedly out the window at a white convertible Mustang that zooms by filled with fun-loving riders. The recording studio mogul, Mr. Hilton, drives a white convertible Mercedes Benz. Hilton drives up as a group of unemployed musicians wait for a quick audition. He listens to their song, turns them down and drives on as Ivan stands in the background looking on.

The signifier of the white convertible, whose drivers seek to possess the power and success for which Ivan craves becomes a central factor in understanding the film's narrative structure. When Ivan's opportunity arrives finally, he, too, must be in the driver's seat of the particular automobile. At the hotel parking lot, he commandeers a white convertible Chevrolet Impala, holding the white-suited, white cork-hat attired hotel attendant at gun point. The white convertible is a signifier that Ivan is forbidden to express; however within the film's narrative system, he is destined to possess it. Possession of the white horse within the system of narrative realism can signify only his death. When Ivan transgresses the fixed social positions and relations of society and seeks to reformulate the structures of the unconscious by moving from the position of the onlooker—that is, the passive object of power, to intrude upon a seemingly sacred rite; that is, the power and control of the white convertible—he must be punished.

The signification of whiteness in *The Harder They Come* functions as a prominent hermeneutic feature of the film's structure of suspense. Upon Ivan's arrival in the city, he asks for directions to get to Milk Lane, which we learn is his mother's address. But when we read Milk Lane within the context of the other signifiers of whiteness that emerge throughout the film and which help determine its narrative outcome, we witness how social signification influences filmic signification, for Ivan's narrative quest is structured within the codes of power and powerlessness and dominant ideological positions of society.

The repeated shots of Ivan positioned as the outsider pushes the narrative along a structure of social relations based on a system of social signification equivalent to the paradigm of powerful-powerless. The film utilizes windows, fences, natural barriers and other boundaries or demarcations to forcefully construct this visual motif. As the outsider, Ivan (the country boy) is unskilled and suffers constant rejection. When he seeks work at a construction site, he is kicked off and pushed further into the underground. The urban environment is cold and alien, with scenes of raucous poverty and human scavengers who survive off the dump heaps of Kingston's shanty towns. Ironically, the soundtrack appears to plays a wicked game actually inspiring Ivan to his fated confrontation with the law.

> You can get it if you really want;
> But you must try, try and try, try and try;
> You'll succeed at last.
> Persecution you must bear;
> Win or lose, you got to get your share,
> Got your mind set on a dream,
> You can get it though hard it may seem now.
>
> Rome was not built in a day;
> Opposition will come your way.
> But the harder the battle you see,
> It's the sweeter the victory.

In the film, the sound signifiers are highly developed and sophisticated in their signification of the plight of the powerless in society. The soundtrack thematizes and actually presents a complex and progressive commentary that the film's visual language has not mastered. For example,

> 007, Oceans eleven
> Dem a loot, dem a shoot,
> Dem a wail, shanty town.
> Dem rude boys gone pon vacation.

When the lyrics of the sound signification are juxtaposed with Ivan's struggle and the concrete circumstances of his existence, the result is irony, as in *Many Rivers To Cross.* The soundtrack proclaims: "Stop that train, I want to get off." But the narrative refuses to stop; rather, it catapults Ivan into the life against which the sound signifiers caution. The soundtrack informs: You can get it, if you really want it. Ivan really wants it, but he can't get it. The only sweet victory for him in the end is the manner of his death—he dies fighting. But his death is a setback because he dies as a result of delusional hallucinations interspersed with scenes from a Western movie, an illusory reality. In this sense, the filmic signification plays a cruel game, for it lifts the hopes of society's sufferers, but offers no consolation and makes no gains. The system of narrative realism draws on diverse sources, which in themselves offer a progressive social critique. But when they are incorporated within the filmic signification of the narrative, their meaning is redefined within the ideological structures that reproduce realist film language.

NARRATIVE REALISM AND THE REPRESENTATION OF WOMEN

So long as Ivan remains within the strictures of his prescribed social position, a certain social equilibrium is maintained. Dominant political and economic relations are reaffirmed. But Ivan is a rebel, who is in necessary conflict with established authority. When Preacher takes Ivan in, he demands his soul for God. Preacher is a signifier for authority, he is a possessive figure, the keeper of the moral and legal order and the controller of sex. Ivan's quest for sexual and political freedom is met by Preacher's wrath. Preacher is disgusted with Ivan's lifestyle and warns the young rebel that he "should be reading the Bible and praising the Lord." Preacher finds Ivan in the church late at night rehearsing a secular song. Ivan's act is a desecration of the church. Whereas Preacher has bought what Ivan describes as pie-in-the-sky religion, characterized by orgiastic services, heart-rending sermons and rhythmic music, Ivan's religion is the expression of his freedom and the search for social justice. Although the narrative develops the differences between Preacher and Ivan in terms of a conflict of social values and religion, when preacher finds Ivan in the church singing popular music late at night, immediately he storms into Elsa's room, awakens her to interrogate her on who let Ivan into the church. Yet, the narrative shifts attention away from Ivan's entry into the church to that of sex and control of the female.

Preacher: You gave him the key to my church, why?
Elsa: I had to give it to him.
Preacher: What else did you give him?
Elsa: Nothing! ... I gave him nothing.
Preacher: You're lying.
Elsa: No.
Preacher: You've been fornicating with him.
Elsa: No.
Preacher: You gave him your lips.
Elsa: No.
Preacher: You gave him your body.
Elsa: No ... No ... (She weeps)

Whereas the narrative offers concrete items over which the men argue and fight, nonetheless, the significant tension arises in relation to the position of women and when men negotiate the lives of women. In an early scene, Longo tells Ivan that Preacher has been tending Elsa's garden for a long time and if Preacher does not pick the fruit, he will because he is entitled to possess women. Later, Ivan mutilates Longo's face. When Preacher confronts Elsa about giving Ivan entry to the church, his exchange disintegrates into charges about fornication.

The representation of women in *The Harder They Come* provides another example of the way narrative realism is an ineffective means for reformulating an alternative film language. The film actually reproduces a reactionary ideology regarding the social positioning of women in its narrative. Who are the women in *The Harder They Come*? The narrative is motivated by Ivan's grandmother's death, which functions as the catalyst for his move to the city. The hero's mother opposes his desire to emancipate himself from a life in the country for a dead-end life in the city. Ivan's encounter with his mother Daisy upon his arrival in the city is characteristic of the tension involving the representation of women in the film.

Daisy: What happen to de place?
Ivan: Grandma sold de place before she die.
Daisy: And what happen to de money?
Ivan: She say she wanted a big funeral.
(Ivan gives her the remaining money from the property)
Daisy: Tis only this leave ...? How you going get back tonight?
Ivan: I not going back.
Daisy: What you going to do then? Yuh can't stay here, yuh know ... because I can't help yuh.
Ivan: I staying in town.
Daisy: Yuh think town is easy? How yuh going to live?
Ivan: I could make a record. I can sing, yuh know mama.
Daisy: Yuh tek this thing for joke.
Ivan: Well, I can get a job then.
Daisy: What kind of job you can get outside of turn criminal.
Ivan: Why you say a thing like that? Why you say a thing like that 'bout me?
Daisy: ....Go back to country.

At best, we can say that Daisy is pragmatic and displays a maternal urge to protect her son. However, pragmatism is more concerned with adjusting to the practical problems of everyday existence as opposed to seeking out opportunities for change.

Another female image is presented in the character of the suburban middle-class housewife who lounges in a verdant social setting oblivious to the poverty that pervades the world around her. She is isolated, insulated, dependant and romanticized. She has no sympathy for the suffering of the poor. Ivan approaches as she relaxes in an easy chair. He is positioned outside the hedge and is physically separated from her.

Ivan: How do you do?
Woman: What you doing here?
Ivan: I'm looking for work, ma'am.
Woman: I don't have any work to give you.
Ivan: I can wash your car, you know ma'am.
Woman: My husband gets the car washed downtown.
Ivan: I can do the gardening, you know ma'am.

Woman: We have a gardening service to do that.
Ivan: I can do anything you know ma'am ... anything.
Woman: Look, there's nothing you can do for me ... nothing.
Ivan: Give me ten cents ma'am.
Woman: What's the matter with you young, healthy boys. All you know is beg, beg, beg. That's all you can do is beg. How did you get in here anywhere?
Ivan: The gate was open.
Woman: Well, when you go outside, you make sure you lock the gate behind you.

The spectrum of female characters is completed with Pinky—Jose's companion—who lures Ivan into a police trap by granting him sexual favors. The police close in on Ivan as the couple have sex.

A summary of the representation of women in *The Harder They Come* reveals how Ivan's grandmother's death throws his life into crisis by catapulting him into the jungle of the city. His mother cannot help him in his time of need. Ivan pleads for help from a well-to-do housewife, who turns him away and berates him for his poverty. Ivan falls in love with Preacher's ward, Elsa; she gives him the key to the church where the Preacher catches him rehearsing a "profane" song. While on the run, Jose's companion leads him into a police trap. Finally, Elsa turns Ivan over to the authorities, and he is surrounded and killed by the army. The women in *The Harder They Come* function to legitimize the very status quo the hero sets out to overcome because their signification either thrusts Ivan into crisis or is developed in opposition to his struggle for freedom. What we learn about women in this film is that they are pragmatic, unquestioning of their social dependence and God-fearing.

The difficulty with the filmic signification of women in narrative realism is in the way we conceive of film: does the film reflect life and its social relations objectively? Or does it provide a critique of society in an attempt to produce knowledge with which we can change our social reality? The filmic signification of women in narrative realism reifies their political marginalization and functions as fodder for foregrounding a male-oriented narrative and the main character's heroic struggle. Ivan's conflict with Elsa illustrates the problem:

Ivan: You want me to go and beg work for $10.00 a week for the rest of my life. I tried that. I'd rather die. I don't want to. I'm going to make it.
Elsa: Ivan, ... You're a dreamer.
Ivan: Me, a dreamer? Who's a bigger dreamer than you? ... Always talking 'bout

> milk and honey in de sky. But no milk and honey no in de sky. Not for you, not for me ... (It's) right down here, and I want mine now, tonight.

The dramatic requirements of the narrative position women in subordinate and in stereotypical terms. Toward the end of the film, Elsa reveals to the Rastafarian Pedro that, "Every game I play, I lose." This certainly is a fitting epithet to describe the position of women in society and their representation in the narrative realist film. Although this paradigm of filmic signification contains some progressive tendencies, it fails to proceed beyond stereotypes and the limitations imposed by the dominant world view. Narrative realism seems incapable of radically transforming the popular signification of women. As an expressive form, it does offer elements of resistance, but it is extremely limited in its ability to reformulate new meanings and social positions.

THE IMPLICATIONS OF NARRATIVE REALISM FOR ALTERNATIVE CINEMA

The implications of narrative realism are vast. Its filmic signification conditions a limited view of the world and of social relations, which then ironically masquerades as truth; not ideology; as fact, not fiction. Although some reformulations of realism present a progressive critique of society, it is in a vulgar realism that the 'real' is removed from its proper historical context and is used to reproduce the world view of dominant ideologies. Witness the way that movements and institutions of the socially disadvantaged are appropriated either intellectually or commercially by powerful social classes, thereby rendering mute important moments of social critique. The commercialization of reggae music and its adoption as part of Jamaica's national culture by political and economic elites rendered this art form impotent in contrast to its early creativity. As reggae music increased in international popularity and its commercial exploitation intensified, its most creative innovations, which joined social critique with corresponding formal experimentation in the music, were relegated to the background for a popular and catchy beat and digestible social criticism. Early reggae vehicles experimented with modernist forms of antinarrativity in musical expression in which two or more melodic developments could be found in one piece. In addition, the reflexive social critiques of the disk jockeys were superseded by the sexual lyrics of Jamaican dance-hall music.

Popular cinema may tend toward forms of social realism as a means of cinematic expression because it is believed that this narrative realism provides the most poignant expressive language for communicating political ideas and helping to bring about social change. The concern with realism exemplifies but one moment in a political critique of society. It dramatizes social conditions and thematizes the need for resistance, but it steers clear from the more important task of reformulating meanings. But we must ask how is it that a system of signification that emerged within the problematic of contemporary Western society to meet its ideological needs can also serve as a vehicle for those who have suffered as a result of the rise of the Western world. When filmmakers use narrative realism, it is imperative for them to question its system of filmic signification. It becomes crucial to undertake a reflexive critique of realist signification itself, for film not only reflects the conditions of social reality, but also functions to help create and alter reality through the production of its signification and its creation of alternative modes of perceiving, organizing and structuring reality.

Fundamentally, narrative realism is a descriptive cinematic form, which concerns itself with the visible and visual empirical effects of oppression as good subject matter for commercial filmic signification. In so doing, it does not speak to the causes of oppression and the conditions that reproduce it. It visualizes suffering, but offers no perspective of society's oppressed. Henzell is able to push the genre to its limits in *The Harder They Come,* but in so doing aptly dramatizes the limits of narrative realism as an expressive language for the development of an alternative cinema.

The use of film language within narrative realism is driven by the requirements of the narrative. The cinematography and editing are lucid and lyrical. There are some brilliant visual sequences, such as the romantic interlude with Ivan and Elsa on the bicycle along the waterfront, that point the way to an alternative filmic signification. But the film relies primarily on realist framing and compositions, shot-reverse shot patterns and poignant documentary vignettes of urban life. The camera follows the narrative attentively, but does not push it or seek to redefine narrative concerns.

When the system of narrative realism is pushed to its limits, it is possible to thematize the existence of a counter-cultural hero, but a new hero cannot be developed within the terms of this type of filmic signification. Ivan's exhibitionism and fatal confrontation with the law is tantamount to irresponsibility and his acts of resistance take on the intertextual glamour and romance of Hollywood film genres, instead of locating the film's violence in the historic motivation of society's sufferers to redress their deprivation. Without a doubt, the filmmaker offers no sympathies for social elites: they are seen as corrupt and oppressive. In turn, the film also offers no strong sympathies for the oppressed. But the film is most cynical in its refusal to separate the violence of the victim in response to his social condition from that perpetrated by powerful social classes maintaining their social power. Ivan's narrative fantasy desire for the Old West elicits little sympathy for his fate. But the nature of his choice is where the problem lies. The ideology of the narrative claims that given the opportunity, the oppressed will choose to aspire to the conditions and lifestyle of dominant social classes. At best, we live in a world gone mad, in which the victim, no matter how glamorous and romantic, is just as bad as the oppressor.

REFERENCES

Boal, A. (1979). *Theatre of the oppressed.* New York: Urizen Books.

Fanon, F. (1968). *The Wretched of the earth.* New York: Grove Press.

Henzell, P. (Director/producer). (1971). *The Harder They Come* (Film). Island Films.

Thelwell, M. (1992). *The Harder They Come: From Novel to film.* In Mbye Cham (Ed.). *Exiles: Essays on Caribbean Cinema.* Trenton: Africa World Press.

ARGENTINE COMMERCIAL CINEMA: INDUSTRY, SOCIETY AND AESTHETICS, 1983-1989

Alberto Ciria

This paper traces the history of the filmmaking industry in Argentina from 1983 to 1989, during the presidency of Raul Alfonsin. The author examines the industry's economic as well as artistic development emphasizing the production by the most important filmmakers of that period to bring to light the strong influence of American films and filmmaking processes on the evolution of Argentina's domestic cinematographic art and industry.

L'auteur trace le parcours de l'industrie cinématographique en Argentine pendant la présidence de Raul Alfonsin (1983-1989). En faisant le bilan à la fois du développement économique et de l'activité artistique, il insiste sur le travail des réalisateurs les plus en vue pendant cette période pour mettre en relief l'influence du cinéma américain sur l'évolution de l'industrie domestique pendant cette époque.

THE WORLD AND ARGENTINA

MANY TOPICS DEALT WITH in this article are not exclusive to Argentina and its commercial film industry. Increasingly, such topics reflect the globalization of the film business, demonstrated by worldwide acceptance of United States films and Hollywood genres, videos, series and other television programming, satellite technology, enterprises like Ted Turner's CNN (Cable News Network), together with the promotion and advertising of entertainment products, and English as the universal language of film.

Problems related to "national" filmmaking in many developing countries are also frequent in established film industries of Europe. The option of subsidizing domestic industries or allowing a free market logic to prevail in this area, usually implies a flood of United States mass consumption artifacts. By 1989 the seven major Hollywood corporations grossed 43 per cent of their total revenues for distribution/exhibition of films in overseas countries—Japan, France, West Germany, Great Britain, Spain, Italy, Australia, Sweden, Brazil—without including Canada, which remains assimilated within the United States domestic market.

Hollywood's dominance over foreign screens has brought about well-known processes of trivialization and homogenization of content and format, as is the case of action-oriented films with special effects and the manufacturing of global figures such as Sylvester Stallone or Arnold Schwarzenegger. The trend has reached Europe, including the former Eastern bloc countries.

In Latin America, the problems faced by national film industries are not always identical. In Brazil, for instance, there are crucial relations between the film industry and the powerful Globo television network. In Mexico, during the presidency of Carlos Salinas de Gortari (1988-1994), the National Institute of Cinematography (IMCINE) established a policy of co-productions with small private firms usually put together by young filmmakers. For Cuba, seen in progressive quarters as a possible alternative model to standard Latin American commercial cinema, it is important to analyze the impact of its present economic emergency in key areas such as the Cuban Institute of Cinematographic Art and Industry (ICAIC).

ECONOMY AND SOCIETY: AN INDUSTRY IN CRISIS

Since the advent of sound, Argentina has had a lengthy tradition of a commercially viable film industry: *Tango!* (Luis Moglia Barth, 1933) was an early manifestation of the "tango melodrama" genre which dominated local screens, and in turn became a profitable export for the Spanish-speaking market, well into the 1940s. Argentina Sono Film—still in business today—Lumiton and smaller producers consolidated an industrial pattern based on private entrepreneurs drawn from the distribution/advertising fields or from the radio business.

By the early 1950s the populist Peronist regime (1946-1955) and its protectionist policies introduced state subsidies mostly favoring the production of "quickies" and formula films, including a permanent influence of Hollywood paradigms. The Latin American market shrunk for Argentine films, as a partial consequence of United States support for the Mexican movie industry in its expansion through Central America and the Caribbean.

After Juan Perón's overthrow in 1955, the new Argentine cinema developed another industrial pattern: middle-class spectators replaced the more popular audiences of the immediate past, with a newly found taste for *auteur* film. The struggle for credits and subsidies from the state became a constant feature of commercial production and direct or indirect censorship would show time and again its ugly face.

The 1970s, with their dramatic switches of military and civilian governments, showed a decline in quality and quantity of feature film production. By the next decade, and Argentina's return to liberal democracy under President Raúl Alfonsín (1983-1989), there was a certain renaissance of domestic cinema. This was reinforced by the work of filmmaker Manuel Antín who became director of the National Film Institute (INC). The abolition of movie censorship through Law 23.052 and the establishment of a system of film classification according to the age of the viewers, was a decisive step in the process of cultural democratization: 727 Argentine and foreign films had been directly censored between 1968 and 1984.

Other policies of the INC were the imposition of a ten per cent tax on the price of movie tickets to help the financing of new Argentine films; some official support for first-time feature film directors; sponsorship of Argentine films in international festivals; the creation of Argentine to market less commercially viable films in foreign countries; support for professional training, film societies and research. The climate in which the INC worked included "full freedom about [films] themes and complete ideological pluralism" (Antín, 1991, p.216) which remained one of the major achievements of Antín's tenure as the INC director.

One of the aspects of Argentine reality that has made the development of a stable movie industry a difficult proposition is the small size of the domestic market of a country with 33 million inhabitants. Certain journalists have defined the situation during the Alfonsín years as merely "a collection of films" (Oliveri, 1984) rather than a distinct system of production on an industrial basis. Between 1983 and 1989, 47 movie houses were closed in the city of Buenos Aires, 34 in Greater Buenos Aires and 206 in the province of Buenos Aires, according to INC statistics. The following table shows the decline in attendance for the same period (figures between parentheses indicate the number of Argentine films released during the year):

SPECTATORS' ATTENDANCE AT ARGENTINE AND FOREIGN FILMS FROM 1983 TO 1989[1]

Year	Films	Spectators	Percentage of Spectators
1983	Argentine (19)	8,260,533	16
	Foreign	44,737,763	84
	Total	52,924,307	100
1984	Argentine (24)	12,201,058	19
	Foreign	51,156,421	81
	Total	63,357,479	100
1985	Argentine (23)	7,510,107	14
	Foreign	47,259,166	86
	Total	54,781,273	100
1986	Argentine (36)	11,867,457	22
	Foreign	43,202,480	78
	Total	55,070,237	100
1987	Argentine (33)	7,556,937	20
	Foreign	30,938,594	80
	Total	38,395,531	100
1988	Argentine (28)	4,641,398	16
	Foreign	23,739,231	84
	Total	28,380,629	100
1989	Argentine (12)	1,207,117	5
	Foreign	23,790,639	95
	Total	24,997,756	100

The industrial prospects of Argentine cinema were crushed by successive economic crises during Alfonsín's term of office (including bouts of hyperinflation), and uneven competition with foreign films on domestic screens, especially United States products. Hollywood films and their advertising, videos and a growing cable television industry were greeted with enthusiasm by Argentine upper and middle classes while regular television channels kept on providing massive entertainment to popular sectors.[2] There was also a long-standing technological dependence on Unitede States supplies. Problems brought about by the importation of raw film and key elements for its processing were compounded by frequent rises in the values of the American dollar.

By the late 1980s the average production costs of a feature film, with a crew belonging to Union of the Argentine Film Industry (SICA),[3] were $US400,000. The figure could not be earned on the domestic market with less than 500,000 tickets sold. In spite of subsidies and loans from the INC, which ended up representing increasingly smaller proportions of total budgets, the production of quality Argentine films became problematic.

In those years, and also after 1989, a trend toward co-productions made inroads in local filmmaking to complement venture capital that occasionally invested in the movie business. Examples of foreign partners were European television, particularly Spanish (TVE), Italian (RAI) and English (Channel Four), as well as Cuban (ICAIC) and private producers from the United States, Canada and Brazil.

The experiences with TVE and Channel Four, a specialized cultural outfit with private financing, have been generally positive. Here there is less pressure for script changes/final cuts as a condition of partnership, as is usually the case with U.S investors. Also, the system of pre-sale in several markets tends to favor Argentine filmmakers, because it also allows them access to domestic television audiences of TVE and Channel Four. But the results of other co-productions have not been so favourable. Filmic hybrids have emerged with a minimum common denominator of plot and acting (*road movies,* for instance), and the use of English becoming mandatory.

The screening of films brought about other problems. The ten per cent tax on tickets was frequently evaded by movie-house owners, compounding the INC's lack of resources to support filmmaking and to monitor the fiscal obligation. Also, by the end of Antín's tenure, exhibitors were violating the law by refusing to comply with screen quotas for Argentine films, which the state was not particularly willing to enforce. Thus, many producers became debtors of the INC for credits that had not been repaid, while lack of funds restricted the number and amount of new INC loans.

During the 1980s Argentine commercial cinema was well-represented at international festivals[4] and through isolated productions, in selected world markets, particularly film art circuits and other equivalents in Europe and the United States. But, significantly enough, for the Argentine mass media the two events that helped to bring world recognition to the new Argentine cinema were the Hollywood Academy's Oscar for best foreign film awarded in 1986 to Luis Puenzo's *La historia oficial (The Official Story)* (1984), and Argentina's participation in the satellite television broadcast of the 1990 Oscar ceremony.

The Oscar to Puenzo was considered by local media almost like a national victory, an overdue cultural recognition by Hollywood of the quality of Argentine films. It also helped *La historia oficial* at the box-office in Argentina and paved the way for a successful international run on screen and video. Few voices were raised against domestic triumphalism: one exception was the respected cultural critic Homero Alsina Thevenet, who stated that this kind of award does not really help to build up a viable local industry or bring back lost audiences to the movie houses on a permanent basis (Thevenet,1986, pp.56-58).

By 1990, the crisis in the Argentine cinema industry was self-evident, and the contrast between Buenos Aires elites in the Teatro Colón and a handful of strident supporters of local filmmaking, stationed in the opera house's vicinity, seemed quite symbolic. On the one hand, there were multinational forces of globalization and standardization of people's tastes, and on the other, union representatives of different sectors within the movie industry committed to the preservation of a cinema that can contribute, even if occasionally, irreplaceable elements of cultural-national identity.

All this was taking place on the night of March 26, 1990, when Buenos Aires Channel 11 received via satellite and broadcast to the whole country, television images and sounds originating in the Los Angeles Music Centre. Thus Buenos Aires was linked with Sydney, Moscow, Tokyo and London. Originating at the Salón Dorado of the Teatro Colón, the world saw and heard Norma Aleandro, *La historia oficial*'s star, and Hollywood icon Charlton Heston engage in a brief banter before announcing Oscars for best documentary and short films, unknown to a huge majority of Argentine spectators because these kinds of productions are not shown commercially by local exhibitors.[5] Meanwhile, communications technology, sponsored by multinational corporations doing business in Argentina (as it was reported during the event), changed Oscar-night for Argentine audiences into a colorful display of women's fashions. A leading playwright and scriptwriter commented, ironically: "We are somebody because Hollywood TV is watching us" (Goldenberg, 1987).

SOME AUTEURS AND TRENDS

In the period under consideration (1983-1989), Argentine commercial cinema was characterized by the fact that, with the INC's fundamental support, more than 30 directors shot their first features. Those filmmakers—coming from the thinning ranks of the industry, film schools, and television advertising—were living proof of a system unable to provide them with opportunities to continue their professional careers. Jorge Polaco, with three features released between 1985 and 1989, was one of the few exceptions to the rule. Another newcomer, Alejandro Agresti, used the co-production system to make idiosyncratic films: the process culminated with *Luba* (1990), an Argentine film shot in English and produced in Holland. Some directors were able to continue previous activities, like Héctor Olivera, Fernando Ayala, María Luisa Bemberg, Raúl de la Torre, Alejandro Doria and Alberto Fischerman.

Fernando Solanas (b. 1934) was, during the Alfonsín years, the best known director, mostly on the basis of the militant film *La hora de los hornos (Hour of the Furnaces)* (co-directed with Octavio Getino, 1966-1968), widely circulated in foreign specialized circuits. Solanas' European exile during the 1976-1983 dictatorship brought about deep aesthetic changes and adaptations of his Peronist ideology to the realities of Argentina's democratization. After 1989, he became a leading critic of neo-conservative policies implemented by President Carlos S. Menem (successor of Alfonsín). This experience consolidated Solanas' decision of filming not only for the Argentine market but also for the international circuit of independent films.

Solanas wrote and directed *El exilio de Gardel (Gardel's Exile)* (1985), an Argentine-French coproduction. His *tanguedia*—a mixture of tango, comedy and tragedy—had at least two major audiences in mind. The Argentine one, where the collective imaginary of France/Paris has deep roots in history and popular culture,[6] received the film as a multifaceted story of political exiles in Paris interspersed with their staging of a musical show with allusions and references to domestic history and mores. The international audience especially in Latin America and Europe, considered *El exilio de Gardel* a sophisticated version of the tango tradition along the lines of modern musical comedies.

In *Sur (South)* (1988), another coproduction with France with a one million dollar (US) budget (the INC contributed $US117,000), Solanas showed the face of internal exile—*los que se quedaron*—but he kept on exploring the ideology and programs of Peronism, the quasi-mythical world of tango, and the recovery of a collective past unknown to new generations. The plot centres on Floreal, who returns to his neighborhood in 1983 searching for his wife Rosi and his infant son, after having been a prisoner of the military regime for five years. The long night will mix the living and the dead—as is the case with Negro, who was killed by a para-police squad but returns from the grave to become, at times, *Sur's* narrator the past and the present, reality and fiction. Negro advises Floreal, by the end of the film, to return to his family and understand what Rosi went through during his absence. Finally the couple are reunited. (Appropriately, *Sur* is framed by vintage tangos like "Sur," "Garúa," "María," "La última curda").

Sur is one of those films that became a cultural event, a necessary reference to relevant issues of the post-1983 period in Argentina. Solanas, in an extended conversation with Horacio González published in book form as *La mirada* (1989), has explained the creative process of the film, his aesthetic and political influences, his shooting techniques, and his personal position vis-à-vis the plurality of meanings in *Sur.* In opposition to classical Hollywood models, Solanas wants "to break the linear narrative, not only to mix the times but to merge past, present and future; lived scenes, scenes that are being lived and scenes that one is afraid of or wants to live," and to "constantly break and mix genres and languages" (Solanas in González,1989, pp.31-32).

On its Argentine release, *Sur* prompted polemics in the media allowing intellectuals to discuss national issues such as the prospects of a truly national cinema, Solanas' interpretation of the 1976-1983 dictatorship, his re-evaluation of the Peronist legacy, and the role of tango in his artistic thinking. The director loves, and has a background in, music, including tango, a "nostalgic myth" which he employs as a "musical-dramatic structure" (Solanas in González, 1989, pp.193-194).

While some critics, inside and outside Argentina, questioned precisely the excessively nostalgic and sentimental mode of Solanas' *Sur* and its lack of linkages to the present, the filmmaker himself has given a two-part answer to his quest. Politically, he became a severe critic of President Menem's structural adjustment policies while accusing him of betraying the ideology of "historical Peronism." He was the victim of a shooting attack in 1991, and ran for Parliament in 1992 and 1993. Artistically, he made a new film, *El viaje [The Voyage]* (1992), mixing freely the theme of a search for the father, the recovery of Latin American roots and a political satire of a Doctor Rana, a didactic prototype of neo-conservative rulers in Latin America and the Third World.

Eliseo Subiela (b. 1944) had a background in literature and advertising. *Hombre mirando al Sudeste (Man Looking Southeast)* (1986) was his locally financed second feature—the first was made in 1980—and it showed the director's familiarity with Argentine literature: Robert Arlt, Adolfo Bioy Casares and Julio Cortázar's classic *La invención de Morel* (1940).

The film tells the story of psychiatrist Julio Denis (played by Lorenzo Quinteros) and his enigmatic patient Rantés (Hugo Soto), who contributes to the personal and professional frustration of the psychiatrist. Rantés, who has suddenly appeared in a Buenos Aires municipal hospital, possesses extrasensory faculties and spends hours standing still on the hospital's ground and "looking Southeast" ("I receive and transmit information").

Denis is shown to be a divorced father with small children, and an amateur saxophone player: he remains quite sceptical about psychiatric treatments at the hospital that do not cure patients. The doctor is obsessed with understanding Rantés, to find out if he is mad, a great con artist, or if he really comes from another planet, having been sent by unknown masters to discover the complexities of the human brain. Beatriz, a mysterious woman who may or may not be Rantés' outerspace companion, complicates the issue of the patient's origins by claiming that Rantés is a man of many trades and a reformed alcoholic. Among the memorable episodes of the film, Rantés, Beatriz and Dr. Denis go out to attend an open-air concert in which the orchestra plays Beethoven's Ninth Symphony. Rantés ends up by conducting the musicians while the audience joins in a collective dance. Through Subiela's cross-cutting, the spectator sees the hospital patients also dancing to the Ninth, which is heard on the sound-track.

Meanwhile, the hospital's director diagnoses Rantés as a "delirious paranoid," and the change in his medication provokes an organic deterioration that soon ends in Rantés' death ("Doctor, Doctor, why have you abandoned me?", Rantés asks the psychiatrist with obvious Biblical echoes). The patients react to Rantés' death with the hope that he will take them away in a spaceship. Dr. Denis, who has made love to Beatriz but rejected her when she confessed to being an alien, now waits for her return. He has kept a torn photo of Rantés and Beatriz: who are they? (Who are we?)

Hombre mirando al Sudeste is a film that can be analyzed from a variety of perspectives. In Argentina, for instance, it was interpreted as the story of an escaped *desaparecido* who fakes his true identity and finds shelter in the hospital. When the film was released in United States and Canada, its advertising called it "an *E.T.* for adults," a reference to Steven Spielberg's 1982 *E.T.: The Extraterrestrial,* in the search for a specialized audience that enjoys auteur, intimist films instead of American science-fiction productions full of special effects.

Subiela's next film, *Ultimas imágenes del naufragio (Last Images of the Wreckage),* first shown in Argentina in 1990, was produced by the director's Cinequanon corporation with additional financing from TVE, which controlled exhibition rights for Spain and Latin America excluding Argentina, Uruguay and Paraguay, but did not interfere with writer/director Subiela's creative freedom. (The original treatment of *Ultimas imágenes* was developed in Robert Redford's Sundance Institute). The film is an extended flashback of "survivor" Roberto (Lorenzo Quinteros), an insurance salesman who wants to write a great novel, and his relationships with a very strange family.

Roberto first meets Estela (Noemí Frenkel), who fakes suicide attempts to attract clients for her activities as a prostitute. He pays the woman to tell him her life history, which will be written into the book. Soon Roberto will meet Estela's mother, who presides over a fatherless decadent family which includes Estela's three brothers: Claudio, who obsessively erases words he will not use any more; Mario the artisan who is building a plane in the backyard; and José, who has chosen to be a petty criminal.

Roberto faces a crisis in his marriage, and starts a relationship with Estela. As an aspiring novelist, or substitute father, he is fascinated by José's life and prepares guidelines for future holdups, but he cannot prevent the thief's death in one such operation. Roberto helps Mario to fly in his homemade plane, and sees Claudio and his mother leave for the Interior to try to find a father and a husband. Finally, Estela is reunited with Roberto, now interested more in life than in writing. The spectator soon realizes that the film is an extended flashback by Roberto addressed to his and Estela's infant son, a not too original variation of a well-known Hollywood formula.

Subiela himself has emphasized thematic continuity between *Hombre mirando al Sudeste* and *Ultimas imágenes del naufragio*: his obsessions with madness, love and death. Argentine critics underlined the literary hommages to Arlt in the second film, and also parallels between a fatherless family and a country deprived of stable leadership, as if it were possible to talk of affective and political wreckages. The narrative, with a non-naturalistic love story and excentric characters, was perceived to be full of ambiguities, and was even considered as "a metaphor on the disintegration of the Argentine middle class" (Núnez, 1990, p. 12). Foreign critics, however, questioned in *Ultimas imágenes* what they considered trivial references to Pirandello and his notions of reality and fantasy, the obscurity of many dialogues and a lack of empathy with the male lead Roberto, who is not really explained dramatically as a real or potential writer.

The tendency started by Subiela with these two films was followed by *El lado oscuro del corazón (The Dark Side of the Heart)* (1992) and its prolongation of hommages to the director's favorite writers—this time Oliverio Girondo, Mario Benedetti and Juan Gelman—to tell the idiosyncratic love story of a poet and (again) a prostitute. This cinematic excursion of Eliseo Subiela has strong links with "magical realism" in Latin American fiction, underlining the filmmaker's attachment to a literary-fantastic cinema pioneered in Argentina by Manuel Antín.

Luis Puenzo (b. 1946) had a long career as director of television commercials, and some experience in feature filmmaking during the 1970s. His most successful film up to the present remains *La historia oficial* (1984), with a script co-authored by Puenzo and Aída Bortnik. This "story of a consciousness that awakens," applauded at film festivals and in the *film d'art* circuit, draws part of its appeal that it adhered conventions of Hollywood cinema.

The film is the story of Alicia (Norma Aleandro), a well-to-do woman who teaches Argentine history at a secondary college (Buenos Aires, early 1983, during the last stages of the military dictatorship), and her husband Roberto (Héctor Alterio), an executive with links to North American multinationals and local generals. They seem a happy couple, and have adopted a five-year old daughter, Gaby.

However, the apparently normal world soon begins to crumble, and Alicia will experience doubts about situations once believed to have been straightforward. Through a woman friend, Ana (Chunchuna Villafañe), herself a past victim of illegal arrest, torture and forced exile, she learns how many newly-born children were separated from their birth mothers and sold or given to childless couples. Then, in her classroom, Alicia is confronted by teenaged students who reject the country's official history[7] and state that its real history "is written by assassins." In the streets Alicia sees the Abuelas de Plaza de Mayo [Grandmothers of May Square] demonstrating for the return of "disappeared" grandsons and granddaughters to their natural families.

The woman starts a pilgrimage that takes her to physicians, priests and public officials to try to find the truth about Gaby's real identity; she is no longer satisfied with Roberto's explanations about the adoption, and his present reluctance to clarify these facts. In the process, Alicia meets one of the Abuelas, Sara (Chela Ruiz), who may or may not be Gaby's own grandmother. Her advice to Alicia is to keep on looking for the truth about Gaby, instead of crying.

Roberto is shown to have been cheated by his former business associates, and in a confrontation with Anna it is also suggested that he may have informed on the woman. Alicia, after having been inspired by the Abuelas' mobilization, faces her husband. Roberto threatens to take Gaby away from her and brutally attacks his wife. Alicia puts an end to the marriage, and takes refuge with Gaby in the home of her understanding in-laws.[8]

La historia oficial was co-produced by Puenzo and Progress Communication from the United States. It's success led to the hiring of Puenzo and Bortnik by Jane Fonda Productions to adapt Carlos Fuentes' novel *Gringo viejo* to the screen: Puenzo directed *Old Gringo* and Columbia Pictures distributed it.

With a budget of $US25-35 million, the film was shot in Mexico—on location and in the Churubusco studios—and star producer Fonda exercised her right to the final cut. *Old Gringo,* the 1989 film, bombed at the box-office in the United States.

Most of the explanations suggested that its "revolutionary" themes frightened potential spectators, especially those of a Conservative political persuasion, but it must not be forgotten that over 20 percent of *Old Gringo*'s dialogue was in Spanish, and it is well-known that United States mass audiences do not like to read English subtitles.

The film, technically proficient in the Mexican Revolution's war scenes, deals with the relationships of Old Gringo Ambrose Bierce (played by Gregory Peck), a great writer; Harriet Winslow (Jane Fonda), a governess hired by the powerful Miranda family from Chihuahua; and revolutionary General Tomás Arroyo (Jimmy Smits), illegitimate son of the landholder who commands a column loyal to Pancho Villa sent to occupy the hacienda. *Old Gringo* oversimplifies Fuentes' text when dealing with a United States writer (Bierce) who disappeared in the real world of the Mexican Revolution: the film concentrates on a sentimental triangle carved by Harriet and her affection for Bierce's father figure as well as her erotic passion awakened by Arroyo.

In this case, both Argentine and Canadian critics dealt harshly with *Old Gringo* on the grounds that it was essentially a "Hollywood blockbuster," but not everything is afflicted with banality in the film: the attack by villistas on the Miranda mansion ("We are all Villa!" cries General Arroyo); the former indentured peasants entering the big house for the first time; and the "revolutionary justice" decreed by Pancho Villa, are three positive examples.

Luis Puenzo's next film, *The Plague* (1992), co-produced by Argentina, Great Britain and France, was ignored by European critics in that year's Venice Film Festival. His adaptation of Albert Camus' novel *La Peste* to a Latin America under the rule of military Juntas was dramatically top-heavy in spite of its international cast: William Hurt, Sandrine Bonnaire, Robert Duvall.

Carlos Sorín (b. 1944) has a background in film studies and advertising in Argentina and Latin America, and since 1968 he has been associated with underground/experimental cinema as director of photography of several unreleased or unfinished films.[9]

La película del rey (The King's Movie) (1986), Sorín's first full-fledged directorial effort, was a prototypical auteur movie. It mixed the fascinating true story of Orélie Antoine, who around 1860 proclaimed himself "King of Araucania and Patagonia" (and lived many adventures among the natives of Southern Argentina), with the problems of location-shooting a basic plot. A distant cousin of Francois Truffaut's *La nuit américaine (Day for Night)* (1973), *La película del rey* made forceful parallels in a personal cinematic language between the French adventurer's passion for power and glory and the passion for movies by authentic filmmakers.[10]

The script by Sorín and Jorge Goldenberg, borrowing at times from the language of commercial television, provides the spectator with some data on the events surrounding the King of Patagonia, while introducing the members of a film crew prepared to shoot a feature based on that story. Economic problems plagued director David Voss (Julio Chávez) and executive producer Arturo (Ulises Dumont), to the point that the production ended up being made on a cooperative system; furthermore, non-professional actors are cast as characters of this film-within-the-film.

Crew and actors travel by train to Patagonia, and start shooting from a base on an orphanage run by nuns. In a most appealing way, Sorín presents many personal and professional issues related to this kind of low-budget production; financial difficulties with banks and official institutions; drunkenness and homosexuality in the cast; the director's breakup of a liaison with a Brazilian actress who lacks a role in the film; ingenuity in solving production dilemmas; rebellions of actors and technicians demanding to be paid, and so on.

David rejects Arturo's practical advice and carries on with his vital and filmic folly. The film-within-the-film, though, collapses due to a variety of causes, and director and producer are seen returning by train to Buenos Aires, still talking about the movies. David daydreams about a new production on a little-known figure of Latin America's 18th century. Life and movies go on and on.

La película del rey, produced by Carlos Sorín with some financial support from the INC, had a budget of some $US360,000, and was well received in international festivals. While acknowledging his initial success, Sorín was aware of the problems faced by an auteur cinema like his own, that attempts to penetrate world markets with films that do not copy formulas or glorify special effects. There are great difficulties in "placing peripheric cinema in the world's present markets, especially when one has a disadvantage: not being able to speak English" (Sorín, 1987, p.44). The filming and distribution of Sorín's second feature, *Eversmile, New Jersey,* shot also on Patagonian locations in 1988 and distributed in American and Canadian markets in 1991, would confirm that evaluation.

Originally, the script by Sorín, Goldenberg and Roberto Scheuer looked promising: within the "road movies" genre, the production told the story of an "odontological prophet" with a fundamentalist intent on defeating cavities as if they were "humankind's number one enemy" (Sorín, 1988, p.56). The original character of the dentist with a mission appealed to actor Daniel Day Lewis, and his early commitment to the project facilitated a coproduction between Los Films de Camino Production (Sorín and Osvaldo Kramer) and J & M Entertainment, with offices in London and Los Angeles, a corporation specialized in making and selling films for an international market. Unfortunately, *Eversmile, New Jersey* became a middle-of-the-road filmic hybrid, illustrating some pitfalls common to this sort of coproduction.

The film is unfocused and loosely episodic. *Eversmile, New Jersey* does not clearly state its intentions, so the spectator has difficulties empathizing with the "travelling dentist" Fergus O'Connor (Day Lewis). We meet Fergus and his motorcycle, crisscrossing Patagonia with evangelic fervor, another stage of a South American mission. His mobile consulting outfit is financed by a Foundation for the Development of Dental Consciousness, headed by an American woman philanthropist. The dentist's obsessive goal is to eliminate cavities in all Patagonians, even if that means abandoning his own wife.

Fergus is seen recruiting a young dental assistant, Estela, who helps him treat schoolchildren, shepherds, village people, even monks. To fight the Devil's cavities they will use Eversmile toothbrushes, freely distributed by Fergus. After several unconnected episodes that show Fergus' opposition to establishment dentistry, our hero finds out that the Foundation's president has discontinued funding due to a sudden change in the causes to be sponsored. Now the Foundation will concentrate on the protection of panda bears. The dentist and Estela exit by motorcycle toward a predictable horizon, with a renewed faith in modern technologies that will eliminate bacteria forever.

Another director to emerge from the 1983-1989 period is Miguel Pereira, a graduate from London's International Film School. His first feature *La deuda interna* (1988)—distributed in world markets as *Verónico Cruz*—had a combined financing from the INC, the Argentine province of Jujuy, an interprovincial cooperative Yacoraite film Limitada, a small British producer (Mainframe Film), television's Channel Four and the British Institute.

The plot is simple. By 1964, in a lost village of the Argentine Northwest high plateau, the Puna of Jujuy, a woman dies giving birth to her son Verónico Cruz (Gonzalo Morales). The father goes off to work in the sugar cane fields and leaves the baby in the care of a grandmother. Verónico grows up to become a sheep shepherd and a part-time agriculturalist, and time and again searches for his identity in old family papers.

The new school teacher (Juan José Camero) opens the doors of reading and imagination to Verónico who likes comics portraying feats of the British Royal Navy. He dreams of ships sailing on the distant Southern sea, freighters, passenger ships and rich people's yachts. The teacher and Verónco soon become friends.

The consequences of the 1976 military takeover in Argentina reach the Puna in due course.[11] A radio broadcasts the junta's communiqués from Buenos Aires; three Argentine soldiers arrive in a camouflaged pick-up, tear down portraits of President Isabel Perón, Perón himself and Evita Perón, and delegate all authority in the local police constable: politicians are out.

The boy's grandmother dies, and Verónico goes to live with the teacher. The constable is under orders to confiscate "political books" and forbid the isolated village's inhabitants to listen to "Communist radios," attitudes which indicate the dictatorship's cultural repression. In a letter to the teacher, Verónico's father remembers his life as a logger, a cane-cutter and a worker at the Zapla steel mills, where he also belonged to the union. The writer is aware of the dangerous times and the risks of becoming another *desaparceido,*" so he asks the teacher to tell his story to the boy but insists that Verónico remain in the village because it is his place of birth.

On holidays, Verónico and the teacher travel to Jujuy, the provincial capital, to look for the boy's father. The teacher is questioned at the police station, and warned about becoming involved with "subversives." Back in the village, Verónico will remember the urban landscape—even his first exposure to television—as being part of an Argentina unknown in the Puna.

By 1982, the teacher—from his new posting at Humahuaca—fails in his attempt to reach Verónico by mail. During the turbulent weeks of the Falklands/Malvinas war he follows on television the rambling speeches of dictator General Leopoldo Galtieri, the triumphalism of journalists and the torpedoing of the cruiser General Belgrano with hundreds of Argentine casualties. After the end of the war, the teacher goes back to Verónico's village. A neighbor shows him a letter from Verónico with an autographed photo of himself and several other conscript seamen ("The lads from the *Belgrano*").

Winter is ending at the Puna, and Juanita—seen previously as a schoolmate and friend of Verónico—is pregnant with his posthumous child: the life and death cycle is on again.

To Argentine audiences and critics, this film represented a very different perspective from the emphasis on the city of Buenos Aires manifested in a majority of old and new domestic productions. Within the limits of its linear metaphors taken from the Interior of Argentina, the audience saw what takes place in faraway centres of power where rural existence can be burdensome. Miguel Pereira's personal cinema combines a regional perspective with artisan filmmaking. It points to feasible, small-scale solutions for Third World countries to questions posed by the already mentioned process of globalization and homogenization in the film business.

During 1983-1989, in the middle of a serious economic-financial crisis, the Argentine movie industry managed to produce a variety of films which synthesized major trends and issues. The five filmmakers briefly analyzed here represent the positive aspects of ideological and aesthetic pluralism that characterized those years.

Fernando Solanas dealt with the multifaceted Peronist movement, the tango tradition, interpretations of the past, external and internal exiles. Foreign audiences usually appreciated the elements of tanguedia and musical numbers in both *El exilio de Gardel* and *Sur,* while domestic critics and intellectuals engaged in politico-cultural polemics about Solanas' artistic and ideological goals.

Eliseo Subiela prolonged another Argentine tradition of a literary cinema, used the family as a microcosm of the country, and in general favored a metaphorical approach to reality, which can be also illustrated with the works of other promising Argentine directors.[12]

Luis Puenzo is a representative of Hollywood influences on narrative conventions, and therefore a polar opposite of Solanis. The "seal of approval" of a Hollywood Oscar legitimized for an international public a well-made political melodrama (La historia oficial). Puenzo, later became a contract director in the United States and participated in international production deals (*Old Gringo, The Plague*), by no means an isolated example in the global business of the movies.

Carlos Sorín's two films exemplify a crucial dimension of that globalization. *La película del rey* was a refreshing auteur movie, a low-budget production with a high content of creativity, while *Eversmile, New Jersey,* in similar locations, remained merely a formulaic, run of the mill artistic hybrid.

The economic-financial crisis already mentioned has increased since 1989 and it affects the remnants of what decades ago was a thriving movie industry. Only a few films are released every year (13 in 1993, for instance), coproductions with important guest foreign actors (Marcello Mastroianni, Vanessa Redgrave) are periodically launched, the state's protection of independent filmmaking has decreased under the neoconservative economic policies (another case of "structural adjustment") of President Carlos S. Menem, and Argentine spectators tend to favor American blockbusters rather than domestic films.[13]

Apparently, then, the Argentine situation, remains an appropriate case to further explore the issues surrounding nationalism and internationalism in global filmmaking and global distribution.

ENDNOTES

1. *Humor.* Buenos Aires, 277, October 1990.
2. *Los Top Ten Videos* in video rentals for the city of Buenos Aires, in September 1988, were nine United States films with the exception of the Australian-made *Crocodile Dundee* (Clarín, Buenos Aires, September 9, 1988).
3. The union was a holdover from the era of several operating studios and a labour-intensive film technology: it was not readily amenable to structural changes in the production of commercially viable movies.
4. Argentine films won over 200 awards in a variety of film festivals between 1983 and 1989, as documented by Antín, "Hoy estreno: 'país sin cine'," pp.2119-2122.
5. The author watched the television broadcast of the Oscars in Buenos Aires, March 26, 1990; see also *La Nación,* Buenos Aires, March 27, 1990.
6. Jose de San Martín, Argentina's national hero, died in France in 1850; tango lyrics are full of references to Paris, and so are many films form the 1930s and 1940s; the tango's major star, Carlos Gardel (1890-1935), was almost certainly born in France; cultural and intellectual relations between Argentina and France have usually been very close, etc.
7. In Spanish, *historia* has two different meanings: "history" and "story": the Argentine title alludes to the first, easily understood in the domestic context; the English title refers to the second meaning (*La historia oficial* and *The Official Story,* respectively).
8. Particularly for Argentine audiences, the generational conflict (and opposing morals) between Roberto and his father, an old Spanish Republican immigrant, complement the film's thriller structure. See Foster, *Contemporary Argentine Cinema,* 52.
9. The most important one was *La Nueva Francia [The New France]* (1972) by Juan Fresán and Jorge Goldenberg, which inspired in due course Carlos Sorín's *La película del rey.*
10. A brief historical background for this film in María Rosa Lojo, Antoine I, rey de Araucania y Patagonia, *Clarín,* July 25, 1991.
11. Miguel Pereira skilfully uses the blood motif (a puma attacking the sheep, the slaughtering of cattle) as a premonition of the military's brutality.
12. Such as the first feature film by Tristán Bauer, *Después de la tormenta [After the Storm],* shot in 1989 but released in Argentina during 1991. It mixes poetic and documentary approaches to deal with key issues like deindustrialization and unemployment, tertiarization of former workers into low-paying menial jobs, family and generational crises, etc., without preaching economic or moral reductionisms.

13. A solitary exception was *Tango Feroz [Ferocious Tango]* (1993), Marcelo Piñeyro's first feature, that attracted over a million spectators in two months, and was the object of an extensive and intensive marketing campaign among teenagers and young adults.

REFERENCES

Antín, M. (1991, November/December). Hoy estreno: 'país sin cine', *Propuesta y control* XV. 19, 2116.

Avellaneda, A. (1986). *Censura, autoritarismo y cultura: Argentina 1960-1983.* 2 vols. Buenos Aires.

Barnard, T. (Ed). (1986). *Argentine cinema,* Toronto: Nightwood Editions.

Beceyro, R. (1989, December). El repliegue. El cine argentino en 1989. *Punto de vista,* 36, pp.33-36.

———. (1994, August 26). Cine argentino inédito. *Clarín.*

Ciria, A. (1990). Roberto Cossa: el teatro histórico, la historia teatral, *Canadian Journal of Latin American and Caribbean Studies,* 15(29), pp.129-148.

Couselo, J.M., et al. (1984). *Historia del cine argentino.* Buenos Aires.

Eisner, K. (1991, September 27/October 4). Movie review, *The Georgia Straight.* 21.

Fabrikant, G. (1990, June 25,). Hollywood takes more cues from overseas, *New York Times,* A1,C12.

Feinmann, J.P. (1993, July 17). Tener o no tener cine, *Página/12.*

Foster, D.W. (1992). *Contemporary Argentine cinema.* Columbia.

Fusco, C. (1987-88). The Tango of aesthetics and politics. *Cineaste,* XVI, pp.1,2,5.

Getino, O. (1988). *Cine latinoamericano, economía y nuevas tecnologías.* Buenos Aires.

Godfrey, S. (1992, March 28). Behind the big screen. *The Globe and Mail,* A1,A6.

González, H. (1989). *La mirada: Reflexiones sobre cine y cultura.* Buenos Aires.

Johnson, B.D. (1989, October 16). The Great divide. *Macleans,* 61.

King, J. (1990). *Magical reels: A history of cinema in Latin America.* London.

King, John and N. Torrents (Eds). (1988). *The garden of forking paths: Argentine cinema.* London: British Film Institute.

Loja, M.R. (1991, July 25). Antoine I, rey de Araucania y Patagonia. *Clarin.*

Marimón, A. (June 1988). "Sur, una película feliz." *La ciudad futura,* 11, p.23.

Meson, D.L. (1986). The Official story. *Cineaste,* XIV, pp.4,31.

Moncalvillo, M. (April, 1987). "Carlos Sorín, el realizador de *La película del rey. Humor,* 194, p.44.

National Film Institute (1989, November 1989). Reflexiones, *Sobre cine argentino,* p.1.

Núnez, M. (1990, April 6). Sueños de sobreviviente. *Página/12.*

Olivieri, R.G. (1984, November 18). Ilusiones que matan al cine. *Tiempo Argentino.*
Schnittman, J.A. (1984). *Film industries in Latin America: Dependency and development.* Norwood, NJ.
Thevenet, H.A. (1986, July). Del Oscar a la eternidad. *El Porteño,* V, pp.5, 56-58.
Torrents, N. (1993). The cinema that never was. In C.M. Lewis and N. Torrents (Eds.). *Argentina in the Crisis Years (1983-1990): From Alfonsin to Menem.* London.

INTERVIEWS

Goldenberg, J. (April 7, 1987), Buenos Aires.

CHAPTER VI

RETHINKING IDENTITIES

IDENTITY AND DIFFERENCES IN THE CARIBBEAN DIASPORA: CASE STUDY FROM METROPOLITAN TORONTO[1]

Daniel Yon

The first part of the paper points to the conceptual difficulties inherent in the study of identity. The second part draws on a specific ethnographic study of identity negotiation among Caribbean-Canadian youth in Metropolitan Toronto to illustrate that the tension between essentialist and contextual meanings of identity are not as oppositional as they may be theorized. There is no crisis of identity brought about by modernization and migration, as linear models might have us believe. The study reveals the relational nature of identity seen as a dialectical process of mapping new experiences and aspirations onto older identities and experiences. In the context of Toronto, this "global city" where the mix of peoples leads to an "ethnic flux" rather that a "melting pot," ethnicity assumes a variety of forms and subjective meanings over time.

Les difficultées conceptuelles qui soustendent la notion d'identité sont soulevées dans la première partie de cette étude. Il s'agit, ensuite, d'examiner les résultats d'une recherche ethnographique sur la négotiation identitaire. A partir des entrevues avec des jeunes Canadiens/caraïbéens domiciliés à Toronto, l'auteur veut montrer que la tension entre les définitions essentialistes et les tenants d'une théorie basée sur l'importance du contexte culturel, n'est pas nécessairement conflictuelle. Dans le cadre de Toronto, cette «ville mondiale» où un mélange de peuples aboutit à un flux ethnique plutôt qu'un creuset, les notions d'identité et d'ethnicité reflètent une variété de formes et de significations subjectives.

THE ISSUE OF IDENTITY, and the questions it evokes, occupies a central place in social, political and cultural theory in the closing decade of the 20th century. In positing this development, in the words of Stuart Hall (1989) as "the question of identity," I draw attention to the contestation and struggles over what it means to talk about identity and to the identifications that are invoked in the process of talking and writing. The theoretical and other developments leading to the present centering of identity in theory and politics are multiple. They include intense debates around issues of nationalism, ethnicity, race, class, sexuality. This paper acknowledges the significance of these debates and their importance as sites within and around which identity is negotiated. However, attention is drawn to the challenge posed by the fluid and often contradictory ways by which these and many other sites of identification are engaged. In so doing, the dialogical and sometimes antagonistic processes that constitute identity negotiation are highlighted.

In emphasizing continual processes of identification I stress that identities are never ahistorical. Instead they are contextual, contingent and negotiated both within and in relation to a variety of discourses as well as in disparate material conditions and unequal relations of power. I use power not simply to reference Marxian notions of relationship to the means of production or as that which is invested evenly within categories of race or gender, but as Foucault suggests, as a "multiplicity of force relations immanent in the sphere in which they operate.... Power is everywhere; not because it embraces everything but because it comes from everywhere.... It is the name that one attributes to a complex strategical situation in a particular society" (1990, pp.92-30). For example, my friend's recent pronouncement, "I did not have an ethnicity until I came to Canada," speaks cogently to the power relations and a discourse of multiculturalism within which "ethnicity" is produced. It also speaks to the unequal relations subsumed in notions of "dominant culture" against which "minority cultures" are produced and sustained in this discourse.

Kobena Mercer (1990) reminds us that identity only becomes an issue when it is in crisis. The "crisis," to which Mercer refers, partly addresses the various disjunctions experienced and articulated in late modernity between "individual identities" and what is imagined by the concept "cultural identity." Thus, while under pre-modernity, assumptions are made about the anchoring of individual identities in the traditions and structures of community, modernity witnessed a fracturing of the notions of continuity, coherence and stability that were assumed in these relationships. Continuity, coherence and stability are displaced by notions of disruption, contradition, ambivalence. Fluidity and change now stand in where fixity in the relationship between individual and imagined cultural identities—collective identifications—were assumed.

In alluding to the various developments that help us to read these conditions, I draw attention to two of several factors that have led to the disruptions in the ways that identity is practised and theorized. These factors are, first, the assertion of "difference" within communities, and, second, the various developments that are subsumed in the concept "globalization." What these features of late modernity mean for identity and culture is discussed in the first part of this paper. Also addressed is the link between concerns with identity and anthropology's continuing debate around the meaning of culture. The latter part of the paper draws on my larger ethnographic project on identity negotiation among Caribbean and Caribbean-Canadian youth in Metropolitan Toronto to show how notions of fluidity, ambivalence as well as questions of globalization and difference are played out.

DIFFERENCE AND GLOBALIZATION

The "difference" that I am referring to in this paper is not simply that which is imagined when one talks about say, "the Carribbean community" or specific collectives within what Anderson (1983) describes as "imagined communities." Such difference, often spoken of synonomously as "different cultures" is imagined as pre-given ethnic traits, heritage, customs, experiences. This difference is about how people live and how the representations of those lifestyles differ from others. It is this kind of difference which underlies beliefs in cultural pluralism embodied in the "Canadian Ethnic Mosaic" and relies on what Toni Morrison (1993) calls an "economy of stereotypes" to make it intelligible. The intelligibility of the knowledge that is produced and circulated about these "different cultures" is largely dependent on imagined pre-given "dominant cultures" against which "minority cultures" can be read.

The difference that I draw attention to in this paper extends the normative notions of culture—embodied in beliefs and practices—by drawing attention to how the representations through which these "cultures" are imagined, negotiated and mapped often in in very ambivalent ways. This use of difference unsettles tendencies to fix identities on the overarching categories of race, ethnicity, class, gender, sexuality, which have all been foregrounded as celebrated sites of identification in recent times. Extending the older primary categories of race and class has opened up opportunities for acknowledging multiple subject positions, but in so doing frequently asserts new kinds of certainity about what these categories mean. The difference that is taken up in this paper therefore borrows from Rutherford and disrupts some of the certainty assumed in categories such as "cultural identity," "racial identity," "sexual identity." Instead, difference is taken up as "a motif for that uprooting of certainty ... an experience of change, transformation and hybridity ... a critique of essentialism and mono-culturalism, asserting the unfixed and 'overdetermined' character of identities" (1990, p.10). As will be demonstrated below, this assertion of difference is about working both within and against the categories (black; Caribbean; black-Canadian) through which identity is negotiated. This difference urges us to look not simply at the properties that distinguish the group, spoken of as "different cultures," but also at how the cultural properties are produced and negotiated. It also speaks to the ways by which the difference that is articulated as ethnic property are also displaced by the subjects who are imagined and "Othered" by those categories.

The second concept, globalization, has come into increasing use in the closing decade of this century. It references the transnational flow of goods, labour, and information in a multimedia world; culture and communities becoming de-territorized; the growth of transnational identities; the dominating influence of multinational corporations. These developments have had a significant impact on how space and time is imagined and theorized, as discussed below. Globalization has provoked a growing body of anthropological works concerned with how these developments are played out in local contexts (Appadurai, 1992; Hannerz, 1992; Basch, Shiller and Szanton-Blanc, 1994). A significant theme that emerges in these and the present work is the sense in which the local is also global. Communities previously imagined as bounded entities are now best conceptualized as deterritorized and cultural fixity conceptualized through hybridity and diaspora. These concepts address changes to the ways that social relations are organized and the ways by which culture is continually being reproduced. Globalization and these attendant concepts thus form the backdrop against which the ethnography addressed in this paper was undertaken.

Among the multiple and varied changes that have been ushered in by globalization is the increasing influence of market forces and the mass media in negotiating and commodifying social identity. Subsequently, the "practice" of identity as Friedman (1990, p.327) puts it, has come to encompass practices of consumption and production. One of the effects of the proliferation of media images and the imagined possibilities they evoke is that personal narratives setting out to fix identities have also been troubled. In the same context, Kellner speaks of a "post-modern identity" being produced as maps are redrawn in peoples' heads and as a multiplicity of identities "mingle and overlap with great fluidity" thereby making "increasingly anachronistic" claims to fixed subjects (1992, p.169). Extending sites of identification and imagined possibilities further complicate assumptions about coherent relationships between individual and cultural identity. They make for a more complicated process of identity negotiation as multiple identification compete, compliment and even collide and contradict, as is shown below.

CULTURE AND IDENTITY

Identity is itself a cultural construct. It is used to impute meaning on human diversity. In the process of imputing meaning, categories such as race and ordering (in the case of race thereby producing racism) are produced. As a specific cultural construct, conceptual difficulties are encountered when identity is applied arbitrarily and cross-culturally without specifying what is being addressed. Furthermore cross-cultural studies of "self" and "personhood" suggest important difference in how persons and self are conceived in different societies around the world (Kirkpatrick and White, 1985; Lutz and White, 1986). These factors contribute to ways by which identity is contested. Contestation is also tied up with the problems of reification in social science; that is how we turn the fluidity and complexity of social phenomena into an object of study. Talking and writing about identity is thus intimately connected to the problems of writing culture and the "crisis of representation" that this entails (Marcus and Fisher, 1986).

Much of the tension that is produced in talking and writing about identity comes from what I will crudely describe as two inter-related uses and meanings of the concept. On the one hand there is a meaning that recognizes the highly contextual, relational, contingent and dynamic nature of identity. This understanding of identity as process is illustrated by the material drawn on below. On the other hand this position is often set in tension by a more essentialist understanding, that is, beliefs in an identity that is fixed and rooted in the various imagined "natural" categories, such as the often cited race, gender, class, "community." Cultural identities, within the latter framework, are seen as fixed and embodied in groups which are produced by history. Debates about culture and identity thus become debates about marginalization and cultural appropriation. Essentialist notions follow the logic of identity building as a linear process through which the "disjunctions" causing "identity crisis" may be resolved. This logic also seeks to resolve or domesticate antogonistic positions that may emerge even among those who share histories of discrimination and displacement. Perceptions of identity as a dynamic process, on the other hand, recognize processes of identification whereby self is continually being identified in relation to Others. Cruder notions of reductionism—identity reduced to multiple categories of race, ethnicity, gender, etc.—become more problematic. Identity is seen as emerging through the mapping of discourses. Furthermore, viewed as a process of positioning in relation to different cultural representation, as well as racist practices, studies of identity negotiation also entail a "politics" of identity (Yon, 1991).

The tension between essentialist and contextual meanings of identity manifests itself in the research this paper addresses. I argue, however, that these two categories of meaning are not as oppositional as is often argued. Furthermore, the challenge of reconciling the tension is particularly pronounced among those who speak from those whose histories and experiences have been marginalized and erased through the exploitative experiences of colonialism and racism. These conditions have created a climate in which a discourse about "reclaiming" history and a search for "authentic" identities take place. The African proverb, to the effect that stories about deeds of bravery will always be told about the hunters until the lions have their own story-tellers, speaks to the importance of this process. Gayatri Spivak (1990) coins the phrase "strategic essentialism" to acknowledge the necessity for closures around such categories as ethnicity in order to redress past injustices and present unequal power relations.

Ethnic and other forms of "cultural" identities are premised on beliefs in a shared history. What a contextual and historical notion of identity does is to make the case for thinking about how interpretation and representations of the past are made and produced. In doing so, essentialist claims to a "true" or "authentic" identity are problematized. Furthermore by thinking about cultural identity as an issue of representation, authenticity itself is troubled. As Chambers (1990, p.6) notes, representation involves repression: "Some things are shown, others hidden; some things said, others unsaid. For in every representation the object represented is initially cancelled and then replaced, represented, in another context and language." Similarly Williams guards against what she describes as "identity formation plans" frequently implied in ethnicity. These plans, she warns, are often "intent on creating a putative homogeneity out of heterogeneity through the appropriative process of transformist hegemony" (1989, p.439).

Debates and concerns about questions of identity in late modernity also parallel debates in anthropology about the meaning of culture. Populist perceptions of culture as confined to reified traditions, beliefs, practices and achievements are challenged and rendered inadequate. Culture goes beyond the reified and static traditions to include the everyday processes, practices and experiences in which people are engaged. At the same time, mass media influences play an important role in blurring traditional distinctions that are made between "popular" and "high" culture with one now intercepting and overlapping the other. Culture, like identity itself, is no longer conceptualized as a static entity but as continually being made and re-made. Rattansi (1992, p.4) reminds us that culture cannot be understood simply as that which expresses the identity of a community but rather the *processes,* categories and knowledge through which communities become defined (my emphasis).

The stress on context and process in thinking about identity challenges the established logic which speaks of an "identity crisis" coming about as traditional ways of living in the world disintegrate under the impact of modernity and modernization. Such a logic is inadequate for grappling with multiple, fragmented and sometimes contradictory identities whereby negotiating disjuntions are an integral part of the process of becoming. Similarly, explanations caged in the language of binary opposites are also made much less certain. Feathersone (1990) reminds us that binary opposites such as homogeneity and heterogeneity, integration and disintegration, unity and diversity can no longer address the complexity of the new social relations we are witnessing. Furthermore, the assertion of "difference" along gender, sexual, ethnic or other lines does not imply social disintegration in the same way that the identities forged around "pop" and mass-mediated forms of culture such as "Hip Hop" or "Roots" do not imply the abandonment of ethnicity or other sites of identification. As is illustrated below, one can be "West Indian" in a variety of different ways and with a variety of other identities simultaneously. The "differences" that are asserted are not necessarily in opposition *to,* but rather *within* "cultural" identity.

The global developments associated with late modernity also open new challenges for re-conceptualizing old notions of space and place. Rodman (1992) makes the case for viewing "place" as politicized and cultural constructs rather than as locales in which identities are contained. This holds true for Caribbean people in ways that different narrative of places in the Caribbean get constructed as sites of social and political identification in the diaspora. The name Jamaica, for example, can evoke both nostalgic and political sentiments simultaneously. Furthermore, old ideas about the spacial ordering in the Caribbean are undermined as people in the diaspora become physically close in highrise apartment blocks. Social networks are formed within these spaces. However, individuals might also be socially distant because the transnational social networks transcend earlier traditions of social networks being bounded within limited spaces. Giddens (1990) reminds us that the structures around which place has been traditionally constituted are no longer organized in a specific locale. The local and the global have effectively become inextricably intertwined compressing significantly how time-space is imagined. Social relations have become "disembedded ... lifted out from local contexts of interaction ... (and) restructured across indefinite spans of time-space." (1990, p.2) Appadurai uses the prefix "scapes," as in "ethnoscapes," to reminds us that the relationships and conditions which our cultural studies address, like landscapes themselves, never look the same from every angle. Instead, different actors bring different meanings to the contexts in which they act, and they inflict specific histories on the different landscapes or "ethnoscapes" which they produce (1991).

Hannerz (1992) distinguishes between two distinct "camps" which have emerged in debates about cultural consumption, globalization and the different sorts of global flows associated with it. On the one hand, the "radical diffusionist," following Wallerstein's World Systems Theory, emphasizes the hegemonic effects of the unequal flow of culture from the centre to the periphery in processes of homogenizing differences. The second view, supported in this paper, extends this argument laying emphasis on how cultural interaction generates new identities and new forms of "creolized" culture. This view of the social effects of globalization does not deny the factor of power and the differential power relations that are implied in Systems Theories (Wallerstein, 1978). However, it emphasizes the creativity and role of human agency in the production of new cultural forms within those uneven relations of power. Thus Hall notes how identities are transformed in the course of an unfolding of new dialectics in two forms of global culture, namely, "increasingly defensive corporate forms of nationalism that accompanies the building of national cultural identity which erects barriers around itself," which, he argues, "struggles with a second form of global culture the global post-modern which is trying to live with and at the same time, overcome, sublate, get hold of and incorporate difference" (1991, p.33). The consequence of the interplay of these two expressions of culture is that globalization does not simply eradicate differences. But differences are negotiated, commodified and marketed in late modernity.

Globalization has produced significant changes in the relationships between anthropologist and those they seek to study. Fabian notes the effects of electronic information in breaking down old relations between anthropology and its object: "between the West and it's Other" which have traditionally been conceptualized not simply as difference, but also "distance in space and time." (1983, p.147). Globalization has made redundant the privileging of stable and bounded communities. It is not simply the locality, economy or national state which frames identity. Instead, these overlap and intercept with the global context, media, popular culture, and, as Lash and Friedman (1992, p.25) remind us, with "the ethnographer him/herself, the subjects own self-reflexivity" in efforts to define identity.

What then are some of the immediate implications that stem from the foregoing discusion for a study of identity and difference within the Caribbean diaspora? First, it continues to allow for the commonly recognized normative difference in the sense of linguistic, political, and cultural practices that exist among the different communities both in the Caribbean and in the diaspora, but draws attention to the processes by which these differences are produced. At the same time it acknowledges the commonalities produced by shared experiences of colonialism, migration and racism. However, it also troubles the authority that may be produced in attempts to prescribe what is implied in a "Caribbean" or "West Indian" identity. It draws attention to how commonalities and differences are re-presented and re-told in different places in processes of talking and writing. It acknowledges a dialogic relationship between a number of axes operating simultaneously. For example, as Hall (1990, pp.234-235) puts it, between "difference and rapture," between the "presence and absence" of Africa and the "refusal and recognition" of the European presence. The discussion also draws attention to the ways by which patterns of identity shift as new sites of identification are explored and old identities are continually re-produced and transformed in the diaspora.

ETHNOGRAPHY: NEGOTIATING CARIBBEAN IDENTITIES IN THE DIASPORA

The histories of Caribbean immigration to Britain and Canada are connected in a number of ways. First the increasing scale of immigration from the Caribbean to Canada in the late 1960s coincided with the closing of the doors in Britain when a series of restrictive immigrations acts were introduced as postwar labour demands receded and as the definition of what it means to be British changed. In the same period, the discriminatory legislation which disadvantaged Caribbean people was repealed in Canada and the result was a significant increase in the hitherto highly restricted rate of immigration from the Caribbean. A second way in which these two countries' histories are connected lies in the significant numbers of Caribbean immigrants or children of immigrants who, dissatisfied with conditions in Britain,[2] undertook a second migration in search of better opportunities in Canada. Third, research points to evidence of "racialization" of Caribbean people occuring in the fields of immigration and employment, as is the case in Britain. A detailed discussion of this history is beyond the scope of this paper. Suffice to point out that the history of migration also put in place a tradition of family separation and reunions, of stresses and strains, struggles and celebrations which together constitute a shared history that shapes specific social relations and common identifications.

The same history also means that family structures have become transnational. For example, in a focus group discussion with eight Caribbean youths, four spoke of living with their respective mothers in Toronto, while their fathers reside in Miami, New York, Chicago and Kingston, respectively. Family networks and relationships form triangular patterns linking Canada, the United States and the Caribbean. There are also ties with England, a country which continues to evoke a certain awe and fascination. Thus we see in the global city of Toronto, as in New York City (Sutton, 1987), transnational Caribbean socio-cultural systems challenging established notions of incorporation into culturally plural societies. The advances in communications and other dimensions of globalization enable Caribbean diasporic identities to be constantly renewed and reconstituted under localized and distant influences simultaneously.

ON IDENTITY AND PLACE

A brief description of a research site follows to illustrate the significance of place in constituting identity. "Site" is not used to refer to a bounded place in which the ethnography is contained; instead, it is used to describe a symbolic place that becomes a specific site for the play of difference and identification.

The place is a tiny strip of Metropolitan Toronto known as "Little Jamaica," but in circles where the implications of Jamaican hegemony are resisted, it is known quite simply as "the Strip." This is one of many areas in the city known for its "ethnic distinctiveness." Stores display tropical fruit and vegetable; barrels used for shipping goods to the islands line sections of the pavement; community newspapers offer special flight deals to the Caribbean; a notice in a popular shop-come restaurant announces "same day remittance." The area represents the classic "locally situated expression of distanciated relations" (Giddens, 1990, p.9). Much of the music that hails from the record shops is produced in Kingston and other places in the Caribbean as well as England and the United States. At the same time the "Roots" and "Hip Hop" fashions symbolize a culture which is becoming more and more international commodifying Malcolm X and other symbols of resistance in the process. The area's distinctiveness within this "global city" confirms Hall's (1991, p.62) claim that global processes do not simply roll over everything to create homogeneity or similarity, but negotiate particular spaces and mobilize identities in dialectical processes instead.

A Black Canadian, born of Jamaican and Guyanese parents in Toronto, tells me that "this is the place I go to feel at home." For him feeling at home entails, "checking out the 'roots fashions', eating 'down home cooking' and seeing the black youth 'hang out'." However, the sense of identity and belonging which is evoked by this symbolic and localized sense of community is at the same time ambivalent. "I couldn't live there," he tells me, "I can't really relate to how you're suppose to behave, the macho stuff and all that." Similarly, a second respondent, born in Canada of Trinidadian parents, describes how he used to go to the same area for "that sense of rootedness" but laments that he is not "really" at home there: "They tell you you're not black and all that because of the way you walk, so you 'become black' and move on." Thus, while identity and community is affirmed in this specific locale and the global connections it subsumes, affirmation is not simply a process of investing oneself with the symbolism it implies. It is also about self-reflection on the Other that is made of oneself within this space; it is about negotiating difference, multiple identities and lifestyles *within* that community. The difference being negotiated is affirming and antagonistic simultaneously. Affirmation is in fact partially produced through antagonism. Identity is hereby being forged by taking on what it means to be black while displacing this meaning at the same time.

The sense of difference within identity which is played out here in the mapping of discourses should not be conceptualized as binary opposites as in notions of "the community" versus "the individual." Instead, it is difference and identifications that retain the roots of the former self in the process of moving towards encapsulating another. The respondents in this study confirm the sense of contradiction, ambivalence and conflicting desires which collide as overlapping identity discourses, situated in different times and places, compete and compliment one another. A senior high school student who emigrated from one of the smaller islands of the Caribbean at the age of nine to join her father in Canada makes claims to "keeping her heritage" while going on to point out:

> (B)ut I am not (West Indian) because I am not there any more and I doubt if I would go back there to live. I am Vincentian first and foremost and then I am living in this society. I am adapting whatever Canadian society is. You become so accustomed to another way of life and I find it too difficult to change again.

She also talked about the different social relations (and social isolation) which stem in part from a sexual orientation which is not perceived as mainstream. What transpires is not a sense of being caught between two worlds but situated among many discourses and the feeling of ambivalence that this evokes is a common theme in the narratives that respondents articulate. Thus expressions of pride about group identity, symbolized by speaking Patois and other Creolized languages, must also be balanced with a similar pride which is expressed about speaking "Canadian." This is not a "crisis" of identity brought about by modernization and migration as linear models might have us believe. It speaks to the nature of late modernity and the contingent and relational nature of identity this implies. It is also an integral part of the dialogical process of mapping new experiences and aspirations onto older identitications and experiences.

ON IDENTITY POLITICS

Identification and processes of identity construction do not take place in a vacuum, but are, instead, implicated in discourse and therefore, as argued about, within multiple structures of power. Thus we see Caribbean black subjectivities and identities being forged as a reaction to marginality, exclusion, racism and Eurocentricism and to differential incorporation into the Canadian "multi-cultural ethnic mosaic." As new identities are forged following immigration, traditional class barriers which are pervasive in the Caribbean become blurred, at one level, but they do not disappear at personal levels. The question, "Which school did you go to back home?" is commonly posed to "situate" fellow islanders in more ways than one. On the other hand, class is completely displaced by race when this section of the community becomes criminalized by racist practices of law enforcement officers.

Discussions with young people who came to Canada in the 1980s as sponsored dependents also dramatize a growing black consciousness following the transition from a milieu in which blackness is dominant to a more heterogeneous multicultural society in which "whiteness" dominates. Thus a male Jamaican-born respondent spoke of not really having an identity before leaving Jamaica at the age of 14. He was referring to not being conscious of blackness and "getting into roots," as he put it, until he became Other in Canada. A female elaborated upon similar changes she was conscious of:

> When I was in Jamaica you didn't really care who you are. I now know more about who I am and my culture and stuff and I appreciate myself more for being black....When I was there I felt black as being negative. Now I am positive and thankful for being black.

As conversations dig deeper, however, it become obvious that despite formal claims to positive consciousness, the dialogue with blackness is complex and imbued with ambivalence and denial. Franz Fanon's *Black Skin, White Masks* offers useful insights into the pathological nature of this denial and the ways by which blackness which is constructed as evil Other is internalized to become the object of oneself. The preoccupation with "shade-ism" as one respondent puts it, is also derived in part from what Gordon Lewis (1987) calls the tradition of "pigmentocracy" which has been a marked feature of Caribbean history and which remains a salient factor today. Thus the student who speaks about being "positive and thankful for being black," in a later part of the conversation and after a long pause and giggle also pointed out that the thing she "really admires in life" is seeing black and white together. Gender factors enter into this: "If I walk down the street and see a White guy with a Black guy I admire it. Sometimes I don't always like it when I see a Black guy with a White girl." Similarly, a student who embraces black consciousness and who lectures many of his fellow students against "altering their Africanness" by straightening their hair and using make-up, nevertheless also smugly talks about the "neat" way he was able to settle into Canada because of his "light" complexion. A third student who was born in Grenada, on the other hand, was less subtle about his feelings when he confided in me about how he glances in the mirror and wishes he was a little lighter.

Conversations thus confirm that forging collective black consciousness, common identifications and negotiating identity around "race" entails "positioning" not only in relation to dominant whiteness but also in relation to the various definitions of blackness. There is internal resistance to the sanctions that are implied in name-calling such as "White Wash," "Oreo Cookie" (black on the outside and white on the inside) in the same way that there is resistance to the stereotyping and tendencies to treat this section of the community as a homogeneous block by the community at large. A Saint Lucian born student who lived her first five years in the city of Edmonton notes:

> In Toronto I automatically have to be black. Like I find myself trying to talk like them and not trying to sound too correct. I don't know what being black is yet. I think it is being what you think you are and I know that I am black so that is being black.

Caribbean diasporic identities in Toronto have become increasingly politicized around issues related to black representations (and the lack of them) in the media, in school curricula. We also witness the emergence of "black activism" which is prompted by experiences of racism and marginalization. Identities that are formed around this activism, and those that are formed in reaction to them, contest older identities that are formed around island associations. These new identities also attempt to universalize blackness: "What do you mean 'Jamaican-Canadian?" one respondent reacted, "I am a black man of African descent.... Africa is like the compass providing armour. Canada is a home 'in a way' because the world is a house and Canada is a room where the heating is best."

However, efforts to universalize blackness are counter-balanced by continuing island loyalties and there is internal resistance to the homogenizing tendencies implied in notions of "the black Community." This challenge also comes from a peculiar cultural distinctiveness of being "in-between," neither assimilated nor isolated. Homi Bhabha's (1990) concept of a "third space" is useful for understanding how this "in-betweenness" displaces the histories that constituted it and allows for other positions and possibilities to emerge. This third space opens up radical possibilities for asserting differences. It is from this cultural space that individuals stand to challenge what Mercer (1988) coins "the burden of representation," that is the burden of always having to speak as delegate, presenting "positive images" on behalf of the community in which one's experiences are constituted. The internal critique of community and the challenge to essentialism that this implies is not the same as destructive criticism which creates divisions, erode community politics and retard community advancement. Instead it challenges, in the words of Cornel West (1990), assumptions of older anti-racist emancipatory politics about what the "real black community" is. Critique and the challenges to essentialism also confirm that what Giddens (1991) describes as "emancipatory politics" and "politics of life-style" may actually coexist in the same moment.

SUMMARY AND CONCLUSION

The various dimensions of globalization in the closing decade of the 20th century open up important challenges for studies of identity. I have drawn attention to the significance of "strategic essentialism" which is contingently deployed by marginalized groups in efforts to carve out identities for social and political purposes. This process is vital for addressing injustices. The importance of this practice is acknowledged and the creative works that are currently being produced "from the margins" further bears witness to its potential for creativity. However, the above discussion also cautions against the dangers that are inherent in attempts to fix and prescribe identities in these processes.

Identities are never mirror images of the bounded and "imagined" community in which they are constituted. Instead, the forgoing ethnographic details speak to the sense in which they are negotiated and constructed through ambivalence. New identities are continually forged dialogically from the interplay of being black, young, gendered, sexualized, Caribbean, Canadian and global all at the same time. The symphonic interception and collisions of these various "sites" of identification guard against tendencies to over-determine identities by privileging one "site" over the others.

An understanding of identity as process, which is argued for in this paper, is of special significance for educators and it challenges beliefs in a search for positive images that "reflect" the identities of the learners they serve. It guards against ethnic and racial essentialism which compromise differences within identities. Despite the specific and located context in which self-identity is forged, that context cannot be divorced from the broader global influences that are played out within it. Thus notions of cultural identities as coherent units are also challenged by the research addressed here. The case is also made for a shift to the interface between the global and located as a specific focus for engaging questions of identity.

ENDNOTES

1. This is a revised version of the paper entitled "Popular Culture, New Sites of Identification and New Challenges for Multicultural Curriculum Innovations" presented at the Annual Conference of the Canadian Association for Latin American and Caribbean Studies, Culture and Development: Rethinking Modernity. Ottawa, October 21-24, 1993. It also draws on two earlier papers, "Globalization, Identity and the Caribbean Diaspora: Notes for Curriculum Planning and Development," presented at the Annual Conference of the Caribbean Studies Association, Kingston and Ocho Rios, Jamaica, May 24-29. 1993; and, "Identity and Difference, a Case Study of Identity Construction Among Caribbean Youth in Metropolitan Toronto," presented at the Annual Conference of the American Anthropological Association, Association of Black Anthropologists' invited symposium, "Contact Culture: In Search of Hemispheric Americana," San Francisco. December 2-6, 1992. These works draw on my larger ethnographic project which addresses identity negotiation among high school students.
2. For a comparison between Britain and Canada see Anthony Richmond (1988); for racial discrimination in the field of employment in Toronto see Frances Henry and Effie Ginsberg (1986); for racialization of immigration from the Caribbean see Vic Satzewich (1989).

REFERENCES

Anderson, B. (1983). Imagine communities: Reflections on the origin and spread of nationalism. London: Verso.

Appadurai, A. (1992). Disjuncture and difference in the global cultural economy. In M. Featherstone (Ed.), *Global culture: Nationalism, globalization and modernity.* London: Sage Publications.

———. (1991). Global ethnoscapes, notes and queries for transnational anthropology. In *Recapturing anthropology: Working in the present.* New Mexico: School of American Research Press.

Basch, L., Glick Schiller, N. and Szanton-Blanc (Eds.). (1994). *Nations unbound: Transnational projects, postcolonial predicament and deterritorialized nation-states.* Amsterdam: Gordon and Beach.

Bhaba, H.(1990). The third space. Interview with Homi Bhaba. In *Identity, community, culture, difference.* London: Lawrence Wishart (pp.207-21)

Chambers, I. (1990). *Border dialogues, journeys in postmodernism.* London, New York: Routledge.

Fabian, J. (1983). *Time and the other: How anthropology makes it object.* New York: Columbia Press.

Fanon, F. (1986). *Black skin white masks.* London: Pluto.

Featherstone. M. (Ed.). (1990). *Global culture: Nationalism, globalization and modernity.* London: Sage Publications.

Foucault, M. (1990). *The history of sexuality, an introduction.* New York: Vintage Books, Random House.

Friedman, J. (1990). Being in the world: Globalization and localization. In *Theory, Culture and Society,* 7.

Giddens, A. (1990). *The consequences of modernity.* California: Stanford University Press.

———. (1991). *Modernity and self-identity: Self and society in the late modern age.* California: Stanford University Press

Hall, S. (1989). Ethnicity: Identity and difference. *Radical America,* 23(4).

———. (1990). Cultural identity and diaspora. In *Identity, community, culture, difference* (pp.222-237). London: Lawrence and Wishart.

———. (1991a). The local and the global: Globalization and ethnicity. In A. King (Ed.), *Culture, globalization and the world system.* Binghamton: State University of New York.

———. (1991b). Old and new identities, old and new ethnicities. In A. King (Ed.), *Culture, globalization and the world system.*

Hannerz, U. (1992). *Cultural complexity: Studies in the social organization of meaning.* New York: Columbia University Press.

Henry F. and Ginsberg, E. (1986). *Who gets the work? A test of racial discrimination in employment.* Toronto: Urban Alliance on Race Relations and the Social Planning Council of Metropolitain Toronto.

Kellner, D. (1992). Popular culture and the construction of post-modern identities. In S. Lash and J. Friedman (Eds.) *Modernity and Identity.* Oxford, Cambridge: Blackwell.

Kirkpatrick, J. and White, G. (Eds.). (1985). *Person self and experience.* Berkley, London: University of California Press.

Lash, S. and Friedman, J. (1992). Introduction: subjectivity and modernity's other. In S. Lash. and J. Friedman (Eds.) *Modernity and identity.* Cambridge, MA; Oxford: Basil Blackwell.

Lewis, G. (1987). *Main currents in Caribbean thought.* Baltimore: John Hopkins Press.

Lutz, C. and White, G. (1986). The anthropology of emotions. *Annual Review of Anthropology,* 15, pp.405-36.

Marcus G. and Fisher, M. (1986). *Anthropology as cultural critique.* Chicago and London: University of Chicago Press.

Mercer, K. (1988). Diasporic culture and the cialogic imagination. In M. Cham and C. Andrade-Watkins (Eds.), *Black frames: Critical perspectives on black independent cinema.* Cambridge, MA: MIT Press.

———. (1990). Welcome to the jungle. In *Identity, community, culture, difference.* London: Lawrence and Wishart.

Morrison, T. (1990). *Playing in the dark, whiteness and the literary imagination.* New York: Vantage Books, Random House.

Rattansi, A. (1992). Introduction. In *Race, culture and difference.* London: Sage Publications.

Richmond, A. (1988). Caribbean immigrants in Britain and Canada: Socio-economic adjustment. *International Migration,* 26(5), pp.365-86.

Rodman, M. (1992). Empowering place: Multilocality and multivocality. *American Anthropologist,* 94(3), pp.640-656.

Rutherford, J. (1990). A place called home: Identity and the cultural politics of difference. In *Identity, community, culture, difference* (pp.9-27). London: Lawrence Wishart.

Satzewich V. (1989). Racism and Canadian immigration policy: The government's view of Caribbean migration, 1962-1966. In *Canadian Ethnic Studies,* 21(1), pp.77-97.

Spivak, G. (1990). *The post-colonial critic: Interviews, strategies, dialogue.* New York, London: Routledge.

Sutton, C. (1987). *Caribbean life in New York City.* New York: Centre for Migration Studies of New York.

Wallerstein, I. (1978). World systems analysis: Theoretical and interpretative issues. In B.H. Kaplan (Ed.), *Social change in the capitalist world economy.* Beverly Hills, CA: Sage.

West C. (1990). The new politics of difference. In R. Ferguson (Ed.), *Out there: Marginalization and contemporary culture.* Cambridge, MA: MIT Press.

Williams, B. (1989). A class act: Anthropology and the race to nation across ethnic terrain. *Annual Review of Anthropology, 18.*

Yon, D. (1991). Schooling and the politics of identity: A study of Caribbean students in a Toronto high school. In H. Diaz et al. (Eds.), *Forging identities and patterns of development.* Toronto: Canadian Scholars Press.

L'EXPRESSION D'UNE IDENTITÉ À TRAVERS LA POÉSIE ET LES CHANSONS AU NICARAGUA

Milagros Ortiz

Cette étude a pour objet d'élucider l'identité du métis nicaraguayen en analysant son expression populaire dans la poésie et les chansons. Cette identité comporte deux dimensions: *l'indien en moi* et *l'indien des autres*. La première dimension se retrouve presque exclusivement dans le discours poétique, où «l'indianité» se définit par l'exaltation de l'héroïsme autochtone et la sublimation de la défaite par la victimisation ou la mise en valeur de la notion de l'indien naif, située dans un passé mythique. La deuxième définition situe l'indianité dans le présent mais elle est manifestée par les expressions de révolte. Il existe, cependant, une expression artistique de l'indianité qui revendique *l'indien en moi* dans le présent. Cette identité a été nié aussi bien par le gouvernement révolutionnaire que par les gouvernements pré-révolutionnaires mais les deux conceptions identitaires s'avèrent extrêmement problématique.

We can learn more about the identity of the Métis of Nicaragua by analyzing their forms of popular expression: poetry and songs. This identity has two dimensions: the «Indian within» and the «Indian without». The first definition of identity relations belongs almost exclusively to poetic discourse where being «Indian» is defined by exalting heroic deeds of the indigenous population, as well as by sublimating defeat by victimizing or extolling the indigenous Indian of a mythical past. The second definition locates «indianity» in the present but it is found in expressions of revolt. There is, however, an artistic expression of «indianity» which identifies with the «indian within» in the present. But it is this notion of identity which was rejected by both the revolutionary and the pre-revolutionary governments. In fact, both conceptions of Métis identity are extremly problematic.

CET ARTICLE TENTERA de répondre aux questions que se posait le poète Pablo Antonio Cuadra: «*¿Sería el Nicaragüense un hombre dividido por la duda?*», «*¿o es el nicaragüense la fusión de antagonismos, la unificación de contrastes?*» (1978, p.20).[1] Au départ, nous nous butons à un premier problème : de quel Nicaraguayen parle-t-il ? Les conflits armés apportent une partie de la réponse, car ils ont laissé voir qu'il existe plus d'une seule identité nicaraguayenne. Nous tenterons ici de répondre au poète en analysant des chansons et des poèmes provenant des Nicaraguayens de la majorité *ladine* «Métisse»,[2] le peuple qui se retrouvent sur la Côte pacifique où il contrôle l'appareil d'État. Ses chansons et poèmes sont des manifestations artistiques importantes de sa culture populaire et de son discours identitaire.[3]

Quelle est la place de l'Indien dans l'identité du Nicaraguayen Métis? Nous proposons que cette identité a deux dimensions: «l'Indien en moi» et «l'Indien des Autres». Dans la première dimension il y a une indianité révendiquée autant à un niveau d'identité individuel que collectif. Mais elle est située dans un passé révolu et transmise par les discours officiels et poétiques. Dans la deuxième dimension, l'indianité est niée mais utilisée pour identifier d'autres membres du même groupe ethnique. Elle est plutôt refletée par un discours «populaire» et son espace temporel est le présent.

Le corpus d'extraits a été puisé au répertoire des auteurs les plus connus et consiste en des chansons ou poèmes composés entre la fin du XIXe siècle et la période précédant la révolution.[4] Les métaphores et les mécanismes de symbolisation seront relevés afin de cerner les thèmes pertinents pour notre enquête. Dans un premier temps nous allons expliquer en quoi consiste «l'Indien en moi» qui se dégage des poèmes, ensuite nous aborderons «l'Indien des Autres» qui se dégage des chansons.[5] Finalement, nous exposerons quelques exeptions qui contredisent certains aspects de ces deux dimensions et concluerons avec une hypothèse sur la question.

PREMIÈRE DIMENSION: «L'INDIEN EN MOI»

Cette dimension, inhérente à notre appartenance ethnique comme «Métis» et présente dans la dichotomie Indien-Espagnol, est caractérisée par une exagération des éléments provenant de ce que nous croyons être la culture espagnole, aux dépens des éléments autochtones aussi bien sur le plan culturel que génétique. Néanmoins, certains éléments autochtones sont séléctionnés afin d'être utilisés pour légitimer la structure du pouvoir actuelle. «L'Indien en moi» est caractérisé aussi par une exaltation de certains traits qui lui sont attribués. L'Indien dont on parle est celui des temps pré-colombiens ou de l'époque de la Conquête, il est *l'ancêtre mythique,* fabriqué pour justifier la présence d'une classe au pouvoir qui paradoxalement n'est souvent pas autochtone.

Cette volonté d'exagérer l'influence espagnole au Nicaragua et de diffuser l'idée d'un métissage biologique largement répandu est prôné dans les discours historique et officiel (lesquels, étant donné le contexte politique sont presque les mêmes). Ce même message se retrouve dans la poésie. Ainsi, un éminent folkloriste nicaraguayen nous dit que: «... *la mezcla de lo indio con lo español fue casi total, sobre todo en la cultura popular. Quizá ello sea debido a que tal mestizaje cultural se realizó simultáneamente con lo racia* » (Perez Estrada, n.d., p.21). Les exemples comme celui-ci, pris d'un manuel destiné aux écoles secondaires sont nombreux. «*Indios e hispanos participaron en el proceso de fusión de dos literaturas—la culta y la popular—para formar una tercera de rasgos comunes y acusados* » (Matus Lazo, 1977, p.18). C'est uniquement cette définition de «soi» qui est diffusée à la population par l'État, par le biais du programme de l'enseignement de l'histoire et de la littérature du ministère d'Éducation publique et bien évidemment, par les politiciens.[6]

Cependant, la réalité est toute autre. Il n'y a pas eu un tel métissage généralisé au Nicaragua, car le nombre de conquistadores et de colons espagnols étaient extrêmement réduit. Même au niveau populaire, (comme c'est le cas pour d'autres Latino-Américains), on retrouve cette exagération qui consiste à mentionner un «ancêtre blanc» réel ou fictif, de n'importe quelle origine.

LE DISCOURS POÉTIQUE

Les discours historique et officiel maintiennent une relation dialectique avec le discours littéraire. Il reflète presque exclusivement ce que nous appellons ici la dimension «l'Indien en moi». Au Nicaragua il y a deux courants poétiques: le Modernisme, d'inspiration cosmopolite dont Ruben Darío était la célébrité internationale; et le mouvement Vanguardia, qui surgit en s'opposant au premier, avec Cuadra et Coronel Urtecho, dans un effort désespéré de trouver une «identité nationale».[7] Pour comprendre les dynamiques de ces mouvements nous reprenons ces propos de Zolberg:

> L'oeuvre d'art fait l'objet de constantes réinterprétations, elle est continuellement réévaluée; l'analyse de ces réceptions successives met en lumière l'interaction existante entre des éléments des contextes artistique, politique et économique. (cité par Couture, 1990, p.164)

En effet, on a dit de la poésie de Darío que: «*sa racine était profondément espagnole*» (Saenz et Velasco, 1965, p.415), alors que Cuadra nous dit: «*Yo diría más bien que lo permanente en la poesía de Rubén es su misteriosa obsesión de raíz indígena por concebir la unidad como dualidad*» (Cuadra, 1978, p.26). Aussi, comme Whisnant (1992) le souligne, Darío est au centre des manipulations idéologiques de la part des pouvoirs politiques.[8]

La Vanguardia a le mérite d'être le précurseur quant à la valorisation d'un language et d'une littérature qui se veulent un reflet d'une réalité propre. Cependant, comme Vilas a noté, ce mouvement littéraire est aussi réductioniste et ethnocentriste que le modernisme de Darío: d'une part l'Indien est le Métis, et d'autre part, le Nicaraguayen est Métis (Vilas, 1990, p.203-204). Pour les deux mouvements, l'indianité est réliée à un métissage et à un passé, mythique. Les extraits de poèmes suivants montrent l'image de l'Indien dans le discours poétique, image ambiguë caractérisée à la fois par une exaltation de son héroïsme (le héros rebelle, fort et courageux), et par la sublimation de la défaite face aux conquérants par le biais de la victimisation à travers le martyre ou la naïveté. A notre avis, cette ambiguïté révèle une des sources du malaise identitaire des Métis nicaraguayens: l'intériorisation de la Conquête comme un passé historique non résolu.

EXALTATION DE L'HÉROÏSME AUTOCHTONE

Tout d'abord, il y a l'exaltation de l'héroïsme autochtone selon lequel l'Indien est conçu comme «rebelle», «altier» ou «glorieux», entraînant l'exaltation du métissage qui en est le résultat.

> *Juntas las testas ancianas ceñidas de líricos lauros*
> *y las cabezas jóvenes que la alta Minerva decora,*
> *así los manes heroicos de los primitivos abuelos,*
> *de los egregios padres que abrieron el surco pristino,*
> *sientan los soplos agrarios de primaverales retornos*
> *y el rumor de espigas que inició la labor triptolémica.*
> *Un continente y otro renovando las viejas prosapias,*

en espíritu unidos, en espíritu y ansias y lengua,
ven llegar el momento en que habrán de cantar nuevos himnos.
(*Ruben Darío,* 1989 :329)

(Sont réunies les têtes d'antan, ceintes par des lauriers lyriques
et les jeunes têtes que la haute Minerva décore
ainsi, les âmes **héroïques** des **primitifs aïeuls,** [héroïsme, ancêtres]
des **pères illustres qui ont ouvert le sillon original,** [ancêtres]
sentent les souffles agraires des retours printaniers
et la rumeur des épis qui a été initié par le travail triptolémique.
Un continent et l'autre renouvelant les vieux lignages [métissage]
unis en esprit, en esprit et en désir et en langues
ils voient arriver le temps quand ils vont chanter de nouveaux hymnes).

... «*... escribí un poema en que quise resumir ... la ironía y el drama de ser nicaragüense*».

Yo pelié con don Gil en la primera
guerra nicaragüense. De muchacho era indio,
y español al unísono me herían.
Tengo el grito bilingüe en las dos fosas
porque me dieron flechas en el lado blanco y balas
en mi dolor moreno.
El hijo de Septiembre. (Cuadra, A., 1978, p.15).

(J'ai combattu aux cotés de Don Gil
dans la première guerre nicaraguayenne. De jeune j'étais Indien
et **l'Indien et l'Espagnol me blessaient à l'unison** [métissage, dualité]
j'ai le **cri bilingue dans mes deux gorges**
parce que j'ai reçu des **flèches dans mon flanc blanc**
et **des balles dans ma douleur cuivrée**).

Baja como bajaste sobre el cerrito un día;
que besen nuestra tierra tus morenitos pies;
que Nicaragua toda palpita de alegría,
y que nuestra alma indígena, castellana y bravía [...]
Nicaragua ante la Virgen de Guadalupe, Coronel Urtecho, J. (Peña, 1964, p.93).

(Descends comme un jour tu es descendue de la coline
que tes petits pieds basanés baisent notre terre
car tout le Nicaragua palpite d'allégresse
et que notre âme **indienne, castillane et altière** [...]).

SUBLIMATION DE LA DÉFAITE À TRAVERS LA VICTIMISATION

Dans ces extraits il y a donc l'exaltation à la Rousseau de l'Indien, qui fut victime du martyre et du Destin Divin. Mais comme on exalte en même temps le métissage, les conquérants n'incarnent pas le Mal: ils sont représentés comme «forts», «ambitieux» et «féroces», ce qui permet de sublîmer la défaite des Indiens, dans ce qui fut rencontre de deux héroïsmes.

Cuando en vientres de América cayó semilla
de la raza de hierro que fue de España,
mezcló su fuerza heroica la gran Castilla
con la fuerza del indio en la montaña.

!Pluguiera a Dios las aguas intactas
no reflejaran nunca las blancas velas;
ni vieran las estrellas estupefactas
arribar a la orilla tus carabelas.
(*Ruben Darío,* 1989, p.399)

(Quand **la semence a pénétré les ventres d'Amérique**
venant **de la race de fer qui fut celle d'Espagne,**
la grande **Castille** unit sa **force héroïque**
à celle de l'Indien de la montagne.

Qu'il plût à Dieu que les eaux intactes
jamais ne reflètent les voiles blanches;
ni vissent les étoiles surprises
arriver au rivage tes caravelles.

Audaz y fuerte era el rudo Conquistador; su coraza
sudaba fuego; el recuerso todavía comenta
el atrevimiento imposible de sus épicos saltos,
y sobre todo, su lógica estaba audazmente sentada
en dos inflexibles premisas: su ambición y su espada.

El Indio era libre y salvaje; tenía dos brazos
constelados de heroicos tatuajes; se erguía en su frente
un hirsuto penacho de plumas; comía las frutas
del trópico dulces y los sangrientos despojos
de los vencidos, y su alma estaba estrellada en el bronce
que funde la Gloria en el crisol del Martirio.
(Cortés, 1931, p.VIII et IX).

(Le rude conquérant était **audacieux** et **fort**
il suait le feu, on en parle encore
de l'**incroyable bravoure** de ses assauts épiques
mais surtout, sa logique était audacieusement
assise sur deux implacables prémices: **l'ambition et son épée.**

L'indien était **libre** et **sauvage;** il avait deux bras
étoilés de tatouages héroïques; dans son front se dressait
un panache hirsute de plumes; il mangeait les fruits
des douces tropiques et les restes sanglants).
des vaincus et son **âme était fondue dans le bronze**
qui fond la **gloire** dans le **creuset du martyre**).

SUBLIMATION DE LA DÉFAITE À TRAVERS LA NOTION DE NAÏVETÉ

Cette dernière répresentation fait appel à une légende concernant le cacique dont le pays a pris son nom: Nicaragua. Il est demeuré prototype de l'Indien naïf qui reçut les conquérants en amis et leur offrit des cadeaux, préparant ainsi sa prope défaite. Mentionnons que l'historiographie actuelle y voit plutôt une stratégie de résistance, une ruse qui visait à gagner du temps devant des ennemis redoutables (Arellano, 1990). Avec Darío, cette naïveté devient un trait du caractère national qui persiste devant les envahisseurs du XXe siècle, à côté d'un héritage syncrétique.

Eres los Estados Unidos
eres el futuro invasor
de la América ingenua que tiene sangre indígena,
que aun reza a Jesucristo y aun habla español.

Mas la América nuestra, que tenía poetas
desde los viejos tiempos de Netzahualcoyotl, (...)
A Roosevelt, 1904. Darío, R. (Ruben Darío,1989: 339)

(Toi, les Etats-Unis
tu es le futur envahisseur
de **l'Amérique naïve** qui **a du sang indien**
qui prie encore Jésus et qui parle encore espagnol.

Mais, notre Amérique, avait des poètes [ancêtres mythiques]
depuis les temps de Netzahualcoyoyl, [...]).

DEUXIÈME DIMENSION: «L'INDIEN DES AUTRES»: SATIRE, VICTIMISATION, RÉVOLTE

En examinant la deuxième dimension de cette ambiguïté identitaire, nous découvrons qu'il y a un Indien bien vivant parmi nous, mais personne ne se l'approprie. L'expression de cette identité s'est faite à travers les dictons ou proverbes, le plus souvent satiriques. Le parler nicaraguayen est rempli d'expressions comme: *Te sale lo indio* («Tu deviens méchant»), *Es lo peor poner un indio a repartir la chicha* («Tu deviens prétentieux comme un Indien qu'on a chargé de répartir la bière de maïs»). Cette fois, on le voit, les marqueurs d'indianité sont inversés et deviennent négatifs; c'est seulement la nuance qui varie: méchanceté, sotise, saleté ou paresse (Ortiz, 1992). Cet Indien est forcément «l'Autre».

On retrouve cette image négative dans les chansons contestataires, écrites par des Métis. Elles sont l'expression artistique qui reflètera le mieux les caractéristiques de la deuxième dimension. Si, dans la poésie écrite l'Indien est souvent un héros, ici il est l'anti-héros: il est essentiellement souffrance, passivité, pauvreté et retard. Il est identifié au monde rural de l'arrière-pays.

Certaines chansons soulignent, de manière satirique et comique, le malaise identitaire actuel de l'Indien. Mais la plupart exploitent le thème de la tristesse et traitent des pénibles conditions sociales et matérielles de l'Indien et du paysan, en utilisant indifféramment ces deux catégories ou en y référant par le biais des métaphores. Voici la réinterprétation du passé par un vieil homme: «Ponían música triste a su vida porque su vida era triste. Como no sabían leer ni escribir le ponían música a sus sentimientos, a sus pesares, y a sus dolores. Y así, de generación en generación se fue transmitiendo esta música» (Mazurcas, valses y polkas, 1990, p.16).

Comme l'a affirmé Vilas, cette image de l'Indien inclut le Métis, non plus défini par un syncrétisme de deux cultures, mais bien par la *perte* d'une identité en même temps que d'un patrimoine. Le paysan et l'artisan, et aussi l'homme de la ville (donc la grande majorité de la population) ont perdu leur langue tandis que leur culture et leur structure sociale et économique propres ont déjà disparu ou sont en train de disparaître (Vilas, 1990, p.209). Nous observons ici une relation de classe masquée par l'ethnicité, car l'Indien est le pauvre, le paysan,[9] et celui que en parle le fait à la troisième personne.

En su voz hay un lamento
que sale desde el fondo de su corazón;
con sabor de sufrimiento
amargo reflejo de su situación>
Lo ven como a un extranjero
en esa tierra suya que un día perdió:
y se regresa callado, camino del monte
de donde salió
pobre indio de mi tierra[...]
Queja india, Krüger, E.
(*Cancionero Popular,* p.133).

(Dans **sa** voix on entend une **lamentation**
qui sort du fond de **son** coeur
avec une **saveur amère de souffrance**
reflet amère de sa situation.
Il est vu comme un **étranger**
sur sa terre qu'un jour il a perdue
et il retourne **silencieux,** vers la brousse
d'où il vient
pauvre indien de mon pays [...]).

Por los senderos del campo	Sur les sentiers des champs
llevas cargando tu pena	tu marches portant **ta peine:**
tu pena de amor y llanto	elle est faite d'amour et de **pleurs**
en tu vientre de arcilla y tierra	**dans ton ventre d'argile et de terre**
Tu tinajita redonda que llevas año	**Ta marmite** ronde que tu portes
con año	année après année
de la semilla que siembra	de la sémence qu'a semée
el campesino en su pobreza.	le paysan dans **sa pauvreté,**
choza de paja, silencio	hutte de paille, ***silence***
sólo el rumor de la selva	on entend juste la rumeur de la forêt
tus lágrimas son de barro	**tes larmes sont de terre cuite**

María Rural, Siú, A. (*Cancionero Popular,* p.160)

A la Candida Martinez	Candide Martinez
un guardián la conminó	un garde l'a ménacée
vení chavala, le dijo,	il lui dit: viens ici fillette
lavame este pantalón	lave mon pantalon
la cipota campesina	**la jeune paysanne**
fue mancillada ay nomás,	**a été violée à l'instant même**
y Tacho desde un afiche	et Somoza riait du haut
reía en el taquezal.	de l'affiche pendue sur le mur
Retoñaban los quequisques	les «quequisques»[10] bourgeonnaient
estaba la milpa en flor	**le champ de maïs fleurissait**
cuando a la pobre Matilde	**quand la pauvre Matilde**
la patrulla la agarró	a été prise par les militaires
la indita abortó sentada	et à cause de leurs interrogatoires,
con tanta interrogación	**la petite indienne a avorté,** assise
me lo contó la quebrada	C'est la rivière qui descend du Septentrion
que baja del Septentrión.	qui m'a tout raconté.

Las Campesinas del Cua, Cardenal, E., (Mejía. Godoy, C., musique et intérprétation, *Cancionero Popular,* p.161).

Mais la passivité de la victime peut se muer en révolte, quand elle prend conscience de l'explotation et de l'oppression.

A mí me gusta vivir en libertad
aunque tenga mucho más que trabajar
y quisiera yo encontrar al que inventó
que la finca debe ser de algún patrón.

Y le enseñaría yo a ese carajo
cuanto vale mi trabajo, sin contar mi soledad;
y le enseñaría yo a ese soquete
con la palma del machete que lo ajeno no hay que dar.

El arriero, Zapata, C. (*Cancionero Popular*, p.135).

(J'aime vivre en liberté
même si je dois travailler beaucoup plus
et je voudrais pouvoir trouver celui qui a inventé
que la ferme doit appartenir à un patron

Et je lui apprendrais à ce type
combien vaut mon travail ainsi que ma solitude
et je lui apprendrais à cet imbécil
avec la lame de ma machette,
qu'on ne doit pas donner ce qui appartient à d'autres).

Ces trois dernières chansons sont typiques d'un genre qui a été extrêmement populaire au Nicaragua, surtout dans les années soixante-dix, *la nueva canción*. A la différence du discours strictement poétique, il n'est pas question de héros dans ces chansons. Par le jeux des métaphores on construit une image d'un Indien moderne, qui est la victime : sa vie n'est que souffrance et il n'a ni pouvoir politique ni contrôle sur son destin. La victimisation ici est double : celle vécue auparavant aux mains des conquérants et celle de la dictature. Le passé se conjugue au présent.

Les femmes sont victimes des militaires, elles se font violer et maltraiter atrocement. Les hommes ne sont pas là pour les défendre (l'armée les aurait emmenés dans un avion et les aurait fait disparaître). Cette féminisation de l'Indianité victime s'enracine aussi dans une légende d'origine. On raconte qu'au Nicaragua, les Espagnols n'ont pas trouvé assez d'or et ils ont envoyé les hommes dans les mines d'or du Pérou (Arellano, 1990). Voici la version historique de la part du cacique des Nicaraguas : «*Nosotros ya no éramos dueños de nuestras esposas, ni de nuestros hijos, ni de ninguna de las cosas que antes teníamos*» (Arellano, 1990, p.94). Les hommes apparaissent comme des victimes inoffensives d'un pouvoir militaire. Cette chanson de protestation réactualise donc, dans le contexte de la dictature de Somoza, la mémoire collective de ce qui est arrivé pendant la Conquête.

SUR L'IDENTITÉ

¿Dónde está el indio? preguntan	Où est l'Indien? demandent
las señoras del balcón.	les dames du balcon
Está en la caballeriza.	—Il est dans les écuries
ahí está el indio pelón.	il est là cet Indien tondu.
¿Es un indio todo indio	**—Est-ce un Indien bien Indien**
o un indio medio español?	ou un Indien à moitié Espagnol?
Es un español todo indio,	—C'est un Espagnol bien Indien,
un indio todo español.	**un Indien bien Espagnol.**
¿Es un español o un indio?	**—Est-ce un Espagnol ou un Indien?**
Es un indio como yo,	**—Il est Indien comme moi,**
español como todo indio,	**Espagnol comme tout Indien**
tan español como yo.	**aussi Espagnol que moi.**

Villancico indio, Pasos A.J. (Peña, 1964, p.293)

Cette chanson met en évidence la relation de classe qui se déguise en relation ethnique d'une manière plus directe, car les femmes sur le balcon sont appelées des «dames», alors que l'on se réfère à l'Indien comme un «tondu». On voit ressortir surtout toute la question de l'ambiguïté identitaire en même temps qu'on aborde l'obsession de faire ressortir les racines espagnoles avec une certaine ironie.

Soy Granadino, nací en Nandaime	Je suis de Grenade, je suis né à Nandaime
de Zapatones jamás usé caites,	d'une famille qui portait des chaussures
	je n'ai jamais porté des sandales
	indiennes

bajo a la población, no me paro	je descends au village et je ne m'arrête pas aux carrefours:
en las esquinas, no me gusta que	je n'aime pas qu'on me dise
me digan que yo soy un indio	que je suis un Indien
sin educación	qui n'a pas de bonnes manières

El nandaimeño, Zapata, C. (*Cancionero popular,* p.146)

Sur le mode ironique, cette chanson exprime mieux que les autres le renversement identitaire : «l'Indien des Autres» est forcément «l'Indien en moi» même si on prend bien soin d'éviter tous les marqueurs extérieurs de l'indianité. On affirme l'existence d'une indianité dans le présent, ce qui contredit le discours poétique.

L'EXPRESSION ARTISTIQUE À CONTRE-COURANT

Contrairement aux chansons précédentes, qui réaffirment l'indianité présente par la satire, celle qui suit le fait sur le mode sentimental : l'Indien est heureux à cause de la production de son champ, l'Indienne, à cause de la reproduction. Il y a d'autres chansons comme celle-ci, elle ne constitue nullement une exception, mais comme elles ne se prêtent pas à l'utilisation idéologique, les moyens de diffusion au pays ne leur ont pas accordé autant d'importance. À la campagne, les paysans chantent plutôt à l'amour.

el invierno floreció	La saison des pluies a fleuri
y la tierra embarazada	et la terre enceinte
busca tu interrogación	cherche tes questions
pero ya no encuentra nada	mais elle ne trouve rien.
que el indio es feliz	que l'Indien est heureux
ya sonríen las mazorcas	les épis sourient maintenant
con sus dientes de maíz	avec leurs dents de maïs
la mujer también	la femme aussi
mece su emoción	berce son émotion
hubo cosecha de maíz	il y a eu récolte de maïs
hubo cosecha de amor. (bis)	il y a eu récolte d'amour.

El Calabazo, Mantilla, F. G. (*Cancionero popular,* p.144)

Ce genre de poésie avait été jetté aux oubliettes et, il y a de deux raisons importantes pour avoir gardé dans l'oubli cette littérature nicaraguayenne écrite entre le XIXe siècle et le premier quart de XXe siècle (Cerutti, 1970, p.34). On y fait allusion à l'expulsion des marines américaines, ce qui est suffisant dans le contexte de la dictature Somociste; par ailleurs, son contenu érotique n'était admissible ni à l'époque où ils ont été écrits ni avant la révolution. L'érotisme était rejeté autant par les autorités religieuses et politiques que par la société. Et il est fort probable que le ministère de l'Éducation du gouvernment actuel ne diffuse pas cette littérature à cause de ses liens étroits avec l'Église catholique, même si la révolution a amené des revirements en ce qui concerne l'expression de l'érotisme.

Vanegas, lui aussi exalte la force et l'héroïsme de l'Indien. Cependant, il le situe dans le présent, contrairement à la poésie et aux chansons qui avaient été diffusées. Et qui faisaient de l'Indien un martyre ou une victime passive. En outre, ce poète réclame une nouvelle identité en revendiquant «l'Indien en moi», l'Indien du présent, être dynamique faisant partie de la réalité. En somme une identité que les gouvernements nicaraguayens, pré-révolutionnaires, révolutionnaires ou post-révolutionnaires, ne sont pas disposés à transmettre.

Tiende, Rebeca, el cántaro moreno
a mi boca reseca, de argamasa
indígena, *que el sol tirano abrasa,*
y haz que ***el barro se me vuelva bueno.***

(Vanegas, 1968, p.77)

(Rébecca, tend ta cruche brune
à mes lèvres désséchées, d'argile
autochtone, qu'un soleil tyrannique fait flamber
et fait que la glaise me devienne douce).

Dejé de estar bordando
un encaje de llanto a mis ensueños
y descubrí una mina
de bronce
en mis adentros.

(J'ai arrêté de broder
une dentelle de larmes à mes rêves
et **je découvris une mine**
de bronze
dans mes entrailles).

(Vanegas, 1968, p.1)

El indio no puede vivir maniatado
y siempre que quieren tenerlo enjaulado
se muere el QUETZAL.
Eso es muy antiguo, me dicen. No es cierto.
Yo canto: !es eterno! Los indios no han muerto.
Ronca el atabal.

Y el bronce indio refleja la gloria
porque el indio sabe que siempre a su lado vendrá la victoria.(...)

(L'Indien ne peut pas vivre ligoté
et quand on veut le garder emprisonné
il meurt, le QUETZAL.
C'est lointain et révolu me disent-ils. Non, vous avez tort.
Je chante: **c'est éternel! L'Indien n'est pas mort.**
ronfle l'atabal).

Huyó la manada
de bizontes rubios, herida, diezmada,
sin aves de acero y el rabo entre las piernas.
¡Sólo quedó el indio rebelde y altivo
como un volcán vivo
tallado en las propias montañas eternas!

(Vanegas, 1968, p.55-59).

(Le troupeau de bisons blonds fuit
bléssé, décimé, puis il est parti
sans leur oiseaux en acier, la queue entre les jambes,
seulement l'Indien est resté, rebelle et orgueilleux
tel un volcan actif
taillé sur les montagnes éternelles).

CONCLUSION

Nous avons vu que la poésie et les chansons des Nicaraguayens métis de la Côte pacifique manifestent un malaise d'identité dans les deux dimensions exposées précédamment. Au lieu d'exprimer une *fusion* parfaite de deux cultures, elles présentent la *confusion.* Dans «l'Indien en moi», l'Indien n'y est plus actuel et dans «l'Indien des Autres», l'Indien existe encore mais on le renie pour soi même. La chanson satirique soulignera la fausseté du paraître; la chanson contestataire tentera de dépasser la contradiction en décrivant l'Indien comme éternelle victime capable de révolte; tandis qu'une veine lyrique peu connue le chantera sous l'angle de la passion amoureuse.

La négation de «l'Indien en soi» est une conséquence nécessaire si on retient l'observation de Cuadra, pour qui le Nicaraguayen [le Métis] *au singulier* se considère intelligent. Mais lorsque l'individu qualifie sa collectivité, il considère son groupe stupide (Cuadra, 1978, p.60). Les explications sont tautologiques, les Métis attribuent la responsabilité aux piètres gouvernements et Cuadra lui-même nous parle d'une sorte de «naturel autocritique». Mais il y des éléments théoriques qui tentent d'éclairer le phénomène identitaire au Nicaragua, entre autres, ceux de Cross :

> *L'Indien intériorise-t-il au sein de ses catégories originelles des catégories qui lui sont étrangères et qui sont contradictoires par rapport aux premières. En intériorisant cette altérité irréductible à ses propres normes l'imaginaire collectif se donne à voir comme une matrice appelée à ne produire que des figures hybrides. Implantée dans la conscience, l'altérité ne saurait en effet s'y dissoudre.* (Cross, 1991, p.49)

Ainsi, nous adhérons à l'idée que l'interprètation d'une réalité est un processus aussi dynamique que la construction d'une identité : l'histoire explique le présent, mais on interprète le passé, on le construit en fonction du présent, on le réinterprète, on le reconstruit. Or, avec les valeurs *machos* et évolutionnistes des Métis, l'intériorisation de la défaite des Indiens face aux Espagnols ne peut que provoquer un profonde malaise.

En effet, elle se fait en assumant que les Mangues ou Chorotegas et les nahuats ou Nicaraguas, les deux cultures principales de la Côte Pacifique à l'arrivé des Espagnols (Arellano, 1990), ont manqué de courage et/ou intelligence, ce qui a été cristalisé dans l'image du cacique Nicaragua. De plus, la culture autochtone du Nicaragua se trouve constament minimisée car elle est placée au bas de l'échelle évolutionniste : à cause de sa défaite et par le manque de structure étatique qu'avaient les cultures autochtones au Mexique et au Pérou.

Les doutes sur le courage des Indiens hantent surtout une élite qui répugne à s'identifier avec de tels vaincus. Cette élite se cherche donc un discours nationaliste. Ce qui correspond à une quête d'identité populaire. On essaie alors d'exorciser ces doutes par l'exaltation des qualités qui ont, soit disant, manqué aux indiens. Les moyens sont nombreux : distortion de la réalité historique, exagération de la présence espagnole, victimisation par l'exaltation du martyre ou d'une bonté qui va jusqu'a la stupidité. Le débat sur l'Indian de la Cônquete et sur l'Indien pré-colombien, sert d'alibi au vrai débat—à peine amorcé—sur l'identité actuelle des Nicaraguayens.

NOTES

1. Ma gratitude est grande envers le professeur Pierre Beaucage, ses commentaires ont enrichi ce texte. Je tiens également à remercier Mme. Norma de Ortiz, ma mère, pour m'avoir procuré les livres dont le corpus de poèmes a été tiré, mes amis Jocelyn Tousignant et Jean Jacques Dubois pour m'avoir offert le livre *El Nicaragüense.*
2. Les études de P. Beaucage (1985) La jeune fille, la fleur et l'orphelin, in *Recherches Amérindiennes au Québec,* XV(4), 79-90, et celles de Jarden J.P. (1982) Littérature antillaise d'expression française et identité culturelle, in *Anthropologie et Société,* 6(2), 59-69; nous montrent la pertinence de l'analyse de la poésie ou des chants pour la compréhénsion de l'organisation sociale et de l'identité.
3. En ce qui a trait à la chanson, voici les propos d'un chansonier de village: "Ahora ya tengo 71 años pero cuando era joven, ho había ni radio ni roconolas, por eso todo el mundo sabía tocar la guitarra" (Mazur., val., y polk., 1990, p. 16). Mais dans la campagne profonde où j'avais été en 1981, c'est encore le cas et les paysans se réunissent souvent pour chanter accompagnés des petites guitares à trois ou quatre cordes, assez rustiques, qu'ils fabriquaient eux-mêmes. Quant à la relation entre la poésie, voici la remarque très juste de Whisnant: "... *tiny nation that since the days of "el divino Rubén" has envisioned itself becoming a nation of poets*" (Whisnant, 1992, p.43). Même nos voisins du sud nous perçoivent ainsi (Cuadra, 1978, p.79). Par ailleurs, Cuadra et l'ex-président Ortega, malgré leur divergences idéologiques sont d'accord à ce sujet.
4. Cette période comprend l'émergence d'un nationalisme libéral au XIXe siècle et sera marquée par la dictature somociste à partir des années trente.

5. Il faut noter cependant que malgré des différences très marquées qui se dégagent de deux manifestations artistiques, il y a un rapport entre les deux. Ceci est un fait inhérent au processus de création : les poètes écrivent les paroles de certaines chansons, des poèmes sont mis en musique ou des chansoniers composent des poèmes originaux. Aussi, le mouvement Vanguardia et le contexte politique révolutionnaire ont favorisé le déchaînement de la création des chansons contestataires.
6. Voir la Constitution promulguée par le gouvernement sandiniste.
7. Voir Whisnant.
8. Voir Whisnant qui souligne l'utilisation idéologique dont Darío et son oeuvre ont été l'objet par les gouvernements nicaraguayens avant, pendant et après la révolution.
9. Wolf affirme que «dans l'Amérique centrale, le préjugé des castas, comme aussi à l'égard des Indiens, reste un préjugé social», (Wolf, 1962, p.208).
10. Tubercule de la famille des euphorbiacés, semblable au manioc.

RÉFÉRENCES

Arellano, J.E. (1990). *Nueva Historia de Nicaragua.* Managua: Fondo Editorial CIRA.

Cancionero Popular. Managua, Nicaragua. (n.d.).

Cerutti, F. (1970). La vida, la obra y los tiempos de Félix Medina []. *Revista Conservadora del pensamiento centroamericano,* 115, 33-41.

Cortés, S. (Édit.). (1931). *Tardes de Oro.* León, Nicaragua.

Couture, F. (1991). Vera L. Zolberg, *Constructing a Sociology of the Art.* [Compte rendu]. *Cahiers de recherche sociologique,* 16, 164-166.

Cuadra, P.A.(1978). *El nicaragüense.* (8e édition). Costa Rica: EDUCA.

(1985). Situación de la Cultura. *Revista Conservadora del pensamiento centroamericano,* 168, 91-104.

Matus Lazo, R. (1977). *Literatura española e hispanoamericana* []. Managua: Ministerio de la Educación Pública.

Mazurcas, valses y polkas. (1990, Juillet). *Enlace,* 1(1), 14-17.

Ortiz, M. (1992). *Ethnohistoire et identité: les Miskitos de Nicaragua.* Mémoire inédit, Université de Montréal, Montréal, Québec, Canada.

Peña, E. (1964). *Castellano Básico.* (12e édition). Managua: Ministerio de la Educación Pública.

Perez Estrada, F. (n.d.). *Estudios del Folklore nicaragüense.* Managua, Nicaragua: Tipografía Brenes.

Ruben Darío. Poesía. (1989). Managua: Editorial Nueva Nicaragua.

Sáenz de Urturi, M. et V. Mateo Velasco. (1965). *Historia de la Literatura.* Madrid: Ediciones S.M.

Vanegas, Alí. (1968). *Bronce Indígena. Poemas.* (Nicaragua, dessin de couverture par Cuadra, H.R.).

Vilas, M.C. (1990). *Del colonialismo a la autonomía: modernización capitalista y revolución social en la Costa Altlantica.* Managua: Editorial Nueva Nicaragua.

Whisnant, D.E. (1992). Ruben Darío as a focal cultural figure in Nicaragua: the ideological uses of cultural capital. *Latin America Research Review,* 27(3), 7-49.

Wolf, E. (1962). *Peuples et civilisations de l'Amérique centrale, des origines à nos jours.* Paris: Payot.

BEAUTIFUL LIES: LEGITIMATION OF THE NATIONAL IDENTITY IN TWO SERIES OF INDIANIST POEMS OF THE DOMINICAN REPUBLIC, 1877-1882

Catharina Vallejo

Four of the first texts published in the Dominican Republic are Indianist. This paper concentrates on two of these works: *Fantasías indíjenas* by José Joaquin Pérez (1877), and *Anacaona,* the long narrative poem by Salomé Urena (1880); both deal with events that took place soon after Columbus' arrival in Hispaniola in 1492. The literary expression of Indianist themes, which uses various legitimation techniques, presents a Eurocentrically Romantic version of the glorious beginnings of the Dominican people. These discourses, however, which ignore the events of the intervening 350 years, do not take into account the contemporary social reality of the 19th century, as well as the Dominican national identity.

Parmi les premiers textes publiés dans la République dominicaine, quatre d'entre eux sont de caractère «indianiste». Cet article étudie deux de ces oeuvres : les *Fantasías indíjenas,* de José Joaquin Pérez (1877) et *Anacaona,* le long poème narratif de Salomé Urena (1880). Il s'agit des événements qui ont eu lieu dès l'arrivé de Christophe Colomb en 1492. L'expression littéraire des thèmes indianistes, qui s'appuie sur des techniques de légitimation, présente une version eurocentrique et romantique des origines glorieuses du peuple dominicain. En passant sous silence les événements des prochaines 350 années, ces textes déforment la réalité sociale du XIXe siècle ainsi que l'identité nationale dominicaine.

THE APPEARANCE OF FOUR MAJOR literary works in the space of five years in Santo Domingo between 1877 and 1882 marks the first flourishing of Dominican literature.[1] Until that time, except for short stories and some legends in verse, only one book-length literary work had been published in the city, an anthology of Dominican poetry in 1874.[2] The *Fantasías indíjenas* by José Joaquín Pérez, of 1877, is the first volume of poetry published in Santo Domingo by a Dominican author; in 1879 Manuel de Jesús Galván published Part I of the first novel with a Dominican theme, *Enriquillo* (completed in 1882); in 1880 the *Sociedad amigos del país* (which served as a centre for writers' meetings and readings) sponsored the publication of the *Poesías* of Salomé Ureña de Henríquez and, finally, in 1882 the same *Sociedad Amigos del País* published the drama in verse *Iguaniona,* written by Javier Angulo Guridi in 1867.

It is remarkable that these first forays into local publication should be Indianist[3] in character; three of the works are entirely Indianist and the fourth, Salomé Ureña's *Poesías,* contains an extensive poem, "Anacaona," on the same theme. In this paper I will concentrate on "Anacaona," as well as on the *Fantasías indíjenas* of José Joaquín Pérez, and show that expression of the Indianist themes came about as an ideological need for legitimizing a national identity in a discursive process which inevitably manifests contradictions in its literary expressions.[4]

Literature, as Foster has remarked, can be viewed as particular versions of the "'(re)writings' of the ideological patterns" (1990, p.10) of the time and space in which they are produced, by formulating them through the presentation of events and characters. Literary narratives constitute "semiotic transformations of the ideological and sociocultural structures of a society" (Foster, 1990, p.10). This process, in turn, transforms—by confirming or denying—these same ideological patterns. In the Dominican Republic, literature was one of the major practices which served the ideology of the Dominican Republic elite in the establishment of its hegemony during the 1870s and '80s.

The country had suffered major political and social upheavals since the beginning of the 19th century. The territory had declined in power and prestige during the more than 300 years of Spanish colonization. In 1804 the western half of the island obtained its independence as Haiti, which invaded the eastern half in 1822 and occupied it for 22 years. During that time, universities were closed, newspapers heavily censured or prohibited, and all forms of Hispanic cultural expression were forbidden.

The independence, achieved in 1844, lasted until 1861 when, amid continued fear of renewed invasions from Haiti, President Pedro Santana requested annexation to Spain, in the face of protests from liberal elements in the country. This annexation lasted until 1865, when the Second Republic was proclaimed. During the following years, the threat from Haiti diminished, to be replaced by the increasing involvement of the United States in Caribbean affairs, and renewed fear of loss of sovereignty. Throughout, the country was generally ruled by a succession of *caudillos,* or local leaders; *caudillismo* was seen by the liberal elite as one of the most serious problems for the country's progress (Moya Pons, 1981/1983).

In that same period, the country underwent profound economic changes. The re-establishment of the importance of sugar, a shift of economic dominance from the north to the south, regionalism, subsequent cultural and social fragmentation and a struggle between conservative and liberal elements, between cuasi-feudalism and pre-capitalism, between the old-style regional *caudillismo* and the new intellectual nationalism, were all factors that contributed to these changes (Moya Pons, 1981/1983 and Franco, 1977). By the mid-1870's, the liberals (in Santo Domingo it was the "Blue Party", or simply *los azules*), were able to concentrate power and government in Santo Domingo—which around 1865 had a population of 6,000 (Domínguez, 1977)—whose ruling class constituted an almost entirely white, liberal, and highly culture-conscious bourgeoisie.

In a process common to all Spanish-American countries shortly after obtaining their independence, the governing liberals of Santo Domingo, being keenly aware of the recent history of their country, felt a strong need to establish a positive national identity for the Dominican people. In other countries this desire was expressed especially through the novels, some of which are now often called "foundational fiction."[5] The research on Dominican literature presented here indicates that the foundational aspect is also present in Dominican poetry of the era,[6] in which the ideological patterns of the State are confirmed and perpetuated. The official ideological patterns of the State seek to impose a coherent worldview which ignores or alters the conflicts that beset the society by interpreting it in terms of one dominant concept, in this case, the forging of a national identity founded on the heroic characters and deeds of the Indians of Hispaniola.

The world outlook of the liberals during the early 1870s was still essentially Romantic in nature, manifested both in the politics and in the intellectual and cultural activities. Although Romanticism was adapted to local circumstances to a certain degree—as it was in all Latin America—it was still strongly Eurocentric in nature. Thus, Romanticism's interest in the past, in myths and mysteries, in the exotic, in the strong belief of the power of the individual and subjective feelings, would form the basis of a national identity through identification with heroic figures, who would glorify the past.

During the later 1870s, Positivism became important in the country; it was stimulated by Eugenio María de Hostos, a Puerto Rican thinker exiled in Santo Domingo for several years. Positivists believed their philosophy to be a social science that would attain progress through order. Education and the encouragement of a scientific outlook were considered important aspects of public policy, thus building a national consciousness with a view to the future and to a secular society based on order and reason.

It is readily apparent that the two philosophies that were the foundation of the national consciousness are sharply contrasting. However, Dominican intellectuals allowed the contradiction; in fact Salomé Ureña and José Joaquín Pérez wrote poetry which show that both ideologies were significant for the cultural elite.[7] The present study concentrates on the Romantic aspect of the ideological climate in Santo Domingo, with its exploration and mythification of the past. The literary formulation of a national history allows this history to be remade according to ideological conditions. Thus, Dominican history is poeticized and confirmed as the foundation of a progressive and "positive"[8] future. In his letter to Javier Angulo Guridi, author of *Iguaniona* (a letter later published as "Prologue" to the work), José Joaquín Pérez writes that "this past is there, with the immobile solemnity of its fearsome mysteries, waiting for its ashes to be reanimated by the life-giving breath of thought" (Pérez in Angulo Guridi, 1882/1953, pp.xii-xiii)—a reanimation to be effected by the works of the Dominican poets.

The creative consciousness of the writers reflects the past as a mirror which reproduces events that took place 350 years before—ignoring the intervening period—and which is meant to be a model for the Dominican people in their present. This national and sociocultural consciousness would thus create the people as Dominican subjects, in both senses of the word: subject to the Nation (its citizens) and Subjects of the nation (its people).

With respect to the Indianist texts studied here, it must be remembered, in a first instance, that the Indian presence in Hispaniola had been eliminated as a cultural and racial entity within 50 years of Columbus' arrival, and that the Indian traditions did not contribute to the formation of Dominican culture (see for example Cassá, 1974). However, in the 1870s the recent past of the Dominican Republic offered no possibility for the glorious past and sacred origins needed for a positive national consciousness. This past, including its cultural consequences, such as the presence of and contribution by Africans—brought to the island since the early 16th century—was thus ignored or erased.[9] In fact, the African ethnic had been a strong, continuous and lasting presence in the Dominican Republic since that period. The disregard of this ethnic group by the intellectuals comes to the fore in a peculiar and paradoxical manner in José Joaquín Pérez's work. He introduces his *Fantasías indíjenas* by a sentence which, according to him, was the "war hymn of the ciguayan Indians who inhabited the Island" (1877/1989, p.35): *Igi aya bongbé*. The spirit of this sentence, which is translated as "death rather than slavery" (*primero muerto que esclavo*), pervades many of the poems of the volume. However, there is considerable controversy over whether these are, in fact, native Indian words, or words belonging to an African language.[10] In explicit terms, the African presence is completely ignored in the historical literature of this elite.

The works of Ureña and Pérez deal with the era immediately following the discovery of America, up to the first few years of the 16th century. In his *Fantasías,* Pérez presents all the major Indian chiefs or *caciques* of the island and their (its) history; 14 lyric poems and a legend in prose deal with Guarionex, Gucanagarí, Cotubanamá and other figures both historical and legendary. Ureña (1880/1989) poeticizes the life of Anacaona—the cacique Caonabo's wife—who was killed in the massacre of Jaragua in 1502.

In order to establish the myths of the indigenous history as the first stage of the Positive progressive history of the Dominican people, the poets try to relate this past to their present, and describe their own era as nostalgic and elegiac, a time which contemplates the tombs and the slavery of history. This past is seen in strongly Eurocentric terms, as is clear from the reference to the "lowly Redeemer" in this passage from "Guarionex" by José Joaquín Pérez:

> The traveller who today crosses the domains over which the great *cacique* Guarionex one day extended his power and glories battling the bold conqueror, sees the Holy Mount which holds a sanctuary at its top, in memory of the exploits which gave victory to

indolent Spain and to the cross of the lowly Redeemer. At the foot of this simple monument lie the remains of a noble race, to whose name memory links heroic traits of genial virtue (p.58).[11]

The relation between the greatness and glory of the *cacique* and the virtues of the Christian Redeemer is clear; so is the implied martyrdom of the Indians.[12] In addition, it is evident that the relation established between the past and the present is expressed as landscape, and not through the inhabitants or their customs—both discontinous with the present of the poet. Pérez wrote in his Prologue to the first edition of Galván's *Enriquillo* in 1882:

Our land ... keeps within its mountains and valleys, in its rivers and torrents, in each stone and each tree trunk and each drop of water, some history of pain and tribulations, which we must evoke so that the world may know the secrets of things not imagined in all of the course of the historical ages (1882/1966).[13]

The poet has to anchor himself in Dominican soil—landscape and earth—in order to see his relation with his mythified past, dead and buried there.

Octavio Paz has pointed out that the Romantic ideology, as is the case with all revolutionary movements, tended toward instituting a mythical past and a sacred origin (1950/1970). Thus, rather than being "indigenist" as they profess to be, these Romantic poems constitute a search for the beginnings of a Dominican identity, and its legitimation in consecrating the Indian chiefs of Quisqueya as mythical heroes. At the same time, this concept of a mythical past conformed to the Positivist idea of the first stage in the spiritual development of humanity being the mythological. In this way the two conflicting ideologies are unified into a coherent whole.

The creation of a unifying ideological project can only occur under the aegis of an enormous textual production, as Foster has pointed out (1990). It is astounding to see the quantity of intellectual works produced by the small literate elite during that period; its members wrote and published drama and poetry, several novels, and innumerable articles about local customs; there were at least seven newspapers and two intellectual societies in the city. In addition to this production Dominican intellectuals commented, prologued, published and, in general, publicized (and so intended to popularize) each other's work(s).[14] The existence of these practices confirms Goldmann's precept that written discourse, though signed by one person, is the product of a mentality that transcends the individual.[15] This process of production and repetition of the ideology constitutes aspects of the ritualizing (and therefore institutionalizing) of the ideology (see Althusser, 1970). The transmission and diffusion of the ideological—contradictory—"truths" were aimed at creating a Dominican citizenry from an amorphous mass whose only allegiance had been more to a regional *caudillo* than to a national president.

Various types of justifications are offered by the poets to emphasize the authenticity of the texts in order to legitimize the legends presented in the works as the true and important history, in which from the beginning the Dominican people were sacrificed and victimized by the Spaniards. The vagueness of information about dates and names (Anacaona's daughter, for example, is called either Higuemota or Higuenamota by the various authors), does not interfere with the truth that the poems convey. The essential characteristic of myths, that their events are conceived as social paradigms, comes to the fore here, the paradigm being the betrayal and extinction of the indigenous people, victims sacrificed at the hands of the Spaniards. This is a more essential truth, in the mythification, than the exactness of dates, names and places. It matters little, therefore, that the heroes are not historical. Iguaniona, for example, is a character invented by Angulo Guridi; she is praised by José Joaquín Pérez as "the heroic virgin, the sublime woman who carries incarnate within her destiny the destiny of her country. I seem to see in her the image of the country itself" (in Angulo Guridi, 1882/1953, pp.xiii-xiv).[16] By legitimizing the literary discourse, the authors thus at the same time legitimize history itself, filling its gaps with paradigmatic values and constructing the mirror of ideology.

Salomé Ureña offers a list of vocabulary and Indian names at the end of her poem; for example she uses *areíta* (taíno for song), *arijuna* (stranger), *bohío* (house), *diumba* (dance), and *Quisqueya* (1880/1989). José Joaquín Pérez's poems have footnotes—provided by the author—considered to be necessary to explain the context of each character, to translate the fairly numerous indigenous words used and to legitimize the information presented with quotes from "authorities."

This use of legitimizing texts, both historical and literary, presents certain paradoxes. There are references to works by Columbus, by Father Las Casas; references to a biography of Las Casas, to Juan de Herrera's *Décadas,* and also to works by Lamartine and Washington Irving. The foundation of the national myth of Santo Domingo, therefore, is based on Eurocentric Romantic traditions. The writers found it necessary to provide vocabulary lists, for example, because the language was exotic, even for Dominicans.

The works establish a clear dualism between Good and Evil, a binary opposition which necessarily classifies the Indian as Good and the Spaniard as Evil. The characters of the *caciques* are modified by means of a positively charged lexicon; in Pérez's poetry, they are "indomitable," "happy," "noble" (p.35), "powerful," "courageous," "genial," "virtuous," "rich," "beautiful" (p.36), "intrepid," "heroic," "great," "faithful," "meritorious" (p.37), "free" (p.38), and, finally, also "oppressed," "martyrs," and "sacrificed" (p.73). These characteristics are attributed to all *caciques,* without differentiation. Not even Guacanagarí, the *cacique* of the Marién region who allied himself with the Spaniards and so caused the loss of his territory and his people, is reviled. In the poem "Guacanagarí at the Ruins of Marién," Pérez does not use a negative or accusatory lexicon, but gives the poem an elegiac and nostalgic tone by making it Guacanagarí's lament: "Reckless accomplice of the wanton power that in the name of God's love lied, I live weeping, like an obscure serf, when I believed myself to be master of all" (p.75).[17] As has been noted by Max Henríquez Ureña (1945/1966), Pérez's contemporaries would not have failed to note the parallel between Guacanagarí's predicament and that of Pedro Santana, the beloved Dominican *caudillo* and President who in 1861 had allied himself with Spain by requesting and obtaining annexation, thus annulling the so strongly fought for independence of the Republic. The relation established between the Indian past and the Dominican present remained positive, however, as it was reinforced by the noble quality which, because of ideological considerations, must be attributed to the Indian, and by the high regard in which Santana was held, due to his personal magnetism and the heroic deeds performed before his treasonous act.

The glorification of the *caciques* (Indian *caudillos*) by the authors, themselves part of the elite of their own times, reinforces the elitist climate of the literary and ideological discourse. These Indianist texts are directed to other intellectuals, members of the elite; not to the *people,* but to the *nation,* which was defined by the very same elite. To a certain extent then, the texts also reinforce the spirit of *caudillismo* which had so plagued Dominican politics after independence.

The noble attributes of the *caciques* are equally applied to the Indian race as a whole, contrary to most Indianist works, in which the race is generally villified as barbarous, although particular individuals—often *mestizos*—may be seen positively (one thinks of Tabaré in *Tabaré* or of Cumandá in *Cumandá*). The suffering of the Indian people, borne nobly, is continuously exalted in the Dominican poetry.

The Spaniards, by contrast and with some few particular exceptions, are presented (for example in Pérez), as: a group of "parvenus" (p.38), "a bloodthirsty horde" (p.40), "perfidious and deceitful" (p.39), "lustful and thirsty for vile gold" (p.51), "ambitious" (p.52), "hypocritical" (p.54), "indolent" (p.58) and "cruel" (p.69). Christopher Columbus is the only Spaniard glorified as "immortal genius," and "intrepid mariner" (p.43).

In the texts of both Ureña and Pérez, the Indians are central and individualized in the narration; although objects of the narration, there is consistent focalization on the Indians who, moreover, often express themselves through direct speech. For example, in Ureña's poem, Anacaona laments the absence of Caonabo, who has been taken to Spain as prisoner: "Weeping, alone, I spent nights, days; but the hope of seeing him again calmed my agony. However, the *arijuna* crossed the ocean in his big, strong canoe, and my Caonabo was taken to faraway regions" (p.216).[18]

José Joaquín Pérez's presentation of the amorous discourse of an Indian couple—the songs of a "He" and a "She"—can be seen as another example of direct speech; in addition, however, these poems evoke the style of European Romanticism:

> Your eyes are so languid, beautiful Indian maid that I adore, that for them I would give my bow, my crown and my treasure! Red corals as your lips, feathers of brilliant white swans I would give you, my beauty, for necklaces, for a diadem in your hair.... etc. ("Él", p.132).[19]

This catalogue of the beautiful traits of the beloved is characteristic of the love-poetry of Spanish-America during the 19th century, which presents the emotions of courteous love in the rhetoric of European literary tradition.

There is thus an effort on the part of the authors to present the Indians as subjects of their own discourse; the Indians as subjects are construed as mirrors to foment the idea of Dominicans as subjects with the same positively charged qualities as the Indian. The Spaniard is presented as the stranger (*arijuna*), the Other. Columbus, for example is always called by his Indian name, Guamiquina, as is the Virgin Mary, who is called Altabeira (as in "La ciba de Altabeira" by José Joaquín Pérez). All the Indians have proper names, even the women (who are numerous), for example Toella, Vahaní, Flor de Palma, Anacaona.

There is emphasis on the fact that this indigenous race lived in a paradisal landscape, an Eden seen by Ureña as primitive, then lost, with the arrival of the Spaniards (1880/1989). Pérez sees the landscape as "joyful" (p.111), and as a space where the Indian race lives in freedom; he specifies the land of the Indians as a "Quisqueyan paradise" (p.50) and "sacred soil" (p.37). In Perez's work there are various references to a "native Eden" (pp.86, 105), an image which, on the one hand, recalls the utopian view of America held by the discoverers and their era and, on the other, is a reminder to the Dominican people that this paradise is their native land. The native Eden described by Ureña and Pérez recalls the *locus amoenus* common to Romantic European literature and 18th century images of *le bon sauvage;* the Indians spend their time singing and dancing:

> Again and again, in *diumbas* and games and songs, the flock solemnized its rituals and altars.... Girded with beautiful flowers, the Indian virgins dance and sing the *areítos* of the ritual in sweet voices, happy and ingenuous (Ureña, pp.178, 181).[20]

Through this image of Eden, the authors incorporate the Indian into the European tradition, and into Dominican history, an incorporation which in itself constitutes another form of legitimizing the discourse. This act, however, results at the same time in the negation of the indigenous culture, traditions and people, as founding elements of Dominican society. The Indian is a scapegoat on a mythical level, a sacrificial lamb that will permit the beginning of renewed life, necessarily discontinous with the indigenous past. Indeed, the texts themselves present the Indians as discontinuous; they all die and there is no one left to establish a link between the past and its future.

The project on the part of the Dominican poets to legitimize the indigenous past as the glorious beginnings of Dominican history by means of their writings, remains at the margin of this history through the paradoxes which are implicit in their very discourses. These are Eurocentrically Romantic and literary and, therefore, contradictory to the contemporary social reality around them, as well as to the very concept they wished to promote, the Dominican national identity. The revitalization of the forgotten and disdained Indian past, which could be seen as an effort to revindicate this Indian, has instituted the latter as a myth in the past of the Other, in an exotic native Eden which had been extinguished and could hardly participate in a dynamic present in a Dominican Republic urged to be positive and progressive.

It is evident that the ideology presented was the dominant ideology of Santo Domingo culture during the period in question. All writers mentioned here had strong ties to the government and were active in state institutions (they held Government posts, founded schools, newspapers, etc.). The texts they wrote, published and publicized were models of reality in that they (re)produced, and so confirmed and institutionalized it in a certain way, reflecting and betraying this reality at the same time. In 19th-century Dominican Indianist works, literary conventions and rhetoric constituted an effective way of constructing the mirror of ideology, but it is at the same time a transparent glass which allows its contradictions to be seen.

ENDNOTES

1. This essay represents an elaboration of a paper read—in Spanish—at the Conference of the Canadian Association for Latin American and Caribbean Studies in Ottawa, Canada, in October of 1993, with the title "Mitificación de la historia como legitimación de la identidad nacional: una paradoja discursiva-ideológica en dos obras 'indigenistas' del siglo XIX en República Dominicana." This research is part of a larger investigation into the ideological contradictions of literary expression in 19th-century Dominican literature. Quotes from the Spanish texts have been translated for the purposes of this essay.
2. The *Lira de Quisqueya* (*Quisqueya* was taken to be the Indian—Taíno or Ciguayo—name for the island of Hispaniola).
3. In this paper the term Indianist will refer simply to a preoccupation in the works with native Americans—in this case the Indians of the Island of Hispaniola. Note that the *Fantasías indíjenas* by José Joaquín Pérez is also the first collection of poems with a coherent Indianist theme based on legends and traditions to be published in Spanish America. See Max Henríquez Ureña (1945/1966).
4. The contradictions are inevitable, of course, since ideology—as defined by Althusser (1971, p.162)—is the representation, in this case in the literary practice, of the *imaginary* relation to the real conditions of existence; hence his concept of ideology as "beautiful lies" (p.163).
5. In *Foundational Fictions* (1991), Doris Sommer has formulated the paradoxes presented in *Enriquillo* by Manuel de Jesús Galván in this respect, and David William Foster has worked on the theme in *The Argentine Generation of 1880: Ideology and Cultural Texts* (1990).

6. The poetry material of this essay can be said to be narrative although it has equally great lyric qualities, as will become evident.
7. This significant presence of both Romantic and Positivist ideologies provides interesting topics for the study of Salomé Ureña's poetry; she proves to move towards the margins of both, being patriotic in her "Romantic" compositions (which present her personal, intimate feelings), and personal in her "Positivist" works (which purport to invoke the patriotic, public spirit).
8. The use of the term *positive* in the discourse of the era generally refers specifically to a mode of thinking which accords with the Positivist philosophy.
9. Doris Sommer has elaborated this problematic, both for Santo Domingo and for Uruguay, in analyses of *Enriquillo* and *Tabaré,* respectively.
10. Max Henríquez Ureña states that there do not appear to be authentic *taíno* words in the phrase (p.286); Carlos Pérez (pp.89-95), also maintains that it is African.
11. "El viajero que hoy cruza los dominios / do el gran cacique Guarionex un día / su poder y sus glorias extendía, / combatiendo al audaz conquistador, / ve el Santo Cerro que en su cumbre ostenta / un Santuario, en memoria de la hazaña / que diera el triunfo a la indolente España / y a la cruz del humilde Redentor."
12. José Martí's letter to Manuel de Jesús Galván, praising the latter's novel *Enriquillo* makes this relation explicit: "How this *Enriquillo* seems like Jesus!" (Martí, "Prólogo" to Galván's Enriquillo, p.9). In that same text, Martí writes that the novel is not "historical legend, but a new and enchanting way to write our American history."
13. "Nuestra tierra, ... guarda en sus montes y en sus valles, en sus ríos y en sus torrentes, en cada piedra y en cada tronco y en cada gota de agua, alguna historia de dolor y de tribulaciones, que debemos evocar para que el mundo sepa los secretos de cosas no imaginadas en todo el trascurso de las edades históricas."
14. The *Sociedad Amigos del País* must be considered an important institution of the ideological apparatus. Examples of the activities of its members abound, but the following will suffice with respect to just those authors dealt with here: José Joaquín Pérez wrote prologues to the works of Galván and of Angulo Guridi (as well as for others); Salomé Ureña wrote a poem to José Joaquín Pérez that served as the prologue to the *Fantasías Indíjenas;* Javier Angulo Guridi, his brother Alejandro, Salomé Ureña's husband Francisco Henríquez y Carvajal, her brother-in-law Federico Henríquez y Carvajal, and Manuel de Jesús Galván were all writers and involved in newspaper publishing.
15. See, for example, *Pour une sociologie du roman,* Paris, Gallimard, 1964.
16. Woman-women's image play(s) an important role in the shaping of the national consciousness during this era, a contradictory role shaped by the contradictions of the Positivist and Romantic outlooks. This subject will be dealt with in a forthcoming study.

17. "Guacanagarí en las ruinas de Marién": Cómplice incauto del poder protervo / que en el nombre de Dios amor mentía, / llorando vivo como oscuro siervo / cuando dueño de todo me creía ...
18. .... preso Caonabo, llorando a solas / pasé las noches, pasé los días; / pero calmaba mis agonías / grata esperanza de verle al fin. / Mas en su fuerte grande canoa / cruzó los mares el arijuna, / y mi Caonabo fue sin fortuna / llevado lejos a otra región ...
19. Son tan lánguidos tus ojos, / bella indiana que yo adoro, / ¡que por ellos diera mi arco, / mi corona y mi tesoro! / Rojos corales como tus labios, / plumas de cisnes de albos destellos / te daría, hermosa, para collares, / para diadema de tus cabellos.
20. .... y en diumbas repetidas / y juegos y cantares, / su culto y sus altares / solemnizó la grey / ... / Ceñidas de lindas flores / van las vírgenes indianas, / y los areítos del culto / con voz dulcísima cantan / alegres y candorosas /.../

REFERENCES

Alcántara Almánzar, J. (1989). Prólogo. In J.J. Pérez, *Fantasías indígenas y otros poemas,* pp. 9-27. Santo Domingo: Corripio.

Althusser, L. (1971). Ideology and ideological state apparatuses. *Lenin and philosophy and other essays,* pp. 127-186. New York: Monthly Review Press.

[Angulo] Guridi, J. (1882/1953). Iguaniona. Drama histórico en verso y en tres actos. Ciudad Trujillo: Eda. Montalvo.

Cassá, R. (1974). *Los taínos de la Española.* Santo Domingo: Ed. de la UASD.

Castellanos, J. (Ed.) (1874). *Lira de Quisqueya. Poesías dominicanas.* Santo Domingo: Impr. de García Hermanos.

Céspedes, D. (1989). Salomé Ureña o la metrificiación de una ideología: el positivismo. In Salomé Ureña, *Poesías completas,* pp. 7-55. Santo Domingo: Corripio.

Domínguez, J. (1977). La economía dominicana durante la Primera República. In T. Mejía-Ricart (Ed.), *La sociedad dominicana durante la Primera República* (1844-1865), pp.85-108. Santo Domingo: UASD.

Foster, D.W. (1990). *The Argentine generation of 1880. Ideology and cultural texts.* Columbia and London: University of Missouri Press.

Franco, F.J. (1977). Clases, grupos y conflictos sociales en el marco histórico de la independencia dominicana. In T. Mejía-Ricart (Ed.). *La sociedad dominicana durante la Primera República (1844-1861),* pp. 47-76. Santo Domingo: UASD.

Galván, M. de J. (1879-1882/1966). *Enriquillo* (7th ed.). Santo Domingo: Ed. Librería Dominicana.

Goldmann, L. (1964). *Pour une sociologie du roman.* Paris: Gallimard.

Henríquez Ureña, M. (1945/1966). *Panorama histórico de la literatura dominicana* (2nd ed.). Santo Domingo: Julio Postigo Eds.

Hoetink, H. (1972). *El pueblo dominicano 1850-1900.* (2nd ed.). Santiago de los Caballeros: Univ. Católica Madre y Maestra.

Martí, J. (1882). Prólogo. In Manuel de Jesús Galván, *Enriquillo,* p.9. Santo Domingo: Ed. Librería Dominicana.

Moya Pons, F. (1981/1983). *Manual de historia dominicana* (7th ed.). Santiago de los Caballeros: Univ. Católica Madre y Maestra.

Paz, O. (1950/1970). *El laberinto de la soledad.* México: FCE.

Pérez, C. (1970). Notes. In J.J. Pérez, *Fantasías indígenas.* Santo Domingo: Univ. Nacional Pedro Henríquez Ureña.

Pérez, J.J. (1882/1953). Prólogo. In J.A. Guridi, *Iguaniona,* pp.xi-xix. Ciudad Trujillo: Montalvo.

———. (1882/1966). Prólogo. In M. de J. Galván, *Enriquillo,* pp.3-7. Santo Domingo: Impr. de García Hermanos.

———. (1877/1989). Fantasías indíjenas. In *Fantasías indígenas y otros poemas,* pp.35-168 . Santo Domingo: Corripio.

Sommer, D. (1991). *Foundational fictions.* Berkeley: University of California Press.

Ureña de Henríquez, S. (1880/1989). Anacaona. In *Poesías completas,* pp.176-248. Santo Domingo: Corripio.

CHAPTER VII

HISTORICAL PERSPECTIVES

HISTOIRE ET LITTÉRATURE : LA REPRÉSENTATION DE L'ANNÉE 1938 DANS DEUX ROMANS CHILIENS[1]

José Del Pozo

Parmi les romanciers chiliens de la génération de 1938 qui ont écrit sur un fond historique de leur pays, deux d'entre eux font l'objet d'une analyse ici, pour dégager les rapports entre le travail du romancier et celui de l'historien. Les événements de 1938, c'est-à-dire, la victoire du Front populaire au Chili ainsi que la guerre qui se déroulait en Espagne au même moment, se retrouvent dans les romans de Fernando Alegría et Guillermo Atías, sujets aux relectures et aux représentations qui conviennent au travail du créateur. Ces différentes interprétations de l'histoire nous montrent que la vision du romancier peut devenir, à son tour, une source d'inspiration pour les historiens.

Two Chilean novelists from the generation of 1938 are examined in the light of their creative relationship with historical fact. The events of 1938: the victory of the Popular Front in Chile and the war taking place at the same time in Spain, are both reinterpreted in the novels of Fernando Alegría and Guillermo Atías. These different rereadings of history also show us that the writer's vision of the past can become, in its turn, an inspiration for historians.

*

LA PRODUCTION DES ÉCRIVAINS chiliens dans le domaine du roman historique, malgré l'héritage laissé par Blest Gana depuis la publication de *Durante la Reconquista* (Pendant la reconquête) à la fin des années 1890[2] est assez mince. Ceci contraste avec la fécondité de ce courant dans d'autres pays latino-américains. Mis à part la guerre civile de 1891 qui donna lieu à la publication de plusieurs ouvrages, les autres faits historiques n'ont pas eu le même impact au niveau littéraire (Zamudio, 1973, p.20).

Les événements de l'année 1938 ont cependant suscité un certain intérêt chez les écrivains: au moins deux parmi ces derniers, et pas les moins connus du pays ont choisi d'écrire sur ce sujet. Ces auteurs sont Guillermo Atías et Fernando Alegría. Il y avait certes, de quoi les émouvoir : 1938 avait été l'année de la victoire historique du Front populaire, qui portait pour la première fois dans l'histoire du Chili sur une alliance des partis du centre-gauche; en même temps avait eu lieu la dramatique tentative de coup d'état par les national-socialistes chiliens, qui s'était soldée par un bain de sang.[3] Devant cette période riche en événements, les écrivains ont réagi en choisissant divers aspects de la réalité et en accordant une signification différente aux faits et aux personnages historiques. Cet ensemble d'ouvrages nous permet d'explorer les rapports entre la littérature et l'histoire.

Comment définir le roman historique? Selon certains, il ne suffit pas que l'oeuvre littéraire porte sur le passé pour faire partie de cette catégorie; il faut de plus, que les faits historiques réels constituent le sujet central du roman. Les personnages fictifs ou semi-véridiques auraient comme fonction de mettre en valeur la partie proprement historique. Autrement dit, le contexte historique ne devrait pas servir uniquement de toile de fond aux personnages (Sanchez 1968, p.333).

Un deuxième critère réside dans une certaine distance qui doit exister entre l'auteur et les événements historiques traités. Par exemple, même si le roman *A través de la tempestad* (A travers l'orage) du Chilien Luis Orrego Luco porte sur la guerre civile de 1891, il ne constitue pas un roman historique, puisque l'auteur vécut lui-même cette époque. Le même raisonnement s'applique au roman bien connu de Mariano Azuela, *Los de abajo* (Ceux d'en bas), sur la révolution mexicaine. Dans ce cas et dans bien d'autres, il faudrait plutôt parler de roman politique (Sanchez 1968, p.436).

Dans la perspective de cet article, ces considérations ne sont pas de nature à exclure Atías et Alegría. En ce qui a trait au premier argument, c'est bel et bien la réalité historique qui constitue la raison d'être de leurs romans. Quant au deuxième, il pourrait s'appliquer aux deux auteurs chiliens qui ont écrit sur 1938, puisqu'ils furent contemporains de cette époque, même s'ils ont rédigé leurs oeuvres une vingtaine d'années plus tard.

Mais cet argument ne suffit pas pour les disqualifier: en effet, ce qui m'intéresse n'est pas de déterminer si leurs romans sont historiques ou politiques, mais plutôt de discuter leur apport au travail de l'historien.

On ne peut pas demander aux écrivains même si certains se sont appuyés sur une documentation assez solide—d'apporter de nouvelles informations sur l'époque qu'ils décrivent. Par contre, leurs romans peuvent permettre de «mieux voir ce qui est déjà connu» (Daspré, 1975, p.239). Dans la mesure où un écrivain crée des personnages fictifs incarnant des traits propres à des personnages réels, il nous permet de réfléchir sur le passé, de voir sous de nouveaux angles la signification des événements et d'imaginer de nouvelles orientations de recherche. Ceci est particulièrement vrai lorsqu'il s'agit de 1938. En effet, aussi surprenant que cela puisse paraître, les événements de cette année, qui ont été utilisés à profusion dans la propagande électorale de plusieurs partis dans les années ultérieures, n'ont pas vraiment fait l'objet de recherches systématiques par les historiens. La vision des romanciers peut donc s'avérer féconde comme source d'inspiration pour les historiens.[4]

Enfin, le roman historique, avec la création de héros et de mythes, contribue aussi à forger la mentalité du public et arrive ainsi à mieux définir l'identité nationale. Ce dernier trait a d'ailleurs été identifié comme l'un des plus importants du roman historique latino-américain (Jitrik, 1986, p.16-17). Comme nous le verrons, l'oeuvre littéraire produite autour de 1938, incorpore de diverses façons ces trois aspects.

LA «GÉNÉRATION DE 1938»

Les auteurs qui nous intéressent ici partagent une série de caractéristiques, la première étant le fait qu'ils ont été profondément influencés par les événements de 1938. Cette symbiose historico/littéraire est tellement importante que les critiques ont constitué la «génération de 1938». Même si certaines sources indiquent une autre année comme point de référence chronologique,[5] tous sont d'accord pour identifier certains traits communs chez les écrivains qui font partie de ce groupe : l'influence du marxisme, la prédominance des thèmes urbains, la sensibilité aux problèmes sociaux, l'importance accordée aux héros collectifs et la tentative de «surmonter l'expression régionaliste, par le biais d'un réalisme populaire, qui visait une projection universelle» (Promis, 1977, p.99-100). Le plus connu parmi ses représentants, Fernando Alegría, abonde dans ce sens, en affirmant que sa génération se distinguait pour avoir «incorporé à la littérature certaines couches de notre société qui avaient été ignorées par les écrivains et avoir considéré les luttes pour l'émancipation politique et économique de la classe travailleuse» (Alegría, 1962, p.116). Ceci s'explique, selon l'auteur, par l'influence de la révolution russe, de la révolution mexicaine et surtout de la guerre d'Espagne qui avaient profondément marqué sa génération et ce, tant sur le plan esthétique que politique.[6]

La préférence pour les thèmes urbains n'était pas un phénomène entièrement nouveau dans la littérature chilienne. Des écrivains tels qu'Eduardo Barrios, Augusto D'Halmar et Alberto Romero avaient décrit la misère des habitants des *conventillos* de Santiago durant le premier tiers du siècle.[7] Mais ils cherchaient surtout à explorer les aspects extérieurs de la vie de leurs personnages, en insistant sur leur façon de s'habiller, le type de nourriture qu'ils consommaient, leur langage et leur logement; de plus, la narration était rendue à travers un personnage qui ne faisait pas partie de ce même milieu. Ceci faisait en sorte que «ce qui était accessoire devenait le thème fondamental d'un espace qui était décrit par quelqu'un qui était étranger à ce monde». (Guerra, 1987, p.107)

Par contre, la génération de 1938 cherchait à donner une perspective intérieure au monde qu'elle décrivait, en essayant de créer des personnages plus authentiques et en utilisant souvent des souvenirs personnels, puisque les écrivains de cette génération provenaient du même milieu social qu'ils évoquaient dans leurs romans.(Guerra, 1987, p.107).

Il fait souligner une autre distinction importante entre les écrivains de 1938 et leurs prédécesseurs. Parmi ces derniers, quelques-uns avaient déjà choisi des ouvriers comme protagonistes. Néanmoins, ces personnages n'étaient identifiés ni à un parti politique ni à une idéologie particulière. Ils incarnaient le sentiment de protestation ouvrière à son état brut. On en trouve un bon exemple dans le roman de Manuel Rojas, *Punta de Rieles* (Croisement de voies ferrées). L'un des personnages principaux, Romilio Llanca, ouvrier itinérant, parle de lui-même dans les termes suivants :

> La politique ne m'a jamais intéressé. Etre député ou même sénateur, comme d'autres l'ont fait, des ouvriers comme moi, qui une fois rendus au Parlement cessent de se comporter comme des travailleurs et deviennent des bourgeois, cela ne va pas avec moi. Ce que j'aime c'est la lutte dans les syndicats, sans chercher la transformation de la société, comme les anarchistes, ni chercher à remplacer les patrons dans la direction des entreprises, comme les socialistes et communistes ... Je me suis promis que je ne serai jamais

autre chose qu'un ouvrier ... Devenir patron ou un agent intermédiaire, ça non, jamais, car je cesserai d'être ce que j'aime. (Rojas, 1963, p.47-48)

L'approche des représentants de la génération de 1938 est toute autre. Dans leurs romans, les personnages adoptent des attitudes politiques beaucoup plus définies. Cela peut s'expliquer par le décalage des générations : contrairement à Rojas, ces écrivains ont grandi à une époque où les partis politiques—surtout ceux de la gauche—sont bien établis et constituent les canaux d'expression habituels pour ceux qui adhèrent aux idéaux de la classe ouvrière.

Ils sont nés à l'époque de la première guerre mondiale. Ils appartiennent à la classe moyenne et sont allés à l'Université. Parmi eux, Fernando Alegría s'est le plus illustré. Diplômé de l'Institut Pédagogique de l'Université du Chili, il est parti pour les Etats-Unis dans les années 1950 où il devint professeur. L'engagement politique constitue un autre trait commun. Le premier ouvrage de Fernando Alegría, publié en 1938 lorsque son auteur n'avait que 20 ans, était une biographie d'Emilio Recabarren, le fondateur du Parti communiste au Chili. Quant à Guillermo Atías, il a milité dans le PC sans s'afficher ouvertement car il était employé dans une banque et le Parti a préféré qu'il ne révèle pas son engagement politique.

Ces écrivains appuyèrent ouvertement la candidature de Salvador Allende en 1970. Atías a même écrit un roman engagé durant l'Unité populaire, *Y corría el billete ...* (Et l'argent circulait en abondance), publié par Quimantú, la maison d'édition du gouvernement.[8] Alegría continuait à vivre en Californie où il résidait depuis longtemps.

On retrouve ces mêmes traits dans la plupart des autres écrivains de cette génération.[9] Ces antécédents permettent de mieux comprendre les raisons du regain d'intérêt pour le roman historique ou politique : il n'y a pas de doute que la décision d'écrire au sujet des événements qui constituaient un repère important dans l'histoire de la gauche chilienne correspondait à un engagement politique de la part de l'écrivain et faisait partie d'une tendance grandissante dans l'espace culturel chilien en faveur des forces qui ultérieurement allaient porter Salvador Allende au pouvoir.[10] Ainsi, on peut affirmer que la production littéraire au sujet des événements de 1938 représente un apport important en vue de définir l'identité nationale chilienne à travers un nouveau prisme.

FERNANDO ALEGRÍA : LA VIOLENCE AU CHILI ET DANS LE MONDE DES ANNÉES 1930

Le roman d'Alegría, *Mañana los guerreros* (Les guerriers viendront demain) publié en 1964, mentionne l'influence de l'Espagne, mais il accorde beaucoup de place aux événements de l'histoire chilienne qui aident à comprendre 1938. Cependant, leur déroulement n'a pas lieu uniquement pendant l'année en question. Il y a plusieurs références au passé, dont l'impact de la crise mondiale de 1929, qui aident à comprendre le présent. Les personnages principaux sont des jeunes en train de décider leur orientation politique et personnelle et qui sont en quelque sorte en confrontation avec la génération précédente.

Les protagonistes sont un couple de jeunes étudiants, Juan Luis et Elisa, dont les parents habitaient en province et avaient joui d'une bonne situation économique jusqu'au moment de la crise. A partir de 1930 cependant, leur situation économique s'était détériorée : ils avaient perdu les terres qu'ils possédaient dans le sud et avaient été contraints à quitter Santiago, où ils s'efforçaient de cacher leur pauvreté. Cette mise en situation est importante, car elle nous montre Juan Luis et Elisa comme des jeunes qui s'opposent à leurs parents, en partie à cause du fait que ceux-ci semblent appartenir à une génération qui a échoué.

Ce fossé apparaît dans un dialogue entre Juan Luis et son père. Celui-ci parle avec fierté des valeurs de sa génération, du Parti radical, de la classe moyenne et des actions des «nobles combattants» qui avaient contribué par une grève à la chute d'Ibáñez en 1931.[11] Mais le jeune Juan Luis a gardé un souvenir bien différent des événements. Pour lui, cette époque n'était pas celle d'un «noble combat» mais plutôt celle des gestes de vengeance d'une foule déchaînée qui s'en prenait aux carabineros[12] pour exprimer sa joie devant la chute de la dictature. Il se souvient de ce qu'il a vu de ses yeux d'enfant :

> C'étaient des personnes mal habillées, des chômeurs en haillons, avec des foulards sales autour du cou, quelques ouvriers qui montraient une froide détermination dans leurs visages, des jeunes avec un regard fou, prêts à tout, quelques visages criminels, des annonceurs de journaux, des voleurs ... (Alegría, 1964, p.108)

Ces gens s'étaient lancés contre un *carabinero* sans défense

> ... acculé au mur, avec son uniforme déchiré, à bout de souffle, qui nous regardait avec les yeux d'un animal encerclé ... Il tomba à terre sous les coups de la foule, qui l'acheva avec une barre de fer, avec laquelle ils ont déchiqueté son crâne. (Alegría 1964, p.108-109)

Cette violence de l'année 1931 s'ajoute à celle qui provenait de la vieille Europe, la guerre civile espagnole et les tueries nazies. Cette vague déferle sur le Chili et provoque une nouvelle explosion de violence : Grove menaçait de tuer les oligarques (Alegría, 1964, p.72), les nacis[13] étaient à l'origine des attentats à la bombe qui ont causé la mort de plusieurs vendeuses de pâtisserie dans une station ferroviaire,[14] les batailles à tirs de revolver entre les nacis et les marxistes étaient fréquentes[15] et le leader naci, Jorge González von Marées tirait une balle de pistolet sur le président Arturo Alessandri en pleine séance du Parlement (Alegría, 1964, p.163).

Dans ce contexte, des jeunes tel que Juan Luis, étaient des «guerriers» qui avaient, comme point commun, la haine et le désabusement. Plus encore, ils étaient

> des terroristes, dévorés par l'angoisse d'une vie de quartier sans espoir, qui marchaient avec le veston déchiré et les pantalons frippés et sortaient au centre-ville pour s'attaquer aux *carabineros,* démolir les statues devant l'Université et conspirer dans les restaurants.[16]

Certains d'entre eux, comme Mario, le frère d'Elisa, adhèrent au parti naci, dont l'activité leur donnaient «une sensation d'exaltation, avec l'uniforme, la chemise, les bottes allemandes, les défilés, les cris de guerre et la matraque ...» (Alegría, 1964, p.184).

Chez Elisa, l'esprit guerrier se manifeste dans sa décision d'avoir l'enfant qu'elle attend de Juan Luis, même si elle n'est pas certaine de se marier avec celui-ci et en dépit de l'opposition de sa famille. Pour Juan Luis, la rébellion implique la recherche des héros du passé : il s'identifie à Martín Rivas, qu'il perçoit comme «un guérillero ou un terroriste, quelqu'un qui prit d'assaut une maison à la hauteur de son talent, qui s'empara de la femme qu'il méritait» (Alegría, 1964, p.133). II admire aussi Carrera, Bilbao et Alessandri le Lion, «avant que celui-ci ne tombe sous l'influence de ses amis bourgeois». Pour lui, ces personnages incarnent aussi le patriotisme, car ils se sont battus pour la liberté.[17] Il compte leurs luttes aux actions contre le fascisme : lui et ses amis veulent «imposer au reste du monde l'image de notre patrie, l'imposer dans un geste héroïque, montrer comment dans ce dernier coin de la planète on gagnait la bataille contre le fascisme» (Alegría, 1964, p.200).

Juan Luis trouve son idole en 1938 dans la personne de Pedro Aguirre Cerda, le candidat du Front populaire :[18]

> Cette année, notre héros était un homme petit de taille, la peau foncée, le visage marqué par la petite vérole, avec une petite moustache et une cigarette dans le coin de sa main, qui aimait le vin, quelqu'un qui parlait d'une voix rauque, comme dans les routes de province ... don Pedro aimait aussi sa patrie. (Alegría, 1964, p.199)

Vers la fin du roman, il est question de la tuerie de jeunes nacis, qui avaient échoué dans leur tentative de coup d'état, peu avant l'élection présidentielle. Parmi eux se trouvent Mario et Lucho, frères d'Elisa. L'auteur décrit l'angoisse de Mario durant cette journée. Lorsque l'aventure tourne mal, il espère s'en tirer en vie : «je pensais que, au pire, on serait passés à tabac par la police, nous resterions ensuite en prison pendant quelques semaines et ensuite ce serait l'exil» (Alegría, 1964, p.244). Mais bientôt il devient évident que la situation est grave. Yuric, l'un des leaders, les informe que personne ne viendra les aider : «croyez-moi, nous avons perdu. Les *carabineros* ont enfoncé les portes de l'Université à coups de canon ... il y a plusieurs morts. Les militaires qui avaient promis de nous appuyer n'ont pas respecté leur parole» (Alegría 1964, p.248). Ensuite, c'est le massacre : les jeunes nacis se rendent à la police, on les concentre dans l'édifice de l'Assurance-travail (*Seguro obrero*) où ils sont froidement assassinés par les *carabineros.* La description de ces événements sanglants occupe plusieurs pages du roman.

Dans les jours qui suivent, les personnages réfléchissent sur la signification de cet épisode. Si certains pensent que «ce fut une affaire des bourgeois», Juan Luis a une autre opinion. Il se rend compte que

> Parmi les soixante-et-un nacis assassinés il y avait trois mécaniciens, un coiffeur, un électricien, un plombier, un dessinateur, deux chauffeurs, un employé de boulangerie, plusieurs ouvriers sans qualification, vingt-sept employés de bureau, seize étudiants et un avocat. (Alegría 1964, p.259)

Malgré cette tragédie, l'élection présidentielle a lieu normalement le 25 octobre, au milieu du printemps austral. Il n'y a plus de batailles à coups de revolver, mais une mobilisation de la gauche en vue de contrer les tentatives de fraude de la droite qui cherche à acheter le vote des électeurs pour faire triompher son candidat, Gustavo Ross. Le Front Populaire gagne par une étroite majorité et une manifestation de masses a lieu au centre-ville. Les partisans de Ross «sont restés chez eux, la carabine de côté, à se livrer à des prières ou tout simplement à attendre» (Alegría 1964, p.271). La violence semble chose du passé. C'est la raison pour laquelle l'auteur termine son livre sur la note suivante :

> Demain, les guerriers marcheront sans armes dans les rues de la ville. Et au lieu de porter des casques, des boucliers et des drapeaux, ils porteront les fruits de l'été chaud. Ils marcheront à travers les villes, illuminées par une éclatante lumière, alors que les morts, couverts par la verdure, leur parleront d'une voix tranquille. Et nous allons répondre à leurs salutations et à leurs questions avec la voix que la renaissance de la vie nous a donnée. (Alegría, 1964, p.273-274)

Les événements de 1938 sont présentés comme le résultat d'un ensemble de circonstances, dont l'origine se trouve autant au Chili qu'à l'étranger. En outre, l'auteur cherche les antécédents historiques dans l'évolution du Chili depuis la dictature d'Ibáñez, dont la chute avait déclenché une période agitée qui persista durant le gouvernement d'Arturo Alessandri.[19] Ceux-ci aident à mieux comprendre l'ambiance qui prédominait en 1938, le but de la lutte politique de l'époque et l'état d'esprit des contemporains. On y trouve aussi des références explicites à des faits et personnages réels de cette époque, tels Pedro Aguirre Cerda, Carlos Ibáñez, Alessandri, Grove, González von Marées, Yuric et Ross. Enfin, les personnages ne sont pas tous reliés aux mouvements de la gauche. L'attrait du nazisme transparaît chez plusieurs des protagonistes, principalement dans le cas du jeune Mario.

Ce qui impressionne le plus dans le livre c'est sa section finale. Comme on l'a vu plus haut, l'auteur laisse entendre qu'avec la tenue de l'élection présidentielle le Chili a laissé derrière lui la vague de violence. Il est également vrai qu'à partir de 1938 toutes les élections se sont déroulées normalement et que les résultats ont été respectés jusqu'en 1973. Mais il est vrai que le roman n'aide pas à comprendre comment le climat de violence qui avait prédominé jusque-là disparaît subitement et pourquoi les jeunes guerriers mettent de côté leurs armes pour se consacrer à des activités paisibles. Dans ce sens, Alegría pose un problème qui demeure sans réponse.

GUILLERMO ATÍAS : UNE VISION RÉTROSPECTIVE ET DÉSABUSÉE DE L'EXPÉRIENCE DU FRONT POPULAIRE

Le roman d'Atías, *A la sombra de los días* (A l'ombre des jours) se démarque nettement des autres écrits dont il est question ici. L'action de son récit s'étend alternativement sur deux périodes chronologiques : 1938 et la fin des années 1950. Cette technique permet à l'auteur de situer les événements de 1938 dans une perspective historique, et de se livrer à une réflexion sur la signification de cette expérience pour la gauche chilienne, une génération plus tard.

Les trois personnages principaux, deux hommes et une femme, forment un triangle complexe. Les deux hommes militent politiquement dans des camps opposés : Mauricio Gálvez est un haut dirigeant du Parti socialiste; Lambert est un jeune professeur de français qui malgré lui devient militant nazi. Sara, pendant quelque temps la femme de Lambert, devient plus tard la maîtresse de Mauricio. L'auteur a donné beaucoup moins d'importance à son personnage. Puisqu'elle ne s'intéresse pas à la politique, sa fonction semble se limiter à servir de lien entre les deux hommes, qui autrement n'auraient rien en commun.

Atías cherche les origines des événements de 1938 dans les années précédentes. Lambert est originaire d'une province du sud; son père, de souche suisse-allemande, possédait une petite industrie de sciage, mais l'avait perdue à cause de la crise économique. C'est alors que l'on décida que le jeune Lambert irait à Santiago pour faire ses études, mais étant donné la situation difficile de ses parents, il avait très peu d'argent en arrivant dans la capitale. Il s'assimile alors aux nombreux pauvres de la ville: «en 1933, les chômeurs faisaient légion à Santiago».[20] Ce détail est important, car c'est cette situation précaire qui oblige Lambert à accepter l'aide économique de son oncle, Alfred Lambert, un ardent militant naci. L'oncle l'invite aussi à assister à des soirées chez lui, où l'on discute de politique. Lambert se voit ainsi amené à adhérer au Parti naci, même s'il ne ressent aucun enthousiasme pour cette cause.

Les pages consacrées à cette expérience donnent lieu à des descriptions animées. L'un des passages les mieux réussis est la description d'une scène dans un restaurant lorsque Lambert est témoin d'un incident provoqué par des jeunes militants qui, cherchant à provoquer et à conscientiser les clients font irruption dans établissement :

> Ils étaient quatre, portant des chemises brunes, des ceintures en bandoulière, des casquettes et des petites matraques dans leurs poignets.Ils avancèrent parmi les tables, à un moment où le local était bondé de clients. Une fois assis à une table proche de celle de Lambert, l'un d'eux avait crié «Vive le Chili!», avec l'assentiment de ses camarades ... S'adressant au garçon de table d'une voix haute et forte, pour que tous les clients les entendissent, ils commandèrent des boissons gazeuses, afin de susciter la surprise de la clientèle, qui ne consommait pas de telles boissons à cette heure-là de la nuit.... Celui qui semblait être le leader du groupe commença par la suite un discours dans lequel il dénonçait les habitudes vicieuses du peuple chilien, qui se trouvait, disait-il, empoisonné par l'alcool.[21] L'avenir de l'Amérique latine et du Chili, pays de blancs, ne pouvait pas être confié à une race en décadence par l'ivrognerie». (Atías, 1965, p.68-69)

L'épisode se termine par une bagarre entre les clients et les jeunes; Lambert intervient pour aider un des nacis qui a été blessé, et cette intervention resserre les liens entre Lambert et son oncle. Plus tard, il tombe amoureux de Sara, la secrétaire d'un haut dirigeant du parti. Comme Lambert, la jeune femme n'est pas liée aux nacis par conviction idéologique. En effet elle affirme : «je les trouve sympa parce qu'ils sont totalement fous» (Atías, 1965, p.94). Les amoureux n'hésitent pas à se servir de l'argent de l'oncle pour fréquenter les restaurants et les hôtels. Finalement, ils se marient et l'auteur nous dit que des militants nacis en uniforme ainsi que des membres du corps diplomatique allemand sont présents à la cérémonie.[22]

Par la suite, Lambert participe à diverses actions de provocation en milieu ouvrier et de sabotage contre des entreprises américaines. Il est aussi du groupe qui se lance dans l'aventure du coup d'état du 5 septembre 1938. Les dirigeants du parti avaient fait croire aux participants qu'une partie de l'armée et le général Ibáñez étaient avec eux; pour cette raison, lorsque des militaires viennent les encercler au siège central de l'Université du Chili, ils se rendent en disant que «nous n'avons pas d'ordres de tirer sur l'Armée qui est notre allié potentiel» (Atías, p. 204). Mais les militaires les amènent vers l'édifice de l'Assurance-travail, où les *carabineros* déclenchent le massacre que l'on connaît. L'auteur fait en sorte que Lambert soit l'un de ceux qui a la vie sauve.

L'autre personnage central, Mauricio Gálvez, est moins élaboré. L'auteur nous donne très peu d'informations sur lui avant 1938. En quelques lignes, il raconte que Gálvez avait été dirigeant universitaire socialiste et qu'il avait fait par la suite une brève carrière dans le parti. Au moment où le Front populaire gagne l'élection avec Aguirre, il est membre du comité central. L'auteur dit comment Mauricio abandonne vite ses idéaux révolutionnaires pour se servir du pouvoir à des fins de promotion personnelle. Il accède à un poste important dans l'administration publique et obtient un appartement de luxe, situé en plein centre-ville, bien équipé, «que tous convoitaient, comme si c'était un petit paradis» (Atías, 1965, p.14-15). Le parti, en 1939 est décrit comme une organisation hétérogène dont faisaient partie des anciens trotskystes et des anarchistes. Plus grave encore, les hauts dirigeants avaient cessé d'être à l'écoute des militants de la base. Pour illustrer ce fait, l'auteur raconte une scène dans laquelle un représentant du syndicat des opérateurs de tramway essaie sans succès de se faire entendre par les membres du comité central. Il avait besoin de l'appui des autorités du parti pour la grève que lui et ses camarades allaient déclencher. Mais les dirigeants préfèrent écouter les propos d'une poétesse socialiste vénézuélienne, de passage au Chili :

> une femme aux yeux radieux et dont la voix avait des accents tropicaux.... Ensorcelés, les cinq socialistes chiliens l'écoutaient sans sourciller, même si ses propos allaient à l'encontre des thèses marxistes orthodoxes. (Atías, 1965, p.106)

Ces souvenirs reviennent une vingtaine d'années plus tard. En 1963, Mauricio a abandonné la vie de militant; il fait un voyage dans une province du sud afin de rencontrer Sara, qui a quitté Lambert et qui est devenue sa maîtresse depuis des années. En arrivant au village du rendez-vous, Mauricio est reconnu par un libraire qui se met à lui parler des idéaux de 1938 et du désenchantement qui suivit. «Et notre cher Front populaire? Il n'a été qu'une étape romantique, un échec ... et maintenant, on veut répéter la même histoire» (Atías, 1965, p.114).[23] Le libraire poursuit son accusation contre la gauche : celle-ci, dit-il, ne s'est pas renouvelée, elle utilise des mots d'ordre dépassés en continuant de rendre hommage à l'URSS, alors que «la nouvelle vague s'implante dans notre cour, chez les ouvriers industriels» (Atías, 1965, p.125).[24] De mauvaise humeur, Mauricio admet que le libraire a raison.

De retour à Santiago, Mauricio vit une autre expérience qui lui montre à quel point ses idéaux sont derrière lui. Dans un café, il a une discussion improvisée avec un groupe de jeunes qui se moquent de lui à cause de son âge, puis lui font sentir leur désintéressement face à la politique. Les parents de plusieurs d'entre eux avaient été militants communistes ou socialistes et certains avaient même souffert la répression de 1948.[25] Cependant, la seule passion des jeunes c'est le soccer. L'un d'eux dit :

«Nous autres, on ne fait pas de politique, on n'aime pas ça. Qu'est-ce que nos parents y ont gagné? Ils sont foutus, comme le père de Juan» (Atías, 1965, p.134).

A la fin, Mauricio prend la décision de rompre avec Sara et de réintégrer le parti. Dans les dernières pages, l'auteur nous livre une longue réflexion de Mauricio sur la signification historique du Front populaire: si cette expérience a échoué, «c'est parce qu'il s'agissait seulement d'une stratégie antifasciste ... nous avons laissé intact l'appareil institutionnel de la bourgeoisie» (Atías, 1965, p.220). Il dit aussi que, malgré tout, «en 1938 nous avons livré de bonnes batailles ...» (Atías 1965, p.221).

La nouveauté chez Atías c'est la vision rétrospective qu'il offre sur l'expérience du Front populaire, grâce au récit à travers le temps. Dans cette optique, le personnage clé est celui de Mauricio Gálvez. Curieusement, même si le personnage de Lambert est beaucoup plus élaboré sur les plans humains et psychologiques, il l'est beaucoup moins au niveau politique. En effet, l'auteur consacre peu d'espace au nazisme et à des questions telles que les raisons de la croissance de cette idéologie dans les années 1930. Une autre lacune, plus importante encore, c'est l'absence quasi totale de références au Parti communiste. De fait, Atías choisit de se concentrer uniquement sur le cas du Parti socialiste, comme si cette formation était la seule de la gauche chilienne. Lorsqu'il mène le récit aux années 1960, une autre lacune de taille apparaît : la révolution cubaine n'est même pas mentionnée.[26]

Le message prédominant du récit d'Atías est que toute adhésion à une cause de jeunesse, peu importe laquelle, sera suivie d'une désillusion. C'est peut-être à cause de cela que les trois personnages sont peu attrayants : ils ont des personnalités faibles, incohérentes sur le plan idéologiques et ils entretiennent des relations affectives maladives, qu'eux-mêmes ne réussissent pas à expliquer. Si ce roman constitue un apport novateur aux rapports entre la fiction et l'histoire, il présente en même temps plusieurs zones d'ombre en ce qui a trait à l'analyse historique, et le ton global de l'ouvrage laisse un goût amer.

Si on compare les romans examinés ici avec d'autres ouvrages traitant du même sujet en Amérique latine, force est d'admettre que leur contribution est d'une portée limitée. Les personnages principaux proviennent tous de la classe moyenne et l'action des romans se rédoule principalement dans ce même milieu. On n'y trouve pratiquement aucune tentative d'incorporer des personnages d'autres couches de la société : les possédants autant que les ouvriers ou paysans sont exclus de l'univers exploré.

Une discrimination semblable est à signaler en ce qui concerne les femmes qui font des apparitions plutôt marginales. Enfin, aucun des romans ne réussit à créer des personnages épiques qui suscitent l'adhésion enthousiaste du lecteur. Ils se situent loin des créations d'un Jorge Amado ou d'un Mario Vargas Llosa qui décrivent des univers riches en personnages de toutes les origines sociales.

Une deuxième observation s'impose ici. Comme ces romans s'inspirent d'un réalisme social ou du roman historique traditionnel, le récit est linéaire. Il n'y a pas ce que certains appellent "conscious distortions of history, through omissions, anachronisms and exaggerations" (Menton, 1993, p.22-25). Il n'y a pas non plus trace d'une vision imprégnée d'ironie (Singler, 1993, p.41). Bref, on est loin de ce qu'on appelle le «nouveau roman historique latino-américain» (Menton, 1993, p.14-38).

Malgré ces partis pris, ces romans peuvent contribuer à l'oeuvre de l'historien sur cette période de la vie socio-politique du Chili. Leur contribution se situe au niveau de l'interprétation des faits autour de l'an 1938. Ainsi, ces écrits incitent le lecteur à se demander jusqu'à quel point la guerre civile espagnole et l'antifascisme ont joué un rôle dans la formation et la victoire du Front populaire. Les rares auteurs qui se sont penchés sur cette question sont de l'avis que l'apparition du Front s'explique essentiellement par des facteurs de la politique interne chilienne. La décision du Parti radical de retirer son appui au président Alessandri et de chercher l'alliance avec les Partis socialiste et communiste aurait été, selon certains, un facteur clé (Stevenson, 1942). L'antifascisme aurait joué un rôle purement secondaire, malgré l'existence au Chili d'un Parti national-socialiste.

Le du roman d'Alegría pourrait aussi amener les historiens à faire des recherches sur un sujet qui demeure à peu près inexploré : la situation des jeunes. Comment ce groupe percevait-il la politique dans les années agitées de 1930? Etaient-ils vraiment des «guerriers» ou s'agissait-il de la même attitude anticonformiste ou rebelle que l'on retrouve dans n'importe quelle génération de jeunes confrontés à un tournant de l'histoire? Par ailleurs, comment expliquer la terrible tuerie des nacis en 1938? D'après certains, il s'agirait d'un épisode qui n'a pas son égal dans l'histoire du Chili. Selon Ricardo Donoso il y a eu d'autres faits sanglants, telles que les exécutions durant la guerre civile de 1891 et l'assassinat de Manuel Rodríguez, l'un des héros de l'indépendance. Cependant, il affirme que «aucun de ces épisodes ne porte la marque de la férocité et de la lâcheté des événements du 5 septembre 1938 ... ce fut un crime qui dépasse la psychologie nationale, fruit de l'hystérie» (Donoso, 1954, vol.2

p.258). Cependant, la question demeure entière : comment expliquer la décision de faire massacrer ces jeunes sans défense? Peut-on l'attribuer à la crainte d'Alessandri de subir l'affront d'une deuxième défaite, comme le suggère Donoso (Donoso 1954, p.259)? Il faudrait peut-être chercher la réponse dans la mentalité des *carabineros,* qui avaient gardé dans leur mémoire les persécutions dont ils avaient été eux-mêmes victimes à la fin de la dictature d'Ibáñez comme on l'a vu dans le roman d'Alegría.

Enfin, ces romans aident à poser des questions au sujet de l'avenir. Comme l'affirme Alegría, «une année n'a pas de commencement», ce qui a fait dire à un critique que «ce qui se passe au cours d'une année a ses racines dans les années précédantes et a des répercussions dans les années ultérieures» (Lipp, 1972, p.108). Même si Alegría et d'autres auteurs situent leurs récits en 1938, la projection des événements de cette période va beaucoup plus loin. C'est le sujet qu'a exploré Atías et qui permet de toucher à une question de la plus grande importance : quel fut l'impact de l'avènement du Front populaire sur le devenir de la gauche chilienne? Sans doute, son roman reflète une vision péjorative de cette expérience. Cette opinion partagée par plusieurs, n'a toutefois pas dissuader la gauche en 1946, de reprendre la même politique, ce qui devait s'avérer un échec pire que le précédent. En dépit du résultat, lors des campagnes électorales d'Allende en 1964 et 1970 on faisait référence à 1938 sur un ton positif.

Finalement, le roman d'Alegría suggère un sujet de réflexion utile quant à l'interprétation de l'histoire : comment et pourquoi le Chili, pays qui a connu autant de bouleversements dans les années 1930, devient-il, tout à coupe un pays assagi en 1938? Question d'autant plus importante que cette stabilité institutionnelle deviendra le trait le plus connu du Chili (du moins jusqu'en 1973) et constituera le principal aspect de la culture nationale. Il faudrait peut-être ajouter ici une autre considération à l'analyse : le non-dit, l'omission, le refus de parler de certains sujets. On peut ainsi proposer que la stabilité du Chili représente un facteur de son trajet historique tellement évident, et donc fortement intériorisé par les écrivains, qu'il n'était plus nécessaire d'en parler et donc ils l'ont tout simplement tu.

NOTES

1. L'auteur désire remercier Mario Ferrero, critique de littérature chilien et la professeure María Cristina Pons, de l'Université de Californie à Los Angeles, pour leurs remarques et leurs informations.
2. Ce roman met en vedette la lutte des patriotes chiliens contre les Espagnols durant la phase de reprise du contrôle du pays par les partisans de la monarchie, entre 1814 et 1817.
3. La victoire du candidat du Front, Pedro Aquirre, constitue un point tournant dans l'histoire du Chili : pour la première fois depuis la formation du pays, la droite perdait le pouvoir et les forces marxistes participaient au gouvernement.
4. Les seules études existantes sur l'expérience du Front populaire sont déjà anciennes et pas très satisfaisantes : celles de Stevenson (1942) et de Super (1975). Deux autres ouvrages abordent partiellement cette époque : Drake (1978) et Potashnik (1974).
5. Promis (1977) parle de la «génération de 1942».
6. (1969) «La maraton de Fernando Alegría». *Ercilla* 1969 n.1773 p.50-53, sans auteur.
7. Eduardo Barrios (1884-1963); Augusto d'Halmar (pseudonyme, 1880-1950) et Alberto Romero (1896-197?). Leurs ouvrages les plus représentatifs à cet égard sont *Un perdido* (1917), *Juana Lucero* (1902), et *La viuda del conventillo* (1932), respectivement.
8. Dans ce roman, Atías décrit les agissements des anciens patrons d'une usine, récemment nationalisée par le gouvernement d'Allende, qui essayaient de corrompre certains travailleurs de l'usine afin de provoquer le chaos économique et l'éventuelle chute de l'Unité populaire.
9. Parmi les plus connus des écrivains de la même génération de 1938, il faut mentionner Volodia Teitelboim (né en 1916), sénateur et secrétaire général du Parti communiste, auteur du roman *La semilla en la arena* qui traite de la répression anticommuniste de 1948; Reinaldo Lomboy (1910-1974), auteur de *Ranquil,* qui décrit la tuerie des paysans dans cette localité du sud du pays en 1934.
10. La présence d'intellectuels identifiés au marxisme et aux partis de la gauche était assez importante dans les années 1960 et au début des années 1970, que ce soit dans les milieux littéraires, scientifiques ou académiques. Le recteur de l'Université du Chili, élu en 1963, Eugenio González, était un ancien sénateur socialiste; il avait fait incursion dans la littérature, avec deux romans sur l'époque de la dictature d'Ibañez.
11. Carlos Ibañez (1877-1960) : général de l'armée de terre, président dictateur du Chili entre 1927-1931 et président démocratiquement élu entre 1952 et 1958.

12. Au Chili, le mot «carabinero» désigne la police. Ses membres furent l'objet d'agressions en 1931 parce que l'institution était très liée à Ibañez, qui l'avait crée en 1927.
13. Le mot «naci» était utilisé au Chili pour désigner les membres du Mouvement nacional socialiste. A ne pas confondre avec «nazi» même si les deux mouvements avaient des points communs.
14. Francisco Lomeli (1983), *La novelística chilena de Carlos Droguett,* Madrid, Ed. Playor, p.41
15. L'autuer se trompe ici en faisant croire que le Parti naci chilien avait un appui important de l'ambassade allemande. Selon un spécialiste américain, le nacisme ne fut pas soutenu par les allemands parce que ce mouvement ne partageait pas la doctrine raciste de Hitler. Cf. Potashnik [1974]
16. On parle de la Démocratie-chrétienne qui était en train de s'implanter dans le milieur ouvrier à cette époque.
17. Les personnages mentionnés ici sont José Miguel Carrera (1785-1821), héros de l'indépendance; Francisco Bilbao (1823-1857), leader libéral qui a participé à la rébellion contre les conservateurs en 1851, et Arturo Alessandri (1868-1950), deux fois président du Chili, membre du Parti libéral. Quant à Marin Rivas, il s'agit du héros du roman d'Alberto Blest Gana, publié en 1862. Ces deux dernières références ont de quoi surprendre. S'il est vrai que le président Alessandri avait été élu la première fois en 1920, avec un certain appui populaire, lors de son deuxième mandat (1932-38) il avait agi d'une façon assez conservatrice. Quant à Martin Rivas, plusieurs ont signalé qu'il s'agit d'un héros bourgeois qui participe à la révolution de 1851 du côté des rebelles mais qui, une fois accepté par la famille de Leonor, la riche héritière dont il était amoureux, n'hésite pas à collaborer aux affaires de son beau-père.
18. Pedro Aguirre Cerda (1879-1941), militant du Parti radical et président du Chili (1938-41), décédé avant de terminer son mandat. Malgré sa popularité, il était un riche homme d'affaires et il avait accepté contre son gré l'appui du Parti communiste à son élection.
19. Parmi les faits qui contribuèrent à l'instabilité durant le deuxième gouvernement d'Arturo Alessandri figurent la tuerie des ouvriers agricoles de Ranquil en 1934, la répression lancée par le gouvernement contre la grève des cheminots de 1936 et la fermeture de plusieurs journaux et revues de l'opposition.
20. Parmi les faits qui contribuèrent à l'instabilité du pays durant le deuxième gouvernement d'Arturo Alessandri figurent la tuerie des ouvriers agricoles de Ranquil en 1934, la répression lancée par le gouvernement contre la grève des cheminots de 1936 et la fermeture de plusieurs journaux et revues de l'Opposition.

21. Durant une bonne partie du XXe siècle, il y eut de fréquentes dénonciations de la part de groupes d'ouvriers et de différentes organisations contre l'alcoolisme et contre les producteurs de vin, accusés d'être les responsables de ce vice.
22. L'auteur se trompe ici en faisant croire que le parti naci chilien avait un appui important de l'ambassade allemande. Selon un spécialiste américain, les Chiliens ne furent pas soutenus pas les Allemands parce que leur mouvement ne partageait pas la doctrine raciste de Hitler. cf. Potashnik 1974.
23. L'auteur fait allusion ici au fait qu'en 1963 les Partis socialiste et communiste se préparaient à affronter l'élection présidentielle de 1964, en alliance avec d'autres formations non-marxistes, ce qui rappelait l'expérience de 1938.
24. On parle ici de la Démocratie-chrétienne, qui s'implantait dans le milieu ouvrier à cette époque.
25. Il s'agit de la répression lancée par le président radical Gabriel González Videla contre le Parti communiste, qui pourtant avait contribué à son élection en 1946 et qui avait occupé quelques ministères dans le premier cabinet du nouveau gouvernement. Le PC chilien allait demeurer dans l'illégalité jusqu'en 1958.
26. Cette omission est assez surprenante, puisque le ton désabusé de l'auteur à l'égard de l'expérience du Front populaire pourrait signifier le rejet de la voie électorale, l'attitude qu'un certain nombre de militants socialistes et communistes commençaient à défendre au début des années 1960. La plupart d'entre eux, motivés par l'expérience cubaine, songeaient à d'éventuelles actions armées pour prendre le pouvoir. Si Atías était déçu par la stratégie électorale, il ne semblait pas pour autant partisan de la voie armée.

RÉFÉRENCES

ROMANS

Alegria, F. (1964). *Mañana los guerreros.* Santiago, Editorial Zig-Zag.
Atias, G. (1965). *A la sombra de los días.* Santiago, Editorial Zig-Zag.
Delano, L.E. (1964). *El rumor de la batalla.* Santiago, Editora Austral.
Droguett, C. (1953). *Sesenta muertos en la escalera.* Santiago, Editorial Nascimento.

OEUVRES CRITIQUES

Alegria, F. (1962). *Literatura chilena del siglo XX.* Santiago, Zig-Zag.
———. (1983). *Una especie de memoria.* México, Editorial Nueva Imagen.
Blanco, G. (1965). «A la sombra del 38», *Ercilla,* 22-12-65, p.39-40.

Daspre, A. (1975). «Le roman historique et l'Histoire», *Revue d'histoire littéraire de la France,* n.2\3, p.235-244.

Donoso, R. (1954). *Alessandri, agitador y demoledor.* México, Tierra Firme, 2 tomos.

Drake, P. ([1978). *Socialism and Populism in Chile,* 1932-1952. Chicago: The University of Illinois Press.

Guerra, C.L. (1987). *Texto e ideología en la narrativa chilena.* Minneapolis MI: The Prisma Institute.

Jitrik, N. (1986). «De la historia a la escritura: predominios, disimetrías, acuerdos en la novela histórica latinoamericana», (ed.) Balderson, D. *The Historical Novel in Latin America.* Gaithesburg, Ediciones Hispamerica, p.13-30.

Lipp, S. (1972). «Fernando Alegría, guerrero optimista», in Giacoman, H. (1972). *Homenaje a Fernando Alegría.* New York: Las Américas Publishing, p.96-109.

Lomeli, F. (1981). «Encuentros con Carlos Droguett», *Literatura Chilena.* Creación crítica. Vol.5, n.3,, julio-septiembre, p.25-29.

———. (1983). *La novelística chilena de Carlos Droguett.* Madrid: Ed. Playor.

Menton, S. (1993). *Latin America's New Historical Novel.* Austin: The University of Texas Press.

Potashnik, M. (197). *Nacismo: National socialism in Chile, 1932-1938.* Thèse doctorale inédite, dép.d'Histoire, University of California, Los Angeles.

Promis, J. (1977). *La novela chilena actual.* Buenos Aires, F. García editor.

Rojas, M. (1963). *Punta de rieles.* Santiago, Editorial Zig-Zag.

Sanchez, L.A. (1968). *Proceso y contenido de la novela hispanoamericana.* Madrid, Gredos.

Singler, C. (1993). *Le roman historique contemporain en Amérique latine. Entre mythe et ironie.* Paris: L'Harmattan.

Stevenson, John. (1942). *The Chilean Popular Front.* Westport: University of Pennsylvania Press

Super, R. (1975). *The Chilean Popular Front. Presidency of Pedro Aguirre Cerda.* Thèse doctorale inédite, dép.d'Histoire, Arizona State University.

Zamudio, J. (1973). *La novela histórica en Chile.* Buenos Aires, Ed. Francisco de Aguirre (éd.originale 1949).

LA GUADELOUPE DANS L'IDÉARIUM ET LES STRATÉGIES DU DÉCOUVREUR : NOUVELLES APPROCHES

Alain Yacou

C'est à la providentielle île de Caloucaera (Guadeloupe) que Colomb donne le nom symbolique de Santa Maria de Guadalupe. Terre pressentie en quelque sorte, cette île peuplée de Caraïbes a joué un rôle de premier plan dans la consolidation de l'idéarium du Découvreur. Elle devient très vite un élément clef de la géostratégie de l'Amiral dans sa dimension à la fois économique et politique.

In a highly symbolic gesture, Christopher Columbus gave the name of Santa Maria de Guadalupe to the providential island of Caloucaera (Guadeloupe). This land, originally populated by the Caribe people, was soon to play an important role in consolidating the great project of Discovery as it rapidly became a key economic and political element in the Admiral's geostrategy.

*

C'EST LE 4 NOVEMBRE 1493 que Christophe Colomb découvre, comme on sait, l'île que les Indiens caraïbes appelaient Caloucaera et qu'il baptise du nom de Sainte-Marie de la Guadeloupe suivant la promesse qu'il avait faite aux Hiéronymites du monastère du même nom en Espagne.

C'est très exactement à l'embouchure de la rivière du Grand Carbet dans la partie Sud de l'actuelle commune de Capesterre Belle-Eau (Sud-est de la Guadeloupe proprement dite) qu'eut lieu le tout premier débarquement des Espagnols dans l'île principale des Caraïbes.

C'est donc en cet endroit que s'est déroulé ce qu'il est convenu d'appeler la rencontre des Deux Mondes, laquelle tourna très vite au choc des Deux Mondes en terre guadeloupéenne, la responsabilité de Colomb nettement engagée en l'espèce.

Dès cette époque, la Guadeloupe, terre pressentie en quelque sorte, va jouer un rôle éminent dans la consolidation de l'idéarium de Christophe Colomb où religiosité et savoirs scientifiques se côtoient. Plus encore, la Guadeloupe devient un élément-clef de la géostratégie du Découvreur dans sa dimension à la fois économique et politique.

IDÉARIUM

S'agissant d'abord de l'idéarium, on ne saurait passer sous silence, le lien étroit qui unit le Découvreur à la Vierge de Guadeloupe. A force d'insister sur le rôle qu'ont joué des Franciscains du monastère de la Rábida, où Colomb a fait des séjours somme toute techniques entre 1485 et 1492 et qu'une riche iconographie a vulgarisés, on a fini par sous-estimer ou même oublier les visites qu'il a effectuées au monastère de Guadalupe avant et après 1492 (Ramos, 1985, p.13-32).

Au demeurant, l'habile Gênois, qui est admis à la Cour dès le 20 janvier 1486, ne put guère que calquer sa démarche sur celle des souverains, Isabelle de Castille et Ferdinand d'Aragon. Or l'un des passages obligés, étape par excellence même des deux monarques sur la route qui les mène, depuis la Cour, qu'elle fût en Castille ou en Aragon, aux différents champs de bataille contre les Maures d'Andalousie, est le monastère hiéronymite de Guadalupe. Là, les souverains tiennent le prieur informés des progrès de la guerre. Ils y puisent eux-mêmes les secours de la Foi et ils ne font pas mystère de leur affection à l'endroit des hiéronymites (de Armas, 1974, p.132).

Pour ce qui est de Christophe Colomb, c'est là, à notre sens, qu'est née ou a pris corps la dévotion mariale qu'on s'accorde à lui reconnaître. Est-il besoin de rappeler ici que la Vierge de Guadalupe était la grande protectrice des armées chrétiennes en lutte contre les Maures, tout comme elle l'était des navigateurs qui devaient affronter les périls de l'Océan? Pour un dévot aussi fervent que ne l'était Christophe Colomb, c'est forcément à ses yeux de l'intercession de la fameuse Vierge Noire, dont il a imploré les secours, que dépendait à tous les égards la réussite de son projet.

Toutefois, ce qui est surprenant, c'est que Christophe Colomb ait attendu le second voyage (1493-1498) pour baptiser du nom de Guadeloupe, une des îles qu'il avait «découvertes». Il avait eu tout le loisir de le faire—si l'on ose écrire—entre le 12 octobre 1492 et le 13 janvier 1493, au cours du premier voyage. On ne saurait se satisfaire ici de l'hypothèse suivant laquelle l'Amiral aurait perdu de vue la Vierge de Guadalupe et que tout à la griserie de sa découverte il aurait tout bonnement oublié la promesse faite aux moines hiéronymites. Partant, nous en déduisons que dans ses stratégies, la dénomination «Guadalupe» a été réellement réservée pour un second voyage dont la finalité était distincte du premier. Maintenant le hasard veut que la chaîne montagneuse de l'une des îles qu'il aperçoit le 4 novembre au matin ressemble à la Sierra de Guadalupe en Extrémadure. Il est même, providentiellement, une imposante cascade qui jaillit de la cime du mont le plus élevé et qui n'est pas sans rappeler, à une autre échelle, le spectacle du ruissellement des eaux de la rivière Guadalupe, là-bas en Espagne! On connaît la suite.

C'est dire que le mot Guadeloupe est un concept-clef de l'idéarium colombien, qui renvoie en définitive à la partie secrète de l'entreprise, celle-là même qui avait emporté l'adhésion des Souverains catholiques contre l'avis de la junte de savants présidée par Hernando de Talavera et commise tout exprès pour expertiser ledit projet.

On sait que l'idée soutenue par Colomb de gagner l'Orient par la voie occidentale n'était pas neuve dans la seconde moitié du XVe siècle. Mais, nonobstant l'erreur bien connue suivant laquelle il en était arrivé à conclure qu'une petite étendue de mer séparait l'Espagne de l'extrémité de l'Asie, on pouvait lui reprocher à bon droit que quelle que soit l'étendue de cette mer (la Mer Ténébreuse, l'Océan Atlantique), on ne pouvait la franchir en droiture pour gagner la terre ferme orientale, les Indes, comme on disait. Sans doute qu'en bon Portugais qu'il était devenu, Colomb n'a pas révélé aux savants incrédules qui l'ont écouté en Castille, la connaissance parfaite qu'il avait de l'existence d'un certain nombre d'îles situées sur le chemin entre l'Europe et l'Asie. N'avait-il pas d'ailleurs réservé la primeur de ses informations aux Rois catholiques eux-mêmes qui, dans une lettre du 16 août 1494, le félicitent en des termes qui ne laissent pas d'intriguer :

> Il nous semble que tout ce que vous nous aviez dit au début, que vous pourriez atteindre, l'a été en sa plus grande partie, comme si vous l'aviez vu avant de nous le dire. (Fernández de Navarrete, 1825, p.393)

Outre les rumeurs et les indices qu'il aurait pu recueillir à Porto Santo, ces renseignements il les avait reçus directement ou indirectement, lors de son séjour au Portugal, du savant humaniste Paolo del Pozzo Toscanelli. Au surplus, il reste toujours l'hypothèse très ancienne, mais aujourd'hui réactualisée, du secret de Colomb, à savoir les révélations qu'il aurait eues d'un pilote, *Le Pilote inconnu* ou le prédécouvreur le «protonauta», comme l'écrit Juan Manzano y Manzano dont nous reprenons ici la leçon (Manzano y Manzano, 1989, p.493).

Dans cette optique, l'Amiral n'aurait rien ignoré de la route ou de la distance entre l'Europe et les îles situées à l'entrée des Indes comme il l'écrit. Au demeurant, n'avait-il pas prétendu dès le premier voyage que ces îles se trouvaient à quelque 750 lieues des îles Canaries. C'est précisément au cours du second voyage que ces assertions seront vérifiées par tout l'équipage, marins et capitaines, que l'Amiral tenait réellement sous son charme. Un point sur lequel les témoignages sont unanimes retient d'abord l'attention : c'est que, partie de Cadix le 25 septembre 1493, et après une escale technique du 2 au 13 octobre, l'imposante flotte de dix-sept navires, aux ordres de l'Amiral de la Mer Océane, aurait rejoint les îles des Cannibales, comme on disait, en quelque vingt jours et de façon déconcertante. C'était, écrit le Dr. Chanca, comme si l'Amiral connaissait parfaitement la route. Et Scyllacius, suivant de près Guillermo Coma, de renchérir :

> Très peu de nous savaient où ils étaient arrivés, à la différence du Préfet (l'Amiral) qui n'ignorait rien de toutes ces choses (...); ce dernier savait très bien l'endroit précis et la zone du ciel où se trouvait ces (sept) îles. (Varela, 1982, p.187)

Fait plus troublant, que rapporte encore Scyllacius : alors que pour comble d'infortune il apparut que l'on avait consommé toute l'eau disponible, l'Amiral serein «tel Moïse, guidant les siens», soulignait-il, avait consolé tout son monde en assurant que dans l'espace de trois jours au plus, on verrait apparaître une nouvelle terre qu'ils aborderaient par une côte tranquille où l'on apercevrait, promettait-il, les eaux cristallines de fleuves limpides. Or c'est ce qui arriva, non point dans la petite île de Marie-Galante où eut lieu un premier débarquement le 3 novembre mais à la Guadeloupe le lendemain.

De la sorte, on peut avancer que si le but du premier voyage était d'atteindre Cathay (la Chine) et Cipango (le Japon) à des fins politico-religieuses de contournement de l'Islam bien évidemment, pour des raisons de commerce avec l'Orient, les objectifs du second comportent une dimension scientifique on ne peut plus manifeste. De fait, en empruntant délibérément une route différente de celle du premier voyage, comme le lui permettait, il est vrai, la *bulle Intercaetera* du Pape Alexandre VI—laquelle mettait fin à l'hégémonie portugaise dans l'Atlantique—

Colomb peut, cette fois, vérifier à bon droit la localisation des îles (les petites Antilles) dont il aurait connu à l'avance l'existence et qu'il savait peuplées de Caraïbes aux dires des Indiens Taïnos qui sont ses hôtes dans l'île Espagnole (Ayti) en décembre 1492.

Il se trouve par ailleurs que c'est dans l'île de la Guadeloupe, en novembre 1493, que Colomb aura confirmation de la bouche des Indiennes taïnos, captives des Caraïbes, de l'existence plus au sud d'une masse continentale que le Pilote inconnu ou prédécouvreur aurait également abordée (Nagy, 1984, p.83). Il s'agit, selon la théorie de Colomb, de cette seconde «Terre Ferme» (la tierra firme de ACA) située au sud de la terre ferme d'Asie connue (la tierra firme de ALLA), un autre monde en quelque sorte, inconnu des Européens. C'est bien évidemment cette masse continentale—«la quatrième partie du monde», aujourd'hui l'Amérique du Sud, que l'Amiral va toucher avec beaucoup d'aplomb au cours de son quatrième voyage en 1498 mais que sa vie durant, il situera en Asie.

En tout état de cause, arrivés à la Guadeloupe dans la matinée du 4 novembre 1493, Christope Colomb et les siens n'en repartiront que le 10 sans avoir pu percer le secret de l'île, comme on disait; en d'autres termes nul ne put savoir s'il s'y trouvait de l'or. A défaut de métal précieux, on pouvait néanmoins s'émerveiller devant les richesses végétales et ornithologiques de l'île principale des Caraïbes. A cet égard, des témoins autorisés (le docteur Alvárez Chanca qui était médecin de l'expédition, Guillermo Comas que Scyllacius plagia avec son assentiment, et Michel Cuneo) ont dressé dans leurs écrits respectifs de précieux inventaires de la faune et de la flore guadeloupéennes de l'époque.

GÉOSTRATÉGIE

Par cela et en raison de la localisation de la Guadeloupe à l'entrée des Indes, Colomb va lui conférer un rôle prépondérant dans sa géostratégie selon ce qui en apparaît dans la lettre qu'il adresse aux souverains à la fin de janvier 1494, document exceptionnel retrouvé il y a cinq ans à peine et conservé aux Archives des Indes à Séville (Colomb, Lettre de 1494).

La vision que l'Amiral nous y donne de la Guadeloupe renvoie immanquablement à ses conceptions sur le commerce lointain et à sa double culture d'agent de commerce gênois et de navigateur portugais. Certes, on sait qu'en sa qualité de vice-roi des Indes pour le compte des Rois Catholiques, Christophe Colomb se trouve à la tête d'une formidable expédition de colonisation—on disait peuplement—et d'occupation territoriale sur le modèle castillan de la «Reconquista». Mais il est juste de souligner qu'il n'avait pas renié pour autant son propre modèle, celui des comptoirs en bord de mer à la manière des Portugais sur le pourtour de l'Áfrique en direction des Indes, où celui des enclaves comme celles que jadis les Gênois avaient établies pour y accueillir à bon compte les caravanes de marchands d'Orient.

De la sorte, obligé d'assumer la conquête pour ainsi dire des grandes Antilles, en tout cas de l'île Espagnole—assimilées à des terres asiatiques—et de promouvoir l'évangélisation des indigènes, Christophe Colomb s'en tient en ce qui concerne la Guadeloupe à son propre modèle qu'il transpose ou adapte en érigeant l'île principale des Caraïbes en escale technique et en lieu de ravitaillement pour les vaisseaux espagnols à l'entrée des Indes.

Un passage de la lettre déjà mentionnée qu'íl adresse aux Rois Catholiques s'avère particulièrement significatif à cet égard. Ainsi alors même qu'il exerce, comme on le verra, des représailles d'importance contre les Caraïbes qui se refusaient à tout contact avec lui, Colomb écrit de la façon la plus intéressée qui soit :

> Je ne brûlai point leurs maisons pour que nous puissions en profiter quand nous repasserions par là car elles sont sur le chemin de Castille. (Colomb, lettre de janvier 1494, fol. n.4 verso et n.5 recto)

Lorsqu'en 1496 il retourne en Espagne, Colomb fait de nouveau voile vers la Guadeloupe pour y recueillir du pain de cassave et faire provision de bois et d'eau. Ouvrons d'ailleurs ici une parenthèse pour dire qu'à cette occasion, Colomb s'est livré cette fois là mais en vain à des tentatives de séduction des Caraïbes à des fins d'órganisation de son ravitaillement sur la base du troc (H. Colomb, 1986, p.165-166). S'inaugure dès lors une tradition. Ainsi, sans l'assentiment de ses propres habitants, l'utilisation de la Guadeloupe comme escale technique fît école. Colomb en personne revint à la Guadeloupe dans le même but au début de son quatrième et dernier voyage en juin 1502. Plus encore, sur les six grandes expéditions organisées par la couronne espagnole, dans le dos de l'Amiral en quelque sorte, entre 1499 et 1502 trois au moins firent escale à la Guadeloupe (Yacou, 1992, p.232-233).

GÉOPOLITIQUE

Enfin, sous l'angle géopolitique, la Guadeloupe constituait aux yeux de Colomb un enjeu capital au moment où commençait l'implantation des Espagnols dans les îles. Colomb n'avait-il pas pressenti qu'une grande rivalité allait opposer ces derniers aux Caraïbes qui exerçaient une manière d'hégémonie dans la mer des Antilles?

De fait, peu de temps après son arrivée en Guadeloupe, il avait appris de la bouche des captives taïnos que la plupart des guerriers caraïbes étaient partis en canots pour se livrer à des opérations ordinaires de razzia contre les Indiens taïnos de l'île de Boriquen (Porto Rico) dont elles étaient elles-mêmes originaires. En somme, la Guadeloupe constituait depuis longtemps une des grandes bases de repli ou d'offensive des Caraïbes. Il fallait donc mener contre eux une guerre préventive et exemplaire, dans l'esprit de Colomb, pour apparaître de surcroît comme des libérateurs aux yeux de toute l'ethnie taïno. Il suffisait pour ce faire de trouver un «casus belli» convenable.

Dès les premiers jours de l'escale à la Guadeloupe, les marins descendus à terre,à l'embouchure de la rivière du Grand Carbet, rapportèrent à l'Amiral les preuves de l'anthropophagie à laquelle se livraient les Caraïbes aux dépens de leurs prisonniers taïnos. Colomb d'abord sceptique n'y ajouta foi que lorsqu'il put recueillir de la bouche des femmes taïnos que les Caraïbes retenaient en captivité en Guadeloupe, avec des jeunes hommes taïnos. Dès lors Colomb s'employa à montrer de façon saisissante la barbarie desdits Caraïbes et à stigmatiser les excès dont ils étaient les auteurs à l'endroit de leurs captifs :

> On vit peu d'hommes et on en prit peu; ils s'enfuirent tous dans les bois, et à cause de l'épaisseur de ces derniers on ne put reprendre que des femmes. Lesquelles me disaient qu'on les avait amenées d'autres îles, et à mon avis ils les tenaient en esclavage et pour concubines; elles me disaient également avec des paroles et par signes qu'ils avaient mangé leurs maris, et à d'autres leurs fils et leurs frères et qu'ils les obligeaient à les manger elles-mêmes. Je trouvai aussi quelques jeunes hommes qui avaient été pris de même et à qui ils avaient coupé le membre; je croyais que c'était par jalousie au sujet des femmes, mais ils ont coutume de faire cela pour qu'ils engraissent comme on le fait en Castille aux chapons qu'on mange lors des fêtes; quant aux femmes ils ne les tuent jamais. Je trouvai dans leurs maisons des paniers et des grands coffres remplis d'os humains et des têtes accrochées dans chaque maison. (Colomb, Lettre de janvier 1494, fol: 4 verso).

C'est donc sur le fondement de l'ignominie, à ses yeux, des moeurs des Caraïbes, que Colomb va élaborer une savante stratégie d'élimination, et à tout le moins d'abaissement, de ces derniers.

De la sorte, dès le tout premier contact avec les Caraïbes dans leur île principale, Colomb leur déclare une guerre sans merci en se livrant à des actes de dissuasion significatifs, à commencer par une tentative de réduction de leur rayon d'action. Nous n'en voulons pour preuve que ses propres déclarations toujours dans sa lettre de janvier 1494 aux Rois catholiques :

> Leurs canots sont très grands et plus longs que des fustes, et mieux faits que ceux des gens qui sont plus à l'ouest, et je les brisai tous, petits et grands; je fis de même dans tous les autres lieux; j'avais l'intention de le faire aussi dans chaque île, et j'avais grand désir de les explorer toutes. (Colomb, 1494 fol.5 recto)

C'est aussi à la Guadeloupe que l'Amiral, qui tient les Caraïbes pour les ennemis naturels des chrétiens, inaugure la pratique de la déportation des Indiens en Espagne suivant la doctrine qu'il a exposée dans le fameux *Mémoire* que le capitaine Torres devait remettre aux Souverains toujours dans l'année 1494 :

> Vous direz à leurs Altesses que pour le plus grand bien des âmes desdits Cannibales et même des Indiens d'ici, il m'est venu à l'esprit que plus loin on les enverra, mieux cela vaudra. (Estorach, Lequenne, 1991, p.37)

A cet égard, est particulièrement illustratif des objectifs politiques de l'Amiral l'épisode du rapt, en Guadeloupe, d'un petit enfant caraïbe abandonné par les siens dès le premier jour de l'arrivée des Espagnols à l'embouchure de la rivière du Grand Carbet, et auquel des matelots avaient rendu visite chaque jour durant l'escale à la Guadeloupe :

> Je le fis donner à une des femmes qui étaient parties de Castille pour venir ici, précisait-il aux Souverains; il est des nôtres aujourd'hui, il jouit d'une bonne santé et il parle dans notre langue qu'il entend merveilleusement. (Colomb, 1994 fol. 5 recto)

Il y avait là un langage convenu, un code pour tout dire, dont la clef nous est fournie dans le *Mémoire* déjà cité que l'Amiral remit à Antonio de Torres. Colomb insiste sur la nécessité de former des interprètes indiens pour répandre la bonne parole dans un dessein évident d'assimilation, susceptible en tout cas de façonner la configuration psychologique des Indiens et de les transformer en de dociles métis culturels pour les besoins de la cause.

En guise de conclusion, on peut remarquer d'abord que l'idée majeure de Christophe Colomb d'ériger la Guadeloupe en une base de ravitaillement fut reprise par les gouvernants espagnols sous une forme amenuisée, il est vrai, celle de l'aigouade pour les galions de S.M.C. tout au long du XVIe siècle.

A l'inverse, la pratique instaurée par l'Amiral de raids contre les Caraïbes dans leur île principale à des fins s'assujetissement ne donna point les résultats escomptés. Au demeurant, la réponse des Caraïbes aux actes de piraterie perpétrés contre eux fut d'organiser des expéditions d'envergure contre les établissements espagnols de Porto Rico qui mirent en péril l'entreprise coloniale : il est particulièrement significatif à cet endroit que les indiens taïnos de Porto Rico et Caraïbes de la Guadeloupe, ennemis invétérés d'antan, firent cause commune contre les envahisseurs européens. (Yacou, 1992, p.273).

Dans ces conditions, la volonté d'anéantir les Caraïbes qui se fait jour, côté espagnol, se solda par une série d'échecs à commencer par la toute première tentative, en 1515 où Juan Ponce de Leon, le conquistador de Porto Rico qui avait été nommé «Capitaine de l'armada contre les Caraïbes», perdit l'honneur en Guadeloupe suivant le mot infiniment juste du chroniqueur Pierre Martyr d'Anghiera (Décadas del Nuevo Mundo, 1989, p.382).

Ce n'est donc que sous les coups conjugés des aventuriers français et anglais que prend corps au XVIIe siècle l'entreprise d'abaissement des Caraïbes que l'Amiral de la Mer Océane avait appelée de ses voeux dans un dessein qui ne fait pas mystère.

RÉFÉRENCES

Colomb, C. (1493). *Lettre à Santangel.* Madrid, 1994, Anaya, Ed. Ismael Espinos.

———. (1494). *Libro Copiador* Testimonio Compañía Editorial.

Colomb, H. (1986). *Christophe Colomb raconté par son fils.* Paris, Librairie Académique Perrin.

Décadas del Nuevo mundo. (Vol.II, 1989) Santo Domingo, Circulo Bibliófilos.

Estorach, S., et Lequenne, M. (1991). *Christophe Colomb. La découverte de l'Amérique.* (Vol.III Ecrits et documents : 1492-1506. Paris. La Découverte.

Fernandez de Navarrete, M. (1825). *Colección de los viajes et descubrimientos que hicieron por mar los Espanoles desde el siglo XV : Vol.1.* Madrid, Imprenta Real.

Gil, J., et Varela, C. (1982). *Cartas de particulares a Colón y relaciones coetáneas.* Madrid. Alianza Editorial.

Manzano y Manzano, J. (1989) *Colón y su secreto : el predescubrimiento.* Ediciones de Cultura Hispánica.

Ramos, D. (1985). Las visitas de Colón a Guadalupe y el cumplimiento del voto de viaje de retorno. *Revista Guadalupe,* no. 675.

Rumeu de Armas, A. (1974). *Itinerario de los Reyes Católicos.* Madrid. Consejo Superior de Investigaciones Científicas.

Szaszdi Nagy, A. (1984). *Un mundo que descubrió Colón. Las rutas del comercio prehispánico de los metales.* Valladolid. Casa Museo de Colón.

Yacou, A. (1992). *Christophe Colomb et la Découverte de la Guadeloupe.* Paris. Editions Caribéennes.

CHAPTER VIII

TOWARD AN ELECTRONIC HOOD

NAVIGATING THE TEXT: AN EXPLORATION IN COMPARATIVE CROSS-CULTURAL EPISTEMOLOGY

Cecilia Taiana

This paper is a preliminary exploration of the use of hypertext and its capability of identifying and opening up embedded epistemological traditions present in the text. Two academic outlines for introductory courses in psychology, one from Carleton University (Ottawa, Canada) and one from the University of Buenos Aires (Argentina), have been chosen to illustrate the interaction between the reader, the hypertext links and the processing activity. The paper shows a specific facet of cross-cultural analysis where the text becomes a third social actor in the triadic author-text-reader relationship.

Cette étude constitue une exploration préliminaire de l'hypertexte et de ses capacités d'identifier les traditions épistémologiques inscrites dans le texte. A partir de deux descriptions pour un cours de psychologie de première année, proposées par l'Université Carleton (Ottawa, Canada) et l'Université de Buenos Aires (Argentine), l'auteur explique une méthode d'analyse transculturelle, en mettant en évidence les éléments socio-sémiotiques du texte dans le contexte d'une discussion sur la création et l'utilisation de l'hypertexte.

*

THIS PAPER IS AN EXPLORATION of the use of hypertext and its capability of identifying and opening up embedded epistemological traditions present in the text. Two academic course outlines, one from Canada and the other from Argentina, have been chosen to illustrate the discussion.

Several researchers have noted the importance of the role of the reader in the process of producing meaning (Jonassen, 1993; Eco, 1992; Derrida, 1976, 1978). This relationship between the author, the text and the reader is further complicated by the use of hypertext. Ted Nelson (as cited in Landow, 1992) coined the term hypertext in 1965, defining it as "non-sequential writing-text that branches and allows choices to the reader, best read at an interactive screen ... a series of chunks connected by links which offer the reader different pathways."

This paper attempts to stimulate an increased interest with the text as a third social actor in the triadic author-text-reader relationship and the significance of the cross-cultural analysis of the text in the discussion on the creation and use of hypertext techniques. On this socio-semiotic aspect of the text and its ramifications, Donald Bruce (1993) notes that "the first problem is that the epistemological and indeed ontological status of the electronic text must be rethought in the ways it differs from more traditional notions of text ... the one side of the coin is thus of a theoretical nature" (p.358). Similarly in *Order and Coherence in a New Medium,* John Slatin (1991) states with reference to the electronic text: "A new medium involves both a new practice and a new rhetoric, a new body of theory" (p.4).

THEORETICAL CONSIDERATIONS

As a non-linear, web-like organizing technique, hypertext creates a structure that reflects the cognitive system[1] of the hypertext's author (Edwards, 1994). Irrespective of electronic hypertext's debatable, comparative superiority over the established paper medium—a subject much under discussion in the psychological and non-psychological literature—to hypertext a text implies a purposeful intervention, a fragmentation, an interruption of the semantic narrative established by the author of the text. The basic assumption underlying "hypertext techniques" is, according to P.A. Kommers, "that texts can be parsed into self-contained paragraphs which can be read and interpreted independently" (1992). However, before any drastic intervention takes place it is necessary to reflect on the nature of the text and its relational structures. In his discussion of the linearity of the text, Peter Whalley (1993) refers to text linguists, such as Grimes (1975) and de Beaugrande (1980), who have shown how, under a superficially linear form, authors may create complex relational structures. According to Paul Edward (1994), this "myth" of linearity is also undermined by Saussure's observation that the text is not a stable entity in the first place. On the same topic, Saussure coined the phrase "self-activating field" to describe a text (as cited by Edwards, 1994). It appears that current hypertext designs would not only benefit from a richer appreciation of the variety of reading strategies that people can adopt, as argued in the literature currently published by psychologists,[2] but also and more fundamentally, from a more thoughtful understanding of the semantic organization of knowledge embedded in the text and the social, political and cultural intertextuality from which the text emerges. According to Roland Barthes (1979), "the text is held in language" and it is dependent for its meaning on other texts and on activating the idea of play, of dislocations, overlapping, variations and silences. All texts in his view, whether scientific or literary, are constituted as:

> the activity of associations, contiguities, and cross-references coincides with a liberation of symbolic energy.... Every text, being itself the intertext of another text, belongs to the intertextual, which must not be confused with the text's origins; to search for the "sources of" and "influence upon" a work is the myth of filiation. (Barthes, 1979)

It could be posited that the text is already hypertext to its own intertextuality and to its own articulation of cross-referencing and silences. As described by Barthes (1979) and Foucault (1977, 1980) the notion of "intertextuality" names the necessary reliance of any given text on many others for the construction of its meaning. If we accept this premise, using hypertext to unravel the inheritance of the text creates a sense of the immanent presence of other levels, thus creating a whole new level of content represented in the cognitive map of the structure, and of the knowledge present or absent in the text.

The discussion that follows constitutes preliminary considerations associated with the use of hypertext links as tools to identify and open up embedded epistemological traditions present within the text as part of a systematic cross-cultural analysis of the text. For this purpose, I have chosen two Introduction to Psychology course outlines offered in two universities, in different countries: Introduction to Psychology, as taught at the Department of Psychology, Carleton University, Ottawa, Canada, and Introduction to Psychology offered to psychology students in the Faculty of Psychology, University of Buenos Aires, Argentina.

The task is to imagine the possible types of queries that would constitute the methodological steps towards a cross-cultural analysis of the text, in other words to reveal the intensive and multi-levelled cross-referencing that makes "a text a fundamentally social and interactive category" (Edwards, 1994). As Bolter (1991), Edwards (1994) and Landow (1992), among others, have noted, this argument stresses that at both the cognitive and social levels all texts are hypertexts, webs of signification whose contents are open for constant revision, reinterpretation and extension.

A key notion for these post-structuralist authors for the understanding of the text is the notion of the palimpsest,[3] the parchment of medieval scribes whose original writing was rubbed out again and again and again for reuse. The key meaning of palimpsest is that althought the tablets have been inscribed upon over and over again, the previous texts are never perfectly erased and still partly visible (p.89). Like palimpsests, texts for the deconstructionist, contain the dim but still legible traces of other texts from whose resources they are built. Layers of meaning may be peeled away, always revealing other layers beneath them. David Bolter (1991) argues that hypertext is the perfect palimpsest.

NAVIGATING THE TEXT

Every course outline could be conceived as a "labyrinthine of inferential relations"[4] within an encyclopedia of knowledge. They are part of the universe of human culture with its network of interpretations and interpretants and as such they "only register 'truths' but, rather, what has been said about the truth or what has been believed to be true" (Eco, 1986).

Reading texts, which in this case are academic course outlines, is a matter of reading them in the light of other texts, people, historical events, as a context in which to place other texts. The use of hypertext seems to offer a useful tool to create a cross-cultural analysis of the text, and hence to explore the labyrinth of the inferential relations of the intertextuality of these two texts.

In thinking about how to hypertext the course outlines, (to their intertextual field) a number of methodological considerations come to mind. The course outline is a particularly succinct expression of a more voluminous content; as such it can offer a point from which to begin fanning out into intertextuality. Given the succinctness and introductory nature of these two course outlines it can be assumed that the authors included what they considered fundamental to the discipline.

The headings of the course outlines from Carleton University and the University of Buenos Aires were chosen as the "experimental" texts to examine the conjectures about psychology, as a discipline, which are put forward by professors to their students at an introductory level.

The following represent some of the initial and more generic methodological questions to be answered:

1/ Can course outlines help us understand the epistemological traditions followed by the authors?

2/ What steps or methodological path should we follow to open up a text to its intertextuality?

3/ To what extent are the two outlines chosen representative of psychological traditions of their country of origin?

4/ Are they representative only of their universities? Or the professors chosen?

5/ Would an external analysis of the course outlines, i.e., to examine the history of "migration" of theories and practices provide a partial explanation of the reasons why we found certain practices and theories, and different conceptualization of this field in different parts of the world?

6/ What factors/contexts have influenced the prosperity, or otherwise, of those traditions after migration?

7/ Can we detect the "palimpsest history" conveyed by the course outline?

8/ Can hypertext links and webs provide us with an appropriate tool for this job?

9/ What kinds of queries would we formulate to open up the text to its intertextuality and cultural inheritance?

10/ Sample of possible specific queries:

- a) number of pages in the course outline dedicated to different areas within psychology;
- b) which concepts are omitted in one outline and present in the other;
    - i with high frequency;
    - ii with low frequency;
    - iii can some of the techniques used by the stylo-statisticians to investigate the relationship between the frequency and topography of repeated lexical items in literary text be useful for the present analysis? (Frautschi and Thoriron, 1993)
- c) have the authors dedicated a similar number of pages, proportional to the whole, to the same areas of specialization?
- d) within each chapter, is the topic preceding and following the discussion on a particular topic the same in both outlines? In other words, what is the sequence of presentation the authors have deemed optimal? Is there a logic to this sequential arrangement? How is it different in both outlines?

e) which suggested/required readings complement the units/chapters described in the course outlines?
f) how different/similar is the citation map for each unit/chapter?

HEADINGS OF COURSE OUTLINES

Carleton University	**University of Buenos Aires**
Introduction to Psychology	Introduction to Psychology
The Scope of Psychology	1. Epistemological foundations: theoretical concepts pre-dating the emergence of a general psychology.
1. The Beginnings of Psychology Structuralism Functionalism Gestalt Psychology Early Behaviorism Early Psychoanalysis	2. The configuration of the intra-intersubjective: the concept of personality.
Current Perspectives in Psychology Behavioral Perspective Biological Perspective Cognitive Perspective	3. The capacity to know the world: the fact of perception.
Psychodynamic Perspective Social Perspective Comparing Perspectives	4. The capacity to transmit information and to construct a symbolic universe.
Psychology—Research and Practice Research Psychologists Practicioner Psychologists Complementary roles of Science and Practice	5. The capacity of problem solving, problem anticipation and of adapting to changing situations. The phenomenon of thought and and the construction of culture.
Boundaries and Frontiers	
2. Research Methods in Psychology	

3. Evolution, Heredity and Behaviour

4. Biopsychology and Consciousness

5. Sensation and Perception: Basic Principles and Visual processes.

6. Sensation and Perception: Audition, the Somatosenses, Smell and Taste.

7. Learning and Behavior Analysis

8. Memory

9.Thinking and Language

10. Motivation and Emotion

11. Life-Span Development

12. Gender Development and Sexual Behavior

13. Intelligence

14. Personality

15. Psychological Disorders

16. Therapy

17. Social Psychology

18. Life-Style, Health and Survival

6. The capacity to accumulate, retrieve and forget information. The phenomenon of memory and forgetfulness.

7. The maintenance and change of the intra-intersubjective system. The concept of instinct and the phenomenon of learning.

A first reading of these headings indicates different intertextual fields surrounding the construction of these courses to introduce students to the study of psychology. The reading of both outlines prompts the question: How could the content of two courses with the same title be so disparate/dissimilar? Although both courses are designed to introduce the discipline of psychology to uninitiated students, the authors of these course outlines define by implication the foundations of psychology from radically different perspectives.

A closer reading yields further differences of approach when introducing similar concepts. For example, in the University of Buenos Aires course outline the theories of perception are placed within the context of transitional spaces and its relational conceptualization, while in the Carleton University outline "perception" is the only area that receives two full chapters, both titled "Sensation and Perception," one focusing on principles and processes, and the other on senses and sense systems.

Another effect of these different perspectives is revealed in the presentation of the different schools within psychology that the authors chose for the reader. These schools are addressed individually under one heading in the Carleton University course outline, while in the University of Buenos Aires outline they (the schools of psychology) are included primarily for their specific contributions and perspectives on the larger issues described at the level of chapter headings. This seems to indicate a different inferential labyrinth, the authors' disparate reasoning as to the constitutive nature of these schools, (i.e., their origins and raison d'être).

It would be a mistake to assume that simply introducing better technology into "the text" can better explain the text or educate the reader. Long and hard thinking has to be put into effective ways of providing the reader with the epistemological knowledge to be able to analyze the classification systems used to organize the expert knowledge surrounding the text. However, on a preliminary basis, the two course outlines described in this paper prompted many questions, which could, if systematically pursued and examined, provide the basis for the unravelling of the intertextual field surrounding the text. To be able to recognize, to paraphrase Barthes, the field activated by the text.

Prior to the creation of hypertext links several key questions must be answered regarding the specific classification systems[5] in use, in both countries, for the organization of the knowledge in psychology. The best place to start is not obvious. The mental dialogue of the hypertext designer might read something like the following:

> I would like to query the word psychology in the title of the course outline. Should I start with the modern definition of psychology? Or should I combine historical and present-day definitions? How do I incorporate the dynamic aspects of the chronology of knowledge, that would allow me "to explore how the horizons and contents of a field change with time. (Veltman, 1984)

"What do I consult? Where do I go? How many reference sources do I consult? If I choose encyclopedias, which encyclopedias? How many? Encyclopedias of disciplines or general knowledge encyclopedias? For example, I could access the *Encyclopedia of Psychology.* There are also the dictionaries of psychology, and an *Encyclopedia of Psychology and Philosophy.*"

"How far back do I go? Am I interested in how these definitions have changed? In which languages? Are the definitions in English and Spanish likely to be different? If I look the definitions up in the dictionary and encyclopedia and find that there are several different definitions, what do I do? Do I analyze their differences or do I draw out their similarities? Are these differences and similarities associated with countries/languages and/or dates of publication?"

"Could cultural dictionaries (glossaries arranged according the epistemological traditions) be useful? Should these glossaries be cross-referenced through the use of a word finder as part of the cross-cultural analysis of the text? Annotated glossaries, that is glossaries that provide the reader with the geneology of an specific school and/or epistemological tradition in psychology could provide the basis of 'search groups'."

A preliminary review of two encyclopedias yields interesting differences. The *Espasa-Calpe Encyclopedia,* published in Madrid in 1958, brings an extensive and detailed description of the contributions made to psychology by the Scholastic philosophers (14 pages double columns, single spaced). While the *Macmillan Encyclopedia,* published in New York in 1964, limits its description of this school of thought to a mere one and a quarter pages. In the Spanish historical account of the discipline, the impact and subsequence responses to Kant's critique of psychology and its epistemological impossibility is proposed as one of the grand epistemological dividers. This finding deserves further exploration and it might offer a partial explanation for the different rooting of the logico-positive paradigm of psychology in the Spanish- and English-speaking cultures.

FUTURE CONSIDERATIONS

The use of hypertext and the existence of electronic texts have compelled us to look at the text in ways that are similar to the "world-wide network of digital imagining systems"[6] which are in the opinion of Mitchel "swiftly, silently constituting itself as the descentered subject's reconfigured eye" (1992).

There are new interconnections and similarities of effects in the way we assembly contexts when using the digitalized image and the way we have replaced the traditionally rigid and stable printed texts by fluid, ad hoc, recombinable electronic hypertext links.

Understood as a tool, hypertext is made to accomplish our purposes as authors, and in this sense it represents our desires and intentions. Hypertext authors extend the understanding of the text to create new semantic configurations beyond presumed certainties and intentional opacity. Hypertext readers would be allowed to disarticulate—and perhaps even destroy—the authority of the author and dissolve the centrality of the author's interpretation, which appears to be the homological counterpart of what in the visual arts literature is termed "the fictional assemblage, the insertion of counterfactual texts, as part of the creation of filtered versions" (Mitchel, 1992). The use of hypertext could be compare to the use of filters in the digitalized visual arts. Filters are devices for picking and choosing, for retaining things you want while getting rid of things you don't. It could be argued that hypertext is in effect—adapting Mitchel's words—the choice of "filtering strategies"; or in the words of this author the "digital *bricolage* of the text."

The electronic manipulation of the text is subtly and constantly altering our perceptual senses. The serial and linear logic of print gives way to the study of configurations and the recognition of patterns. In this environment it is useful to think of technologies, as Marshall McLuhan proposed in his book *Understanding Media* in 1963, as forms of art. This power of the arts to anticipate future social and technological developments, by a generation and more, has long been recognized. Discussing this idea McLuhan describes the arts as prophetic, and he contrasts this concept with the popular idea of the arts as mere self-expression. "Technologies begin to perform the function of art in making us aware of the psychic and social consequences of technology.... Art as means of training perception and judgement" (McLuhan, 1963, p.ix).

Three artists' interactive work appear in *Artintact 1,* the first issue of Artists' Interactive CD-ROM Magazine from ZKM, a multifaceted institute in Karlsruhe, Germany, which has ambitions, according to a reviewer of *Wired* magazine (July, 1995), to be the Bauhaus of the digital age. One of the more complex works included in the CD-ROM is "The Exquisite Mechanism of Shivers" by an American artist Bill Seaman. Thirty-three sentences are broken into remixable, recombinable groups of phrases, so that the reader can produce absurdly poetic lines like "An ephemeral certainty triggers an enigmatic arrangement to escape the changing ramifications of a resonant desire." Videoclips associated with each phrase (panning landscapes, close-up of machinery) allow sentences to be played as movies. The curious associations produced by jumbling video, sound, and text create an endless multimedia update of the surrealist game "Le cadavre exquis." The disc comes embedded in a handsomely designed book containing learned commentary on the works in English and German. This piece, plus two others, which all began as installations, have been reworked into intellectual meditations on the nature of seeing, reading, and the use of hypertext.

"Verdades y Ficciones/Truths and Fictions," a journey from documentary to digital photography, by Mexican-American artist, Pedro Meyer is a CD-ROM of provocative, beautiful and haunting manipulated images and texts. The artist juxtaposes images and texts from different cultures that transform and mix literal images. His creative process is made part of the product step by step, and the critics' opinions of the product are also made part of the product.

At present, this project is still "work in progress" with no final theoretical or methodological answers. The discussion in this paper begins to address an aspect of the literature that seemed neglected in the literature on hypertext written by psychologists.

A fully developed project encompasses the incorporation of multimedia links with visual, graphic and audio "intertextualities" integrated as part of a new textual configuration.

Many people in computing still subscribe to a relatively outdated notion of "text," inherited from earlier critical traditions, a notion which appears self-evident and ahistorical, but which is, of course, historically, culturally and institutionally contingent.

This paper proposes that major advances in conceptual navigation require a model that acknowledges the intertextual nature of the text as central to infobase design. To relate the text to its particular conjunction of socio-historical factors and hence to consider its cultural and historical inheritance, i.e., its socio-semiotic framework, is a pre-requisite for the understanding of the semantic structure of the text and its hypertexts.

The conceptual convergence demonstrated by the interrelationships between such disciplines as informatics, cognitive psychology and literary theory could bring new insights into the cross-cultural analysis of the text.

ENDNOTES

1. Jonassen (1993) defines semantic networks as conceptual representations of what we know. Learning , according to this conceptualization, is the mapping of subject matter knowledge (usually possessed by the expert) onto the learner's knowledge structrure (p.155).
2. The interaction of the reader and the hypertext links, and the nature of this processing task, have been studied from a psychological perspective by several authors in the recent years. Patricia Wright's (1993) article is an excellent illustration of this potential "two-way traffic." She focuses particularly on theories of reading strategies and argues that reading and information retrival tasks in hypertext offer psychology a testing ground for theories which attempt to integrate the more fundamental cognitive processes such as memory, attention and comprehension (p.5). Another aspect of hypertext addressed by the literature is its potential pedagogical impact and the opportunities to use hypertext as a mediator in the learning process. Wright (1993) and Jonassen (1993) addressed the psychological aspects of hypertext primarily from the perspective of the reader and writer, the educator and the learner, the information builder and the navigator, the designer and the user, the scientist and the subject. The text itself receives little attention in this literature; it is assumed to be transparent and non-intentional.
3. Christine Brooke-Rose (1991) in *Stories, Theories and Things* provides an interesting discussion of the concept of palimpsest and palimpsest histories, as part of the intrinsic relational property to the text, conceived as a system of cross-referencing for the reader who wants to read actively rather than passively.
4. See Umberto Eco, *Semiotics and the Philosophy of Language,* 1986, Bloomington, IN page 73, as cited by Richard Rorty in *Interpretation and Overinterpretation* by Umberto Eco (1990), Cambridge University Press.
5. With the use of System for Universal Media Searching (SUMS) as a method for electronic navigation and authoring tool, the analysis of epistemological traditions of course outlines will expand its scope and depth of analysis by allowing the

user/reader to have multivalent access to materials in infobases of libraries all over the world. In Kim Veltman's opinion:

> It is feasible to create a multivalent system which permits comparison of classification methods, definitions, and allows one to trace where a particular book has been arranged in different places in different systems. A given book can serve to reflect changing cultural viewpoints involved in the organization of knowledge. (1984, p.62).

The basic questions of Who?, What?, Where?, How?, Why? would open up the exploration of a variety of indexes in the field of knowledge catalogued under psychology and related descriptors. The three domains of knowledge proposed by Kim Veltman (1994) could be used to organize further contents found and to catalogue new aspects of this corpus of knowledge previously undocumented. In SUMS a distinction is made between three basic domains of knowledge: pointers, objects and interpretations. See Kim Veltman (1994) *A System for Universal Media Searching (SUMS)* for definitions and examples. Meters are tools for conceptual navigation; they are limited to ten levels or choices but subsets can be expanded as necessary. The idea of meters as tools for conceptual navigation is another aspect of SUMS that would allow the creation of different levels of access to present the cumulative nature of learning to the reader/student. The same course outline could then be designed for the introductory level as well as for the fourth-year level. Given the multi-media authoring capability of SUMS it would be possible to produce a CD-ROM containing the specialized knowledge in the field of psychology, in its different cultural and intertextual contexts. By complementing SUMS with the text analysis capabilities of Folio Views, a comparative analysis of the organization of levels as used in Folio Views, where "levels" in the case of the course outlines would be the chapters and subtitles within chapters, could yield interesting insights on the structure of levels of abstractions proposed by the authors of the course outlines. Folio Views is an information management sofware package that permits the user to acces, create, edit, distribute, share and update information electronically.

6. In W.J. Mitchel (1992) *The Reconfigured Eye,* we find a detailed discussion of the historical moment created by the digitalized image and the nucleus this technology provides for new forms of social and cultural practices that mark the begining of a new era of artistic exploration. See pages 20, 85, 95 and 199.

REFERENCES

Barthes, R. (1979). From work to text. In Josee V. Harari (Ed.), *Textual strategies: Perspectives in post-structuralist criticism,* pp.73-81. Ithaca NY: Cornell University Press.

Bolter, D.J. (1991). *Writing space: The computer, hypertext, and the history of writing.* Hillsdale NJ: Lawrence Erlbaum.

Bruce, D. (1993). Towards the implementation of text and discourse theory in computer-assisted textual analysis. *Computer and the Humanities* 27, pp.357-364.

De Beaugrande, R.A. (1980). *Text, discourse and process.* Norwood NJ: Ablex.

Derrida, J. (1976). *Of grammatology* (Gayatri C. Spivak, Trans.). Baltimore MD: Johns Hopkins University Press.

Derrida, J. (1976). *Writing and difference.* Chicago IL: University of Chicago Press.

Eco, U. (1991). *Interpretation and overinterpretation.* Cambridge: Cambridge University Press.

Edwards, P. (1994). Hypertext and hypertension: Post-structuralist critical theory, social studies of science and software. *Social Studies of Science,* 24, pp.229-278.

Encyclopedia Universal Illustrada, Espasa-Calpe, Madrid, 1958.

Encyclopedia of Philosophy. (1967). New York: Macmillan.

Fautschi, R. and Thoiron, P. (1993). Towards a narra-topography: A pilot study applied to Marguerite Duras' Novel *Moderato Cantabile. Computer and the Humanities,* 27, pp.235-247. Netherlands: Kluwer Academic Publishers.

Foucault, M. (1977). What is an author? (Donald F. Bouchard and Sherry Simon, Trans.) In Bouchard (Ed.) *Language, Counter Memory, Practice.* Ithaca NY: Cornell University Press, pp.113-138.

Foucault, M. (1980). *Power/knowledge: Selected interviews and other writings,* (Colin Gordon, Trans.) New York: Pantheon.

Grimes, J.E. (1975). *The thread of discourse.* The Hague: Mouton.

Jonassen, D.H. (1993). Effects of semantically structured hypertext knowledge bases on users' knowledge. In C. McKnight, A. Dillon and J. Richardson (Eds.) *Hypertext, A Psychological Perspective.* Great Britain: Ellis Horwood.

Landow, G.P. (1992). *Hypertext: the convergence of contemporary critical theory and technology,* Baltimore MD: Johns Hopkins University Press.

Mitchel, W.J. (1992). *The reconfigured eye. The visual truth in the post-photographic era.* Cambridge MA: The MIT Press.

Veltman, K. (1984). Multidimensional bibliography and classification, *Eroffnungs Vortrag: Anwendungen in der Klassifikation.* Proceedings 8 Jahrestagung der Gesellschaft fur Klassifikation eV, Ed. Rolf G. Hensler (Teil I), (Hofgeismar, 1984), Frankfurt, Indeks Verlang, 57-75. Studien zur Klassifikation, Bd.14sk 14, p.62.

Veltman, K. (1993) (in press). *Conceptual Navigation: Views beyond Windows,* Sistema Terra, Rome.

Veltman, K. (1994) (in press). A system for universal media searching, (SUMS), *Computers and the History of Art.* London, England.

Whalley, P. (1993). An alternative rhetoric for Hypertext. In C. McKnight, A. Dillon and J. Richardson (Eds.) *Hypertext, A Psychological Perspective.* Great Britain: Ellis Horwood.

Wired Magazine, July 1995.

Wright, Patricia (1993). To jump or not to jump: Strategy selection while reading electronic texts. In C. McKnight, A. Dillon and J. Richardson (Eds.) *Hypertext, A Psychological Perspective.* Great Britain: Ellis Horwood.

NOTES ON CONTRIBUTORS

Stella Algoo-Baksh received her early education in Trinidad and Tobago. She completed her doctorate at Memorial University of Newfoundland in 1991 and has taught in the English Department of Memorial since that time. Her research is in the area of Canadian and post-colonial literature, and she is the author of the book *Austin C. Clarke, A Biography* (1995).

Carolyn Allen is Assistant Lecturer in English at the University of the West Indies (Mona). She works on comparative studies in Caribbean literatures in English, French and Spanish. Her doctoral thesis was on the poetics of creolization.

Nara Araújo is Professor of Caribbean and Comparative Literature at the Universidad de la Habana, Cuba. Her research and publications deal specifically with feminist theory and Caribbean women's narrative, and Caribbean literature in general. She has lectured in France, Brazil, Canada, Jamaica and Mexico. Her publications include *Vision romantica del otro* (1993). She has received the Palms of the French Academy.

Maria-Inés Arratia, born in Chile, has her Ph.D in Social Anthropology from York University and is currently at CERLAC (Centre for Research on Latin America and the Caribbean) at York University. Her publications, research and work experience are in the field of symbolic anthropology and deal with questions of development, knowledge systems and intercultural education, especially in the Southern Andean region.

Gage Averill is an Assistant Professor of Ethnomusicology at Wesleyan University, a columnist for *Beat Magazine,* associate editor of the *Yearbook* *for Traditional Music* and director of the Pandemonium Steelband (U.S.A.). He was member of the O.A.S. 1990 electoral mission to Haiti and is currently finishing a book on the subject of Haitian music and politics.

Pierre Beaucage enseigne au Département d'anthropologie de l'Université de Montréal. Il a obtenu son Ph.D en anthropologie sociale à la London School of Economics. Ses recherches publiées portent sur les économies autochtones, les problèmes de développement rural, les perceptions et pratiques concernant l'environnement et les mouvements amérindiens contemporains.

Frederick Ivor Case is Professor of African and Caribbean literatures at the University of Toronto. He is currently Principal of New College at the University of Toronto, where he publishes and lectures on literature, culture, race and ethnicity.

Embert Charles is former director of the Folk Research Centre in Saint Lucia. He has done extensive research on folk culture and popular music in the Caribbean.

Alberto Ciria is Professor of Political Science at Simon Fraser University, Vancouver. He has done much research in the area of culture and has published extensively on Argentinian cinema.

Austin Clarke was born in Barbados and came to Canada in 1955. He completed his studies at the University of Toronto's Trinity College. His long list of novels and short stories, published in this country, confirms his status as one of Canada's important writers and critics. He is currently living in Toronto.

David Craven, Professor of Art History at the University of New Mexico, has published three books, several monographs and over 70 articles in journals from the United States, Canada, Belgium, German, England, Nicaragua, Spain and elsewhere. His publications include *The New Concept of Art and Culture in Nicaragua Since the Revolution in 1979* (1989). At present, he is preparing a book on art, cultural policy and revolutionary movements in twentieth-century Latin America.

Anny Dominique Curtius, originaire de la Martinique et installée à Montréal depuis 1990, est titualire d'une maîtrise en littérature comparée de l'Université de Montréal. Actuellement, elle prépare une thèse de doctorat sur *Manifestations religieuses et espace littéraire antillais.* Ses recherches portent également sur le cinéma africain et l'épistémologie d'une littérature africaine.

Cyril Dabydeen won the Sandbach Parker Gold Medal in 1964, the highest prize for poetry in Guyana. He emigrated to Canada in 1970 and since then has published in numerous journals and reviews throughout North America, the Caribbean and Europe. In 1985, he became the poet laureate of Ottawa and he currently teaches English at the University of Ottawa.

José Del Pozo, né au Chili, habite le Canada depuis 1974. Il est actuellement professeur d'histoire latino-américaine à l'UQAM. Il a publié *Rebeldes, reformistas y revolucionarios,* una historia oral de de la izquierda chilean en la época de la Unidad popular (Santiago, 1992). Il est co-éditeur d'un ouvrage collectif, *Le Chili de 1970 à 1990* et directeur exécutif de la *Revue canadienne des études latino-américaines et caraïbs.*

Gustavo Esteva is a Mexican scholar-activist who describes himself as a deprofessionalized intellectual and nomadic story teller.

Jorge Etcheverry is a Chilean born poet who currently lives in Ottawa. His book *The Escape Artist/El evasionista* was published by Ediciones Cordillera in Ottawa, 1981; *La Calle* was published in Sin Fronteras, Chile, 1990. His anthology *Northern Cronopios: Chilean Novelists and Short Story Writers in Canada* was published in Ottawa by Split Quotation in 1993. He has lectured in England, Cuba and Canada and has published poems, short stories and articles in Canada, Cuba, the United States, Mexico, Chile and Spain.

Honor Ford-Smith is the founding artistic director of the Sistern Theatre Collective of Jamaica and co-author and editor of *Lionhert Gal: Life stories of Jamaican Women.* She is also an actress and poet and has published works in anthologies of Caribbean poetry. She is currently working on her PhD at the Ontario Institute for Studies in Education in Toronto.

Cecil Foster came to Canada from Barbados in 1979. He has written for the *Toronto Star, The Globe and Mail* and is currently an editor at the *Finanical Post.* His two novels have won him great critical acclaim: *No Man in the House,* Random House in 1991, and *Sleep On, My Beloved,* Random House 1995.

Annemarie Gallaugher is a Ph.D candidate in the York University Graduate Program in Music. Her research interests include the politics of ritual and celebratory expression and issues of representation and identity in ethnography with particular reference to the Caribbean area.

Hugh Hazelton grew up in Chicago, but has lived in Canada since 1969. He has traveled extensively in the Americas, Australia, India, and Africa. His three collections of poetry include *Sunwords, Crossing the Chaco,* and *Ojo de papel.* Co-editor and principal translator of *Compañeros: An Anthology of Writings about Latin America* (Cormorant, 1991), he currently teaches Spanish translation at Concordia University in Montreal.

Alberto Kurapel, agrégé de l'Ecole de Théâtre de l'Université du Chili, vit à Montréal depuis 1973. Il a fondé la *Compagnie des Arts Exilio,* groupe de Théâtre-Performance latino-américain. En tant que concepteur scénique, comédien, auteur, compositeur et chanteur, il a participé à des Festivals de théâtre nationaux et internationaux, a publié des oeuvres poétiques et dramatiques et a fait des microsillons de poésie québécoise traduite en espagnol.

Dany Laferrière came to Canada from Haiti in 1976. Currently, he lives in Miami but appears regularly on Quebec television as art, literary and film critic. Winner of the Grand Prix du Carbet in 1991 for his novel *L'Odeur du café,* he has published six novels in French with VLB Editeurs in Montreal and his works have been translated into English by Coach House Press, Toronto.

Jean-Louis de Lannoy is Associate Professor of Sociology at the University of Toronto. He is co-author, with G. Perez Ramirez of *Estructuras demograficas y sociales de Colombia,* and author of *Condiciones de vida en America Latina,* as well as a number of articles on various apsects of ideology in Mexico (indianism, student activism, fascism) and on liberation theology.

John A. Lent is Director of Third World Media. He has been studying Asian and Caribbean mass communications since the 1960s and is one of the major authorities on Communications in the Caribbean. He is the author or editor of 47 books and monographs among which are *Caribbean Popular Culture, Caribbean Mass Communications* and a four-volume bibliography on comic art worldwide, which was recently awarded the Ray and Pat Browne Best Book in Popular Culture prize.

Pedro A. Noguera is Assistant Professor in the Division of Social and Cultural Studies at the School of Education at the University of California Berkeley. An American of Jamaican and Trinidadian background, he received his Ph.D in Sociology from Berkeley. He has done extensive research and field work in Granada, Belize, El Salvador and Nicaragua.

Naïn Nomez now lives in Chile after being exiled for 12 years in Canada. Poet, professor and critic, he has published in Canada and in Chile including *Paises como puentes levadizos,* in Santiago, Chile 1986, translated by Christina Shantz as *Burning Bridges* and published in Canada by Cormorant Books in 1987. His anthologies include *Chilean Literature in Canada/Literatura chilena en Canadá,* Cordillera 1982; *Pablo de Rokha: Neuva antología y poesia chilena contemporánea,* Santiago de Chile, 1992.

Marie-José N'Zengou-Tayo est haïtienne et professeure adjointe au Département de français de l'University of the West Indies, sur le Campus de Mona, Jamaïque. Sa thèse de doctorat (Université Charles de Gaulle, Lille) a porté sur Julien Green. Actuellement, elle travaille principalement en littérature comparée sur les romans antillais francophones.

Milagros Ortiz a obtenu sa maîtrise en anthropologie à l'Université de Montréal. Son mémoire portait sur l'ethnohistoire et l'identité chez les Miskitos du Nicaragua. Dans le cadre de ses études de doctorat elle effectue présentement des recherches sur la condtion des jeunes autochtones urbains au nord-est de la Colombie britannique.

Sylvie Perron teaches Spanish at McGill University where she is currently working on her Ph.D in Hispanic Literature. Her thesis deals with the "Exiled" in Hispanic literature from the Middle-Ages to the present.

Lady Rojas-Trempe was born in Peru. She teaches Spanish in the Department of Modern Languages and Literatures at the University of Ottawa. She is Coordinator of the Canadian Literary Centre for Research on Latin American Women Writers. Her publications range from poetry to scholarly work on literature.

Alvina Ruprecht is Associate Professor of French at Carleton University and Director of the Centre d'analyse des littératures francophones/créolophones des Amériques (CALIFA). Her research and publications are in the area of contemporary French, Caribbean and Quebec theatre and literature. She has also published articles on Mass Communications and popular culture in Guadeloupe and is currently preparing a book on ritual theatre in Quebec.

Makeda Silvera is a poet who lives in Toronto. She is the founder and director of *Sister Vision,* a Toronto-based publishing house specializing in the publication of works by women of colour.

Cecilia Taiana lectures on cross-cultural analysis of social policies and practices in the School of Social Work at Carleton University. She grew up in Buenos Aires, and studied in Paris, London and Ottawa. She is presently preparing her doctoral dissertation on cross-cultural analysis and the use of new technologies; she is currently developing multimedia educational courseware at Carleton University. She has published articles on the nature of the therapeutic alliance in cross-cultural counselling.

Pablo Urbanyi, writer of Argentinian origin, has published several novels and volumes of poetry in Argentina, including *En ninguna parte,* published in 1981 in Buenos Aires and then in English in 1982 (Toronto) under the title *The Nowhere Idea* and in French, *L'Idée fixe* in Montreal, 1988. A selection of his short stories was published in Hungary, *A hagyatek* (A Legacy). He received an award from Planeta, the Argentinian publishers, for his latest book, *Silver.*

José Leandro Urbina, came to Canada in 1977. His book of short stories *Las Malas Juntas,* published by Ed. Cordillera in 1978, appeared in English as *Lost Causes,* with Cormorant Books in 1987, and again with Planeta in 1993. His novel *Cobro revertido* was shorlisted in the 1992 Planeta international competition in Argentina. Published in Chile the same year, it won the prize of the Chilean National Book Council for the best novel published in 1992.

Alfonso Quijada Urías, from El Salvadaor and now living in Vancouver, has published ten books of poetry and short stories in El Salvador, Honduras, Cuba, México and the United States. His work has been translated into English, French, Dutch, Russian and Italian. His volume of short stories *The Better to See You,* translated by Hugh Hazelton, was published in 1993 by Cormorant Books.

Catharina Vallejo, born in the Netherlands, is currently Assistant Professor of Spanish at Concordia University in Montreal. She has published books and articles on the contemporary Spanish-American short story, Spanish-American Romantic poetry and contemprary Spanish-American literature. She is currently working on a study of the image of women in the identity discourse of the 19th-century Dominican Republic.

Sylvia Wynter is Professor Emerita of Spanish, Portuguese and Afro-American Studies at the University of California at Stanford. She is the author of one of the first novels by a Caribbean woman writer, *The Hills of Hebron* (1962). She is a well respected writer and critical thinker, and the author of numerous books and major essays on postmodern theory including "1492: A New World View," in *Race, Discourse, and the Origin of the Americas,* The Smithsonian Press, 1995.

Alain Yacou is Professeur of Hispanic Caribbean Studies and Caribbean History at the l'Université des Antilles et de la Guyane, Guadeloupe. He is currently the director of the Doctoral Programme (DEA/Caraïbe Amérique du Sud et du Nord) at the Centre d'études et de recherches caraïbéennes) CERC. He has published extensively on Caribbean history with special emphasis on Cuba. He is the editor of the journal *Espace Caraïbe.*

Carole D. Yawney is Associate Professor of Anthropology at Atkinson College, York University. She has been an active researcher of Rastafari since 1970 and has had field experience in North America, the Caribbean, and the United Kingdom. She is recognized as one of the foremost specialists of Rastafari culture in North America.

Gladstone L. Yearwood is Associate Professor of Media Studies at North Carolina Central University, Durham. He is a graduate of New York University's Institute of Film and Television. He is the editor of *Black Cinema Aesthetics: Issues in Independent Filmmaking* (Ohio University Centre for Afro-American Studies, 1982) and has written on black cinema in the United States, the Caribbean and Canada.

Daniel Yon is Assistant Professor with a cross-appointment in the Department of Anthropology and the Faculty of Education, York University. He teaches on the anthropology of race and racism. His current research project explores issues of globalization, identity, diaspora, multiculturalism and their implications for pedagogy.